D1248496

★ ★ ★

RICHARD S. EWELL

CIVIL WAR AMERICA
Gary W. Gallagher, editor

★ ★ ★

RICHARD S.

EWELL

A Soldier's Life

Donald C. Pfanz

THE UNIVERSITY OF NORTH CAROLINA PRESS
CHAPEL HILL AND LONDON

BOOK CLUB EDITION
Manufactured in the United States of America

The paper in this book meets the guidelines for
permanence and durability of the Committee on Production
Guidelines for Book Longevity of the Council on Library Resources.

Library of Congress Cataloging-in-Publication Data
Pfanz, Donald.
Richard S. Ewell: a soldier's life / by Donald C. Pfanz.
p.   cm. — (Civil War America)
Includes bibliographical references and index.
ISBN 0-8078-2389-9 (cloth : alk. paper)
1. Ewell, Richard Stoddert, 1817–1872. 2. Generals—Confederate
States of America—Biography. 3. Confederate States of America.
Army—Biography. 4. Virginia—History—Civil War, 1861–1865—
Campaigns. I. Title. II. Series.
E467.1.E86P44   1998
973.7′3—dc21   97-21473
CIP

Frontispiece: Richard S. Ewell (Library of Congress)

02 01 00 99 98   5 4 3 2 1

TO MY PARENTS,
Harry and Letitia Pfanz,
whom I love and admire

Contents

Maps

★ ★ ★

Illustrations

★ ★ ★

Preface

During its four-year existence, the Army of Northern Virginia had seven infantry corps commanders: James Longstreet, Stonewall Jackson, John Gordon, A. P. Hill, Jubal Early, Dick Anderson, and Dick Ewell. The first five have received wide attention; Anderson and Ewell, by contrast, have been all but ignored. In the 130 years since the Civil War, Ewell has been the subject of just two biographies: Percy G. Hamlin's standard, *"Old Bald Head,"* published in 1940, and Samuel J. Martin's more recent *The Road to Glory*. Hamlin's work provides an overview of the general's life, but it lacks depth. Martin's book probes more deeply into Ewell's Civil War career, but it fails to utilize many important primary sources.

My first goal in writing this book is to provide a complete and detailed account of Ewell's life. Biographies of Civil War generals all too often focus exclusively on the war years, glossing over the subject's life before and after the conflict. While the Civil War was certainly the defining event of Ewell's life, it encompassed just four of his fifty-five years. The other periods of his life also deserve attention. As an officer in the First U.S. Dragoons, Ewell participated in two famous cross-country expeditions, fought in the Mexican War, and played an instrumental role in the settlement of the American Southwest. He crossed paths with Kit Carson, was an adversary of Cochise, and served in Mexico with the likes of Philip Kearny and Robert E. Lee. After the war, Ewell moved to Tennessee and created one of the finest stock farms in that state. His career peaked between 1861 and 1865, but it did not begin and end there.

My second goal is to provide a balanced view of Ewell's personality. Douglas Southall Freeman has done more than any other individual to shape the public's perception of Ewell's character. In his classic work, *Lee's Lieutenants*, Freeman portrays Ewell as a quirky and hot-tempered (if lovable) eccentric, known as much for his cussing as for his fighting. His description is not so much wrong as it is incomplete. By stressing the general's idiosyncrasies, Freeman obscures the fact that Ewell was an intelligent, hard-working professional who knew his business and did it well. He was an officer who led by example. At Cross Keys, Port Republic, and a half-dozen other battles besides, he was in the thick of the combat. Two injuries, four dead horses, and an untold number of close calls attest to his bravery under fire.

Ewell was a high-strung individual and often lost his temper in times of extreme stress. Otherwise, he was an eminently likable man. His offbeat sense of humor, unaffected manners, and kindness toward others won him many friends. Dr. Hunter McGuire referred to him as "brave, chivalrous, splendid, eccentric Dick Ewell, whom everybody loved," and others echoed that sentiment.[1] Ewell's most admirable trait, perhaps, was his modesty. Although he led the successful charge at Port Republic, encouraged his men by his bravery under fire at Gaines's Mill, and rallied his troops at Fort Harrison, you will see no evidence of it in his official reports or in his personal correspondence. Ewell lavished praise on his subordinates, but he never sought it for himself. In an army brimming with ambitious officers, he stands out for his genuine modesty.

Finally, I have sought to reexamine Ewell's military career in light of modern scholarship. Again it was Freeman who set the tone for subsequent interpretations of Ewell's generalship. Freeman considered Ewell to be an able subordinate but felt that he lacked the capacity for independent command. He based his judgment on the postwar writings of men such as Jubal Early, Isaac Trimble, and John Gordon, who criticized Ewell and others in order to bolster their own reputations. Freeman accepted their self-serving comments at face value, as have most historians since then.

An analysis of Ewell's career, however, shows him to have been a remarkably talented officer who knew how to handle troops in combat. In addition to being a stubborn fighter, he was an able administrator and arguably the best marcher in the army. Recent tactical studies confirm his ability. In the Shenandoah Valley and the Wilderness, at the Seven Days and Second Winchester, he performed well and sometimes brilliantly. Even his performance at Gettysburg does not appear to have been as flawed as previously thought; certainly it was no worse than those of Lee, Longstreet, Stuart, or A. P. Hill. As to his supposed incapacity for independent command, one needs only to examine the record. Of the four major engagements in which Ewell exercised field command, he won decided victories at three: Cross Keys, Second Winchester, and Fort Harrison. The remaining battle, Sailor's Creek, found him overwhelmed by a Union force more than twice his size. Even then he surrendered only after his corps was surrounded. That is not to say that Ewell made no mistakes. He stumbled at Gettysburg, his tactics at Groveton lacked imagination, and his performance at Spotsylvania was riddled with flaws. But when weighed against his many accomplishments, these short-comings appear small. When the balance sheet is tallied up, Ewell's successes as a general far outweigh his failures.

★ ★ ★

Acknowledgments

In writing this book, I have received help from countless individuals and institutions. First and foremost I wish to thank my father, Harry W. Pfanz, who read and reread the manuscript, weeding out errors and offering valuable suggestions for its improvement. As a preeminent authority on Gettysburg, his insights and suggestions regarding that pivotal battle were particularly helpful. No less important was his encouragement throughout the writing of this book. Because of his support, "the world waits" for *Ewell* no longer.

Robert K. Krick of Fredericksburg, Virginia, was also instrumental in the completion of this book. He passed along to me dozens of Ewell-related items over the years, then meticulously read through the manuscript, pointing out errors and polishing the prose. This book would be poorer if not for his considerable efforts.

Gordon Rhea proofread the chapters on the battles of the Wilderness and Spotsylvania Court House. Just as important, he offered valuable advice on eliminating awkward expressions, unnecessary words, and superfluous phrases. The text is cleaner and more concise because of his suggestions.

Historians Chris Calkins, John Hennessy, Robert E. L. Krick, and George Stammerjohan graciously took time to read over individual chapters of the manuscript. They passed on to me arcane information about the general that they uncovered while pursuing research of their own. George, in particular, went out of his way in sending me information about Ewell's service in the Old Army.

While a historian at Manassas National Battlefield Park, Robert E. L. Krick did some fine research on General Ewell's wounding. He sent me some interesting correspondence between Ewell and Lawrence O'Bryan Branch not found in the *Official Records*, as well as other bits of information gleaned in his research. He also provided information regarding the members of Ewell's staff.

Throughout this project I received the support of many of Lizinka Campbell Brown Ewell's descendants, particularly Dace Farrer of Prospect, Kentucky; James A. Lyon of Chattanooga, Tennessee; the late Susan B. Lyon of Murfreesboro, Tennessee; Lucia Brownell of Birmingham, Alabama; Lizinka Benton of Houston, Texas; Cathy Charnley of Atlanta, Georgia; and the late Lizinka Mosley of Nashville, Tennessee. I also wish to express my gratitude to members of the Ewell family, particularly Mrs. Nathaniel McGregor Ewell Jr. of Charlottesville, Virginia, and Judge John Ewell of Front Royal.

My colleagues in the National Park Service have been a constant source of help and support. In addition to those mentioned above, I wish to thank Noel Harrison, Keith Bohannon, Paul Shevchuk, David Sherman, and Jimmy Blankenship, all of whom have sent me Ewell items over the years.

General Ewell suffered from a number of illnesses throughout his life. Doctors Joseph C. Greenfield Jr., Marvin Rozear, and G. Ralph Corey of the Duke University Medical Center analyzed the general's various symptoms and proposed theories concerning his medical condition. If Ewell had had such a talented medical team on his side after the Civil War, he might have lived a quarter-century longer.

Individuals at various libraries graciously gave of their time. My thanks go to John White at the Southern Historical Collection of the University of North Carolina; Dr. Richard Sommers of the U.S. Army Military History Institute at Carlisle Barracks, Pennsylvania; Michael Musick and his coworkers at the National Archives; John Coski and Robert Hancock at the Museum of the Confederacy; Robert DePriest and Ruth Jarvis of the Tennessee State Library and Archives; Mr. Worley and Ms. Dodd of the Hopewell, Virginia, Library; Marie T. Capps and Suzanne Christoff at the United States Military Institute; Corey Seeman of the Chicago Historical Society; and Margaret Cook of the College of William and Mary. John Hogan of the Prince William Mapping Agency; Betty Loudon of the Nebraska State Historical Society; Charles W. Turner of Lexington, Virginia; James Hoobler of the Tennessee Historical Society; and Carol Friedman of Fairfax County were also helpful in my research, as were Dr. Linda A. McCurdy of Chapel Hill, North Carolina, and June Cunningham of the Virginia Military Institute Museum. Archivist James J. Holmberg deserves special mention for alerting me to the presence of the Brown-Ewell Family Papers owned by the Filson Club.

In the course of my research I was fortunate to visit many sites associated with General Ewell's life. I would like to thank the following individuals for kindly permitting me to visit their property: Dr. William E. S. Flory of Bel Air, Audrey

Weichman of Stony Lonesome, William O. Hutchison and Rumsey Light of Auburn, Ed Davies of Dunblane, and Dr. and Mrs. Walter Brown of Spring Hill.

Terry Jones of Northeast Louisiana University provided me with much useful information on the Brown family, while Christine McDonald, Jill K. Garrett, and Dr. William Haywood of Columbia, Tennessee, kindly sent me information about General Ewell's postwar life in Tennessee.

Constance Wynn Altshuler offered several helpful suggestions for sources about Ewell's life in the Southwest. By like token, Harry Myers of Put-in-Bay, Ohio, was gracious in answering questions about Ewell's life at Fort Scott. Mildred Tyner of Culpeper, Virginia, kindly permitted me to consult a letter written by General Ewell that is in her possession.

Ed Raus and the late John E. Divine accompanied me on a very informative tour of the sites associated with Ewell's wounding and amputation. Other historians from whom I have received assistance and guidance in my research include authors Clark B. Hall, Burke Davis, Robert Garth Scott, Noah Andre Trudeau, Joseph Glatthaar, Patricia Hurst, and William D. Matter.

I also wish to express my appreciation to Wallace A. Hebert of Columbia, Tennessee; Robert and Karen Amster of Petersburg, Virginia; William H. Willcox of Washington, D.C.; Stephen L. Ritchie of Muncie, Indiana; Gray Golden of Austin, Texas; and Theodore P. Yeatman of the Tennessee Western History and Folklore Society in Nashville, Tennessee.

Ed P. Coleman of Petersburg, New Jersey, skillfully produced the maps in this book. I appreciate his patience and hard work. I also wish to thank editors David Perry, Ron Maner, and Stephanie Wenzel, series editor Gary W. Gallagher, and other individuals at the University of North Carolina Press for making this book a reality.

Finally, I wish to thank my wife, Betty, whose love, tolerance, and good nature is a constant source of wonder and inspiration to me.

★ ★ ★

RICHARD S. EWELL

CHAPTER I

Stony Lonesome

Across the rolling plains of northern Virginia a new morning dawned. It was a soft spring day in May: bright, cool, refreshing. In the pastures cows nibbled quietly at the grass, while across the land farmers hitched up their plough horses for another day's labor. The year was 1861.

At a farmhouse ten miles west of Manassas, a forty-four-year-old man bid his brother and sister farewell and rode off to war. He carried little in the way of personal baggage, for by profession he was a soldier and accustomed to traveling light. Richard Stoddert Ewell had been an officer in the U.S. Dragoons for more than twenty years. In that time he had served primarily at frontier posts in the West, where, as he claimed, he had learned all there was to know about commanding fifty dragoons and had forgotten everything else.[1] Those who knew him might have added that he was one of the army's most competent and experienced Indian fighters.

This time, however, Dick Ewell would not be fighting Apaches but U.S. soldiers. Virginia and other Southern states had recently seceded from the Union, throwing the country into civil war. It was a prospect Ewell abhorred. Like most Regular Army officers, he felt a strong loyalty to the flag that he had long and faithfully served. His ties with the United States seemed as strong as life itself. To break them, he later wrote, "was like death to me."[2] Yet strong as was his allegiance to the national government, his allegiance to Virginia was stronger still. After painful deliberation he cast his lot with the South. Once he made the decision, he did not look back. The tocsin had sounded, and Dick Ewell, like his forefathers in earlier wars, could not ignore its call.

The Ewells were Virginia planters of English stock. Outside London, in Surrey County, stood an ancient Saxon village named Ewell, and there, according to tradition, the family took root.[3] James Ewell left England about the time of the

English Civil War and emigrated to Virginia's eastern shore. A brickmaker by trade, James settled at Pungoteague and became a "man of substance." He married a woman named Ann and left seven children.[4]

Among James Ewell's many offspring was a boy named Charles, who became a brickmaker like his father. Charles moved across the Chesapeake Bay to Lancaster County.[5] At a small inlet later known as Ewell's Bay, he established "Monashow," a plantation where he probably grew tobacco and other crops suited to the soil. Charles married Mary Ann Bertrand. The union produced seven children, including three boys: Charles, Bertrand, and Solomon. The youngest son, Solomon, inherited his father's estate and went on to found the "Lancaster" branch of the Ewell family. His brothers, Charles and Bertrand, moved up the Potomac River to Prince William County and established the family's "Prince William" line.[6]

Charles built "Bel Air" plantation in 1740.[7] During his life he was a vestryman in the local parish and served as an officer in the Prince William militia. Charles's wife, Sarah Ball, was a first cousin of George Washington's mother, Mary Ball. Of the couple's four children, three survived to maturity. Their only daughter, Mariamne, married Dr. James Craik, who became chief physician and surgeon of the Continental Army. Craik is best remembered for his close association with Washington, who referred to him in his will as "my compatriot in arms, an old and intimate friend." When Washington died at Mount Vernon in 1799, Craik was one of three doctors at his bedside.[8]

Besides Mariamne, Charles Ewell had two sons who survived to maturity. Both took wives within the family. His oldest son, Jesse, married his first cousin Charlotte Ewell in 1767. Jesse's younger brother went one better. Col. James Ewell of "Greenville" married his double first cousin, Mary Ewell, and when she died, he took another first cousin, Sarah Ewell, as his second wife.

Jesse inherited Bel Air. Following the pattern of public service set by his father, Jesse served as an officer in the county militia and was a vestryman in Dettinger Parish. As a young man he attended the College of William and Mary, and while there, he became a close friend of his Albemarle County classmate Thomas Jefferson. The two men remained friends until Jesse's death in 1805. They corresponded frequently, and Jesse occasionally hosted Jefferson at his home. During the Revolution, Jesse was a colonel in the militia, though his regiment apparently never saw combat. His silver-hilted rapier was later given to his grandson Richard Ewell, who wore it during the final years of the Civil War.[9]

The marriage of Jesse and Charlotte Ewell resulted in no fewer than seventeen children. One daughter, Fanny, married the Reverend Mason Locke Weems,

Col. Jesse Ewell of Bel Air
(Alice M. Ewell, Virginia Scene*)*

The hilt of Col. Jesse Ewell's sword from the American
Revolution. General Ewell wore the sword during the
last half of the Civil War. (Judge John Ewell)

Bel Air, the home of Col. Jesse Ewell (Donald C. Pfanz)

the author of a popular early biography of Washington. "Parson" Weems's stories of young Washington cutting down the cherry tree and throwing a coin across the Rappahannock, though probably fictional, have long been part of American lore.[10]

Fanny's younger brother Thomas, born in 1785, was Charlotte Ewell's fourteenth child.[11] Thomas had a brilliant but erratic mind and a fiery, restless disposition. As a young man he studied medicine under Dr. Benjamin Rush at the University of Pennsylvania. Following his graduation in 1805, Thomas received an appointment as a surgeon in the U.S. Navy through the influence of his father's friend Thomas Jefferson. He served first at New York City's naval yard and later at Washington, D.C.[12]

For Thomas medicine was more than a profession; it was a challenge. A daughter recalled that he "disliked the practise of medicine, unless the case was an exciting one, such as to call out all his powers of analysis in the symptoms and cause of disease, and the discovery of new and better modes of treatment." His quest for knowledge sometimes got him into trouble. On one occasion he was nearly mobbed by an angry crowd for dissecting the brain of a deceased patient without the consent of the man's widow.[13]

Thomas published the results of his investigations in five books spanning almost two decades. Some of his theories were far ahead of their time. In his book *Discourses on Modern Chemistry*, for instance, he promoted the use of chemical fertilizers, soil testing, and insect control to increase crop yield and advocated conservation techniques to prevent the destruction of American forests. Some of his ideas spawned controversy within the medical community. His book *Letters to Ladies*, remembered one descendant, "shocked the 'delicate and refined females' of that day by attributing their fainting fits, tears, and tantrums to illness of body and not to sensibility of soul." Pre-Victorian America was not yet ready to accept such progressive thinking.[14]

Only once did Thomas Ewell make a literary venture outside the field of science. That occurred in 1817 when he edited the first American edition of philosopher David Hume's *Essays*. Like everything to which Thomas Ewell set his hand, the book inspired controversy. The Catholic and Episcopal Churches had proscribed Hume's books, and Ewell was publicly censured for publishing them. The doctor was unrepentant. Although a devout Episcopalian, he found Hume instructive and believed the general public, like himself, could read books and extract what was valuable "without being affected by the dross contained in them."[15]

On 3 March 1807 Thomas married Elizabeth Stoddert in Georgetown. James and Dolley Madison attended the ceremony. In 1808 Elizabeth delivered a daughter, whom she named Rebecca Lowndes in honor of her mother. Other births followed: Benjamin Stoddert in 1810, Paul Hamilton in 1812, and Elizabeth Stoddert in 1813. A fifth child died in childbirth, but by the summer of 1816 Elizabeth was again pregnant. On 8 February 1817 she gave birth to her third son, a boy whom she named Richard Stoddert after a deceased brother.[16]

Richard first saw light at his mother's childhood home, "Halcyon House," at the southwest corner of Thirty-fourth Street and Prospect Avenue in Georgetown. Built by Elizabeth's father in 1785, the large brick building, with its rolling terraces and panoramic view of the Potomac River, was one of the oldest and grandest houses in town. Wrote one historian, "No site could have been fairer and the house, as Major Stoddert built it, was worthy of the site."[17]

Richard retained no memories of his birthplace. When he was just one year old, his family moved to Philadelphia, where his father attended a series of medical lectures at the University of Pennsylvania. The Ewells returned to the District of Columbia in 1819 and moved into a new two-story brick house on the west side of President's Square across from the White House. At that time Washington was still sparsely populated, and only two other buildings stood on the block:

*Halcyon House, the Georgetown home of Benjamin Stoddert and
the birthplace of General Ewell (Library of Congress)*

St. John's Church and Commodore Stephen Decatur's house. Decatur was mortally wounded in a duel with Commodore Barron a short time after the Ewells'
arrival. The Ewell children watched as his near-lifeless body was carried back to
his house.[18]

The Ewells had been in Washington just one year when Thomas's health began to fail. Apparently the doctor's brilliance and eccentricity had led to excess.
He became an alcoholic and suffered bouts of depression. The fortune he had
amassed dwindled, and his successful medical practice languished.[19] In 1820 the
Ewells left Washington and moved to "Belleville," a 1,300-acre farm in Prince
William County, Virginia. Because of its rocky soil and isolated location, family
members took to calling the property "Stony Lonesome," a name that stuck.[20] In
addition to Stony Lonesome, the Ewells owned four one-half-acre lots and a large
house in Centreville, Virginia, called "Four Chimney House."[21] They continued
to retain possession of their Washington home, which they rented to top government officials for as much as $600 a year.[22]

Four Chimney House in Centreville, Virginia, once owned by the Ewell family
(Library of Congress)

The Ewells were slaveholders. Census records for 1830 show two black females living at the house.[23] One of these was Fanny Brown, better known to the family as Mammy. Fanny was not actually a slave. She had been acquired as chattel by Benjamin Stoddert, but Thomas Ewell later freed her from bondage after she successfully nursed him through a dangerous fever. Fanny accompanied the Ewells to Stony Lonesome, where she managed the poultry, did the cooking, and performed other routine chores around the house. To the children she was both a comforter and adviser, and they loved her like a mother. No one dared take liberties with Fanny, however, not even Mrs. Ewell. More than once, when Elizabeth rebuked her or offered some unintentional slight, Fanny packed her bags and walked out the door. But she never made it past the front gate. Moved by the tears of the Ewell children, who followed her weeping to the road, she always changed her mind and came back—"just to spite Mistis," she claimed.[24]

Two servants, three houses, and an abundance of land gave the family an aura of wealth that it did not possess. Like many Virginians the Ewells were land poor; that is, they owned large amounts of land but had little money. A vigorous man might have scratched out a living for himself and his family under such conditions, but Thomas Ewell was no longer a vigorous man. Dissipation had sapped his strength. For six years he led what one family member described as a "chequered life," struggling unsuccessfully against both alcoholism and poverty.[25]

As Thomas's finances declined, the size of his family increased. After Richard's birth in 1817, Elizabeth delivered four more children. A girl named Charlotte died as an infant, but the other three—Virginia, Thomas, and William—survived, adding more mouths to an already hungry family. To support his growing clan, Thomas turned once more to medicine. In 1824 he published *The American Family Physician*, a popular guide to medicine. That same year he applied for a vacant chair on the faculty of the University of Virginia's medical school. He wrote to both Thomas Jefferson and James Madison asking for letters of recommendation. Ewell's dependence on alcohol was well known, however, and apparently neither man replied. It was his last attempt to pull himself out of poverty. In 1826, at age forty, Thomas succumbed to his disease, leaving behind a grieving wife and eight children.[26]

Richard was nine years old when his father died. The two had never been close. Richard's youth, his father's alcoholism, and the large size of the family had created a chasm that was never bridged. Benjamin Ewell later confessed that as a boy he never felt his father's proper care, and his brother might well have said the same. In all of his subsequent correspondence, Richard never once made reference to his father.[27]

He was much closer to his mother, Elizabeth Stoddert Ewell. Elizabeth had an ancestry even more illustrious than that of her late husband. Her great-great-grandfather, Benjamin Tasker, had ruled for twenty years as president of Maryland's Proprietary Council; a great-uncle, Samuel Ogle, had been a three-time governor; and two other great-uncles, Daniel Dulany and Benjamin Tasker Jr., had held the important post of provincial secretary.[28]

Elizabeth's father, Benjamin Stoddert, had been a major of cavalry in the Continental Army. A crippling wound at the battle of Brandywine in 1777 incapacitated him for field duty, but he continued to serve his country as secretary to the Board of War. After the Revolution, Stoddert moved to Georgetown, built Halcyon House, and opened a tobacco export company. Over the next decade, as Georgetown blossomed into a major port, Stoddert's business prospered. His company hired on additional ships and opened branch offices in London and Bordeaux. Within a decade he became one of the young republic's foremost merchants.

In 1798 John Adams appointed Stoddert to be the country's first secretary of the navy. The United States was then on the brink of war with France, and it was

*Benjamin Stoddert, first U.S. secretary of the navy and grandfather
of General Ewell (Library of Congress)*

Stoddert's responsibility to create a national navy to protect the country's coast.
He succeeded brilliantly. In just three years he purchased land for six navy yards,
acquired fifty ships, and recruited 6,000 sailors, including a corps of talented
young officers that included David Porter, Isaac Hull, Oliver Perry, and Stephen
Decatur. The naval victories later achieved by the United States in the War of 1812
resulted in large measure from the groundwork laid during Stoddert's administration. Stoddert remained in office until 1801 and served a brief stint as secretary

*Charles Willson Peale painted this portrait of Benjamin Stoddert's children at
Halcyon House in 1789. Ewell's mother, Elizabeth, is on the left; Lizinka's mother,
Harriot, is in the wagon; and Benjamin Stoddert Jr. (d. 1834) is at the right.
(Dumbarton House Collection, Headquarters of the National Society of the
Colonial Dames of America, Washington, D.C.)*

of war before returning to private life. Financial distress dogged his remaining
years. Unwise land transactions at home and disrupted trade abroad caused his
business empire to crumble. He died in 1814, a poor and embittered man.[29]

Elizabeth was Benjamin Stoddert's eldest daughter. Described as a woman "of
stern character modified by charity," she demanded a great deal of her children.
Though a critical nephew once characterized her as "a great slattern—morally,
intellectually, and physically," her children remembered her better qualities: her
courage, high principles, and devotion to family. Born at Halcyon House in 1784,
Elizabeth moved with her parents to Philadelphia in 1798 when her father became
secretary of the navy. While there, she attended an elite girls' school and mingled
with the foremost families in America. Aaron Burr, Harry Lee, Oliver Wolcott,
and other prominent figures frequented the Stodderts' Philadelphia home; so,

too, did President John Adams and his wife, Abigail, who once brought plum cake for "Betsy" and the younger Stoddert children.[30]

Elizabeth never let her children forget their distinguished heritage. She regarded the family's narrow circumstances as merely a temporary condition and had no intention of allowing her children to "settle into a state of vulgarity" with their "rough uncultivated neighbors." Disdaining outside assistance, she put her children to work. While she and her daughters taught school in Centreville, the boys ran the farm.[31]

Despite the family's best efforts, poverty hovered at its doorstep. Supper often consisted of nothing more than a piece of cornbread, and some days not even that. More than once the children went to bed hungry. In an effort to alleviate her family's financial distress, Elizabeth sought vocations for her children outside the home. In 1828 Benjamin left to attend the U.S. Military Academy at West Point, New York. About the same time Paul Ewell started attending medical lectures at Columbia College in Washington. Rebecca lived with relatives in Bladensburg, Maryland, and taught music at a nearby school. Mrs. Ewell arranged to have her second daughter, Elizabeth, teach school in Maryland, but the girl declined the offer, "alledging that she had rather be at the wash tub at home, then live away."[32]

Paul pursued a career in medicine, but he died in 1831 from a liver infection or possibly typhoid. His family buried him in Centreville beside his father. A few days after Paul's death, a human skeleton was found hanging inside a deserted house near the Ewells' property. The family thought that someone had placed the bones there as a malicious prank, but they later discovered that the skeleton had belonged to Paul himself, who had been using it in his medical studies. Richard and a neighbor took down the offensive object and buried it. The shock of this untimely discovery threw Mrs. Ewell into a fitful illness that lasted for weeks.[33]

With Paul dead and Ben at West Point, Richard became the head man of the family. He took the responsibility seriously—too seriously, in the opinion of his older sister Elizabeth. "Richard is master and thinks himself mistress too," she wrote Ben. "You would be amused to see the air with which he struts along." With more charity she added, "He is very useful though and a good boy."

Richard was just fourteen when his brother died. Even at that young age he had developed certain character traits that would mark his personality in years to come. In him one could see the practical, precise mind of his grandfather Benjamin Stoddert and, negatively, the cynicism and sharp tongue of his mother, Elizabeth. The similarities to his deceased father were more pronounced still. Richard possessed Thomas Ewell's violent temper, high intellect, nervous energy, and love of alcohol. Fortunately he escaped most of his father's excesses, but he did not escape his father's eccentricity—at least not entirely. Generations of in-breeding among the Ewells had given the whole family a certain imbalance of mind; just how much may be judged by the fact that Dick was regarded as the only normal member of the clan.[34]

The family's poverty and the responsibility of managing the farm left their stamp on Richard's personality. He was more mature, disciplined, and serious than other boys his age. Although he never developed polished manners, young Ewell learned things of greater importance: integrity, industry, and honesty. Thanks to his mother he also learned humility. "It was a disgrace to push," she would lecture, "except at work."[35] Like his mother, Ewell had a sharp tongue and spoke his mind freely. A story from his early life tells of him receiving a Bible from his Sunday School teacher, Nelson Lloyd. When he accepted the gift without a word, his mother felt constrained to prompt, "Aren't you going to thank Mr. Lloyd for it?" The blood probably rushed to her face when her son answered, "I never asked him for it."[36]

Although rough around the edges, Richard had a good heart. When just thirteen years old, he rode to a neighboring town with his brother Tom to sell the farm's produce at market. Night overtook the boys as they were coming home, forcing them to seek shelter under a tree. It was early spring, and as the temperature dropped, Tom became chilled. To protect him from the damp night air, Richard took off his coat and placed it over his brother's shoulders. "Tom was sickly," he later explained, "and Mother would be uneasy." The two boys reached home the next day safe and sound.[37]

Richard's most conspicuous attribute as a boy was his bravery. One day, at the age of eighteen, he was working in the fields when he saw a rabid dog headed toward the farmhouse. Thinking quickly, he unhitched the plow, leaped onto the horse, and followed the frothing dog, shouting warning to everyone it approached. Members of his family took alarm and fled inside the house, all except his eleven-year-old brother, William, who was in the orchard and unable to reach the building. When the dog headed toward his brother, Dick galloped ahead and placed the frightened lad safely on a fence. The dog chased a few chickens around the yard, then headed to the next farm.

Though his own family had escaped danger, Dick continued to pursue the animal. His neighbors fled inside and barred the door as the dog approached. Dick dismounted in front of their house and calmly demanded a rifle. One man started to shove a gun out the door but pulled it back and slammed the door shut when the dog suddenly rounded the corner. Dick was left to contend with the animal alone, unarmed and dismounted. Fortunately the dog did not attack. As it moved off, Ewell persuaded his craven neighbors to crack the door and give him the gun. He then tracked the dog on foot to a nearby mill and killed it. His courage throughout the episode was surpassed only by his presence of mind. Rather than trying to anticipate the movements of the dog, he had wisely followed it, giving warning to all it approached. His mother, who witnessed the scene, confided to Becca that "he was as cool as a cucumber all the time."[38]

Working on the farm left Dick little time to pursue an education. Instead Rebecca taught him to read, write, and cipher at home, utilizing books from their father's large and diverse library. Not until he reached age seventeen did Dick attend school, and even then for just a year. In 1834 his mother scraped together enough money to send him to school at the Fitzhugh home in Fauquier County. There he studied the classics under the Reverend Mr. Knox, a teacher of some local distinction. He later attended classes with his brother Tom at Greenville, the Prince William County home of his relative James Ball Ewell. Dick proved to be a capable, if uninspired, student. While conceding that neither Dick nor her other brothers excelled in their early studies, Elizabeth Ewell later recalled that all the teachers "liked our boys and were proud of them."[39]

Elizabeth Ewell Sr. wanted Dick to have more than a basic education; she wanted him to attend college and enter a profession. In 1834 she began to make inquiries about enrolling him at the U.S. Military Academy. If Dick's courage suggested a military career, the family's pecuniary situation demanded it. Traditionally, appointments to West Point went to the descendants of Revolutionary War veterans who could not otherwise afford a higher education. There was no tuition, and cadets received a nominal salary to help cover necessary expenses. For the Ewells and other families struggling to make ends meet, the academy offered an excellent education at no cost. Ben had gone to West Point in 1828 and had graduated third in his class. Might not Dick do as well?

Mrs. Ewell's initial efforts to get her son an appointment bore no fruit, however, and as summer passed into fall, family members began to despair of his chances. Tasker Gantt, for one, believed nothing short of a miracle could secure his cousin's appointment. Even the members of Dick's immediate family began to discuss other possibilities for his employment. His sister Elizabeth piously voiced the hope that he would study divinity, while his mother made arrangements to send him west to study law if his application failed.[40]

Despite such precautions, neither Dick nor his mother ceased battling for his appointment. In an effort to better her son's chances of being accepted to West Point, Elizabeth enlisted the support of two prominent Tennessee relatives, her brother William Stoddert and her brother-in-law George W. Campbell.

Campbell's influence was particularly important. As a former member of Congress, ambassador to Russia, and secretary of the treasury, he wielded great influence in Washington. Early in 1835 Campbell took his nephew to see President Andrew Jackson, a fellow Tennessean. After a brief interview, Jackson wrote Dick a recommendation to present to Secretary of War Lewis Cass.

Cass promised to give Ewell an appointment if he could secure the nomination of his local congressman, Joseph W. Chinn. Ewell returned a few weeks later with Chinn's nomination in hand and reminded Cass of his promise. By then, however, all the vacancies for that year had been filled. Perhaps there would be room next year, he suggested. The boy bridled. Cass had promised him an appointment for the current year, he insisted, not the next. Cass laughed and referred him to the army's chief engineer, Gen. Charles Gratiot, who had immediate authority over the military academy. Gratiot received Ewell kindly, but he could not offer him any encouragement. The 1835 appointments had already been made; the boy would have to wait another year.[41]

Dick's mother and sister used the time to make Dick the shirts and quilts he would need if he went to New York. As spring approached, the family anxiously scanned the mail looking for confirmation of Dick's appointment. It arrived in March 1836. Ewell wasted no time drafting a letter of acceptance. At the bottom of the page Elizabeth Ewell signed her consent, binding her son to five years' service in the U.S. Army.

The die was cast; Dick was to be a soldier. In early June he left Stony Lonesome for West Point. Behind him he left the farm, his family, and his friends—everything he had known up to that time. The curtain had fallen on the first chapter of his life; a new chapter was about to begin.[42]

CHAPTER 2

West Point

West Point, New York, is a place of great beauty and history. The town stands on a grassy, level plain 150 feet above the Hudson River surrounded by the rugged hills of the New York highlands, a strategic feature in the latter years of the American Revolution. There Polish engineer Thaddeus Kosciuszko had constructed fortifications designed to block the incursion of British ships up the Hudson. His defensive system had centered on Fort Clinton, a structure that protected the great iron boom that extended across to Constitution Island. No less important was Fort Putnam, which guarded Fort Clinton and its auxiliary redoubts against attack from the rear. By 1836, however, these were relics of a distant past. The stone citadels once so critical to American liberty had fallen into disuse and become ruins.

From their granite rubble rose the buildings of the U.S. Military Academy. The academy was then in its fourth decade, having been established by Congress in March 1802. Four massive stone structures dominated the scene: a mess hall, an academic building, and two cadet barracks. North of these stood a broad forty-acre field used by the cadets for drill and parade. To the south and west were the houses of instructors and other small buildings. A Greek Revival chapel, under construction on the southeast corner of the grounds, and a hotel overlooking the river rounded out the small military community that for the next four years would be Dick Ewell's home.

The young Virginian arrived at West Point in mid-June 1836 and took his place beside the other boys in his class. He quickly struck up acquaintances with fellow Virginian George H. Thomas and Thomas's roommate, William Tecumseh Sherman, known familiarly as "Cump." Other members of his class included George W. Getty, William Hays, Bushrod R. Johnson, Paul O. Hébert, Stewart Van Vliet, and Israel B. Richardson.[1] Ewell gained friends quickly among his new associates, who affectionately called him "old Dick." He was particularly close to

Sherman, whom he later described as being "in every sense a gentleman[,] generous & high toned." Ewell liked to fish while at West Point, but it is said he would never go without Cump.[2]

At the same time Ewell was forging friendships with his classmates, he was renewing ties with his brother Benjamin. After graduating from West Point in 1832, Ben had stayed on as an assistant professor of mathematics. In that role, according to his brother, Ben soon gained a reputation for being "the best Mathematician on the Point and the most intelligent man." Ben was serving on the faculty when Dick arrived. Although seven years separated the two brothers, they bore a striking resemblance to each other, a circumstance that in one instance resulted in Ben being ordered to his quarters "in no very gentle terms" by a cadet officer who mistook him for Dick. The mistake would not be repeated. On 30 September Ben resigned his commission in the army and moved to York, Pennsylvania, to accept a position as assistant engineer of the Baltimore and Susquehanna Railroad.[3]

The highly structured lifestyle of West Point left little time for Ben and Dick to get reacquainted. After passing the entrance examination, Dick donned the "cadet gray" and took his place in the battalion. For the next two months he and other cadets camped outdoors, where they received instruction in the art of practical soldiering. From dawn until dusk they marched, drilled, and paraded to the barked commands of company officers. At night the cadets took turns walking guard. The smallest infraction, Ewell found, was grounds for demerits. "The duties here are much more arduous than I had any idea of," he confessed. "We have to walk post eight hours out of the 24, 4 in the day and 4 in the night, and if we do not walk constantly or if we speak to any person while on post we are reported and get 8 or 10 demerit."[4]

The cadet battalion was divided into four companies of approximately seventy cadets each. Members of each company lived together, drilled together, and usually ate together throughout their four years at the academy. Upper-class cadets appointed as officers were responsible for the good conduct and discipline of the cadets in their company. Ewell was assigned to Company A, which in 1836 counted among its officers Joseph Hooker, John Sedgwick, P. G. T. Beauregard, and Henry Halleck. Among the upperclassmen in the company who held no rank were Jubal Early and Henry Hunt. Sherman, Thomas, and Getty initially were assigned to other companies, but each would transfer into Company A before graduation.[5]

The two-month encampment ended on 31 August, when cadets struck their tents and moved into barracks in anticipation of the new academic year. Three days earlier they closed out the summer with a traditional end-of-season ball. Ewell did not attend the dance, but he described it for his sister Rebecca nevertheless. "There was a splendid ball given here on the 28th. It was given in the Mess Hall which was adorned with wreaths, flags of the different European nation[s], muskets, and swords and presented a most beautiful appearance. The Hall is very large as you may suppose for the whole Corps to dine in at once, but it was crowded to overflowing with visitors. I was on guard," he wrote, "and of course could not attend and would not if I could. Fire works were kept up untill [*sic*] a late hour some of which were most beautiful. It was a close night and the rockets would often go above the clouds before they burst, giving them the same tints as the sun in the morning."[6]

Summer balls provided rare enjoyment in the otherwise hard life of a cadet. The War Department intentionally made life difficult to build character, foster esprit de corps, and accustom cadets to the hardships of a military regimen. Housing was crowded and spartan. As a member of Company A, Dick resided on the east side of the North Barracks. His furniture consisted of a chair, washstand, mirror, and leather trunk. No paintings or other forms of ornamentation were permitted. Cadets slept on pallets spread out on the floor until 1839, when authorities issued iron bedstands. Officers frequently inspected the rooms, and if they were not in "a state of perfect cleanliness and order," cadets went on report. Something as small as hanging a hat on a peg rather than a hook might result in demerits.[7]

In his first year as a cadet, Ewell shared his cramped quarters with at least two other cadets, both members of his own class. One was Reuben P. Campbell of Statesville, North Carolina; the identity of the other is not known. Campbell was one and a half years Ewell's junior—a "genial, noble, warm-hearted" chap—the sort who never excelled on the drill ground or in the classroom but was a general favorite in the corps. He and Ewell got along famously, remaining friends for life. "Between these congenial spirits there always existed the most sincere and cordial friendship," a former cadet later remarked. Ewell was an earnest student, and he was glad he had been put in a room with cadets of his own class rather than upperclassmen. To Ben he wrote, "It has been the most fortunate thing for me in the world that I did not room with any old Cadets[.] there are several here who will be deficient on that account[.] they are always frolicking and spreeing instead of studying."[8]

Dick was less satisfied with West Point's food. The fare served at the dining hall was repetitive and far from appetizing. Meals typically consisted of boiled beef, boiled potatoes, and boiled pudding. Sanitation frequently was lacking. Cadets customarily received tough meat, sour molasses, and rancid butter. One student found a nest of mice in his pudding, and another discovered a comb! A few lucky cadets secured a place at the table of Mrs. Amelia Thompson, the widow of a Revolutionary War veteran, who ran a boarding establishment on the grounds. Perhaps through the agency of his brother, Ewell received one of these coveted spots when he arrived at West Point and maintained it throughout his four years at the academy.[9]

The cadets' schedule was tightly structured. Every minute of the day was closely regulated, allowing cadets no opportunity to get into trouble or, for that matter, to have fun. Regulations prohibited drinking, smoking, chewing tobacco, playing cards, or cooking. Even visiting the rooms of other cadets outside prescribed hours was forbidden. Those who broke the rules risked being reported and getting demerits. Teenage boys naturally bridled against such restrictions and broke them when they thought they could get away with it. Sherman became famous throughout the corps for smuggling food out of the mess hall and hosting furtive "hash bakes" in his room at night. Others risked immediate expulsion by slipping off post to enjoy a glass of "flip" at Benny Havens's tavern.

Ewell did not visit Benny Havens's, or if he did, he was never caught. He received comparatively few demerits, most for venial offenses. Instances of scuffling in the ranks, inattention at drill, and absence from reveille were minor stains on an otherwise respectable record of conduct. In his first year Ewell amassed 56 demerits, 55th best of the 211 cadets in the corps. His demerit count increased to 70 in his second year, then settled down to 41 and 46 demerits, respectively, in his final two years. Never did his conduct approach the 200-demerit limit, nor did it adversely affect his final class standing.[10]

Discipline relaxed to some extent on the Sabbath. Church attendance was mandatory. In the morning cadets marched to chapel, where they sat for two hours on backless wooden benches. The minister conducted a high-church Episcopal service, a liturgy, observed Sherman, "in which but a few take interest, much less join in heartfelt devotion." Far from exhibiting religious fervor, many cadets took advantage of the relaxed supervision at church to study their lessons and chew tobacco. Spitting tobacco juice during the service became so common by Ewell's final year that the superintendent had to issue an order requesting cadets to refrain from the practice because it was leaving stains on the floor. Ewell had been raised in a devout Episcopal household and was more pious than most of his comrades. Though military life would slowly erode his faith, at West Point he still held dear those convictions he had learned in his youth.[11]

Once the church service ended, cadets had the rest of the day to themselves. With no money to spend and nowhere to go, they quickly became bored. Some checked out books from the library. Others hiked to Fort Putnam or one of the many other nearby places that offered a panoramic view of the Hudson River Valley. The only organized club activity permitted at the academy was the Dialectic Society, a group of some four dozen cadets who met to debate current issues. Perhaps because he had an interest in debate or perhaps just because there was nothing better to do, Ewell joined the society.[12]

Ewell soon adjusted to military life and gained many friends among his new classmates. Life at the academy took on a brighter hue. By November he was able to write, "I like W. Point much better than I did some time ago and shall be very well contented if I get along in my studies. If I do not get along the fault will not be in my not studying."[13]

Classes for Ewell began on 1 September 1836. Unlike other American colleges, which emphasized the humanities, the U.S. Military Academy stressed mathematics, science, and engineering in order to prepare its students for a military career. The curriculum was challenging: nearly half of those who entered West Point with Ewell in 1836 would not graduate four years later.[14]

Each cadet took the same courses. Each course was divided into sections, with each section containing five to ten cadets. The most gifted students in a subject occupied the first section, which was taught by the professor. Less gifted students occupied the lower sections, which were taught by assistant professors. In this way cadets could progress at a pace commensurate with their ability.[15] Students learned by means of daily recitations. Twice a year, in January and June, they stood before an academic board to be examined. Their score in a subject was multiplied by a factor ranging from one-half to three corresponding to the topic's relative importance in the curriculum. Important subjects, such as engineering or natural philosophy, were weighted heavily; less important topics, like drawing or chemistry, had a lower factor. Cadets' scores were tabulated, then placed on a published list in order of merit. The General Order of Merit was then determined by adding together the scores for each of the individual classes. The General Order of Merit was of great importance, for it would later be used to determine which branch of service a cadet entered. The higher a cadet's final standing, the better assignment he would receive.[16]

Cadets in the Fourth Class, or "plebes," took only two classes in the fall, French and mathematics. The French lessons focused on grammar and translation, their purpose being to teach cadets to read French scientific and military books that would later be used as texts in other courses. The mathematics course began with algebra and was taught by Lt. William W. S. Bliss, an affable young man who, Ewell claimed, sometimes set "the whole Section to laughing at his grimaces." Like the course in French, Bliss's mathematics classes would be the foundation for future courses.[17]

Ewell began his studies with trepidation, for he knew that he had come to West Point with less education than most of his classmates. New England cadets seemed to have had the best training. "I have no hopes of getting a good standing at this place," Ewell lamented. "The Plebe class consists in all off [sic] nearly 150 and is said to be the most intelligent class that has been here for many years. There are several Yankees here who know the whole mathematical course; of course, they will stand at the head of the Class. A person who comes here without a knowledge has to contend against those who have been preparing themselves for years under the best teachers and who have used the same class books. The Yankees generally take the lead in almost every class."[18]

Despite his pessimistic predictions, Ewell did well. Having studied algebra in Virginia, he breezed through the first weeks of recitations and was placed in the first section of his class beside Sherman, Thomas, and Van Vliet. As the fall term progressed and new material was introduced, however, Ewell found the going tougher. Classes, he confessed to Ben, were "no joke," and he feared he would do poorly. He stayed up half the night studying by the dim light of coals glowing in the heating grate.[19] His perseverance paid off. At the end of January exams, Dick stood fourth in math, seventh in French, and third in general merit. He realized he would not be able to retain that position, however, and warned his mother not to boast to relatives and neighbors.[20] As anticipated, Dick fell off the pace in the spring, dropping to sixteenth in math and eleventh in French, despite such close application to his studies that he actually impaired his health. In general merit he plummeted to twelfth.[21]

With the end of the school year at hand, the members of Ewell's class put aside thoughts of books and blackboards and began looking ahead to their second summer encampment. "Our class have [sic] been debating how to spend the encampment in the most enjoyable manner," wrote Sherman. "They have concluded to spend it in the usual manner, that is, buy a library and have a dancing school. . . . I was put on the library committee—will have nothing to do with dancing."[22]

Unlike his classmate from Ohio, Ewell chose to enroll in the dancing school. He did satisfactorily until it came time to waltz. He repeated the steps over and over, but, try as he might, he could not master them. Finally the exasperated instructor threw up his hands in disgust and declared Ewell's case hopeless—the clumsy Virginian simply could not learn the dance! Stung by his failure, Ewell went back to the barracks and practiced the steps until he had them down pat. When he returned to the class one month later, the instructor was so astonished by his progress that he exclaimed, "Mr. Ewell, you are the best waltzer at the Point!" Elizabeth Ewell believed the success that crowned her brother's efforts pleased him more than the compliment to his skill.[23]

While at West Point, Ewell kept abreast of events in Virginia through family correspondence. Letters from home were his greatest source of pleasure, and he usually answered them as soon as he received them. Frequently his letters touched on the subject of love. No romance within the family circle escaped his peppery humor. Concerning the marriage of an elderly uncle, he wrote Ben, "What do you think of Mr. Ewell's marriage? I expect there will be another lot of young cousins in a few years. I'll bet the lady has twins the first offstart. The old man had lived single so long when I left home that he could not come within 20 steps of a lady without grinning from ear to ear and casting sheep's eyes at her." When his cousin and fellow cadet, Levi Gantt, returned to West Point after a visit to Stony Lonesome, Ewell wrote, "Miss Gray must have made a good impression on him, he has not done talking of her yet. I would not have believed that any woman could have made such a change in him. It looks more like magic than anything I ever saw. Formerly, the only way in which he ever showed his admiration for one of the fair sex was by abusing the fortunate lady most unmercifully. But Miss Gray appears to have lighted a flame which he does not try to conceal, with even this artifice."[24]

Of his own social life Ewell said little, probably because there was little to tell. During his first semester at school he wrote Ben, "I have seen very few handsome ladies since I have been here and have had nothing to do with them, which I believe is a very good thing as I am apt to think of them rather than of algebra." Three years later, in response to his mother's recommendation that he return to Virginia and pursue the affections of a local girl, Ewell wrote, "I am very much obliged to you for your information and advice concerning Miss Susan Macrae, but unfortunately I made a vow many years ago that I would never marry, and my resolutions have been confirmed by my maturer deliberations. You know there are two kinds of persons who never get married; one kind includes those who never 'fall in love,' the other (to which I belong) those whose hearts are very susceptible, yet owing to this quality are too tender to retain an impression long enough for it to lead to any dangerous consequences." For the time being, at least, the susceptible young cadet would remain a bachelor.[25]

Two months of drilling at the summer encampment brought Ewell to the advent of his second academic year. The 1837–38 curriculum again included French and mathematics, but it added a new course: drawing. Like all West Point courses, the drawing classes were utilitarian in their application, being designed to teach the cadets skills they would later need to execute maps and sketches to accompany military reports. For two years the course was to be Ewell's nemesis. He had absolutely no artistic aptitude, and his class rank dropped to thirty-third in that subject. Fortunately he continued to hold his own in mathematics and French, so despite a poor showing at the easel, he still ranked thirteenth in general merit by the end of the year.[26]

Traditionally cadets received a two-month furlough at the end of their second year. It was the only time during their four years at West Point that they were allowed to leave the post. Most took advantage of it to return home and visit their families. Ewell, however, elected to remain at West Point. The reason, quite simply, was money. Like most cadets, he had found it impossible to make ends meet, and by the end of his second year he found himself "a good deal in debt." Unable to pay for the trip home himself and unwilling to impose on the meager finances of his family, he regretfully declined his furlough and remained at the academy. While his classmates boarded ships that would take them home to family and friends, Ewell stayed behind to prepare for his third, and saddest, summer encampment.[27]

The 1838 encampment was not without its advantages, however. In addition to the added prestige due to a member of the Second Class, Ewell had the honor of being appointed third sergeant of his company. Cadets received such appointments based not on academic performance but on general deportment and soldierlike attention to duty. As a rule, corporals were selected from cadets of the Third Class, sergeants from those of the Second, and commissioned officers from those of the First. Cadet officers supervised other students in their company and assisted the faculty in maintaining discipline. As third sergeant, Ewell also acted as a guide and file closer during parade exercises and helped drill younger cadets. On 25 March 1839, for instance, as sergeant he was appointed to command a squad of eight cadets in the "School of the Soldier." Among those serving under him in that exercise were Robert S. Garnett, John M. Jones, and Don Carlos Buell. Being an officer was not all glory, however. With the honor came added responsibility. On 11 August 1838 he was placed under tent arrest for two days for allowing disorderly conduct among the cadets at his mess table.[28]

The summer of 1838 brought transition not only in Ewell's status at West Point but in the leadership of the academy itself. Five years after making Maj. Rene E.

West Point, ca. 1840 (Special Collections, U.S. Military Academy, West Point, N.Y.)

DeRussy superintendent, the War Department replaced him with Maj. Richard Delafield. DeRussy's ouster came as a result of his lax management. Discipline in the corps had declined significantly during his tenure, so much so that even Ewell remarked that matters seemed to be "going down hill with increasing velocity." The secretary of war apparently agreed, and on 1 September 1838 put in Delafield.[29]

Forty-year-old Richard Delafield was a New Yorker by birth. He had graduated from West Point in 1818 at the head of his class and as an army engineer had spent most of his career constructing fortifications near New Orleans, Louisiana, and at Hampton Roads, Virginia. Delafield was a short, stocky man with dark hair and a prominent nose. Energetic and active, he quickly restored West Point's iron discipline and initiated a series of sweeping reforms that echoed from the parade field to the mess hall. Although Ewell believed that it was "better for the inst that the Supt should have a character for strictness," most cadets disapproved of Delafield's unyielding discipline. Even the local inhabitants seemed intimidated. To Ben, Dick wrote, "The people about here are as much afraid of him as if he had absolute authority; none of the old women will make pies for cadets, within five miles around, some of them are even afraid to make them for their own use lest they should be suspected. Godfrey, our shoemaker, refused the other day to make three holes in a leather strap for pants, because it was customary to make but two. Money is of less service here than any place I ever saw," he added, "inasmuch as nobody will sell without the permission of the Supt. 'A new broom sweeps clean.'"[30]

Delafield's changes seemed to touch every aspect of the cadets' lives. Ewell was critical of his wide-ranging reforms, though he did favor certain changes, notably those pertaining to the mess hall. Early on, the young cadet had fallen into debt trying to satisfy an appetite that, he claimed, "would enable me to give a good account of an ox." Delafield not only improved the quality of the meals but cut their price nearly in half. "If we had always had him," Ewell admitted, "I would be out of debt, which I am far from being as it is." Lowering the prices of meals was just one measure by which the new superintendent strove to keep the boys out of debt. Forbidding needless expenditures was another. On 3 October 1839 Ewell wrote to his mother, "Major Delafield would not give me a dictionary because I am in debt, although it would be of immense advantage to me."[31]

Ewell's classmates returned from furlough on 31 August 1838 and commenced their fall studies the next day. Cadets considered the third year's curriculum the most difficult at West Point. The class in drawing continued, while chemistry and natural and experimental philosophy replaced mathematics and French. Chemistry included subjects that today would be classified under the heading of physics. Natural and experimental philosophy covered topics such as mechanics, acoustics, optics, and astronomy. In both subjects Ewell did well, ranking eighth in chemistry and fifteenth in natural and experimental philosophy. He felt he should have received a higher grade in chemistry, but as he explained to Ben, "it would have been contrary to the nature of things to put the 'big bugs' down for one whose standing in other branches was as low as mine. This, however, did not give me much uneasiness as I studied it rather to gratify my inclinations than for standing." If chemistry proved to be Dick's best subject, drawing continued to be his worst. In his third year he dropped to forty-third, just three from the bottom of his class. His lack of skill in that field reduced him to fifteenth in the General Order of Merit.[32]

By the start of his final year at West Point, Ewell had developed into not only an impressive student but an impressive soldier. He had a natural inclination for military life that his superiors recognized. As summer ushered in his last encampment, Dick received promotion to lieutenant of Company A, which was commanded by Stewart Van Vliet. James Longstreet, a Third Class cadet, was a corporal in the company. As a lieutenant Ewell assisted the company commander in his duties, inspected the barracks, and commanded platoons at drills. Among the many new cadets he drilled, and perhaps "devilled," was "Sam" Grant, a shy, stoop-shouldered lad from Ohio.[33]

In the summer of 1839 President Martin Van Buren, Secretary of War Joel R. Poinsett, and Gen. Winfield Scott visited West Point. The Corps of Cadets received them with honors.[34] Visiting dignitaries pricked Ewell's interest but seldom impressed him. One year earlier, Prince Joinville had come to West Point. "I believe a good many wished him safe at home," the Virginian wrote after describing the uncomfortable three-hour display staged for the prince's benefit. "He looked very much like a plebe though better dressed than the generality of animals, but just as awkward and unpolished. He did not at all come up to my idea of him. I was perfectly willing however to take the trouble of the review in order to have my curiosity gratified."[35]

Dignitaries were not the only curiosities at West Point that summer. In August, Delafield purchased twelve horses for the academy and introduced classes in riding.[36] As a member of the oldest class, Ewell was among the first to ride. He had grown up around horses and sat well in the saddle. Those who knew him later claimed he was "a horseman of unsurpassed excellence." Though not as handsome as some equestrians, "he had no peer for skill or management of a horse."[37]

Before the riding classes had ended, the fall curriculum started anew. Fourth-year students took five courses: mineralogy and geology, ethics, infantry tactics, artillery, and military and civil engineering. Civil engineering was covered in the fall, and military engineering in the spring. Crammed between the two was a brief, nine-hour session titled "The Science of War." This was West Point's most famous course and, from the cadet's standpoint, the most interesting. It covered a wide range of military topics from outpost duties to the organization of armies. The course culminated in grand tactics and strategy. As a member of the first section in engineering, Ewell received instruction directly from its professor, Dennis Hart Mahan.[38]

Mahan was the most renowned member of the West Point faculty. His texts on engineering and fortifications were famous throughout the Western world. Small in stature and aloof in bearing, he was respected by his students but never loved. One student described him as "the most particular, crabbed, exacting man that I ever saw. He is a little slim skeleton of a man and is always nervous and cross." In his classes Mahan preached the principles of Swiss military theorist Baron Henri Jomini, which stressed the importance of secrecy, speed, and maneuver in combat. So fascinated was Ewell by Mahan's lectures that he checked out a two-volume military study, *The Science of War*, the only time in four years that he withdrew a book from the school library.[39]

Ewell maintained his high standing during his final academic year, finishing tenth in mineralogy and geology, sixteenth in ethics, twentieth in infantry tactics, eleventh in artillery, and twelfth in engineering. At the end of four years he stood thirteenth in general merit among the forty-two cadets who graduated in his class, seven behind Sherman and just one behind Thomas.[40]

With his days at West Point nearing an end, Ewell had to plot his future course. His mother urged him to resign from the army and teach school in Virginia, but he rejected her advice as impractical. "I think I have nearly as much aversion to that life as yourself," he wrote her in reference to the army, "but you know that the education that we get here does not qualify us for any other than a military life, and unless a man has money, he is forced to enter the army to keep from starving." He wrote to Ben in a similar, if more humorous, vein. "I have no particular wish to stay in the army," he asserted, "but a positive antipathy to starving or to doing anything for a living which requires any exertion of mind or body" prompted him to do so.[41]

Determined to pursue a military career, Ewell had to decide which branch of the service to enter. He did not care for the artillery and had not graduated high enough in his class to be an engineer. This left the dragoons, marines, and infantry. The dragoons reportedly had better officers and more pleasant duties than some of the other branches of service, but they invariably occupied frontier posts, miles from civilization. The infantry also occupied western posts, which Ewell liked, but "not so far as to be out of the world" as to be cut off from society, as was the case with the dragoons. The marine corps also had its points. As a grandson of Benjamin Stoddert, Ewell had a natural "inclination for the sea"; moreover, the marine corps commander was so anxious to get West Point graduates to enter the corps that he was supposedly offering them their pick of assignments. Dragoons, infantry, or marines? Ewell's choice would affect his whole career. "You may see I am like an ass between 3 bundles of hay and all light on the subject would be of invaluable service to me," he told Ben. After much deliberation Dick chose the dragoons.[42]

The prospect of leaving West Point gave Ewell anything but pleasure. He confessed to Ben that "although I have suffered some pain and mortification since I have been here, yet the pleasures have more than counterbalanced the sorrows, &

it is hard to leave forever those with whom (in the language of one of our 4th of July toasts) we have shared the hardships of the camp and the terrors of the Blackboard." [43] But the event could not be postponed. On 1 July 1840 Ewell graduated from the U.S. Military Academy and was brevetted a second lieutenant in the First Dragoon Regiment. As he stepped aboard the ship that would carry him away, the popular West Point tune "Army Blue" may have come to mind. The lyrics that once held such hope and promise, however, now must have inspired doubt and foreboding.

> We've not much longer here to stay,
>   For in a year or two,
> We'll bid farewell to "Cadet Gray,"
>   And don the "Army Blue." [44]

CHAPTER 3

Not above His Merit

The rolling fields and broad vistas of Stony Lonesome must have been a refreshing sight to Dick Ewell after living for four years in the New York highlands. He had left the farm a rough country boy of nineteen and returned a proud, disciplined officer of twenty-three. Much had changed in his absence. Ben was married and residing in York, Pennsylvania; Tom was the president of a small academy in Tennessee; and Elizabeth had converted to Catholicism and moved to Georgetown, where she would soon take the vows of a novitiate. Sadly, Virginia was dead. The youngest of the Ewell daughters had succumbed to dysentery in 1837 and now lay buried beside her father and brother Paul in the family cemetery at Centreville. Dick may have visited the plot on his way home.[1]

Mrs. Ewell, Rebecca, William, and Fanny Brown still remained to welcome the young soldier home. The three women had changed little. Not so William, who had grown from a boy into a handsome young man of sixteen. At his mother's urging, he had dropped his father's surname and had taken to calling himself simply William Stoddert, a measure Elizabeth had at one time advocated to her other sons without success.[2]

Dick remained on leave at Stony Lonesome until the end of the summer, when he reported for duty at Carlisle Barracks, Pennsylvania. Tom thought his brother would have done better in another profession. "He would have made a good farmer but a better merchant," Tom predicted. "He has a calculating head, would have been frugal cautious & industrious. If he had, as originally intended, come to the West, he would have certainly been a richer & probably a happier man; the congeniality of his pursuits & his disposition would have made him contented, but the life of an officer will not please him."[3]

En route to Carlisle, Dick stopped at York, where he had the pleasure of meeting his new sister-in-law, Julia McIlvaine. To his disappointment, Ben was not at home. Dick returned to York two months later and spent a day with Ben, Julia, and the entire McIlvaine family. Present at the gathering were Julia's two sisters, Jane and Sarah, whom Dick considered the "two most strikingly pretty sisters I have ever seen." Jane, in particular, impressed him as "the handsomest lady I ever saw," though Ben believed Sarah the more captivating of the two. In matters of personal taste, Dick was the soul of tolerance. As he told Becca, "Doctors you know will differ." Before meeting Julia's family, Dick had lodged at a "filthy hog hole of a German Dutch tavern," which so aggravated him that he nearly left town without visiting either Ben or the McIlvaines. But he later confessed that "after changing my lodgings and seeing the ladies I would have been willing to have remained there a week instead of the day to which I was limited."[4]

Duty, however, required his immediate return to Carlisle Barracks. The army used Carlisle as a training site for dragoon officers. By 1840 there were two dragoon regiments in the army, numbering 750 men apiece. They wore sky blue trousers and navy blue jackets trimmed in orange. For weapons they carried percussion cap pistols, single-shot carbines, and heavy sabers known by the soldiers as wristbreakers. Such, at least, was the ideal. Rarely did their weapons meet this standard. As late as the 1850s, when regulations called for Sharps Carbines and Colt Revolvers, Ewell's command still carried a heterogeneous collection of firearms that one soldier described as no better than "old rattletraps."[5]

Capt. Edwin V. Sumner commanded at Carlisle Barracks. A veteran of the Black Hawk War, Sumner was an exacting disciplinarian. "He was of the old school," remembered one soldier, "rugged and stern, honest and brave, had a good conscience, was devoid of sensibility, detested frivolity, was austerely sober, and always reminded me of Cromwell's best puritan soldiers." Although many considered Sumner to be a martinet, he impressed Ewell as both a capable officer and "an excellent man." By October Dick expressed himself "very much pleased with Capt Sumner, who is strict with himself as well as with us."[6]

Sumner cracked the whip over his young officers. Each day the routine was the same: stable call between reveille and breakfast, drill and recitation in tactics until dinner, then more drill and stable duty until retreat. Ewell found the duties "constant and laborious," but he did not complain. Indeed, he told Rebecca that "so far from disliking the duties I would not care if they were increased as I spend the time more agreeably." Even the onset of winter did not interrupt the stringent routine. With some pride Ewell wrote, "We never think of stopping our drills for the cold. Capt Sumner says for his own comfort he wishes the thermometor [*sic*] would always remain 20° below zero so that common mortals have no chance with him. Thus far, thank my stars, I have been able to stand as much cold as others and think I can continue to do so."[7]

Social events tempered the hardship. Shortly after Ewell's arrival, Sumner threw a party for his officers, to which he invited Carlisle's most eligible belles. Ewell looked forward to showing off his waltzing skill, but he was doomed to disappointment. "I was near shocking the delicate nerves of one of the young ladies past recovery by asking her to waltz," he reported to Rebecca. "She told me with quite a tragedy queen air that the ladies of Carlisle never waltzed. I came within an ace of telling her the anecdote in Peter Simple where the breast of the turkey would not go down. The young ladies here are too puritanical to dance though they have no objection every now and then to a little flirtation and gossip." For all their faults, Ewell admitted a certain weakness for the girls, most of whom were of German descent. "There are some very pretty women among them," he confided, "and quite the first circles too. If it were not for an insurmountable prejudice I have to every thing which has the smallest claim to be called Dutch I should certainly fall in love with some of their pretty faces."[8]

Time might have overcome his prejudice, but on 20 November he received orders to report to Company A, First U.S. Dragoons, at Fort Gibson in what is now eastern Oklahoma.[9] Fort Gibson was one in a string of posts that stretched from Minnesota to Louisiana, delineating what military authorities optimistically termed the "permanent Indian frontier." West of this imaginary boundary, so the theory went, Indian tribes such as the Choctaw, Creek, and Cherokee could live without the threat of white encroachment on their land. East of it, white settlers could live and work without fear of Indian attack. The army's task was to patrol the fragile thousand-mile border and maintain peace.[10]

Ewell remained at Fort Gibson only a few days. His company had been reassigned to Fort Wayne in Cherokee Territory, and after a brief rest he joined it there. He arrived just six days before Christmas. What he saw must have disappointed him. The fort was nothing more than a collection of huts on a flat, desolate prairie. Less than 100 men occupied the post, and the nearest town— Bentonville, Arkansas—was twenty-five miles distant. The post's small size and isolation did have one advantage, though: it offered Ewell a wide range of responsibilities. In addition to his normal company duties, Ewell was the post quartermaster and commissary of subsistence. In the absence of superiors he sometimes also acted as post commander. "I like the duties very well," he told Ben, "except that my time hangs heavy on my hands and I am sometimes a little in the humour for society, although the last penchant comes less often every day."[11]

One duty Ewell did not relish was dealing with local contractors, whom he found ignorant and boorish. They "look upon an Officer as something infinitely below themselves unless they want to get a contract or something of that sort in which case their attentions and civil[i]ty become almost aweful [*sic*]," he told Rebecca. "I have the misfortune to be acting Quartermaster and have to make purchases, &c. and I assure you I find their impertin[en]ce at times unbearable. They will sit in my room for hours at a time very often before they will tell their business and quit although I have an office for their express benefit." As for hints about leaving, he fumed, "you might as well try them upon a runaway horse[.] take up a book or leave the room [and] they will wait as cool as a cucumber until you are through with the book, or for that matter inter[r]upt you with some such question as, 'Well do you know any news about more forces coming out here[?]' repeated for perhaps the twentieth time[.] The brutes actually put me in a furor sometimes."[12]

Fort Wayne was under construction when Ewell arrived. Company officers shared a small block of quarters containing three rooms and two kitchens.[13] To cook his meals and groom his horses Ewell purchased a young slave named Arthur. At one time he contemplated hiring a soldier to do the work, but he considered a slave more economical. He bought the fourteen-year-old black youth in the spring of 1842 for $600 with the understanding that at the end of two years the boy's previous owner could buy him back at the original purchase price. Either way, Ewell felt that he could not lose by the bargain. "A servant costs me about $12 a month," he explained to Rebecca, "so that you see I shall get at the rate of 25 per ct for my money & will make $300 by the transaction even if the negro is redeemed which is hardly probable as I think times will [then be] harder even than they are now. I am not able to more than half pay for him now & will borrow the rest." Apparently Ewell never questioned the morality of owning a slave. Indeed, he informed his sister that "as soon as I shall have squared myself [financially] with reference to the boy I believe I shall endeavor to purchase a woman."[14]

Some officers had wives to do the household chores, though few were so fortunate. At West Point Ewell had vowed never to marry, but a year of isolation on the prairie tempered that conviction. With a twist of humor he told Rebecca, "I really think if you can find any person about Stony Lonesome who would like a military life and who is fair to look upon that I would quit the lonesome life of a bachelor. Should you find one that you think would answer and that you can recommend you can give a letter of introduction and send her out. Maybe as there is a large lot to pick from you had better send a half a dozen so I can take my choice."[15]

A broad selection was a luxury that Ewell did not enjoy on the frontier. Eligible females west of the Mississippi River were scarce, and women with claims to beauty were practically nonexistent. "This is the worst Country for single ladies I ever saw in my life," he complained. "They are hardly allowed to come of age before they are engaged to be married however ugly they may be. . . . I have not seen a pretty girl or interesting one since I have been here."[16]

Some officers chose to marry less desirable women for lack of better; others kept Cherokee mistresses. Ewell rejected both options. He believed that a marriage borne of desperation would eventually end in grief. Reflecting on one such marriage, he wrote, "It is the fate of many officers who pass the ordeal of the world to fall a victim at an isolated post to a very inferior stock. It reminds me of a saying . . . 'Who knows the luck of a lousy calf that lives all the winter but to die in the spring?'"[17] As to keeping a Cherokee mistress, he refused to do so "both on account of my purse and taste. Occasionally a good looking half breed may be seen, but generally they are a dirty set and all have a smoky odor about them which is particularly disagreeable to me."[18]

He therefore continued to bide his time until a suitable partner came along. His loneliness at times must have seemed unbearable. At one point he jokingly told Rebecca that he had considered joining the Campbellite church just to shake hands with the girls. He only desisted when he discovered that "some of them had been crying and I believed wiping their noses without their hdks. [handkerchiefs], which is considered quite the thing here." Even on the frontier, Dick Ewell had his standards.[19]

The prospects of Ewell finding a bride in the West were poor, for he was not the most eligible bachelor. A low-grade officer of limited means, he had developed a distinct lisp and already was growing bald. "How does Richard contrive to please the ladies if he retains his peculiarities of articulation?" asked Tom in a letter home. "Young Love, a cadet from Nashville, said last summer on hearing me, 'Why you talk just like Old Dick.' So I presume my respected brother like myself says 'stho' when he wants to say 'so.'"[20]

Ewell apparently did not consider these anomalies a social barrier. In letters home he never made reference to his speech impediment and mentioned his loss of hair only once, and that in a humorous context. "I found not long since that all my hair was coming out and was obliged to shave my head to keep what little I have left from following suit, with, I believe, the desired effect. As there are no wigs to be had, I am obliged to wear a black silk skull cap. It would have made you laugh to have seen the people in the Court house stare when I took off my hat. I really believe they thought I had been shaved for some misdemeanor or other." His unadorned pate gave rise to a lasting nickname within the company. Thenceforth the men knew him affectionately as "Bald Head Ewell."[21]

Forces of a more fundamental nature meanwhile were at work shaping Ewell's personality. The strong religious faith instilled in him by his mother was slowly but noticeably eroding. Subtle changes in this direction may have first appeared at West Point, but they did not become manifest until he reached the Plains. Ewell maintained a bedrock faith in God, but organized religion no longer played an important role in his life. He did not own a Bible, and although he still attended worship services when possible, his devotion increasingly became one of form rather than of substance.[22]

The natural skepticism of youth, the nefarious influence of military life, and the lack of organized religion on frontier posts all played a part in his religious decline. More destructive still was the corruption he witnessed among Christian missionaries in the West. Itinerant preachers labored among the Indians in service to God. Unfortunately many also served themselves. Wife beating, fornication, theft, and adultery were just a few of the abuses Ewell attributed to the class. It was no wonder, then, that he expressed disapproval when informed that his brother William intended to become a missionary. "I was quite shocked at the thought of William's turning Missionary," he wrote. "I have seen so much injury done the Indians here by them that I am rather skepti[c]al as to their utility. Some of the greatest scamps we have are Missionaries."[23]

Whereas some men found solace in religion, others found it in a bottle. Ewell had a fondness for liquor and drank heavily while in the Old Army, though not to the dereliction of his duties.[24] The same cannot be said for Fort Wayne's commander, Capt. Isaac P. Simonton. Simonton was an alcoholic with a violent temper. In 1841 a subordinate officer preferred charges against him for intoxication and ungentlemanly conduct. A second officer then accused Simonton of snapping a carbine at him and attempting to run him through with a bayonet. In the resulting court of inquiry Ewell appeared as a witness against Simonton. The captain denied the charges, claiming that Ewell and the other officers at the post had formed a combination against him. Simonton's sudden death in February 1842 brought the issue to a close. With his demise Capt. Benjamin D. Moore became Company A's new commander.[25]

Alcoholism was not confined to the officer corps. Enlisted men regularly slipped across the border into Arkansas to visit grog houses that specialized in cheap liquor. Cherokee Indians also frequented such places, and when the two groups met, there was trouble. Late in 1841 Ewell attended the civil trial of four soldiers accused of killing an Indian in a drunken brawl. To his disappointment all four men were acquitted.[26]

Disturbances of this nature resulted in a decision by the War Department to abandon Fort Wayne in favor of a new post to be called Fort Scott located in Osage country, 100 miles north. Ewell was not pleased by the transfer, which would cost $4,000 and entail several months of work. The only ones who would benefit from the move, he told Rebecca, were the local inhabitants, who would turn a profit by hiring out their wagons and teams for transport.[27]

Captain Moore rode ahead to begin work on the new post in May 1842, leaving Ewell at Fort Wayne to supervise the transportation of public property. By the time the junior officer rejoined the company, construction of Fort Scott was well under way. The new post stood 100 miles south of Fort Leavenworth, near the spot where the Fort Leavenworth–Fort Gibson military road crossed the Marmaton River. The compound was laid out in the shape of a square and, like Fort Wayne, had no stockade. In appearance it was more like a village than a fort.[28]

Companies A and C of the First Dragoons initially manned Fort Scott alone, but in the fall a company of infantry arrived, increasing the garrison to 220 men. Ewell reached the fort in mid-July and was appointed post commissary. Occasionally his duties required him to go on detached service, but he spent most of his time on post. The presence of Federal troops had effectively quelled disturbances between the Osages and the settlers, making life at Fort Scott, in the estimation of post quartermaster Thomas Swords, "dull, very dull."[29]

That changed in 1843 with the advent of two mounted expeditions. In the spring Capt. Philip St. George Cooke received orders to escort a party of Mexican traders from Fort Leavenworth to Santa Fe. Company A was ordered to supply a platoon of men for the mission. Much to his disappointment, Ewell was not selected to take part in the expedition. Instead Company A's new commander, Capt. Burdett A. Terrett, chose to lead the detachment himself, leaving Ewell and the balance of the company at Fort Scott. Late that summer, however, Cooke announced his intention to lead a second caravan of traders to Santa Fe, and this time Terrett picked Ewell to command Company A's complement of troops.

Cooke's expedition assembled at Council Grove on the Santa Fe Trail, 120 miles northwest of Fort Scott. Council Grove was a heavily wooded oasis on an otherwise flat, untimbered prairie. Its trees were fed by the waters of the Neosho River, a clear and rapid stream. To all appearances the place seemed healthful, but the wet bottomlands harbored mosquitoes. Ewell reached Council Grove on 28 August, three days ahead of the main body of troops. While waiting for the others to arrive, many men contracted malaria, including Ewell, who would suffer from its effects for the rest of his life.[30]

Cooke reached Council Grove from Fort Leavenworth on 31 August, bringing troops from Companies C, F, and K. Detachments from Companies E and H stationed at Fort Gibson joined the expedition later. Having received timely notice of Cooke's approach, Ewell drew up his platoon to greet the captain. By then 140 wagons had assembled for the journey, to which were added hundreds of mules and oxen. Bad weather plagued the expedition from the start. Cold rains poured down day after day, transforming dry prairie roads into bottomless quagmires. The caravan slowed to a crawl. During the first twelve days it covered only 87 miles; after five weeks it had added only 126 miles more. "How depressing the circumstance!" despaired Cooke on 23 September, "—rain and frost, in a desert without fuel; —forage fast going the way of all grass; and no power to recede or advance, for the caravan is again stuck in the mud." Two days later there was a severe frost that caused terrible suffering among men and animals alike. For Ewell, however, hardship brought opportunity. When Ewell's superior officer fell ill from exposure, Cooke placed the young Virginian in charge of a squadron.[31]

By the fourth week out, the forage was nearly exhausted and food supplies had dwindled to the point that the men had to be put on half-rations. The cold and winds alone increased. Ahead lay the Arkansas River, the recognized boundary between Mexico and the United States. Sixty miles beyond that lay the Cimarron River. For Cooke the Cimarron River represented the Rubicon. If he crossed it, there would be no chance of returning to Kansas before winter. He would have no choice but to winter at Bent's Fort and return to Council Grove in the spring. On the other hand, if he turned back before reaching Santa Fe, the traders would be exposed to attack from Indians and freebooters. Cooke decided to go on.[32]

His decision met with the unqualified approval of his troops, who longed to visit the fabled city of the Southwest and dance the fandango with its beautiful raven-haired women. "Our spirits were raised to many degrees above boiling," Ewell wrote, "when, as if the devil had placed them there for our sins," they found fifty Mexican dragoons drawn up at the river's edge. The soldiers were part of a 500-man force sent by the Mexican government. Cooke gladly turned responsibility for the traders over to the Mexicans and led his men back to Council Grove. For Ewell and the other American soldiers who wished to see Santa Fe, it was bad luck indeed.[33]

No longer encumbered by the traders' slow-moving wagons, the dragoons reached Council Grove in just two weeks. Bad weather continued to plague the

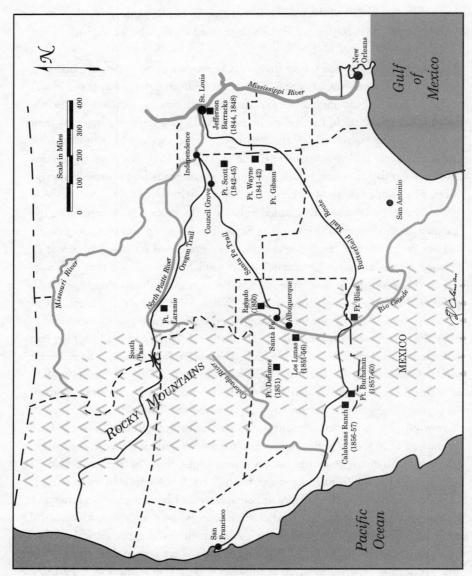

Gulf
of
Mexico

New Orleans

Mississippi River

St. Louis

Jefferson
Barracks
(1844, 1848)

Independence

Ft. Scott
(1842-45)

Ft. Wayne
(1841-42)

Ft. Gibson

San Antonio

Council Grove

Santa Fe Trail

Butterfield Mail Route

Oregon Trail

North Platte River

Missouri River

Ft. Laramie

Rayado
(1850)

Albuquerque

Ft. Bliss

Rio Grande

South Pass

ROCKY MOUNTAINS

Colorado River

Santa Fe

Ft. Defiance
(1851)

Los Lunas
(1851-56)

Ft. Buchanan
(1857-60)

MEXICO

Calabasas Ranch
(1856-57)

Pacific
Ocean

San
Francisco

The West

Scale in Miles

0   100   200   300   400

expedition, and fodder grew scarce. By 5 October the prairie grass failed altogether. The dragoons had to leave the Santa Fe Trail and march cross-country to the Arkansas River in order to obtain forage for their horses.[34]

The soldiers meanwhile subsisted on elk, buffalo, and other game. Near Ash Creek they encountered a herd of buffalo so vast, claimed Cooke, that they blackened the landscape with their numbers and shook the earth with their momentum. Ewell was "astonished with the novelty & grandeur of the sight," more so than he "conceived possible for a person of my phlegmatick disposition." He told Ben, "If you stand in the back door at home (whence there is the largest view) you cannot see land enough whereon to place the buffaloe I have seen at one coup d'oeil. You are aware that on the Prairie you can see at times ten or fifteen miles from the effects of Mirage, but there were points on the trace whence the bare Prairie could not be seen, hill after hill covered with buffaloe ad infinitum."[35]

One night a herd of bison stampeded toward the dragoons' camp, threatening to trample the soldiers to death. Thinking quickly, Cooke formed his men in a wedge in front of the wagons and ordered them to fire. Some of the foremost buffalo slumped dead on the ground, but those behind continued forward. The dragoons fired a second blast into the oncoming beasts, then a third. Bodies of dying animals lay piled up in a bloody heap just twenty feet in front of the blazing guns. The buffalo could take no more. Like water parted by the prow of a ship, the herd veered to the right and left to avoid the wall of flame. The camp was saved.[36]

The dragoons had to pass through one final ordeal before the expedition ended. Just outside Council Grove a prairie fire broke out near the camp. Fueled by high grass and gusting winds, the fire swept toward the camp, threatening its destruction. The soldiers rushed out with blankets to fight the flames, realizing, said Cooke, that the "provisions, baggage, everything, depended on success." After an exhausting battle of several hours, they succeeded in repelling the fire.[37]

The jaded horsemen trotted into Council Grove on 18 October 1843, more than six weeks after they had set out. Ewell left the main body at the Fort Leavenworth–Fort Gibson military road and led his detachment back to Fort Scott. In the course of the expedition he and the other troopers had traveled more than 700 miles and had been exposed to everything from snow to prairie fires. Of the many officers who participated in the expedition, Ewell alone received special mention in Cooke's report. "Lieut. R. I. Ewell has had during the fall a command—that of a squadron—much above his rank, but not above his merit."[38]

CHAPTER 4

A Man Much Esteemed

November 1843 found Dick Ewell back at Fort Scott, engaged again in the mundane administrative duties that comprised a large part of an officer's life. The excitement of the Santa Fe expedition made the isolated post seem dull by comparison. Hunting wolves relieved Ewell's tedium to some extent; conversing with the ladies at the post allayed it even more. Of the two species, Ewell found the wolves the most amiable. "We have three ladies at present here—two married," he told Ben. "A person would think they ought to be very intimate, whereas they do not visit. Napier says war is the natural state from man to the lowest insect; it seems to apply most particularly to the womankind."[1]

By this time Ewell had served in the West for nearly three years. Although his rank had not changed in that time, his reputation in the First Dragoons had grown considerably. He was recognized throughout the regiment as an officer of solid ability and enjoyed the good opinion of his superiors and the friendship of his peers. Few officers were more popular. Lt. J. H. K. Burgwyn, meeting Ewell in 1841, pronounced himself "much pleased" with the West Point graduate and esteemed him "quite an acquisition to the regt." A later visitor to Fort Leavenworth found Dick to be a general favorite among the officers there.[2]

He was less popular among the rank and file. His language and conduct toward his men, by his own admission, were sometimes severe. Later he would learn "that kindness gives a far more perfect control over the human as well as brute races, than harshness and cruelty," but that was in the future. In 1843 he demanded obedience; he did not inspire loyalty. Even so, at least one private at Fort Scott later recalled "many kindnesses" he received at the balding Virginian's hands.[3]

At Christmas Ewell left Fort Scott and accompanied Lt. John Love of Company C and another officer to Fort Leavenworth. While there, the three men attended a ball—"a pretty unique sort of affair it would be thought in Va.," Ewell assured his brother, "but quite elegant out here." Unfortunately the female company left much to be desired. There were few single girls over the age of thirteen at the party, and the older girls were generally unattractive. At one point an acquaintance introduced Ewell to an excessively heavy woman named Mrs. Pye. Ewell had no choice but to dance with her. "I got so mad before we sat down that I was in a perfect fever," he fumed. "She would not begin to dance untill I would tell her what to do & then she would keep dancing untill the musick began for the next couple. It was just as much as I could do to keep myself from shoving her along & I have no doubt she thought she was quite a Fan[n]y Elssler."[4]

Disappointing as it was, the trip to Fort Leavenworth whetted Ewell's appetite for civilization. He considered applying for a furlough, but with Captain Terrett on detached service and Lt. William Eustis on extended sick leave, he realized his request would be denied. Instead he applied to Col. Stephen Kearny for recruiting duty at Jefferson Barracks, Missouri. Jefferson Barracks was a larger post than Fort Scott, and it stood just ten miles from St. Louis, the most populous city west of the Mississippi. Kearny approved the application, and on 3 May 1844, after Terrett returned, Ewell headed east.[5]

Jefferson Barracks did not live up to Ewell's expectations; in fact, he found it "a most disagreeable Post." To his surprise the place was practically devoid of troops. The Fourth U.S. Infantry, which garrisoned Jefferson Barracks, had recently transferred to Fort Jessup, Louisiana, leaving the former post almost deserted.[6]

Lt. Ulysses S. Grant belonged to the Fourth Infantry. Grant was on leave when his regiment received its marching orders and therefore had not accompanied it to Louisiana. When he returned to Jefferson Barracks, he reported for duty to the senior officer at the post, which at that time happened to be Ewell. The dragoon remembered Grant from West Point, where they had been on friendly terms. After scanning the younger officer's papers, Ewell wrote an order authorizing Grant to join his regiment at Fort Jessup. When the Ohioan asked for a few days' extra leave before starting south, Ewell kindly granted the request. Grant never forgot the brief interview or the piping lieutenant from Virginia. "This was the same Ewell who acquired considerable reputation as a Confederate general during the rebellion," he later noted in his memoirs. "He was a man much esteemed, and deservedly so, in the old army, and proved himself a gallant and efficient officer in two wars—both in my estimation unholy." The next time the two officers met it would be as adversaries on the field of battle in the second of those unholy wars.[7]

Ewell repented having come to Jefferson Barracks. He had done so to enjoy a fuller social life, "but instead of being the pleasant Fort I had anticipated," he grumbled, "it is as lonesome as Fort Scott." Only a few "grass widows" of the

Fourth Infantry remained, and in Ewell's opinion they made "very poor company." They were "always grumbling about their Husbands," he wrote, so much so that he found it "quite a bore to call." [8] The ladies' constant complaints momentarily dampened Ewell's ardor for marriage. He told Ben that he "never saw a place so well calculated as Jeff. Brrks is, at present, to cure an Officer of a matrimonial disposition." Col. John Garland's daughters were exceptions to the rule. Ewell found the sisters "devilish pretty." Unfortunately they were both engaged, one to Lt. George Deas of the Fifth Infantry and the other to James Longstreet, who was then a lieutenant in the Fourth Infantry. "Except the Miss Garlands," Ewell lamented, "I have not seen a pretty girl or interesting one since I have been here." [9]

To escape the dull company of the post, Ewell made frequent trips to St. Louis. He made acquaintances among the military families there and visited his cousin Thomas Tasker Gantt, who was a prominent businessman in the city. In October Ewell accompanied Colonel Kearny to a "tea fight," an affair, he explained, in which "there was no dancing, but the company was expected to amuse itself by flirtations, &c. &c." The young lieutenant enjoyed a delightful evening, despite the absence of beauty among the female guests. "I do not think I ever saw a more homely set together," he commented with evident disappointment. The host's daughter was the exception. "Whether it was because her father was immensely wealthy or she really was so," wrote Ewell, "I thought I had not seen a more interesting looking young lady for a good many years." [10]

The life of a social blade suited Ewell to a tee, but it strained his modest budget. As the frugal Virginian dryly noted, a trip to St. Louis "being attended at all times with a certainty of spending a small amount & the possibility of spending a good deal, is not always agreeable." Since graduation he had struggled to stay out of debt, but without success. To make ends meet, he often found himself dependent on loans from Ben. His brother obliged him but cautioned him to practice economy. The advice was unnecessary. In October Ewell assured his brother that he was "economising [sic] as much as possible in order to lay up some money to go on furlough next Spring. Had I been left at Fort Scott I would have been able to save by that time nearly if not quite $800." As it was, he had to ask Ben for another $50. [11]

He was more successful in recruiting new soldiers than in saving money. He filled his quota in short order and by the fall of 1844 was ready to return to Fort Scott. On 16 October, however, he learned "in a kind of half official way" that Kearny intended to keep him at Jefferson Barracks through the coming winter, "an arrangement," wrote Ewell, "which, but for the expense, I should consider as very fortunate. The only thing that I care about is that I shall not have as much money to spend when I have a furlough as I would had I remained at Fort Scott. . . . This place is so expensive that I am sometimes afraid I will not have money enough to pay my expenses next spring, though I think I can afford to live on bread & water for one month." 12

As it turned out, Ewell wintered at neither Fort Scott nor Jefferson Barracks. Before the year ended, he received orders to report to Louisville, Kentucky, for more recruiting duty. It was a brief but pleasant assignment. "I am perfectly delighted with Louisville," he told Ben, "& the only drawback to my pleasure is the anticipation of having to return to the frontier to fried bacon and Indians." While in the city, Ewell entertained Henry Clay Jr., a son of the 1844 presidential candidate. His most cherished visit, though, was from his brother Tom, whom he had not seen since 1836. "It was to me like meeting with a stranger in whom one is interested & whose character is a matter of interest," he wrote Rebecca. Dick went to meet Tom at his hotel, but Tom had gone to get his trunk. Dick went out to find him. He eyed everyone he passed on the street until finally he spotted a young man, about six feet tall, with "fine eyes" and a slight stoop, that he thought might be Tom. He was correct. "He is a noble minded fellow & as talented [as] Mother ever anticipated he would be in her most sanguine moments," Ewell told his sister. "He excels in conversation & I should think must be a most excellent speaker." Dick later affirmed that he "never saw a person whose colloquial and other talents made a stronger impression on me." 13

Tom's trip to Louisville was nearly his last. Shortly after his arrival he contracted erysipelas, or "black tongue," as it was commonly known, a disease that inflamed the skin tissue. According to Dick, "Tom's face was swelled so much that he could not see & from the constant application of diluted lunar caustic was as black as Othello. The attack was accompanied with delirium & for several days while at its worst he was in great danger of his life. He left perfectly recovered but weak from abstinence during the attack."

Dick did not let his brother's indisposition interfere with his social calendar. "There are some beautiful girls in this place & nothing but poverty prevents my falling desperately in love," he told Becca. "I regretted very much that Tom's Phis [i.e., face] did not recover sufficiently for him to visit some of the ladies as his wit would have delighted them." One young lady in particular captured Dick's fancy. Though prudence forbade the mention of her name, he did not hesitate to enumerate her qualities—and faults—to Becca: "to state the question mathematically she is plus 4 or 5 negroes & an old uncle who has many more[,] a pretty good education & much reading[,] black eyes & beautiful hands—minus[,] she walks badly[,] once had dirty finger nails (important to know whether by scratching herself or not, but did not like to ask), is short & not a belle. She is a pious Catholic," he continued, "& declare[s] she is going into a nunnery, but I suppose that you would put [that] down to her credit[,] though to tell the truth I always thought a[t] church She was too fond of looking at the beaux to be much taken by the service." [14]

Peculiar gaits and dirty fingernails notwithstanding, Ewell maintained a high opinion of Louisville women. "As unsophisticated a personage as myself would most certainly fall a victim were it not that one heals the wounds left by another," he joked. One morning, while Dick was penning a letter to Ben, a waiter delivered a bouquet of flowers to his room. With it was a card that read, "From a friend, a Cincinnati bouquet." Ewell explained to his brother the flowers had been sent by a widow who "has been sparking me and who at present is on a visit to [Cincinnati]. She is rich and is engaged to be married but like most Widows is fond of a flirtation." With a blissful sigh he added, "These ladies do certainly plague one out of his life." [15]

Had he been free to indulge his inclinations, Dick undoubtedly would have stayed in Louisville until he had sparked or been sparked by every lady in the city. But the army had other ideas. With cold indifference to his social agenda, it abruptly transferred the amorous lieutenant to recruiting duty in Madison, Indiana, on 10 April 1845. He stayed there for just one month before returning to Fort Leavenworth to take part in a mounted expedition. On the way he stopped briefly in St. Louis to see Ben, who happened to be visiting Tasker Gantt. While there, he spent an evening in the company of a St. Louis belle "whose father has an income of $40,000 & he is daily adding to it." So, at least, reported the pragmatic Mrs. Ewell, who, like her son, took great interest in such matters. [16]

Ewell reached Fort Leavenworth toward the middle of May and found the post buzzing with activity. Colonel Kearny was preparing for what was to be one of the epic marches in American history. Kearny planned to escort emigrant parties along the Oregon Trail to South Pass in the Rocky Mountains, then return to Fort Leavenworth by way of Bent's Fort and the Santa Fe Trail. The purpose of the expedition was to impress the Plains Indians with a show of force, thereby deterring future attacks on American travelers. [17]

The Army assigned five dragoon companies to take part in the expedition— nearly 25 percent of its total mounted force. Four companies—C, F, G, and K— came from Fort Leavenworth. The fifth—Ewell's Company A—rode out of Fort Scott. Each company brought 50 men for a total of 300 rank and file. Among

Stephen W. Kearny (courtesy, the Arthur H. Clark Co., from Eugene Bandel,
Frontier Life in the Army, 1854–1861 *[Glendale, Calif.: Arthur H. Clark, 1932])*

those participating in the march were Capt. Philip St. George Cooke of Company K, Lt. Philip Kearny of Company F, and Ewell's friend from Company C, Lt. John Love. Lt. William B. Franklin of the Topographical Engineers went along to map the route. Unlike in the 1843 expedition, Ewell did not lead his company's complement of men. That honor went to Capt. William Eustis, the new company commander.[18]

The dragoons set out on 18 May 1845. Each company rode horses of a distinctive color: black for Companies A and K, bay for C, chestnut for F, and gray for Company G. The dragoons rode two abreast with a 100-yard interval between companies in order to avoid each other's dust. Each day the companies alternated their place in the column, enabling each to enjoy a place at the front. The spectacle of 300 dragoons stretched out along the prairie in line of march, said one witness, made for a scene "exceedingly picturesque and beautiful."[19]

Kearny set a course for the Platte River. Near the Platte he planned to pick up the Oregon Trail, which he would follow to Fort Laramie and to South Pass. The first night out an alert sentinel awakened the dragoon camp with the cry, "Company A—horse loose!" Eustis, Ewell, and others in the company scrambled to their feet and chased the animal through the tall, wet grass while their comrades in other companies roared in laughter. They laughed even louder after Eustis and his discomfited men captured the horse; it belonged to Company K.[20]

For six days the dragoons pursued their course without seeing a single party of emigrants. Finally on 24 May scouts spotted a long train of white-topped wagons moving west on a distant ridge. Word of the sighting caused a stir in the dragoon ranks. "We felt the same interest and excitement which a passenger, who has been long at sea, would experience as the cry 'Sail ho!' would greet his ears from the look-out aloft," wrote J. Henry Carleton. The wagons belonged to pioneers from Missouri, the first of many such groups the soldiers would encounter. In all, Kearny estimated that 850 men, 475 women, 1,000 children, 460 wagons, 7,000 cattle, and 400 horses and mules journeyed to South Pass that spring.[21]

The dragoons reached the Platte River and followed its sandy course west toward the Rocky Mountains. For two and a half weeks they traversed the prairie, sometimes under a scorching sun, sometimes in drenching rains. On 10 June the dragoons passed Court House Rock, described by Cooke as "a hill, or immense mound, which strongly resembles such a building, with wings; the sides are near a cream color, with apparently, a black roof." Later that day the column came within sight of Chimney Rock, a volcanic mass that from a distance looked "like the mineret [sic] of a mosque, or the smoke-pipe of a steamer." Several officers clambered up its rocky slopes and enjoyed a view of "surpassing loveliness." The last major landmark encountered by the dragoons was Scott's Bluff, a height rising 200 feet above the surrounding plain. To Cooke it seemed like a "Nebraska Gibralter," while to another pioneer it looked like "an immense castle . . . with battlements, towers and redoubts flanking it on all sides." [22]

The dragoons reached Fort Laramie on 14 June. They rested there for three days, then pushed on to South Pass. While at Fort Laramie, Kearny and his officers met with several Sioux tribes. Kearny told the Sioux that the Oregon Trail must be left open to emigrants and warned them against the use of whiskey. The Indians made a suitable reply, after which Kearny passed out gifts. As a climax to the day's events, the dragoons fired off a howitzer. [23]

On 17 June Kearny left Fort Laramie for South Pass with four companies. Ewell's Company A remained behind to guard government property until the rest of the regiment returned. Although they welcomed the extra rest, company members must have felt disappointment at not reaching the Rocky Mountains. Kearny returned to Fort Laramie on 13 July, picked up Company A, and headed home by way of the Santa Fe Trail. To reach the trail, he led his men south in a line parallel with the Rocky Mountains until he struck the Arkansas River. He followed the river downstream to Bent's Fort, where he picked up the trail. From there it was a straight line home. The jaded troopers reached Fort Leavenworth on 24 August 1845, having ridden 2,066 miles in just ninety-nine days. [24] Company A covered the 100 miles from Fort Leavenworth to Fort Scott in less than a week, and the men were back at their regular duties by early September. Ewell returned from the long march fevered and fatigued. Like many others, he placed himself on the sick rolls as soon as he reached Fort Scott. [25]

Ewell had been away from Fort Scott for fully sixteen months as a result of recruiting duty and the South Pass expedition. In that time he had sold Arthur, his only slave, whom he found to be "an incorrigible young scamp." He intended to buy another slave at the first opportunity, but not a boy, he insisted, "for I have had enough of them but some old man of 30 or 40 who might be depended on." He had hired a dragoon to do the chores in Arthur's absence, but the man was just not working out. "He made up my bed the other day with a comfortor [*sic*] between the sheets," Ewell complained. "On which side of the former he intended me [to] sleep I have no idea." [26]

The soldier's cooking was no better than his housekeeping. Ewell told his sister Rebecca about the visit of a married officer. As the man was leaving, Ewell's soldier-servant brought in two raw tomatoes, an onion, some salt, six cold sweet potatoes, and two small pieces of beef. Ewell invited his guest to stay for dinner, "thinking he would be as likely to sit in the fire," but to his surprise the officer sat down and pitched into the tomatoes. "Married men, on all such occasions, generally hurry off, on the first intimation of a meal," Ewell explained. "The only indiscretion of the kind I ever saw before was followed by an attack of indigestion which lasted the rash man a week."[27]

Some of the officers' wives, taking pity on the bachelor, sent him gifts of food and buttermilk. He reciprocated by bringing them grouse and other game that he bagged. Ewell always took his dogs with him when he went hunting. Curiously, he named each of the three animals after a brother or sister. "Bet. Bill & Tom are each paragons of sense & hunting qualities & each have a striking fancy for monopolizing . . . the best part of the fireplace," he informed Becca.[28]

In October 1845 Ewell received a leave of absence to visit his family in Virginia. He hoped to be home by Christmas. "What would be the chance of collecting some of the beauty & fashion of P. Wm. [Prince William County] at Stony lonesome [at] Christmas & having a regular blow out to a real fiddle[?]" he asked Rebecca. "It has occurred to me while writing this & I think it would be glorious[.] If it were necessary you might intercede with some young lady for a Dragoon & we might enliven the occasion with a wedding but let her not have large hands & feet which I abominate." Ewell left Fort Scott on 4 November. Though he did not know it at the time, he would never return.[29]

En route to Virginia, Ewell stopped at St. Louis to see his cousin Tasker Gantt. He then took a steamship to Nashville, Tennessee, to visit his Uncle George and Aunt Harriot Campbell. While on the ship, he suffered an attack of neuralgia in his head and eyes. He became so ill that he had to check into a hotel and summon a doctor as soon as he reached Nashville. The physician cupped him and applied other remedies in an effort to ease the pain, but without any obvious benefit to the sufferer. When the Campbells heard of Dick's condition, they took him to their home and nursed him back to health. In a few weeks he was well enough to travel, but the illness had depleted his meager funds and put him well behind schedule. He would not make it home in time for Christmas after all.[30]

From Nashville Ewell traveled to Jackson, Tennessee, to see his brother Tom and to visit the widow of his deceased uncle, William Stoddert. The Stodderts had taken Tom into their home late in 1836 in order to alleviate Elizabeth Ewell's financial burden. With financial help from the Campbells, they had seen to it that Tom had received a good education. Dick never forgot their generosity toward his brother. Many years later he told his niece that the Stodderts "treated your Uncle Tom in time of need with more kindness and forbearance than would have been shown, I fear[,] by any of us to any one in the world. . . . No Mother or Sister could have been more kind and forbearing than they were towards Tom."[31]

His brother had made the most of the opportunity the Stodderts had provided him. After graduating from Nashville College in 1840, he pursued a career in law, and just two years later he ran for a seat in the state legislature. Though he lost the election, he maintained his high standing among Democratic leaders in the state. At the age of twenty-two Tom was selected by his party to be an elector in the presidential campaign of 1844. But despite his thriving law practice and bright political future in Tennessee, he was anxious to go west. At the time of Dick's visit, Tom was planning to move to Texas, an idea his brother endorsed. Tom never left Tennessee, though. Before he could get away, national events carried him in a different direction.[32]

Dick left Jackson, Mississippi, in mid-December and set sail for Richmond, Virginia. He had suffered from malarial chills and fevers since returning from the South Pass expedition, and the long ocean voyage further impaired his health. By the time he reached Richmond, he was sick and had only fifty cents to his name. He had intended to take the stage from Richmond to Prince Edward County, Virginia, to visit his brothers Ben and William, but the stage left before he arrived. There would not be another one for two days. Rather than wait, he proceeded by coach to Stony Lonesome. A chill came over him just a few miles from his destination, and he had to stop overnight at a neighbor's house in Greenwich. The next day—New Year's Eve—his family fetched him home and put him to bed. So began his long-awaited homecoming.[33]

Ewell's mother, Elizabeth, and sister Rebecca successfully treated his cold with large and frequent doses of quinine, though Dick ascribed his improvement to the fact that he refrained from eating sausage at breakfast. As soon as he was back on his feet, he began making social rounds and accepting invitations to parties. At one gathering a widow grabbed his arm and would not let him go. Thereafter he shunned her. The beautiful Miss Powell of Middleburg was more to his liking. A friend believed that Dick was smitten by her charms, hardly a novel charge considering the amorous lieutenant's widespread sentiments.[34]

Ewell spent several days of his vacation in Washington, D.C. There is evidence that he may have met with Tom's friend President James K. Polk while there. He may also have taken the occasion to visit his sister Elizabeth, who was teaching school in Marlborough, Maryland. In her youth she was considered "intelligent, agreeable, and good looking," but her melancholy disposition and the want of a sizable dowry had discouraged serious suitors. Her conversion to Catholicism greatly distressed her mother. For many years the younger woman served as organist in Trinity Catholic Church, directing the choir and performing the masses of classical composers. She remained in Georgetown until her death in 1891.[35]

Late in January Dick Ewell's malaria returned with a vengeance. Relatives noted his hollow cheeks and sunken eyes and privately commented that his nervous system seemed "much deranged." His mother dosed him heavily with quinine, but it did little good. Twice Dick had to apply for an extension of his leave. Eventually he overcame the disease, but its wasting effects—exhibited in his thin body and pinched features—stayed with him for the rest of his life.[36]

When Ewell returned to duty on 1 May 1846, it was as a first lieutenant. He had received the promotion the previous September, but he probably did not hear the news until he reached Virginia. With his advancement came a transfer from Company A to Company G.[37] Ewell did not join Company G, however— at least not right away. While on leave, he applied for temporary duty with the Coast Survey, and he served in that department until 19 May.[38]

The Mexican War cut short Ewell's assignment with the Coast Survey. In 1845 America's long-simmering dispute with its southern neighbor came to a head. President Polk annexed the independent Republic of Texas and sent General Zachary Taylor into territory claimed by Mexico near the mouth of the Rio Grande. Mexican troops attacked Taylor on 24 April 1846. Seventeen days later Polk declared war.[39]

Congress appropriated $10 million for the war and called for 50,000 volunteers. Ewell was transferred from the Coast Survey to recruiting duty in Ohio. He set up a recruiting station at Cincinnati, then moved on to Columbus and Zanesville. Finding that recruiting stations had already been established in those cities, he set up shop in Chillicothe. He rode south to Portsmouth to determine the feasibility of a recruiting center at that point, then headed west to Newport, Kentucky, to procure clothing for the recruits. By 20 June he was back at Chillicothe.[40]

While passing through Dayton, Ohio, Ewell learned that Col. Stephen Kearny had ordered Lt. John Love to close his recruiting station and rejoin the regiment. Kearny was preparing to lead the dragoons to Santa Fe. Like all young officers eager for glory, Ewell did not want to miss the action. On 4 June he asked the adjutant general for permission to join Company G.[41]

The adjutant general took no action on his request. Ewell was disappointed, but he did not give up. Lt. Philip Kearny's Company F was then at Jefferson Barracks. Kearny had orders to join Taylor's army on the Rio Grande, and he was short an officer. At Ewell's request, Kearny had Ewell assigned to temporary duty with his company. "He could not have confer'd a greater favor upon me," Ewell wrote his mother, "as otherwise I should have been sent to Fort Leavenworth, on very disagreeable duties & have run great risks of being sick, besides the morti-fication of being at a garrison in time of war." [42]

Ewell reported to Kearny at Jefferson Barracks late in August 1846, bringing with him twenty-seven men he had recruited at Chillicothe. [43] For five weeks Kearny and Ewell drilled the troops to prepare them for the coming campaign. Training came to an abrupt halt on 5 October when the company received orders to go to Point Isabel, Texas. Within twenty-four hours it was on a transport head-ing down the Mississippi River. "We left Jeffn. Barracks on tuesday, the day after our orders were recd. with 91 men, armed & equipped for [one] years service in the field," wrote Ewell, "& when you take into consideration that our own private affairs had to be attended to, as well as public, & that the men & horses had to be provided for, you will see that Lt. Kearny . . . deserves great credit for promp[t]ness & energy." [44]

After a brief stopover in New Orleans, Company F landed at Point Isabel, Texas, at the mouth of the Rio Grande. It halted there briefly before joining Tay-lor's army at the front. For the first time Ewell faced the prospect of combat. Six years of military service had trained him thoroughly in the art of marching, drilling, recruiting, and army administration. How he would respond to the chal-lenge of battle remained to be seen.

CHAPTER 5

To the Cannon's Mouth

By the time Company F reached Point Isabel in November 1846, the American government had blockaded the Mexican coast and launched two major campaigns. In the West Col. Stephen Kearny had marched toward Santa Fe with the First Dragoons, bent on claiming the New Mexico and California territories for the United States. At the same time Gen. Zachary Taylor had advanced into north-central Mexico, defeating the Mexican army at Palo Alto and Monterrey. Taylor then camped at the city of Saltillo. In December Company F joined him and took part in several routine scouting expeditions. Ewell brought a servant with him.[1]

Kearny's and Taylor's campaigns, though highly successful, failed to crush Mexican resistance. For the war to end, America would have to capture Mexico City. Gen. Winfield Scott was selected to lead the expedition. He planned to land his army at Vera Cruz on the Gulf Coast and advance to Mexico City over the National Highway. Taylor dispatched Gen. William J. Worth's division from Saltillo to reinforce Scott's army. Company F rode with Worth. In the upcoming campaign, it would have the honor of acting as Scott's mounted escort.[2]

Scott organized his 10,000-man army into four divisions led by Generals Worth, David Twiggs, Gideon Pillow, and John A. Quitman. While waiting for the campaign to begin, Ewell renewed acquaintances with old friends, including his cousin Levi Gantt. Dick had not seen Levi since they had parted at West Point five years earlier. At one point it was doubtful whether his indolent cousin would graduate from the academy, but he did and was now a first lieutenant in the Seventh Infantry.

Dick also saw his brother Tom, who was a first lieutenant in the First Mounted Rifles. When he was not drilling, Tom took time to visit his brother at Palo Alto. "I found Dick, looking rather badly," he reported to Ben, "for he has been quite sick this Winter—however the prospect of getting knocked on the head at Vera

Cruz cheers him up. He complains of not hearing from Virginia for I don't know how many months." Dick's company moved to the mouth of the Rio Grande on 15 February 1847. Ten days later it boarded a ship for Vera Cruz. The ship lay off the coast for a week before finally setting sail for Mexico.[3]

A rough four-day voyage along the Gulf Coast brought the fleet to Vera Cruz. After a reconnaissance, the American army put ashore three miles south of the city. The Mexicans did not contest the landing. Scott secured the beachhead, unloaded supplies, and surveyed the Mexican position. On 16 March he invested Vera Cruz and brought up siege batteries to batter the city's walls. After a four-day bombardment, the Mexicans surrendered the city. The American army marched into Vera Cruz on the twenty-ninth with bands playing. Success had crowned its first efforts.[4]

The prevalence of yellow fever along the coast prompted Scott to move inland at the earliest opportunity. Ewell was among those who fell victim to the disease, but he refused to take himself out of action. "During the almost entire campaign, Captain Ewell, although suffering with ague & fever, was never out of his saddle when an enterprise was to be undertaken or deeds of daring to be performed," Scott wrote with approval.[5]

The American army started down the National Highway toward Jalapa on 8 April, the first step on the road to Mexico City. Scott and his staff left Vera Cruz four days later with Company F as their escort.[6] Ahead, Gen. Antonio Lopez Santa Anna blocked the highway at a mountain pass called Cerro Gordo. A river protected one of Santa Anna's flanks, and high hills the other. The highway passed through the center of his line and was exposed to Mexican batteries posted on either side. Scott and his officers examined the position closely, looking for a suitable point of attack. Tom Ewell found it. While scouting on the right, he discovered a mountain road that led to Santa Anna's flank. On 17 April Twiggs's division, using that road, attacked Mexican batteries at La Atalaya, one of two hills anchoring Santa Anna's left flank. The next morning Twiggs captured Telegraph Hill, the remaining enemy position. Tom Ewell led his company into battle each of the two days and was the first man to enter the Mexican works on Telegraph Hill. He cut down the first enemy soldier he met with his sword and had raised his arm to strike down a second when he was shot through the stomach.[7]

Scott had held Company F in reserve throughout the battle, but when Twiggs swept the Mexicans from Telegraph Hill, the horsemen charged forward in pursuit. At the base of the hill Dick ran into Levi Gantt, who told him of Tom's injury. Dick found his brother on the ground surrounded by a crowd of officers. He knelt at Tom's side and examined the ghastly wound. The bullet had entered

Tom's stomach one inch from the navel and had halted near the spine. Tom asked Dick to write home and told him that he had given his watch and purse to Major Loring. He observed that his wound was fatal but claimed he would rather die than continue to suffer. Dick could not stay to hear more. The dragoons were in pursuit of the Mexican army, and duty demanded that he return to his company. With unspeakable emotion, he left Tom in the care of others and galloped away.

Dick returned at 7:00 P.M. As he approached the place where Tom lay, a doctor confirmed that his brother's wound was mortal. Dick found Tom resting easily, "calm as though he were going to prepare for sleep." Earlier Winfield Scott had paid the dying man a visit. "Dick, did you hear what General Scott told me?" Tom asked as his brother knelt by his side. "'Mr. Ewell, you are an honor to your name, an honor to the service to which you belong.'" Tom's smile faded as he described the morning's attack and the circumstances surrounding his injury. In a soft voice he expressed the wish that his great suffering might be an expiation for his sins. Dick stayed with his brother throughout the long night. After midnight Tom observed that his legs were becoming numb. A short time later he placed his hand on his thigh and said, "That leg has assured the ball," referring to his impending death. His breathing became easier, and sometime after 1:00 A.M., with his brother at his side, Tom Ewell quietly breathed his last.

Dick procured some rough planks and nails and fashioned a rude coffin. With the help of three other officers, he buried Tom where he had died. That had been Tom's wish. Having completed that sorrowful task, Dick walked to the spot where Tom had received his injury. The hill was covered with corpses. Dick picked his way through the carnage, then returned to camp. It was a cruel introduction to war.[8]

The American army did not remain long at Cerro Gordo. As soon as possible it moved on to Jalapa, then to Puebla. Scott halted there for ten weeks to await supplies and reinforcements from Vera Cruz. Ewell escorted wagon trains to and from the port city during the lull. "This country is to all intents & purposes conquered," he declared in a letter home. "No Army or anything else. St. Anna is a wanderer & though he may raise 1 or 2000's to attack a baggage train [he] cannot raise another formidable Army unless with most extraordinary assistance from our bad management. We have only to send home the volunteers & keep possession for a year or two & extend our laws to make this a part of the United States." The young imperialist concluded on a personal note: "The chances are slightly in favor of my being a Captain at this time."[9] As it turned out, he was wrong both as to his own promotion and as to the strength of Santa Anna's army.

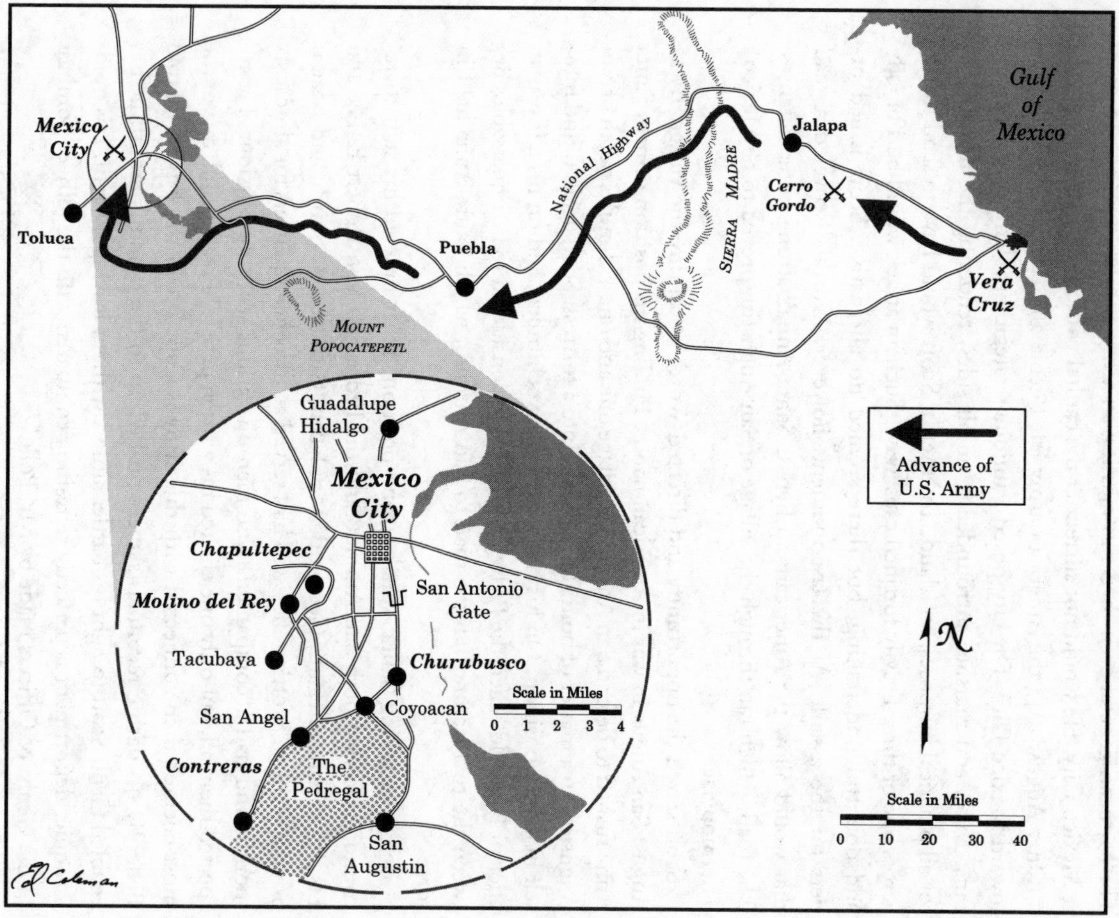

Mexican War

Gulf of Mexico

Vera Cruz

Jalapa

Cerro Gordo

SIERRA MADRE

National Highway

Puebla

MOUNT POPOCATEPETL

Mexico City

Toluca

Advance of U.S. Army

Scale in Miles
0   10   20   30   40

Scale in Miles
0   1   2   3   4

Mexico City

Guadalupe Hidalgo

San Antonio Gate

Churubusco

Coyoacan

Chapultepec

Molino del Rey

Tacubaya

San Angel

The Pedregal

Contreras

San Augustin

E. Coleman

The Mexican general even then was massing an army of more than 25,000 men at Mexico City. He would not surrender the capital without a fight.

On 7 August 1847 the American army left Puebla and continued its advance toward Mexico City. The city posed a unique strategic problem for the Americans. Lakes and marshes surrounded it on all sides, rendering the metropolis, for all practical purposes, an island. To enter it, Scott would have to send troops across one of three heavily fortified causeways. Such an attack would be a bloody and doubtful undertaking, but there seemed no alternative. Scott issued orders for the assault. At the last moment, however, Worth discovered a road that would allow the Americans to bypass Santa Anna's strong outer defenses. The road, which ran through the village of San Augustin, proved to be Mexico's Thermopylae.[10]

Scott seized the opportunity and directed Worth to capture the village. By 17 August San Augustin was in American hands. Finding his position turned, Santa Anna rushed to defend San Antonio, a village one and one-half miles north of San Augustin. In a matter of hours he turned it into a fortress. Scott again found himself in a tight position. On his right was Lake Xochimilco, and on his left was an ancient lava field called the Pedregal. Both were considered to be impassable. Between the two features ran the road to San Antonio, which Santa Anna held in force.[11]

Before attacking Santa Anna's strong position, Scott ordered his staff to reconnoiter toward both San Antonio and the Pedregal. Capt. Robert E. Lee and Lts. P. G. T. Beauregard, George B. McClellan, Gustavus W. Smith, and Isaac I. Stevens were on Scott's staff. Ewell had served at army headquarters for almost six months and had accompanied these men on various scouting missions. He respected them all, but only one elicited his written praise. "I really think one of the most talented men connected with this army is Capt Lee of the Eng's," he told Ben. "By his daring reconnais[s]ances pushed up to the cannon's mouth he has enabled Genl. Scott to fight his battles almost without leaving his tent. His modest, quiet deportment is perfectly refreshing compared with the folly & bombast of the Genls. & Officers made by Mr. Polk."[12]

Lee and Beauregard led the 18 August reconnaissance toward the Pedregal, supported by Kearny's troopers and two companies of infantry commanded by Lt. Col. William M. Graham. As the party approached the volcanic formation, it was shot at by Mexican soldiers concealed among the rocks. It was Ewell's first time under fire. "It was some time before I could clearly comprehend," he reflected, "but presently a horse in [the] ranks tumbled over, shot through the heart, & I could hear the bullets striking the ground around us & singing over our heads." Kearny sent Ewell with half the company to turn the Mexicans out of their position. Finding themselves flanked, the Mexicans withdrew, leaving eight or ten dead and about as many prisoners in American hands.[13]

Once the Mexican skirmishers retreated, the engineers began their reconnaissance. Again fortune smiled on the American army. Lee and Beauregard discovered a path through the Pedregal that led to the town of Contreras. Scott ordered yet another turning movement. On 19 August, while Worth demonstrated in front of San Antonio, Pillow led his men across the Pedregal to Contreras. He attacked the Mexicans there and put them to flight. Pillow's success turned Santa Anna's position and opened the road to Mexico City. With American troops in his rear, Santa Anna evacuated San Antonio and fell back to Churubusco.[14]

While Worth engaged the Mexicans at San Antonio, Twiggs and Pillow pressed forward toward Churubusco in an effort to cut off their retreat. The road from Contreras to Churubusco ran through Coyoacan. There the road forked. The left branch went to Churubusco, while the right branch led to Santa Anna's rear at San Antonio. Scott sent Lee with Company F and a company of mounted rifles to scout the San Antonio road. Pillow's division followed him while Twiggs moved on Churubusco. When Lee reached San Antonio, he found the Mexicans in full retreat toward Churubusco, pursued by Worth. Pillow's division and Company F joined the pursuit.[15]

Twiggs, Worth, and Pillow assailed the Mexican army at Churubusco and routed it. Kearny pursued the Mexicans with Company F and three other dragoon companies. With some difficulty he edged his men forward through the debris of battle and crossed the Churubusco River bridge. Col. William S. Harney, the army's cavalry chief, ordered him to push on after the Mexicans. Led by Company F, Kearny's dragoons thundered down the causeway, riding down all who stood in their way.

Ahead, at the entrance to the San Antonio Gate, stood a Mexican redoubt mounting two guns. "The gate was a good deal obstructed," remembered Ewell, "& we pushed them so rapidly that they got into the water on each side of the road—began firing upon us & to some effect too. When we approached the gate I saw the crow[d] before us open as if by one movement & then saw a piece of artillery frowning over the works." Without waiting for their own men to clear the way, Mexican gunners poured canister into the milling crowds of soldiers crowded about the gate. Kearny leaped from his horse and, shouting for his men to follow, rushed into the battery. It was then that Ewell discovered, to his horror, that Kearny's forces had dwindled to a mere handful of men. "Col Harney had ordered the recall to be sounded in the rear," he explained, "& as it took some time for the information to get to the head of the column, they not being able to hear in all the noise & confusion, we were engaged while the rear was retreating. Col. Harn[e]y had refused to lead the charge & of course should not have interfered as it was out of his power to control after we passed him." [16]

Kearny and Ewell found themselves inside the enemy works with just five officers and a dozen privates. They had no choice but to retreat. At peril to their lives, they left the battery and scrambled back down the narrow causeway. Canister from the Mexican guns shredded their ranks. Ewell escaped injury but had two horses shot from under him, "one by a Musquet [musket] from the side of the road, the other by a canister shot through the neck." The second animal was able to bring him back at a walk. Kearny did not fare so well. During the retreat a canister ball shattered his bridle arm, making it impossible for him to guide his horse. Ewell seized Kearny by the waist and brought him safely off the field. "Only a miracle saved Capt. K & myself," he commented. With Kearny disabled, Ewell assumed command of Company F.[17]

The defeat at Churubusco left the Mexican army in disarray. Had Scott pressed his advantage, he might have captured Mexico City at once. Instead he unwisely halted his advance and opened peace negotiations with the Mexican government. For two weeks American troops waited just outside the city walls while the talks dragged on. "The opinions regarding peace are as diverse as they would be on the subject of rain next week," Ewell wrote his mother. "In the mean time we are kept waiting around the suburbs of the city in the most disagreeable state imaginable, not permitted to enter & very much an[n]oyed with ennui & fleas." He addressed his letter "3 miles from the Halls," presumably in reference to the Halls of Montezuma.[18]

While the American army waited outside Mexico City, Santa Anna prepared his army for the next wave of American attacks. Hostilities resumed on 8 September when American troops seized Molino del Rey, a mill southwest of the capital. Four days later, American artillery opened a furious bombardment on Chapultepec, a castle that guarded the southwest approaches to the city. American troops assaulted the fortress the next day and captured it in a brief but bitter struggle. In the fighting Levi Gantt was killed.[19]

Gantt had visited Ewell at Tacubaya shortly before his death. He was in low spirits. He had volunteered to be a member of the party that was to storm Chapultepec's walls that morning, and he did not think he would survive. He came to bid his cousin farewell and to give him directions concerning his affairs. After ten minutes Levi returned to his command. He died a short time later from a musket ball in the chest.[20]

Thanks to the sacrifice of Gantt and others, Chapultepec fell to the Americans. At 8:00 A.M. Scott triumphantly entered the city's Grand Plaza, accompanied by the dragoons. The troops cheered and the bands played "Yankee Doodle" as the commander in chief rode up and down the dressed lines of his victorious army. Dismounting, he joined his generals inside the royal palace to draft an order announcing the victory. After six months of hard campaigning, Mexico City belonged to the Americans.[21]

Dick did not learn of Levi's death until the ceremony at the city square had ended. The next morning he interred his cousin's corpse in the churchyard at Tacubaya. Levi's death must have been quite a blow to Dick, coming as it did on the heels of Tom's demise. Dick had known Levi since childhood and had been his chum at West Point. In the weeks before his death, they had been as close as brothers. Dick told his mother, "Our intercourse had been very intimate whenever we had come together, which was the case at Monterrey, Vera Cruz, Jalapa, Puebla, & more particularly between the battles of Contreras & Cha[pultepe]c. His sympathy for the loss of [Tom at] Cerro Gordo was invaluable to me & . . . in a great measure [served] to bring us closer than we had ever been before."[22]

Mexico City's capture ended the war for all practical purposes, but a peace treaty was still months away. Until then, the Americans became an army of occupation. It was an enjoyable assignment. When they were not engaged in their military duties, soldiers enjoyed theaters and bullfights and dated the city's dark-eyed señoritas. Like most soldiers, Ewell found Mexico City a beautiful and fascinating place. He picked up some Spanish while there, but if he wooed any Mexican women, he did not record the fact. Ewell was one of 150 officers that founded the Aztec Club, a fraternal organization formed in October 1847 to perpetuate the names and deeds of those officers who took part in the Mexican War.[23]

The army maintained strict discipline throughout the occupation, but crimes occurred nonetheless. In a letter to his mother Ewell described how four officers and eight soldiers had broken into a Mexican house, robbed it, and murdered the owner. One of the thieves was later arrested and turned state's evidence against his accomplices. Within a few hours they were all behind bars. "It is very much to be hoped that the whole batch will be hung," Ewell wrote.[24]

Ewell remained in command of Company F until 22 December. At that point he took command of Company K, which had lost all of its officers. Not long after, he learned that he had been breveted captain "for gallant and meritorious conduct in the Battles of Contreras and Churubusco."[25]

Ewell kept active during the occupation, conducting routine patrols, carrying dispatches for General Scott, and escorting wagon trains between Mexico City and Vera Cruz. During one trip to the coast he was stung in the leg by a large scorpion. "He had stung me twice below the knee," Ewell told his mother, "without causing as much discomfort as if it had been a bee, though some Mexs. gave me a horrid account of what was to take place in a few hours. I think this shows fairly the exaggeration that exists about this country. . . . I have been almost equally disappointed in every thing I have seen from this to [Mexico] City." That included the inhabitants. "A more stupid, begotted [sic] race cannot easily be imagined," he wrote critically. "Almost half of every City I have yet seen is in ruins & though there is an immense population of beggars but a small part of the land is under cultivation."[26]

Ewell joined a 2,000-man expedition sent to capture the city of Toluca, thirty miles west of the capital, in January 1848. Before the Americans reached Toluca, a delegation of citizens met them and offered to surrender the city. "They had prepared quarters in anticipation, & recd. us as long expected guests," Ewell wrote. He personally carried news of Toluca's surrender to General Scott at Vera Cruz and dined at the general's table. He then returned to Toluca, where he remained throughout the remaining months of the occupation.[27]

The relatively easy garrison duty at Toluca should have benefited Ewell's frail health, but it did not. As winter set in, his malaria returned. Gen. William O. Butler offered him a three-month leave of absence to recover his health, but Ewell felt he should remain on duty. Dragoon officers were scarce in Mexico, and he had a rare opportunity to hold a command above his rank.[28] In any event, it looked like the occupation would soon be over. The United States and Mexico signed a peace treaty on 2 February 1848. It only remained for the governments of both countries to ratify the document to end the war. "To use a common expression here," Ewell wrote to his mother in April, "peace stock is very high. Genl. Scott told me that he had very little doubt but that the Mexican Congress would immediately agree to the treaty, particularly as the modifications were agreeable to all parties." Scott was correct. Both governments ratified the treaty, and in June the American soldiers boarded ships bound for the United States. After twenty months at war in a foreign land, they were going home.[29]

Company G soon found itself once more amid the familiar surroundings of Jefferson Barracks. When he was able to break away from work, Ewell visited friends and relatives in St. Louis. Acquaintances were struck by his cadaverous appearance. Tasker Gantt noticed that Dick was "extremely thin" and that his health was "shattered." As usual the culprit was malaria. Many soldiers had returned from the war slightly debilitated, but "in his case," wrote Gantt, "the ill-condition of the system was of longstanding before he went to Mexico, and now in place of the intermittent fever which formerly attacked him, he is severely afflicted with neuralgia. . . . Neuralgia is a very common form of intermittent fever—just as headache is one of the most frequent symptoms of dyspepsia." Ewell's disease was so severe that he applied for a leave of absence and even considered resigning from the service altogether. He feared that returning to frontier duty would seriously impair his health, as it had at Fort Wayne and Fort Scott. Rather than remain in the army, he told Gantt that he wished to raise livestock at Stony Lonesome or some other farm in Maryland or Virginia.

Gantt persuaded Ewell not to resign, arguing that farming in the East was unprofitable and offered no mental challenge. He advised his cousin to remain in the army, where he had "the solid advantage of a good income and an honorable position." Gantt enlisted Ben Ewell's help in talking Dick out of leaving the army. "Dick has not a very contented spirit," he wrote, "at least he has never been content since I have known him. . . . Pray consider closely this matter carefully before you see Dick, and the more facts you have to offer him, the greater the amount of deterring examples you can parade for the purpose of making his soul afraid within him, the better."[30]

Ewell left Missouri in August 1848 on a leave of absence and headed home to Virginia. By the time he reached Stony Lonesome, he was "in a very critical state. . . . Fits of nausea came constantly on & he was just on the verge of inflammation of the stomach," wrote his brother William. "He had an attack [of] Chol[ora] Morbus one night. This was a result of torpidity of the liver for which I prescribed blue pill which[,] however, he would not take until the Doctor seconded me." At the advice of an army physician, Dick visited Warrenton Springs to avail himself of the waters. Later he went to Washington to have a tooth plugged.[31]

As Ewell's health improved, he began taking an interest in Stony Lonesome's management. He had decided opinions about livestock and agriculture, and he shared those ideas with William, to the younger man's delight. "He reasons & talks without appearing to have the idea that I am a perfectly worthless child," William noted with pride, and "I am pretty determined to show him that he is not mistaken." Living at home with his mother and older sister Rebecca, William knew what it was like to be henpecked. Dick initially escaped the ladies' barbs, but William knew that would not last. As he told Ben, "The last [person who] comes is & has been from time immemorial [*sic*] treated to all the [attention] until by some base construct about the seven[th] or eight[h] day he shows himself unworthy of the high honor & trust reposed in him & is himself served up in small bits."[32]

But Dick was not easily pinned down. In addition to his trips to Washington and Warrenton Springs, he went hunting with friends, attended a dance at Mount Vernon, and traveled to Williamsburg to see Ben. While in Williamsburg he and Ben went to see the Eastern Lunatic Asylum. "There might be many worse things than a berth in the asylum," mused Dick as he gazed at the building. Ben nodded his head in agreement, adding that the asylum might be a good place for their whole family.[33]

Dick's leave expired in October, and on the twenty-seventh he reported for recruiting duty at Carlisle Barracks. It was an easy assignment featuring regular hours and little responsibility. When he was not in the office, Ewell hunted partridge and cast his line for trout. In the evening he attended parties and paid social calls on ladies in the town. Like a child in a candy store, he declared, "If I only knew how to choose[, I] might yet get suited to a fraction." Ewell invited his mother to pay him a visit, but she declined.[34]

While at Carlisle Ewell became embroiled in two matters pertaining to rank. The first episode involved an officer named James W. Schaumburgh. Schaumburgh had been a first lieutenant in the First Dragoons until 1838, when he had been forced to resign because of ungentlemanly conduct. Officers in the regiment considered him a blackguard, and when he later sought reappointment at his former rank, they opposed him. Ewell led the charge. Although he had never met Schaumburgh, he would stand to lose by his reappointment. Promotion in the army was by seniority. If Schaumburgh was reinstated, Ewell would be knocked one peg lower on the army roster. For six years, beginning in 1844, the Virginian's correspondence is sprinkled with references to Schaumburgh's appointment and the dragoon officers' efforts to head it off.[35]

The Mexican War brought a temporary suspension of Schaumburgh's suit, but once the conflict ended, he renewed his claims. The matter came to a head in March 1849 when the Senate passed a resolution favorable to Schaumburgh. Believing the Louisianian's reappointment would be an injustice to himself and other officers who would "suffer by the loss of Rank attendant upon his return," Ewell rode to Washington on 26 March to bring the matter to the attention of the secretary of war.[36]

At Baltimore he ran into a friend who informed him that Schaumburgh was staying in Washington. Schaumburgh was a brawler. Once the nature of Ewell's trip became known, the man warned, Schaumburgh might seek Ewell out and try "to make a personal affair of the business." He might even go so far as to challenge Ewell to a duel. This was something the Virginian had not counted on, and he paused to consider his next step. He did not seek a confrontation with Schaumburgh, but neither would he avoid one. After thinking the matter over carefully, Ewell determined to call on Schaumburgh as soon as he reached the city, "tell him as quietly as possible the object of my visit to the District and if possible to avoid any difficulty with him." Considering Schaumburgh's belligerent reputation, that was not likely. Ewell confessed to Ben that he "felt very uneasy from the want of some sensible friend in case I should meet with insult &c from him to assist me in steering between the two dangers of caution on the one [side] and rashness on the other side."

He need not have worried. When he called on Schaumburgh, the Louisianian refused to see him. Puzzled but relieved, Ewell proceeded to the War Department to discuss Schaumburgh's suit with Adj. Gen. Roger Jones and Secretary of War George W. Crawford. He then carried his appeal to President Zachary Taylor. Although Schaumburgh's case had not yet reached his desk, the president assured Ewell that he considered Schaumburgh out of the service by his own actions. Ewell replied that the officers of the regiment "only asked for a fair showing before any action in the man's favor should be taken by the executive." Taylor promised that this would be done.[37]

Ewell remained in Washington for two days, then spent five days at Stony Lonesome. He returned to Carlisle late on 3 April "tired to death." As he passed through Washington on his way back to Carlisle, he stopped once more to see Schaumburgh. Again the Louisianian refused to see him. "I rather think he was sick," Ewell opined. "The plan he has adopted is to remain quiet untill the Senate meets again. . . . We shall see what we shall see." In the end Ewell's efforts and those of other officers prevailed. Schaumburgh did not receive the appointment.[38]

Emboldened by his success in the Schaumburgh affair, Ewell challenged the War Department on another matter of rank less than two weeks later. On 20 April he wrote for information relative to Lucius B. Northrup. The War Department had recently promoted Northrup to captain in the First Dragoons, even though he had been sick or absent from the regiment for more than three years, a period that happened to coincide with the Mexican War. Had he done any duty in that time? asked Ewell. Would he ever serve with the regiment again? "My object in asking for the above information," he stated, "is to bring Capt Lucius B. Northrup's case before the President of the U.S. as I was particularly aggrieved by his reappointment." Ewell had every right to feel aggrieved, for he was at the head of the promotion list and as such was entitled to the captain's vacancy awarded to Northrup. In this instance, however, his protests failed. Senator Jefferson Davis of Mississippi exerted influence on Northrup's behalf, and as a result the War Department sustained his promotion. Ewell considered Northrup's appointment "the greatest act of injustice" he had experienced in the Old Army, and he never entirely forgave Jefferson Davis for it.[39]

Promotion deferred was not promotion denied. Capt. William Eustis resigned from the regiment that summer, and on 4 August Ewell filled his vacancy as captain of Company G. Even so, he thought he deserved more. After the Mexican War the War Department had distributed brevets liberally to deserving and undeserving officers alike. In retrospect Ewell felt shortchanged. "I wish I had known in time that there was to be such an overwhelming quantity of Brevets made out," he grumbled, "& I certainly should have tried hard for another & might have got it. Many are Brevetted who staid at home the whole time in command of single companies, one man for taking care of [General] Worth's family &c."[40]

Ewell transferred to recruiting duty in Baltimore prior to receiving his promotion. Recruiting was rather dull as a rule, but he did not complain. It allowed him to remain in the East for a while, something that was necessary if he was to regain his health.[41] A recruiting officer's duty was simple enough. He informed young men about service in the dragoons, enrolled interested candidates, made sure they passed a proper physical examination, and arranged for their transportation to the training facility at Carlisle Barracks.

Such duty generally excited little controversy. On at least three different occasions, however, Ewell had to explain his actions to his superiors. In most instances the controversy centered around the enlistment of minors. Typical was the case of James H. Coulter. In March 1850 Coulter appeared at the recruiting office eager to enlist. Ewell eyed him from head to toe and curtly asked his age. Coulter stammered that he was twenty-one (the minimum age of enlistment). When Ewell did not believe him, Coulter produced a written statement to that effect purportedly signed by his mother. Ewell doubted the document's authenticity but signed Coulter up anyhow. Within a few weeks the boy became disillusioned with army life and sought to escape his military obligation by charging that he was underage. When the matter was brought to Ewell's attention, he produced the boy's papers. If the written statement about his age was correct, Coulter had no grounds for complaint, Ewell said. If the paper was false, Coulter was liable to prosecution for submitting a forged document. Presumably Coulter remained in the army.[42]

Ewell's most serious case involved a man named David Johnson, who enlisted in the summer of 1850 only to desert three months later. In a letter to the War Department, Johnson justified his conduct by charging that Ewell had forced him to join the army against his will. According to Johnson's sworn statement, he fell in with Ewell along the road, and they later checked into the same hotel. The next morning Ewell appeared at Johnson's door with a bottle of wine laced with drugs. After two drinks, said Johnson, he passed out. By the time he regained consciousness, he was on a train bound for Carlisle Barracks. When Johnson complained, Ewell pulled from his pocket an enlistment paper with his signature on it. Ewell had quietly and effectively shanghaied him. Such was Johnson's story. If true, it represents the only recorded instance of improper conduct in Ewell's career. That Johnson did not submit his protest for three months, however, suggests that he concocted the tale to justify his desertion. Officials in Washington apparently thought so, for Ewell never received a reprimand for the incident.[43]

Robert E. Lee happened to be serving in Baltimore at the same time that Ewell was on recruiting duty there. Ewell found the colonel and his family "a most agreeable set." He was even more impressed with the Lees' houseguest, Miss Britannia Peter of New York. "I have s[e]ldom seen so agreeable and interesting personage," he confided to Rebecca. "Her highest praise though is to mention that Col. [Lee] admires her excessively[,] and the Colonel does."[44]

The highlight of Baltimore's social season was a medieval tilting tournament hosted by the Carroll family at Doughregan Manor. Capt. John B. Magruder was the Carrolls' guest of honor. Ewell attended the event as a "knight" and matched his lance against those of fellow officers, among them perhaps Lts. Ambrose Powell Hill and Henry Hunt, both of whom were on duty in the city at that time. The winner of the competition received a prize from the hand of Miss Louise Carroll, "the lovely debutante daughter of the house." Although Ewell failed to capture the prize, he enjoyed himself thoroughly.[45]

Until this time, Ewell's adult life might have been described in two words: soldier and socialite. To these he now added a third dimension: businessman. The lieutenant saved a good deal of money in Mexico, and for the first time in his life he had capital to invest. He wasted no time in seeking to multiply his assets. At first Ewell considered investing in a risky speculative venture in California, but in the end he invested with Ben in the stock market.[46] His success in business surprised no one who knew him. As early as 1840 Tom Ewell noted that his brother had the calculating mind of a merchant, and ten years later even so shrewd a businessman as Tasker Gantt had to admit that Dick showed "a very pretty turn for stockjobbing & fancy operations."[47]

As 1849 drew to a close, Ewell paid a holiday visit to his relatives in Virginia. While staying with Ben, he took a particular interest in a certain Miss Tucker, whom he had at one time dubbed "the prettiest girl in Williamsburg." She cannot have made too great an impression, however, for six weeks after his return to Baltimore, Ewell told Rebecca that he was "perfectly devoted to at least a dozen" Maryland girls. That very evening, he informed her, he was scheduled to ride with a young lady "worth $200,000 and 'lovely as the day.'" He added rapturously, "I expect I shall not be able to think of anything below the moon for the next 6 days." It was ever Ewell's fate to leave a city before he could develop any serious attachments, though, and so it was now. In April 1850 he transferred from Baltimore to Richmond, Virginia.[48]

Before leaving Baltimore, Dick transacted an important piece of business. On 16 May he sold his interest in Stony Lonesome to his brother William for $1,200. After the death of Thomas Ewell Sr. in 1826, the farm had been split into six equal shares and divided among his children. Dick received one share of the property and purchased his brother Tom's share after the Mexican War. Thus by 1850 he held title to one-third of the family estate. The sale of his shares to William was a pivotal point in Ewell's life, for it showed that he had abandoned the idea of starting his own farm and had committed himself to a military career. It also marked a watershed in his personal life. In parting with the land, he severed his last tangible link with his father, a man whom he hardly remembered and never really knew.[49]

Ewell reported for duty in Richmond around the first of June 1850. He was there just two months when he was ordered to join his company in New Mexico. Ewell dropped off a detachment of new recruits at Carlisle Barracks, then headed to Fort Leavenworth, arriving in time to join a party going toward Santa Fe. Ben may have accompanied him as far as Nashville.[50]

At Fort Leavenworth Ewell took charge of 160 recruits headed to Santa Fe. The new soldiers were an unruly bunch. Before reaching Jefferson Barracks, they had roughed up the officer who had charge of them simply because he had ordered roll to be called. Ewell put an end to such behavior at once. In doing so he received little help from the other officers present, who, he reported sourly, "lay in bed untill 7 & remain under shelter of their arbor all day" to escape the sun.[51]

Ewell and his recruits left Fort Leavenworth on 15 August 1850. With them rode Capt. Abraham Buford of the First Dragoons, Lt. Alfred Pleasonton of the Second Dragoons, and Lt. Henry Heth of the Sixth Infantry. Ewell fell ill with dysentery soon after the journey commenced and had to turn the command over to Buford.[52] Two days out of Taos, New Mexico, the party met Kit Carson and a group of ten dragoons. Carson had received information that a man named Fox and several accomplices intended to rob a caravan of wagons traveling east on the Santa Fe Trail. Carson was riding hard to overtake them. By then Ewell had recovered from his illness, and he volunteered to join Carson with twenty-five men. Proceeding by forced marches, the military posse caught up with the wagon train near the Cimarron River and placed Fox under arrest before he could hatch his plot. The unusual episode marked the beginning of a friendship between Ewell and Carson that lasted for many years.[53]

Ewell reached Santa Fe on 23 October. For seven years he had dreamed about the city. Now, as he looked about him, he beheld unpaved streets, squalid tenements of baked mud, and a poor, uneducated populace. Over all there burned a relentless, scorching sun. Was this the city of gold, New Mexico's fabled metropolis? Ewell's heart must have faltered at the sight. Had he known how long he would be stationed in the Southwest, it might have ceased beating altogether.[54]

CHAPTER 6

Rayado and Los Lunas

Brig. Gen. Stephen Kearny seized New Mexico in 1846, and the Mexican government formally ceded the territory to the United States one and one-half years later in the Treaty of Guadeloupe Hidalgo. It was a dry, rugged expanse of picturesque deserts broken by high, tree-topped mountains. The region had a poor Mexican population of some 60,000 people, mostly small farmers and ranchers who scratched out a living along the Rio Grande and its tributaries. Above them, in the mountains, lived the Indians. By 1850 an estimated 40,000 Native Americans lived in and around New Mexico, about half of whom belonged to hostile tribes such as the Utes, Navajos, and Apaches. These tribes subsisted in large measure by plundering one another and their Mexican neighbors.[1]

It was the duty of the U.S. Army to protect the Mexican inhabitants and any new American settlers from Indian attack. To accomplish this task it assigned twenty-one companies to the territory. They were grouped administratively into the Ninth Military Department, later renamed the Department of New Mexico, with headquarters at Santa Fe. The army scattered troops up and down the Rio Grande in an effort to protect its many settlements. When Dick Ewell reported for duty at department headquarters in October 1850, he received orders to take command of Company G at Rayado, taking with him fifty-three recruits then at Las Vegas, New Mexico. Rayado was a two-company post on a tributary of the South Fork of the Canadian (or Red) River. On the map it stood eighty miles northeast of Santa Fe and just forty miles east of Taos. In reality it was much more distant, being separated from those towns by the 13,000-foot Sangre de Cristo mountain range. The post, which occupied a strategic location near the spot where the Santa Fe Trail's eastern branch met the Bent's Fort road, boasted Kit Carson among its residents.[2]

Ewell reached Rayado on 30 October 1850 and reported to Bvt. Maj. William N. Grier of Company I. Ewell may have remembered Grier from West Point, where Grier had briefly served on the faculty. Academics had not suited Grier, however, and at his own request he had been reassigned to the frontier. At Rayado he commanded 131 men, divided in roughly equal fashion between Companies G and I.[3]

Like many western posts, Rayado had no stockade. Officers posted guards in case of an attack, but the chances of Indians assaulting a military post were slim. As long as soldiers remained within sight of the post, they were relatively safe. If they ventured farther away, however, they took their lives in their hands. Just four months before Ewell's arrival a soldier from his company had been murdered near the fort by a Jicarilla Apache warrior.[4]

Danger was just one of many negative aspects of a soldier's life. For an enlisted man in the Regular Army, hardship was routine and comforts were few. Loneliness, monotony, harsh discipline, bad food, low pay, and poor living conditions led some men to drink and others to desert. The army exacerbated the soldiers' plight by failing to pay them promptly. "It has been nearly 3 months since we have been paid at this Garrison," Ewell complained to headquarters in June 1851, "& for the men it is unfortunate. Tobacco is a necessary & the temptation to sell clothing or public property in their charge is very much increased when the Pay Master's appearance is a rare or uncertain event. The uncertain movements of troops make it more difficult to obtain credit, except at exorbitant prices." He urged the department to pay the soldiers their back pay in small increments over a long period of time rather than in one lump sum. The more ready cash they had, the more likely they were to desert.[5]

In an effort to clamp down on desertion, Ewell urged the immediate trial of three men accused of that offense in April 1851. "There is some reason to expect more attempts at desertion as the Spring opens," he wrote, "and the speedy trial and punishment of these men might have a salutary effect. To be kept confined for several months as have been the two men tried in March would be fully as injurious as their escape." Ewell had little patience with deserters. On more than one occasion he enclosed with the list of charges a letter to the commander of the department recommending that those who fled his company receive the full penalty of the law. So that the effect of their punishment would not be lost on the others, he posted the results of court-martial proceedings for all to see.[6]

Though a strict disciplinarian, Ewell was fair and sometimes clement. When three of his men languished in prison for four months awaiting trial for a minor offense, he requested that the charges against them be dropped, explaining that their confinement was "at least as severe punishment as they would have received from a court martial." In April 1852 Ewell released a prisoner early because of good behavior, and on another occasion he recommended that a man sentenced to five months' imprisonment and a dishonorable discharge for heavy drinking have the last month of his sentence revoked. "The effect of his sentence is only a warning to others as far as the confinement," he explained. "The Discharge is an incentive & my recommendation is made in that view." Despite his efforts to shore up sagging discipline in the company, alcoholism, theft, and desertion remained high. At times he had as many as 15 percent of his men confined in the guardhouse awaiting trial.[7]

On 16 December 1850 Ewell sat on a general court-martial board at Las Vegas, New Mexico, with Lt. John Buford of the Second Dragoons and four other officers. The court tried seven cases involving ten men and found each defendant guilty. In the first case a soldier from Company F, First Dragoons, and two accomplices were convicted of desertion, unsoldierlike conduct, and disobedience of orders. The court decreed that the men receive fifty lashes apiece with a rawhide whip, forfeit their pay and allowances, have their heads shaved, and be drummed out of the service. The actual sentence was not nearly so harsh. In the end the court reduced the soldiers' punishment to the forfeiture of pay and allowances.

Half the cases tried by the court involved drunkenness. In four of the five cases the men charged were from Ewell's own Company G. Their sentences varied depending on the specific nature of the offense. In three of the cases the men received monetary fines and were ordered to stand on the head of a barrel six hours a day for up to thirty days. A more serious offender forfeited $10 of his pay and was ordered to be bucked six hours a day for thirty days. A soldier convicted of "habitual drunkenness" received the harshest penalty. The court ordered him to forfeit all pay and allowances, have his military buttons and lace cut from his uniform in the presence of his command, have his head shaved in disgrace, and be drummed out of the service. In a moment of leniency, however, it allowed the man to keep his hair.

The final two cases involved robbery and theft. A soldier convicted of robbing a store was sentenced to stand on the head of a barrel three of every four hours from reveille to tattoo for twenty-five consecutive days and forfeit $700 in pay. The court ordered a defendant convicted of stealing and selling the clothing of a fellow soldier to refund the money he had received for the stolen goods, pay a fine equal to the amount of the lost clothing ($7.64), and be bucked for six hours a day for fifteen days.[8]

Court-martial duty comprised only a small part of Ewell's time. He spent many more hours engaged in escort duty and scouting. During his first three years in the West, Ewell was in the saddle approximately 30 percent of the time. Much of that he spent chasing the Jicarilla Apaches, a tribe that occupied the northeast corner of the territory. Establishing a post at Rayado had curbed Jicarilla raids on settlers and wagon trains in that region, but it had not stopped them altogether. In a dispatch dated 6 June 1851 to the department's assistant adjutant general, Lt. Lafayette McLaws, Ewell reported that Jicarilla warriors had been seen in large numbers crossing the road between Rayado and Taos heading north. "The Indians are in all probability on their way to the head waters of the Red (Canadian) & Vermijo Rivers, their old haunts. . . . Their position would enable them to unite with the Utahs & fall at a moments warning upon trains or small parties on the Bent Fort or Semirone [Cimarron] road," Ewell warned. "I would therefore respectfully request that Lieut. [J. H.] Whittlesey with 'G' Company, belonging to the garrison of this Post, may be returned here as by both routes trains are expected during the present month & at present I could not detach a large enough command." Ewell's dispatch to McLaws underlined a problem common among companies at western posts: namely, it took so many men to properly garrison a post that frequently there were not enough left to employ against the Indians.[9]

Military leadership in New Mexico changed abruptly in July 1851 when Ewell's old mentor, Edwin Sumner, took command of the department. Sumner, now a brevet colonel, came to Santa Fe with orders to reduce military expenditures. He began by removing troops from the cities. Prior to his arrival many soldiers in the department lived in towns at great expense to the government. Sumner ordered his officers to move their posts into the country, where they would be in a better position to protect the settlements and more effectively block Indian incursions into Sonora, Mexico. He also ordered the garrisons to become more self-sufficient. No longer would the government provide soldiers all of their food, forage, fuel, and shelter. Now the men would have to help grow their own crops, gather their own forage and fuel, and build their own posts. The free ride was over. In the future the soldiers of the Ninth Military Department would have to pull their own weight.[10]

Sumner passed through Rayado on his way to Santa Fe. While at Rayado, he notified Ewell of his intention to break up the post and move its troops to a new camp on the Canadian River. He asked Ewell to examine the proposed site. Ewell did so and on 17 July filed his report. In it he gave his opinion that the Canadian River was too small, too slow, and too unreliable at that particular point to support a post. Furthermore, local supplies of grass and fuel were insufficient to support even one company of dragoons, much less two. In short, he recommended against establishing a post there.[11]

The garrison instead went to San Domingo, where Sumner was gathering troops for an expedition into the mountains west of the Rio Grande. Until 1851 the United States had pursued a conciliatory policy toward the Indians of the Southwest, but that was about to change. When Sumner came to New Mexico, he brought with him authorization from the War Department to chastise hostile tribes.[12] It was the type of order the old soldier liked, and he wasted no time putting it into effect. His target was the Navajos, who continued to raid towns and attack wagon trains despite the army's repeated warnings.

In August Sumner led his men deep into Navajo territory to seek out and punish the offenders. But he learned, as had others before him, that the Indians were not easily brought to bay. Weeks of hard marching failed to turn up a single Navajo, while injuring dozens of dragoon horses. In Ewell's company alone, twenty-six animals broke down. Sumner halted the fruitless march and returned to the Rio Grande. Behind he left five companies and a military post that he named Fort Defiance.[13]

Ewell's Company G was one of the five companies initially stationed at Fort Defiance. For three months it remained on duty there, escorting wagon trains to and from the fort. Forage at Fort Defiance was not sufficient, though, and in December Ewell received orders to move his company to Los Lunas, where grass was more plentiful. Los Lunas stood on the west bank of the Rio Grande, approximately twenty-five miles south of Albuquerque, in an area traversed by Mogollon, Jicarilla, and Mescalero Apaches. It was the smallest post in the department, manned by Ewell's company alone.[14]

In accordance with Sumner's policy of economy, Ewell purchased supplies from local sources when he could do so at a savings to the government. In one instance he bought ten head of cattle at $22 apiece, while a couple hundred miles to the south, at Fort Fillmore, government agents were paying almost twice that price. Horses were his biggest concern. In a single year hard service had cut in half the number of mounts in Ewell's company. By 1852 he had only thirty-six serviceable animals, approximately one for every two men in his command. Horses and mules were at a premium in the West, and despite Ewell's efforts to overcome the shortage, he found it almost impossible to keep his company adequately stocked.[15]

He had better luck feeding his troops than mounting them. In the spring of 1852 Company G planted a garden at Los Lunas on land donated by local farmers who benefited from the army's protection. Ewell cleared a large tract and planted onions, beets, and cabbages. He also rented a vineyard and purchased

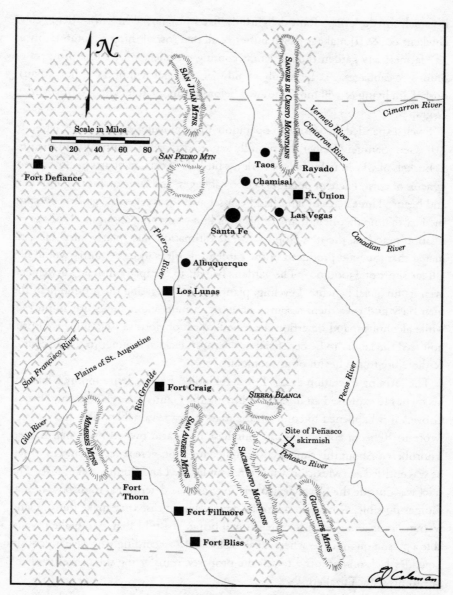

New Mexico, 1850–1857

livestock for the post. "I am delightfully fixed just now," he wrote Ben, "cows chickens &c & [I] make my own butter & all that sort of thing as comfortably as any farmer; My garden though late is coming on finely with a fine prospect of onions & cabbages. . . . I am only afraid Col. Sumner will find out how luxuriously I am living & will move me away before I reap the full benefit of my garden & grapes." [16]

Ewell expanded his farming operation the following spring. In a letter to Adj. Gen. Samuel Cooper, he proudly reported that his company had planted 25 bushels of wheat, 12 bushels of barley, 5 bushels of oats, 12 quarts of clover seed, 12 acres of corn, 1 acre of potatoes, 3,000 cabbages, and large quantities of onions and beans. Three acres of land had been set aside as a vegetable garden. Despite the fact that neither he nor any of his men knew anything about local soils or irrigation practices, the 1853 crop by Ewell's estimation was "pretty fair." He estimated that the food produced in the garden "at prices in this country would not fall far short of $3000.00." The garden's benefit to company morale outweighed even its financial benefits. Leveling, planting, and irrigating the ground kept the men busy and gave them a source of extra revenue. Company spirit improved, while alcoholism and desertion decreased. With obvious satisfaction Ewell pronounced the labor "to be beneficial in the most decided manner to the discipline & therefore to the health of my company." [17]

The farming operation at Los Lunas rekindled Ewell's desire to buy a farm of his own. He expressed an interest in buying the Gantts' Maryland farm, "Brook Grove," if it happened to come on the market at a reasonable price, and he later wrote to Rebecca concerning the purchase of a farm owned by a man named Thornberry. About this time he also applied for a 160-acre parcel of land to which he was entitled as a Mexican War veteran under the Land Bounty Act of 1850. The tract was outside the New Mexico territory, and he determined to dispose of it as soon as possible. "I have come to the conclusion in case they make out my land warrant at once, to sell it for what it will bring," he told Ben. "To make it valuable a person ought to be where it can be located." Accordingly he gave his cousin Lowndes Jackson authority to sell the property, transferring the proceeds of the sale to his sister Elizabeth. [18]

Real estate might be a good investment even if one did not intend to farm. When land values in the Williamsburg area increased, Dick chided Ben, who had been a professor of mathematics at the College of William and Mary, for not having the foresight to capitalize on the situation. "What a pity that you didnt profit by the rise in land in your vecinity [sic]. it is never a matter of chance, this sort of thing & if you would only reason as clearly [on this] as on Newton's Theorem for the Binomial it might put more dollars in your pocket." As for himself, it was not a lack of foresight but funds that kept him out of the real estate market. "Land offers greater inducements here to purchase than anywhere I have seen but lack of mon[e]y cramps my genius," he wrote during a visit to Williamsburg in 1856.[19]

Money was never far from Ewell's thoughts. Perhaps because of his poverty as a child he attached great importance to wealth, and he never ceased to search for financial independence. He conservatively invested his money in stocks and deposited it in bank accounts, using trusted cousins such as Lowndes Jackson, Tasker Gantt, and William Reynolds as his financial agents. By 1854 he had sent $2,000 to Reynolds alone. To his chagrin his cousin failed to invest the money promptly. "It will be too bad if he leaves it any time unemployed as I hate to lose the interest," Dick wrote to Ben. "Better a bad speculation than none at all."[20]

Naturally Ewell sought to get the best return on his investment. In 1854 he wrote to his friend and former West Point classmate William T. Sherman, who was then employed at a banking house in St. Louis. He had heard a rumor that Sherman was taking money from officers at a heavy interest and wanted to get in on the deal. "I would like to put in $8000," Ewell eagerly wrote to his brother Ben, but I "have but 6000. could you put in the two either on my security & a fair interest or at your own risk & profit[?] Answer by return of mail."[21]

Later, when Ewell learned that bankers in California were offering interest at 3 percent per month, he again turned to Ben for financial support. "I have not mon[e]y enough . . . to make it worth while, but I really believe an independence might be had in that way. Would you add $2000. to mine in case anything of the kind should be attempted?" he asked. "If you can advance a sum & we operate through Tasker, both of us may profit. I would prefer to get the money from you on interest," he wrote. "After a few m[o]nths I will have a thousand dollars. If you could borrow 2 or 3,000 at 6 per cent we would do a good business." Ewell was a prudent investor but hardly a timid one. He thought nothing of risking his all— and more than his all—to finance an attractive business proposition. He frequently proposed borrowing money to fund his business ventures and in one instance went so far as to suggest that his brother Ben mortgage the family farm.[22]

The West offered unlimited opportunities for those with capital and a little imagination. Several times while in New Mexico Ewell joined others to supply sheep to California, and in each instance he doubled his investment. "Could I have gone into it myself I would now have been rich," he claimed. "Money is to be made with capital & labor but it is not the one thing needful." Sheep were not the only animals in demand on the West Coast. From Kit Carson Ewell learned that large dray horses were selling for $800 to $1,200 apiece in California.

A person who could successfully drive a herd of such animals across the plains to the coast stood to make a fortune, and Ewell was just the man to try. "What can such horses, the coarser the better, be bot for in the States?" he inquired of Ben. "By taking ambulances which double their cost, Corn for the whole journey via N.M. [New Mexico] can be taken, leaving in Sept.[,] wintering here[,] & reaching San F. in April. Suppose you go into it. I will go from here with you. We would want 30 to 40 horses[,] 10 men[,] & 5 ambulances."[23]

The plan for taking horses to California never panned out, but Ewell had several other irons in the fire. By 1852 he wished to go east and personally check on his investments. Unfortunately circumstances made that impossible. His lieutenants were on leave or detached service throughout much of 1852 and 1853, and he could not leave his command. But he did not complain. In fact, since coming to Los Lunas his subordinates had been so worthless that he looked on their absence as a happy event rather than otherwise. He was entirely without officers, he told Ben, "& if they will only keep away, will please me much. My 1st Lt. [Clarendon J. L.] Wilson . . . is when sober an excellent Officer, but unfortunately is a confirmed Sot & sets such an example to my men that my trouble is doubled when he is present. At the same time he has performed no duty since joining—either drunk or sick[.] I would like to have an active Officer with the Comp'y so that in due season I might go on leave of absence & attend to my private affairs. I have money enough in Reynolds hands to make it worth my while to look after it." Wilson's illness was more serious than Ewell imagined. The lieutenant died in February 1853, again leaving Ewell the only officer at the post. Seven months later 2nd Lt. Isaiah N. Moore arrived at Los Lunas. Unlike Wilson, Moore was a sober and efficient officer. His presence freed Ewell from much of the post's administrative drudgery.[24]

One duty that Ewell could not escape was his obligation as a host. People traveling up and down the Rio Grande frequently stopped at Los Lunas. As the post's ranking officer, Ewell suffered "the annoyances of a Tavernkeeper" trying to feed and shelter them. "I have been entertaining with great want of interruption for the last 6 m[o]nths," he grumbled to Ben. "Today I have been pestered by a Mexican for several hours[,] a Dutch Jew merchant[,] & lastly an Irish carpenter." So great was the burden of feeding these people that in August 1852 he asked Colonel Sumner to designate Los Lunas a "permanent" or "fixed" post, which would entitle it to double rations.[25]

Some of Ewell's visitors were officers traveling to or from the states. Among those headed east was Capt. Abraham Buford. "He came out with me in 50.," Ewell recalled, "without much money, but several fine blooded horses & great skill in cards. He won on one horse race $1800. & by judicious sales of his horses & good luck at cards goes home with 2 yrs pay due & about $8000 in cash. . . . Buford as you may suppose is hardly calculated to shine in any ball room except a Mexican fandango, where he seems in his element. Here the natives call him, Hellroaring Buford. He is over 6 feet & out of proportion large in other respects."[26]

Maj. Oliver L. Shepherd of the Third Infantry stopped at Los Lunas in July 1852 with his fifteen-year-old Mexican bride. Ewell saw immediately that the marriage was in trouble. "They stopped here during the heat of the day," he told Ben, "& the prospect ahead for him made me feel melancholly [sic]. He is a fool & coarse brute & neglects this girl very much. There were scoldings & disputations when they got into the carriage & temper in the greatest abundance. She, raised among those whose virtue was very easy, young & neglected by her husband, who is crass & not agreeable in his Dep[ortmen]t. has as I can see hardly one chance in fifty of keeping within bounds," Ewell predicted. "The first sproutings looked almost ready to burst forth. I have no doubt when he finds the horns full grown he will make a devil of a fuss just as if they were not entirely owing to his own stupid & brutal course. As we sow so must we reap." Hispanic women had a reputation for marital infidelity. Even so, Ewell had no objection to an officer marrying one, provided the man "never was so imprudent as to return home at unreasonable hrs or when not expected."[27]

Indians as well as husbands might appear when and where they were least expected. On 8 January 1853 Apache warriors broke into a corral at Los Lunas and stole four horses and mules. Ewell followed the culprits 120 miles east to the Plains of St. Augustine, following the tracks left by the stolen animals. At that point the ground froze solid, and the tracks were lost. The trail had literally grown cold. Ewell knew before setting out that pursuit would be fruitless, but he gave chase anyway, he said, to appease the local populace and "to acquire some knowledge of the country" in that direction, "as on former occasions I could not procure guides." He returned to Los Lunas on the nineteenth, having been in the country for nine days with just six days' rations. Though hardly a friend of the Apaches, in this instance Ewell was not inclined to take a harsh view of the offense, since he believed it was born of necessity. "The depradations [sic] are committed for the sake of food," he wrote department adjutant Samuel D. Sturgis, "the apaches being said to be in a starving condition."[28]

The Navajos had also committed many depredations that year. In order to punish them, the army determined to send a large force into their homeland. It had tried a similar tactic in 1851 without success, and this time it fared no better.

For four weeks in July and August 1853, U.S. forces marched back and forth across the countryside near Fort Defiance without encountering a single hostile Indian. Much of the time it rained. But for Ewell, at least, the expedition was not a total failure. During the brief campaign he was able to explore various trails, which he later included in a map that he sent to headquarters.[29]

In November 1853 the War Department issued Company G Sharps Carbines so that it could test them under actual field conditions. (Prior to this the company had carried a variety of weapons, including Harpers Ferry Rifles, musketoons, and Hall's Carbines.) After a six-month trial Ewell reported that the Sharps Carbine was far superior for "mounted service, taking also into consideration the liability to fight on foot, to any firearm I have ever seen. It is fired far more rapidly than Hall's Carbine or the service Rifle, with equal accuracy below two hundred yards, and rapidly increasing superiority ahead that distance. I have seen no appearance after a great deal of trial, of their getting out of order, nor is it rendered unserviceable by rapid firing." Although Ewell gave the weapon high marks, he suggested two modifications: graduating the sight to show elevation and placing the swivel nearer the butt of the gun. "As far as concerns my own company," he concluded, "these defects are not of sufficient consequence to delay furnishing the weapon, as the company would be doubly efficient with Sharp's Carbine than with the present arm."

He was less complimentary about Maynard primers, which the army had also asked him to test. The primer's tape, which was similar to a roll of caps in a cap pistol, failed to catch fire two out of every three times, he reported, and occasionally several caps exploded at once. Moreover, he predicted that the primer would not withstand moisture or hard service. He concluded by expressing his decided preference for percussion caps.[30]

The Sharps Carbines arrived at an opportune time, for in 1854 Indian uprisings erupted all across the territory. Three tribes were primarily responsible: the Utes, the Jicarilla Apaches, and the Mescalero Apaches. In January Ewell led a thirty-day march into the Sierra Blanca, east of the Rio Grande, to suppress the Mescalero Apaches, who had been stealing livestock in the area. As usual the Indians got wind of the expedition and disappeared without a trace. In his report to headquarters Ewell laconically noted, "We met no Indians & nothing of particular moment occurred on the march."

The account he gave his sister Rebecca was less brief. "Since the 16th of Dec. I have been leading a very active life, marching several hundred miles through the mountains & travelling on horseback at more than the usual rates. To day I returned from Sante [*sic*] Fe, 66 miles[,] making it in about 8 travelling hours. Within three days I start for Fort Union[,] 200 miles off[,] to be absent untill nearly the end of the month—very probably to start on a Campaign half way to California on my return. I like this way of doing business very much as it keeps me in better health, & keeps one from thinking." Although he wrote this in jest, there was truth in what he said. Ewell had a high-strung, nervous temperament and was never happier or healthier than when physically active.[31]

The trip to Fort Union may have had some connection with expeditions then being launched against the Utes and the Jicarilla Apaches in the northeast corner of the territory, near Ewell's former post at Rayado. Military operations against the tribes escalated that summer with the arrival of David Meriwether, New Mexico's new territorial governor. Meriwether was no stranger to the frontier, having been a trapper before moving east to pursue a successful career in Kentucky politics. At age fifty-three he returned to the West to take charge of New Mexico's affairs.[32] The new governor brought a carrot-and-stick policy toward the Indians: he would give gifts to those tribes who agreed to live in amity with the U.S. government, but he would chastise those who persisted in their hostile actions. The instrument of his wrath was Bvt. Brig. Gen. John Garland of the Eighth Infantry, who had recently replaced Edwin Sumner as commander of the department.[33]

Garland vigorously campaigned against the Utes and Jicarillas throughout 1854. In October he ordered Company G to advance northward along the western edge of the Sangre de Cristo Mountains toward Chamisal. A Mexican settler named Chacon agreed to act as Ewell's guide. Chacon led Company G from one Indian campsite to another, but it did not see a single Indian. Ewell's practiced eye told him the campsites were not fresh, and at the end of two days' search he ordered his company back to Santa Fe. In his report to Garland Ewell expressed the opinion that there had been Apaches in the Chamisal area, "but not so recently as supposed by Mr. Chacon. The people of that vicinity seem to be on the most friendly terms with the Indians." As a footnote he added that "Mr. Chacon seemed to be in earnest in searching for the Indians, but his conduct occasionally was such as to countenance a report I heard since i.e. that he is not always sane."[34]

Other units would have to defeat the Utes and Jicarillas; Company G would strike its blow against the Mescaleros. Like the Jicarillas farther north, the Mescaleros had been in open rebellion against the U.S. government throughout 1854. Meriwether reported that they were "robbing and murdering our citizens whenever a favorable opportunity presented itself." The Mescaleros numbered just 900 people, but they inspired terror far out of proportion to their modest numbers. Led by the fierce warrior Santa Anna, they ravaged the country east of the Rio Grande, attacking settlements along the Pecos River and falling on wagon trains on the roads between Texas and New Mexico.[35]

In December 1854 Mescalero warriors stole 2,500 sheep from a ranch on the Pecos River. Ewell rendezvoused with troops from Fort Fillmore at the Bonito River and pursued the Indians into the Sacramento Mountains. On the night of 17 January 1855 the Mescaleros attacked Ewell's force at the Peñasco River. After a brief exchange of arrows and firearms, the Indians set fire to the grass around the camp. The dragoons would not budge. The next morning Ewell pursued the natives up the Peñasco into the Sacramento Mountains. The Mescaleros disputed his advance from every rock and ravine. Undeterred, Ewell threw forward a heavy skirmish line and continued his advance. It was tough going. "The country was broken into high hills with deep ravines crossing the line of march," Ewell remembered. "Lt. Moore with some of the best horses gave chase to some Indians on the first open ground, but a winter march of 450 miles had reduced the horses too much to catch the Indians on their fresh animals."

The Mescaleros' boldness convinced Ewell that he was getting close to their village. He pushed after them as rapidly as possible in the hope of bringing them to battle. "During the day some fifteen of them were shot from their horses & carried off by their comrades," Ewell wrote, "leaving the ground marked by their blood & at one time after the fall of the boldest they collected on a high hill to set up a lamentation, afterwards becoming bolder in their attacks."[36] At 3:00 P.M. he reached the abandoned Mescalero camp. Five hundred yards away stood a second collection of abandoned lodges. Ewell sent Capt. Henry W. Stanton forward to investigate. When Stanton reached the huts, he saw some Indians in the distance and rashly pursued them. As he and his party were returning, the Mescaleros ambushed them, killing Stanton and two others. Ewell heard the shots and immediately sent Moore to Stanton's support, but it was too late. The Mescaleros fled at Moore's approach, leaving the corpses of their three victims behind.

Ewell buried the bodies and again took up pursuit. The exhausted condition of his horses and the inability of the guides to track the Indians, however, doomed the effort to failure. On 20 January 1855, having passed the headwaters of the Peñasco, the dragoons ceased their pursuit and returned to the Pecos River. On the way back down the mountain, they halted to collect the remains of their fallen comrades. Animals had torn the bodies from the grave and had partly devoured them. The soldiers burned what flesh remained on the corpses and carried the bones away. A two-week march brought them back to Los Lunas on 8 February. Their six-week odyssey was over.[37]

The fighting along the Peñasco River, though minor in terms of casualties, was seen as a victory. Seven Mescalero warriors had been killed, including Santa Anna. It had been Ewell's first experience fighting Indians, and he had acquitted himself well. His success in tracking the Mescaleros to their stronghold and his aggressive yet prudent pursuit up the mountain marked him as a frontier officer of promise. His accomplishments were not lost on his superiors. In his report to Washington, General Garland announced "with feelings of more than ordinary satisfaction the result of Captain Ewell's expedition in pursuit of the Mezcalero Apaches." The campaign, he reported, "redounds greatly to the credit of this well tried, gallant and valuable officer. But for the impatience of one of his officers, smarting under disappointment in the Mexican war, it is believed that not a man of the command would have been killed."[38]

Stung by their defeat, the Mescaleros plotted revenge. Two weeks after Company G's return to Los Lunas, fifteen Apache warriors attacked the dragoons' grazing camp, twenty-five miles east of the post. Four soldiers were wounded. Ewell happened to be in Santa Fe on business at the time. Lieutenant Moore, commanding in his absence, sent a party in pursuit, but the assailants escaped. Ewell later visited the four wounded soldiers at the post hospital in Albuquerque. Cpl. Thomas C. Ringgold had received eight wounds in the attack and was on the point of death. Ewell brought the young man a letter from his father. When Ringgold died, the captain sent the father a letter of condolence.[39]

The Mescalero attack on the dragoon grazing camp was the last defiant act of a defeated tribe. Ewell's successful invasion of the Mescaleros' homeland, coupled with other setbacks that winter, compelled the tribe to sue for peace. In June 1855 Ewell escorted Governor Meriwether 200 miles up the Rio Grande to Fort Thorn to meet with Mescalero leaders.[40]

One month later Ewell accompanied Meriwether and Garland to Black Lake, near Fort Defiance, for a meeting with the Navajos. Approximately 2,000 Indians attended. When the two sides could not reach an agreement, the Navajos broke off the negotiations. That night, according to Pvt. James A. Bennett, Ewell learned that the Indians planned to attack the outnumbered U.S. negotiating party at dawn. He sent one of his soldiers back to Fort Defiance for help, telling him, "Go as soon as God will let you, and tell the Commanding Officer at the fort to send me some help or we will all be killed in the morning."

Ewell and the other soldiers spent an anxious night preparing for an attack and praying that the reinforcements would arrive in time. "The first signs of day had just begun to appear," remembered Bennett, "when was heard a more welcome sound than music: the rumbling of cannon wheels over the solid rock road. When it was just light the full 75 men of the Artillery Company came charging into our camp. *No attack was made.*" Seeing that they could not successfully attack the U.S. party, the Navajos returned to the negotiating table. Four days later they signed an agreement.[41]

Altogether Meriwether negotiated treaties with six hostile tribes that year. He personally carried the documents to Washington that fall for ratification. Ewell escorted the governor as far as Fort Leavenworth and then went on a sixty-day leave of absence. It was his first extended leave in ten years.[42]

In 1855 the army expanded, adding two regiments of cavalry and two of infantry. Ewell hoped to get a major's commission in one of the two new mounted regiments, and he encouraged Ben to go to Washington to lobby on his behalf. He offered to reward his brother's efforts with $1,000 if he got the commission, and to pay his expenses if he failed. "Wonders are sometimes done by spending a little money judiciously among the proper agents," he wrote. "One thing I will swear & that is that you will theorise [*sic*] beautifully whether you do anything or not."[43]

Ben brought Dick's suit to the attention of Gen. Winfield Scott, who agreed to write a testimonial on his behalf. In the end, though, the competition was too keen. Several brevet colonels, numerous brevet lieutenant colonels, and a legion of brevet majors all vied for the same few positions. "Capt Richd. Ewell had no show in that crowd," a Washington insider told Ben. "You have seen the appointments—all good men, who had done the state service. . . . Richd. Ewell is a first rate man & officer," he continued. "But that crowd were to strong for him, in age, length of service, & brevets. . . . Ewell must say not 'Sparta has many a worthier son,' but in the language of t'other poet, 'other not abler soldiers.'"[44]

On the heels of this disappointment a letter arrived from Tennessee offering Ewell a job as a plantation manager. The position promised a good salary, social opportunities, and an agrarian lifestyle—everything he professed to want. Ewell scanned the letter again until his eyes came to rest at the signature on the bottom of the page. There, written in a firm but delicate hand, was a name he knew all too well: Lizinka Campbell Brown.

★ ★ ★ CHAPTER 7 ★ ★ ★

A Belle of the First Water

Lizinka Campbell Brown was Dick Ewell's first cousin, both being grandchildren of Benjamin and Rebecca Stoddert. The secretary and his high-born wife had reared nine children, four girls and five boys. Each of the girls had married, and three had had children. Elizabeth, the eldest, became the bride of Thomas Ewell; Harriot had married Tennessean George Washington Campbell; Nancy wed Marylander Thomas Gantt and was the mother of Dick Ewell's cousins Levi and Tasker Gantt; and Rebecca had married Maj. David Hubbard of Alabama and became stepmother to the children of her husband's previous marriage.[1]

Lizinka was the daughter of Harriot Stoddert and George W. Campbell. Campbell was one of Tennessee's leading men. After three terms in the U.S. House of Representatives, he had served briefly as a judge on Tennessee's Supreme Court of Errors and Appeals, as U.S. secretary of the Treasury, and as a member of the U.S. Senate. In 1818 President James Monroe appointed Campbell minister to Russia. By then he and Harriot had three young children: George, Benjamin, and Elizabeth.[2]

Judge Campbell and his wife reached the Russian capital of St. Petersburg in 1818. For the couple it was to be a city of tears. Just months after their arrival a typhus epidemic swept through the capital, taking the lives of their three children. The parents were distraught. In their grief they received consolation from Czar Alexander I and his wife, Lizinka. The royal pair had recently suffered the loss of a son and could therefore sympathize with the Campbells' anguish.

For the American couple joy followed despair. Later that year Harriot Stoddert gave birth to a young boy, whom she named George in memory of her eldest son. On 24 February 1820 she bore a second child, whom she christened Elizabeth McKay after her deceased daughter. That was the girl's name on paper. In honor of the Russian empress, the Campbells called the little girl Lizinka.[3]

81

Like Dick Ewell, Lizinka retained no memories of her birthplace. Just four months after her birth the Campbells left Russia and returned to the United States, settling in Nashville. There, amid central Tennessee's green, rolling hills, the little girl grew to adolescence. Apparently she suffered some misfortune in her youth. Rebecca Ewell critically remarked in 1831 that her eleven-year-old cousin was "a very good child, tall of her age, but too fond of talking—has a scarred Neck from the burn Anna gave her and a crooked arm, but is pretty well looking. George is a fine looking boy, but is much more intractable than she." The deformities mentioned by Rebecca Ewell either healed or were so slight as to escape notice, for no one else ever mentioned them. In fact, Lizinka grew more beautiful each year, fulfilling her Aunt Elizabeth's prediction that she would be "a belle of the first water."[4]

Lizinka was as talented as she was pretty. As befitted the daughter of a former senator and foreign minister, she received a first-rate education. Rebecca Ewell reported in 1835 that her fourteen-year-old cousin "plays finely on the piano, very well on the harp, sings, speaks French, [and] is learning Italian. . . . She is very pretty they say," sniffed the older girl, "and of course has every advantage that wealth can procure. Aunt Nancy says she has the reputation of more wealth than she really possesses. Such she supposes is the reason of the attention she receives."[5]

Rebecca and the other members of the Ewell family knew Lizinka well. In 1832 President Andrew Jackson appointed Judge Campbell to serve as one of three commissioners to settle spoliation claims under the Treaty of Indemnity with France. For a time the judge and his family moved to Washington, D.C.[6] Lizinka cut quite a figure in the capital city—too much so in the opinion of some of her relatives. Ben Ewell believed his teenage cousin was "much too young to go into company at all" and certainly into such fast company as the nation's capital afforded. "A winter at Washington is enough to turn the head of a much older belle," he asserted. "Her health too must suffer much by the dissipation, and although she may not feel it now she will hereafter—a girl of sixteen ought to be at school. If she is not completely spoiled she must be superhuman."

As if to confirm the family's apprehensions, Lizinka was the subject of a letter that appeared in the Washington newspapers. In it the author referred to her as "the fair representative of Tennessee" and proceeded to voice his esteem in lyrical verse. He was not alone in his admiration. Many men came to pay their respects to Lizinka, some drawn by her beauty and charm, others by her wealth. It seemed only a matter of time before a legitimate suitor would step forward and ask for her

Lizinka at age thirteen (Tennessee State Library and Archives)

hand in marriage. "Do you know whether or not she had any offers in Washington?" Ben inquired of Rebecca. "Among so many sighing swains some surely ought to have been in earnest."[7]

There was at least one: Dick Ewell. Ewell had become well acquainted with his clever, agreeable cousin during her frequent visits to Stony Lonesome, and before long he fell desperately in love with her. Considering the genetic fondness Ewell men historically had displayed toward their female cousins, he could hardly have done otherwise. At first family members did not know what to make of the budding romance. Elizabeth Ewell, writing in the spring of 1835, had to admit that she could not tell how the two stood as a couple. But as the months passed, Dick's attentions toward his cousin became more pronounced. Mrs. Ewell was delighted by the prospect of such a match, though she thought Dick stood little chance with the girl. She was right. In 1836 Dick left Virginia for West Point, and three years later Lizinka married James Percy Brown.[8]

Brown was a handsome man—urbane, well traveled, and intelligent. Though trained in the law, he did not have an active practice, preferring to dabble in politics and manage his cotton plantation in Mississippi. Brown's polished manners and winning charm swept Lizinka off her feet, and in April 1839 they were married. A few months later, in New York, Dick Ewell announced his intention to remain a bachelor.[9]

Lizinka's marriage produced three children—George Campbell, Percy, and Harriot Stoddert—but it failed to produce sustained happiness. Brown mistreated his wife and eventually took his own life, leaving Lizinka a widow at age twenty-four. The years only added to her sorrow. In 1848 her father died, and five years after that Lizinka's only brother, George, and son Percy passed away. Percy's death was particularly trying. The ten-year-old boy fell while climbing a tree at Lizinka's Spring Hill plantation and impaled himself on a wooden stake. To the horror of his frantic mother, his life could not be saved.[10]

The deaths of her father, husband, brother, and son left Lizinka utterly bereft but extremely wealthy. Estimates of her property ran as high as $500,000. Her father had amassed quite a fortune in his lifetime, and when he died, his estate was divided between George and Lizinka. George's death in 1853 left Lizinka heiress to her father's entire fortune, including several lots in Nashville and St. Louis, more than 15,000 acres of land scattered throughout Tennessee, and some $50,000 in investments. In addition to these assets, she and her children received some 2,700 acres of land in Mississippi from the estate of James Percy Brown. Lizinka suddenly found herself one of the wealthiest women in Tennessee and perhaps the nation.[11]

Lizinka as she appeared at the time of her first marriage (Dace Brown Farrer)

Dick Ewell learned of Lizinka's misfortunes from relatives. For several months he did not write to her, believing her pain "must be so great that sympathy would appear like mockery." The vast amount of property that she owned, he reasoned, would help assuage her grief, for "the management of it will occupy her so much that her mind will not be able to contemplate her misfortunes. I believe from what I have seen of her that in the end she will be a happier person than ever before, not of course because she has the property but because the duties it will entail, will keep her mind employed." [12]

Lizinka was not able to manage such extensive holdings, though, and she had to turn to her cousins for help. Tasker Gantt became her business manager and adviser, and she asked Dick Ewell to take over management of her Spring Hill plantation. For Ewell it was the opportunity of a lifetime. He would have a chance to manage a large farm and at the same time earn a handsome salary. Best of all, he would be close to Lizinka, whom he still held in warm regard. From the start, however, Ewell determined that personal feelings should play no part in the decision. "Any disposition that I might have to accept Cousin's L's [*sic*] offer would spring more from the admiration that I have always had for her than from any idea of getting rich," he told Rebecca, "& philosophically speaking this very admiration would be the best reason for not accepting. . . . I don't think there is any likelihood that I shall resign." Still it was an attractive offer, and when Ewell took a leave of absence in late 1855, he decided to look into it further.[13]

On his way east he visited Tasker Gantt in St. Louis. Ewell told his cousin in "very emphatic language of the irksomeness of his situation in that semi-barbarian country"—meaning New Mexico—enumerating "many particulars of the annoyance & disagreements to which he was there subject." On a more wistful note, Ewell spoke of his taste for agriculture, expounding at length on the various ways he would seek to increase the productivity of Lizinka's farm should he accept the position as manager.

Ewell's words convinced Gantt that he intended to accept Lizinka's offer. In a letter to Lizinka, Gantt assured his comely cousin that Dick took "a rational and perfectly commercial view of the matter . . . and that if he should at any time think he has made a bad bargain, will blame no one but himself. . . . He says he would not hesitate to accept your proposal if you were a man, but he fears to take advantage of a poor weak woman in the matter of a bargain. I begged him to believe he might with propriety treat you like a man. He is very far above any of his family in common, healthy sense."[14]

Dick toured Spring Hill with Lizinka that fall, but in the end he decided against taking the position. Gantt had hoped Dick would take the job, and he was angered when he did not. He blamed Dick's decision on Rebecca Ewell's baneful influence over her brother and on Dick's weakness of character. "Prepared as I was for the vacillation and indecision of Dick Ewell, I am nevertheless astonished at what you tell me," he told Lizinka. "You have done well to put an end to the treaty. No good could come of it. I had no notion that Dick took counsel of Becca. I do not like a man's taking counsel of anyone but his own mind, after he is turned of thirty. . . . Does it seem as if Dick was mocking when he spoke of wanting the opinion of Becca Ewell?" he asked. "Upon my word, I would as soon take that of a child ten years old as either Becca's or Ben's. Dick's judgment is really sounder than either, or would be if he were consulted as to the case of a third person. It is chiefly the agonies of indecision which rack him and make him act so foolishly," Gantt declared. "Yet he is a good soldier, I believe. I have heard so from many officers. It is clear that he could never rise above a very subordinate place however. When executing orders given by a superior, no doubt he would do well. If it became necessary to decide between a certain sacrifice and a possible or probable great recompense, he would be paralysed. I am amazed at Becca's allusions to Dick's sentiments or supposed sentiments towards you," he concluded. "My opinion of Becca's taste & judgment has at no time been flattering: but I own myself much disappointed in Dick. . . . One's respect is necessarily impaired by such weakness and want of poise as he has shown." [15]

Thinking that Dick may have refused the offer because he did not wish to be considered her "overseer," Lizinka revised the terms of her offer in an effort to make it more palatable to him. Instead of being the farm manager, she proposed that Dick lease her land and servants for a period of six years. In return she would receive half the farm's profits. She made the offer for purely pragmatic reasons, she asserted, and urged him to accept or reject it in like spirit without any personal consideration toward herself. "Now look on this calmly as a business matter and if you think you can make by it I will be very glad you should accept it, but remember there is to be no favor on either side. I make the proposition to you, as on mature consideration the best way I can get my business managed— if you accept it do so . . . because on the whole it promises more for the future than anything else." [16]

Ewell rejected this offer, too. Although he never gave any reason for his decision, Rebecca believed that his tender feelings for Lizinka weighed heavily in the matter. William Stoddert offered a different explanation entirely. He maintained that his brother liked the army and that he never had the remotest intention of resigning. "If Mrs. B. had given him the farm he might have considered it," the younger man speculated. "My opinion is that Mrs. B. was in a measure aware of his attachment to army life as he was not himself. I say he never intended. I only mean he would not. A more variable, uncertain person I never saw. But to all great & important things he is constant." [17]

Lizinka was disappointed that Dick would not lease her property, but she bore him no hard feelings. In fact she remained "excessively anxious" about his welfare and sought to boost his career by securing him a major's commission in the Paymaster's Department. As she explained to her uncle Maj. David Hubbard (a former member of Congress), the department carried ten majors on its rolls who were selected by the secretary of war from captains in the Regular Army. After Dick had gotten his major's commission, she believed that he could easily transfer back to line duty, which was his great desire. "His reasons for not applying to you for your influence in his promotion are natural enough," Lizinka explained, "that you have already exerted it for him, that he has no opportunity & expects to have none to return the obligation, & that were he known to apply for the exertion of political influence in his favor & fail to obtain it, his position in the army would be rendered unpleasant thereby."[18]

Ewell may have been reluctant to use political influence to advance, but Lizinka was not. In addition to contacting Hubbard, she wrote to her friend Senator Andrew Johnson, General Winfield Scott, and several other prominent individuals on Ewell's behalf. Ironically, Ewell claimed he did not want the paymaster position. That was just as well, since the secretary of war did not offer it to him.[19]

Ewell left Lizinka in November 1855 and traveled to Stony Lonesome to visit his mother, Rebecca, and William. Twice he rode to Georgetown to visit his sister Elizabeth at the convent, but each time he returned without seeing her.[20] Ewell spent much of his leave in Williamsburg visiting Ben. At age forty-five, Ben was Dick's eldest brother and closest companion. Ben had resigned from the army in September 1836 to accept a job from Isaac R. Trimble as principal assistant engineer of the Baltimore and Susquehanna Railroad. But education was in Ben's blood. After just three years with the railroad, he had moved to Virginia and taught mathematics, first at Hampden-Sydney College, then Washington College, and finally the College of William and Mary. In 1854 William and Mary's Board of Visitors appointed Ben president of the college. By then his wife was no longer with him. A few years after their marriage Julia grew violent. Her wild speech and uncontrolled temper ultimately led to the Ewells' separation. The blow fell hardest on their daughter Lizzie, who divided her time between the homes of her estranged parents.[21]

Dick Ewell stayed with Ben and Lizzie for three months, until his leave ended, then returned to New Mexico. With him went his brother William. William was the most peculiar of the Ewell children. As the youngest, he had always been his mother's favorite. In deference to her wishes, he had dropped his surname and took to calling himself simply William Stoddert. He chased after girls in his younger days, but stronger convictions ultimately drew him in a different direction. After graduating from Hampden-Sydney College and Union Theological Seminary, William donned the robes of a Presbyterian minister.[22]

As he increased in years, William began exhibiting signs of eccentricity, the result of his family's chronic inbreeding. En route to New Mexico, Ewell and his brother stopped at St. Louis to see Tasker Gantt. After spending an evening or two with his cousins, Gantt pronounced William to be "one of the most unbalanced men I ever saw—his mind was, as far as I could judge, constantly under the influence of a notion that he was being watched and must for his own protection not be natural, but perform a part." Gantt thought William not only paranoid but immature. "He is a child in fact, although more than thirty years old, and will I dare say be a child in most things at 50. But he has not the appearance of a sane being to me. There is no repose, no balance about him." [23] Balanced or not, William was an amiable traveling companion, and Dick was glad to have him along.

Dick and William left Gantt and rode to Fort Leavenworth, where Ewell took command of a detachment of recruits heading to Santa Fe. Governor Meriwether, having completed his business in the East, returned to New Mexico with Ewell's party.[24] After dropping Meriwether off at Santa Fe, Ewell and his brother continued down the Rio Grande to Los Lunas, where Ewell reported for duty on 1 May 1856. The post was not at all what William expected. He had imagined Los Lunas to be an isolated spot in the middle of the desert; instead he found it to be a busy place visited by numerous travelers.

As commander of the post, Dick shouldered the responsibility of entertaining visitors. He handled that chore with considerable grace, if not complete sincerity. William had frequent opportunities to watch him in action. "His manners are most attractive," William informed Rebecca. "He gives every one the idea he is their particular friend & this by mere manner. . . . So Gov. M. thought, yet when alone 'Brute & guts' were app[el]lations not rarely applied. . . . The best sample of him I saw the other day. A man came to the gate & called for fear of the dog. He saw him & said, 'I wish he would eat your heart out,' but went out, brought him in, gave him some seed, & really went to trouble about him which no one else would have done. He has a kind & generous nature but a bitter heart." [25]

Dick Ewell led a busy life at Los Lunas. Because it was a small post, he had direct responsibility for many functions that at a larger post might have been delegated to subordinate officers. Except perhaps for the social obligations incumbent on him as the post commander, Ewell preferred it that way. High-strung and hyperactive by nature, he thrived on the long hours required by Los Lunas's demanding regimen. In addition to conducting drills, enforcing discipline, and handling matters of routine administration, he participated in courts-martial and boards of survey and took part in escort duty, scouting expeditions, and other forms of detached service.

When there was any prospect of combat, Ewell led the patrols in person. Such was the case on 14 May 1856, when reports reached him that Indians were plundering settlements along the Puerco River, northwest of Los Lunas. He immediately mounted all available men at the post—in this case only twelve dragoons—and took up pursuit. As usual, he was too late. By the time he reached the scene, the marauders had long since disappeared. Ewell interviewed victims of the attack, identified the culprits as Mimbres Apaches, and returned to the post, his force being inadequate to pursue the Mimbres into their own territory.[26]

The ride to the Puerco River marked his last scout in New Mexico. In July the War Department split up the First Dragoons, transferring three companies to the West Coast and ordering four others to the newly acquired Arizona territory.[27] Company G belonged to the latter group. It left Los Lunas for good on 22 September. In some respects it must have been a sad parting. The company had made many improvements to the post, including the construction of a ninepin bowling alley and the cultivation of a flourishing garden. With it the company took what was described as "a large valuable Library" and a fund of no less than $25,000 that, in the opinion of one historian, made it "the wealthiest and probably the most comfortably provided company in the department."[28]

William went to Fort Union to serve as a minister rather than accompany Dick to Arizona. Having been raised in a contentious household, he felt right at home among the fort's thirteen families, which quarreled among themselves "like so many sitting hens." The constant nagging he witnessed there and at home may well have soured him toward marriage, for he remained a bachelor the rest of his life, despite rumors that linked him to Miss Green, a woman whom Dick uncharitably described as "many years his senior; much poorer than Job's turkey and not much smarter." William remained at Fort Union for three years, after which he packed his bags and returned to Virginia, leaving the frontier and spinster Green behind.[29]

Dick meanwhile was carving out a reputation for himself in southern Arizona, arguably the most desolate and dangerous section of the country. In addition to the Mexican and American settlers, the territory supported a healthy population of murderers, cutthroats, and thieves who had fled to Arizona to escape justice in California, New Mexico, and Sonora. Law enforcement in Arizona was practically nonexistent. "There was hardly a pretense at a civil organization," wrote contemporary historian Raphael Pumpelly. "Law was unknown, and the nearest court was several hundred miles distant in New Mexico. Indeed, every man took the law into his own hands, and the life of a neighbor was valued in the inverse ratio of the impunity with which it could be taken. . . . Murder was the order of

the day." Independent sources bear out Pumpelly's assertion. Local newspaper accounts of the period routinely contained tales of robberies and gunfights. One
Tucson cemetery contained the graves of forty-seven white men, only two of
whom had died of natural causes. In such a rough-and-tumble society, army
officers like Ewell sometimes had to assume the role of both civil and military
administrator.[30]

As a rule, however, the army had more than enough to do keeping the local Indians in line without worrying about the Mexican and American settlers. Most
Indians in the territory were friendly toward the U.S. government. Then there
were the Apaches. Fierce and warlike, they lived by plundering Mexican settlements. The Apaches were divided into numerous bands scattered throughout
New Mexico and Arizona. Altogether they numbered no more than 8,000 souls,
but as one historian noted, "the havoc they created was out of all proportion to
their population."[31]

To limit the havoc, the army sent Company G and three other dragoon companies to Arizona. Commanding the force was Maj. Enoch Steen, an officer
whom Ewell characterized as "the greatest liar & scamp in the world, and a miserable old 'sitting hen.'" Steen gathered his command near Fort Thorn on the Rio
Grande before beginning his 340-mile trek to Tucson on 19 October 1856. Steen
had orders to establish a military post in Tucson. If he found the public buildings
there inadequate to quarter his troops, he was to select an alternate location from
which he could protect Mexican settlements in the Santa Cruz Valley.[32]

Steen examined Tucson but found insufficient water, shelter, and forage to
support a large military post. Instead he established his command at Calabasas
Ranch, sixty miles south of town. He called the new post Camp Moore. Calabasas
stood near the confluence of the Santa Cruz River and Sonoita Creek, ten miles
from the Mexican border. From an agricultural standpoint, it was superior to
Tucson, containing excellent pasturage for grazing and a dark, rich soil for farming.[33] Unfortunately, the site did not meet the approval of Col. Benjamin L. E.
Bonneville, the acting department commander. Bonneville believed a military
post at Calabasas would foster settlement across the border in the Mexican
province of Sonora while exposing Tucson to Apache raids. In a sharply worded
order, he directed Steen to abandon Calabasas and establish a new post "at or near
Tucson" in accordance with his earlier instructions.[34]

Steen sent parties of men back to Tucson to look for a suitable spot for the
post, but they had no success. There simply was no place near the town capable
of supporting a large military post. As an alternative, Steen had Ewell make a reconnaissance in the direction of the San Pedro River, forty-five miles east. The

balding captain was familiar with that region, having recently spent ten weeks there supervising the construction of a road. After examining the area, he recommended that Steen establish a post at Ojos Calientes in the Sonoita Valley, twenty-five miles northeast of Calabasas. The site offered abundant fuel, forage, and water for the squadron, he reported; moreover, it was healthy, twenty miles closer to Tucson than Calabasas, and in the heart of Apache territory. A post there, Ewell asserted, not only would hasten settlement of the Sonoita and San Pedro Valleys but also would afford protection to silver mines near the Calabasas Ranch and block Apache incursions into Sonora.[35]

Farmers and merchants in Tucson objected to the new location. With some justice they claimed that Ojos Calientes, though technically closer to Tucson than Calabasas, was actually farther away, since the Santa Rita Mountains stood between it and Tucson. Instead of protecting them, they argued, the post would increase their danger by forcing marauding Apaches to detour around Ojos Calientes, thereby approaching closer to Tucson. Ewell brushed aside their objections, stating bluntly that "the only sufferers by our absence [in Tucson] would be the whiskey sellers & those who hope to profit from the dissipation of the Soldiers." Steen apparently agreed. In March 1857 he approved Ojos Calientes as the new site for the post.[36]

Steen hoped that a military post in the Sonoita Valley would deter Chiricahua Apache raids north of the border. The Chiricahuas routinely conducted raids into Sonora and Chihuahua, Mexico, but in recent years famine had prompted them to attack settlements in New Mexico and Arizona too. That could not be tolerated, and in April 1857 Bonneville ordered Steen to mount a large-scale expedition against the Chiricahuas. When Steen fell ill at the last moment, command of the detachment fell to Ewell.[37]

Ewell left Calabasas on 3 May, directing his course northeast toward the Chiricahua Mountains. With him rode Lts. Alfred B. Chapman and Benjamin F. Davis and 103 rank and file of the First Dragoons, plus packers, herders, and other support personnel. Lts. Isaiah N. Moore and Horace Randal were then serving on a court of inquiry in Albuquerque but would join the column with fifteen additional men when the court ended.[38] Ewell established camp in the Chiricahua Mountains on 12 May and the next day started with Chapman and sixty-five men for a seven-day ride around the southern end of the range. He saw no Apaches, but that did not discourage him. As he later admitted, the outing was "rather spent in exploring than scouting" for Indians, "as I had no one who had ever seen that country, or any means of following a trail."

Ewell must have seen something that intrigued him, for he at once set out on a second expedition that approximated the earlier route. This time he had more luck. The second night out the Chiricahuas fired a single shot into his camp—a warning for the dragoons to turn back. The next morning Ewell came upon a small herd of twenty horses. He secured the animals and was about to follow their trail back to the Apache camp when a band of Chiricahuas appeared waving a white flag. The Indians dispatched a captive Mexican boy to the dragoons with what Ewell cynically described as the Apaches' "usual professions of friendship, when they are in trouble." Unswayed by the Indians' declarations of peace, he issued orders for an immediate attack. The Apaches tried to resist, but as the dragoons clambered up the steep face of the mesa, they wisely withdrew. During the commotion the Mexican boy slipped away and rejoined his captors.[39]

Ewell bivouacked that night on an open plain, carefully establishing pickets around the camp. During the night the Chiricahuas fired shots and set fire to the grass nearby. Ewell burned a ring around the camp to keep the fire out and slightly shifted his position. Unaware that the soldiers had moved, the Chiricahuas crept forward and received a surprise volley that sent them scampering to cover. That ended the attack. The Apaches struck again the next night but inflicted no greater casualties than before.[40]

While Ewell pursued the Chiricahuas among the mountains, Bonneville was mounting an even larger expedition against the Mogollon Apaches, who lived along the Gila River. He ordered Ewell to join his force. Ewell gave up his pursuit of the Chiricahuas and headed north toward a depot that Bonneville had established along the river to supply the coming expedition. On the way he encountered Lt. Alexander M. McCook and a detachment from the Third Infantry. Ewell took command of both forces and led them through the Burro Mountains to the point of rendezvous.[41]

Ewell and McCook reached the Gila River Depot on 8 June. They bivouacked there for several days while the remaining units of Bonneville's command trickled in. Ewell was pessimistic about the expedition's chance for success. Over the years he had had little luck tracking Apaches with small bodies of dragoons, and he had no reason to think that a large column, burdened with a wagon train and footsore infantry, would do any better. The time would be better spent working in the company garden. "I am very tired of chasing a parcel of Indians about at the orders of men who dont know what to do or how to do it if they knew what they wanted," he complained. "I would prefer the less romantic but hardly less inhuman business of raising potatoes & cabbages. I say hardly less inhuman

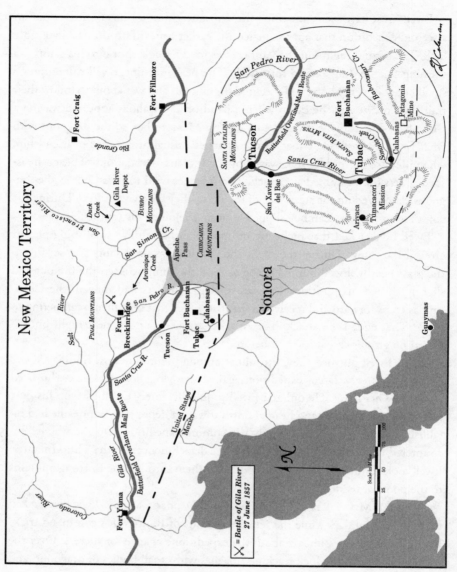

New Mexico Territory

Arizona, 1857–1860

X = *Battle of Gila River 27 June 1857*

because going as we now are about starting in a 'Solumn' (solid) Column of 600 men, we will not be apt to see Indians[,] & mules & horses will be the only sufferers."[42]

Other officers shared his pessimism. Lt. Henry M. Lazelle of the infantry caustically described Bonneville's expedition as "originating in the bombastic folly of a silly old man already in his dotage, and thus far conducted with a degree of stupidity almost asinine." It angered him to think of "our slow motioned and heavily laden Infantry, toilsomely dragging its lengthy and sluggish columns over the burning plains, its troops choking with dust finer than ashes, and its animals suffocating, and dying under their heavy burdens from want of water."[43]

Bonneville divided his command into two columns commanded by one-armed Col. William W. Loring of the Mounted Rifles and by aging Lt. Col. Dixon S. Miles of the Third Infantry. Miles's column had 412 men, which he divided into two wings, one led by Ewell, the other by himself.[44]

Miles left the depot on 13 June and headed northwest. Three days into the campaign, Mexican guides spotted some Apaches near the San Francisco River, twelve miles away. Miles sent Ewell ahead with a mixed force of 120 infantry and dragoons to strike the Indians before they could escape, while he and the remainder of the column followed with the baggage.[45] Ewell followed a rocky trail to Duck Creek. Finding no Indians there, he pushed on to the Nigrita River. Miles and Loring caught up with him there on 20 June. The army rested on the Nigrita for a day before continuing its march. Loring now took the lead.[46]

As Bonneville advanced deep into Apache territory, he became timid. "Col. Bonneville is in a perfect 'tremble of anxiety,'" wrote Lt. John DuBois of the mounted rifles. "A little smoke frightens him to death & then to hear him explain all his reasons to the cooks, in his 2nd childhood's prattle, is certainly less ludicrous than pathetic. I am anxious for some success but feel that accident alone can compensate us for the honest efforts neglected. Capt. Ewell is my only anchor of hope now." To make matters worse, Bonneville was at odds with Miles and Loring. For two days the army remained camped on the Nigrita while the three commanders bickered over what course to pursue. Their hesitation only heightened DuBois's disgust. "If any success is found, Capt. Ewell or Luck will be the sole cause," he confided to his diary. "Have been in Capt. Ewell's camp today," he added, "& like them better every time we meet."[47]

Bonneville finally decided on a course of action. Dividing his army, he sent Loring's column into the White Mountains and directed Miles to march toward the Gila. Miles's guides reported a Mogollon Apache village ahead. Ewell rushed

Battle of the Gila, 1857 (Arizona Historical Society, Tucson)

forward with a light column of eighty infantrymen, thirty mounted riflemen, and sixty dragoons to attack the settlement, but he found only nine women present. The men had escaped.[48]

Ewell set out after the Apaches and sent back a message urging Bonneville to follow. One mile from the village, Ewell's Pueblo scouts encountered the Apaches. A fight ensued, prompting Ewell to send forward Lieutenant Chapman with twenty men to support the scouts. The Apaches withdrew. For the rest of the day, Ewell's party groped ahead, pausing neither to eat nor to rest. That night, as

the soldiers made camp, they heard music not more than 300 yards away. Ewell planned a dawn attack, but by morning the Indians were gone. After a hasty breakfast of horseflesh and rice, the soldiers continued their relentless advance, determined once and for all to bring the Apaches to bay.[49]

Bonneville continued to limp behind Ewell with the main body of troops. Annoyed by his subordinate's aggressive pursuit of the Apaches and fearful of attack, he threatened to turn back.[50] Ewell met with Bonneville and persuaded him to follow the Apaches for just a few days more. Reluctantly, Bonneville agreed. On

27 June the army continued its march, with Ewell again taking the lead. The feisty captain set his course toward the Gila. Pueblo scouts fanned out in front of the column to gather information and prevent an ambush. As they approached the river, the Pueblos encountered unmistakable signs that the Apaches were nearby. Ewell galloped ahead with his dragoons, leaving orders for the infantry to follow as rapidly as possible.[51]

The horsemen came within sight of the Gila at 4:30 P.M. On the banks of the river was the object of their expedition: an Apache village. Incredibly, the residents had not received warning of Ewell's approach. Some forty warriors and their families were still in camp. Ewell took in the situation at a glance and ordered Lt. Isaiah Moore to charge. The shock of Moore's unexpected attack scattered the Indians, who fled into the thick brush that lined the river's banks.

Rather than dismount and fight at a disadvantage, Moore wisely led his men across the Gila, thereby cutting off the Apaches' retreat. "This well timed movement went far towards securing the decisive results," Ewell reported with approval. As his infantry came on the scene, Ewell had them flush the Indians who remained hidden along the river's edge. Bonneville and Miles arrived with reinforcements after the battle was over. As they paused to catch their breath, Ewell hurried forward to attack another nearby village. He was too late. The inhabitants had heard the sound of his earlier attack and had fled their homes before he arrived.[52]

The battle of the Gila was a stirring success. At a cost of just two officers and eight men wounded, Ewell had defeated an Apache band, killing at least twenty of their warriors and taking forty-five women and children prisoner. More important, he had destroyed the Indians' villages and crops, exposing the survivors to starvation in the coming winter. At Ewell's urging, Bonneville plunged deeper into enemy territory, seeking other settlements to destroy. "Capt. Ewell again goes in advance," DuBois noted contemptuously, "while our Colonels remain safely in rear protected by more than one hundred fighting men. *Vive la bagatelle.*"[53]

Stunned by their defeat, the Apache band sued for peace. Bonneville agreed to treat with them, but as the meeting was about to take place, Loring's column appeared, causing the Indians to scatter. When they did not return, Bonneville led his column back to the Gila River Depot.

Ewell was hailed as the hero of the campaign. Bonneville praised the Virginian in his report and called him "my active man on all important occasions." Miles credited him with "planning the battle and breaking the enemy." Ewell's highest accolades came from department commander Bvt. Brig. Gen. John Garland, who, in a report to the secretary of war, complimented the dragoon captain's "gallantry and sound judgment." He was the only officer to receive such notice.[54]

Clouding Ewell's otherwise glorious victory was the fact that he had attacked the wrong people. His object had been to punish the Mogollon Apaches; instead he had attacked their distant cousins, the Coyoteros. This caused only passing embarrassment. Soon after, Apache agent Michael Steck uncovered evidence indicating that the Coyoteros had taken part in attacks on travelers and had recently harbored Mogollon Apaches, including the man who had murdered the popular Navajo agent Henry L. Dodge.[55] Given those facts, the army's assault seemed like just retribution.

The expedition made Ewell's reputation. Thereafter he was recognized as one of the department's premier Indian fighters. To those who had followed his career, his success came as no surprise. Time and again—on the Plains, in Mexico, and in the Southwest—he had proved his mettle and established his credibility. As an officer, he had come of age.

CHAPTER 8

Fort Buchanan

During Ewell's absence on the Gila River expedition, Maj. Enoch Steen had established a new military post at Ojos Calientes, which he named Fort Buchanan in honor of the country's new president. Ewell received orders to report to the post as soon as the expedition ended. There was some urgency to the order. Mexican troops reportedly had crossed the border into the United States and killed four Americans. Ewell remained only briefly at the fort. In August 1857 he attended a court-martial at department headquarters in Santa Fe, some 500 miles away. While there, he picked up money for the troops at Fort Buchanan, some of whom had not been paid in more than a year. It is little wonder that morale at the post often sagged.[1]

Ewell remained at Santa Fe for two months waiting for the trial to convene and for the money to arrive from the states. To pass the time, he went hunting. He bagged approximately 100 birds, including snipe, ducks, geese, and crane, which he distributed among the officers' families. His greatest acquisition, though, he informed his niece Lizzie, "was of a lot of potatoes, an article in great demand in N.M. and which are more welcome to the ladies here than compliments even would be."[2]

Lizzie was one of Ewell's most frequent correspondents, though her letters to him were never as frequent or as long as he thought they should be. In one instance he playfully chided her for trying to make one letter serve for both him and William. "The last letter I have had the felicity of seeing of yours was dated the 7. July & as no names are mentioned in it, I am in a state of great doubt for whom it is intended," he wrote her. "As it was enclosed to William my own private opinion is that it is an artful dodge to make one letter answer for two persons[,] you thinking as it will do for either him or me that both will claim it. You deal in generalities that will do equally well for him or me. However, as it is the last of the month & I believe the last letter has been received by me (I wont say that I owe

Lizzie Ewell, the general's niece (Hamlin, Letters)

you one as you cant pretend to strike a balance with one in 'high official position')[,] I will condescend to pass over the apparent attempt to humbug your two
respectable Uncles."

When it came to writing, Ewell's young relatives gave as good as they got. In a
reply to a taunting letter from her "Dear Uncle Dick," Lizinka's spirited eleven-
year-old daughter, Harriot, wrote, "You are well aware that I did not promise to

give you my daguerreotype or my hair and I am not going to do it. . . . And as to my going to Williamsburg with you it was absolutely preposterous."[3]

While at Santa Fe, Ewell heard that the War Department had introduced camels to a post in Texas as a substitute for horses. Ewell—ever looking for an edge over his Apache tormentors—wanted to be in on the ground floor of the novel experiment. He sent a letter to Washington officially requesting that camels be sent to Fort Buchanan, a point that he considered "well adapted to their use." He wished to use the camels to pursue Apaches across Arizona's arid, rocky terrain, where horses and mules could not readily go. If possible, he wished to experiment with both "express" and "burden" camels, but if restricted to only one type, he preferred express camels "as most likely to be of important service." The department quartermaster who endorsed the request stated that he knew of no officer "who will take more interest in the subject and who will exercise better judgement in the management of the camels than Capt. Ewell." In the end, nothing came of the request. The army asked for funds to purchase 1,000 additional camels, but Congress refused. The Camel Corps was put on hold.[4]

Ewell's court-martial duty ended in November, and he returned to Fort Buchanan with Lt. Orren Chapman of Company B. The two men stopped at Albuquerque to pick up a detachment of recruits, then continued down the Rio Grande to Fort Craig. They found the post in a state of unusual excitement. Indians had just attacked a ranch three miles from the post. When troops arrived on the scene, a hand-to-hand fight had ensued. Lt. William W. Averell, an officer fresh out of West Point, led the U.S. detachment. Ewell stepped forward and placed his hand on Averell's head. "Young man, there is a brevet hanging over your head," he said generously, "I have been scouting for Indians all my life without any luck and here you are a fortnight in the country and make a strike in sight of your Post." Averell was flattered by the veteran's attention, noting that "Captain Ewell and 'old Chap' delighted us with their visit until next day."[5]

Ewell and Chapman reached Fort Buchanan the day after Christmas, their journey having been retarded by a freak storm that dumped three feet of snow on the desert floor. The post stood in the Santa Rita Valley, about twenty-five miles north of the Mexican border. Marshes surrounded it on three sides, exposing the garrison to malaria. In the opinion of critics, the post stood too far from Tucson to prevent Apache raids on that town, too far from the Overland Mail route to afford it proper protection, and too far from the Apache heartland to act as the army's forward base of supply in offensive operations.[6]

Fort Buchanan's design was as bad as its location. Bvt. Lt. Col. Isaac Van Duzen Reeve of Company B, Eighth Infantry, who briefly commanded the post, declared that it occupied "ten times the ground it ought to, being on & around a side hill of considerable abruptness—and does not admit of any considerable improvement in a military point of view—the buildings being located with great irregularity & irrespective of defence." The buildings themselves were badly constructed and of the most temporary nature. Inspecting Fort Buchanan in 1859, Col. Joseph E. Johnston observed that the officers' quarters and post hospital had been built of adobe, but that the other buildings were no more than "logs, or wooden slabs, set on end in the ground & the intervals closed with mud," most of which had fallen out, making them too drafty in winter yet not sufficiently ventilated in summer. "Fortunately very little labour, or, it is to be presumed, money, has been expended upon them," he added dryly.[7]

Fort Buchanan stood in the middle of one of the richest mining regions of the country. The mountains of the Southwest contained large deposits of gold, silver, and copper, some of which, Ewell claimed, would break the Rothschilds. As an amateur chemist, he took great interest in the area's mineralogy. By March 1858 he had converted his quarters into a laboratory for testing mineral ore. "My room is completely filled with chemical machinery," he wrote Lizzie, "& my table boasts of Several crucibles & books; blow pipe, scales, charcoal, supports & at least 6 different kinds of minerals. Maj. Steen left a piece of mineral with me which he thought was rich but appeared ordinary to me. He begged me for a long time to try it & at last thinking of 'fool for luck' did so & found it very rich then reduced some & found it worth at the rate of two dollars the pound of ore—ten cents is considered good from the same amt of ore."[8]

Ewell's interest in mineralogy eventually took a more substantive turn. In May 1858 he joined James W. Douglass, Richard M. Doss, and Lts. Isaiah N. Moore, Richard S. C. Lord, and Horace Randal to open a silver mine just a few miles from the border. They called it the Patagonia Mine. The group reputedly bought information about the mine's location from a Mexican herder for a pony and a few other small articles. Ewell had high hopes for the mine. He told Lizzie that it "promises to rival any that can be mentioned. We propose to take out a fortune in silver & another in stocks to be sold when all the silver is extracted. You might create a sensation by proclaiming yourself the niece of a bachelor who owns part of a silver mine. . . . I am puzzled to know what I shall do with so much mon[e]y," Ewell drolly mused, pondering the riches that would soon come pouring in, "whether to make the Pacific rail road, buy New York City or what. May be you can give [me] some useful hints."[9]

Before the mine could turn a profit, there was much to do. The owners had to sink shafts, build furnaces, buy equipment, and hire laborers. To meet the

Patagonia (later Mowry) Mine, where Ewell hoped to make his fortune
(Browne, Adventures*)*

expenses for such work, Ewell had to invest nearly every dollar available to him. He did so gladly, believing the mine's profits would more than make good the investment. And so they did. As work on the mine progressed, the price of shares doubled, then doubled again. Ewell's hopes climbed in proportion to the mine's value. "It is the darkest, gloomiest looking cavern you can imagine," he fairly chortled to Lizzie, "about 50 feet deep with prospects looking quite bright. I have been offered $1000, for my interest, having at that time expended about $100, so if we fail the croakers cant say it was an absurd speculation. You may rest assured that your Uncle is living very economically not to be obliged to give it up for want of funds. . . . If I can clear by the mine $10,000. I shall take up my line of march for the states & settle down." As if shocked by his own optimism, Ewell added cautiously, "It sometimes almost gives me the chills for fear that it may turn out a failure—more from the wise 'I thought so' of friends than the loss of the money." 10

If the mine failed to turn a profit, Ewell told Lizzie he would quit the army and buy land on San Francisco Bay. "Probably that would be a better spot to revive the former glories of the Ewells than the worn out lands of Prince William," he conjectured. If, however, the mine brought him the fortune he anticipated, he promised to take Lizzie to Europe. To prepare her for the trip, he proposed sending her to school at his own expense, throwing in a little pin money besides. "I shall want whoever goes with me to be accomplished[,] elegant[,] easy in manner[,] & with good teeth and a knowledge of the languages," he teased his niece. "Who knows with so many accomplishments but you may captivate a beggarly French or Italian Count. If the mine fail[s,] the accomplishments may be shown off to advantage at a post where the ladies spend their leisure playing cards and quarrelling." 11

Until Ewell's speculation paid off, he had to endure the day-to-day ennui of garrison life. To pass the time, he read Shakespeare, studied French, wrote letters, and played cards with Fort Buchanan's quarreling ladies. Nothing seemed to help; the boredom grew more oppressive each day. "This place is dull beyond anything I ever imagined," he grumbled. "Nothing going on. I try to work myself tired in the company garden so as to sleep away some of the time but it wont do." 12

Scouting expeditions helped break the grinding monotony. By 1858 Apache attacks near Fort Buchanan had become so common that Steen felt obliged to keep parties of dragoons in the field. "The Indians are constantly committing depredations in the valleys of the Santa Cruz and Sonoita," he complained. "They come in small stealing parties of from 5 to 8 on foot at night [and] drive off the stock. On being closely pursued by citizens or soldiers, they leave that portion of the stock that cannot travel with celerity and make a run for the mountains, when it is impossible to trail them." In Ewell's opinion it was not a lack of opportunity but a lack of will that inhibited pursuit of the marauders. "The Indians are around us robbing all the time, but without any prospect of rousing the Fabius who commands us, so as Mars is out of fashion we will worship Plutus." 13

By "Fabius" Ewell was probably referring to Bvt. Maj. Edward H. Fitzgerald. Fitzgerald took command of Fort Buchanan in the spring of 1858 when Steen contracted a skin disease and left Arizona on an extended leave of absence. As it turned out, Fitzgerald's health was no better than Steen's had been. The new commander suffered from hemorrhaging of the lungs, and after just four months he too left the territory on an extended leave of absence. The change of climate did him no good; he died of tuberculosis two years later.[14]

Fitzgerald left Fort Buchanan on 15 August accompanied by Lt. Isaiah Moore, who was going to the states on recruiting duty. Moore had been Ewell's right-hand man for five years. With his departure Ewell and Lt. Richard Lord were the only officers in the company present for duty. Lord was a married man and occupied separate quarters, leaving Ewell to maintain a "bachelors hall" by himself. To keep him company, he invited Lizzie to stay with him for a while. He was in need of a good housekeeper, Ewell quipped, and wished to give her the right of first refusal. The offer was not without a condition. Before coming to the post, Lizzie had to promise "not to marry some young, poverty stricken, conceited Lieutenant who would expect my best cow & probably old Hester to cook and then grumble if he could not borrow chairs, tables, spoons, plates, Towels, napkins, &c. &c. as well as pestering me with your quarrels."[15]

In subsequent letters Ewell changed the tack of his humor 180 degrees and suggested that Lizzie visit him at Fort Buchanan specifically to find a husband among the post officers. Admittedly the pickings were rather slim. "There are two bachelors here now," he informed her. "One an Irishman Doctor U.S.A. red head & hot tempered as possible and the other a Lieut. from Ohio who, on a march we made together, some time since, when he catered, provided, to my dismay, nothing but a big hog which we were to eat fresh. I suppose in honor of his native state. It is needless to say that I did not fatten on that trip. They would not be very good catches."[16]

Fitzgerald's departure left Ewell in command at Fort Buchanan. In the latter half of 1858 he led several minor excursions into the mountains in an effort to intimidate the Apaches. He was frequently in the saddle for days at a time, trying to chase down marauding Indians who terrorized settlers or ran off stock. During one scout, Ewell and his men halted by a stream to rest. "I lent one of the Soldiers some fishing lines," the hungry leader recalled, "& very soon he made his appearance with a fine string of fish which I duly admired. He walked off with them & just as I had worked myself in a fury at his impudence he came back with one nicely cooked & hot in the frying pan. I have thought better of soldiers ever since."[17]

By his own admission Ewell was "fond of good eating," and he usually managed to dine well, even during an active campaign. He had no superior when it came to roasting a partridge or broiling a quarter of venison over an outdoor fire. When in the more congenial surroundings of his quarters, he frequently took a glass of sherry or Spanish madeira with his meals and polished them off with a piece of fruit. Ewell claimed the fruit took "the taste of grease out of his mouth." He took special delight in sucking on grapes, which he first pitted and peeled, leaving "nothing but liquid to swallow." [18]

A sick stomach often compelled Ewell to adopt a bland diet. When he reached middle age, he developed dyspepsia, or what physicians today might call chronic esophagitis and gastritis. In the summer months his breakfast consisted simply of lettuce, cucumbers, or cole slaw topped with a vinegar and oil dressing, plus a biscuit and a cup of coffee. For dinner he added soup to the menu. Yet sometimes he found that hard to keep down. "I can not eat boiled cabbages and was made sick the other day by toast and coffee," he complained. "You may be sure you eat too much particularly if your food comes up. Being hungry is no sign as the stomach is a muscle which is stronger from exercise and demands its habitual allowance [of] exercise although the rest of the system be well enough with less. The stomach is not provided with brains to know what is sufficient for the health of the other parts." [19]

Ewell penned his gastronomic philosophy for the benefit of Lizzie, who had recently complained of gaining weight. As a dutiful uncle he sought to advise her on this point. "I have been earnestly racking my brains since the receipt of your letter asking for a prescription against, or rather for[,] obesity with which you are threatened. I saw a few days since that it was fashionable and maybe your anxiety was all pretended & nothing more than a modest way of letting it be know how elegant[,] fashionable, & plump you had become. . . . If you really desire to grow thin," he suggested, "you will have to use a great deal of forbearance & self-denial in the winter. In the summer if you should happen to have a dislike to any dish— fat meat for instance—a hearty meal in the warmest part of the day will keep you from increasing in weight for at least one week. Swallowing a fly is also good. . . . If you dont eat you cannot fat[t]en & after all this & exercise are the only panaceas." Ewell then revealed some of his own dieting secrets. "I find the ownership of an interest in a rich mine, which the people are too lazy to work has a good effect," he told Lizzie. "Walking with small gravel in your shoes, having a pin sticking in your flesh, making yourself ridiculous at a party & see the people laughing, get into another row in church & have it published. . . . In short anything to keep you fretting are valuable helps." [20]

Indians kept Ewell fretting. At times he found the friendship of peaceable tribes as intolerable as he did the Apaches' hostility. A case in point were the Pimas, who lived on the Gila River just below the mouth of the San Pedro. The Pimas were an industrious people who lived by agriculture and wove fine blankets of cotton. But they were also avaricious and prone to petty theft. In November the tribe sent a delegation to Fort Buchanan to request arms, ammunition, blankets, and other provisions from Ewell. "I took pains to explain to the chief by himself that I had no authority to give clothing," the captain fumed, "but made him a present of some cotton for himself. This morning he came back with the same string of wants, winding up with the information that he had given away the cotton & wanted some more. Not taking any notice, he walked off in high dudgeon looking as though he felt himself very much outraged. It is the most provoking thing in the world to have business with these people who are compounds of children & foxes." [21]

By 1859 the Pinal Apaches were Ewell's greatest concern. On 27 January 1859 Pinal warriors attacked three U.S. soldiers on furlough from Fort Buchanan. They killed two of the men, but the third escaped. In response to this and other outrages, Ewell proposed leading a punitive expedition into the Pinals' homeland, on the San Pedro River east of Tucson, but a shortage of horses and other supplies prevented him from doing so. He had 170 men at Fort Buchanan and 50 more recruits were on their way. To mount this force Ewell had only 108 horses, 12 of which were unfit for service. Without at least 24 more horses, and preferably 50, he told his superiors, he could offer no more than token resistance to Apache raiders. Ewell also reported serious shortages of horseshoes, cavalry boots, uniform drawers and socks, ammunition, and subsistence. "I am [as] helpless without these supplies as if I were without horses," he complained. [22]

Before Ewell could deal with the Pinals, the Chiricahua Apaches began to act up. The Chiricahuas lived near Apache Pass, 100 miles east of Fort Buchanan. Their leader was Cochise, soon to be the most famous of all Apache chiefs. The Chiricahuas habitually conducted raids on Mexican ranches south of the border, but beginning in 1858 they started raiding Mexican ranches in Arizona as well. In January 1859 Ewell accompanied Dr. Michael Steck, the U.S. Indian agent, to a meeting with Cochise. Steck insisted that depredations north of the border must stop. He promised to bring Cochise and his people food and gifts twice a year if they complied with his demand; otherwise they risked reprisals from the U.S. Army.

Cochise had nothing to gain by starting a war with the United States and pledged his cooperation. As a token of his good intentions, he returned some livestock that his people had stolen and turned over a Mexican boy that they had recently captured on a raid to Sonora. For several months Cochise kept his promise, limiting his raids to ranches south of the border. When Apaches outside his clan stole some livestock in his absence, he personally rode to Fort Buchanan to proclaim his innocence to Ewell, knowing that he might be blamed. On another occasion, when a group of his own people stole eighty or ninety mules from the Sonora Exploring and Mining Company without his knowledge, Cochise apologized and ordered the animals to be returned.[23]

Although Ewell had neither the manpower nor the resources to suppress Cochise, his presence at Fort Buchanan helped to curb the Chiricahua chief's forays. Later officers were not so successful. After Ewell left Arizona, soldiers of the Seventh Infantry hanged members of Cochise's family, causing the Apache to go on a violent rampage. "A better understanding was reached a few years after," wrote one soldier, "through the exertions of officers of the stamp of Ewell, who were bold in war but tender in peace, and who obtained great influence over a simple race which could respect men whose word was not written in sand."[24]

Ewell's influence over Cochise and other Apache leaders was not so obvious at the time. By the fall of 1859, depredations in the Fort Buchanan area had become almost a daily occurrence. Many local residents failed to see that Ewell or any other officer in the army was doing much about it. The editor of the Tucson *Arizonian*, writing in the fall of 1859, complained that despite a burgeoning immigrant population and a successful mining industry, Arizona had "less actual military protection than we had at the time they were first ordered into this Territory." While Fort Buchanan's troops stood by "merely as disinterested observers," Apaches committed daily robberies, attacked travelers, and threatened the local mines. The journalist blamed the garrison's "apparent unconcern" less on the soldiers themselves than on the military authorities in New Mexico, whose "gross negligence" he found intolerable.[25]

No one understood better than Ewell the grave difficulties involved in fighting the Apaches and the post's inability to overcome them. In addition to the crippling lack of supplies described earlier, Fort Buchanan suffered from impossible logistics and insufficient manpower. It all boiled down to a matter of simple arithmetic: the post had only two companies of men to protect an area of several thousand square miles. To compound the problem, the dragoons had to guard the Overland Mail line. "Should all the available force be sent after any one of these tribes," Brevet Lieutenant Colonel Reeve explained, "it would bring down a war of destruction upon this greatly exposed mail route, and it would be impossible to give it protection. I do not see, therefore, any course to be pursued for the present, but the highly objectionable one of *temporizing*."[26]

Too weak to wage war against the Apaches and too distant to be reinforced by other forts in the territory, Fort Buchanan became a paper tiger. The dragoons might occasionally intimidate the Indians, but they could never defeat them. In the words of mine owner Sylvester Mowry, "The small cavalry force in the Territory, although most ably handled by Capt. R. S. Ewell, . . . was entirely unable to make a campaign with decisive results against the Indians."[27] By 1859 even Ewell would have had to concede that he was right.

Bvt. Lt. Col. Isaac Van Duzen Reeve assumed command of Fort Buchanan in March 1859. Reeve brought with him Company D of the Eighth Infantry to replace Company D of the First Dragoons, which had transferred to Fort Fillmore. The dragoons' departure left Ewell's Company G the only mounted unit at the post.[28]

Reeve's arrival gave Ewell a welcome opportunity to take leave. For three and one-half years the captain had stubbornly refused to quit his post, and the fatigue was starting to show. He appeared haggard and tired, and he frequently fell victim to malarial chills and fevers. As soon as Reeve arrived, Ewell applied for a sixty-day leave of absence. He notified headquarters that he intended to spend his leave in the vicinity of the post, so "that in case of movement of the troops I could easily join my Company."[29]

Ewell's careworn appearance that spring resulted as much from grief as from fatigue. A few weeks earlier he had learned of his mother's death. Elizabeth Ewell had passed away on 18 January 1859 at Williamsburg, Virginia, where she was residing with Ben and Lizzie. In deference to Ben, William and Mary's Board of Visitors established a cemetery on the college grounds for deceased faculty members and their families. Elizabeth Ewell was the first person interred there. Dick often discussed placing a proper monument over his mother's grave, but he never did so. Her plot remains unmarked to this day.[30]

His mother's death threw Ewell into a depression for several weeks. He was unable to speak of her passing until May 1859 and then only to members of his immediate family. In a letter written on the nineteenth of that month, he consoled Lizzie for their mutual loss. He assured the teenage girl that her grandmother had been very fond of her. "One advantage about youth is, that these losses do not make a lasting impression compared with the grief of greater age & it is a law of nature that at your time of life the usual gayety [sic] is soon resumed. As for myself I endeavor to occupy my mind as much as possible in my usual business, as it hardly shows any very sensible course to neglect one's duty for no good."[31]

Ewell deferred taking leave until summer in order to avoid being at Fort Buchanan during the "sickly season," the period between July and September when malaria gripped the post. Several soldiers had died from the disease, and

Several members of Ewell's family are buried in the faculty cemetery at the
College of William and Mary (Donald C. Pfanz)

Ewell himself had suffered from its ill effects the previous summer. "I have been living so far in fear and trembling on account of the intermittent fever. So far I have escaped although nearly half of the command is on the sick report," he wrote Lizzie in August. With the sickly season not yet half over, he was not inclined to press his luck. Taking advantage of his leave, he departed the fort and its pernicious swamps and spent a few weeks in the neighboring area.[32]

Ewell spent much of his leave at the Patagonia Mine. In recent months the enterprise had faltered, and his once-high expectations had fallen in proportion. The problem, as he saw it, was simple: the mine lacked a good manager. When time permitted, he oversaw the operation himself, but he could not always be there. Ewell asked his brother William and a cousin to manage the mine for him, but both men declined. His cousin had other irons in the fire, and his brother begged off on account of failing health. Ewell accordingly found himself in a fix. "It is astonishing among the number of beggarly acquaintances and relations one possesses how impossible it is to get hold of one to do any thing," he grumbled.[33]

Violence plagued the troubled mine. In May 1859 some American roughnecks horsewhipped some Mexicans. The Mexicans retaliated by murdering one of the

Americans. The Americans thereupon vowed to drive all Mexicans from the territory. They began by brutally attacking innocent Mexican workers at Patagonia Mine. They killed two of the workers, badly wounded two others, and drove the rest across the border into Sonora. Work at the mine ground to a halt.

Reeve sent Ewell with thirty dragoons to quell the violence, granting him authority to use whatever force was necessary to accomplish that mission. The mere appearance of troops restored order to the agitated region. Later a civilian posse rounded up five of the worst offenders and brought them back in irons to the fort. "There is no civil authority in the Territory," Ewell commented, "& the military have assisted the law & order portion in preserving order. I think one part of these murderers were induced by the hope of driving off all Mexican labor & forcing the people to hire Americans at their own price. Americans here ask $40. per month for common field labor. Two or three of these men have shed so much blood at different times that they seem to be urged on like the tiger to murder without cause."[34]

Indian raids compounded the Patagonia Mine's problems. Three times that summer Apaches attacked the mine, stealing its mules and killing at least one worker. Despite these calamities, Ewell still clung to the hope that the mine would make him rich. His fortune would be made, he believed, "if the abominable Indians would only stop stealing . . . but at present the Mexican expression of doubt suits better than any other, that is, pero, quizas, Quien sabe (but perhaps, Dont know)."[35]

Whatever hopes Ewell had that the mine would succeed vanished when Elias Brevoort got involved in the business. A Dutch merchant and erstwhile army sutler, Brevoort bought out two of Ewell's co-owners in the winter of 1858–59, thereby acquiring a controlling interest in the mine. Ewell admitted that Brevoort was a good businessman, but he considered him a poor judge of men. Under Brevoort's leadership, production at the mine sank to an all-time low. Ewell became so disgusted with Brevoort's mismanagement that he determined to sell his interest in the mine rather than to continue doing business with him. He sold his shares on the open market for $4,000, a modest price considering that he and the other owners had been offered $25,000 in cash for the mine just one year earlier. But prospects had been brighter then; the mine's production had been increasing and its future seemed promising. Now, with mining operations in disarray, it was a buyer's market, and Ewell had to sell his shares at a discount.

Ewell rued the loss. Had Brevoort managed the mine better, he believed they could have sold it for $100,000. He was not far off the mark. Brevoort shortly sold the shaft to Capt. Henry T. Titus, who immediately turned it over to Sylvester

Mowry for $25,000. Under the supervision of Mowry's brother, the mine eventually showed a profit of almost $1,300 a day and, in doing so, made its owner a rich man.[36]

Under other circumstances Ewell might have been that man. As it was, he had to be content with a captain's pay. He supplemented his income by raising cattle. Sometime after coming to Arizona, Ewell purchased several head of cattle that he kept in a corral near Tucson. Although the Apaches periodically ran off some of the stock, the herd grew steadily and yielded a good profit. "You see that I am full of the spirit of speculation and if the Indians did not come down occasionally I would be well off in herds at least," he told Rebecca.[37]

Ewell lost some of his profits betting on horses. Charles H. Tompkins, a dragoon in Company F, recalled that the captain "owned first rate horses, and used to run all the races." One such competition took place on 24 September 1859 at Fort Buchanan. Three horses entered the contest: "Tar River," owned and ridden by Ewell; Dr. Hughes' "Lightning"; and Dr. Irwin's "Rascal." A correspondent of the *Weekly Arizonian* covered the race: "After a false start the horses got off, but as Tar River bolted off the track into the crowd, the race was left between the other two. Rascal won—beating Lightning about three hundred yards in one mile. Capt. Ewell ran Tar River afterwards," the journalist reported, "over the same course and made the mile in one minute and fifty-five seconds—three seconds less than the time occupied by Rascal—which only shows that had not Capt. E's horse bolted, there would have been a well-contested race between Tar River and Rascal, as the latter horse was not let run at full speed in the last half mile of his race against Lightning, who was beaten early in the run." [38]

Other horses disappointed Ewell, too. Brig. Gen. G. Moxley Sorrel remembered in later years that Ewell "never tired of talking of his horse 'Tangent,' . . . who appears to have never won a race and always to have lost his owner's money. But the latter's confidence never weakened and he always believed in 'Tangent.'" Although Ewell would have lost his shirt as a jockey, Sorrel proclaimed him to be "without a superior as a cavalry captain." [39]

Some of the hardest riding that Ewell did was in pursuit of deserters attempting to escape to Mexico. On Thursday, 14 October 1859, two soldiers fled Fort Buchanan on Ewell's best horses. Ewell was absent the day they made their break, and by the time he started after them, they had a thirty-six-hour lead. Accompanied only by a guide, Ewell pursued the fugitives across the border. He captured one of the men near the town of Bajarito, Sonora. He found the body of the other dangling by his neck from a tree. The man had used his handkerchief as a noose. Ewell did not think he had been murdered "because a Mexican would not have

thrown away his handkerchief but would have stabbed or shot him. They murder, each the other (Americans & Mexicans) on this and the other side of the line
without the slightest remorse and as if they wanted to see which was the most
atrocious." Ewell reached Fort Buchanan with his prisoner at 8:00 A.M. Tuesday,
having covered 250 miles in just sixty hours.[40]

Three weeks after that episode, Ewell returned to Sonora as an emissary of the
U.S. government. Mexico was in political turmoil, and its central government
maintained only nominal control over the outlying provinces. Local strongmen,
known as caudillos, stepped into the political vacuum and battled one another for
control. In Sonora, Governor Ignacio Pesqueira held the reins of power. Pesqueira
had antagonized authorities in both Washington and Mexico City by repudiating
a contract made between the Mexican government and an American company to
have Capt. Charles P. Stone survey and map Sonora's public lands. When Stone
arrived in Sonora in March 1858, Pesqueira ordered him to leave. Tensions between the United States and Sonora escalated to the point that some of the more
hawkish members of Congress advocated annexing Sonora by force.[41]

Adj. Gen. Samuel Cooper directed Ewell to call on Governor Pesqueira to
protest Stone's expulsion "as a gross infraction of treaty obligations existing between Mexico and the United States." Ewell's selection was an honor. In transmitting the order through Reeve, Cooper affirmed that Ewell was chosen "for this
delicate and responsible duty from his know[n] intelligence and discretion."
Ewell caught up with Pesqueira in November 1859 at the Sonoran port of Guaymas.[42] He found Capt. William D. Porter of the U.S. sloop-of-war *St. Mary's*
there on the same mission as himself. Ewell called on Porter, and together they
went to see the governor. The meeting was a mere formality. Prior to Ewell's arrival, Porter had met with Pesqueira, and the governor had agreed to permit Stone
to conduct his survey. The matter having been "amicably adjusted," Porter advised Ewell to let the matter drop, rather than reopen the subject with an additional protest. Ewell wisely concurred and returned to Fort Buchanan.[43]

On his way back to the United States, Ewell was arrested by Mexican officials
in Hermosillo and charged with stealing a mule. The captain volunteered to bring
the claim to the attention of proper U.S. officials, presuming the Mexicans could
substantiate the charge. In the interim, he even offered to pay the claimant the
full value of the mule out of his own pocket—but to no avail. A judge confiscated
the animal and insisted that Ewell post bail before leaving town. In an effort to
gain some sort of diplomatic immunity, the captain showed the judge his written
orders from the War Department. The magistrate pushed the papers aside with

the comment that "he did not care" and "that he would do the same if I was the President of the United States."

Ewell found the judge's conduct offensive and considered "the affair as wantonly insulting, & a gross attempt at extortion." Unable to leave the town, he sent a message back to Porter at Guaymas, explaining the facts of the case. "Captain Porter took very decided measures," he gratefully reported, "demanding and receiving my immediate release, a full apology, with the offer of escort, or anything I might require for my journey." Despite the hostility of Hermosillo's local officials, Ewell was pleased to report that the Mexican citizens as a whole disapproved of his detention and even offered to pay for the mule themselves. "During my whole trip to Sonora the most perfect good will was constantly shown by the Mexicans to myself & party."[44]

Ewell returned to Fort Buchanan by the end of November. Three weeks earlier, in response to repeated depredations by the band, Reeve had invaded the Pinal Apaches' homeland along the San Pedro River. He failed to bring them to battle. Undaunted, Reeve returned to Fort Buchanan, resupplied his troops, and took them out again. Ewell had returned from Sonora by then and accompanied the second expedition.[45]

The first day out, 14 December 1859, Reeve attacked a Pinal village and routed its inhabitants. He killed eight warriors, wounded a ninth, and captured twenty-three others—mostly women and children. Ewell was the only soldier injured in the battle, suffering a slight wound to the hand. Ignoring the injury, he continued with the column toward the San Pedro. For twenty days the soldiers searched the mountains in vain for other Pinal villages. Cold rains and snows finally forced them to turn back. On 3 January 1860 the weary column slogged into Fort Buchanan, bringing the three-week, 350-mile ordeal to an end. It was Reeve's last expedition. Two weeks later he fell ill and went on an extended leave of absence, leaving Ewell in command of Fort Buchanan once more.[46]

The Pinal and Chiricahua Apaches soon began stepping up their attacks. In July 1860 Ewell met Cochise and 150 of his people at Apache Pass to demand that they return some stock stolen from a ranch near Fort Buchanan. When the Chiricahua leader produced some second-rate animals, Ewell refused to receive them. He insisted that the Indians restore to the owner the same high-quality stock that they had stolen. When they demurred, Ewell "gave them notice that he would proceed to force them to terms." He allowed Cochise and his people to leave the parley area, then started after them with seventy-five dragoons and several volunteers. But though he was in the field for more than two weeks, Ewell could not bring the Chiricahuas to bay. "Not a single engagement took place," a local news-paperman noted with disappointment, "no prisoners were taken, and the campaign was a complete failure." No one blamed Ewell, for everyone recognized the impossibility of his task. "None who know Capt. Ewell question his zeal or energy in pursuing and punishing Indian marauders whenever he is promptly informed of their thefts," affirmed the editor of the *Weekly Arizonian*.[47]

Some of the most interesting (if not always the most believable) stories about Ewell during this period come from James Tevis's *Arizona in the '50's*. Tevis was a Virginian working in Arizona. When Ewell learned that Tevis was from the Old Dominion, he graciously invited him to share his quarters at Fort Buchanan. Over the next few weeks Tevis became well acquainted with Ewell and with his housekeeper Hester, whose name he incorrectly remembered as Nancy. Hester was an old family slave whom the captain supposedly had brought with him from Virginia. "No mother could have had more affection for her child than Nancy had for the Captain," he recalled. "It was quite amusing to hear her scold him sometimes for not taking better care of himself. All guests of the Captain were well treated by her. Nancy often said she hoped and prayed to live to see the day when the Captain would take her back to good 'Old Virginny' again. I think she got her wish."[48]

Hester was a fine cook. She filled Tevis's plate with numerous dishes, including vegetables grown in the post garden. When Tevis examined the garden, he found that it contained every vegetable imaginable except Irish potatoes, which had never been cultivated successfully in that part of the country. "It was thought then that they could not be grown," he commented. "Captain Ewell, however, kept on experimenting until he succeeded in raising fine ones. I think he was the first man to do so in the territory."[49]

While at Fort Buchanan, Tevis and a group of several dragoons set out to capture the "Phantom Steed." This wild, iron-gray horse was a legend in the Southwest. It was frequently seen but never captured, leading to speculation that it was actually a ghost. When chased, it seemed to observers to simply trot away without even breaking into a gallop. The horse had been seen near the San Pedro River, and Tevis and his companions determined to rope it and bring it back to the post. Ewell advised them not to go, but they would not listen. "Well," said Ewell, "I will tell you how it will all end, for instead of your getting the wild horses, you will all come back on foot, at least those of you who are fortunate enough to live to get back. You will not be there long until the Indians will see you, and if they don't kill you, they will take your horses."

The party set off the next morning. "The Captain paid us the high compliment of calling us a lot of damned fools," Tevis recalled. "He said he had a great notion of taking the troops and going out there at his leisure, so he could be on hand when the Indians rounded us up. Then he would not have to make a forced march to get there when we sent to him for aid." Tevis and the soldiers laughed at his concern. As they sat around the fire that night, the adventurers referred to Ewell as "an old fogey, old military crank, and an old fool." One remarked that the captain acted as though they had never seen Indians before. But Ewell was right. As he predicted, the men failed to find the Phantom Steed, and the Apaches stole their horses.[50]

Tevis sometimes watched Ewell drill the troops. "The Captain used to attend to the drill in person, and when vexed he was not very particular about his language and would 'cuss' the soldiers very lustily; but no other man dared do it in the Captain's presence," noted Tevis, "for he loved his soldiers and, although he talked roughly to them, he always took care that they were made as comfortable as possible, and his soldiers all liked him."[51]

One day Ewell was teaching a group of fresh recruits how to mount a trotting horse bareback. Among his pupils was a man who had enlisted while under the influence of alcohol. He had seldom been on a horse, much less one in motion and lacking a saddle. Time and again the man tried to leap on the animal's back, but each time he failed. Finally the captain's patience snapped.

"Clear out of here!" he roared. "Go to Sonora! Get out of my sight! Go to the stables and take the best horse and skip! Take your horse off the drill ground this instant!"

The man quietly led his horse to the stable while Ewell proceeded with the exercise. Later Ewell stopped in to check on his favorite racer and found its stall empty. When he demanded an explanation, the stable guard informed him that the chastened recruit had taken the animal out for exercise.

"Exercise? Hell and damnation!" cried Ewell. A bugler blew "Boots and Saddles," and within minutes the enraged captain was pounding down the road hell bent for leather with a party of coughing dragoons in his dusty wake. But the deserter reached Mexico before being overtaken. Livid at the loss of his best horse, Ewell returned to Fort Buchanan and personally interrogated each member of his company about the incident. "Strange to say, not one of the troop would admit that he saw the man ride off," Tevis commented, "and the stable guard said he thought the man was only going to exercise the horse; but from a conversation I heard afterwards, a great number of them saw him go away, and they thought it would be a good lesson to the Captain."

That was not the end of the story. After reaching Sonora the soldier became engaged to the daughter of a Mexican aristocrat. The don opposed the marriage but agreed to consent to it on one condition: that the suitor return to the United States and bring back a letter from Ewell attesting to his good character. The father naturally assumed that the man would refuse to go for fear of being clapped in irons for desertion. He was therefore astonished when his daughter's suitor agreed to the condition. Rather than go directly to Ewell, the dragoon rode to a gin shop near Fort Buchanan and asked its owner to intercede for him. Instead, the owner turned him in to collect the reward. The tavern keeper's perfidy angered Ewell more than the loss of his horse. Privately, he wished to let the soldier go, but his hands were tied; the man was in the guardhouse and would have to be tried for desertion. Or would he? The next day Ewell called Tevis into his office and showed him a letter of recommendation that he had written for the young man. Tevis read the note—"good enough to tickle the vanity of any man who wanted to [be] called father-in-law," he remembered—but questioned its value under the circumstances.

"What the devil is the use of that letter to the poor fellow now, since he is in the guardhouse?" he asked.

"Well, I have now done my duty as far as the letter is concerned," Ewell replied, adding enigmatically that he hoped it might be of use to the man after all. Two days later the man escaped from the guardhouse under mysterious circumstances and fled to Mexico, where presumably he presented Ewell's recommendation to his fiancée's father and was married.[52]

Ewell's most celebrated episode in Arizona involved the rescue of eleven-year-old Mercedes Sias Quiroz. On 17 March 1860 Ewell received word that Pinal Apaches had attacked a lumber camp in the Santa Rita Mountains and abducted Mercedes and twenty-three-year-old Larcena P. Page. The Apaches had frequently stolen livestock in Arizona, but never before had they taken hostages. Report of the abductions threw the region into a panic.

Realizing that pursuit of the Apaches would probably result in the two women being murdered, Ewell opened negotiations with the captors. The Pinals claimed to have killed Larcena Page, but they agreed to exchange Mercedes for two dozen Pinal women and children being held at Fort Buchanan. Ewell agreed to their terms and effected the exchange at Aravaipa Canyon, northeast of Tucson. A few days later Larcena Page stumbled into the lumber camp from which she had been abducted, having survived thirteen wounds and fourteen days in the snow-clad mountains.[53]

The event's happy conclusion coincided with Arizona's constitutional convention. On the third day of the session, Ewell rode into Tucson with Mercedes. Citizens poured into the town plaza to embrace the little girl and to bless the man who had delivered her from danger. In appreciation for successfully negotiating Mercedes's release, delegates granted Ewell an honorary seat on the convention floor, issued him a formal vote of thanks, and named one of the territory's original four counties after him. In the evening they held a "grand military ball" in his honor.[54] Ewell viewed the proceedings with amusement. "The people made a great fuss about the child," he explained to Lizzie some days later, "and not knowing how to thank Providence for the safe recovery, vented their gratitude in making a fuss over me. . . . The fact is, they had not time to think over the matter, being taken as it were, by surprise."[55]

In the wake of the abduction the army decided to abandon Fort Buchanan and establish a new and larger military post at the junction of the San Pedro and Aravaipa Rivers, in the heart of the Pinal Apache territory. Ewell inspected the site in May 1860 and christened it Fort Aravaipa, a name his superiors changed to Fort Breckinridge. Its purpose was to curb depredations by the Pinal Apaches and their kinsmen, the Tontos, who lived farther north. Ewell anticipated the move to Fort Breckinridge with anything but pleasure. "The annoyances of moving [are] coming at the worst time," he carped. "My military duties have been of a more active nature and I have great horror of those details." He particularly disliked the spit-and-polish "grand military etiquette" that usually accompanied larger posts. "I suppose coats will have to be buttoned and minutia of equal importance as if the safety of the world depended upon the amount of useless annoyance they can give," he predicted.[56]

Ewell never found out, for in September 1860, while Fort Breckinridge was still under construction, he received orders to report to Fort Bliss, Texas, for court-martial duty. He left Arizona in feeble health, having just suffered through his third sickly season. Soon after reaching Fort Bliss, Ewell put himself on the sick list. He told Lizzie that he had been "very ill with vertigo, nausea, etc., and now am excessively debilitated[,] having occasional attacks of the ague."

In contrast to the chills and fevers of previous seasons, the current attack took the form of violent headaches and a sick stomach. Ewell became so ill that on 29 October he applied for an extended leave of absence with permission to leave the department. It was no longer simply a matter of choice, but of necessity. "It is not likely that I could stand another season in Arizona," he confided to Lizzie, "as I would be much more debilitated than before and the last one nearly did the business."[57] To his request for leave Ewell appended written statements by two army surgeons recommending that he leave the territory as soon as possible. Despite the obvious urgency of the request, his commander, Col. Thomas T. Fauntleroy, refused to grant it until the trial concluded. Fauntleroy's decision ultimately compelled Ewell to ride an additional 275 miles, for in January the trial moved from Fort Bliss to Albuquerque.[58]

While the court was in session, news arrived that South Carolina had seceded from the Union. Few doubted that the result would be war. "Every one here is on the tenter hooks of impatience to know what the Southern States will do," Ewell told his niece. "Officers generally are very much averse to any thing like civil war, though some of the younger ones are a little warlike. The truth is in the army there are no sectional feelings and many from extreme ends of the Union are the most intimate friends."

For Southern officers, torn between loyalty to their native state and loyalty to their country, the prospect of war was particularly unsettling. Ewell was no exception. Although opposed to secession, he realized that Virginia's fate must be his own. Characteristically, his first concern was economic. "I look to the business with particular dread because every cent I have in the world may be lost in [the] distress and trouble of civil war," he wrote with evident concern. "I fear that there is a possibility of being left without a cent in case of great troubles."[59]

Ewell started for the states on 31 January 1861, as soon as the court-martial board had wrapped up its business. Although he feared war was inevitable, he was careful not to violate his commission by committing any act of disloyalty toward the United States. In fact, while passing through Texas, Ewell volunteered to help fight a group of secessionists who were threatening to attack a Federal post. He was little better than an invalid by then. The difficult trip across Texas had shattered his frail health, and the subsequent voyage to Virginia nearly did him in. He arrived at Stony Lonesome a thin, pale, sickly man. When his sister Rebecca saw his wasted condition, she lamented that "Richard has come home to die."[60]

Under her care, however, Dick slowly improved. In March he requested and received a ten-month extension of his leave on the grounds that he was still ill and did not wish to return to Arizona until fall, when the sickly season had passed. In his own mind, however, he was uncertain whether he would ever return. As his health improved, he began taking a hand in the farming operations at Stony Lonesome, and he strongly considered staying there for good.[61]

Fate determined otherwise. On 12 April 1861 Confederate forces in Charleston, South Carolina, fired on Fort Sumter, compelling the surrender of the Federal garrison. Three days later President Abraham Lincoln proclaimed the Southern states to be in revolt against the national authority and asked the loyal states to supply 75,000 troops to suppress the rebellion. Virginia responded by throwing its allegiance to the South. The nation was at war.

To the end, Ewell hoped that the Union might be saved. "If there were anything I had to dread & regret in 61 it was this war," he later remarked. "I was too sick & too busy sowing guano & timothy, &c. to think much about it, but I clung to the last ray of hope like a drowning man to straws." With dissolution of the Union now certain, his duty was clear. On 24 April he resigned his commission in the United States Army and tendered his sword to Virginia. "It is hard to account for my course," he later explained to a former comrade-in-arms, "except from a painful sense of duty; I say painful, because I believe few were more devoted to the old country than myself. . . . It was like death to me." [62]

As was the case with most men, Ewell's decision to support the South was a matter of simple loyalty: "I had to fight with or against my state," he declared, and he chose to fight with it. To do otherwise would have pitted him against his family, neighbors, and friends. Still, it was a difficult decision. He had everything to lose and nothing to gain in a civil war. "By taking up the side of the South I forfeited a handsome position, fine pay and the earnings of twenty years hard service. All the pay I drew in four years in the South was not as much as one year's pay in the old army," he later wrote.

As for the charge that he threw his support to the Confederacy in the hope of military advancement, Ewell denied it. "Had I been ambitious there was not much cause for expecting favor from Mr. Davis," he asserted, citing as evidence the influence used by the new Confederate president in Lucius Northrup's behalf in 1849. Ewell put aside personal considerations, however, and girded himself for the coming conflict. "Sacrificing every earthly hope for principle," he mounted his horse and rode to Richmond, where new duties, new adventures, and possibly new laurels beckoned. [63]

CHAPTER 9

No Orders, No Orders

Even as Dick Ewell resigned his commission in the U.S. Army, Virginia was preparing a place for him in its provisional army. On 25 April 1861 the Advisory Council of the State of Virginia nominated the former dragoon as a lieutenant colonel of cavalry, a recommendation approved by Governor John Letcher, who sent it on to the state legislature for confirmation. That same day Letcher, at the advice of the Advisory Council, appointed Ewell to serve on a joint commission "to name all efficient and worthy Virginians and residents of Virginia in the Army and Navy of the United States, for the purpose of inviting them into the service of Virginia in accordance with the ordnance of convention adopted April 17, 1861." Others appointed to the six-man body included Gen. Joseph E. Johnston and Col. John B. Magruder of the army and Capts. Samuel Barron, Robert B. Pegram, and Sydney S. Lee of the navy.[1]

Ewell's tenure on the commission was brief. At the end of April he rode to Ashland, a dozen miles north of the capital, to take charge of a camp of cavalry instruction that had been established at the local racecourse. The track had been selected because it had facilities for horses. Inspecting the grounds on 1 May Ewell noted that there were sixty stalls, each 10 by 12 feet, extending over an area of 1,000 yards. He had no intention of using the stalls for the horses, though; he intended to quarter his troops there. By assigning 5 men to a stall, he figured he could shelter up to 300 men in the stables. In addition, there were other buildings nearby that might be used as a hospital, officers' quarters, storehouses, and additional barracks. Altogether they might accommodate 800 men.[2]

He would need all that space and more. Within the week, mounted units from counties throughout central Virginia began to arrive at Ashland in such numbers that Ewell could not house them. He applied in vain for permission to rent buildings in the area. Instead, the Quartermaster Department began construction of additional barracks at Ashland. Until they were finished, Ewell would have to make due with what he had.[3]

Arms and ammunition were in even greater demand than quarters. Imported weapons from Europe had not yet arrived in substantial numbers, and the South had few weapons of its own. As a result men came to camp armed with an odd array of antiquated weapons brought from home. In many cases, they brought no arms at all. Ewell made repeated applications to the authorities in Richmond to supply him with rifles, but to no avail; there simply were none to spare.[4] Cartridges were almost as rare as rifles. In a letter almost pleading in tone, Ewell assured his superiors that any ammunition sent to him would not be squandered. "I do not propose issuing the cartridges if furnished except a *very few* for target practice, merely to insure that every man can load & fire his piece. By examining the notes on this requisition you will see that one company as armed at present could not take the field & many men of these companies are without arms."[5]

Despite the lack of arms, ammunition, and quarters, Ewell did his best to mold the recruits under his charge into soldiers. For two hours each morning he conducted mounted drill on the racecourse grounds. In the afternoons he had foot drill and inspected arms. A dress parade at sunset brought the day to an end. The young men grumbled at Ewell's strict discipline. Many voiced regrets at having joined the army at all, but that was to be expected; the transition from civilian to soldier was seldom smooth.[6]

Although there were no Federal troops within fifty miles of Ashland, Ewell set pickets around the camp. No one could come or go without proper authorization—even Ewell himself, as events proved. Pvt. George Cary Eggleston remembered his first encounter with the lieutenant colonel. Eggleston was standing guard at a gate and had orders to permit no one to pass his post. Ewell appeared "dressed in a rough citizen's suit, without side-arms or other insignia of military rank" and undertook to pass through the gate. Eggleston ordered him to halt, and when Ewell threatened to ride over him, Eggleston drew his pistol and threatened to shoot him if he resisted. He then placed Ewell under arrest and summoned the officer of the guard. "Ewell was livid with rage," remembered Eggleston, "and ordered the officer to place me in irons at once, uttering maledictions upon me which it would not do to repeat here."

The officer of the guard refused to remove Eggleston from his post, much less arrest him. "The sentinel has done only his duty," he asserted, "and if he had shot you, Colonel Ewell, you would have had only yourself to blame. I have here your written order that the sentinels at this gate shall allow nobody to pass through it on horseback, on any pretense whatever; and yet you come in citizen's clothes, a stranger to the guard, and try to ride him down when he insists upon obeying the orders you have given him." Ewell realized that the officer was right. After he had cooled down, he called Eggleston to his tent, apologized for his behavior, and offered him a position on his staff. Still rankling from his earlier tongue-lashing, the private declined the offer, though it convinced him that "in spite of his infirm temper, Ewell was capable of being a just man, as he certainly was a brave one."

The story had a sequel. In late 1864 Ewell, then in command of the Richmond defenses, received a dispatch informing him of an engagement between Mackey's Point and Pocotaligo. The South Carolina names were unfamiliar to him, and he asked those with him if any happened to know their locations. Eggleston was present and gave him the information he sought. Ewell eyed the young man intently and asked, "Aren't you the man who came so near shooting me at Ashland?"

Eggleston replied that he was.

"I'm very glad you didn't do it," piped Ewell.[7]

Ewell's assignment at Ashland ended on 19 May when he received orders to report to Culpeper Court House to assist in the instruction of cavalry. Though he had been at Ashland for less than three weeks, he had gained the respect of many officers there. One, Capt. Williams C. Wickham of the Hanover Dragoons, wrote to Richmond on 20 May recommending that Ewell be promoted to colonel, a measure that authorities may have already considered.[8]

Ewell reached Culpeper around 24 May, the day Federal forces occupied Alexandria, Virginia. The troops at Culpeper were immediately ordered north to reinforce Brig. Gen. Milledge L. Bonham at Manassas Junction. The South Carolinian had two regiments of infantry. He placed one at Centreville and the other at Mitchell's Ford on Bull Run. When Ewell reached Manassas Junction, Bonham put him in charge of his cavalry and ordered him to establish an outpost at either Germantown or Fairfax Court House, whichever he deemed best. Ewell chose Fairfax.[9]

Fairfax Court House was located just fourteen miles west of Alexandria on the Little River Turnpike. In the center of town, on the south side of the turnpike, stood the courthouse; directly across from it was the hotel. Zion Episcopal Church stood approximately 500 feet west of the hotel, on the turnpike; a Methodist church was roughly the same distance south of the hotel, on the road to Fairfax Station.[10] Two companies of horse numbering sixty men apiece occupied the town: Capt. J. Shackleford Green's Rappahannock Cavalry and Capt. William W. Thornton's Prince William Cavalry. Both units were poorly armed and even more poorly disciplined. Green's men lodged in Zion Episcopal

Church, while Thornton's made their quarters at the courthouse. Ewell took a room at the hotel, adjacent to Thornton's company.[11]

One week after Ewell arrived in town, Fairfax Court House became the scene of one of the war's earliest skirmishes. At 3:00 A.M. on 1 June, a detachment of Company B, Second U.S. Cavalry, surprised and overwhelmed Confederate pickets one mile east of town. Ewell first learned of the attack from a breathless courier who galloped into town shouting in Paul Revere fashion that "the Yankees were coming." Ewell summoned Thornton to his room, but before he could issue any orders, Union horsemen came pounding down the turnpike, firing wildly to the right and left. They met no resistance; the Confederate cavalry had fled at their approach without firing a shot.[12]

Thornton dashed off to rally his company, while Ewell threw a coat over his nightshirt and went to find the Warrenton Rifles, an infantry company that had arrived in Fairfax Court House earlier in the day. By then the main body of Union horsemen had passed through town. A single soldier had remained to watch the street. Ewell deftly evaded the man and slipped across the turnpike to the courthouse, thence up a side street toward the Methodist church, where the Warrenton Rifles had taken their quarters. Fearing that he might be taken prisoner if the enemy discovered his rank, he removed his coat and cast it aside.[13]

As Ewell approached the church, he spotted some fifty members of the Warrenton Rifles attempting to form themselves into a line. He hurried over to take command of them. Ewell was a stranger to the company, having been out on a scout when it had arrived. Dressed only in a white nightshirt, he looked more like a scarecrow than an officer, and one man questioned his right to command them.

"What, sir, do you dispute my authority?" exclaimed Ewell.

"I do, sir, until I know you have a right to exercise it," the soldier replied.

It was an awkward situation and might have gotten worse had a voice in the darkness not settled the matter. "Men, this is Lieutenant-Colonel Ewell, your commanding officer, a gallant soldier, in whom you may place your confidence." It was William "Extra Billy" Smith, the former governor of Virginia, who happened to be lodging in town for the night. He and Ewell were old acquaintances. With Smith's help, Ewell got the Rifles into line and marched them back to the turnpike. He placed them behind a stone wall adjacent to the road to await the enemy, who would have to pass back down the road in order to return to their own lines.[14]

Ewell had barely completed this task when the Union cavalry reappeared, galloping east along the turnpike. The Rifles held their fire until the Federals were within range, then loosed a straggling fire that drove the enemy back down the

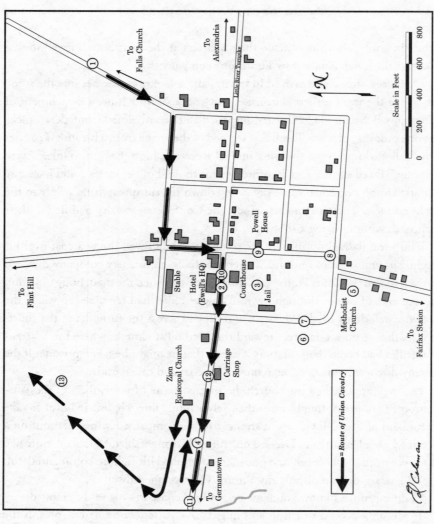

Fairfax Court House

1. Union cavalry fire on Confederate pickets posted on Falls Church Road.
2. Prince William Cavalry attempts to form on turnpike in front of the courthouse.
3. Rappahannock Cavalry forms in yard behind courthouse.
4. Federals ride through town, routing Prince William Cavalry and pursuing it westward out of town on Little River Turnpike.
5. Marr forms line in clover field with right resting near Methodist church.
6. Marr is killed in clover field between Methodist church and turnpike.
7. Rappahannock Cavalry scatters southward after being mistakenly fired at by Warrenton Rifles.
8. Smith reforms Warrenton Rifles at corner.
9. Ewell leaves hotel, evades Union soldier in turnpike, and throws off coat at Powell House before joining Smith and Warrenton Rifles at corner.
10. Ewell and Smith lead Warrenton Rifles to turnpike, where they fire on returning Federal cavalry.
11. After rebuff at courthouse, Federals reform at creek west of town.
12. Warrenton Rifles advance to carriage shop and repulse two Union charges. Ewell is wounded.
13. Federals retreat through fields north of town.

William "Extra Billy" Smith (Library of Congress)

road. The bluecoats re-formed and came on again. In the darkness it was impossible to see the riders' uniforms. The Confederates hesitated to fire for fear the horsemen might be their own cavalry returning to town. In order to confirm the riders' identity, Ewell stepped forward to challenge them.

"Who goes there?"

"Cavalry," came the reply.

"What cavalry?"

In answer, the Union leader fired his pistol at Ewell, grazing him in the shoulder near the neck. The Warrenton Rifles responded with a volley that caused the dragoons to retreat up the turnpike once again. This time they did not return. Having failed twice to break through the Confederate line, they elected to ride around Fairfax Court House instead, making their escape through the fields north of town.[15]

Ewell was unaware that the Federals had fled and readied his men to meet another assault. A soldier, noticing his injury, asked if he was much hurt. "None of your damned business!" snapped Ewell. "Take your place in the ranks!" Brig. Gen. Samuel Wragg Ferguson later laughed when he heard the story. "I have often pictured to myself the old soldier, mad as a hornet at being taken by surprise and his command thrown into confusion and smarting too with a wound, having a raw recruit interrupting him with his sympathy," he chuckled. The soldier did not find it so amusing. Repeating Ewell's response to an acquaintance a short time later, the offended man remarked, "You know, sir, that was not only impolite, but very profane." And so it was.[16]

During the skirmish Ewell dispatched a courier to Fairfax Station for reinforcements. Two companies of cavalry arrived about sunrise in response to his call. Although the Federals had been gone for at least two hours, Ewell sent the gray horsemen in pursuit. He directed one company to follow the invaders' trail while the other company took a different route in the hope of intercepting them. Neither party was successful.[17]

Ewell meanwhile tallied his losses. The Federals admitted losing one man killed, three wounded, and three captured, plus the loss of numerous small arms and horses. By comparison, Ewell reported one man killed, one wounded, and five captured. The sole Confederate fatality had been John Quincy Marr, the thirty-six-year-old captain of the Warrenton Rifles, who was struck in the heart by a stray shot early in the fight. Soldiers discovered his body shortly after dawn lying in a clover field south of town, his sword clutched firmly in his right hand. Aside from Marr, Ewell was the only Southerner injured. His wound kept him from taking the saddle for several days and marked him as the first Confederate field officer to be wounded in the war.[18]

The skirmish at Fairfax Court House, though insignificant by later standards, was a major news event at that time and gave Ewell a measure of fame. Not all of the publicity was favorable. The Richmond *Enquirer* claimed that Ewell had posted his pickets defectively, thereby allowing himself to be surprised. Available evidence, however, indicates that Ewell properly posted his men, though perhaps in less force than was necessary under the circumstances. The real problem seems to have been the men themselves. Inexperienced, undisciplined, and poorly armed, the Confederate pickets stood little chance of delaying a determined charge by a superior force of well-armed, battle-toughened Regulars. General Bonham appreciated the difficulties under which Ewell labored and later praised him for his efforts. Reporting Ewell's wounding to authorities in Richmond, he remarked, "Not only on this occasion, in the face of the enemy, but at all other times he has exhibited promptness, energy, and gallantry in the discharge of his duties."[19]

Ewell was too busy to take notice of either praise or criticism. Throughout early June, refugees from Alexandria poured into his lines bearing exaggerated tales of atrocities committed by Union soldiers against defenseless citizens. Such reports persuaded him that the Southern cause was just. "I believe we are in the right," he told Lizinka with halting conviction, "I trust so. Our soil is invaded with the most barbarous threats too often carried into execution & there is nothing to be done but what we do."[20]

The refugees brought intelligence of a military build-up along the Potomac. According to one credible source, the Union Army of the Potomac planned to attack Confederate troops near Manassas within five days. Ewell passed this information on to Bonham, who put little stock in the report. Nevertheless, Ewell remained on the qui vive, determined not to be caught off guard again. "I have been expecting an attack ever since," he wrote Lizinka shortly after the 1 June fight, "& have not had 2 nights sleep as I keep dressed all night & have to be up at 3 o'clock A.M. I have 700 men here & there are 1000 & 7 pieces of Artillery at Centreville." The weight of responsibility was beginning to show. "It seems to me with the excessive worry & fatigue having no officer of experience to answer all complaints & to whom all apply &c that I would give anything for a few days rest of mind & body," he complained.[21]

Ultimately the long hours and nervous strain took their toll. Throughout the summer Ewell was ill with chills and fevers. All the while his responsibilities grew heavier. On 17 June he was promoted to brigadier general and placed in charge of three infantry regiments: Col. Robert E. Rodes's Fifth Alabama, Col. John J. Seibels's Sixth Alabama, and Col. Isaac G. Seymour's Sixth Louisiana. The promotion came as a surprise to Ewell, though not necessarily a pleasant one. "I wonder if you were as much astonished as I was at my promotion?" he asked Bonham. "I assure you it is a matter that gives me no rejoicing as the responsibility is painful, particularly in my present state of health." Fear for his reputation may have had as much to do with Ewell's reluctance for promotion as fear for his health. "You are surprised . . . at my want of any desire for rank," he wrote Lizinka several months later, "but I have very little confidence in the style of our troops[,] the manner they are disciplined &c. &c. and one hazards more than life with them. Want of success of course is laid to the fault of the leaders."[22]

On 1 June Gen. P. G. T. Beauregard replaced Bonham as commander of the Manassas line. Beauregard's victory at Fort Sumter had made him the hero of the South. His transfer to Virginia was welcomed by the people of the state, including Ewell, who considered the Creole "a host in himself."[23] Beauregard commanded six brigades: Bonham's, Ewell's, Philip St. George Cocke's, James

Longstreet's, David R. Jones's, and Jubal A. Early's. Beauregard established his
main line along Bull Run, east of Manassas. He advanced Bonham, Cocke, and
Ewell beyond the run to observe the enemy and provide early warning of an attack. Bonham held Fairfax Court House, supported by Cocke at Centreville.
Ewell was five miles south of Bonham at Fairfax Station. If threatened by a superior Union force, Bonham had orders to fall back toward Mitchell's Ford, drawing the Federal army after him. Ewell was to cover Bonham's right, retreating
"over a rather rough and difficult country road to Union Mills Ford." [24]

The Army of the Potomac began its long-awaited advance on 16 July 1861, forcing Bonham back toward Centreville. Bonham notified Ewell that he was falling
back, but the message miscarried. As a result, Ewell found his brigade nearly cut
off. A skillful delaying action by Rodes on the Old Braddock Road, however, enabled Ewell to withdraw to Union Mills in accordance with Beauregard's earlier
instructions. As Ewell retreated, he felled trees across the road to impede the enemy and destroyed the railroad bridge over Bull Run. [25]

At Union Mills, Ewell held the right end of the Confederate line. Early's
brigade supported him. To Ewell's left, covering the upstream fords, were Jones,
Longstreet, Bonham, and Cocke. Ewell occupied a two-room wooden house on
the hillside overlooking the Union Mills Ford. Supporting his line was a howitzer
battery commanded by Lt. Thomas L. Rosser of the Washington Artillery, a crack
unit from New Orleans. [26]

Ewell anxiously awaited the enemy's appearance. On the morning of the eighteenth, Union soldiers dressed in Zouave uniforms emerged from the woods opposite Union Mills Ford and drew water from a tank beside the railroad tracks.
Rosser eagerly sought permission to shell them, but Ewell told him to wait. As
Rosser's men nervously fingered their lanyards, a teenage girl rode toward them
across the field. She came from Fairfax Court House and claimed to have information important to the Confederate cause. The soldiers took her to see Ewell,
who was with Maj. John B. Gordon of the Sixth Alabama observing the place-
ment of Union batteries across the run. Gordon remembered the earnestness with
which the girl delivered her message. "She was profoundly impressed with the belief that she really had something of importance to tell. The information which
she was trying to convey to General Ewell she was sure would be of vast import
to the Confederate cause, and she was bound to deliver it." Ewell listened to her
story, then pointed toward the Union batteries visible across the stream.

"Look there, look there, miss! Don't you see those men with blue clothes on,
in the edge of the woods? Look at those men loading those big guns. They are go-

ing to fire, and fire quick, and fire right here. You'll get killed. You'll be a *dead damsel* in less than a minute. *Get away from here! Get away!*"

The young lady glanced impatiently at the cannons but did not pay them the slightest heed. The general marveled at her courage. "He gazed at her in mute wonder for a few minutes," wrote Gordon, "and then turned to me suddenly, and, with a sort of jerk in his words, said: 'Women—I tell you, sir, women would make a grand brigade—if it was not for snakes and spiders! They don't mind bullets—women are not afraid of bullets; but one big black-snake would put a whole army to flight.'"[27]

Not long after the courageous girl had departed, artillery fire erupted two miles upstream at Blackburn's Ford. It continued from noon until 4:00 P.M., accompanied now and then by the rattle of musketry. To soldiers unaccustomed to war, it seemed as though a full-fledged battle was in progress. Excitement ran high in the Confederate camp. Ewell kept his brigade under arms, but the Federals opposite his position remained quiet. Later, news arrived that Longstreet had repulsed a Union assault. The Confederates danced and shouted with joy in the belief that they had won a major victory. Ewell knew better. At Blackburn's Ford the Union army had simply been testing the Confederate line. The real fighting still lay ahead.[28]

On 19 July 1861, the day after the Union demonstration at Blackburn's Ford, a twenty-year-old Tennessean named George Campbell Brown stepped from the train at Manassas Junction carrying a large, heavy trunk. Stopping a soldier, he asked directions to General Ewell's headquarters. Brown's face fell when the man informed him that Ewell's brigade was at Union Mills, five miles down the track. He looked despondently at his burden. The young man had no horse, and it would be manifestly impossible for him to carry the trunk such a long distance without one. He finally decided to leave the trunk at the station and set out on foot. He would come back for the trunk later.

Brown had gone only a short distance when three soldiers overtook him. One of the soldiers had the other two under guard and was taking them to their camps. Brown joined the group and chatted pleasantly with the man in charge until gradually it dawned on him that he was under guard as well! His arrival at the station had aroused suspicion, and an officer there had charged the soldier to keep an eye on him. As Brown and the soldiers made their way toward the front, a group of riders in plain dress galloped past them in the opposite direction, headed toward the junction. "There goes Genl. Ewell now," said the guard. Brown looked intently at the horsemen. He had met the general five years earlier, but he no longer recognized him.

Brown and the soldiers trudged the remaining distance to Union Mills, where the man in charge turned Brown over to Lt. John Taliaferro, an aide-de-camp on Ewell's staff. Taliaferro was a gawky, freckled-faced, ex-plebe fresh out of West Point, but to Brown he seemed "most majestic & terrific in his military power." Brown introduced himself and said that he had come to Virginia at General Ewell's invitation to accept a position on his staff. Brown and Ewell were relatives, he explained, Brown's mother, Lizinka Campbell Brown, being the general's first cousin. Taliaferro invited Brown inside the farmhouse that Ewell was using as his headquarters. The building had nothing in the way of "military display & splendor" about it; on the contrary, it struck Brown as being rather "simple & rough." [29]

The same might be said of Ewell himself. Chronic illness and hard service on the frontier had left him with a gaunt body and a pale, haggard face. Brown studied the general closely when he entered the room an hour later. He described him as "a medium-sized & plain man, with well-shaped, spare figure & face much emaciated by recent sickness but indicative of much character & genius." Specifically, Ewell stood five feet ten and one-half inches tall and weighed 140 pounds. Though not as neatly dressed or as well groomed as some officers, he had a military bearing that impressed everyone who saw him as "being every inch a soldier." Ewell was not a handsome man; his ears and nose were large, and wrinkles seamed his wizened face. He seemed much older than his forty-four years. If he had a striking feature, it was his piercing gray eyes, which observers invariably likened to those of an eagle or a woodcock. [30]

Like Brown, most people recognized in General Ewell a certain quality of genius—an offbeat kind of genius perhaps, but genius nonetheless. Maybe it was his head. Since leaving West Point in 1840, Ewell had lost most of his hair, and he now displayed a gloriously smooth crown. Dark brown locks of medium length and brushed forward at the temples wreathed his dome and tumbled over his jaws in the form of fierce, bristling sideburns, culminating in a bushy moustache and fluffy tuft of beard. When once asked to explain the contrast between his bald head and heavy beard, Ewell said that he supposed that it resulted from the fact that he used his head more than he did his jaws. [31]

The general did not notice Brown at first, and Taliaferro had to alert him to his presence. Ewell seized his relative by the hand and exclaimed, "Well, Campbell, I am sorry you have come." The greeting took Brown aback. Thinking that Ewell might have selected someone else to fill his position, he stammered that he too

Campbell Brown, 1866 (Tennessee State Library and Archives)

was sorry if his presence caused the general any embarrassment. Ewell laughed and explained that he only meant that there was a battle pending and that he had hoped Brown might not arrive until the danger was past. But as he was there, Ewell laughed, it could not be helped. To get his young kinsman started, Ewell loaned him a horse and arranged a billet for him at headquarters. From that day the two men became inseparable companions.[32]

Brown's arrival helped to flesh out Ewell's meager staff. Col. Charles H. Tyler headed the staff in rank, if not in character. Authorities in Richmond had assigned him to be Ewell's adjutant, unaware perhaps that Tyler was a drunkard and utterly worthless as an officer. Because of Tyler's inefficiency, Ewell relied heavily on his other adjutant, Lt. (later general) Fitzhugh Lee. Lee was the grandson of "Lighthorse Harry" Lee, the Revolutionary War general, and in Ewell's opinion was more like his grandfather than any other member of the Lee family. Unlike Tyler, Fitz Lee had joined Ewell's staff by mutual consent. Hardworking and efficient, he served Ewell well during the early months of the war. Other members of Ewell's military family included brigade quartermaster Capt. Charles H. Rhodes, volunteer aide Robert F. Mason, Taliaferro, and Brown, who was commissioned a first lieutenant and appointed to be Ewell's aide-de-camp. These six officers, plus a civilian clerk named Edgar A. Hudnut, comprised the general's entire staff in the summer of 1861. Not until fall would he be assigned a commissary officer or a surgeon.[33]

Ewell was in earnest when he told Brown that a battle was pending. That very day Gen. Joseph E. Johnston's Army of the Shenandoah began arriving at Manassas from the Shenandoah Valley. Once Johnston's entire army had arrived, he and Beauregard planned to join forces and attack Brig. Gen. Irvin McDowell's Union army across Bull Run.[34] In the meantime Beauregard's troops remained on edge in the expectation that McDowell might strike first. For one man, the nervous strain was too much. On 19 July Lt. James A. Clendening of the Sixth Alabama rushed into Ewell's headquarters and announced that the Federals had thrown two pontoon bridges across Bull Run at Yates's Ford, three miles below Union Mills. The story seemed incredible, but it could not be ignored. Ewell sent a courier to army headquarters to inform Beauregard of the report and had one of his staff accompany Clendening back to Yates's Ford to confirm the sighting. The report was false. Clendening had imagined the whole thing!

Ewell sent a correct statement of the facts to headquarters, but not before Beauregard had ordered Early to the threatened point. Ewell meanwhile placed Clendening under arrest and opened an investigation. Clendening's superiors testified to his good character but admitted that his family had a history of insanity. After consultation with doctors, Ewell determined that the rigors of camp life and intense mental excitement had resulted in Clendening's temporary derangement. He released the lieutenant from arrest and suggested that he resign from the service. Clendening did so, "intensely grateful" to Ewell for not preferring charges against him.[35]

Beauregard meanwhile formulated a plan of action. He confidently expected the Federals to advance down the Warrenton Turnpike and attack the left end of his line near the stone bridge that spanned Bull Run. When they did, he would counter by throwing the right wing of his army across the stream and striking Mc-

Dowell's left flank and rear near Centreville. Ewell would open the attack, supported by Jones, Longstreet, and Bonham on his left and by Theophilus Holmes's brigade in his rear.[36]

At 5:30 A.M., 21 July, Beauregard ordered Ewell to hold himself "in readiness to take the offensive on Centerville at a moment's notice," taking care to "protect well your right flank against any attack from the eastward." Beauregard declared his intention "to take the offensive throughout my front as soon as possible."[37] While awaiting the order to advance, Ewell took breakfast with Gordon. "Come and eat a cracker with me," the gruff veteran offered, "we will breakfast together here and dine together in hell." The native Georgian considered the invitation neither inspiring nor appetizing, but he nevertheless joined the general, whose spirits, he remembered, "seemed to be in a flutter of exultation."[38]

McDowell beat the Confederates to the punch. In the morning blue-clad infantry splashed across Bull Run at Sudley Springs, turning Beauregard's left flank. From his position at Union Mills, Ewell could hear "the booming of artillery and the faint discharge of musketry far up the run toward the turnpike," but he could only guess at its meaning. The sound grew louder each minute. Why did Beauregard not send word to advance? An aide arrived from army headquarters, but he brought no orders.[39] Ewell fretted and fumed. In the morning he sent Gordon across the run to feel the enemy. By the time the Georgian returned, Ewell was "in an agony of suspense. He was chafing like a caged lion," remembered Gordon, "infuriated by the scent of blood. He would mount his horse one moment and dismount the next. He would walk rapidly to and fro, muttering to himself, 'No orders, no orders.'"[40]

Gordon regarded Ewell as one of the most unusual men he had ever met. "He was a compound of anomalies, the oddest, most eccentric genius in the Confederate army," he asserted. But he also had a hot temper and a sharp tongue. "No man had a better heart nor a worse manner of showing it. He was in truth as tender and sympathetic as a woman, but, even under slight provocation, he became externally as rough as a polar bear, and the needles with which he pricked sensibilities were more numerous and keener than porcupines' quills."

Gordon was not the only one to notice this contrast in Ewell's personality. Prior to the Mexican War, Tom Ewell wrote that Dick "had the sharpest tongue and softest heart" of anyone he knew. The general's future stepdaughter, Harriot Brown, likewise recognized the difference between the inner and outer man. "So far from being an eccentric, cynical mountibank [sic], Gen. E. was of all the men I have ever known, the most single hearted, earnest and unaffected," she wrote. "Beneath a rough exterior he hid as warm, chivalric & generous a heart as ever

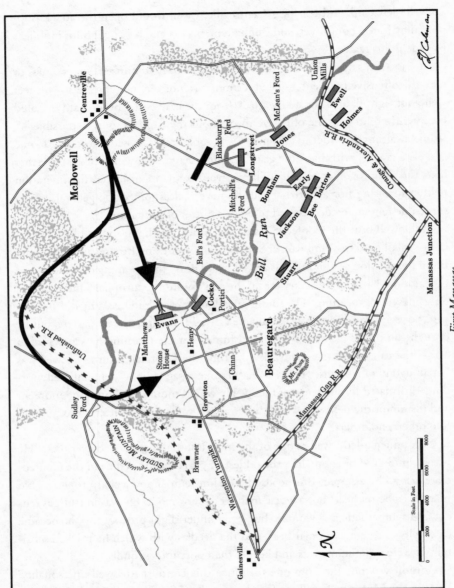

First Manassas

beat in human bosom. . . . Ewell would not willingly have done . . . any man an injustice."[41]

The general sometimes had trouble making himself understood in the heat of battle. "His written orders were full, accurate, and lucid," recalled Gordon, "but his verbal orders or directions, especially when under intense excitement, no man could comprehend. At such times his eyes would flash with a peculiar brilliancy, and his brain far outran his tongue. His thoughts would leap across great gaps which his words never touched, but which he expected his listener to fill up by intuition, and woe to the dull subordinate who failed to understand him!"

What happened next was vivid proof of Gordon's assertion. Having failed to hear from Beauregard, Ewell ordered Gordon to send him a courier at once "with sense enough to go and find out what was the matter." Gordon sent a man from the Governor's Guard, a mounted company that boasted some of Virginia's most intelligent and accomplished young men. The soldier found Ewell at his head-quarters, impatiently awaiting his arrival. "Before this inexperienced but promising young soldier had time to lift his hat in respectful salutation," remembered Gordon, "the general was slashing away with tongue and finger, delivering his directions with such rapidity and incompleteness that the young man's thoughts were dancing through his brain in inextricable confusion. The general, having thus delivered himself, quickly asked, 'Do you understand, sir?' Of course the young man did not understand, and he began timidly to ask for a little more explicit information. The fiery old soldier cut short the interview with 'Go away from here and send me a man who has some sense!'"[42]

Ewell sent members of his own staff to contact Jones, on his left, and Holmes, in his rear, to see whether they had received any orders. Between 9:00 and 10:00 A.M., before the staff officers returned, a courier arrived from Jones, bearing a copy of a 7:00 A.M. dispatch that Jones had received from Beauregard. The order directed Jones to advance and stated that Ewell had been directed to do likewise.[43] Ewell immediately pushed his troops across the run and started for Centreville.[44] He had no sooner started than Col. A. R. Chisolm of Beauregard's staff brought news that the Union army had turned the Confederate left flank. Fighting was heavy and the issue was in doubt. Beauregard ordered Ewell to fall back to his former position at Union Mills Ford.[45]

Ewell returned to the ford as instructed. Throughout the early afternoon he waited for orders while the battle raged a few miles away. "We went back to our little house on the hill side & the troops to their bivouacs," remembered Brown, "and waited through the long July day with only an occasional flutter of couriers or Staff, listening to the distant & heavy firing . . . with nerves at such high tension that every moment we seemed to hear the guns come nearer & nearer. We gradually learned the state of affairs . . . and we began to comprehend that only in case of our defeat or as a forlorn-hope to prevent it, could we expect to share in the combat."[46]

Finally, at 3:00 P.M., after what must have seemed an eternity, Ewell received verbal orders to attack a Union battery opposite McLean's Ford, one mile upstream.[47] He again threw his brigade across Union Mills Ford and marched to meet the enemy. Rather than take the road to Centreville, as he had done before, Ewell turned left and followed a side road that paralleled the stream. He was just about to come to grips with the enemy when Joe Johnston ordered him to recross Bull Run and march with all haste to the stone bridge. A staff officer asked what such an order implied. "It meant that we are whipped," Ewell replied. The thought of losing the battle sickened the old warrior. "My feelings then were terrible," he recalled, "as such an order could only mean that we were defeated and I was to cover the retreat."[48]

For the fourth time that day Ewell's men splashed across Bull Run. The Sixth Louisiana led the march to the stone bridge, about six miles away. Its members— mostly Irishmen—moved with enthusiasm and confidence, hopeful that they would finally see action. They covered more than four miles in an hour, outdistancing the regiments that followed. Twice they had to halt until Rodes's Alabamians could catch up.[49] Two Union rifled guns took the brigade under fire as it passed behind Mitchell's Ford, but they overshot the road and no one was hurt.[50]

Ewell sent Fitz Lee ahead to tell Beauregard that his brigade was on the way. Robert Mason accompanied Lee, Ewell grimly remarking to Lee that "if one of us got killed, there would be still a chance of the message getting to Army Hd. Qrs. at the hands of the other."[51] As his brigade neared its destination, Ewell personally rode forward to acquaint himself with the terrain and to get instructions. He found Johnston and Beauregard at the Lewis house. By then the sun was setting and the firing had ceased. His troops had arrived too late.[52]

The Union army, after achieving success early in the day, had been routed and was in headlong retreat toward Washington. Ewell wished to pursue the enemy, but Beauregard sent him back to Union Mills to investigate a report that Union forces had crossed the run there and were advancing on the Confederate supply base at Manassas Junction. The report was untrue, and at 9:00 P.M. Ewell's brigade settled into its old camp at Union Mills Ford, having marched more than a dozen miles to no purpose.[53]

After the battle Ewell encountered Jefferson Davis. The president was exuberant at the outcome of the day's fighting and confidently predicted that it would seal the South's independence. Ewell disagreed. The battle was just the first in a long and doubtful struggle, he said. There was only one measure that would ensure independence: freeing the slaves and arming them in defense of the country. The suggestion shocked Davis. It was madness to even suggest such a thing, he exclaimed. It would revolt and disgust the entire South. "May be so," replied Ewell, *but it will paralyse the North.*" The scheme was flatly impossible, Davis maintained. Who would command a brigade of Negroes? "I will," said Ewell. No, said the president, it was simply impossible to even dream of such a thing. With that the discussion ended. Ewell never raised the topic again.

Ewell told Tasker Gantt of the conversation in 1866, and Gantt in turn told Henry Hunt. Gantt had no doubt that the story was true. "I think you know Dick Ewell," he told Hunt. "He was one of the men who were incapable of telling a falsehood, or of coloring the truth. He could not invent or utter a lie of vanity." Jefferson Davis, however, flatly denied that the conversation ever took place. In a letter to Campbell Brown written long after the war, he insisted that the notion of arming the slaves was unheard of in 1861.

One might be inclined to dismiss Gantt's story were it not for a letter written by Ewell to his niece Lizzie: "It is astonishing to me that our people do not pass laws to form Regiments of blacks. The Yankees are fighting low foreignors [*sic*] against the best of our people, whereas were we to fight our negroes they would be a fair offset & we would not be as now fighting kings against men to use a comparison from chequers." This letter was written on 20 July 1862, one year after Manassas and eighteen months before Maj. Gen. Patrick Cleburne made a similar proposal to division and corps commanders in the Army of Tennessee. In suggesting that the South arm its slaves, Ewell and Cleburne displayed a good grasp of military strategy, but none at all of political reality. Not until it had been bled dry by four years of war could the South bring itself to adopt such a desperate measure. By then it was too late—the war was lost.[54]

Ewell submitted his report of Manassas on 24 July 1861. That day or the next he heard that Beauregard was angry with him for not carrying out his 21 July order to advance on Centreville. Ewell's temper flared. How could he obey an order that he had never received? Then and there he sat down and wrote Beauregard a letter reviewing his actions during the battle and listing every dispatch that he had received or sent. He denied having received an order to advance on Centreville and challenged Beauregard to send him a copy of it "as well as the name of the courier who brought it." My object in writing to you, he told Beauregard, was "to ask you to leave nothing doubtful in your report both as regards my crossing in the morning and recall, and not to let it be inferred by any possibility that I blundered on that day."

Ewell's letter put Beauregard on the spot. Not only had he failed to make a copy of the order, but he was unable to identify the courier he had sent to deliver it. He had no choice but to back down. In a kindly worded letter written the following day, Beauregard assured Ewell that he did "not attach the least blame to you for the failure of the movement on Centreville" and promised to set the record straight in his battle report. When the report appeared several weeks later, however, it passed over the incident in a "vague & unsatisfactory" manner. Ewell pronounced himself "greatly disgusted, seeing the probability that nine out of ten who read it would still impute blame to him where in fact it belonged to Beauregard."[55]

He was not far off the mark. As the thrill of victory subsided, the Southern people examined the battle more closely and realized that the Confederacy had squandered an opportunity to crush the Union army. For many, Ewell became a scapegoat. The Savannah *Republican*, for instance, told its readers that for unknown reasons Ewell had not carried out Beauregard's order to attack, suggesting that if he had, the Federal army would have been destroyed. The editor of the Columbus, Georgia, *Sun* went so far as to insinuate that Ewell was guilty of treason, although he later retracted the statement when called on to furnish authority for the remark.[56]

The public censure he received as a result of Beauregard's report hurt Ewell deeply, and he determined never to serve others in the same way. "He was ever after so careful of the feelings of his subordinates that he refrained from stating positively & decidedly what he knew to be true," a family member later recalled, "but in his Reports gave to the General Commanding, the facts, and left to him the task of judging. In this I think he erred but it was the error of a great soul."[57]

Rather than seek vindication for his conduct at Manassas himself, Ewell enlisted Capt. George F. Harrison of the Goochland Light Dragoons to be his advocate. Harrison resigned his commission in October. Before Harrison left the army, Ewell summoned him to his headquarters and handed him some papers. "Captain," he said, "I learn that some of the newspapers in the far South are imputing responsibility to me for the failure of our army to make the attack at Manassas as contemplated. Now, of course, I can publish nothing at this time. But you are going home, through Richmond, and may, sooner or later, hear the subject discussed. Have an accurate copy made of this correspondence between General Beauregard and myself, and take it with you, that you may have it in your power to vindicate me." Harrison copied the papers and later used them to defend his deceased chief when the Manassas controversy resurfaced in 1884.[58]

On 31 July 1861 Ewell wrote to Lizzie about the battle. He described his role in it, then jokingly apologized to her for not being able to "gratify your taste for blood and your ambition by any account of glory that I was to have reaped." In a more serious vein, he added, "We should feel deeply our gratitude for the victory, for the march of the enemy was as a swarm of locusts, burning and destroying. They drove peoples stock into their pens merely to butcher them, leaving farmers without a live animal on their farms. The private memoranda found on the field speak of their depredations on the route." If Ewell wrote heatedly on the subject of Union pillage, he had good reason. Stony Lonesome stood just ten miles from the battlefield. The farms despoiled by the Union army belonged to his family, friends, and neighbors. For him and other northern Virginia residents, the war had become a very personal affair.[59]

CHAPTER 10

Hope and Love and Devotion

In the days after the battle of First Manassas, Johnston's and Beauregard's armies merged. Johnston, as senior officer, assumed command of the combined forces. Ewell had lost confidence in Beauregard since the 21 July battle, and he was pleased to have Johnston in charge. He had known Johnston in the Old Army and had great respect for his ability. Moreover, he liked the man. Johnston had a personal magnetism that inspired loyalty in subordinates, and Ewell was no exception. Although he served under several renowned officers in the war, none captured his devotion as completely as did Joe Johnston.

In late July 1861, while Johnston settled into his new duties, Ewell took advantage of the lull in military operations to visit other brigades. An Englishman fighting with the army recalled that the Virginian stopped by his camp that summer in the company of James Longstreet and Nathan G. Evans. The three generals "were dressed as citizens, with heavy black felt hats on, and except pistols in their holsters, were unarmed and unattended." Throughout the visit Ewell actively inspected the brigade's camp arrangements, only pausing now and then to look toward Manassas with his glass.[1]

One day Campbell Brown brought his chief information that there was honey for sale at a farm three or four miles distant. Ewell determined to get some. It was an uncomfortably hot day, and when he reached the farm, he asked for a glass of buttermilk. The farmer's wife stepped inside to get it. While she was gone, the general picked up a pair of large scissors and started to cut his hair without the benefit of a mirror or any other guide except his fingers. The woman returned before he finished. Putting the scissors aside, Ewell drank the buttermilk, then galloped off with the hair on half of his head still uncut. Several days passed before he completed the job.[2]

Toward the end of July Ewell's brigade shifted its camp from Union Mills to the mouth of Pope's Head Run. It stayed there only a few days. In mid-August

Johnston pushed forward his main line from Bull Run to Fairfax Court House, and the brigade moved up to Sangster's Crossroads, one and one-half miles south of Fairfax Station. Ewell made his headquarters in a small grove of blackjack oaks next to an unfinished house. Brown remembered the site "chiefly . . . for the yellow jackets that infested our table whenever we had honey or sugar on it." Although most members of the staff had sense enough to leave the yellow jackets alone, John Taliaferro persisted in slapping at them as they buzzed around the table. Taliaferro was never known for his common sense, Brown mused, having "the heart of a lion" and "the brains of a sheep."[3]

The Confederate army remained inactive for several months. Too weak to attack the Union army at Alexandria, Johnston had to be content merely to observe the enemy. To get early information about Union movements, Confederate spies infiltrated enemy lines. The most intriguing of Ewell's informants was a spy named Marshall. Brown first saw him at one of the outposts: a short, handsome man dressed in coarse clothing and riding a shabby horse. With an air of quiet confidence, Marshall passed a few private words with Ewell and handed him a soiled scrap of paper. The general examined its contents and had Brown write the mysterious stranger a pass enabling him to enter or leave Confederate lines at any hour, day or night. From that time on Brown held Marshall in awe, as one might regard the dashing hero of a romance novel. Not so Ewell, who put little faith in the spy and quickly grew disgusted with his worthless reports.[4]

The Army of the Potomac, now under Maj. Gen. George B. McClellan, showed no disposition to attack, and as summer moved toward fall, both sides settled into the dull routine of camp life. In August Brown described for his aunt "the wonderful state of idleness" at brigade headquarters. "Just now Gen. Ewell is lying listlessly on his couch studying tactics, a member of his Staff is writing home, another sitting about, doing nothing, another lying upstairs reading a novel, & I am trying to find something of interest to tell you."

To help pass the time, Ewell toured the Manassas battlefield with Capt. (later Gen.) Samuel Wragg Ferguson of Beauregard's staff. Ferguson pointed out the position of various batteries on Henry House Hill and took his guests to a cedar post that marked the location of Brig. Gen. Bernard Bee's death. Although the battle was not yet a month old, the area had revived remarkably. To those who gazed across the rolling field, Brown recalled, "it was hard for the mind to conceive that anything like war had ever disturbed the quiet of that little green meadow."[5]

The battlefield tour, while providing a pleasant diversion, could not compare with the celebrated visit of the Cary girls. Constance Cary of Alexandria and her cousins Hetty and Jenny Cary of Baltimore presented as pretty a trio as could be found in the South. Fitz Lee and Maj. Benjamin H. Greene, Ewell's new commissary of subsistence, met the girls at a party hosted by Brig. Gen. Arnold Elzey and invited them to dine at Ewell's headquarters. The Carys arrived the next day, escorted by their brothers. The ground was muddy, and as the girls alighted from their vehicle, Lee stepped forward. With an allusion to Sir Walter Raleigh, he threw a beautiful blanket onto the ground for them to step on. The cream of the joke, chuckled Brown, was that the blanket belonged to Taliaferro, "who looked ruefully on while Fitz with charming nonchalance turned aside their apologies & regrets for the treatment of his blanket."

The officers and their guests had a rollicking time. At dinner Lee and Greene concocted a mixture of sugar and water, flavored it with a few tablespoons of whiskey, then playfully offered it to the ladies as a sample of camp spirits. Word of the incident got out, and soon the army was whispering that the Carys had gotten drunk while imbibing whiskey with Ewell's staff. This was not true, of course. As one officer noted, the girls were "so intoxicated by flattery & attention as to need no other stimulant." The Carys' giddy behavior that day lent credence to the story. Connie was particularly rambunctious. After dinner she delighted her admirers by firing a pistol, then later, when a Confederate regiment marched by, she mounted a stump beside the road and regaled the passing troops with the "Marseillaise." Campbell Brown described the evening as "one of the maddest frolics I ever saw."[6]

Ewell's brigade remained at Sangster's Crossroads until October, when Johnston, having failed to receive sufficient reinforcements to attack the Federals, withdrew the army to Centreville. Ewell's men resumed their former position at Union Mills.[7] The brigade's composition changed that summer, when the Twelfth Alabama and the Twelfth Mississippi joined the unit and the Sixth Louisiana left it, giving the brigade a total of four regiments.[8]

Up to that time, each brigade had been independent and reported directly to the army commander. But as the number of brigades grew, Johnston reorganized the army into two corps of two divisions each. Beauregard commanded the First Corps, which comprised Earl Van Dorn's and James Longstreet's divisions. Gustavus W. Smith temporarily commanded the Second Corps, made up of his own division and that of E. Kirby Smith. Ewell initially belonged to Van Dorn's division, but on 6 November he received orders to turn his brigade over to Robert Rodes and report to Gustavus Smith. This seems to have been done in order to provide a brigade for Rodes, whose promotion Ewell had long recommended.[9]

Smith placed Ewell in command of the Stonewall Brigade, which had been without a leader since Maj. Gen. Thomas J. "Stonewall" Jackson's transfer to Harpers Ferry. It was one of the shortest assignments of the war. Jackson requested the services of the Stonewall Brigade at Harpers Ferry a couple of days later, and Johnston, unwilling to lose Ewell's services, gave the brigade to Richard B. Garnett. Johnston then reassigned Ewell to Longstreet's old brigade, consisting of the First, Seventh, Eleventh, and Seventeenth Virginia Regiments and the Loudoun Artillery.[10]

Ewell commanded Longstreet's brigade throughout the winter of 1861–62. He pitched his tent in Centreville, just a few hundred yards from Four Chimney House, his family's former home, which Johnston and Gustavus Smith now occupied as a headquarters. Visits to the house by Ewell brought back bittersweet memories of his poverty-stricken youth. "I was a long time yesterday in our old house in Centreville," he wistfully told Lizinka, "and thought much over old times, when I went often to bed on a piece of corn bread & of your tears at Mother's being obliged to keep school. Yet those were probably as happy as any days Mother had passed to that time. Since then with money for every want I have passed no happier."[11]

One day Ewell walked with Campbell Brown to Four Chimney House to ask Johnston where he wished him to place his brigade in the event of an attack. They found the commanding general standing outside talking to Smith. Ewell introduced Brown to the generals, and the four men strolled over to the earthworks. At one point Johnston halted and pointed toward a small hollow well sheltered from Union artillery fire. "There is a place whose perfections I was noticing today," he exclaimed. "Do you see what a perfect cup it is & how it seems made to hide a regiment or two in? I shall expect you to put one or two of yours there in reserve to reinforce either side, if we have an action here." Ewell told Brown to commit the ground to memory, as he might be called on to lead troops across it under fire.

The officers retired to General Ewell's tent and talked about old times. Ewell complained that his wounded shoulder still pained him. "Why, you may expect it for some time yet," said Smith. "Do you know, it is only a few years since my wound in Mexico ceased troubling me." Johnston agreed, observing that a man suffered the effects of a gunshot wound for about seven years, more or less, then generally got over it entirely. He spoke of a wound he had received in Mexico, noting that it had caused him little pain at first, but that it nearly killed him in the end. "I suppose that hurt you more than the other," Ewell commented, pointing to a scar on Johnston's head, that the latter had received during the Second Seminole War. "Yes," Johnston replied, "when I got this, I was running towards the Indians & fell in a heap, feeling as if my whole head were blown off. I thought I was killed, but finding I did not die, put up my hand & felt my head. I could lay my finger in the place, but found no bones broken, so I got up & went on." [12]

Johnston, Smith, Ewell, and other officers met frequently to swap stories, talk strategy, and renew friendships. At one gathering hosted by Ewell, Capt. G. Woodville Latham of the Eleventh Virginia sang "My Maryland." Beauregard and other officers joined Latham in the chorus, but they were outdone by Longstreet, who mounted a bench and led the group in a final, rousing encore. Not all meetings were marked by such fraternity. At a luncheon hosted by Van Dorn, someone offered a toast to Bee, Bartow, and Fisher, three Confederate officers from the Deep South killed at Manassas. Jubal Early objected to the toast on the grounds that a Virginian was not among those named, provoking a heated discussion. The argument ended with Early and some fellow Virginians stalking angrily from the room. [13]

Ewell's most welcome visitor that winter was his cousin Lizinka Brown. In November Lizinka and her seventeen-year-old daughter, Harriot (familiarly known as Hattie), journeyed to Virginia to see Campbell. They stayed at Stony Lonesome, fifteen miles behind Confederate lines. Ewell had loved his beautiful cousin as a teenager, and he loved her still. In an effort to impress Lizinka, he staged a brigade review in her honor. An army ambulance transported mother and daughter to the event. As the vehicle neared the review site, its back seat tipped over, throwing the women head-over-heels onto the floor. A regiment of soldiers cheered, adding to the ladies' embarrassment. [14]

Despite this mishap Lizinka enjoyed the outing and made many more trips to the army before returning to Tennessee. With each visit she and Ewell grew closer. On 1 December 1861 the general summoned his courage and proposed marriage. Lizinka accepted. The couple kept their engagement a secret to everyone except members of the immediate family, but they could not hide their love. Days later cavalry chief Jeb Stuart noted that "Poor Gen Ewell is desperately but hopelessly smitten." [15]

Hattie initially opposed the union. Rather than drive a wedge between the girl and her mother, Ewell offered to cancel the engagement. "You judge me incorrectly if you think any step, that would estrange the affections of your children from you, or cause their unhappiness would not be as repugnant to me as to yourself," he wrote his fiancée. "I trust that in any way possible you will remove any shadow or worry or anxiety from your child. I should a thousand times prefer to a moments estrangement between you & her that I should confine myself to the recollection of the 1st of Decr. and the almost intoxicating thought of being of

Lizinka as she appeared later in life (Donald C. Pfanz)

interest to you. I say this because I can see no brightness in the future, if accompanied with a cloud to you or her." [16]

Eventually Hattie came around. In the meantime Lizinka's affectionate letters elevated Ewell's spirits to such a pitch that even the prospect of an extended war could not dampen them. "In spite of the clouds gathering over our country I am almost happy," he told her. "Events are fast thickening and I hardly know if every letter may not be the last, for a long time at least, and but that I cannot express myself more strongly than I have or more openly, I would weary you with my protestations. My prayer is that I may prove worthy of the great happiness you have conferred on me & which to my wildest fancies seemed hopeless." For Ewell the future looked bright. "To this time I feel as though all human calculations were overthrown and I have hope & faith in the future. At all events it seems to me that the future has more to look forward to than I ever thought possible."[17]

Ewell could hardly believe that Lizinka reciprocated his love. "I assure myself often that you are carried away in regard to myself by your anxiety for the safety of myself & C[ampbell] and that your love for your son is reflected on me. Still in spite of this I cannot help hoping that the future has happiness in store for me." Their love transcended life itself. "Your expression 'in life or death we shall be united' is to me fraught with promise," he told her, probably quoting one of her letters. "It has seemed that were our union limited to this world that it would be comparatively valueless. During my life I have looked to knowing you & loving you in another world & your letter supports the thought. You may think I am in my dotage but I cannot weigh my words."[18]

An early spring offensive by the Union army in the West threatened to interrupt the lovers' correspondence. In February 1862 Brig. Gen. Ulysses S. Grant captured Forts Henry and Donelson, opening central Tennessee to invasion by Union gunboats. Confederate troops abandoned Nashville and retreated to Mississippi, surrendering Tennessee to the Union. Tennessee's loss sent shock waves throughout the South and filled Ewell's mind with "dismal thoughts & forebodings." Reports from the West were so discouraging that he and other officers at one point seriously discussed emigrating to Brazil.[19]

Blame for Henry's and Donelson's loss fell on the Confederacy's western commander, Gen. Albert Sidney Johnston. Ewell joined the chorus of criticism, stating that Johnston had committed "gross blunders" and had been "badly outgeneraled." But he reserved his most severe criticism for President Jefferson Davis, whom he denounced as both obstinate and meddlesome. So long as the administration continued to support incompetent generals and interfere in military affairs, he privately declared, the South would never be victorious.[20]

Ewell's harsh criticism of Johnston and Davis stemmed in part from his concern for Lizinka. After leaving Virginia in December 1861, she had returned to Nashville, which now lay in the path of the advancing foe. Ewell advised her to flee the city, even though it might result in the confiscation of her property there. "I believe that the rule is general, that where females remain on their property within the enemy's lines, it is respected except slaves. Where property is left, it is taken as evidence of disaffection on [the] part of the owners & abused." If Lizinka chose to leave Nashville, Ewell suggested that she settle somewhere between the Tennessee capital and Richmond, preferably in western North Carolina, which seemed relatively free of danger. He strongly recommended that for her personal safety she seek refuge in a town rather than in the country, where she would be "subjected to insults from small marauding bands of the enemy," not to mention lower classes of Southerners. "The more out of the way a place," he concluded, "the more exposed to outrage as there is less restraint over the parties who spread around." [21]

Ewell sent Campbell to help Lizinka move. "You & your all have been at the service of the cause," he rationalized, "and I consider that I am assisting that in aiding any of our people to secure their means." The general had grown quite attached to Campbell and admitted that he felt "ridiculously lonesome" after he left. [22] Brown reached Nashville before the Union army but too late to help his mother, who had already left the city in the company of her friend Governor Isham G. Harris. She and Hattie traveled to Alabama to stay with the Hubbards. Campbell followed. [23]

Before fleeing Nashville Lizinka transferred title of her house to two Unionist friends in an effort to keep the Federals from confiscating it. As an added precaution she left a note for Generals Grant and Don Carlos Buell asking them, in Ewell's name, to protect the house. Both measures failed. When Union forces occupied the city, they seized the house and turned it over to Lizinka's friend, Andrew Johnson, who was military governor of Tennessee. Johnson and his family used the building as their residence for the next three years, renting it at the modest rate of $1,400 a year. Johnson later claimed he took possession of the house "to save it from falling into the hands of the military authorities," but Lizinka and Hattie thought he had more sinister motives. "Although he had been a friend of my mother's," the daughter insisted, "he resented her loyalty to the South bitterly, and wished to punish her for it. He was unable to forgive people who were above him in the social scale, and it is not at all improbable that he was actuated in some degree by a desire to humiliate my mother." [24]

Lizinka's Spring Hill plantation also fell prey to the advancing Union army. One day after she left the area, Federal troops marched through Maury County, entered the plantation buildings, and seized 10,000 pounds of bacon. Soldiers later bivouacked on the land. Before leaving, Campbell informed his mother, they burned the barn, stole the livestock, and left "our once beautiful farm a desolate wilderness." [25]

By the spring of 1862 Union troops swarmed over western Virginia, Tennessee, and Missouri and gained footholds on the North and South Carolina coasts. Millions of dollars in property had been destroyed; thousands of Southerners had become refugees. The young nation seemed on the verge of collapse. Still Ewell believed the South could prevail if it remained "sufficiently aroused" and did not allow its determination to flag "before the enticements of peace." "If our people are true to the cause they have made there is no fear of the result," he declared. "But they have not yet begun in earnest—mean demagogism & truculent legislation have marked the course of things. May be we will wake up and the true man will appear."[26] Good or bad, he was prepared to face whatever the future might hold provided that Lizinka was at his side. "As long as we are all alive," he assured her, "there is hope & love and devotion."[27]

The year 1862 brought advancement for Dick Ewell. In January Gens. P. G. T. Beauregard, Earl Van Dorn, and Kirby Smith transferred to other theaters, prompting a major reorganization of the Virginia army. In the ensuing shuffle Joe Johnston promoted Ewell to major general and appointed him to command Smith's "Reserve Division." Ewell hesitated to accept the commission, believing that the division's temporary commander, Jubal Early, deserved the position more than himself. Early, on the other hand, was pleased that the job went to Ewell. "I would be gratified at it," he wrote Col. James L. Kemper, "and I believe every body else would be better pleased than Ewell himself."[28]

Not everyone was gratified by Ewell's promotion. Some believed the position should have gone to Early, Arnold Elzey, Jeb Stuart, or some other officer who had played an instrumental role in the victory at Manassas. Stuart certainly thought so. In a letter to his wife penned the day of Ewell's promotion, the ambitious brigadier confided that "it was whispered in the street that I was to be a *Major Genl.* I have no such expectations but I do know I would make better than some—Crittenden & Ewell for instance."[29]

No one was more surprised by Ewell's promotion than Ewell himself. He knew that Johnston thought highly of him, but he did not think Jefferson Davis would approve the nomination. After all, what had he done to deserve it? On one occasion he startled a subordinate by asking in genuine puzzlement, "General Taylor! What do you suppose President Davis made me a major-general for?" Ten weeks after his promotion, he still referred to himself as "a mere ephemeral production" of the president.[30]

If Ewell did not understand why Davis had made him a major general, others did. Lt. Edward P. Reeve of the First Virginia had occasion to observe the general frequently during the months that Ewell commanded Longstreet's brigade, and

Reeve liked what he saw. The general's industry, fairness, and attention to detail impressed him. Although Ewell was not as popular with the men as Longstreet had been, Reeve considered him in many respects to be Longstreet's superior. "He seems thoroughly interested in his calling," Reeve wrote, "and is very strict and vigilant in his superintendence of everything connected with his command. I have been struck with this at his inspections. He has an eye which nothing escapes and wo[e] to the luckless soldier who endeavours to screen from his observation a rusty musket or any disorder in his equipments. He seems to take in everything at a glance."

To volunteer soldiers unused to military discipline, Ewell must have seemed like a martinet. "He is thought by some to be particular to a fault but it is this I admire him for," continued Reeve. "He was never known to sign any document until he had examined it himself—shrinks from no labor to this end—examines every account, goes over every subtraction and addition until satisfied with their correctness. All this involves an amount of labor which not one Genl. in a hundred will perform but trust to their clerks. Never shows partiality, will correct a fault in a Col. as soon as in a private, in a word attends thoroughly to his own duties and endeavours to make all under his authority do the same." Ewell's "abrupt and sometimes harsh manner" rendered him unpopular with some of his subordinates, but Reeve was not one of them. "I know no man in our Army under whose training I had rather be if I wished to be a professional soldier," he told his wife. "He is more like the duke of Wellington than any man in our Army."[31]

Although Ewell's promotion to major general dated from 24 January 1862, he did not take command of the Reserve Division until late the following month. His new command had three brigades commanded by Arnold Elzey, Isaac Trimble, and Richard Taylor. Elzey, an 1837 graduate of West Point, was a career artillery officer and the division's senior brigadier. During his twenty-three years in the Old Army he had served in the Second Seminole War, the Mexican War, and at various frontier posts. As a brigade commander at Manassas, his attack on McDowell's right flank had helped turn the fortunes of that day and earned for him the sobriquet "the Blucher of the Confederacy." Although hot tempered and sometimes brusque, Elzey was a tough and efficient officer on whom Ewell could rely.[32]

Isaac Trimble commanded Ewell's second brigade. At age sixty Trimble was one of the army's oldest officers. An 1822 graduate of the U.S. Military Academy, he had served as an engineer in the Old Army for ten years before resigning his commission in 1832 to accept a position with the Baltimore and Susquehanna Railroad. When the Civil War began, Trimble became a colonel of engineers and

Arnold Elzey (U.S. Army Military History Institute)

laid out defenses at Norfolk and Evansport before subsequently receiving command of a brigade in Ewell's division. It was the first line command of his career. Though aged by army standards and wholly inexperienced at handling troops, Trimble was a scrapper. His pugnacity led one officer to remark that "there was fight enough in old man Trimble to satisfy a herd of tigers."[33]

Thirty-six-year-old Richard Taylor commanded Ewell's last brigade. Taylor was the son of President Zachary Taylor and a brother-in-law of President Jefferson Davis. As a young man he had studied at Harvard and Yale and in schools abroad. He later owned a plantation in Louisiana and dabbled in state politics. Unlike Elzey and Trimble, Taylor had no formal military training. He had a fascination

Richard Taylor (Library of Congress)

with military history, however, and had studied the campaigns of Napoleon and other great commanders closely. Ewell was among those who benefited from Taylor's vast store of military knowledge, theoretical though it was. "Alleging that he had small opportunity for study after leaving West Point," Taylor wrote of Ewell, "he drew from me whatever some reading and a good memory could supply; but his shrewd remarks changed many erroneous opinions I had formed, and our 'talks' were of more value to me than to him."[34]

Ewell acquired a new staff to go along with his new division. Of the officers who had served with him at Manassas, only Campbell Brown remained. Rhodes had gone to Richmond as an assistant quartermaster, Taliaferro had transferred

Isaac R. Trimble (Library of Congress)

to the artillery, Mason remained the quartermaster of Ewell's old brigade, and Fitz Lee had accepted a lieutenant colonel's commission in the cavalry. Humphrey Tyler had deserted. During the battle of Manassas Ewell had dispatched him with a message to Beauregard, but Tyler failed to deliver the message and did not return. He was spotted the next day at the tent of a sutler before vanishing for good. A Northern newspaper later reported that he had been captured in Cincinnati,

Ohio, while attempting to bring his wife into Confederate lines. No one at head-quarters mourned his loss.[35]

Ewell appointed a number of "very clever gentlemen" to fill the vacancies on his staff. Lt. Col. John M. Jones and Maj. James Barbour became his assistant adjutants general, Maj. Charles E. Snodgrass held the post of quartermaster, Dr. Francis W. Hancock was the division's medical director, Maj. Benjamin H. Greene of Mississippi headed the Commissary Department, and Capt. George W. Christy of Louisiana became Ewell's chief of ordnance.[36] Hugh M. Nelson, Campbell Brown, and Thomas T. Turner served as aides-de-camp. Nelson had commanded a company in the Sixth Virginia Cavalry and was picked up by Ewell when he failed reelection. Twenty-year-old Tom Turner came from a prominent St. Louis family whom Ewell had met while at Jefferson Barracks.[37]

Campbell Brown was emerging as a leading member of the staff in usefulness if not in rank. Ewell had appointed Brown to his staff in 1861 as a favor to Lizinka. Although he was young and inexperienced, he learned quickly, and Ewell came to depend heavily on him. After Fitz Lee's departure in September 1861, Brown ably took charge of the headquarters paperwork and continued to do much of it even after Jones and Barbour came on duty. Ewell rewarded his diligence by appointing him adjutant in July 1862.[38]

In addition to the regular members of his military family, Ewell employed numerous volunteer aides. These men usually served for a limited time, held no rank, and received no pay. William Stoddert occupied such a position for five weeks in the spring of 1862 before leaving his brother to become chaplain of the Fifty-eighth Virginia Infantry. Congressman Ethelbert Barksdale of Mississippi also joined the staff for awhile. Barksdale was the brother of Col. (later Brig. Gen.) William Barksdale and a friend of Benjamin Greene. He volunteered as an aide for two or three months in the spring of 1862 while the Confederate legislature was in recess.[39]

Ewell had been in command of the Reserve Division for just two weeks when Johnston issued orders for the army to fall back to the Rappahannock River, where it would be in a better position to defend Richmond.[40] The move meant abandoning Stony Lonesome and the rest of Prince William County to the enemy. "It seemed a pity to leave the old place to be destroyed by the Yankees," Ewell later reflected, "and to leave old furniture &c hallowed by the recollections of the past to be profaned by their presence. It would be a relief it seems to me, to hear that they had burned the old house down. Wm. was very much tempted to do so & I believe it would have been better."[41]

Ewell blamed politicians in Richmond for failing to adopt measures necessary to sustain the war effort. "When those who hold the power refuse to act," he fumed, "what can be done by the Generals?" He was particularly critical of recent legislation that permitted infantrymen to transfer to cavalry or artillery companies. Had Johnston carried out the War Department directive, Ewell told Lizinka, the "whole Army would have been broken up, except those two branches." He added angrily, "You would be surprised to see the amt. of weakness, favoring & time serving exhibited towards favorites to the injury of any part of the service."[42]

Confederate troops evacuated the Manassas line on 9 March 1862. Stuart's cavalry covered the retreat. It was a dangerous operation, especially for an army inexperienced in such maneuvers. "A retreat is said to be impossible without a disaster," wrote Ewell two days before the movement, "so that this requires very careful management and safety consists in keeping the exact moment concealed."[43] Despite Ewell's misgivings, the operation went off without a hitch. The Union commander, Maj. Gen. George B. McClellan, did not challenge the withdrawal, and the Confederates made it safely across the Rappahannock.

Johnston did not stop there. After concentrating his troops at Culpeper Court House, he continued south across the Rapidan River to Orange Court House, leaving Ewell to guard the railroad bridge at Rappahannock Station. Stuart's horsemen patrolled toward Warrenton.[44] For the next few weeks Ewell made his headquarters at the Cunningham house, northeast of Brandy Station. The owner had left several bottles of old Madeira behind, which Ewell quickly consumed. He cordially invited Trimble to share the last bottle. The old brigadier tried to criticize it, remembered Ewell, "but when I gave its history . . . he discovered new qualities."[45]

Taylor was a frequent guest at the Cunningham house and came to know Ewell well. His book *Destruction and Reconstruction* paints a vivid picture of the general. "Bright, prominent eyes, a bomb-shaped, bald head, and a nose like that of Francis of Valois, gave him a striking resemblance to a woodcock," wrote the Louisianian, "and this was increased by a bird-like habit of putting his head on one side to utter his quaint speeches. He fancied that he had some mysterious internal malady, and would eat nothing but frumenty, a preparation of wheat; and his plaintive way of talking of his disease, as if he were some one else, was droll in the extreme. His nervousness prevented him from taking regular sleep, and he passed nights curled around a camp-stool, in positions to dislocate an ordinary person's joints."

Ewell's idiosyncrasies did not detract from his effectiveness as a soldier. "Superbly mounted, he was the boldest of horsemen," wrote Taylor, "invariably leaving the roads to take timber and water. With a fine tactical eye on the battle field, he was never content with his own plan until he had secured the approval of another's judgment, and chafed under the restraint of command, preparing to fight with the skirmish line." Twice in the Shenandoah Valley, Ewell called the Louisianian to his side "and immediately rushed forward among the skirmishers, where some sharp work was going on. Having refreshed himself, he returned with the hope that 'old Jackson would not catch him at it.' . . . With all his oddities, perhaps in some measure because of them," thought Taylor, "Ewell was adored by officers and men." [46]

Affairs on the Rappahannock remained quiet until 28 March when Stuart reported the approach of Union general Samuel P. Heintzelman's Third Corps. Stuart endeavored to delay the enemy's advance while the Fifteenth Alabama Infantry regiment tore up the tracks north of the river, but Heintzelman overpowered him. Midway through the afternoon the Alabamians scrambled back across the bridge with Stuart's horsemen at their heels. As the last Confederate soldier crossed, engineers put a torch to the bridge, causing it to collapse in a burning heap into the river below. [47] Ewell and Taylor watched the spectacle from a nearby knoll. The Louisianian seemed annoyed. "You don't like it," chirped Ewell. Taylor admitted that he did not. Citing an episode from the Napoleonic Wars, he illustrated how it was easier to defend one bridge than many miles of fordable water. Now it was Ewell who was annoyed. "Why did you keep the story until the bridge was burnt?" he piped. [48]

Ewell put up a show of force, then withdrew the division to a point about a mile from the river. A shell exploded under Elzey's horse as it headed to the rear. The incident demoralized the brigadier terribly, and when he encountered Ewell a few minutes later, he complained at not having been ordered off sooner. "General, what were my men brought out here for?" he demanded. "Ostentation," replied Ewell. "Ostentation h——!" roared Elzey, "I'll take them back to camp." His insubordination provoked Ewell to profanity. With "very plain language," remembered one witness, the general told Elzey that he had ordered him to the rear "as soon as necessary or intended, & that he might have moved more promptly." [49]

Ewell anticipated that Heintzelman might attempt to cross the Rappahannock and had his division ready for action at dawn the next morning. A heavy fog blanketed the river bottom, hiding everything from view. As Ewell and Stuart awaited the Federal crossing, Lt. John S. Mosby brought news that Heintzelman had withdrawn toward Warrenton, leaving only a thin line of Union pickets to guard the river. Stuart immediately started in pursuit and picked up many prisoners. [50]

With the Federals no longer seriously threatening the Rappahannock, Ewell withdrew his division to Brandy Station, leaving only pickets to guard the river. He made his headquarters at the Barbour house, north of the village.[51] Over the next few weeks he constantly drilled his troops, gradually molding them into an effective fighting force. It was not a happy time. Supplies were short and disease ravaged the camps. As rations ran low, soldiers searched for cattle at local farms, but Confederate commissaries had already stripped them clean. Ewell ventured forth on his own private cattle hunt, returning a few hours later with a scrawny cow that he proudly showed to Taylor. It was a fine capture, the brigadier admitted, but hardly enough to feed an entire division. Ewell's triumphant air instantly vanished. "Ah!" he sighed, "I was thinking of my fifty dragoons."[52]

While Ewell was looking for meat to feed his men, McClellan shipped his army down the Potomac River for the purpose of approaching Richmond from the southeast. Johnston started for the Peninsula to head him off. Stuart followed on 8 April 1862, leaving Ewell just two small regiments of cavalry to patrol the Rappahannock line. The Federals took advantage of Stuart's departure to push their pickets as far as the Rappahannock. For a day or two the two sides exchanged fire across the river. "This served to enliven us," remembered Taylor, "and kept Ewell busy, as he always feared lest some one would get under fire before him."[53]

By mid-April the strategic situation in Virginia was looking grim. The Union army had roughly 180,000 men in the state, divided into four major armies: Mc-Clellan's Army of the Potomac, on the Peninsula; Irvin McDowell's Department of the Rappahannock, in north-central Virginia; Nathaniel Banks's Department of the Shenandoah, near Strasburg; and John C. Frémont's Mountain Department, scattered throughout the Allegheny Mountains of western Virginia. Opposing them were 80,000 Confederates. Three-quarters of that force was with Johnston on the Peninsula. The remaining 20,000 were divided among Brig. Gen. Charles Field's brigade at Fredericksburg; Ewell's division near Brandy Station; Stonewall Jackson's Army of the Valley, near Mount Jackson; and Brig. Gen. Edward "Allegheny" Johnson's tiny Army of the Northwest, near Monterey. The Union army's superiority in numbers becomes even more evident when broken down by region:

Peninsula: McClellan (110,000) vs. Johnston (60,000)
Fredericksburg: McDowell (30,000) vs. Field (2,500)
Upper Rappahannock: Abercrombie/Geary (6,500) vs. Ewell (6,500)
Shenandoah Valley: Banks (20,000) vs. Jackson (6,000)
Allegheny Mountains: Frémont (20,000) vs. Johnson (3,000)

The Confederates were heavily outnumbered on every front except Ewell's, where they had roughly even numbers. Opposing Ewell was Brig. Gen. John J. Abercrombie's 4,500-man brigade, guarding the Orange and Alexandria Railroad at Warrenton Junction, and Col. John W. Geary's 2,000 men, working on the Manassas Gap Railroad. Surprisingly, neither Abercrombie nor Geary seemed to pay much attention to Ewell; indeed, Abercrombie did not even know who commanded the Confederates opposite him.[54]

Ewell hoped to attack either Abercrombie or Geary, but before he could do so, the odds turned against him. In early April Brig. Gen. Louis Blenker joined Abercrombie at Warrenton Junction with 9,000 men, increasing the number of Union troops there to 13,500. Blenker was on his way to the Shenandoah Valley to reinforce Banks. As his mostly German division moved through the state, Union soldiers wantonly broke into houses, insulted ladies, and destroyed personal property.[55]

Blenker's depredations sharpened Ewell's aversion to "the Dutch." He had disliked German Americans since his days as a dragoon in Carlisle, a prejudice no doubt heightened by the Schaumburgh affair. Reports of German troops looting his state and insulting its women made him seethe with anger. Ewell decided to take action. In a letter to Charles Field, Ewell suggested that they join forces to attack Blenker's division. Once they had defeated it, they could move north and threaten Washington.[56]

When Field did not respond to the proposition, Ewell sought Jackson's help. Ewell described the enemy's situation with unconcealed contempt. "Their troops are very much scattered and demoralized, are ill-treating the people, robbing and stealing and wantonly killing all the stock," he told Jackson. "Blenker's men are deserting; those I have seen are stupid, ignorant Dutch. These people are committing more wanton injury than they did in the Mexican war, and are as cowardly as villainous." Ewell urged Jackson to join him east of the Blue Ridge for an attack on Blenker, but Jackson rejected the plan because it would have exposed Staunton to capture.[57]

After spending more than two weeks near Strasburg, Banks was showing signs of continuing his march up the Valley. Too weak to offer battle, Jackson prepared to retreat to Fisher's Gap, where he would be in position to check Banks's advance on Staunton. Johnston ordered Ewell to cooperate with Jackson and reinforce him if called on to do so. In the event that Jackson and Ewell combined forces, Jackson as senior officer would take command.[58]

Ewell could not have been happy about the prospect of serving under Jackson. A brutal midwinter campaign in the Allegheny Mountains, a defeat at Kernstown, and the unfair arrest of Brig. Gen. Richard B. Garnett had tarnished the laurels that Jackson had won at Manassas. Moreover, he and Ewell had contrasting personalities. Ewell was excitable and sometimes profane, while Jackson was stiff and pious—the epitome of the "sour Presbyterian" that Ewell had once professed to despise. The only thing they had in common, it seemed, was a common desire to defeat the enemy.[59]

The two men nevertheless tried to work together in harmony. At first their correspondence was downright cordial. Jackson kept Ewell informed of events transpiring in the Valley, and Ewell sent Jackson newspapers and passed along information concerning military events in other parts of the country. Before long, each man was addressing the other as "My dear General."[60]

Confusion about geography hampered their communications from the start. Jackson initially confused Fisher's Gap with Swift Run Gap, fifteen miles farther south. Ewell admitted that he did not even know where Fisher's Gap was, remarking that one gap sometimes had several names. In order to prevent misunderstandings, Jackson sent Ewell a map showing the roads and gaps and asked that Ewell correct it and return it to him. For his part, Ewell asked Jackson to put all instructions regarding important movements in writing and advised him to send an officer to guide his march to the Valley, when and if that became necessary. To make sure important dispatches were not lost en route, as had happened at Manassas, Ewell suggested that Jackson continue to send him couriers until he received a reply.[61]

For a week Ewell and Jackson exchanged dispatches daily, as they ironed out the details of Ewell's march to Fisher's Gap. In accordance with earlier instructions from Johnston, Jackson ordered Ewell to fall back to the Rapidan River along the Orange and Alexandria Railroad, then march to Fisher's Gap via Madison Court House. Since Madison Court House was north of the river, Ewell suggested that it would be faster to march there without going to the Rapidan, but Jackson insisted on following Johnston's orders to the letter. To be on the safe side, Ewell had staff officers examine not only the route to Fisher's Gap but also that to Swift Run Gap.[62]

While Jackson waited for Banks to make his move, new recruits swelled Ewell's ranks. By 16 April his division had increased to 8,000 infantry, 500 cavalry, and 14 guns. Discipline, too, had improved. In less than eight weeks Ewell had brought the division to "an admirable state of efficiency." His men were well drilled, and their morale was high. Ewell's cavalry chief, Col. Thomas Munford, considered the division "equal to any that ever entered either army."[63]

As the strength of his division increased, so did Ewell's impatience to attack the enemy—by himself, if necessary. By then Blenker had disappeared over the Blue Ridge, and Geary had moved to Rectortown. Irvin McDowell's corps, however, was within striking distance. On 16 April Confederate scouts reported between 6,000 and 10,000 of McDowell's men scattered along the Orange and Alexandria Railroad between Catlett's Station and Manassas Junction: 6,000 to 10,000 Yankees—even odds. It was enough! That very day Ewell applied to Adj. Gen. Samuel Cooper and to army commander Joe Johnston for permission to attack McDowell as soon as the Rappahannock River fell to the point where he could ford it.[64]

Approval came quickly. Gen. Robert E. Lee wired Ewell the next day, authorizing him to take the offensive if he was reasonably sure of success and if in doing so he would not jeopardize the safety of his command. Lee was Jefferson Davis's personal military adviser. With Johnston's attention focused on the Peninsula, Lee had the uncomfortable role of acting as intermediary between him and the troops in the central and western parts of the state. Lee stressed that Ewell should attack McDowell only if it did not conflict with Johnston's orders. It did not. Just hours after receiving Lee's telegram, Ewell got qualified approval from Johnston himself for the plan. "The question of attacking the enemy in front of you is one which must be decided on the ground," wrote the army commander. "It would be well to drive him away; you would be freer to aid Jackson, and it might make, perhaps, a diversion in his favor. To decide it you have to consider relative forces, the enemy's position, and the facilities for crossing the river. . . . If you feel confident after considering these things, attack."[65]

Attack! The word was music to Ewell's ears. It was then 17 April. The river was falling; he would cross the next day at dawn. But Jackson had other plans. Before Ewell's troops had fairly started for the river, Henry Kyd Douglas appeared at Ewell's headquarters bearing a dispatch from Jackson. In it Stonewall notified Ewell that Banks had advanced to Mount Jackson; in consequence, the Valley Army was falling back to Swift Run Gap. Ewell was to join him at that point. As Ewell finished reading the dispatch Douglas passed out, overcome by fatigue from his nightlong ride across the mountain. Ewell caught the young man in his arms, dragged him to his own cot, and brought him brandy, coffee, and food. After Douglas had revived, Ewell placed him in an ambulance and sent him to Culpeper, where he rested before undertaking the long ride back to the Valley.

Ewell's treatment of Jackson's one-armed ordnance officer, Lt. Richard K. Meade, was not so kind. Within an hour after Douglas delivered his dispatch, Meade arrived at Ewell's camp bearing a letter from Jackson marked "In haste." The dispatch was identical to Douglas's, except that it had been written six and one-half hours earlier. Meade's tardiness in delivering the note, added to his rather dissipated appearance, suggested that he had been on a spree. Ewell upbraided the hapless lieutenant for his late arrival and criticized him sharply in his next report to Jackson.[66]

Ewell started for Swift Run Gap that afternoon, leaving only a token force to hold the Rappahannock line. So successful was he in masking his withdrawal that Union generals north of the river did not learn of his departure until 29 April, eleven days after he had left. With Meade as his guide, Ewell marched down the Orange and Alexandria Railroad to the Rapidan River. The pious Stonewall suggested that Ewell rest his division Easter Sunday, 20 April, but Ewell was running behind schedule. He disregarded the order.[67]

At the Rapidan River Ewell's men boarded trains for Orange Court House. According to Jackson's instructions, they were to debark at Orange and march west to Liberty Mills (Somerset), where the Stanardsville–Orange Court House Road intersected the Gordonsville–Madison Court House Road. Again Ewell chose to ignore Stonewall's orders. The road from Orange Court House to Liberty Mills was unimproved. Recent rains had rendered it nearly impassable, whereas the road from Gordonsville to Liberty Mills was macadamized and remained in good condition. In distance the two roads were about the same. Ewell therefore led his troops to Gordonsville, a dozen miles farther down the line, taking care to notify Jackson of what he had done.[68]

During the march to Gordonsville, Ewell received a series of contradictory orders from Jackson. Stonewall originally ordered Ewell to Swift Run Gap, but he later changed his mind and ordered Ewell to Fisher's Gap instead. On 19 April Jackson changed his mind again and once more ordered Ewell to Swift Run Gap. Col. Isaac G. Seymour of the Sixth Louisiana Infantry unfairly blamed Ewell for the confusion. "We are all exceedingly dissatisfied with our division Commander Genl. Ewell, who is very eccentric, and seems half the time not to know what he is doing, the consequence, is we are pretty much engaged in undoing one day what we have done the previous one, marching and countermarching but never getting any nearer the enemy."[69]

Banks meanwhile cautiously pursued Jackson up the Valley. By 22 April 1862 he had advanced to New Market and had pushed forward a portion of his command as far as Harrisonburg. Jackson ordered Ewell to move up to Liberty Mills.[70] From there he would be in a position to reinforce the Valley Army via either Fisher's Gap or Swift Run Gap. He would also be near the Virginia Central Railroad should Lee or Johnston summon him to Richmond or Fredericksburg.

Lee was considering both options. Late in April he reinforced Field with Brig.

Thomas J. "Stonewall" Jackson (Library of Congress)

Gen. Joseph R. Anderson's brigade, raising the number of Confederate troops at Fredericksburg to approximately 8,000. Three thousand more were on the way. Lee hoped that Ewell and Jackson together might strike Union troops scattered between Rappahannock Station and Manassas Junction. But if that was not possible, Lee hoped that Ewell could join Anderson at Fredericksburg for an attack on McDowell. As ranking officer, Ewell would take command of the combined forces there.[71]

Before Lee's suggestions reached Jackson, the situation in the Valley began to heat up. On 26 April Union horsemen drove Confederate cavalry to within seven miles of Jackson's headquarters at Conrad's Store. With Banks's army now within striking distance, Jackson ordered Ewell to move up to Stanardsville at the eastern foot of the Blue Ridge Mountains, directly opposite Conrad's Store. Ewell's men passed through Stanardsville early on 27 April and bivouacked west of town. The next day they crept forward to the base of the mountain.[72]

On 28 April Jackson summoned Ewell to his headquarters for their first face-to-face meeting since the campaign began. Jackson felt that Banks was too strong to attack directly, even with Ewell's help. Instead he proposed three alternate plans of action:

1. Strike Banks's lines of communications via New Market with his own and Ewell's forces.
2. Strike Banks's lines of communications via Front Royal with his own and Ewell's forces.
3. Strike Frémont's advance guard west of Staunton with his own and Edward Johnson's forces.

Ewell favored the first option, but Jackson remained undecided. After a day of thought, he made up his mind. Early on 30 April Jackson again summoned Ewell to his headquarters and informed him that he intended to join Johnson in attacking Frémont's troops west of Staunton. Ewell's division would take his place at Conrad's Store, checking Banks's advance up the Valley.

By afternoon Ewell had his troops in motion, toiling westward over the mountain. The months of anxious waiting were past; the Valley Campaign was about to begin.[73]

CHAPTER II

The Road to Glory

Ewell's division crossed the Blue Ridge late on 30 April 1862 and made its camp at Elk Run, a rocky stream at the western foot of Swift Run Gap. By the time the last brigade cleared the pass, darkness had fallen. Cheers went up as the troops discerned the campfires of Jackson's division dotting the valley floor below. Not until morning did they realize that the camps were deserted.[1]

Ewell led the march across the Blue Ridge, establishing his headquarters at the village of Conrad's Store (modern-day Elkton). He stayed at the house of Capt. Asher Argenbright, the same building that Jackson had occupied up to that day. In one of the rooms Ewell's staff officers found a copy of the charges recently preferred by Jackson against Brig. Gen. Richard Garnett. It was a grim reminder of the price paid by those who failed to live up to Old Jack's rigid standards.[2]

Jackson returned to Conrad's Store at 6:00 P.M. for a brief chat with Ewell. He probably reiterated the importance of preventing Banks from reaching Staunton, which would place the Union general squarely behind the Valley Army. Jackson may also have emphasized the need to keep close tabs on Banks in order to prevent him from sending troops to General McDowell at Fredericksburg. Under no circumstances, he stressed, was Ewell to leave the Valley until he returned.[3]

The cordiality that heretofore had marked Jackson's and Ewell's relations was conspicuously absent at Conrad's Store. The two had a falling out, and Ewell took no pains to hide the fact. More than one soldier remembered hearing the former dragoon curse Jackson for disappearing without giving him any orders or any indication as to where he was going. Such complaints, however, were simply not valid. Ewell knew quite well that Jackson had gone to Staunton to join Johnson (though he may not have known Jackson's exact route), and he certainly knew what Jackson expected him to do.[4]

Ewell's resentment probably resulted more from Jackson's attitude than from his secretiveness. As long as Ewell had remained outside the Valley District, Jackson had treated him as an equal. But once Ewell entered the Valley and came under Jackson's authority, their relationship abruptly changed. Jackson no longer treated him like an equal, but as a subordinate. No longer did he confide in Ewell and seek his counsel. Instead he issued Ewell orders and coldly demanded obedience. The change caught Ewell off guard. In time he would adjust to Jackson's peculiar ways, but until then relations between the two remained strained.

Capt. David F. Boyd of the Ninth Louisiana Regiment claimed that Ewell was so disgusted by Jackson that he sought to have him removed. According to Boyd, Ewell sent Brig. Gen. Richard Taylor to Richmond to urge President Davis to replace Jackson as commander of the Valley District. After hearing Taylor's arguments, Davis supposedly decided to send James Longstreet to take charge of the Valley, but before the secretary of war could issue the necessary orders, the Valley Campaign began. Boyd's story is probably not true. Taylor did go to Richmond at this time to brief authorities on the state of affairs along the Rappahannock, but there is no evidence that he sought to have Jackson removed. None of the primary participants—Taylor, Longstreet, Ewell, or Davis—ever alluded to such a scheme, and certainly Jackson never knew of it.[5]

Stress and discontent marked Ewell's stay at Conrad's Store. One day Col. James A. Walker of the Thirteenth Virginia called on him at his headquarters. Hearing that the general was in a towering rage, Walker prudently determined to return at a later time. But before he could escape, Ewell spotted him. "Colonel Walker," the irate veteran began, "did it ever occur to you that General Jackson is crazy?"

Walker had studied under Jackson in Lexington and had once challenged him to a duel. But that had been a decade earlier. With admirable restraint he now replied, "I don't know, General. We used to call him 'Fool Tom Jackson' at the Virginia Military Institute, but I do not suppose that he is really crazy."

"I tell you, sir, he is as crazy as a March hare," Ewell ranted. "He has gone away, I don't know where, and left me here with instructions to stay until he returns. But Banks's whole army is advancing on me, and I have not the most remote idea where to communicate with General Jackson. I tell you, sir, he is crazy, and I will just march my division away from here. I do not mean to have it cut to pieces at the behest of a crazy man."

Leaving Ewell, Walker rode to the headquarters of his brigade commander, Arnold Elzey. Elzey, too, was in a foul humor, having just had a run-in with Ewell. When Walker mentioned that he had just come from Ewell's headquarters, Elzey fairly seethed. "I tell you sir," he said, "General Ewell is crazy, and I have a serious notion of marching my brigade back to Gordonsville."

At that instant a conscript from Walker's regiment burst into the tent and thrust a piece of paper in front of Elzey with the words, "I want you, sir, to sign that paper at once, and give me my discharge. You have no right to keep me here, and I mean to go home." The general was stunned by the unexpected and impudent demand—but not for long. Recovering from his astonishment, he lunged for a brace of pistols that lay nearby. The private took to his heels with Elzey in hot pursuit. The general fired two shots after the man, but both missed. Returning to his tent, the general growled, "I should like to know, Colonel Walker what sort of men you keep over at that Thirteenth regiment? The idea of the rascal's demanding of me, a Brigadier-General, to sign a paper. Oh! if I could have only gotten hold of my pistols sooner."

Walker had to laugh. "Well, I don't know what to do myself," he replied. "I was up to see General Ewell just now, and he said that General Jackson was crazy; I come down to see you, and you say that General Ewell is crazy; and I have not the slightest doubt that my conscript, who ran from you just now, will report it all over camp that General Elzey is crazy; so it seems I have fallen into evil hands, and I reckon the best thing for me to do is to turn the conscripts loose, and march the rest of my regiment back to Richmond."[6]

Walker related a similar story to an acquaintance after the war. In an effort to deceive Banks into thinking he was leaving the Valley, Jackson had sent wagons up into the mountain gaps during the day, then once it became dark, ordered them back to the Valley. Ewell used the circumstance to berate Jackson again as crazy. "Why, Walker, what are we going to do?" he asked the colonel. "He sends these wagons up to the mountains and as soon as it gets dark, he orders them back again. Did you ever see such damn foolishness?" Walker did not answer, and Ewell "went off up the road in high disgust."[7]

Frustration lay at the heart of Ewell's anger. A born fighter, he had been in the Confederate army for a full year and as yet had participated in nothing more than a few skirmishes and artillery exchanges. At Manassas his brigade had sat idle at Union Mills while the rest of the army gained glory on the field of battle. When the action later shifted to the Peninsula, Johnston had left him behind to hold the Rappahannock line. After that Ewell had tried to engineer an attack on Blenker but found no one willing to support him. Then, when he felt strong enough to make the attack on his own, Jackson had thwarted his plans by summoning him to Swift Run Gap. Now that he was in the Valley, he had the thankless task of watching Banks while Jackson and Johnson attacked Frémont. It was enough to make a soldier swear!

And swear he did. Ewell had been an army officer for many years, and according to the Reverend William Meade Dame, "he did not confine himself to the dull neutralities of undecorated speech." Pvt. George Cary Eggleston put it more bluntly. "General Ewell was at this time the most violently and elaborately profane man I ever knew. Elaborately, I say, because his profanity did not consist of single or even double oaths, but was ingeniously wrought into whole sentences. It was profanity which might be parsed, and seemed the result of careful study and long practice." Col. Thomas Munford agreed, saying that Ewell "was a hard old customer and could swear, when he chose to exercise that faculty, in a style that defies description. He spared no one when he was cross, but was nobly generous at all other times." [8]

Ewell directed much of his salty locution toward the members of Capt. Elijah V. White's Thirty-fifth Virginia Cavalry Battalion. The "Comanches," as they would come to be called, had been assigned to Ewell's headquarters as scouts and guides. They found their new chief to be "a stern, fierce old soldier," remembered Lt. Frank Myers, and "were a great deal more afraid of him than of Yankees." As with all his scouts, Ewell insisted that White's men report only what they personally had seen and not to take the word of so-called reliable citizens. Reports had to be accurate and thorough. "One of his abominations was to receive 'don't know' for an answer," wrote Myers, "and before very long every man detailed for duty at the General's headquarters went with fear and trembling, for there were a great many things which they really did not know, and when asked about them they couldn't say anything else." [9] Scouts were only one means by which Ewell gathered information on Banks's army. Spies, cavalry, and a signal station at the southern tip of the Massanutten also kept him apprised of the enemy's movements. [10]

The Massanutten divided the Shenandoah Valley from the narrower Page (or Luray) Valley to the east. It was passable at only one point along its fifty-mile length: New Market Gap near the center of the range. The North Fork of the Shenandoah River drained the Shenandoah Valley; the South Fork drained the Page Valley. The two streams converged at Front Royal and flowed northeast thirty miles to Harpers Ferry, where they emptied into the Potomac River. Of the two valleys the Shenandoah was by far the most developed. Through it ran the Valley Turnpike, which connected the towns of Winchester, Strasburg, New Market, Harrisonburg, and Staunton. The Page Valley had no towns of consequence, except Luray, and its roads were unimproved.

Ewell's camp at Conrad's Store stood at the upper (southern) end of the Page Valley. Banks had concentrated his army at Harrisonburg, at the upper end of the Shenandoah Valley. The Union general could not advance beyond Harrisonburg

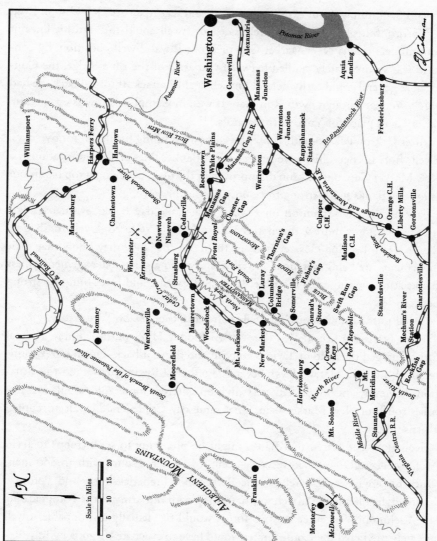

toward Staunton without exposing his flank and rear to an attack by Ewell. Even at Harrisonburg he was not entirely safe, for Ewell could threaten his lines of communication via New Market Gap or Front Royal. Ewell's position, by contrast, was secure. Safely cradled between two arms of the Blue Ridge, the Confederate general could easily defend himself against attack. If forced back, he had only to retreat through Swift Run Gap. It was, in Campbell Brown's estimation, "a very hard place for Yankees to get at us."[11]

After Jackson left Conrad's Store, Ewell heard nothing from him for two days. Ewell wrote his new chief advocating a jab at Banks's lines of communications via New Market Gap, but Jackson disapproved of the plan, believing it too hazardous as long as Banks had a strong force posted near the town.[12]

Jackson reached Staunton on 5 May. That same day Banks evacuated Harrisonburg and withdrew down the Valley. Jackson ordered Ewell to shadow the Federals, keeping close enough to them "so that they may know that their movements are being watched." Ewell was to avoid a general engagement unless Banks attempted to cross the Blue Ridge and Ewell could meet him in a strong position.[13]

Ewell pushed down the Page Valley after the Federals on Wednesday, 7 May. Taylor's Louisiana brigade led the way. At Honey Hill, south of Luray, Federal forces charged the head of Taylor's column and drove it back four miles. A counterattack by Col. Harry Hays's Seventh Louisiana Regiment righted the situation, however, and by dark Ewell's division entered Somerville, a village a few miles south of New Market Gap. That same day Confederate cavalry occupied Harrisonburg.[14]

Robert E. Lee feared that Banks might be preparing to send troops to Irvin McDowell. McDowell had recently occupied Fredericksburg with 30,000 men. Once his engineers had rebuilt the Richmond, Fredericksburg, and Potomac Railroad, he planned to march south, uniting with the Army of the Potomac outside Richmond. Together the two forces would be virtually unstoppable. Ewell privately predicted the Confederates would have to evacuate Virginia by July. Reinforcements from Banks's army would increase the Union odds all the more.

Lee's strategy was to defeat Banks and McDowell in detail before they could unite. Since Banks no longer threatened Staunton, Lee saw no reason for Ewell to remain at Swift Run Gap. On 6 May he urged Ewell to proceed to Culpeper, where he would be in position to intercept any troops that Banks might send to Fredericksburg. He repeated this advice two days later, but this time suggested that Ewell move to the railroad junction at Gordonsville. There he would be in position to strike at Union troops in the piedmont, join forces with Brig. Gen. Joseph Anderson at Fredericksburg, or reinforce Johnston near Richmond.

To strengthen Ewell's hand, Lee placed Brig. Gen. Lawrence O'B. Branch's brigade under his command and sent it to Gordonsville. Lee told Ewell that he wished Branch to remain east of the Blue Ridge "to form a strong column for the purpose of moving beyond the Rappahannock to cut off the enemy's communication" between the tidewater and the Valley. Ewell was not to summon Branch to the Valley unless absolutely necessary. The next day Lee sweetened the pot by sending Brig. Gen. William Mahone's brigade to Gordonsville too.[15] Ewell needed no encouragement to attack the Federals, but he was not at liberty to do so. He had explicit instructions from Jackson to remain in the Valley. If Ewell left the Shenandoah before Jackson returned, Banks might advance to Staunton and menace the Valley Army's rear.[16]

Ewell's impatience for action rendered him extremely cross. Earlier he had posted Trimble's brigade at the crest of Swift Run Gap, keeping Col. William W. Kirkland's Twenty-first North Carolina Regiment at Fisher's Gap, a few miles farther north. When Trimble asked Ewell to send him some mounted men as couriers, Ewell's patience snapped. "Look here!" he said, addressing the division's cavalry chief, Col. Thomas Munford, "send *that old man* Trimble a mounted man or two. Nobody is going to hurt him way behind me, yet he wants some cavalry to keep him posted; and he has a fellow named Kirkland over on the mountain, on picket, who wants *horsemen.* I expect if a fellow in the woods would say boo, the whole crew would get away." Although Munford realized that Ewell "'*had a curious way*' of doing things, and a very free way of expressing himself," he had to admit, "This sounded very 'queer' to me."[17]

Jackson meanwhile united with Johnson and on 8 May defeated Frémont's advance at McDowell, thirty miles west of Staunton. Brig. Gen. Robert H. Milroy commanded the Federal force. Jackson's chief of cavalry, Col. Turner Ashby, brought Ewell news of the battle. Ashby saluted the general and politely asked how he was. "I've been in hell for three days! been in hell for three days, Gen. [*sic*] Ashby," raved Ewell. "What's the news from Jackson?"

"Gen. Jackson says the Lord has blessed our arms with another glorious victory," answered the swarthy horseman.

For the first time in many days, Ewell smiled. Now that Jackson had blunted Frémont's advance, he would be free to return to the Valley. Ewell's couriers, noting the improvement in their chief's disposition, "began to think there might be a warm place somewhere away down in his rugged, iceberg of a heart, and they decided that he wasn't such a savage old bear after all." They were wrong. Instead of returning to the Valley, Jackson pursued Milroy farther into the mountains, making Ewell more cross than before. Among his couriers "it was finally given up that 'old Ewell' didn't love but one thing on earth, and that one thing was 'Friday,' the ugliest, dirtiest and most aggravating and thievish little wretch of an Indian boy in the country."[18]

This is one of the few references to Friday, a Pueblo boy who accompanied Ewell throughout the war. The records list Friday as a slave, but his actual relationship with the general is unclear. Ewell had purchased Friday from an Apache chief in Arizona for $75. He did so in order to save the boy's life, for the Apache chief had threatened to kill him. After that, Friday followed the general wherever he went, providing the eccentric general with an appropriately odd escort.[19]

Ewell learned that Jackson had pursued Milroy into the mountains on 11 May. That same day a Union deserter reported that Maj. Gen. James Shields's division was preparing to evacuate New Market. The capture of Union soldiers carrying three days' cooked rations seemed to confirm the fact. Shields commanded one of Banks's two divisions; Brig. Gen. Alpheus Williams commanded the other. Shields had been covering Williams's withdrawal to Strasburg. With Williams now safely inside Strasburg's defenses, Shields appeared ready to move down the Valley as well. The news put Ewell in a blaze. He saw an opportunity to strike the divided Federal army and wanted to take advantage of it. He was "crazy to attack Shields," remembered Munford, "and though awaiting orders from General Jackson, wrote to ask permission to be allowed to attack him."

Shields withdrew down the Page Valley rather than the Shenandoah, suggesting that he might be headed to Fredericksburg. If so, it was imperative that Ewell intercept his march. But that was up to Jackson, and as Ewell confessed to Branch, he knew nothing of Jackson's plans. "He never tells them, if he has any in advance, untill the moment of execution. Beyond doubt we ought all to be concentrated for the point where we are to act."[20]

Richard Taylor was astonished to learn that Ewell knew nothing of Jackson's intentions. "What!" cried Taylor, "you, second in command, and don't know! If I were second in command I would know!"

"You would, would you?" smiled Ewell. "No, you wouldn't know any more than I do now. You don't yet know the man."[21]

Shields's division broke camp after dark on Monday, 12 May; crossed New Market Gap; and marched down the Page Valley toward Front Royal.[22] Ewell sent Munford to pursue him with the Sixth Virginia Cavalry and two guns. Munford was to build barricades, destroy bridges, feign attacks, and do whatever else it took to impede Shields's march.

Munford departed in the middle of the night. Before going, he stopped by Ewell's headquarters for final instructions. The general, dressed only in a white nightshirt, was in bed. Motioning Munford into the room, Ewell spread a map out on the bare wooden floor. In a moment both men were on their knees. "His bones *fairly rattled*," remembered the startled horseman, "his bald head and long beard made him look more like a witch than a Major-General." Ewell explained the strategic situation and pointed out the positions of Jackson, Shields, and McDowell.

Earlier Jackson had sent Ewell a dispatch proudly announcing that by the blessing of Providence he had captured most of Milroy's wagons. Ewell was not impressed. Waving the paper in front of Munford he cried, "This *great wagon hunter* is after a *Dutchman*, an old fool! General Lee at Richmond will have little use for wagons if all of *these people* close in around him; we are left out here in *the cold*. Why, I could *crush* Shields before night if I could move from here. This man Jackson is certainly a crazy fool, an idiot. What has Providence to do with Milroy's wagon train?" The general leaped to his feet and began pacing the floor. "Mark my words, if this old fool keeps this thing up, and Shields joins McDowell we will go up at Richmond! *I'll stay here*, but you go and do all you can to keep *these people* from *getting together*, and keep me posted—follow Shields as long as it is safe, and *send* me a *courier to let me know the hour you get off*." [23]

As soon as Munford departed, Ewell notified Lee, Jackson, and Branch that Shields had abandoned New Market Gap and was marching toward Front Royal with 7,000 men and thirty-six pieces of artillery. The Union general's probable destination, he reasoned, was Fredericksburg.[24]

Ewell crawled back into bed and tried to sleep. No sooner had he closed his eyes than he heard a saber striking the stairs outside. A moment later a courier knocked at his door looking for Munford. Ewell bid him come in and light a lamp.

"*Look under the bed*," he suggested sarcastically, "—do you see him there? Do you know how many steps you came up?"

"No, sir," the man answered.

"Well I do, by every lick you gave them with that *thing* you have hanging about your feet, which should be *hooked* up when you come *to my quarters*. Do you know how many *ears you have*? You will go out of here less *one*, and *maybe both*, if you ever wake me up this time anight looking for your *Colonel*." The courier made a hasty, and presumably quiet, exit. He begged Munford never to send him to Ewell's headquarters again.[25]

Ewell's aggravation peaked on Tuesday, 13 May. In the morning he got a dispatch from Jackson written from the outskirts of Franklin, nearly 100 miles away. Milroy had made a stand there, and Jackson was considering an attack. Ewell was to stay put until he returned to the Valley or until Banks left it. Jackson did not think the latter possibility very likely. Discounting Ewell's notion that Shields was headed to Fredericksburg, Jackson predicted that Banks would soon retreat farther down the Valley. But what if Banks split his army, keeping one division in the Valley and sending the other away? Jackson did not address that.[26]

Ewell found himself in a difficult position. On one hand, Jackson appeared ready to battle Frémont near Franklin. If defeated, he might call on Ewell to reinforce him. On the other hand, Shields appeared ready to leave the Valley. If that happened, Ewell had to be at Gordonsville to intercept him. He could not be at both places at once, and his orders prevented him from going to either. Jackson had expressly told him to remain in the Valley. If he disregarded those orders, Banks might capture Staunton and cut off Jackson's retreat. The only solution, as Ewell saw it, was for the Confederates to take the offensive in the Valley. If he, Jackson, and Branch united their forces, they could overpower Banks and drive toward Maryland, relieving pressure at other points. Ewell had made this suggestion to Jackson earlier but had gotten no response.[27]

Instead, Stonewall continued to chase Frémont's troops deeper into the mountains, leaving Ewell to watch Banks. That was not Johnston's intention when he had left Ewell to go to the Peninsula a month earlier. "Please remember me to Genl. Johnston & tell him that I wish he would give me an order to do somthing or anything," Ewell griped to Jeb Stuart, adding, "Genl. Jackson seems thoroughly convinced that the world is centered in this valley & would keep me here if Richmond & all the Confederacy were at stake."[28]

For Ewell, the weeks of waiting and uncertainty were becoming unbearable. He vented his frustration to his niece Lizzie: "I have spent two weeks of the most unhappy I ever remember. I was ordered here to support Genl. Jackson pressed by Banks. But the former immediately on my arrival started in a long chase after a body of the enemy, far above Staunton & I have been keeping one eye on Banks & one on Jackson & all the time jogged up from Richmond untill I am sick & worn down. Jackson wants me to watch Banks," he explained, "at Richmond they want me elsewhere & call me off when at the same time I am compelled to remain untill that enthusiastic fanatic comes to some conclusion. Now I ought to be en route for Gordonsville, at this place & going to Jackson at the same time.

That is there are reasons for all these movements and which one is taken makes it bad for the others. The fact is there seems no head here although there is room for one or two. I have a bad head ache," he complained, "what with the bother and folly of things. I never suffered as much from dyspepsia in my life, and as an Irishman would say I am kilt intirely." [29]

Fortunately the worst was past. On Wednesday, 14 May, Jackson notified Ewell that he was on his way back to the Valley. Lee was aware of Jackson's plans and wrote Ewell urging him to remain in the Valley until Jackson returned. Better news followed. On 13 May, after almost a month of silence, Johnston directed Ewell to unite with Jackson in attacking Banks—the very plan Ewell had advocated all along. Johnston admonished Ewell to use all his troops, including those at Gordonsville. If Banks started for Fredericksburg before the Confederates could strike, Jackson and Ewell were to immediately head east to Fredericksburg or Richmond as circumstances might dictate. It was an order that would cause Ewell much uneasiness before the week ended. [30]

For the first time since the campaign began, Ewell's superiors seemed to be of one mind. That was welcome news, but would it last? Ewell was skeptical and for the time being determined to pursue Banks only as far as Luray. "General Jackson's views may change at any moment," he told Branch, "and I won't go too far under present instructions, as I may be wanted elsewhere."

In accordance with Johnston's orders, Ewell ordered Branch to cross Fisher's Gap with his own and Mahone's brigades and join him at Luray, leaving at least two regiments to guard the Rappahannock line. Ewell instructed Branch to carry five days' rations and bring only troops that were armed and ready to fight. Above all, he was to travel light. "You cannot bring tents," he lectured. Tent flies without poles or trimmed-down tents were admissible, but "only as few as are indispensable. No mess-chests, trunks, &c. It is better to leave these things where you are than throw them away after starting. We can get along without anything but food and ammunition." [31]

Ewell practiced what he preached. His division used tent flies rather than tents and carried just two days' rations. As he informed Branch, "We transport here . . . only necessary cooking utensils in bags (not chests), axes, picks, spades, and tent-flies, and the lawful amount of officers' baggage and subsistence stores (80 to 100 pounds), horseshoes, &c. The road to glory cannot be followed with much baggage." [32]

Ewell had learned the value of speed while chasing Apaches across the desert Southwest. It was a lesson that he did not forget. "Time is everything in war," he would say, and rapid marches were more important than "numbers, preparation, armament—more even than all these and all else." Because his division traveled light, it could march up to seven miles in just two hours, a rate that outstripped even Jackson's vaunted "foot cavalry." In an army known for its marching, Ewell's division was second to none.[33]

By 15 May the Confederates were moving toward their assigned objectives like so many gears in a clock. Jackson was slowly making his way through the Allegheny Mountains toward the Valley; Ewell was creeping down the Page Valley toward Luray; Branch was marching toward Madison Court House en route for Fisher's Gap; Munford was east of the Blue Ridge breaking up the Manassas Gap Railroad; and Ashby had occupied New Market and secured possession of the vital gap east of town.[34] As Ewell was leaving Swift Run Gap, he received information that Shields was crossing the Blue Ridge at Chester Gap, east of Front Royal. If true, Johnston's 13 May orders compelled him to head east immediately. Ewell halted his march while awaiting confirmation of the report and told Branch to do likewise.

Jackson meanwhile continued to misread the enemy's intentions. On 16 May he wrote to Ewell informing him that Banks and Shields remained in the Valley and were preparing to reinforce Frémont. The Valley Army was on the point of leaving the mountains and would be moving down the Shenandoah Valley, via Harrisonburg, toward a junction with Ewell. "It may be that a kind Providence will enable us to unite to strike a successful blow," he added.[35] But would Jackson arrive in time? If Shields left the Valley before he appeared, Ewell would have no choice but to head east. In that event the scene of action would shift to Fredericksburg or perhaps to the Confederate capital itself. Ewell urged Jackson to hurry. "On your course may depend the fate of Richmond," he wrote.[36]

His warning came too late. On 17 May Munford confirmed that Shields had left the Valley and was headed toward Warrenton. Ewell had no choice but to follow him. He dispatched a courier with orders for Branch to return to Gordonsville and directed the troops of his own division to start for Fisher's Gap, the first leg on their journey east. He issued the orders reluctantly. Shields's departure had cut Banks's army in half, leaving it vulnerable to attack. Now was the time to strike. A dispatch from Jackson later in the day spelling out his plans for attacking Banks only fueled Ewell's disappointment. Must he leave the Valley? he reflected. Was there no way to salvage the offensive? He had to try. Ewell issued orders to his brigade commanders directing them to stop when they reached the crest of the Blue Ridge. In a separate order he directed Branch to go no farther than Gordonsville. Having thus halted the eastward movement of his troops, Ewell saddled his horse. He was going to see Jackson.[37]

CHAPTER 12

Attack at Daylight

As the sun rose over the Blue Ridge on Sunday morning, 18 May 1862, a solitary horseman rode through the sleeping camps of the Valley Army and drew rein at Stonewall Jackson's headquarters at Mt. Solon, ten miles southwest of Harrisonburg. Dick Ewell had traveled throughout the night to lay before Jackson the dilemma created by Gen. Joseph E. Johnston's order of 13 May.[1]

Ewell met with Jackson in a mill beside Mossy Creek. It was apparent to both generals that Johnston's order to follow Banks's troops across the Blue Ridge did not precisely fit the current situation. Johnston had written the order with the idea that Banks would leave the Valley with his entire force. Like Jackson, he did not take into account the possibility that Banks might split his force, leaving half his troops in the Valley and sending the other half away. To complicate matters further, Johnston's order contradicted recent instructions from Lee that Jackson and Ewell unite and smash Banks's remaining force at Strasburg. The previous night, when he had first learned from Ewell that Shields's division had left the Valley, Jackson had telegraphed Johnston. He informed his chief of Shields's departure and said that he intended to strike Banks at Strasburg if he could retain Ewell's division for that purpose. Without it, he wrote, he would have to remain on the defensive. Johnston had not yet replied.[2]

In the absence of new instructions Jackson and Ewell were on their own. The safest course would have been for one or both of them to leave the Valley and go east in accordance with Johnston's 13 May orders. No one could fault them for that. Yet they both realized that in doing so they would forfeit a brilliant opportunity to defeat Banks and relieve the pressure on Richmond. Jackson had no authority over Ewell in the matter; each man would have to decide for himself what course to take. Jackson made it clear that he still wished to attack Banks but that he could not do so without Ewell's help. Would Ewell support him?

Ewell had no love for Jackson at this point in their relationship (he still harbored strong suspicions that the wagon-hunting deacon was crazy); but he
wanted to fight, and Jackson was offering him that chance. He weighed the consequences of his action, then made his decision: he would remain in the Valley
and fight under Jackson, at least until he heard from Johnston. In return he asked
that Stonewall assume responsibility for his actions, a proposition to which his
comrade-in-arms readily agreed. He had Ewell put his dilemma in writing, then
responded in kind.

> Headquarters Valley District,
> Mount Solon, May 18, 1862
>
> Maj. Gen. R. S. Ewell,
>   Commanding Third Division, Army of the Peninsula:
> General: Your letter of this date, in which you state that you have received
> letters from Generals Lee, Johnston, and myself requiring somewhat differ-
> ent movements, and desiring my views respecting your position, has been
> received. In reply I would state that as you are in the Valley District you
> constitute part of my command. Should you receive orders different from
> those sent from these headquarters, please advise me of the same at as early
> a period as practicable. . . .
>
> T. J. Jackson
> Major-General.[3]

From that day forth, Ewell ceased to berate Jackson and loyally supported him. A
military comradeship was born.[4]

Having secured Ewell's pledge to remain in the Valley, Jackson set forth his
strategy for defeating Banks. His plan was to thunder down the Valley and overpower the Union general at Strasburg or, if he found Banks too strongly entrenched there, to flank his position by way of Front Royal. The Confederates
would concentrate their forces between New Market and Mount Jackson on
Wednesday evening, 21 May. Jackson would come by way of the Valley Turnpike, followed by Ewell and Branch, who would cross the Massanutten at New
Market Gap.[5]

Richard Taylor received an unusual assignment. Rather than cross New Market Gap with the rest of Ewell's division, Jackson ordered Taylor to march up the
Page Valley, swing around the southern tip of Massanutten Mountain, and fall in
behind the troops plodding down the Valley Turnpike. Why Jackson ordered him
to make this long and seemingly purposeless march Taylor could not say. Ewell,

Prayer in Stonewall Jackson's camp. Ewell appears directly below the flag.
(Casler, Four Years*)*

who was more acquainted with Jackson's strange ways, probably did not ask. The consultation over, Jackson invited Ewell to breakfast. Afterward they attended religious services together at the camp of the Twelfth Georgia Infantry. The day was still young when Ewell wearily lifted himself back onto his horse for the fifty-mile ride back to Columbia Bridge. He had not slept in more than twenty-four hours.[6]

Ewell reached Fisher's Gap late that night. The next day he led his division back into the Page Valley, resuming his former position at Columbia Bridge. At his order Branch likewise resumed his march to Madison Court House.[7] The order to Branch was the most recent in a series of contradictory commands the earnest brigadier had received from Ewell in the past three days. He had left Gordonsville with his own and Mahone's brigades on Friday, 16 May, to join Ewell at Luray. In the evening he received orders to halt. Ewell instructed him to resume his march at noon on the seventeenth, but after just three miles those orders, too, had been countermanded, and Branch was told to return to Gordonsville. With mounting frustration Branch turned his troops around and started to retrace his steps when Ewell directed him to suspend his march once more. There was a reason behind each change of orders, of course, but to Branch they seemed the result of fickle minds or worse. "I think this foolish ordering and counterordering results from rivalry and jealousy between Gens. Jackson & Ewell," he wrote his wife. "It is very unfortunate that our Govt is under the necessity of suddenly transforming so many Lieuts. and Captains of the old army into Brigadiers and Major Generals." [8]

By 20 May the offensive was beginning to take shape. Jackson had passed Harrisonburg and was marching toward New Market; Taylor had rounded the Massanutten and was puffing down the Valley Turnpike hard on Jackson's heels; and Branch was on the verge of crossing Fisher's Gap in order to rendezvous with Ewell at Luray. Just as all the pieces seemed to be falling into place, a final obstacle arose. A courier brought Ewell a dispatch from Johnston, notifying him that Branch had been directed to go to Hanover Court House.

That was not the worst of it. In the same dispatch Johnston stated that if Banks had entrenched at Strasburg (which he had), it would be too hazardous for the Confederates to attack him there. In that event Ewell was to head east, leaving Jackson in the Valley to observe the enemy. If circumstances permitted, Jackson and Ewell could strike Shields's division east of the Blue Ridge, but then Ewell was to continue eastward. "We want troops here," he wrote in conclusion, "none, therefore, must keep away, unless employing a greatly superior force of the enemy. In your march communicate with Brigadier-General Anderson, near Fredericksburg; he may require your assistance. My general idea is to gather here all the troops who do not keep away from McClellan's greatly superior forces." Johnston had written this dispatch three days earlier, on 17 May, one day *before* Jackson had sent his dispatch from Mt. Solon. [9]

Again Ewell mounted his horse and went to see Jackson in an effort to salvage the Valley offensive. He found the general at Tenth Legion, about ten miles above New Market. [10] Jackson happened to be standing outside his headquarters when Ewell rode up.

"General Ewell, I'm glad to see you. Get off!" cried "Old Jack" with unaccustomed bonhomie.

"You will not be so glad, when I tell you what brought me," replied Ewell.

"What—are the Yankees after you?"

"Worse than that. I am ordered to join General Johnston." Jackson's face became grave as Ewell produced the order requiring him to leave the Valley. The two men retired to a nearby grove of trees and privately discussed the matter. [11] Johnston's order was clear cut, they agreed, but it was also outdated. His obvious concern was to prevent the Federals from increasing the odds against him at Richmond. Would that goal not be better achieved by Jackson and Ewell defeating Banks? Such a move, followed by a strong demonstration toward the Potomac, would bring Shields's division back to the Valley and might very well paralyze McDowell's whole corps.

This made sense and Johnston would probably approve of it, but there was no time to ask him. It customarily took three days to receive a reply from Johnston, who insisted on transmitting messages via courier rather than by telegraph. Jackson needed an answer that night. The only way to get it was to appeal directly to Lee. Lee did not have any direct authority over Johnston, but as the president's military adviser he possessed a great deal of influence. Until he received Lee's reply, Jackson ordered Ewell to suspend execution of Johnston's order.[12]

A dispatch from Johnston that night confirmed Jackson's and Ewell's decision. Sometime after sending his 17 May order, Johnston had received Ewell's message informing him that Shields had left the Valley and asking for instructions. In reply Johnston had sent a courier to the Valley, advising Ewell and Jackson to use their discretion. If they could successfully attack Banks, they should do so; if not, Ewell should immediately come east. Ewell received Johnston's dispatch on the night of 20 May and immediately forwarded it to Jackson. At last the two generals had the approval they sought.[13]

Ewell returned to the Page Valley to prepare his troops to cross New Market Gap. On the morning of 21 May he summoned Capt. Frank Myers to his tent and handed him a bundle of dispatches with instructions to deliver them to Jackson. Myers had no idea where Jackson was and was afraid to ask. Fortunately he ran into Maj. James Barbour of Ewell's staff, who described the route to him. Ewell must have overheard the conversation because he stepped from his tent before Barbour had finished and said in a quick, spiteful tone, "[Captain] Myers, go to New Market and take the turnpike road to Harrisonburg; be quick now, I want to see you again to-day." Myers found Jackson at Tenth Legion. The general read Ewell's dispatches and sent a reply back with Myers. The captain found Ewell on Massanutten Mountain, his division moving toward New Market Gap. He handed Ewell Jackson's dispatch. Ewell read it, then ordered his division to return to the Page Valley.[14]

Jackson had changed his mind. Rather than attack Banks directly at Strasburg, he had decided to seize Front Royal, thereby turning Banks's position. This strategy offered several advantages: first, it would provide Jackson with a more concealed route of march; second, it would place the Confederates between Banks and Fredericksburg; and third, it would eliminate the need to attack Banks in his strong works at Strasburg. After the war Campbell Brown claimed that Ewell prevailed on Jackson to take this course; Jackson likely came to the decision on his own. He was not one to invite comments from a subordinate, and Ewell was not one to offer unwanted advice. Brown recognized his chief's diffidence as a defect common to the entire Ewell clan. "He sees very plainly the good that might be done by a little more common-sense in the control of our movements, but having formed an idea that his advice will be ungraciously received & perhaps his interference rebuked, he refuses to interpose in any way." [15]

Jackson had considered an advance down the Page Valley as early as 17 May, as is shown by his dispatch of that date directing Ewell to collect boats for a possible river crossing at Front Royal, yet it appears that he did not make a final decision on the matter until 20 May. His determination to attack Front Royal rather than Strasburg was probably influenced by two factors: information from Ewell that only a small Union force held Front Royal, and Johnston's recent injunction not to hazard an attack on Strasburg if Jackson found Banks strongly entrenched there. These considerations, rather than any opinions Ewell may have voiced, probably shaped his strategy. [16]

On Wednesday, 21 May, Jackson's infantry and artillery crossed the Massanutten and joined Ewell's division near Luray, giving the Confederates a combined effective force of approximately 17,000 men and 50 guns. [17] The advance down the Page Valley began the following day. After conferring with Jackson, Ewell took his place at the head of the column. In the absence of Col. Thomas Munford, who was away on official business, Ewell's acting cavalry chief, Lt. Col. Thomas T. Flournoy, led the march. [18]

When the day ended, the Confederates were just ten miles from Front Royal. Jackson had the army strip down to fighting trim. Soldiers were to clean their rifles and cook three days' rations, ambulances and ammunition wagons were to follow their regiments, and excess baggage was to be left in camp. In an effort to discourage skulking during the fight, Jackson ordered two men from each company to be detailed to medical duty. No one else was to leave the ranks for any reason. To make sure that they did not, Jackson ordered company commanders to call roll immediately after the battle and to submit to him the names of all absentees. Having taken these precautions, he turned in to bed. [19]

Friday, 23 May, dawned fair, giving promise of a beautiful day. Ewell reflected the sunny skies with an equally sunny disposition. After enduring three stressful weeks at Conrad's Store and overcoming numerous man-made obstacles, he was finally going to have an opportunity to fight. His division marched at dawn. Taylor's brigade took the lead, followed by Elzey and Trimble. Jackson's division kept pace close behind. [20]

Turner Ashby overtook the column before noon with several companies of cavalry. Jackson ordered the swarthy horseman to capture Buckton Station on the

Manassas Gap Railroad, thereby severing Banks's communications between Front Royal and Strasburg. The Second and Sixth Virginia Cavalry of Ewell's division augmented Ashby's force. The Confederate cavalrymen attacked Buckton Station in the afternoon and, after a sharp skirmish, succeeded in cutting the telegraph wires and destroying a section of the tracks. This action prevented the Union troops at Front Royal from retreating toward Strasburg or from receiving reinforcements from that quarter.[21]

Jackson meanwhile continued toward Front Royal. Realizing that the Federals had pickets on the Luray Road, he shunted his troops onto the Gooney Manor Road, a less-frequented thoroughfare that approached Front Royal farther to the east. Before reaching the town, Jackson ordered Col. Bradley Johnson's First Maryland Infantry to the front. In the coming battle it would have the honor of leading the Confederate attack.[22]

Front Royal lay just ahead. Beyond it the North and South Forks of the Shenandoah merged. The Manassas Gap Railroad crossed the South Fork just above the confluence and followed the North Fork west to Strasburg. From Front Royal a road headed north, crossed both forks of the Shenandoah, then proceeded to Winchester via Cedarville and Nineveh. Jackson's goal was to annihilate the Union detachment at Front Royal and to capture intact the bridges over the North and South Forks.[23]

A few miles south of the town Jackson encountered his first opposition: a Union picket dozing in the spring sun. The man jumped to his feet, fired a single shot, and took to his heels. Confederate cavalry galloped ahead, scooping up the soldier and the other members of his party. As the prisoners passed to the rear, Johnson asked one of them their regiment. "I belongs to de fust Maryland," the man answered. Johnson sat bolt upright in his saddle and, pointing to his troops, shouted for all to hear, "There's the First Maryland!"

The Valley Army was now just outside town. Ahead stood a hospital. Union troops inside the building, seeing the Confederates approach, fired out the windows, wounding six men. Ewell was riding at the head of the column with Johnson. "Colonel, can you take that building?" the general asked. "Yes, sir, in five minutes," Johnson replied. With a shout his troops lunged forward and in half the time promised had the hospital in their possession.[24]

Johnson's Marylanders charged into the town, flushed the Federals from the buildings, and pursued them toward the rivers.[25] Five companies of Maj. Roberdeau Wheat's First Special Battalion, better known as the Louisiana Tigers, supported them on the left. The Union commander, Col. John R. Kenly, rallied his troops on a hill overlooking the South Fork bridges. For two hours Kenly kept his

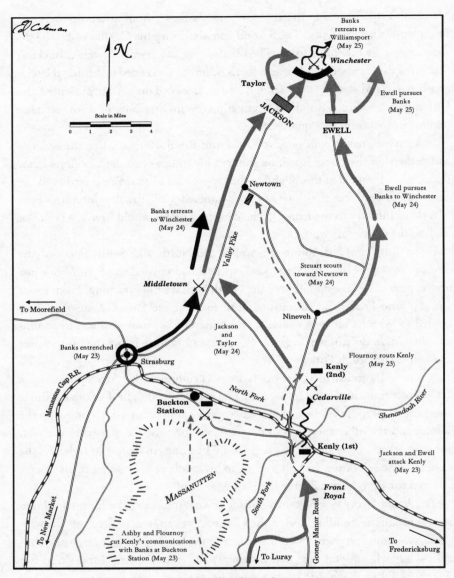

Front Royal and Winchester

assailants at bay, but in time Confederate numbers began to tell. When Kenly learned that Ashby's cavalry had attacked the Union garrison at Buckton Station and would soon be in his rear, he ordered a retreat. At 5:00 P.M. he withdrew his regiment across both branches of the river, igniting the North Fork Bridge behind him. Two guns of Capt. Joseph M. Knap's Pennsylvania battery covered the retreat.[26]

Ewell watched the battle from a point near the front. With him were Capt. Frank Myers and a small knot of couriers. Knap's artillerists spotted the horsemen from the bluffs across the river and opened fire on them.

"What do you mean, sir, by making a target of me with these men!" Ewell demanded of Myers.

"Why, General," replied the startled officer, "you told me to stay near you, and I'm trying to do it."

"Clear out, sir, clear out," Ewell bellowed, "I didn't tell you to get all your men killed and me too!"

Myers did not have to be told twice. Deeming himself discharged of his responsibility, he and his men left Ewell and spent the rest of the day searching the abandoned Federal camps for pistols, sabers, canteens, and other useful equipment.[27]

Jackson and Ewell meanwhile pushed forward in an effort to save the North Fork bridge. By the time they reached it, it was in flames. Col. Henry B. Kelly gallantly led several companies of the Eighth Louisiana Regiment through the river under fire and drove away Union skirmishers posted on the other side, enabling the Confederates to extinguish the fire. In minutes Southern horsemen were clattering across the charred span in pursuit. Flournoy led the way with four companies of the Sixth Virginia Cavalry. He overtook Kenly's force at Cedarville, two miles north of the river. In one of the truly splendid cavalry actions of the war, Flournoy charged Kenly's line and broke it. Kenly re-formed his troops in an orchard to the right of the road, and Flournoy charged again. This time the horsemen shattered the Federal line beyond repair.[28]

Flournoy's success was all the more remarkable because Kenly outnumbered him more than five to one. Ewell, Jackson, and Brig. Gen. George "Maryland" Steuart caught up with Flournoy in time to witness the thrilling spectacle. As a former dragoon, Ewell appreciated the courage and discipline required for such a charge. He later spoke of it "as one of the most gallant affairs he had ever witnessed." Frank Myers, to whom he made the comment, remarked that "no higher praise could be given than to say" that one "fought under the eye of General

Richard S. Ewell, and won his warmest admiration, for, like Jackson, he never bestowed it unmerited, and he meant everything he said." Ewell encountered Flournoy the following day and after expressing regret at the cavalryman's twenty-six-man loss, added feelingly, "But you made a glorious charge." He thereafter referred to Flournoy's regiment as the "Bloody Sixth."[29]

Confederate cavalry spent the rest of the evening rounding up the survivors of Kenly's command. They captured hundreds of prisoners and both of Knap's cannon. Two privates in the Sixth Cavalry brought in one of the pieces. Commandeering a couple of plow horses from a farm, they hauled the piece away under the eyes of Federal pickets and brought it back to Front Royal—"a piece of cool daring hard to match," Ewell wrote with approval.[30]

Jackson and Ewell remained at the front for several hours supervising the pursuit of Kenly's men before returning to Front Royal.[31] Their first engagement together had been an unqualified success. In three hours of fighting they had overpowered and destroyed a sizable Federal outpost, capturing 700 men, 2 cannon, 800 stands of small arms, plus $100,000 worth of supplies. More important, by seizing Front Royal they had turned Banks's position at Winchester, making his strong defenses there untenable.[32]

Although Ewell's division alone participated in the 23 May fighting, he took no credit for the victory. "The attack and decided results at Front Royal," he claimed, "were the fruits of Major-General Jackson's personal superintendence and planning."[33] Yet if Ewell had not masterminded the victory, he had certainly contributed to it. He had advocated an attack on Front Royal and had gathered the military intelligence necessary to carry it out. He had led his division down the Page Valley and supervised its attack on Kenly. After Kenly withdrew across the rivers, Ewell actively joined in the pursuit and supervised the roundup of Union prisoners. For a year he had waited impatiently to get into battle—a year filled with aggravations, frustrations, and disappointments. But in the end the result was victory, and that was worth the wait.

Jackson's victory at Front Royal on 23 May 1862 placed Banks's army at Strasburg in imminent peril. The Confederates stood between him and Irvin McDowell at Fredericksburg; worse, it put Jackson on his flank, endangering his lines of communication with Winchester and Harpers Ferry. The Union commander had four options: he could remain at Strasburg and wait for Jackson to attack him; he could cross Little North Mountain and march west to the Potomac River; he could race down the Valley, hoping to beat Jackson to Winchester; or he could try to outguess his adversary, and when Jackson moved toward Winchester, slip

Ewell of the Valley (Hamlin, Letters)

behind him at Front Royal and move toward Fredericksburg or Washington. Jackson correctly anticipated that Banks would retreat down the Valley, and on 24 May he had his army march toward Winchester. To make sure that Banks did not pass through Front Royal once he left the town, he sent scouts toward Strasburg to provide early notice of any Union movement in that direction.[34]

Ewell spent the evening of 23 May camped north of Front Royal, on a hill beyond Crooked Run. Jackson visited him there, probably to work out the details of a major army reorganization that would take effect the next day.[35] After his victory over Milroy, Jackson had amalgamated Ed Johnson's Army of the Northwest into his command. Johnson's army consisted of two brigades led by Cols. William C. Scott and Zephanier T. Conner and three batteries under Capts. Charles I. Raine, John A. M. Lusk, and William H. Rice. Since Johnson had been wounded at McDowell, Jackson added Johnson's troops to Ewell's command. That increased Ewell's division to four brigades and one regiment of infantry, five batteries of artillery, and two regiments of cavalry—more than 10,000 men.

On the surface it seems odd that Jackson would add Johnson's troops to Ewell's division rather than his own, since Ewell already had far more men than he did. But there was no better alternative. Jackson could not effectively exercise command of both the army and an enlarged division, and he did not yet trust any of his brigade commanders to command a small division, much less a large one. Eventually such a man would emerge, but in the meantime Jackson would continue to exercise direct control over his old division, leaving Ewell to watch over Johnson's men.[36]

Arnold Elzey was the single greatest benefactor of the reorganization. Elzey had started the year with three regiments: the First Maryland, the Tenth Virginia, and the Thirteenth Virginia. In recent weeks, however, the First Maryland and the Tenth Virginia had been stripped from him and transferred to other brigades, leaving him in command of just the Thirteenth Virginia. This was an awkward situation, particularly since Elzey was Ewell's senior brigadier. Ewell therefore added Conner's three regiments to Elzey's brigade. The Forty-fourth, Fifty-second, and Fifty-eighth Virginia Regiments of Scott's brigade were also placed under Elzey's command for the time being, though on paper, at least, they retained a separate identity.[37]

George Steuart also gained in the reorganization. When the First Maryland Infantry was formed in the spring of 1861, Elzey became its colonel and Steuart its lieutenant colonel. After Manassas, Elzey was promoted to brigadier general and Steuart became colonel of the regiment. Steuart was not above a little politicking. In the spring of 1862 he traveled to Richmond and, after conferring with officials

George H. Steuart (Library of Congress)

there, returned to the army as a brigadier general. He brought with him orders from the secretary of war to form the Maryland Line, a mixed force of infantry, cavalry, and artillery made up exclusively of Maryland men. At the secretary's instructions, Jackson transferred the First Maryland Infantry and the Baltimore Light Artillery to Steuart's command. They were to be the nucleus of the Maryland Line, with other units to join it as they came into being.[38] Steuart led the Maryland Line for just one week. On 24 May Jackson placed him in temporary command of Ewell's cavalry. It was a move that was long overdue. Col. Thomas Munford had ably led Ewell's horsemen to that point, but the job by right belonged to a brigadier.[39]

In selecting Steuart for the position, Jackson may have had an eye toward improving the efficiency of his own cavalry more than Ewell's. Col. Turner Ashby, who commanded Jackson's cavalry, was a brave and skillful horseman, to be sure, but in Jackson's view he commanded too many men (twenty-six companies as opposed to the normal ten) and exercised too little discipline.[40] By placing Steuart in charge of Ewell's cavalry, Jackson perhaps hoped that some of Steuart's Old Army discipline might rub off on Ashby. If it did not, Jackson had the option of combining the two cavalry forces, in which case Steuart, as ranking officer, would be in charge.

Ewell's work began when his conference with Jackson ended. During the evening of 23 May he closeted himself in his tent to draft orders for the next day. His staff was absent from headquarters seeing to the disposition of captured prisoners and stores, so Ewell dictated his orders to a cavalry officer. He kept the man busy late into the night.[41] As the evening wore on, Ewell's staff returned, and the general joined them around the campfire. Campbell Brown and his black servant, Willis, were among those present. As Brown closed his eyes to sleep, Willis whispered to him that a man was stealing corn from his saddlebags.

"Who is it, Willis?" asked Brown.

"It's *General Trimble*, Sir," the servant replied.

Brown nudged Ewell, who was seated nearby, and said, "General, look at that old rascal stealing my corn." Ewell watched Trimble for a moment then motioned Willis to come over.

"Willis, go and give my compliments to that gentleman," he said, adroitly avoiding mentioning Trimble's name, "and ask him to put back the corn he took from that horse." Willis dutifully delivered the message. When Trimble indignantly asked who had sent it, the servant pointed to Ewell. Trimble bowed politely, said "Very well," and put back three of the nine ears he had taken. Then, with Ewell and the others still looking on, he proceeded to rifle the corn from a courier's saddlebag instead. As Brown observed, Trimble's horse probably got the largest feed of any animal in camp that night.[42]

The Confederates broke camp by 6:00 A.M. on Saturday, 24 May, and started marching toward Winchester. Ashby's cavalry led the way, followed by Ewell's and Jackson's divisions. Rain developed during the morning, and occasionally it hailed. At 8:00 A.M., after covering a distance of six miles, the column halted for breakfast, its head at Nineveh and its tail beyond Cedarville, five miles to the rear.[43] Jackson rode with Ewell's division. Though rapid, the march lacked the urgency that normally accompanied Jackson's movements. The reason was simple: Jackson did not yet know Banks's location or intentions. In an effort to find answers to those tantalizing questions, he sent scouts toward Strasburg and ordered Steuart to ride to Newtown, nine miles south of Winchester on the Valley Pike. For the moment, he could do no more.[44]

Jackson breakfasted with Ewell at the Mason house, north of Nineveh. Before they left, Steuart sent word that wagons and disabled men were moving down the Valley Pike in the direction of Winchester. Jackson and Ewell barely had time to digest this bit of news before Trimble drew their attention to a column of smoke rising from the direction of Strasburg.[45] Convinced that Banks was fleeing to Winchester, Jackson at noon struck out for the Valley Pike with Ashby's cavalry and Taylor's infantry. He retraced his steps to Cedarville, turned west, and marched by way of a country road to Middletown, six miles north of Strasburg. His own division followed.

If Banks was retreating toward Winchester, as Jackson believed, the Confederates would be in position at Middletown to cut the Union army in two. But if Jackson was mistaken and Banks was retreating across Little North Mountain, he needed his army well in hand to pursue. When Trimble therefore proposed sending Ewell's division (minus Taylor) to Newtown to block the Union army's retreat to Winchester, Jackson ignored his advice. Instead he ordered Ewell to stay at Nineveh, where he could move to Middletown, Winchester, or Front Royal as circumstances required.[46]

When Jackson reached Middletown about 3:30 P.M., he found the Federal wagon train stretched out before him on the Valley Pike. Without waiting for his own division to come up, he pitched into the Union column with Ashby's and Taylor's men. The result was bloody mayhem. "In a few moments the turnpike, which had just before teemed with life, presented a most appalling spectacle of carnage and destruction," he reported with grim satisfaction. "The road was literally obstructed with the mingled and confused mass of struggling and dying horses and riders. The Federal column was pierced."[47]

For an hour and a half Ewell listened to the sound of Jackson's attack, anxiously awaiting orders. At 5:00 P.M. a message arrived from Jackson, notifying him that the Federals were in full retreat toward Winchester. Ewell was to proceed immediately to that point on the Front Royal Road, while Jackson pursued Banks directly on the Valley Pike. "Please report hourly your advance and circumstances," Jackson admonished.[48]

Minutes later a second dispatch from Jackson arrested Ewell's march. A "considerable body of the enemy" had advanced on the Confederates from the direction of Strasburg. Jackson was now uncertain whether the bulk of Banks's army was to his left, toward Strasburg, or to his right, toward Winchester. In either case he might need more troops. Consequently he ordered Ewell to send Elzey's brigade, including Scott's three regiments, to Middletown. Ewell was to stay put with the rest of his force—now reduced to just Trimble's brigade, Courtney's battery, and the Maryland Line—until he received further orders.[49]

By the time Ewell got this message, around 5:30 P.M., the sound of gunfire indicated that the fight was shifting northward. At Newtown, George Steuart had encountered Banks's column and boldly attacked it, capturing some 250 prisoners plus numerous wagons and ambulances before being brushed aside by a brigade of Union infantry. Ewell sent the First Maryland Infantry and Brockenbrough's battery to his support.[50] Steuart's skirmish, taken with other evidence, convinced Ewell that Banks's army was north of Jackson and headed toward Winchester. About 5:45 P.M. he wrote to Jackson suggesting that Trimble join Steuart in attacking the Union column at Newtown. By then Jackson had come to the same conclusion. Rather than have Ewell go to Newtown, though, he directed him to move on Winchester.[51]

Couriers dashed back and forth between the two generals, passing one another in transit. It took approximately an hour to transmit a message between the two generals via Cedarville, and it was almost sundown when Jackson received Ewell's proposal for an attack at Newtown. By then Jackson had chased Banks to Newtown with Capt. William T. Poague's Rockbridge Artillery. Stonewall's infantry had been unable to keep pace, leaving Poague's guns practically without support. Jackson needed fresh troops if he was to keep pace with Banks, and he sent word to Ewell at Nineveh to come to Newtown as proposed.[52]

By the time Ewell received Jackson's dispatch, however, he was no longer at Nineveh. After waiting in vain for marching orders, Ewell about 6:45 P.M. had taken matters into his own hands. "Without instructions my situation became embarrassing," he later explained, "but I decided after consultation with Genl. Trimble & Maj. [sic] Brown of my staff to move on to Winchester." In doing so he was taking a chance, for Jackson had explicitly told him to stay put. Fortunately his decision was quickly validated. Within minutes after Ewell put his troops into motion, a courier delivered Jackson's 5:45 order to march to Winchester. Later a second courier overtook Ewell with Jackson's order to move to Newtown. By then Ewell had gone too far to turn back. He ignored the order and continued to march to Winchester, taking care as always to notify Jackson of his actions. Stonewall approved his course, admonishing him to stay abreast of the Confederate troops on the turnpike. As Ewell's route was the shorter of the two, this required him to travel slowly.[53]

Ewell's force reached the outskirts of Winchester at 10 P.M. Union pickets greeted its arrival with an annoying fire, prompting Ewell to throw out Kirkland's Twenty-first North Carolina Infantry as skirmishers. Kirkland pressed the Federals back toward Winchester and established a skirmish line two miles from town. When Steuart came up later in the night, Ewell had him picket the Berryville and Millwood Turnpikes, which entered Winchester from the east. Skirmishing continued intermittently through the night.[54]

Capt. William C. Oates of the Fifteenth Alabama stated that Ewell considered an attack on the Federal position that night, but this seems unlikely.[55] Having arrived after dark, he had no knowledge of the terrain in front of him, much less the size or position of the enemy. Ewell sent scouts to reconnoiter the enemy position, but the information they brought him must have been sketchy at best. Perhaps his greatest handicap was his ignorance of Jackson's plans. Ewell later wrote that he had "received several messages from Genl. Jackson during the night, but as circumstances had in every case changed the condition of things before their arrival, I was forced to follow my own judgement as to Genl. Jackson's intentions." It was impossible to mistake the import of one message, however. An hour before dawn Ewell received from Jackson a detailed map of Winchester, showing roads, woods, streams, and other prominent features of the area. Beneath the map were the words "Attack at daylight."[56]

A heavy mist made it difficult to tell just when daylight began that Sunday morning. Ewell rode forward to the Twenty-first North Carolina's skirmish line at 5:00 A.M. personally to reconnoiter the enemy position, but the morning fog and the stone fences that crisscrossed the rural countryside obscured his view. Unable to see the enemy, he determined to feel their position with his infantry. At 5:40 A.M. he ordered Kirkland to find the bluecoats and develop their position. The Twenty-first Georgia Infantry followed in support.[57] With a popping of rifles the Tarheels scattered Union pickets on the Front Royal Road and seized a commanding hill at the junction of the Millwood Turnpike, one mile from town. Courtney's and Brockenbrough's batteries unlimbered in the wheatfield that crowned the hill and at 7:00 A.M. engaged Union batteries posted on a ridge west of town. The Fifteenth Alabama and the Sixteenth Mississippi Regiments of Trimble's brigade supported the Confederate guns.[58]

Ewell established his headquarters just behind the guns, where he had an excellent, if rather dangerous, vantage point from which to view the artillery exchange. He was particularly impressed by the conduct of eighteen-year-old Lt. Joseph W. Latimer, who ably commanded Courtney's battery throughout the campaign.

"This young officer was conspicuous for the coolness, judgment, and skill with which he managed his battery," the general noted, "fully supporting the high opinion I had formed of his merits." Brockenbrough, while not enjoying the warm encomiums thrown Latimer's way, nevertheless handled his battery "with energy and effect."[59]

Shortly after Latimer and Brockenbrough went into action southeast of town, Jackson's artillery opened fire from a point on the Valley Pike, a mile and a half to the west. The sound of Jackson's guns dispelled any lingering doubts Ewell may have entertained concerning his commander's intentions, and he proceeded to press his attack with vigor. He dispatched his aide Hugh Nelson to the Valley Pike to communicate with Jackson and ordered the Twenty-first North Carolina to advance up the Front Royal Road. In his report of the battle Jackson praised the North Carolinians' attack as having been "executed with skill and spirit," but in hindsight there appears to have been a good deal more spirit than skill involved. Kirkland was so eager to press his attack that he failed to post skirmishers in advance of his line. As his regiment dashed up the road, it ran headlong into two Union regiments concealed behind a stone wall. The bluecoats poured a point-blank volley into the North Carolinians, felling seventy-five men and repulsing the rest. Kirkland was among the wounded, taking a bullet in the thigh.[60]

As the Tarheels tumbled back toward the hill, other regiments moved to their assistance. The Twenty-first Georgia slipped around to the right and took Kirkland's assailants in flank, prying them from their strong position behind the wall. At the same time the First Maryland Infantry filled the interval separating Trimble's brigade from Jackson's forces on the Valley Turnpike. Ewell admonished Bradley Johnson to establish contact with Jackson as soon as possible. Leaving the Front Royal Road to his right, Johnson led his men through the fields south of town until he reached an orchard that, to his astonishment, he discovered to be behind enemy lines. Although unsure in his own mind whether his men "were prisoners in a big army, or had achieved a grand tactical movement and exploit," he prepared to make the best of the situation. He sent his adjutant back to Ewell with the suggestion that Trimble resume his attack down the road. When Johnson heard Trimble's guns, he "would charge down behind the Union lines and sweep them away from the front attack."[61]

At 7:30 A.M., before Ewell received Johnson's message, a thick fog blanketed the Front Royal Road. The fighting halted for thirty minutes as both sides waited for the haze to clear. It occurred to Ewell that the Federals might take advantage of the fog to escape Winchester by way of the Berryville Road. To prevent this, he sent the Twenty-first Georgia, the Fifteenth Alabama, and the Sixteenth Mississippi Regiments east of town to a position from which they could turn Banks's flank and threaten his line of retreat. Trimble had suggested such a movement earlier that morning. At that time Jackson had not yet come up and the tactical situation was still unclear, and Ewell had refused to do so for fear that the Federals might overwhelm his small force. With Jackson engaging the Federals' attention on the left, Ewell now felt at liberty to order the movement.[62]

When the fog lifted, Ewell found the Union army still in place and disposed to fight. Opposing gunners resumed their duel, engaging one another in one of the most picturesque artillery actions of the war. The exchange of shells against the backdrop of the quiet town, wrote Isaac Trimble, was "as inspiring a battlescene as was ever witnessed." The fire "was incessant and well directed on both sides, displaying a scene of surpassing interest and grandeur on that sunny but far from peaceful Sabbath."[63]

Col. Stapleton Crutchfield, the army's chief of artillery, supervised the firing of Ewell's batteries. Crutchfield appeared at Ewell's headquarters just after the fog cleared, carrying a dispatch from Jackson written several hours earlier. Campbell Brown remembered that it directed Ewell "to go back by Newtown (7 miles off) & crossing over to the Valley Pike at that point, to come up it, as the Enemy were being reinforced at Strasburg!" The order made absolutely no sense, and Ewell ignored it. Instead he planned to press his attack on the Front Royal Road, having secured a better knowledge of the strength and position of the enemy forces that confronted him there. Before he could do so, the clatter of small arms fire called his attention to the Valley Turnpike, where Jackson's attack was reaching its climax. At 8:30 A.M., after an artillery duel of more than an hour, Jackson hurled Taylor's brigade against the Federal right flank and put it to flight. Ewell purportedly cheered himself hoarse as he watched the charge from his hillside perch.[64]

As the Federal line gave way under the force of Taylor's attack, Ewell ordered his line forward. The Twenty-first North Carolina, having recovered from its earlier repulse, pushed straight down the Front Royal Road. The First Maryland, on its left, entered the suburbs south of town.[65] Trimble led Ewell's remaining three regiments east of Winchester in an effort to get behind Banks and cut off his retreat. He struck the Martinsburg Turnpike near Stephenson's Depot, three miles north of town. The Fifteenth Alabama led Trimble's pursuit, at times going at a flat run. Although it covered nine miles in just two hours, the regiment reached the road too late to catch Banks's fleet-footed troops. Trimble claimed that he could have bagged a large portion of the Federal army had Ewell permitted him to move but a half-hour earlier. As it was, most of Banks's troops escaped.[66]

Even if Ewell had allowed Trimble to move earlier, it is unlikely he could have caught the Union army. Banks had a more direct route out of the city, and his troops, unlike the Confederates, were comparatively fresh. If Jackson was to bag the Federals, Confederate cavalry would have to do the job. No one knew that better than Jackson himself, yet when he looked for Ashby and his men, they could not be found. "Oh that my cavalry were in place!" he cried. "Never was there such a chance for cavalry!"[67]

Unable to locate Ashby, Jackson sent his adjutant Sandie Pendleton to order Steuart forward. After a lengthy search Pendleton found the cavalryman placidly grazing his horses in a clover field along the Berryville Road, two and one-half miles from town. Incredibly, Steuart refused to accept Jackson's orders, insisting that they must come through Ewell. Pendleton was stunned. With rising impatience, he explained that Jackson's order was "peremptory and immediate" and must be obeyed. When Steuart still refused to budge, Pendleton had no choice but to ride to Ewell. He found the general two miles down the road directing the pursuit of his infantry. Ewell expressed surprise and irritation at Steuart's "ill-timed scrupulosity" and sent Pendleton back to him with an order to move at once. Steuart did so, pursuing the enemy vigorously to Martinsburg, fifteen miles distant, capturing numerous prisoners and stores along the way.[68]

Why had Ewell not ordered Steuart forward sooner? As a former dragoon, he knew the value of vigorous and immediate pursuit. It seems strange that he would have allowed Steuart's men to remain idle when obviously there was work for them to do. In his memoirs Campbell Brown suggested that Ewell did not consider Steuart's cavalry as being under his command following the 24 May reorganization and therefore did not feel authorized to direct its movements.[69] If so, it was a costly misunderstanding. Steuart's delay in getting started gave Banks an hour's head start, which he profitably used to re-form his demoralized command and put distance between it and its pursuers.

Ewell accompanied Trimble on his roundabout march to Stephenson's Depot, then joined Steuart in pursuit of the Federal army. Confederate troops who lined the road cheered the general as he flew past at full speed, "his head bare and bald, with dark, piercing eye and hooked nose." His appearance, thought one artillerist, was at once "ugly, but oh! so splendid." Presently Jackson, too, galloped past, his ride marked by even greater ovations than those given to Ewell.[70]

Despite Jackson's, Ewell's, and Steuart's efforts, the Union army got away. In a feat of marching rarely matched in the war, Banks's troops covered forty-three miles in less than twelve hours and crossed safely to the north bank of the Potomac River. The Union general put the best face on his flight from Strasburg, reporting to superiors in Washington that his army "had not suffered an attack and rout, but had accomplished a premeditated march of near 60 miles in the face of the enemy, defeating his plans and giving him battle wherever he was found." Jackson's troops, exhausted from several days and nights of hard marching, could not keep pace with the Union army, and Jackson did not try. Once the Federals made good their escape, he put his army into camp near Stephenson's Depot.[71]

The battle had been short. From the time of Ewell's initial advance to the time Taylor swept the bluecoats from the field, just over three hours had elapsed—the same time it had taken to subdue Kenly at Front Royal. In material results, however, the victory at Winchester far eclipsed the earlier battle. At Winchester and Martinsburg Jackson captured 9,354 small arms, two cannon, half a million rounds of ammunition, plus vast quantities of quartermaster and medical supplies. In addition, the Valley Army seized more than 100 head of cattle, 34,000 pounds of bacon, and quantities of flour, salt, sugar, coffee, hardtack, and cheese.[72]

The campaign's strategic results were more impressive still. Jackson's goal had been to hold in the Valley Union troops that might otherwise have been sent east to help capture Richmond. In this he succeeded far beyond his own or anyone else's expectations. When the Lincoln administration learned of Banks's defeat, it postponed McDowell's advance on Richmond and sent Shields and one other division to the Valley. In one brilliant stroke Jackson had denied McClellan the use of 40,000 men and, in doing so, probably saved Richmond from capture. But he did so at grave peril to himself. Determined to crush the Confederates once and for all, Lincoln ordered Frémont and McDowell to converge on the Valley Army from the rear, cutting off their retreat up the Valley. The two Union generals could bring 30,000 and 15,000 troops, respectively, into action against Jackson. Counting Banks's 7,000 men at Williamsport and Brig. Gen. Rufus Saxton's 7,000 men then gathering at Harpers Ferry, the North by late May had nearly 60,000 troops in position to converge on the Valley Army. By contrast, casualties and attrition had reduced the Confederates to just one-fourth of that total. Jackson had stirred up a hornet's nest, and he would now have to deal with the consequences.[73]

CHAPTER 13

A Question of Legs

Unaware that he had already accomplished his goal of diverting Union troops from Richmond, Stonewall Jackson pressed north to threaten Harpers Ferry. Thomas Flournoy's Sixth Virginia Cavalry led the advance, capturing Charlestown, eight miles west of Harpers Ferry, on 28 May. Ewell sent twenty men to inventory the property that Flournoy had garnered. Before wagons could carry the goods away, a Federal force of some 1,500 men sallied forth from Harpers Ferry, recaptured Charlestown, and burned the supplies. Brig. Gen. Charles Winder arrived later in the day and impetuously pitched into the enemy, driving them back to Harpers Ferry.[1]

Brig. Gen. Rufus Saxton commanded the Federal garrison at Harpers Ferry. Saxton had just 7,000 men to defend the river town, and many of those were of an inferior stamp. Jackson hoped to capture Harpers Ferry, if only briefly. On Thursday, 29 May, he moved up to Halltown, three miles from Harpers Ferry, and sent the Second Virginia Infantry across the Shenandoah River to occupy Loudoun Heights.[2]

Before marching to Halltown, Ewell sent Capt. Frank Myers to reconnoiter the town. Myers discovered a sizable force of Union infantry and cavalry on the road to Halltown. When it withdrew toward Harpers Ferry, he and a companion, Ed Oxley, followed close behind. The two men entered Halltown via a millrace, then climbed to the second floor of the miller's house. From there they had a full view of the enemy force in town, which they estimated at not more than one regiment of infantry and 600 cavalry. Having secured this information, they took dinner with the miller and his family, then made their way back to Confederate lines.

Myers and Oxley found Ewell and Jackson together on a hill one-half mile from Halltown and reported their findings. The generals praised the scouts' skill and daring, though Ewell, for one, thought they should have brought the information back without stopping to eat. "But it was too late then," reflected Myers with a smile, "for they had the dinner, and mentally resolved to do the same thing, when the opportunity presented itself, whether the general liked it or not, but they also resolved, in the same manner, not to tell him next time."[3]

For two days the Valley Army skirmished with Saxton's defenders near Hall-town. Union sharpshooters peppered the Confederate artillerists with an annoying fire. A pocket of five sharpshooters was particularly irksome. Ewell had recently distributed twenty new Merrill carbines to the members of his mounted escort for use in scouting details, and the Comanches were eager to put them to use. When they saw the five Federals sniping at the Confederate gunners, Myers and two others asked Ewell for permission to drive them away. The general refused on the grounds that it was too hazardous; but the men persisted, and he finally gave in. "Yes; go on, go on," he sputtered, "but you'll come back faster than you go." And so they did. The scouts picked off three of the sharpshooters, but in doing so they attracted the fire of two infantry companies. Within minutes Myers came racing back to Confederate lines, bullets whistling about his ears. Ewell ordered the artillery to fire into the woods to cover the scout's retreat. Had he not done so, Myers thought, it was unlikely that he would have escaped.[4]

Friday, 30 May, brought an abrupt halt to the Valley Army's offensive. In the morning Jackson learned that Banks had been reinforced and was preparing to advance from Williamsport. More alarming were reports that Shields and Frémont were converging on Strasburg, forty-three miles to Jackson's rear, with a view of cutting off his retreat up the Valley. Shields had 10,000 men; Frémont, 15,000. If either one reached Strasburg before Jackson, he would be trapped in the lower Valley.

The Federals had the inside track. On 30 May Shields occupied Rectortown, thirty-two miles east of Strasburg, and Frémont was at Fabius, forty miles west of the town. The Valley Army, at Halltown, was likewise about forty miles from Strasburg, with the Second Virginia Infantry on Loudoun Heights being several miles beyond that. In the coming race Jackson had the advantage of a good road and level terrain, but he was burdened with 2,300 prisoners, droves of cattle and sheep, and a ten-mile-long wagon train. The Confederate army's fate depended on Jackson reaching Strasburg before Shields or Frémont. In Lincoln's words, the campaign had become "a question of legs."[5]

With the Federals fast closing in around it, the Valley Army started for Strasburg. Jackson ordered Winder's brigade to remain at Halltown until the Second Virginia Infantry returned from Loudoun Heights, then to catch up with the rest of the army. Steuart's cavalry would bring up the rear.[6]

Jackson rode ahead to Winchester, leaving Ewell in charge of the retreat. Mistakes marred the movement. At some point Ewell's ordnance train took a wrong turn and headed toward Smithfield. The general sent a party of horsemen after it only to discover later that the wagons had not left the column at all. The First Maryland Infantry was not notified of the retreat and was nearly left behind. Fortunately Winder encountered the regiment the next day as he was leaving the town and gathered it in. Despite these mishaps and a drenching rain that muddied the roads, the Valley Army made good time. It reached Stephenson's Depot, north of Winchester, shortly after dark, having covered twenty-five miles in ten hours.[7]

After putting the army into camp, Ewell rode into Winchester to confer with Jackson. As he entered the town, a courier brought him a dispatch from Col. Zephanier T. Conner of the Twelfth Georgia Infantry. Jackson had left Conner's regiment at Front Royal a week earlier when the Valley Army marched to Winchester. Conner's dispatch announced that Shields had captured Front Royal and was marching on Winchester. "Unless you can throw re-enforcements here by morning," he wrote in alarm, "all will be gone." Subsequent investigation showed that the colonel had lost his head and abandoned Front Royal without a fight. Ewell considered Conner to be "a brave man, but thrown off his balance by responsibility" and was not inclined to be harsh toward him. Jackson was not so charitable. When he learned of Conner's precipitous retreat, he immediately placed him under arrest. The unfortunate colonel was later permitted to resign.[8]

By sunset, 30 May, the odds had tipped significantly in favor of the Union. Shields had occupied Front Royal, twelve short miles from Strasburg, while Frémont, fighting bad weather and execrable roads, had advanced to Wardensville, twenty miles west of that critical point. By contrast the Valley Army was then at Stephenson's Depot, eighteen miles from Strasburg, and Winder's brigade was still back at Halltown, forty miles away. From the Confederate standpoint, things looked extremely bleak.

Fortunately for the South the Federals squandered their advantage. After boasting to his superiors that he could defeat Jackson without any help, Shields got cold feet and decided to await reinforcements before marching on Strasburg. His division remained idle at Front Royal on 31 May, its only movement being a reconnaissance toward Winchester. Frémont displayed somewhat greater initiative. Prodded by President Lincoln, he pushed through the Allegheny Mountains toward Strasburg, fighting rain and heavy roads all the way. Progress was slow. When the day ended, he was still five miles short of his goal.[9]

Jackson, by contrast, made good time traveling on the Valley Pike. His army marched through Winchester at dawn and at sunset made camp just north of Strasburg. Winder did his best to catch up. Cognizant of their peril, his men marched thirty-five miles on 31 May before collapsing at Newtown, just south of Winchester. "Never was I so tired in my life, as I lied down that night in a hard rain to rest my weary limbs & blistered feet. Under no other circumstances could any of us possibly have held out," remembered Capt. John E. Howard of the First Maryland.[10]

The race for Strasburg came down to the wire. Shields, Frémont, and Jackson were each within a dozen miles of Strasburg when 31 May ended. The one who got the earliest start the next day would probably win the contest. Fortunately for Jackson his opponents were late risers. Frémont did not start for Strasburg until after dawn, and Shields never got started in that direction at all. Incredibly, the blustering Irishman took the road to Winchester instead of the one to Strasburg. By the time his superior, Maj. Gen. Irvin McDowell, discovered his mistake, it was too late to correct it.[11]

The Valley Army, on the other hand, was on the road by dawn. Jackson not only determined to beat his opponents to Strasburg, but he intended to hold it until all of his prisoners, wagons, and troops had passed through. That included Winder's brigade, which was still half a day's march away. Jackson devoted his considerable energies to supervising the movement of the wagon train, leaving Ashby to watch Shields, and Ewell to deal with Frémont.[12]

Ewell had his troops marching by dawn and perhaps as early as 3:00 A.M. In accordance with Jackson's instructions, he followed the wagon train to Strasburg, then turned right onto the Wardensville Road. Five miles out of Strasburg he encountered Frémont's army near Cedar Creek. Skirmishers of Brig. Gen. William B. Taliaferro's brigade sparred with the Federals, while Southern batteries engaged Union artillery from a nearby ridge. Ewell kept the rest of his force out of range of the enemy guns and awaited developments.[13]

There were none. Intimidated by Taliaferro's skirmishers, Frémont refused to budge. The Pathfinder's timid behavior perplexed Ewell, and he went out to the skirmish line to get a firsthand look at the situation. Before doing so, he summoned Dick Taylor. Union artillery fire had played havoc with Taylor's nerves that morning, and by the time he reached Ewell, he was shaking visibly. Taylor apologized for his condition, likening himself to a frightened deer.

"Nonsense!" replied Ewell with a laugh, "'tis Tom's strong coffee. Better give it up. Remain here in charge while I go out to the skirmishers. I can't make out what these people are about, for my skirmish line has stopped them. They won't advance, but stay out there in the wood, making a great fuss with their guns; and I do not wish to commit myself to much advance while Jackson is absent."

Ewell pushed Taliaferro's skirmishers forward to test Frémont's strength. To his surprise the Federals gave ground. "I am completely puzzled," Ewell admitted to Taylor upon his return. "I have just driven everything back to the main body, which is large. Dense wood everywhere. Jackson told me not to commit myself too far. At this rate my attentions are not likely to become serious enough to commit any one. I wish Jackson was here himself." Taylor suggested that he take his brigade around to the right to attack Frémont and thereby discover his intentions. Ewell consented. "Do so," he said, "that may stir them up, and I am sick of this fiddling about." But Taylor could not provoke a battle either; the Union general simply refused to fight. "Sheep would have made as much resistance as we met," Taylor wrote contemptuously. "Men decamped without firing, or threw down their arms and surrendered, and it was so easy that I began to think of traps. At length we got under fire from our own skirmishers, and suffered some casualties, the only ones received in the movement."

Frémont's lack of aggression tempted the Virginian to attack.

"Had Ewell been in command," thought Taylor, "he would have 'pitched in' long before; but he was controlled by instructions not to be drawn too far from the pike." Throughout the morning Ewell held his ground, all the while grumbling about his citrus-sucking commander and his precious "lemon wagons." Stonewall visited him that morning but returned to Strasburg when he saw that his disgruntled subordinate had matters well in hand.[14]

Ewell broke off action with Frémont at noon on learning that Winder had reached Strasburg. He withdrew in the afternoon, rested briefly at Fisher's Hill, then fell in behind Jackson's division, which was making its way up the Valley Pike. For the third day in a row, bad weather hampered the march. A violent storm lashed the army with rain and pelted it with hail. Visibility was almost nil. The darkness was so intense, insisted Taylor, that "owls could not have found their way across the fields." After marching for several hours, the Valley Army finally halted between Woodstock and Maurertown. Steuart covered the retreat, supported by Taylor's brigade and Brockenbrough's battery. That night advance units of Frémont's army surprised Steuart's men at Round Hill, three miles south of Strasburg, and put them to flight. After a week and a half of fighting and marching, battle fatigue was beginning to show.[15]

Sunday, 1 June, marked the end of one race and the beginning of another. Having failed to beat Jackson to Strasburg, McDowell sent Shields up the Page

Valley. He hoped that Shields could slip behind the Confederates at New Market Gap and cut off their retreat, but muddy roads hampered Shields's progress. By the time he reached Luray, Ashby's cavalry had burned the South Fork bridges there. Without pontoons Shields had no way to cross the swollen river. He decided to continue up the Page Valley and cross the South Fork at the next available bridge, near Conrad's Store. So long as the Massanutten and the South Fork divided Shields and Frémont, Jackson could defeat them in detail. The Federals had set a trap for Jackson only to fall into it themselves.

All that was clear in hindsight. At the time, though, Jackson still considered himself very much in danger. As his weary troops retreated up the Valley Turnpike, Brig. Gen. George D. Bayard's Union cavalry nipped at their heels. A West Point graduate and Old Army cavalry officer, Bayard knew his business. He pressed the Confederates day in and day out, giving them no opportunity to rest.[16]

Monday, 2 June, was the most trying day of the retreat. Soldiers, separated from their supply wagons, wandered off the road in search of food. Thousands fell out of the ranks, hobbled by blisters or simply overcome by fatigue. Confederate cavalry helped some of these men to catch up to their commands; others fell behind and were scooped up by Frémont. Continuing rain turned the roads to mud. Wagons snarled and teamsters cursed. Just when matters were at their worst, Bayard pitched into the Confederate rear. For the third time in a week, Steuart was routed. That night, at Ewell's urging, Jackson reshuffled the army, concentrating all of the cavalry under Ashby and placing Steuart in charge of the infantry brigade that to that time had been led by Col. William C. Scott.[17]

The Confederate army made camp that night between Mount Jackson and New Market. Ewell pitched his tent between the two towns, at the point where Valley Pike crossed the North Fork of the Shenandoah River. After dark the river rose. Rushing water surrounded the camp, then flooded it. The general leaped onto his horse "Rifle," pulled Friday up after him, and plunged into the water, leaving his staff to escape as best they could.[18]

The floodwaters that discomfited Ewell materially aided Jackson by blocking Frémont's progress. With Shields bogged down in the Page Valley and Frémont temporarily checked by the swollen North Fork, Jackson felt he could afford to give his men a much-needed rest. He failed to take Frémont's newfound energy into account, however. Union engineers threw down a pontoon bridge after dark, and the next morning Northern troops began pouring across the river. Jackson ordered Ewell to hold back the Federals until the Confederate wagons could get away, but his services were not needed. For the sixth day in a row the heavens poured rain on the countryside. The North Fork rose twelve feet in four hours, forcing Frémont to cut loose his pontoon bridge. Ewell's division returned to its camp just south of New Market. It would get a chance to rest after all.[19]

During the day news of the battle of Seven Pines reached the Valley Army. Gen. Joe Johnston had been seriously wounded in the fighting, prompting discussion among the soldiers as to who would take his place. Some thought it would be Beauregard; others, Jackson. When someone asked Ewell if he knew, the general replied, "No sir; I don't know who will be General Johnston's successor, but I shan't be scared at all if the choice falls on Lee." His comment circulated throughout the army, but it did not generate much enthusiasm. Many of Ewell's men remembered Lee's lack of success at Cheat Mountain in 1861, and they did not want him in charge of the army.[20]

On Thursday morning, 6 June, the Valley Army moved by easy stages to Harrisonburg, then turned southeast toward Port Republic. There, at the headwaters of the South Fork, Jackson would be in position to strike at Shields, Frémont, or both. For the first time in a week the skies cleared. The roads, however, remained muddy. Despite Jackson's precaution of detailing pioneers to each brigade train, Confederate wagons became mired in the seemingly bottomless sloughs. "The wagon train, the wagon train, the great impediment to glory," Ewell was heard to mutter, "it is hanging behind us like a drag."[21]

While swearing teamsters struggled to free the vehicles, Ashby tried to hold back the Federals, who had crossed the North Fork and were coming on strong. A mile outside Harrisonburg, he ambushed a detachment of the First New Jersey Cavalry and captured thirty men, including the regiment's colonel, Sir Percy Wyndham.[22] Even then the Federals did not let up. When he heard that Wyndham had been trounced, Bayard rushed forward the First Pennsylvania Cavalry and four companies of the First Pennsylvania Rifles, better known as the Bucktails because of the fluffs of deer fur that they wore pinned to their caps. Ashby welcomed the challenge. "They have had their way long enough," he remarked to Munford. "I am tired [of] *being crowded* and will make them stop it after today."

Ashby ordered Munford to post two guns in the Port Republic Road at the edge of a wood. A squadron of Munford's men screened the guns in front; the rest of the cavalry remained concealed in woods to the rear. Ashby meanwhile planned to lead a force of infantry through the woods around the Union left. When the Federals rushed forward to capture the guns, he would rip into their flank. Munford would then cap the victory with a cavalry charge down the road. With luck the Confederates might destroy the entire Union detachment. That would teach the upstart bluecoats a lesson![23]

For his plan to work, Ashby needed infantry support. For that he called on Ewell, who was then at Cross Keys. Ewell immediately started back toward Harrisonburg with Taylor. Before they had gone far, they met Ashby coming up the road. In a few words Ashby told them of his plan. Ewell approved and ordered George Steuart to support the cavalryman with his brigade. Ewell, Steuart, and Ashby then rode with the brigade toward the scene of action. "They seemed to be talking very earnestly," noted an infantryman in the Fifty-eighth Virginia, "esp Col. Ashby, who appeared somewhat excited. I thought he was the very picture of a knight, with his long black beard and piercing eyes." Ewell cut a less dashing figure. His presence indicated only "that some serious work was on hand."[24]

Ashby led Steuart's brigade into a dense wood on the right side of the road. At a small clearing Steuart halted the brigade and formed it into a line of battle. The First Maryland, which had been at the end of the column, advanced to the front, taking a position to the left of the Fifty-eighth Virginia. The Forty-fourth and Fifty-second Virginia remained in reserve. Ashby meanwhile briefed Ewell on the tactical situation. "Ashby's dark face [was] afire with enthusiasm," remembered Bradley Johnson. "His hair and head were as black as a crow and his beard grew close up his black eyes, until he looked like a Bedouin chief. He was pointing out the positions and topography, swinging his arm right and left." The cavalryman was in his element, Johnson thought, and clearly enjoying himself.[25]

The sun was setting by the time the Confederates were ready to attack. The First Maryland, on the left, counted 275 rifles; the Fifty-eighth Virginia, on the right, fewer than 200. To even the numbers, Ewell detailed two companies of the First Maryland to act as skirmishers for the Fifty-eighth Virginia. Capt. George W. Booth commanded the skirmish line. As soon as his troops were ready, Booth disappeared into the darkening woods to engage the enemy. He expected to find a thin line of dismounted Union infantry. Instead the Marylander encountered "a well-formed infantry line, sheltered behind a stout fence on the edge of the timber." Ashby ordered the Fifty-eighth Virginia to support Booth's skirmishers, but after tasting the Bucktails' lead, it too fell back. The Virginians kept up a desultory fire but refused to renew the charge.[26]

Ashby was growing impatient. Rather than wait for reinforcements, he led the Fifty-eighth Virginia in a reckless charge directly against the wall. A blast from the Bucktails' rifles stunned the attackers. Ashby's horse crumpled to the ground, struck by two bullets. Its rider sprang from the saddle and continued forward on foot. A moment later he fell dead with a bullet through the heart.[27]

Ewell led the First Maryland and the Forty-fourth Virginia Regiments through the woods to the left of the wall in an effort to pry the Bucktails from their position. The Fifty-second Virginia remained in the rear, having failed to receive the orders to advance. Ewell and Johnson rode at the right end of the First Maryland's line. When the Fifty-eighth Virginia opened its attack, Ewell halted Johnson's men and rode over to the right. He arrived in time to see Ashby fall, though he did not recognize him at the time.[28]

The Fifty-eighth Virginia's attack was in trouble. Putting his spurs to his horse, Ewell returned to the First Maryland and ordered it to advance. "Charge with the First Maryland, Colonel Johnson, and end this miserable affair!" he cried. Johnson led his troops by the right flank up a hill to a point nearly opposite the enemy. He then faced his regiment to the left and charged. A Union volley ripped the regiment at a distance of thirty yards. Before the Bucktails could reload, the Marylanders gained the fence. The bluecoats gave way, retreating in disorder across a 400-yard-wide field. As they fled, Johnson wrote, his men "pelted them with great comfort and satisfaction," killing dozens. The bluecoats fell "as thick as leaves," recalled one trigger-happy Confederate.[29]

The fight lasted less than half an hour. Frémont admitted losing more than forty men in the contest (Ewell thought the number much greater), while the Confederates reported seventy casualties. Despite Ashby's death, Ewell seemed satisfied with the battle's outcome. He was certainly pleased with the First Maryland's performance. "Your men are elegant," he later told Johnson, "only know what to do & they do it."[30]

With darkness settling over the battlefield and Union reinforcements close by, the Confederates hurriedly gathered their casualties and moved off. Ewell personally sought the gallant officer he had seen fall while leading the Fifty-eighth Virginia into battle. Only when he reached the body did he discover that it was Ashby. He had the cavalryman's corpse laid across a horse and carried to Port Republic. Soldiers wept as it passed.[31]

Ewell remained on the battlefield until the last wounded man had been cared for. Because ambulances could not go into the woods, wounded soldiers were placed on horses behind Ashby's cavalrymen. Ewell personally assisted some of the men to mount and brought off one wounded soldier on his own horse. Those men too badly injured to move were left to the mercy of the enemy. Ewell gave some of the soldiers money out of his own pocket to assist them in their captivity. Capt. William W. Goldsborough of the First Maryland never forgot his kindness. He later told a staff officer "that he hadn't cared more for Ewell before than for any other comd'r, tho' he knew him to be a good officer, but that after that evening his Reg't. would have gone anywhere in the world for him, & he loved him."[32]

It was well after dark by the time Ewell left the battlefield. Worried by his prolonged absence, Campbell Brown and Tom Turner rode out the Port Republic Road to find him. They met him a short distance out. He seemed "a little tired & grave," they thought, but otherwise "in fair spirits." As they rode slowly back to camp, he spoke to them about the battle.[33]

Ashby's death affected Ewell greatly. As a former dragoon he fully appreciated Ashby's daring and envied his freedom of movement. Such a man at the head of a small mobile force would be equal to the best division in the army, he told Munford, and he would rather have it. "A man *could do something* without being cramped as I am," he insisted. He told Munford that he was considering asking the War Department to give him such a command or of raising one himself. "You fellows have some fun," he grumbled, "but I am no better than a darned tin soldier. Here I am placed without orders. Yes, no better than a tin soldier."

From Ashby the talk turned to the current military situation. Ewell admitted to Munford that he was uneasy both about affairs in Richmond and in the Shenandoah. Before they left the Valley, they would have their hands full, Ewell predicted. Three days would show that he was right.[34]

CHAPTER 14

The Men Are Willing to Follow Him

Cross Keys, Virginia, was a rural community of rolling fields and scattered farms in 1862, and it remains so even today. Families of English and German heritage shared the land—families with names like Evers, Pence, Nichter, and Rodehoffer. The neighborhood borrowed its name from a local tavern that operated in the area. A country church and its adjoining cemetery stood just down the road. Area residents called the sanctuary Union Church, an incongruous name considering the times, and one that would soon take on new significance.[1]

Dick Ewell's division bivouacked near the church after the battle of Harrisonburg. On 7 June the First Maryland Regiment "sadly and silently" buried their slain comrades under the damp sod of the church graveyard.[2] At Jackson's order, Ewell sent his baggage and trains to the rear at dawn but kept his troops in camp. Jackson had intentionally divided his army. He led his own division to Port Republic to confront Shields, who was moving up the Page Valley, and kept Ewell at Cross Keys, four miles back, to check Frémont. In the words of his chief of staff, Maj. Robert L. Dabney, Jackson "purposed thus to hold both his adversaries at bay, until the propitious moment arrived to strike one of them a deadly blow."[3]

While his troops rested, Ewell conducted a reconnaissance of the Cross Keys area. What he saw prompted him to move the brigades of Steuart and Trimble from Union Church to a ridge already occupied by Elzey and Taylor, one mile south. Frémont sent Brig. Gen. Robert H. Milroy's brigade forward to locate the Confederates late in the day, but the Indiana lawyer did not test Ewell's position. For the first time in two weeks, Confederate guns were silent.[4]

The peace lasted just one day. On 8 June Union cavalry dashed into Port Republic, nearly seizing the Confederate wagon train parked nearby. Jackson happened to be staying in town and narrowly escaped capture by galloping across the North River bridge. Once across, he brought artillery to bear on the town and sent Col. Samuel V. Fulkerson's Thirty-seventh Virginia Regiment charging across the bridge. The Federal horsemen vanished as quickly as they had come.[5]

Before the excitement at Port Republic had subsided, Ewell found himself under attack. At 10:00 A.M. Frémont pressed back the Second Virginia Cavalry and advanced toward Cross Keys. Col. James Cantey's Fifteenth Alabama Infantry stood on picket at Union Church. Ewell told Cantey to hold back Frémont as long as possible in order to give him time to put the rest of his division into line. As an added precaution he sent Captain Myers and another member of the Comanches to the far right to report on any Union movements in that direction.[6]

At the center of the ridge occupied by Ewell's division was a field several hundred yards wide. Ewell posted four batteries in the field, supported by Taylor's brigade, and deployed Steuart and Trimble in the woods to the left and right of the field. Elzey remained in reserve. The Port Republic Road crossed the ridge near Ewell's center. The Keezletown Road crossed the ridge two miles farther west, beyond Steuart's left flank.[7]

At 9:00 A.M. Jackson ordered Ewell to send his best brigade to Port Republic, which was then under attack. Ewell sent Taylor's brigade, his largest. That left him with fewer than 5,000 rifles—half as many as Frémont—and necessitated moving Elzey up to support the guns. Not long after Taylor left for Port Republic, Trimble decided to advance his brigade to a better position one-half mile in front of the main line. Leaving the Twenty-first North Carolina to support Courtney's battery, he occupied the new position at 10:30 A.M. Thus, as the battle began, Steuart held the woods on the Confederate left, Elzey supported the artillery in the center, and Trimble occupied a ridge somewhat in advance of the main line on the right.[8]

Before Ewell had completed these dispositions, Frémont attacked. Col. Gustave P. Cluseret engaged the Fifteenth Alabama at Union Church at 10:00 A.M. Cantey's men stubbornly held their ground, fighting from behind trees near the church and even from behind tombstones in its cemetery. Eventually they were flanked on the right, however, and had to withdraw. Union skirmishers chased the Alabamians back toward Ewell's main line until warned off by Courtney's guns.[9]

Frémont posted his artillery on a ridge opposite Ewell's guns. A spirited cannonade ensued and continued throughout the afternoon. Courtney's battery, located adjacent to the Port Republic Road, remained under fire for five hours. When it exhausted its supply of shot and shell, it resorted to firing canister,

though it was well over half a mile from its target. Like the other Confederate batteries in action that day, it maintained its fire despite taking casualties from Union
artillery on the opposite ridge. At the end of the battle Ewell could truthfully say,
"I was satisfied with them all."[10]

The general made his headquarters immediately in the rear of his batteries,
where he enjoyed an excellent view of the battlefield. There, on the open hillcrest,
Union artillery fire was its most destructive. Within thirty minutes after the cannonade started, Frémont had eight and one-half of his ten batteries in action—
roughly fifty guns in all. The Federal artillery covered a wider front than the Confederates' and thereby achieved a converging fire. A Louisiana officer remembered
it as the most accurate and destructive bombardment he encountered during the
war. "It was a very hot place indeed," agreed a Maryland lieutenant, "a perfect
hail of shell, cannon-balls, and bullets."[11]

Arnold Elzey shared Ewell's exposed position on the ridge. Ewell consulted
with the former artillery captain frequently during the battle, availing himself of
Elzey's "known military skill and judgment." A projectile wounded Elzey's horse
early in the day, and a rifle ball later killed it. The same ball that killed the horse
struck its rider in the leg, forcing him to retire from the field. George Steuart, too,
was a casualty of the artillery exchange. He had to be carried from the field when
a canister ball struck him in the upper chest and penetrated to his back. Elzey returned to active duty within a week only to suffer a more grievous wound at
Gaines's Mill. Steuart remained out of action for a full year, rejoining the army
in time to lead a brigade at Gettysburg.[12]

Campbell Brown also fell victim to Northern gunnery. As he was riding toward
the front, a shell fragment struck him in the shoulder, inflicting a large and
painful bruise. Brown's horse got away from him and trotted over to Ewell's party,
which was about 300 yards off. Brown caught up with it there. When the general
asked him how the horse got away, Brown replied that he had lost her when he
was hit by the shell. Ewell was surprised to learn that his young cousin had been
injured and immediately ordered him to the rear.[13]

Despite the carnage taking place around him, Ewell maintained his sense of
humor. Randolph McKim, a former sergeant of infantry, had been promoted to
lieutenant and assigned to Steuart's staff the day before the battle. Although he
was able to borrow a horse, the neophyte staffer still wore his sergeant's uniform
and had no spurs. During the battle he delivered a dispatch to Ewell, but when
he turned to go, his horse refused to budge. McKim repeatedly dug his heels into
the frightened animal's sides, but without result. "Ha! Ha!" Ewell laughed, "a
courier without any spurs!" McKim's face reddened with anger and embarrass-

ment. But he had no choice but to swallow his pride and adopt the general's suggestion "to go back another way."[14]

Cross Keys was the first significant engagement that Ewell fought on his own. Jackson appeared on Ewell's front toward the end of the bombardment, but he returned to Port Republic when he found that his subordinate had matters well in hand. Before leaving, he offered some advice: "Let the Federals get very close before your infantry fires; they won't stand long." A Maryland soldier who saw the two plainly dressed generals riding together wrote that they looked like "two sad-looking videttes" or "like two countrymen higgling over the price of a horse, or a cow or a bunch of hogs."[15]

Jackson had not been gone many minutes when Frémont launched his attack. The Union general directed his principal assault against the Confederate right, which he erroneously judged to be Ewell's "strategic flank." Brig. Gen. Julius Stahel's brigade of Blenker's division led the attack. Stahel's men were advancing steadily through the woods and fields east of the Port Republic Road when they ran headlong into Isaac Trimble's brigade, concealed at the edge of an open wood. When Stahel's line got within fifty yards of the Confederate line, Trimble gave the order to fire. A volley ripped through the blue ranks, the Confederate brigadier reported, "dropping the deluded victims of Northern fanaticism and misrule by scores." When Stahel failed to renew the attack, Trimble took the offensive, driving his opponent back onto another Union brigade that was marching to his support. Ewell heard Trimble's fight raging on the right and sent Col. James A. Walker with two regiments of Elzey's brigade to reinforce him. With Walker's help, Trimble chased the Federals more than a mile to the Keezletown Road.[16]

Less than a mile away, Brig. Gen. Robert H. Milroy's brigade was testing Ewell's left, perhaps supported by Col. Gustave P. Cluseret's small brigade. Milroy flushed out Confederate skirmishers concealed in the wooded creek bottom and drove straight toward George Steuart's brigade on the ridge beyond. Col. Bradley Johnson's First Maryland Infantry anchored Steuart's flank.[17] Earlier, as the regiment was taking its place in line, Ewell had noticed that some of the soldiers were wearing bucktails in their caps—prizes won at Harrisonburg two days earlier. The notion appealed to him, and he told Johnson, "Colonel, you must carry a bucktail in your colors as your trophy, for you won it on Friday." Johnson promptly secured a bucktail and affixed it to the regimental colors. Thus adorned, the Marylanders went into the battle of Cross Keys, where they helped repulse Milroy's attack.[18]

Ewell's left flank remained his chief source of concern. During the afternoon, Brig. Gen. Robert Schenck's brigade maneuvered into position on Milroy's right,

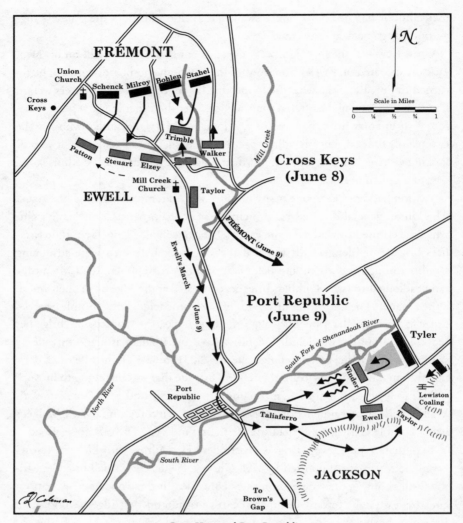

Cross Keys and Port Republic

threatening to outflank Steuart and capture the Baltimore Light Artillery, which anchored his left flank. Ewell recognized (as Frémont did not) that the left flank was his Achilles' heel. When Steuart was injured, he personally took control of that part of the line.[19]

Ewell spent the afternoon buttressing his tender flank against attack. As Schenck lumbered into position opposite his left, Ewell dispatched the two regiments of Elzey's brigade not with Walker to that sector. Later, when Dick Taylor's brigade returned from Port Republic, Ewell detached the Seventh and Eighth Louisiana Regiments to the left to support the Baltimore Light Artillery. Taylor led the rest of his brigade to the right to reinforce Trimble. By the time Taylor reached the front, however, Trimble's attack had played itself out. The doughty Marylander proposed renewing the offensive, but Taylor refused to cooperate. At 4:00 P.M., he led his troops back to camp, having neither seen nor engaged the enemy.[20]

Col. John M. Patton followed Taylor from Port Republic. When Patton reached the field, Ewell sent his small Virginia brigade to the left to bolster further that part of his line. The Forty-eighth Virginia reached the front first. Some of its companies carried rifled muskets; others still used the shorter-range smooth-bores. Ewell ordered the companies with rifles to the front as skirmishers to delay Schenck's advance, while he hastily put the rest of Patton's brigade into line to the right of the First Maryland. When Patton ventured to ask Ewell a question about the position of one of his regiments, the general made an impatient reply. Ewell dismissed the incident from his mind, but not so Patton, who wrote Ewell about it years later. "I forget it," replied the general, "and think it more than likely the chief cause was my habitual annoyance during a fight when my attention was called from important points on which it was necessary to act. Having to decide promptly on the most important steps it was impossible for me to discuss coolly unimportant occurrences."[21]

Even with Taylor and Patton, Ewell found himself outnumbered. He might have found himself overpowered had Frémont not ordered Schenck to withdraw in consequence of Blenker's repulse on the Federal left. The only real threat faced by Ewell during the day thus ended before it began.[22]

Three miles away at Port Republic, Jackson had worries of his own. During the afternoon Shields's infantry appeared at Lewiston, a house more than a mile downriver from Port Republic, placing Union troops squarely on the Confederates' front and rear. Jackson notified Ewell of this development, promising to keep Shields in check if Ewell would hold back Frémont. Ewell assured him that he would do his part. "The worst is over now," he replied in reference to Frémont's attacks, "I can manage him."[23] Ewell had reason to be confident. Despite Frémont's greater numbers, he had failed to dent the Confederate line. Ewell told Dick Taylor "that he felt all day as though he were again fighting the feeble, semi-civilized armies of Mexico."[24]

Having repulsed the enemy at all points, Ewell prepared to advance the left wing of his division and attack Frémont along the Keezletown Road. When Trimble heard the attack begin, he was to pitch into Frémont on the right. The erroneous report of a strong Union column two miles to his left, however, caused Ewell to delay the movement. By the time the troops on his left were in position to make the attack, night had fallen, forcing him to postpone the attack until dawn.[25]

Once the fighting ceased, Ewell rode to Port Republic to confer with Jackson. There he learned that Jackson intended to attack Shields in the morning. Jackson directed Ewell to issue rations to his division that night and have it at Port Republic by dawn. In order to keep Frémont "from advancing upon Port Republic or taking any part in the engagement" with Shields, he ordered Ewell to leave a strong rear guard at Cross Keys. He said nothing about an attack on Frémont.[26]

When Ewell returned to Cross Keys about midnight, he found Trimble waiting for him. The combative brigadier had come to urge him to attack Frémont's troops on the Keezletown Road. When Ewell pointed out the difficulties of a night attack, Trimble begged him to go with him to the picket line and "see how easy it was." Ewell refused. If Trimble wished to attack Frémont, he would have to go to Port Republic and see Jackson about it. Trimble did so, returning some two hours later with instructions from Jackson "to consult Ewell and be guided by him." By then it was 2:00 A.M. or later; sunrise was just over two hours away. Even had Ewell favored an assault, it was too late to make one. For a second time he denied Trimble permission to attack.

Dick Taylor was present and supported Ewell's decision, but Trimble refused to take no for an answer. Like a spoiled child, he continued to argue his point, even going so far as to make the absurd suggestion that his brigade attack Frémont's army alone! Ewell listened with unwonted patience, replying only, "You have done well enough for one day, and even a partial reverse would interfere with Jackson's plans for the next day." Trimble retorted bitterly that they would have Frémont's army pressing them tomorrow if he was not driven off that night, and that it would be better to fight one army at a time. With that the conversation ended.[27]

Despite Trimble's petulant behavior and his submission of a battle report that was critical of both Taylor and Ewell, Ewell graciously gave Trimble credit for the victory at Cross Keys. He listed his own casualties for the battle at 288 and estimated Union losses at "not less than 2,000," a figure almost three times higher than the 684 reported by Frémont. Ewell based his inflated estimate of Union casualties on exaggerated figures contained in Trimble's report. The Federal losses, he reported, "were chiefly of Blenker's division, notorious for months on account of their thefts and dastardly insults to women and children in that part of the State under Federal domination." Blenker's Dutchmen continued to plunder area homes even after their defeat. "They came up spoiling for a fight and a great many of them spoiled after the fight," Ewell commented dryly.[28]

Ewell's division started for Port Republic while it was still dark, leaving burning campfires behind to deceive the enemy. The general personally helped get the troops in motion. An officer in the Thirteenth Virginia Infantry remembered the general riding into camp about 3:00 A.M., just as the men were preparing to draw their rations. "Boys, I'm sorry for you," he told them, "but you must put your utensils back as we have to march at once." Earlier Ewell had assigned Col. John Patton the task of staying behind to delay Frémont. Patton argued that his brigade was too small for the task, and Trimble later convinced Jackson to leave his brigade behind as well. The detachment of Trimble's brigade had no other result, wrote Ewell, "beyond depriving the command of too few to fight Frémont & too many to take from the field of Port Republic." Trimble and Patton had orders to hold Frémont in check, but "if hard pressed, to retire across the North River and burn the bridge in their rear."[29]

Dawn was breaking as Ewell's division approached Port Republic. The village lies between the North and South Rivers, which join there to become the South Fork of the Shenandoah River. To cross the North River, the troops had to use a covered bridge at the northeast end of town. The South River was somewhat shallower. Normally it could be crossed at a ford just upstream from the river junction, but the recent rains had raised the level of the South River past easy fording. To cross the river, a pioneer detachment had placed several wagons end-to-end across the river and covered them with loose planks to create what one soldier termed a "Stonewall Jackson pontoon bridge."[30]

As Ewell's division neared Port Republic, cannon fire echoed from the plain below. The sound acted as a stimulant to the troops, who instinctively accelerated their pace. Passing Taliaferro's brigade, which Jackson had posted on the high ground north of the village, Ewell's men descended the bluff and crossed the North River into Port Republic. Turning left, they negotiated the wagon bridge across the South River. Taylor's brigade crossed without much trouble, but Ewell's remaining brigades did not fare so well. The planks that comprised the bridge flooring had been laid loosely across the wagon's running gear. As the soldiers crossed, the boards shifted and pitched the men into the rushing water. Congestion ensued as the soldiers queued to cross single-file over the few good planks that remained. Ewell paused at the bridge in an effort to untangle the snarl, then rode forward with Steuart's brigade, now commanded by its senior colonel, William C. Scott.[31]

The battle of Port Republic took place on the narrow plain bordering the

Shenandoah's South Fork. Shields's troops, led by Brig. Gen. Erastus B. Tyler, held an admirable position near Lewiston, the country home of Samuel H. Lewis. Tyler's line ran from the Shenandoah River, on the west, across the narrow plain to the wooded foothills of the Blue Ridge, on the east. Six guns posted at an old coal hearth, known as the Lewiston coaling, anchored the left end of Tyler's line and commanded the plain below.[32]

Jackson opened his attack on Tyler just after dawn. He sent Charles Winder's Stonewall Brigade directly against the Union line on the plain and directed Taylor's brigade to capture the battery at the coaling. To reach that point, Taylor had to fight his way through a maze of tangled undergrowth. As he hacked his way toward the front, the Union guns mauled Winder's brigade on the plain.

Ewell took all this in as he led Scott's brigade toward the fighting. The road he took ran along the base of the Blue Ridge Mountains. The plain bordering the South Fork was to his left. When Ewell was within one-half mile of the coaling, he halted Scott's men behind a fence in a dense woods to the right of the road to shelter them from the enemy's fire. By that time the brigade was down to just two regiments. Jackson had seized the Fifty-second Virginia after it crossed the South River and sent it to Winder on the plain. The First Maryland, which had been on half-rations Saturday and had had no food at all on Sunday, had stopped with Ewell's permission to get something to eat on the way to Port Republic and did not cross the South River until the battle was almost over.[33]

Scott's remaining regiments, the Forty-fourth and the Fifty-eighth Virginia, together numbered no more than 273 rifles.[34] Ewell faced them to the left so that they were perpendicular to Winder's line, which was engaged several hundred yards to their front. He had barely completed these arrangements when Winder's men broke ranks and retreated across the plain. The Federal line surged forward in pursuit. As it did so, it moved across Scott's front. Ewell saw his chance. Shouting above the din of battle, he ordered the colonel to remove two fences in his front and to throw his troops upon the enemy's flank.

Scott eagerly obeyed. In stentorian tones he called out, "Men in the front rank, pull down that fence; we will make a charge." In an instant both fences were down, and Scott's men poured across the plain, yelling with all their might— "more to keep our courage up than to frighten the enemy," one soldier candidly admitted. As they left the cover of the woods, they came under fire from the guns at the coaling. Scott's men ignored the fire and unleashed a point-blank volley into the left flank of the onrushing Union line. The attack disconcerted the Federals and caused them to fall back. They soon recovered, however, and drove Scott's Virginians back into the woods with heavy loss.[35]

Ewell rallied Scott's men as they rushed back into the woods, assuring members of the Fifty-eighth Virginia that they had done nobly. He gave no less credit to the men of the Forty-fourth, whose charge, he claimed, had saved the battle.[36] Fortunately the Federals did not pursue them. Just as Scott's line gave way, Lt. Cole Davis of the Rockbridge Artillery halted a brass six-pounder on the plain and fired several rounds into the Union line. His "quickness and decision," noted Ewell, checked the Federal advance "so long that, although Colonel Scott's command was driven back to the woods with severe loss, there was time to rally and lead them to the assistance of the Eighth Brigade."[37]

The Eighth Brigade was Taylor's. After more than an hour struggling through the laurel thickets that blanketed the mountain, the Louisianians had reached the coaling and attacked the Union battery there. Nowhere was the fighting stiffer. Twice the Confederates captured the battery only to relinquish it in the face of determined Union counterattacks. "The opposing forces fired in each others' faces," wrote Pvt. George Neese of Chew's battery. "Bayonets gleamed in the morning sunshine one moment and the next they were plunged into living human flesh and dripping with reeking blood. . . . For a while the hand-to-hand conflict raged frightfully, resembling more the onslaught of maddened savages than the fighting of civilized men."[38]

Taylor rallied his men for one final effort. As he did so, Ewell came crashing through the underbrush, leading the survivors of the Forty-fourth and Fifty-eighth Virginia to his support. The Louisianians greeted Ewell with cheers. Though not given to dramatic speeches, the general gave one now. Pointing toward the coaling, he shouted, "Men, you all know me. We must go back to that battery." The Louisianians rose to their feet shouting and charged the guns joined by Scott's Virginians.[39] Ewell personally led them into battle. "He is a gallant officer," wrote a soldier of the Fifty-eighth Virginia. "I could but notice his coolness in leading us in a charge against the batteries. A shell exploding under his horse he did not even look to see the effect but with his eye fixed steadily on the piece before him moved steadily on. The men are willing to follow him."[40]

When Tyler saw that the coaling was in Confederate hands, he pivoted his line as if to attack it. Taylor watched the maneuver with a mixture of fascination and dread. "Wheeling to the right, with colors advanced, like a solid wall he marched straight toward us," the Louisianian wrote. "There seemed nothing left but to set our backs to the mountain and die hard." Just as all seemed lost, Taliaferro joined Winder and renewed the assault on the plain. Caught in a cross fire between the Confederates at the knoll and those on the plain, Tyler wisely ordered a retreat. The Confederates at the coaling turned the captured guns against their antagonists, Ewell himself helping to operate one of the pieces. Under the battery's withering fire, Tyler's retreat degenerated into a rout.[41]

The guns on the knoll were still smoking when Elzey's brigade, now commanded by Col. James A. Walker, belatedly stumbled onto the scene. At Ewell's order Walker's Virginians filed into place behind Scott's two regiments and started in pursuit of the defeated enemy. A private in the Twenty-fifth Virginia passed Ewell, who was leaning against one of the captured guns, and not recognizing him cried out, "Hello, old conscript; you look like you had captured the battery. Get your gun and come along with us." Ewell smiled at the lad, but said nothing. Some of the young man's friends asked him if he did not know that he had been speaking with General Ewell. "No," he replied, adding that he "did not give a damn."[42]

As the battle entered its final stages, Jackson appeared. Grasping Taylor's hand, he promised to give the captured guns to the Louisiana Brigade. He then joined Ewell, who was standing nearby observing the retreat. Placing his hand on his subordinate's sleeve, Jackson remarked fervently, "He who does not see the hand of God in this is blind, Sir, blind!" Even Dick Ewell might have agreed.[43]

Tyler's stubborn fight thwarted any plans Jackson may have entertained for an attack on Frémont. Sometime around 8:00 or 8:30 A.M. he ordered Trimble and Patton to march to Port Republic, burning the North River bridge behind them. They reached the town at 10:00 A.M., as the battle was ending. When Frémont arrived a short time later, he found the bridge in ruins and both armies gone. The only troops then in sight were Confederate soldiers burying the dead and assisting the wounded. Out of spite or simple frustration, Frémont ordered his batteries to fire on them. Those able to do so scrambled for cover, leaving the wounded on both sides to fend for themselves. In the end, noted one Southerner, Frémont ended up "hurting his Union friends about as much as he did us."[44]

Jackson meanwhile pursued Tyler's defeated force toward Conrad's Store, garnering 450 prisoners, one abandoned cannon, and about 800 muskets.[45] As one might expect from a former captain of dragoons, Ewell took an active part in the pursuit. According to Capt. Henry W. Wingfield, the general's horse had been killed at the coaling, but he found a wagon horse and, using a blind bridle, followed the enemy.[46]

That night the Army of the Valley camped at Brown's Gap, where it was in position to fight Frémont and Shields or to escape across the mountains. Jackson posted his own division on top of the mountain and assigned Ewell's men the steep, muddy slopes, an arrangement that did not sit well with many of Ewell's officers. Jackson and Ewell made their headquarters at the foot of the gap, in what

Campbell Brown described as "a pleasant, little nook, by the side of a cool branch."[47]

Col. Thomas Munford joined Ewell for a late supper. As they relaxed outside his tent, the general turned to his guest and said in his nervous way, "Look here, Munford, do you remember a conversation we had one day at Conrad's store?"

Munford laughed. So many things had transpired since that time, it was difficult to remember specific conversations. "To what do you allude?" he asked.

"Why, to old Trimble, to Jackson and that other fellow, Colonel Kirkland, of North Carolina?"

How could Munford forget? Seldom, if ever, had he heard anyone denounce so many officers in such a short period of time. He replied that he remembered the conversation very well.

"I take it all back," said Ewell, "and will never prejudge another man. Old Jackson is no fool; he knows how to keep his own counsel, and does curious things: but he has method in his madness; he has disappointed me entirely. And old Trimble is a real trump; instead of being over cautious, he is as bold as any man, and, in fact, is the hero of yesterday's fight," he said, referring to Cross Keys. "Jackson was not on the field. They will call it mine," he said modestly, "but Trimble won the fight; and I believe now if I had followed his views we would have destroyed Frémont's army. And Colonel Kirkland, of North Carolina, behaved as handsomely near Winchester as any man in our army, leading his regiment, and taking a stone wall from the Yankees; he is a splendid fellow."[48]

The battle of Port Republic marked the end of the Valley Campaign. Frémont and Shields retreated northward after the battle, leaving Jackson the undisputed master of the upper valley. Once the Federals had left the area, the Confederates moved down the mountain to Mount Meridian. There, according to one soldier, they "enjoyed the luxuries of a good bath, an abundance of food, clean clothes and the rest which we all so much needed."[49]

Ewell took advantage of the lull in military operations to write his reports of the campaign. On 16 June he submitted to Jackson his report on the battles of Harrisonburg and Cross Keys. In it he praised the conduct of his troops, particularly the First Maryland Regiment and Trimble's brigade. He had less favorable words for Capt. Frank Myers of the Comanches. During the battle of Port Republic Jackson had sent Myers to deliver a dispatch to Munford. Myers stayed with Munford for the rest of the day to take part in the pursuit of the Federal army. Ewell scolded him for this, telling Myers that he "was no courier for Gen. Jackson, and that his business was to keep his (Ewell's) Division supplied with couriers, and to obey his orders and nobody else's." The general delivered such rebukes in a forceful manner not soon forgotten. "It is needless to say that the lesson was laid to heart and closely followed thereafter," the chastened officer noted.[50]

During the week Ewell came in for a scolding himself. At some point in the battle of Port Republic he had spotted a Union officer on a snow-white horse recklessly exposing himself to Confederate fire. The officer's courage so impressed him that he told his troops to spare the man's life. Jackson heard of the incident and told his colleague never to do such a thing again. "This was no ordinary war," he explained, "and the brave and gallant Federal officers were the very kind that must be killed. Shoot the brave officers," he advised, "and the cowards will run away and take the men with them."[51]

With that exception, Ewell's conduct throughout the Valley Campaign had been virtually without blemish. "His Division has done more hard work and hard fighting in the last two weeks than any other part of the 'Army of the Valley,'" a soldier-correspondent wrote to the Richmond *Daily Enquirer*. "In sixteen days they fought seven battles, and in every instance were victorious. . . . It is the first time that General Ewell has had an opportunity of showing in battle how skillfully and bravely he could handle an army. Never defeated, never surprised, always at the right place at the right time, he has earned and well merits the title of General."

J. William Jones agreed. "Plain in his dress, quick (and if need be rough) in his orders, prompt in execution, almost reckless in his courage, and stubborn and unyielding in holding any position assigned him, he was just the man whom Jackson needed, in whom he seemed to have the highest confidence, and to whom he was certainly indebted for much of his splendid success."[52]

About the only one who did not praise Ewell was Jackson. In his reports the commanding general mentioned Ewell sparingly and praised him not at all. But Ewell did not complain; he had come to accept Jackson's peculiar ways. In just three weeks he had gone from being Jackson's harshest critic to his most loyal subordinate. When later asked what he thought of Jackson in the Valley Campaign, Ewell responded, "Well, sir, when he commenced it I thought him crazy; before he ended it I thought him inspired."[53]

CHAPTER 15

I Think We Have Them Now!

James Shields was in a fighting mood. Stonewall Jackson had thrashed two of his brigades at Port Republic, but the pugnacious Union general hoped to even the score. No sooner did Erastus Tyler's battered regiments return to Conrad's Store than Shields began making plans to take on Jackson again, this time in conjunction with Frémont. But Lincoln had other ideas. Anxious to get on with the job at hand—capturing Richmond—the president ordered Irvin McDowell to stop pursuing Jackson and return to Fredericksburg. At McDowell's orders, Shields reluctantly withdrew to Front Royal. His retreat left Frémont exposed, and he, too, fell back, leaving Jackson in control of the upper Valley. Shields could not hide his disappointment at the outcome of events. While conceding that Jackson had conducted a skillful campaign, he remained firmly convinced that he and Frémont could have annihilated the wily Confederate if given just a little more time. "The result could not have been doubtful," he reported with evident regret. "Thus lay a kind of fatality." [1]

As the Federals retreated down the Valley, speculation about Jackson's numbers and position reached fantastic proportions. One Union report put the Valley Army at Charlottesville; another had it threatening Frémont; a third placed it near Luray. McDowell did not know what to think. "Jackson is either coming against Shields at Luray, or [Rufus] King at Catlett's, or [Abner] Doubleday at Fredericksburg, or is going to Richmond," he concluded with obvious bemusement. [2]

Lincoln brushed aside such wild reports. With a perception superior to that of his generals, he correctly surmised, "Jackson's game . . . now is to magnify the accounts of his numbers and reports of his movements, and thus by constant alarms keep three or four times as many of our troops away from Richmond as his own force amounts to. Thus he helps his friends at Richmond three or four times as much as if he were there. Our game is not to allow this." [3] Lincoln's solution was to have McDowell resume his advance on Richmond, while Frémont and Banks remained in the Valley to watch Jackson.

The ink on that order was hardly dry when Frémont commenced nagging Lincoln for fresh troops to replace those he had lost in the campaign, a demand the president clearly found annoying. "We may be able to send you some dribs by degrees," he answered, "but I do not believe we can do more." In an earlier dispatch Frémont claimed to have defeated Jackson's entire army at Cross Keys. Lincoln was quick to remind him of this. "As you alone beat Jackson last Sunday I argue that you are stronger than he is to-day, unless he has been re-enforced, and that he cannot have been materially re-enforced, because such re-enforcement could only have come from Richmond, and he is much more likely to go to Richmond than Richmond is to come to him. Neither is very likely."[4]

Lincoln was wrong on both counts. The day that he wrote to Frémont, three Confederate brigades from Richmond reinforced Jackson. Maj. Gen. William H. C. Whiting commanded two of the brigades; Alexander Lawton led the third. Robert E. Lee sent them to Staunton to give the impression that Jackson was going to make another thrust down the Valley. In reality Lee intended to bring the Valley Army to Richmond.[5]

The ruse fooled everyone, including Dick Ewell. Led by Jackson to believe the army would be staying at Mount Meridian for a few more days, Ewell granted staff officers Campbell Brown and John M. Jones a leave of absence to go to Staunton. Jones's nephew and namesake, John W. Jones, accompanied them. "If you gentlemen desire to stay a little over your leave, it will make no difference," Ewell told the departing officers. "We are being largely reenforced, and will rest here for some days, when we will again beat up Banks's quarters down about Strasburg."

Brown and Jones returned a couple of days later to find the army gone—not north toward Strasburg, but southeast toward Waynesboro. The younger Jones asked his uncle why Ewell had lied to them. "Ewell did not deceive us," replied the older man. "He was deceived himself. I am his confidential staff officer and receive all communications that come to our headquarters, and I know, absolutely, that everything that Ewell had received went to show that it was our purpose to move down the Valley again. The truth is, Ewell never knows anything about Jackson's plans until they are fully developed."[6]

Even then Jackson chose to tell Ewell only as much as necessary. On 17 June 1862, without warning, Jackson ordered his subordinate to take his division across the Blue Ridge to Charlottesville. He said nothing of the army's ultimate destination, but Ewell had his suspicions. When Jackson's staff later came to him look-ing for their general, Ewell suggested that they look in the vicinity of Richmond.[7]

Jackson assigned his chief of staff, Maj. Robert L. Dabney, the task of con-ducting the march to Richmond in his absence. He enjoined Dabney to tell no one the army's destination, not even Ewell. Ewell was justifiably angry at his su-perior's secretiveness, viewing it as evidence that Jackson did not have confidence in him. When the army's quartermaster, Maj. John Harman, later appeared privy to Jackson's plans, Ewell lost his temper. "Here, now," he complained to Dabney, "the general has gone off on the railroad without intrusting to me, his senior major-general, any order, or any hint whither we are going; but Harman, his quartermaster, enjoys his full confidence, I suppose, for I hear that he is telling the troops that we are going to Richmond to fight McClellan." Dabney did his best to assuage Ewell's injured feelings, assuring him that he enjoyed Jackson's full confidence. As for Harman, declared Dabney, he was only voicing his opinion; he knew no more than anyone else.[8]

After reaching Charlottesville the Valley Army headed east along the Vir-ginia Central Railroad. Ewell's division led the march as far as Gordonsville. At Walker's Church a group of young ladies gathered to pass out refreshments to the passing soldiers. To keep the women from being jostled, Ewell had them stand inside the churchyard and hand food to the soldiers over an intervening fence. Just two regiments benefited from that arrangement. After that the provisions ran out, leaving the remaining regiments hungry and not a little envious of their com-rades at the head of the column.[9]

Ewell's division reached Gordonsville on Saturday, 21 June. It rested there over the Sabbath, then boarded railroad cars for Beaver Dam Station. The Confed-erates continued on to Ashland, just twelve miles north of Richmond. By now there was no question that the Army of the Potomac was their objective, and the effect was electrifying. "The men were in high spirits at the chance of catching McClellan," noted Campbell Brown.[10]

The Army of the Potomac straddled the Chickahominy River east of Rich-mond. It had five corps, four of which confronted Lee south of the river. Maj. Gen. Fitz John Porter's big Fifth Corps alone remained north of the Chicka-hominy to protect the York River Railroad, McClellan's lifeline to his supply base at White House Landing. Lee planned to attack Porter's isolated corps in over-whelming force and drive it from the railroad, thereby cutting off McClellan from his base and forcing him to fight at a disadvantage. Jackson would open the attack. As he swept down the creek, he would uncover the upper crossings, allowing Daniel Harvey Hill's, Ambrose Powell Hill's, and James Longstreet's divisions to cross to the north side. Once across, the three latter generals would engage Porter in front while Jackson turned the Union general's right flank, prying him out of his entrenched position.[11]

To reach the point of attack, Jackson ordered his divisions to use a single road. Anticipating the congestion that would result, Ewell and another division commander went to Jackson's tent to recommend that they march by separate roads. Jackson promised to consider the matter and notify them of his decision by morning. As the visitors stepped outside, Ewell chirped, "Do you know why General Jackson would not decide upon our suggestion at once? It was because he has to pray over it, before he makes up his mind." A moment later, Ewell's companion discovered that he had forgotten his sword. Returning to Jackson's tent, he found the general on his knees praying for divine guidance, just as Ewell had predicted.[12]

The Valley Army broke camp at 2:00 A.M., 26 June, and proceeded south and east through a barren pine flat known as the Slashes of Hanover. Union cavalry, detecting the Confederates' approach, felled trees, destroyed bridges, and placed other obstacles in their path. By the time Jackson reached the Virginia Central Railroad, at 9:00 A.M., he was six hours behind schedule. Ewell crossed the tracks north of Atlee's Station and turned right toward Shady Grove Church. Whiting and Winder continued east one mile farther to Pole Green Church Road, then turned right and headed for Hundley's Corner.[13]

As he was approaching Shady Grove Church, Ewell spotted a large body of troops one-quarter mile to his right, moving parallel to his line of march. Uncertain as to the identity of the force, he deployed his division to meet the threat. The mysterious troops turned out to be Branch's brigade, which was advancing down the left bank of the Chickahominy to cover Jackson's right flank. Branch rode out to speak with Ewell. Although the North Carolinian had briefly served under Ewell, the two men had never met.[14]

A. P. Hill meanwhile waited impatiently at Meadow Bridge for Jackson to open his attack. Hours passed. At 3:00 P.M., having heard nothing from Jackson since morning, Hill led his division across the Chickahominy and assailed Porter's entrenched line at Mechanicsville. Ewell was near Shady Grove Church when Hill's musketry erupted less than two miles away. "That's the programme!" he exclaimed enthusiastically. "That's the programme! I think we have them now!" Ewell was then bearing down on Porter's right flank and within easy striking distance of it. But rather than attack Porter, Jackson incredibly ordered Ewell to turn east and unite with Whiting at Hundley's Corner. With three hours of daylight remaining and a major engagement taking place nearby, the Valley Army went into camp.[15]

Porter withdrew toward Grapevine Bridge that night. The Confederates took up the chase at first light and overtook him at Gaines's Mill. Lee ordered A. P. Hill to attack at once and sent orders for Longstreet and Jackson to hurry forward their troops. But again Jackson was tardy. Lee ordered him to march to Old Cold Harbor, a crossroads hamlet east of Gaines's Mill, in an effort to cut off Porter's retreat. Jackson started promptly enough but fell behind when he took a wrong turn. Additional minutes were lost when he halted his column to attack a force that did not exist.[16]

A. P. Hill meanwhile was fighting for his life. Porter had skillfully posted his corps behind a marshy tributary of the Chickahominy known as Boatswain's Swamp and had fortified his position with three lines of breastworks. Hill's division struck Porter's line head-on and quickly found itself pinned down in the mire. Jackson, Ewell, and some other officers rode ahead to Old Cold Harbor to examine the ground but had to scatter when Union artillerists took them in their sights.[17]

At Lee's orders Ewell led his division to New Cold Harbor, a point immediately in rear of Hill's beleaguered line. From there a road ran southeast through Boatswain's Swamp to the McGehee house. Ewell threw Elzey's brigade into action to the left of the road to shore up Hill's crumbling left flank. At Lee's command he deployed Taylor's and Trimble's brigades to the right of the road.[18]

Taylor had fallen sick at Ashland, and Col. Isaac G. Seymour commanded his brigade. Seymour led the Louisianians across the swamp, then moved forward to engage the Federals entrenched on the forward slope. Trimble had been following Seymour, but as usual the obstinate old man had gone astray. Ewell had to send a staff officer to turn him around. When Trimble finally appeared, he brought only a fraction of his command. The Sixteenth Mississippi, the Twenty-first North Carolina, and portions of the Fifteenth Alabama had taken a wrong turn, leaving him just the Twenty-first Georgia and a few companies of Alabamians. Ewell preferred to wait until the missing units arrived, but the situation would not admit of delay. Without hesitation he threw Trimble's men into action immediately to the right of the road to plug the gap between Elzey and Seymour. He could put in the rest of Trimble's troops when they arrived.[19]

Ewell crossed the creek in time to witness the Louisiana Brigade's attack. The Tigers' burly major, Rob Wheat, particularly attracted his attention. Ewell remarked that Wheat's large frame made him a "shining mark" for Union riflemen, and he was right. As Wheat charged up the slope, he fell dead with a bullet in the

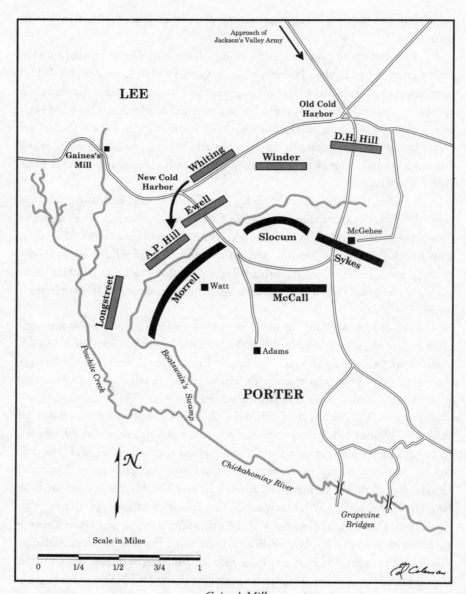

Gaines's Mill

brain. Seymour died just moments later. Unsure whether to charge or to retreat, the leaderless Louisianians did neither. A Union volley settled the question. The blast shivered the brigade's ranks and sent it scampering for the rear.[20]

The Louisiana Brigade's stampede left a dangerous hole in the Confederate line. Ewell extended Trimble's two regiments to the right in a desperate effort to fill the void. For almost two hours the Twenty-first Georgia and the Fifteenth Alabama battled heroically against long odds. Twice Union volleys threatened to drive them back, but each time Ewell kept them at their work, encouraging them, said one man, by "his cool courage and brave example." His presence alone, noted Trimble, "held the men in position for over an hour and a half under this terrific fire."[21]

Leadership availed much; but it could not take the place of men and ammunition, and Ewell was short of both. Some of Trimble's men fired so many rounds that their rifles became too hot to hold. As ammunition gave out, they delved into the cartridge boxes of their dead and wounded comrades. Soon even that ran out. Ewell told the men that help was on the way. Until it arrived, they must hold their ground—at the point of the bayonet if necessary.[22]

For more than an hour Ewell scrambled to find reinforcements. Staff officers galloped to the rear with urgent requests for help. Their efforts finally bore fruit. At 5:00 P.M. Hood's Fifth Texas Infantry came to Ewell's support, and Hampton's Legion appeared on his left. These troops enabled Ewell to hold his ground until Brig. Gen. Alexander Lawton's Georgians arrived. With 3,500 rifles, Lawton commanded the largest brigade in Jackson's army. When he heard that Ewell was in trouble, Lawton led his men into the smoking woods and drove the Federals back. As they passed, Ewell waved his sword over his head and cried, "Hurrah for Georgia!" to which the Georgians responded with a cheer. Lawton paused briefly to confer with Ewell about the situation, then followed his men up the bloody slope. At roughly the same time, Hood's brigade broke the Federal line to Ewell's right and captured a six-gun battery.[23]

With matters on Trimble's front secure, Ewell crossed the New Cold Harbor Road to check on Elzey. Like Trimble, Elzey's brigade had run headlong into Porter's entrenched line and was pinned down. Elzey had been seriously wounded in the face early in the fight, and his men were falling back when Ewell arrived. The Virginian led them back into the deadly, bullet-torn thickets. "Now charge them, boys!" he cried. With a shout Elzey's men clambered up the hill and overran the enemy works.[24] Ewell rode with them. As he struggled up the tangled slope, his sorrel mare Maggie fell dead beneath him. Undaunted, the general scrambled to his feet only to fall again when a bullet glanced off a tree and struck him in the lower leg. The lead pierced his boot but inflicted only a painful bruise.[25]

By sundown, Confederate troops swarmed the ridge recently held by Porter. Ewell had been fighting for four hours and received permission to take his division out of action. He did not permit himself that luxury, however. Instead he stayed on the field until dark, "in order," he explained, "that the troops which came up later in the day might profit by what I had learned of the ground and the position of the enemy." He did more than merely give advice, though. A member of the Stonewall Brigade remembered that the general led them in a twilight charge against the enemy, while Brig. Gen. Maxcy Gregg recalled Ewell ordering a battery to desist from firing on Union troops that he mistakenly took to be Confederates.[26]

At midnight Ewell finally sought rest. He enjoyed a meal with Brig. Gen. Roswell S. Ripley of South Carolina before going to sleep at his New Cold Harbor headquarters. His division had fought doggedly, losing about 800 men, most from Elzey's brigade and from Trimble's Twenty-first Georgia and Fifteenth Alabama regiments.[27] That Ewell himself escaped serious injury was nothing short of a miracle. He had been in the thick of the fighting for several hours, much of the time on horseback. Other officers were not so fortunate. Seymour and Wheat were dead, and Elzey was seriously wounded. Also dead was Col. Reuben Campbell of the Seventh North Carolina Infantry. Campbell had been Ewell's roommate at West Point. He had perished early in the battle, gallantly leading his regiment in an attack ordered by Ewell.[28]

Porter retreated across the Grapevine Bridge during the night, abandoning the York River Railroad to the Confederates. On 28 June Lee ordered Ewell to Dispatch Station to begin tearing up the tracks. Stuart's cavalry headed to White House Landing, which he found in flames.[29]

Col. Bradley Johnson's First Maryland Regiment took position on a hill overlooking Dispatch Station. Johnson directed Ewell's attention to a point across the Chickahominy, where Federal soldiers were engaged in constructing a barricade across the railroad tracks. From where the Confederate officers stood, it was impossible to tell whether the crude work harbored any cannon. Ewell determined to find out. "Colonel, suppose you try those fellows at work there. We'll find out how many guns they have!" Johnson accordingly ran out two guns of Capt. William H. Griffin's Baltimore Light Artillery and opened fire. In an instant, shells from three masked Union batteries screamed over and around the exposed party on the hill. "That'll do," chirped Ewell. "We've found out what we want to know! Some things can be done as well as some others! Capt. Griffin, you will limber up & go to the rear!"[30]

As Ewell was leaving the hill, a Union gunner gave him a parting shot. The ball passed just inches from Ewell's face, causing him to jerk backward, then struck a large pine tree, slicing through it so cleanly that the upper part of the trunk fell straight down and stuck in the ground beside the stump. "Wasn't that beautiful," cried Ewell, "wasn't that well done!" Whether he was referring to the neat way in which the iron missile had cut through the tree or to his own nimbleness in dodging, no one in his cavalry escort knew and none had the courage to ask.[31]

McClellan meanwhile pulled back from the Chickahominy River and retreated south. Lee ordered Ewell to Bottom's Bridge to block the Army of the Potomac if it moved toward Williamsburg. Ewell found everything there quiet. That was not the case across the river, where Maj. Gen. John B. Magruder clawed at the Union army's rear guard at Savage's Station. Ewell heard Magruder's battle and was pondering its significance when he was startled by a series of explosions upriver. Leaving orders for a Louisiana regiment to follow him, Ewell returned to Dispatch Station at a full gallop.[32]

Ewell's first thought was that McClellan was trying to fight his way back to White House Landing by way of the railroad. Instead he found Union troops blowing up supplies stockpiled south of the Chickahominy. Ewell peered down the tracks toward Savage's Station. Across the river stood a train, facing north, apparently blocked by a tree that had fallen across the rails. Smoke billowed from the locomotive's stack. As Ewell, Trimble, and Johnson puzzled over this curious scene, Union soldiers removed the tree, and the train came hurtling down the tracks. Forgetting that the bridge was out, the Confederate officers dove for safety. When the train reached the river, it leaped the tracks and plunged headlong into the water with a terrific crash. Ewell was the first to recover his presence of mind. "That was an ordnance train!" he cried. "Have the troops formed immediately, for the enemy is retreating, and we will be of no further use on this side of the Chickahominy."[33]

Ewell's first instinct was to attack. There was a ford two miles above Dispatch Station. Using the discretion allotted him, he prepared to cross the river and join Magruder's attack on the Union army. Before he could execute this plan, though, Jackson ordered him to march back to Grapevine Bridge. Ewell crossed the Chickahominy after dark. Just across the bridge, a musician in Elzey's Thirteenth Virginia Regiment spotted the general with his pants down picking lice. It was a side of Ewell that few soldiers had an opportunity to see—or cared to.[34]

By now it was clear that McClellan was retreating to the James River. Lee directed Jackson to pursue the Federals toward White Oak Swamp and sent the rest of his army by roads farther west to strike the enemy in flank. At Savage's Station Jackson captured a Union field hospital with 500 attendants and 2,500 patients. Among the hospital staff was a distant relative of Ewell's named Doctor Smith. From him Ewell and Campbell Brown learned that Tasker Gantt was serving as judge advocate on McClellan's staff. Smith assured his Southern relatives that Gantt, though fighting for the Union, still entertained kind feelings toward them. "I told him it was more than they could do for him," Brown wrote to his mother, "at least more than I could." Smith also had news of Rebecca Ewell, who had recently moved to Baltimore to escape the war. Although Becca's going to Maryland effectively severed communication between them, Ewell must have been relieved to know that his sister was out of harm's way.[35]

Jackson pressed on to White Oak Swamp. McClellan had destroyed the bridge and posted two divisions on the opposite side to resist a Confederate crossing. Stonewall brought up twenty-eight guns to dislodge them, but the Northerners stubbornly held their ground. Rather than flank the crossing, Jackson sat down under a tree and took a nap, seemingly indifferent to the battle taking place at Glendale, just a few miles ahead.[36]

Ewell made his headquarters that night at a house recently occupied by Union brigadier general Daniel Sickles. In his haste to retreat, the former Tammany Hall politician had left behind two or three dozen bottles of champagne, which Ewell promptly purchased from the house's owner. He and Sickles differed in many respects, but they shared a common philosophy: no march was so severe nor any campaign so rigorous that an officer could not enjoy a few drinks along the way.[37]

The Federals disappeared during the night, and at dawn Jackson resumed his pursuit. Near Glendale, Brig. Gen. Jubal A. Early reported to Ewell for duty. Early had graduated from the U.S. Military Academy in 1837, three years before Ewell. He had fought in the Second Seminole and Mexican Wars before leaving the military to pursue a legal career near Lynchburg, Virginia. Like his new commander, Early had opposed secession but had remained loyal to Virginia when it sided with the South. A bullet had pierced his shoulder at the battle of Williamsburg in May 1862, taking him out of action. Now, two months later, he was back in the saddle, more eager than ever to fight the Yankees. At Lee's orders he took command of Elzey's brigade.[38]

Early no sooner reported for duty than cannon fire ahead announced that Lee had brought McClellan to bay. The Union general had made his stand at Malvern Hill, a place well suited to defense. Marshy creeks with steep banks protected the Army of the Potomac's flanks, and massed artillery swept the gently sloping fields

Jubal A. Early (Library of Congress)

that fell away from the center of its line. Union gunboats anchored in the James River, a short distance to the rear, added their firepower to the Union defense.[39]

The Confederates approached McClellan's stronghold cautiously. D. H. Hill deployed astride the Quaker Road, opposite the center of the Union line. Magruder slid into place on his right, and Jackson on his left. Jackson deployed

Whiting's division in front, near the Poindexter farm, and kept Ewell's division in reserve near Smith's Shop on the Quaker Road. His own division remained farther back, at Willis Church. As the Confederates filed into position, Jackson took Trimble's brigade from Ewell and sent it to the far left to extend Whiting's line. Later, when a gap formed between Whiting and D. H. Hill, Jackson filled it with the Louisiana Brigade, now temporarily commanded by Col. Leroy A. Stafford. The detachment of Trimble's and Stafford's brigades left Ewell in command of only Early's brigade and the First Maryland Regiment. He put Early in a position to support Stafford and posted the Marylanders west of the Quaker Road, on Early's right.[40]

An artillery exchange preceded the Confederate attacks on Malvern Hill. At one point, as Jackson was helping to post guns near the Poindexter house, a Union shell buried itself in the ground immediately in front of his horse. Ewell was with Jackson at the time. Reaching out, he grabbed the bridle of Jackson's horse and turned the animal aside. The exploding shell covered the officers with dust, but injured no one.[41]

While the artillery duel was in progress, Ewell rode over to the right to see how matters stood on Magruder's front. On his way back he met Lee and Jackson at Willis Church.[42] Lee had hoped to silence the Union artillery on Malvern Hill before making a general assault, but his plan had failed miserably. The few Confederate batteries that managed to get into the fight had been crushed by Union counterbattery fire, forcing Lee to look for other options. Earlier in the afternoon Trimble had discovered what he believed to be a weak spot on McClellan's right. Ewell had passed this information on to Jackson with the recommendation that the Confederates attack that point. As Ewell conferred with Lee and Jackson at Willis Church, he may have reminded them of that opportunity. Lee rode to the left to look into the matter personally. He was considering an attack there when dispatches from Whiting and Magruder indicated that McClellan was withdrawing from Malvern Hill. In an abrupt change of strategy, Lee ordered Magruder to pitch into the Federals. Benjamin Huger and D. H. Hill supported the attack.[43]

Union guns mauled the onrushing Confederate divisions, tearing them to pieces. At Hill's urgent request, Jackson sent Ewell forward with Early's brigade. Rather than taking the Quaker Road, which was scoured by Union artillery fire, Ewell led Early's men through the tangled woods directly in the rear of Hill's position. A creek called Western Run ran through the woods. Ewell rode ahead to find the best way across the creek, leaving Early to bring the brigade forward. Just after Ewell had left, however, a courier who claimed to be acting under his orders

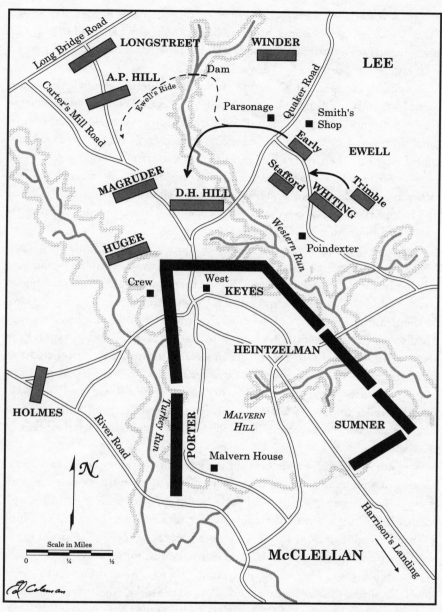

Malvern Hill

approached Early with instructions for him to halt at the edge of the woods. When Ewell returned, he angrily demanded to know why Early had halted. The flabbergasted subordinate replied that he had done so at Ewell's orders. "I gave no such orders!" snapped Ewell. "Forward!" [44]

Early's brigade splashed across the creek, then bore left through the woods toward a farm lane called the Carter's Mill Road. Because horses could not negotiate the stream's steep banks, Ewell and Early had to cross at a dam a short distance upstream. Once across, Early turned south to rejoin his troops. Ewell continued west until he struck the Carter's Mill Road, then followed it south to a pine-covered knoll, where he expected Early's brigade to emerge from the woods. When the brigade did not promptly appear, Ewell dismounted from his horse and plunged into the woods on foot to look for it. He was not successful. Early had veered too far south and was nowhere to be seen.

Unable to find Early or his brigade, Ewell continued to the front alone. When he got there, he spotted Brig. Gen. Joseph B. Kershaw of Magruder's command rallying his brigade. In a few words Ewell explained that he was organizing an attack against the Union line and asked Kershaw to support it. The South Carolinian demurred on account of the small size of his command, but Ewell insisted. He directed Kershaw to place his brigade in a clover field less than 250 yards from the Union guns and wait for further orders. [45] Meanwhile Ewell collared two other regiments and led them in a charge against the Union line near the Crew House. Kershaw noted that the doughty old warrior led the small force "in beautiful order to the attack under a terrible fire of artillery and infantry." But like the assaults that preceded it, Ewell's charge withered under the blasts of McClellan's guns. [46]

The sun set on the chaotic field. In the gathering darkness D. H. Hill found Ewell and advised him not to hazard any more attacks but simply to hold his ground. Ewell agreed. When Jubal Early finally appeared with three of his regiments, Ewell had them lie down in support of Kershaw's thin line. The First Maryland Regiment came up a few minutes later and was placed adjacent to the road as a provost guard to turn back stragglers headed for the rear. [47]

The fighting sputtered to a halt around 8:30 P.M. After things had quieted down, Ewell and Chase Whiting crawled out to the picket line. [48] What they saw, or heard, convinced them that McClellan still occupied Malvern Hill. If he attacked in the morning, they believed, the Confederates would not be able to resist him. D. H. Hill agreed. Although it was then 1:00 A.M., the three generals went to see Jackson. Stonewall listened to their gloomy predictions and assured them that everything would be all right: McClellan would be gone by morning.

He was right.[49] When Ewell visited the front at dawn, Early informed him that McClellan had retreated, leaving only a rear guard to hold the hill. Brig. Gen. Ambrose R. Wright confirmed the report.[50]

The Confederate army was in no condition to pursue. On 2 July it remained in camp while rains lashed the countryside. Ewell took advantage of the lull to grab a nap on the floor of a shanty in front of the position held by Stafford the previous day. The sound of the door opening snapped him back to consciousness. Looking up, he recognized the face of Capt. G. Moxley Sorrel, a distant cousin. As Sorrel entered the room, Ewell pushed himself up from the floor and lisped, "Mather Thorrel, can you tell me why we had five hundred men killed dead on this field yesterday?" That was all, remembered Sorrel; "the soul of the brave General was fit to burst for the awful and useless sacrifice."[51]

Lee started after the Federals on 3 July, but by then it was too late. He had hardly gotten started when Jeb Stuart brought word that the Union army had reached Harrison's Landing on the James River. Lee pursued nonetheless, determined to inflict some parting damage. Jackson marched by way of the Long Bridge Road, but he had to stop to let Longstreet's division pass. Wretched road conditions hampered the Valley Army's progress even more. By the end of the day, it had covered just three miles.[52]

Frustrated by his lack of progress, Jackson ordered his troops to march at "early dawn" on 4 July. Ewell was to lead the march, but when Old Jack reached his headquarters, he found Ewell still asleep. Jackson rebuked him sharply and directed Henry Kyd Douglas to put the groggy general's division in motion at once.[53] This and the minor reprimand that he administered to Ewell for ordering troops to spare the life of the Union horseman at Port Republic are the only recorded instances of Jackson being displeased with Ewell, a remarkable fact in light of Old Jack's strained relations with his subordinates.

The Confederates caught up with the Army of the Potomac that afternoon at Herring Creek, a tributary of the James River. McClellan had entrenched and was waiting for them. Jackson told Ewell to attack but then canceled the order.[54] Ewell's men breathed a sigh of relief. After Gaines's Mill and Malvern Hill they had no stomach for storming strong positions, particularly ones supported by Union gunboats. At least one officer in Ewell's division sent back word that if ordered to attack, his men would not fight.[55]

Ewell reconnoitered the Union position from a knoll at the front. He then sat down on an abandoned crate to catch up on the sleep that Jackson had so rudely interrupted. Pulling his knees up under his chin, he dozed off—but only for a moment. The crack of Union sharpshooters' rifles jolted him awake. One bullet passed between Ewell's foot and thigh, while two others pierced the hat on his head. The general prudently withdrew behind the hill before resuming his nap.[56]

Whiting replaced Ewell's division on the skirmish line on 5 July. By then matters had reached an impasse. McClellan was unwilling to leave his riverside defenses, and Lee refused to attack him there. Not wishing to expose his troops to the region's unhealthy climate, Lee led the army back to Richmond, leaving Stuart to keep an eye on his cautious opponent.[57]

The Seven Days Campaign was over. Strategically it had been a grand victory for the Confederates. They had saved Richmond and had driven the Union army back to its base on the James River. In the process they had captured 10,000 men, fifty-two cannon, and 35,000 small arms. Even so, Lee was not satisfied. His object had been to destroy the Union army, not simply to defeat it. Poor communication and lackluster leadership by key subordinates had thwarted that design. Magruder, Whiting, and Theophilus Holmes had displayed questionable ability; Jackson had lacked his customary aggression; and Huger had been lethargic. A. P. Hill, Longstreet, and D. H. Hill had handled their troops reasonably well, but as soon as the campaign ended, they tarnished their reputations by squabbling amongst themselves. Of the army's nine division commanders, Ewell alone emerged from the campaign with both his personal and professional prestige intact.[58] In the weeks following the campaign, Lee tactfully transferred Magruder, Holmes, Whiting, and Huger to other departments, replacing them with younger and more skillful officers. Ewell survived the winnowing process and by midsummer stood high on Lee's list of generals. His star was clearly on the rise.

CHAPTER 16

A Little More Grape

In the days following the Seven Days, Ewell made his headquarters at Strawberry Hill, four miles north of Richmond. His troops bivouacked nearby along the Virginia Central Railroad. The division had dwindled to fewer than 3,000 men, a far cry from the more than 10,000 rifles Ewell had boasted in the Valley. Most of the missing soldiers were sick. The division had suffered just 987 casualties in the Seven Days fighting, but as Campbell Brown noted, "the seeds of disease sown by the malaria of the swamps carried off a good many more." Ewell was among those who fell victim to the contagion.[1]

Potentially more harmful to the division than malaria was the dissension that was sweeping though its ranks. Despite successes in the Valley and at Richmond, many of Ewell's officers were tired of serving under Jackson. They felt that he was not only too demanding but also too rash. As proof they pointed to his intention of attacking McClellan's impregnable position at Harrison's Landing. Continued service under him, they argued, would ruin the division. A few went so far as to apply to Adj. Gen. Samuel Cooper to have the division taken away from him. Ewell would not hear of it. Pulling himself up from his sickbed, he rode to Richmond to intervene personally with Cooper to keep the division with Jackson.[2]

Ten weeks earlier he would not have made the effort. He had then considered Jackson unbalanced and unpredictable. "He always spoke of Jackson, several years his junior, as 'old,'" remembered Dick Taylor, "and told me in confidence that he admired his genius, but was certain of his lunacy, and that he never saw one of Jackson's couriers approach without expecting an order to assault the north pole." Ewell was even more outspoken in Munford's presence, calling Jackson "crazy," an "old fool," and an "enthusiastic fanatic." Despite these rantings, Ewell had stuck by Jackson. He marveled as his enigmatic chief outfought, outmarched, and outgeneraled his opponents in the Shenandoah Valley. After that he became Jackson's most ardent admirer, even going so far as to adopt some of his chief's peculiar views on health, such as refusing to eat pepper because it produced weakness in the left leg.[3]

Jackson had also gained a high opinion of Ewell that spring. Although he rarely praised his subordinate personally or in official reports, he appreciated his ability. With McClellan no longer immediately threatening Richmond, Jackson proposed that the Confederate government send an army into Maryland to menace Washington, D.C. He had no desire to lead such an enterprise himself, he claimed, suggesting instead that it be led by Lee or Ewell, either of whom he would willingly follow. What greater praise could Ewell receive?[4]

Standing between the Confederates and Maryland was the Army of Virginia, a new entity cobbled together from the discomfited commands of Irvin McDowell, Nathaniel Banks, and John Frémont. Its commander was Maj. Gen. John Pope, a boastful officer who had achieved some success in fighting along the Mississippi River. Pope quickly made himself odious, adopting harsh measures toward the Southern civilians who lived within his lines and by making arrogant proclamations to the eastern troops now under his command. In his first communication to his new army, he claimed to come "from the West, where we have always seen the backs of our enemies." Ewell bristled at the pronouncement. "He'll never see the backs of my troops," the irate general declared. "Their pantaloons are out at the rear and the sight would paralyze this Western bully." After concentrating his army at Warrenton, Pope began creeping south toward the railroad junction at Gordonsville. Lee responded by dispatching Jackson to Gordonsville with his own and Ewell's divisions. His orders to Jackson were clear: "I want Pope to be suppressed."[5]

Ewell's division started for Gordonsville on 14 July. The infantry and artillery traveled by train; the cavalry, by road. The division went without Dick Taylor, who had been promoted and sent west to command the District of Western Louisiana. With Taylor's departure, Ewell lost a capable officer and a trusted friend. He recognized Taylor's genius but confided to friends his fear that the eccentric Louisianian would one day lose his mind. "Most of us are in the estimation of our best friends more or less eccentric," wrote Ewell's brother Ben, himself a rather offbeat character. "So Taylor and Ewell thought Jackson, and so Taylor thought Ewell, and so Ewell thought Taylor, and I have no doubt that if Jackson's mind hadn't been full of more important matters he would have thought so of Ewell and Taylor."[6] Command of Taylor's brigade passed to forty-two-year-old Harry T. Hays of the Seventh Regiment. Hays was still sidelined with a wound he had received at Port Republic. Until he returned to action, Col. Henry Forno of the Fifth Louisiana led the brigade in battle.[7]

Ewell saw his troops off, then rode with his staff toward Gordonsville. En route they stopped at the home of an old farmer. As they sat down to dinner, a bolt of lightning struck a haystack, setting it on fire. The old man looked on helplessly as the flames spread toward his stable. The building was lost, he cried; there was no way to save it. Ewell was more optimistic. He immediately marshaled his staff, and after an hour of hard work, they extinguished the blaze. The stable was safe. In gratitude, remembered Campbell Brown, the owner "fed us all like fighting-cocks & gave us some capital liquor."[8]

Ewell reached Gordonsville on 17 July. That same day Federal cavalry crossed the Rapidan River and entered Orange Court House, eight miles away. Although it was pouring rain, Ewell immediately set out after the Federals with two regiments of infantry and some cavalry. The bluecoats retreated across the river, and Ewell returned to Gordonsville, where he was entertained at the home of Mary E. Barbour, a kind, motherly woman with two unmarried daughters.[9]

Jackson's division joined Ewell at Gordonsville two days later, bringing the number of Confederate troops there to 11,000 men, less than a quarter of the 47,000 men at Pope's disposal. Jackson took the Barbour house as his headquarters and sent Ewell to Liberty Mills, five miles west. Too weak to take the offensive, Jackson drilled his command and waited for a chance to strike.[10]

Ewell used the respite to write to Lizzie. In a recent letter his niece had expressed delight that he had taken part in the fighting around Richmond. Ewell did not share her enthusiasm. "It may be all very well to wish young heroes to be in a fight," he wrote her, "but for my part I would be satisfied never to see another field. What pleasure can there be in seeing thousands of dead & dying in every horrible agony, torn to pieces by artillery &c. many times the wounded being . . . left on the field for 24 hours before they can be cared for?" Ewell had seen enough of such sights. "Since March I have been almost constantly within hearing of skirmishing, cannon &c &c. and I would give almost anything to get away for a time so as to have a little rest," he continued. "I dont know that I ever lived so hardly & so much exposed to every thing disagreeable as during the last few weeks. It is impossible for 20 miles below Richmond to get out of the sight & smell of dead horses. The dead people were pretty much removed, but the Artillery & Cavalry horses killed in the battles lined the roads." Having disposed of McClellan, he explained, the army was now turning its attention to Pope. "The Yankees are now in Culpepper & I learn are systemmatically [sic] destroying all the growing crops and every thing else the people have to live on. Sometimes they ride into the fields & use their sabres to cut down the growing corn. They seem bent on starving out the women & children left by the war."[11]

For the long-suffering residents of northern Virginia, relief was on the way. With McClellan showing no signs of renewing his advance on Richmond, Lee on 27 July dispatched A. P. Hill's division and Brig. Gen. William E. Starke's brigade to Gordonsville to reinforce Jackson. At the same time Jackson's own strength increased as soldiers who had fallen ill during the Seven Days returned to duty. By August he felt strong enough to strike.[12]

Ewell went into the new campaign short one aide. After reaching Gordonsville, Hugh Nelson contracted typhoid fever and died at the home of an Albemarle County relative. The news took Ewell by surprise, for he had no idea that Nelson's condition was so serious. In a letter of condolence to the family, he wrote, "I could not have believed it possible to be so grieved at the death of one, a short time since a stranger, as I am at the afflicting blow that has removed Major Hugh M. Nelson. His devotion to the cause of his country, his bravery, sense, in short his eminent qualities as a soldier and gentleman, have impressed deeply myself, as well as all those brought in contact with him." Incredibly, Nelson was the only man to die while on active service with Ewell's staff.[13]

Ewell could not attend Nelson's funeral because he was then sitting on Brig. Gen. Richard B. Garnett's court-martial board. The board convened at Ewell's Liberty Mills headquarters on 6 August, the day Nelson died. It met to try Garnett on charges preferred by Jackson stemming from Garnett's conduct at the battle of Kernstown. After just one and a half days of testimony, the army went into motion, and the trial had to be suspended. It never reconvened.[14]

Nathaniel Banks was the cause of the trial's interruption. Banks had emerged from the organizational shake-up following the Valley Campaign as a corps commander in the Army of Virginia. In early August Pope pushed Banks's corps up to Culpeper Court House, beyond the supporting distance of the army's other two corps. Jackson saw his chance. On 8 August he led his army across the Rapidan to crush Banks before Pope could reinforce him. Ewell's division forded the river at Liberty Mills, then marched downriver to Barnett's Ford, where Winder and Hill were crossing. A traffic jam ensued at the point where the columns converged. Ewell's division reached the intersection first and led the march to Culpeper under a brutal sun. It bivouacked for the night at Crooked Creek, just eight miles from where it started.[15]

The Confederates continued toward Culpeper the next morning. At a 200-foot monadnock called Cedar Mountain, Union cavalry blocked the road. Ewell ordered his artillery up to shell the horsemen. The Federals scattered but soon returned, leading Ewell to conclude "that the enemy intended to make a stand at this place." He reported his findings to Jackson at the Petty House. Ewell reached the building first and played with some little children on the front porch. Jackson's arrival ended the innocent amusement. In an instant the generals were on their knees poring over maps and papers spread out on the floor. Having determined on a plan of action, they then stretched out for a brief rest before lunch.[16]

It was 1:00 P.M. before Ewell's troops reached the front. Early's brigade led the way. Filing off to the right of the road, it deployed along the lane of the Crittenden family, whose farm rested in the shadow of the mountain. Union artillery fired on the Confederates as they came into range, prompting Ewell's batteries to return fire. Winder came up on Early's left a short time later, adding his batteries to the contest. While Winder was supervising the operation of guns posted near the Culpeper Road, a shell ripped through his side, inflicting a mortal wound. With his demise, Brig. Gen. William B. Taliaferro assumed command of Jackson's division.[17]

Ewell meanwhile led Trimble's and Forno's brigades to the northern toe of the mountain by way of a difficult route along its western slope. Latimer's battery and a section of the Bedford Artillery accompanied the column. Finding that horses could not pull cannon up the steep ascent, Ewell ordered White's battalion and the Twenty-first Georgia to drag the guns to the crest by hand. The mountain offered the Confederates an ideal artillery position, being both above the Federal line and at an angle to it. Ewell posted his guns on a shelf of land halfway down the slope, where they quickly drew the fire of the Union artillery. Trimble and Forno supported the guns.[18]

Ewell communicated with Jackson by means of mounted couriers. At the height of the battle, Stonewall sent his aide-de-camp and brother-in-law, Lt. Joseph G. Morrison, to Ewell with a verbal message. On the way Morrison encountered a Union soldier and defeated him in a hand-to-hand struggle. The encounter so flustered the staffer that when he reached Ewell, he could speak of nothing else. Ewell had to address Morrison sharply to recall him to his duty.[19]

The general showed no greater patience toward a well-dressed officer he found loitering on the mountain. "I say!—you man with the fine clothes on, come here," he shouted. Upon interrogating the officer, Ewell learned that he was a quartermaster who had ridden forward to get a look at the fighting. "Good Heavens, who ever heard of a Quartermaster on a battle field?" exclaimed the general in feigned astonishment. "But since you are here, sir, I'll make you *useful as well as ornamental*." He thereupon handed the man a dispatch to deliver to Jackson, who happened to be at a point of danger on the battlefield. "The gallant Quarter master carried the dispatch," recalled an amused witness, "and brought back old Stonewall's reply, but says [sic] that he suddenly remembered that he had to see after his train and never went near Gen. Ewell during a battle again."[20]

Banks attacked Jackson's line at 5:00 P.M. From his mountain aerie Ewell watched as Brig. Gen. Samuel W. Crawford's brigade pushed through a wheatfield west of the Culpeper Road, routing Taliaferro and turning Early's left flank. Simultaneously, Brig. Gen. Christopher C. Augur's brigade billowed through cornfields south of the road in an effort to outflank Early's right flank near a copse of cedar trees located at the foot of the mountain. Early skillfully maneuvered his regiments to meet these threats, stubbornly holding his ground until reinforcements arrived. Ewell directed his artillery on the mountain to fire into the Federals; otherwise, he could do nothing. Cedar Run separated him from Early and prevented him from sending troops directly to Early's aid.[21]

The attack on Early marked the height of Union fortunes that day. Just when it seemed that Augur and Crawford would sweep the Confederates from the field, A. P. Hill's division arrived and hurled the bluecoats back to Mitchell Station Road. Ewell's division joined the attack. While Early's brigade counterattacked through the cornfield, Trimble and Forno cascaded down the mountain toward the Federal left flank. To those fighting on the plain below, Trimble's advance amid the enemy's bursting shells presented "a magnificent and inspiring sight."[22]

Ewell planned to advance beyond the Mitchell Station Road, then wheel left and roll up the Federal line. But when he reached the bottom of the hill, he found his progress blocked by a millpond. The only line of approach was to the left, across fields swept by Confederate artillery fire. Ewell sent back orders for his gunners on the hill to cease firing, then continued his advance. As he did so, he heard shouting to his left rear. Growing darkness made it impossible to distinguish friend from foe. Ewell prudently halted and opened communication with Early, whose line of march intersected his own. Before Early replied, Jackson ordered Ewell to unite with the left wing of the army. Ewell accordingly pushed on to the Culpeper Road.[23]

Banks's troops were in full retreat. Despite the growing darkness, Ewell ordered a passing battery to give them a parting shot. "A little more grape, Captain, if you please," he shouted to the unit's commander, "for they travel too fast for our boys." In their haste to leave the battlefield, the Federals had to abandon one of their cannon. On the captured weapon was a note left by the lieutenant in charge of the piece complimenting Capt. William F. Dement's battery on its "acurate fireing and distructive shots." Ewell personally delivered the note to Dement, probably adding his compliments to those of the Union officer.[24]

Ewell's impact on the battle had been minimal. Of his three brigades, only Early's had done any significant fighting, and it had operated largely outside Ewell's control. Although newspapers later exaggerated his role in the victory, Ewell knew better. "Where the printed account speaks of Ewell[,] Jackson ought to be substituted," he candidly admitted to Lizinka. "My Division being in advance movements &c were attributed to me that in effect were Jackson's." For Early he had nothing but praise. "General Early is an excellent officer—ought to be Maj. Genl.," Ewell told his Tennessee cousin. "He is dissatisfied as well he may be and talks sometimes of going out to join Bragg. He is very able & very brave & would be an acquisition to your part of the world." [25]

The morning after the battle, Jackson met with Ewell, Hill, and Jeb Stuart beside the Culpeper Road, one-half mile south of Crittenden's lane. Stuart reported that Banks had been reinforced to 30,000 men and that more Union troops were on the way. Unable to resist such a host, Jackson withdrew to Cedar Mountain and ordered his trains back to Gordonsville. The army held its ground an additional day, then followed. [26]

Before leaving Cedar Mountain, Confederate troops buried the dead, cared for the wounded, and collected firearms discarded during the battle. Pope did not hinder them. Instead he requested a truce until 2:00 P.M., 11 August, to bury his dead and remove his wounded. Ewell took advantage of the armistice to chat with acquaintances in the Union army. Early's brigade meanwhile searched the battlefield for Confederate dead overlooked by other divisions. In doing so, they encountered a Union officer on Maj. Gen. Franz Sigel's staff collecting firearms from the battlefield in violation of the cease-fire agreement. Early instantly put a stop to the illicit activity and ordered the arms collected by the Union officer loaded onto Confederate wagons. Ewell fully supported his action. [27]

The Confederate army withdrew across the Rapidan River after dark. To conceal its departure, detachments of soldiers kept campfires burning throughout the night. An unusually large blaze caught Ewell's attention. Riding over, he found two men of White's battalion piling enough hay on one fire to light up the whole hillside. Ewell quickly stopped the soldiers' shenanigans, threatening to "throw a pistol ball among them" if they did not shape up. The offenders privately vowed "to return all the pistol balls he threw them," but they stopped putting hay on the fire. [28]

Ewell had a run-in with White's men again the next day. At midnight he ordered Capt. Frank Myers to take his company to Liberty Mills and hold the bridge there until the infantry arrived. Later he sent a second order, asking Myers to have ten men meet him at a certain road north of the Rapidan. Myers obeyed, but the men took a wrong turn and never reached the general. When Ewell later encountered Myers, he demanded to know why he had not obeyed his order. "I supposed, General," stammered the unfortunate captain. Ewell cut him short. "You supposed," the impassioned general ranted, "you supposed, you say; what right had you to suppose anything about it, sir; do as *I tell you*, sir; do as *I tell you*." [29]

On 12 August the Confederate army crossed the Rapidan River, drawing the curtain on the campaign. Southern casualties numbered approximately 1,400 men, of whom 224 belonged to Ewell. He more than made good his losses by adding Alexander Lawton's Georgia brigade to his division. Lawton had been in Winder's division until that time and became its acting commander on Winder's death. Jackson did not like Lawton, though, and to keep him from retaining command of the division, he transferred the Georgian's brigade to Ewell. It was a clever move, but not effective; within three weeks Lawton secured command of a division anyhow, if only for a brief time. [30]

Two days after recrossing the Rapidan, Ewell received another letter from Lizzie. In it the teenage girl expressed surprise that her uncle had taken part in the Valley Campaign. Ewell hastened to remind her that he "was in every battle in the Valley, commanded at one & inflicted the severest blow on the Feds they had," adding that he was fully as much at risk there as on the Peninsula. Lizzie had asked him to send her some brass buttons as a "trophy" from the Seven Days. Instead Ewell sent her a needle case that he had found on the battlefield, a more appropriate memento for a young lady, he suggested, than the buttons she had requested.

In contrast to his usual writing style, the tone of Ewell's letter to Lizzie was decidedly somber, reflecting his abhorrence at the sights he had witnessed. "I fully condole with you over the gloomy prospects in regard to the war," he remarked bitterly. "Some 100000 human beings have been massacred in every conceivable form of horror with three times as many wounded, all because of a set of fanatical abolitionists & unp[r]incipled politicians, backed by women in petticoats & pants and children. The chivalry that you were running after in such frantic style in Richmond have played themselves out pretty completely," he added, "refusing in some instances to get out of the State to fight. Such horrors as war brings about are not to be stopped when people want to get home. It opens a series of events that no one can see to the end." [31]

The day Ewell wrote this letter, Robert E. Lee arrived at Gordonsville. For more than a month Lee had remained at Richmond keeping tabs on McClellan. With "Little Mac" showing no signs of an advance, Lee boldly moved north with twelve brigades to join Jackson in crushing Pope. For Ewell and many others in the army the commanding general's arrival was reason for added confidence. "Lee is gradually assuming the highest position with us," Ewell wrote Lizinka. "He has no newspaper puffers & therefore his fame is on more solid foundation." One of Lee's first actions was to reorganize the Army of Northern Virginia into two corps led by Longstreet and Jackson. He later designated Longstreet's as the First Corps and Jackson's as the Second. Jeb Stuart remained in command of the army's cavalry.[32]

As Longstreet's brigades filed into Gordonsville, Jackson shifted his troops east to the vicinity of Pisgah Church.[33] Ewell had his troops ready to march at dawn, but by late morning Jackson's marching orders still had not arrived. Encountering an acquaintance, Dr. James L. Jones, at his home three miles from Gordonsville, Ewell chirped, "Doctor, will you please tell me where we are going to?"

"No, General," the physician replied, "but I should like to ask you that, if it were a proper question."

"It is a perfectly proper question to ask," replied Ewell, "but I should like to see you get an answer. I pledge you my word that I do not know whether we are to march north, south, east, or west, or whether we are to march at all or not. General Jackson ordered me to have my division ready to march at early dawn; they have been lying in the turnpike there ever since, and I have had no further orders. And that is about as much as I ever know about General Jackson's movements."[34]

When he finally did get orders to march, Ewell had to follow a long wagon train. It so delayed his march that he did not reach his destination until after dark. Ewell was suffering from a cold that he had caught at Cedar Mountain, and he sought shelter at a house along the road. While there, he wrote Lizinka that the army was moving into position to attack Pope. He predicted "that in a day or two we shall be engaged on a grand scale & the God of Battles alone knows the result." Should a battle occur, he warned, Campbell might be injured or even killed. "I hope & pray that your child may be spared. If God sees fit that it be otherwise, you should remember his virtues, his religion, his merits as reasons which besides Revelation ought to make you hope it is for the best, should he be selected."[35]

Col. Bradley Johnson visited Ewell on the eve of the campaign. Johnson was temporarily without a command. By the end of the Seven Days, his regiment had dwindled to just 150 men. Efforts to recruit new members had been unsuccessful. When the soldiers' terms of enlistment had expired on 7 August, the unit disbanded, leaving Johnson without a job. Ewell wrote to the secretary of war recommending Johnson's promotion. In the meantime he offered the colonel a job as the division's inspector general, a position recently vacated by the ailing John M. Jones. If that did not suit Johnson, Ewell said, he would secure him a position as provost marshal on the staff of Jackson, Longstreet, or any other officer whom Johnson might select. Ewell had need of a provost marshal himself, but he could not offer Johnson a position commensurate with his rank. Johnson thanked Ewell but said he was not looking for a staff position. As he put it, "He had left his home to fight." Johnson got his wish. Within two weeks Jackson appointed him to command a brigade in Taliaferro's division.[36]

Lee would need good officers like Johnson in the coming campaign. Pope then occupied a precarious position between the Rappahannock and Rapidan Rivers. Lee planned to cross the Rapidan, turn Pope's left flank, and pin his adversary against the Rappahannock River. Before he could spring his trap, though, Pope perceived his danger and withdrew across the Rappahannock. The Confederate army crossed the Rapidan at Raccoon and Somerville Fords in pursuit. Ewell's division, now numbering 7,590 men and sixteen guns, halted for the night near Stevensburg, then moved up to Brandy Station. Ewell himself stayed at the Cunningham farm, near the mouth of the Hazel River, where he had made his headquarters prior to the Valley Campaign.[37]

Over the next few days the Army of Northern Virginia (as Lee styled his force) sidled up the Rappahannock River looking for a place to cross. Because the left bank of the river dominated the right bank above Kelly's Ford, the Confederates were unable to force a crossing and had to look for an undefended spot. Ewell's division led the army's advance. On 22 August it crossed the Hazel River at Wellford's Mill and moved toward Warrenton Sulphur Springs. A Union brigade crossed the Rappahannock at Freeman's Ford and attacked the Confederate wagon train, but Trimble and Hood drove it back. "Our men pursued them closely and slaughtered great numbers as they waded the river or climbed up the opposite bank," Trimble boasted. "The water was literally covered with dead and wounded." With typical overstatement he reported inflicting ten casualties for every one he received on a foe three times his size.[38]

The head of Ewell's column was not faring so well. At Warrenton Sulphur Springs the Confederates found the bridge across the Rappahannock destroyed and Union cavalry guarding the crossing. Jackson determined to force a passage. While Lawton negotiated the river at the springs, Ewell sent Early's brigade across a dilapidated dam farther downstream. A hard rain was falling as Early's troops crossed. When asked by Ewell what he should do if the river rose past fording, Jackson replied casually, "Oh, it won't get up, & if it does, I'll take care of that."

Early's brigade completed its passage without incident, but by the time Forno's brigade reached the river at sunset, water was pouring over the dam. Ewell had no choice but to postpone Forno's crossing until dawn.[39]

Until then Early was cut off. Ewell instructed him to conceal his brigade in a pine thicket adjacent to the dam and open communication with Lawton upriver. Since fires might alert the enemy to their presence, Early's men had to spend the night in darkness. Ewell fared no better. Up late attending to business, he fell asleep in a fence corner, the water gathering in puddles about his ears.[40]

By morning the rain had stopped, but the Rappahannock remained too high for troops to cross. To make matters worse, most of Lawton's brigade had re-crossed the river the previous night, leaving Early's troops to face Pope's army alone. Jackson ordered Early to move to a point opposite Warrenton Sulphur Springs and entrench while Confederate engineers built a temporary bridge across the river. If pressed by the Federals, he was to attempt a crossing at Water-loo Bridge, a few miles upriver.[41]

Engineers of A. P. Hill's division labored throughout 23 August to complete the temporary bridge. They succeeded, thanks in part to the collapse of a bridge up-stream that provided them with necessary timber. Rather than withdraw Early, though, Jackson sent Lawton's brigade, two regiments of cavalry, and a section of artillery to reinforce him. Pope, too, brought up reinforcements. During the night Early reported the Federals massing on his front and slowly extending to-ward his left. Jackson ordered Ewell to cross the river at daylight, 24 August, and investigate the situation. If he found the Federals in force, as Early indicated, he was to bring Early's and Lawton's brigades back across the river.

Early was not content to wait until dawn. When informed of Jackson's instruc-tions to Ewell, he sent Ewell a message emphatically stating that the Federals *were* in force and urging Ewell to extricate his brigade at once. If Ewell waited until dawn, he argued, the Federals might shell the bridge and the ford, making retreat or reinforcement difficult. Ewell joined Early north of the river at 3:00 A.M., and after hearing for himself the distant rumble of men and guns, he ordered Early and Lawton to retreat. They completed the crossing just after dawn. Ewell and Early remained on the left bank until Federal skirmishers appeared, then followed their troops across the bridge.[42]

For the next two days Northern and Southern artillerists fired at one another across the river in a noisy but insignificant display of might. One shot threw dirt on Ewell as he stood near the house of Dr. Scott. The grimy general brushed off his clothes and ordered his division under the cover of nearby hills. He then borrowed a towel and walked down to a neighboring creek to wash off. Since most of the soldiers had returned to the commands when the cannonade began, Ewell enjoyed the luxury of a private bath.[43]

Lee meanwhile settled on a bold plan. Leaving Longstreet to hold the Rappahannock line, he would send Jackson's foot cavalry on a wide turning movement aimed at the Orange and Alexandria Railroad, the Union army's line of supply.[44] That cut, the Union commander would have no choice but to retreat toward Washington. A month of maneuvering in central Virginia was about to end; it was time to "suppress" Pope.

CHAPTER 17

Fallen Warrior

The two-day march around John Pope's Army of Virginia was one of Stonewall Jackson's greatest achievements of the war. The movement began at Jeffersonton the morning of 25 August 1862. Breaking camp at dawn, the Confederates marched upriver to Amissville, crossed the Rappahannock River unopposed at Henson's Mill, then proceeded via Orleans to Salem. Ewell's division led the infantry as it often did when speed was required. As usual Jackson told no one of the corps' destination. He directed his division commanders to proceed to specific points, where couriers met them with instructions for the next leg of the march. The Confederates scrupulously avoided main roads, following instead what Campbell Brown called "a series of by-roads and no-roads." They traveled light, taking only a few ambulances and a small ordnance train. In lieu of quartermaster and commissary wagons, which would impede the march, the soldiers carried three days' cooked rations.[1]

The sweating column ground to a halt one mile south of Salem after an exhausting twenty-five-mile trek that even Jackson considered severe. Between the corps and the town stood a low ridge. Ewell's men camped on its slope, away from the town. Except for a few pickets, no one was permitted to go to the top of the hill. To assure secrecy, Jackson prohibited fires and admonished his men against any loud demonstrations.[2]

The Confederates broke camp early on 26 August, hoping to put as many miles behind them as they could before the temperatures rose. Ewell pushed east through Thoroughfare Gap at Bull Run Mountain, then angled south toward Gainesville. Henry Forno's light-footed Louisianians set the pace, while Thomas Munford's Second Virginia Cavalry scouted ahead, picketing all road intersections that the corps would pass. At Gainesville, Jeb Stuart joined Jackson with two brigades of cavalry. With Stuart guarding his right flank and rear, Jackson pressed on with renewed vigor toward his objective, Bristoe Station.[3]

The Confederates reached Bristoe about 6:00 P.M. As they approached, a train roared past, heading east toward Alexandria. The Southerners picked up their pace. Two companies of Union soldiers stood guard at the station, one infantry and one cavalry. Pope had placed them there to defend the railroad against raids by Confederate cavalry; they had no idea that some 25,000 Rebels were nearby. Not until Munford had closed to a few dozen yards of the station did the Federals realize their danger. The combat was short and decisive. Munford charged the depot with 100 men, scattering the Union horsemen before they could form. Union infantry fought briefly from the hotel and other nearby buildings, but they soon recognized the hopelessness of their resistance and surrendered.[4]

While Munford was subduing the depot guard, a second train approached the station, heading toward Alexandria. The cavalrymen hastily threw some ties on the tracks in an effort to derail the train, but the locomotive brushed them aside. At Ewell's orders, Forno's brigade fired a broadside into the train as it sped past. It perforated the engine boiler but failed to disable it. The locomotive wheezed and hissed its way to Alexandria, spreading warning of the Confederates' presence.[5]

Ewell immediately set Trimble's and Forno's men to work tearing up the tracks so that no more trains would elude him. In case any came into sight before the work was finished, he kept a battery at hand to blow them off the tracks. Ewell had no sooner completed these measures than a locomotive appeared, pulling twenty empty cars. When it reached the station, Ewell's infantry fired a point-blank volley into its side, killing the engineer. The train struck the damaged rails and plunged down the steep embankment in a mangled heap. A second train shared the same fate.[6]

Ewell witnessed the destruction from a house 600 yards from the station. He had just left the building when two other trains approached. The Confederates scurried to cover, eagerly anticipating yet another crash, but they were disappointed. Something spooked the engineers, and they stopped well short of the station. A Southerner with some railroad experience mounted one of the captured locomotives and whistled "off brakes," a sign that everything was all right, but this only made the Union engineers more suspicious. They put their trains in reverse and started back to Warrenton. Campbell Brown and Capt. Henry B. Richardson of Ewell's staff tried to overtake them. "Our plan was to shoot the Engineer," explained Brown, "& if there were troops on board to disappear rapidly." Riding at full tilt, Brown pulled alongside the nearest locomotive and leveled his pistol at the driver. He squeezed the trigger. Nothing happened. Again he pulled the trigger; again nothing. The train got up a head of steam and pulled out of sight. Disappointed, Brown gave up the chase. It was the only time in the war that he had drawn his gun in anger, and it had misfired.[7]

Bristoe Station stood just five miles from Pope's supply base at Manassas Junction. Although Trimble's men had already logged almost thirty miles that day, their commander volunteered to press on with two regiments and capture the depot. Jackson approved the expedition but put Jeb Stuart in charge of it. Arriving at Manassas Junction at midnight, Stuart and Trimble overpowered the small guard and captured eight cannon, seventy-two horses, and an immense amount of quartermaster and commissary stores.[8]

While Trimble and his two regiments trudged the dark road to Manassas Junction, Ewell's other brigades bivouacked at Bristoe Station. Ewell put his division in position to resist a Union advance along the railroad and ordered his men to sleep on their arms. In the morning Jackson led Taliaferro's and Hill's divisions to Manassas Junction, leaving Ewell at Bristoe to hold back Pope.[9]

Ewell posted his troops on a ridge just west of the station, facing Warrenton Junction. He deployed Lawton's brigade to the left of the railroad, and Forno's and Early's brigades to the right of it. Munford's Second Virginia Cavalry guarded his flanks. Once his troops were in place, Ewell sent Forno on a reconnaissance toward Warrenton Junction. Before returning, Forno was to destroy the railroad bridge over Kettle Run and tear up as much track as possible. A gun of Capt. Louis D'Aquin's Louisiana Guard Artillery accompanied the expedition. Other troops set fire to the bridge over Broad Run and to the two Union trains that had derailed the previous night.[10]

Not yet comprehending the size or character of the force in his rear, Pope sent nine carloads of troops by rail from Warrenton Junction to retake Bristoe Station. The Union soldiers debarked near Kettle Run, but they returned to Warrenton Station when they found the Confederates in greater force than anticipated. D'Aquin sent the train on its way with a few parting shots. With no other Federal troops in sight, Forno returned to Bristoe Station, leaving the Eighth Louisiana at Kettle Run to damage the bridge as much as possible. The Sixth Louisiana screened the operation from a point west of the bridge. If attacked, it was to fall back skirmishing on the Eighth Regiment. Both regiments would then retreat to Bristoe Station under the cover of Ewell's artillery.[11]

Outside D'Aquin's brush with the enemy, the morning passed quietly. Ewell made a few minor adjustments to his line, sending the Forty-ninth Virginia Infantry to cover the Greenwich Road on the right and advancing the Sixtieth Georgia and one gun to the left of the railroad to support the Sixth and Eighth Louisiana.[12]

In the afternoon Maj. Gen. Joseph Hooker approached Bristoe Station from the direction of Warrenton Junction with one division of Northern infantry. Ewell started his wagon train for Manassas Junction and sent a staff officer to Jackson asking what he should do if the Federals were too strong to resist. Before he received a reply, Hooker attacked the Sixth and Eighth Louisiana Regiments near Kettle Run. The Louisianians fought stubbornly, then fell back to a wooded area about 400 yards from Forno's main line. The Fifth Louisiana helped cover their retreat, while the Sixtieth Alabama of Lawton's brigade incurred heavy casualties south of the railroad protecting Forno's left flank.[13]

So far Ewell had held his own and more, but with Union reinforcements arriving every minute, he began to fear for his division's safety. Immediately to his rear was Broad Run, fordable at only two places. If Hooker managed to turn his right flank, Union batteries could command both crossings. Ewell's retreat might then become a rout. The Virginian therefore determined to cross Broad Run while he could and contest Hooker's advance from the opposite side. He had hardly settled on this plan of action when a staff officer brought a dispatch from Jackson ordering Ewell to avoid becoming entangled with the enemy and to fall back to Manassas Junction if pressed.[14]

Ewell wasted no time ordering a retreat. Lawton's brigade left the field first. It crossed Broad Run at the lower ford, nearest the railroad, and formed a line of battle on the ridge beyond, where it covered the crossing of the remaining two brigades. Forno went next. Breaking contact with the enemy, the Louisianian fell back in good order, passed through Lawton's line, and headed for Manassas Junction. Early was the last to cross. While Walker's Thirteenth Virginia held the Federals in check, Early led his other regiments across the creek and formed a line of battle half a mile behind Lawton.[15]

Capt. William C. Dement's battery followed Early's troops across Broad Run. As it approached the upper ford, Federal infantry threatened its rear. Dement calmly halted his guns and ordered them to fire five rounds apiece into the onrushing blue ranks. Ewell sent his aide Tom Turner in "hot haste" to order Dement off, but by the time Turner reached the battery, Dement had repelled his pursuers and was leisurely heading for the ford. Ewell marveled at the artilleryman's audacity, calling his feat "one of the most daredevil pieces of boldness he ever saw."[16]

Less bold but no less brave was the conduct of D'Aquin's battery. D'Aquin's guns covered the lower ford. As Hooker's infantry came into range, the artillerists opened fire, attracting a firestorm of shot and shell. Ewell was standing with

D'Aquin when a Union projectile screamed past them, killing two of Lawton's men just a few feet away.[17]

Once his division had safely crossed Broad Run, Ewell broke contact with Hooker and headed for Manassas Junction. Early's brigade acted as rear guard. Ewell told Early to hold his ground until ordered back, directing him "to move one or two regiments by flank with colors elevated, so as to present the appearance of the arrival of re-enforcements." The ruse worked. Although Hooker shelled the retreating Confederates, he did not pursue them across Broad Run. At dark Early marched for Manassas Junction, leaving the cavalry to bring up the rear.[18]

Ewell had accomplished his mission in textbook fashion, delaying the Union advance without allowing himself to be drawn into a general engagement. He left few supplies and only a few seriously wounded men. Indeed, wrote Munford, "Genl. Ewell was so anxious to induce the impression that he was not 'running', he required me to carry off the Harness left on the Horses killed by the Enemy's Artillery." Pride steeled Ewell's determination. With Stony Lonesome less than five miles away, he was fighting on home turf.[19]

While Ewell sparred with Hooker at Bristoe Station, the rest of Jackson's corps had spent the day at Manassas Junction gorging on cheese, ham, oysters, and countless other delicacies provided by Pope's sutlers.[20] Ewell's hungry troops eagerly partook of the bounty, then stretched out to rest. For the second night in a row they slept on their arms. A series of explosions brought the men to their feet just after midnight. Mistaking the sound for hostile artillery fire, Jubal Early rushed to Ewell's headquarters to report the corps under attack. Ewell calmed his fears, explaining that Stuart's cavalry had been ordered to burn the depot. Early had heard exploding railroad cars.[21]

Jackson's position at Manassas was dangerous. Pope was on one side of him; McClellan, on the other. If Jackson remained at Manassas Junction, he would be cut off from Longstreet and crushed between these two forces. He accordingly determined to move his corps north of the Warrenton Turnpike, where he would be in position to open communication with Longstreet at Thoroughfare Gap and to strike at Pope's left flank as it advanced up the Warrenton Turnpike toward Centreville.[22]

The march was fraught with confusion. Jackson ordered Taliaferro and Hill to march toward Sudley Spring, but Hill misinterpreted Jackson's vague orders and instead headed for Centreville. Ewell prepared to follow Hill, in accordance with Jackson's orders. Before he did so, he first had to find Trimble, who had wandered off with his brigade. Staff officers eventually found the wayward brigadier at the Lewis House and ordered him to fall in behind Early, who was then crossing Bull Run at Blackburn's Ford.[23]

Jackson meanwhile had learned that Hill and Ewell were heading in the wrong direction. He sent them orders to join Taliaferro on Matthews Hill. By the time Ewell received Jackson's orders, his division had crossed Bull Run. He led Early's brigade up the left bank of the creek and recrossed the stream at the Stone Bridge. Trimble was behind Early, but somehow he became separated from him and veered east toward Centreville, taking Forno and Lawton with him. For the second time that morning Ewell had to send staff officers to get the old man turned around.[24]

By noon Jackson finally had his divisions heading in the right direction. As their troops moved into position on Matthews Hill, Jackson, Ewell, and Taliaferro stretched out in the shade to snatch a few minutes' sleep. Artillery fire brought them back to their feet. Jackson had posted a brigade beyond Groveton, a hamlet two and one-half miles west of Bull Run, to alert him to the approach of Union troops on the Warrenton Turnpike. A Union division led by Brig. Gen. John F. Reynolds had encountered this brigade and was pushing it back. Jackson held no conference and asked no opinions. He had just received a dispatch from Lee notifying him that Longstreet was at Thoroughfare Gap and would cross it in the morning. With the rest of the army within a day's march of him, Jackson rushed to battle. He tersely ordered Taliaferro to "move your division and attack the enemy" and told Ewell, "Support the attack."[25]

Taliaferro led his division west to the vicinity of the John Brawner farm, a homestead that stood north of the Warrenton Turnpike about one mile west of Groveton. Ewell dropped off Early's and Forno's brigades at an unfinished railroad bed, then joined Jackson and Taliaferro near the Brawner farm with his remaining two brigades. By then Reynolds had disappeared to the south, leaving the Warrenton Turnpike void of Union troops. Until others came along, the Confederates could only wait.[26]

It was a scorching hot day, well into the nineties. When Ewell arrived, Jackson and Taliaferro were just polishing off a canteen of buttermilk scrounged from a local farm by cavalryman William W. Blackford. "For God's sake, give me some," cried Ewell, his eyes dancing in happy anticipation of the cool draught. Blackford shook the empty vessel and explained that it was all gone. If the general would detail an orderly to accompany him, though, he would go get some more. Ewell jumped at the offer, proclaiming the elixir "a delicacy not to be despised on such an evening by the commander-in-chief himself."

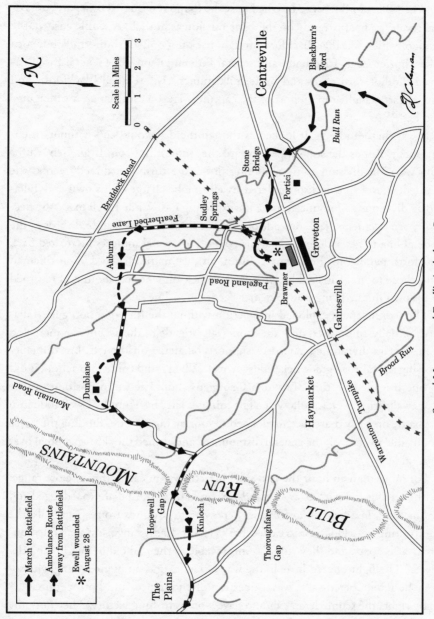

Second Manassas and Ewell's Ambulance Route

When Blackford returned to the house, he found it occupied by a party of Federal cavalrymen, apparently on the same mission as himself. A scuffle ensued, the result of which was that Blackford brought back not only the buttermilk but corn cakes, butter, eggs, fried ham, and several Federal prisoners. "General Ewell enjoyed the hot corn cakes and buttermilk immensely," recalled Blackford, "and had a hearty laugh at my report of the capture. 'Trust a cavalryman for foraging,' said he."[27]

It was then 6:00 P.M. It looked as though the day would end without an engagement. But as the sun dipped toward the western horizon, Brig. Gen. Rufus King's Union division came marching down the turnpike, directly across the Confederates' front. Jackson ordered Ewell to take charge of his own and Taliaferro's divisions and pounce on the unsuspecting foe. While Ewell made the necessary arrangements, Jackson rode out alone to within a few hundred yards of the Federal line to get a closer look at his target. For several minutes he trotted back and forth parallel to the enemy column, an easy mark for any Union rifleman who chose to fire. Satisfied by what he saw, Jackson wheeled about and returned to his own lines. "Bring out your men, gentlemen!" he said.[28]

The Confederates exploded into action with all the fury of a pop gun. Taliaferro initially committed only the Stonewall Brigade to the assault—a mere 800 men. Ewell's division advanced to support Taliaferro on the left, but difficulty crossing the railroad grade delayed its arrival. When it did come into action, it did so one brigade at a time. Lawton's Georgians shouldered into position on the Stonewall Brigade's left, followed a few minutes later by Trimble. Ewell rode into the battle on a bay mare recently loaned to him by Lige White. Finding the horse impossible to control, the general dismounted and turned the skittish animal over to an aide.[29]

For more than an hour the two sides blazed away at each other at close range, neither giving an inch. "It was a stand-up combat," wrote Taliaferro, "dogged and unflinching, in a field almost bare. There were no wounds from spent balls; the confronting lines looked into each other's faces at deadly range, less than one hundred yards apart, and they stood as immovable as the painted heroes in a battle-piece." The fight offered little in the way of tactics and no maneuvering whatsoever, he remembered—"It was a question of endurance, and both endured."[30]

By rights the Confederates should have won a crushing victory. They not only had the advantage of numbers but of surprise. Moreover, they were experienced fighters, whereas most of King's men were not. But the Confederates mismanaged the battle. They failed to attack promptly and to use their advantage in numbers to outflank the Federal line.[31]

Ewell's injury early in the confrontation contributed to the poor result. During the fight Union soldiers in the Sixth Wisconsin Infantry began peppering Trimble's Twelfth Georgia Regiment from the shelter of a wooded ravine beyond the Confederate left. Ewell determined to flush the enemy from cover and led a regiment (possibly the Thirty-first Georgia) into the rocky defile.[32] One of Lawton's men recognized the general and sang out, "Here is General Ewell, boys!" As if responding to the cry, a small party of Federals opened fire on Ewell from the left. The general had dropped to his left knee in an effort to see beneath the low pines surrounding him when the Federals pulled their triggers. A bullet pierced the joint from the top, shattering the patella and the head of the tibia before lodging in the muscles of his calf. Some soldiers of the Fifteenth Alabama, seeing the general fall, stopped firing and offered to carry him to the rear, but Ewell would have none of it. "Put me down, and give them hell!" he reputedly snarled. "I'm no better than any other wounded soldier, to stay on the field."[33]

Campbell Brown was among the first to reach the general. Returning from an errand, he found his chief lying in a small opening among the pines "quite conscious, but in considerable pain." Two badly wounded soldiers lay nearby. Brown hurried off to find a surgeon and to notify Trimble that he now commanded the division. Ewell's two companions meanwhile cried out for help until a litter arrived. Disregarding their own suffering, they insisted that the general be moved first. Ewell appreciated their kindness, but he believed himself too badly injured to be moved. He ordered the litter-bearers to take the other soldiers away and to send back surgeons to operate on his leg.[34]

The physicians arrived a short time later to examine his wound. They concluded that Ewell could be moved safely and even expressed hope that his mangled limb could be saved. The general did not agree. He adamantly insisted that they amputate his leg before moving him. Jubal Early got him to change his mind. Early reached the front shortly before 9:00 P.M. and found his superior lying "on a pile of rocks in advance of his position." Ewell repeated his objections to being moved, but Early persuaded him otherwise.[35] Summoning a few soldiers of the Fifty-eighth Virginia to act as litter-bearers, he had his friend carried to a field hospital a few hundred yards to the rear. Fatigue overcame Ewell, and he fell asleep during the journey. Before dawn attendants carried him to a second field hospital at a house just below Sudley Ford.[36]

Dr. Hunter McGuire, the corps' medical director, reached Ewell late that night. "He was still laboring under the severe shock of the injury when I found him although several hours had elapsed," reported McGuire. "In all gunshot wounds of the knee the shock of the injury is severe, but it was especially great in this instance. The General's health, naturally not very good, was unusually bad at this time. He had also lost a great deal of sleep, and the night he was hurt was compelled to drink a large quantity of strong tea to keep awake."[37]

Ewell rested near Sudley Ford until 8:00 A.M., 29 August, when Pope bent back the left end of the Confederate line and began dropping shells near the hospital. It became too dangerous for Ewell to remain where he was, so members of White's battalion carried him to Arris Buckner's house, "Auburn," nearly four miles behind the lines. Past differences with the general were forgotten as Capt. Frank Myers and his friends bore the crippled figure to the rear. Despite many rebukes they had incurred at Ewell's hands, Myers and the men of his company considered the general "the best friend, of influence, they had in the army" and regretted his injury.[38]

Surgeons removed Ewell's left leg above the knee at 2:00 P.M. that afternoon. In contrast to his attitude the previous evening, Ewell initially opposed the operation, having been informed by one physician that the limb could be saved. "Tell the —— doctor that I'll be —— if it shall be cut off, and that these are the last words of Ewell," he supposedly swore in a moment of passion.[39] Ultimately reason prevailed, however, and the operation took place as planned. McGuire performed the surgery, assisted by the chief medical officer of Ewell's division, Dr. Samuel B. Morrison, and Dr. William A. Robertson of the Sixth Louisiana Infantry. McGuire amputated the leg just above the knee, working as rapidly as possible in order to minimize the loss of blood. Throughout the operation Ewell muttered orders to troops and spoke hurriedly of their movements. He seemed unconscious of pain until McGuire sawed into the bone, when he threw up his arms and groaned, "Oh, My God!"[40]

To remove any doubt that the amputation had been necessary, Robertson took Campbell Brown aside after the operation and in his presence cut open the amputated limb along the track of the bullet. "When the leg was opened," remembered Brown, "we found the knee-cap split half in two, the head of the tibia knocked into several pieces, & that the ball had followed the marrow of the bone for six inches breaking the bone itself into small splinters, & finally had split into two pieces on a sharp edge of bone. These pieces I took out & gave to my Mother, but have always avoided letting the Gen'l know that I had them." Brown and a servant, John Frame, wrapped the bloody limb in an oil cloth and buried it in a corner of Buckner's garden.[41]

For several hours Ewell teetered between life and death. His pulse was weak, at times hardly perceptible. McGuire and other surgeons familiar with his case expected him to die—"a great loss," thought one. At McGuire's instructions Camp-

Dunblane, the home of Dr. Jesse Ewell, where General Ewell was taken following the amputation of his leg (Alice M. Ewell, Virginia Scene)

bell Brown stayed at the general's bedside, administering brandy and water to him every fifteen minutes until his pulse rose. Brown took care not to nauseate the patient or let him fall asleep. Around midnight, a reaction took place. When Morrison examined the general a few hours later, he found Ewell's condition decidedly better, being "pretty well over the first danger from weakness, & in a good condition to encounter the remaining ordinary dangers from amputation."[42]

The general rested at Auburn for a week or more, then was borne by litter six miles to "Dunblane," the home of his cousin Dr. Jesse Ewell. Jesse had lived at Stony Lonesome as a boy and regarded Dick as a brother. He had urged his cousin to come to Dunblane earlier in the week, but the general had then been too weak to stand the journey. But now that the Confederate army was marching into Maryland, leaving northern Virginia vulnerable to Federal forays, it was too dangerous for the general to remain where he was. He gratefully accepted his cousin's invitation.[43]

Overnight Dunblane took on the appearance of a military camp. Foot soldiers pitched tents on the lawn, while mounted troops made camp at Ewell's Chapel, a small sanctuary located at the head of the plantation's half-mile-long drive. "We felt as if all were living at important headquarters," wrote one of the general's female relatives, "and were glad, almost happy. With so many brave hearts and good swords around us we felt safe."[44]

The general stayed in the main house. With him were Dr. Morrison, Campbell Brown, Capt. William F. Randolph of the Thirty-ninth Battalion Virginia Cavalry, and possibly other officers. Mrs. Ewell had placed a large canopied bed in the parlor for her kinsman's use. The parlor entrance was on the left side of the narrow center hall, next to the front door. The men carrying the litter found it impossible to negotiate the sharp left turn into the parlor, but Mrs. Ewell thought of a solution. The hallway ran directly into a spacious room located at the west end of the structure. That room connected to one in the northwest corner of the house, which in turn led to one in the northeast corner, directly across the hallway from the parlor. By going down the hallway into the west room, then making three successive right turns, Ewell's attendants could carry him into the parlor without removing him from the litter.[45]

Family members watched as the soldiers carefully slid their human burden through the narrow passageways. In addition to Mrs. Ewell, a thirty-year-old daughter, Eleanor; a nine-year-old grandson, Jesse; and a two-and-one-half-year-old granddaughter, Alice, lived at the house.[46] "I remember well the maimed figure on the litter, covered with a sheet, and the pale haggard face upon the pillow," wrote Eleanor. "The keen blue eyes were, however, wide open, and seemed to note everything. He spoke not a word, but one had an impression that nothing said or done escaped him." Once the soldiers got General Ewell into the parlor, another problem developed. The bed that Mrs. Ewell had selected for her guest was too big and had to be replaced by the general's own camp bed. While the soldiers made the switch, Mrs. Ewell pulled back the curtains and threw open the windows to let fresh air into the room.[47]

The short journey to Dunblane exhausted the general. For days anxious relatives whispered that he might not survive. But thanks to Dr. Morrison's care and the affectionate nursing of Dr. Ewell's family, his strength increased and he appeared to be out of danger. "All grew more hopeful and cheerful," wrote Eleanor.[48] The general himself attributed his recovery in some measure to grapes and other fruit sent to him by Mrs. George Carter of Loudoun County. Ewell had sent for the fruit shortly after his arrival at Dunblane and washed it down with Richard Cunningham's vintage 1837 Madeira wine. Cunningham had given Ewell several bottles of the wine as a gift in February. Ewell had sent the bottles to Richmond for safekeeping and notified Cunningham that they were there, in case he wished to fetch them. The owner did not reply to the letter, though, and made no effort to retrieve the wine. Since Cunningham had originally presented the bottles to him as a gift, Ewell now sent for them and "used them with great benefit."[49]

The general received excellent care at Dunblane. Dr. Morrison and Mrs. Ewell attended to his needs throughout the day, and Dr. Ewell looked in on him each morning and evening. General Ewell's black valet, John Frame, served him meals. Even Friday had a job to do. The Pueblo boy had the task of fanning his master, wrote Eleanor, but once out of doors, he again became "the little wild 'Injun.' His daring feats of horsemanship, riding without saddle or bridle with arms extended and sometimes standing upright, were the marvel and admiration of our colored people. One evening while at tea I felt my foot twitched under the table and looked down to behold Friday thus impishly amusing himself; but this was an Indian Brave who inspired no fear even when he later crept out." [50]

When not amazing the slaves with his horsemanship or pulling at ladies' toes, Friday probably spent time with nine-year-old Jesse Ewell. Jesse's mother had died earlier, and the boy was being reared by his grandparents at Dunblane. Ewell took such a liking to the lad that he later left him $1,000 in his will. Dr. Ewell put the money toward the boy's "professional education & equipment." [51]

Ewell had plenty of company at Dunblane. Stony Lonesome was less than ten miles away, and as news of his whereabouts spread, friends and neighbors dropped in to pay their respects. Among his visitors were his childhood physician, Dr. Arrel Marsteller, and a member of Congress, Jeremiah Morton. From across Bull Run Mountain came Alfred Randolph, a future bishop of Virginia, and Edward Carter Turner of "Kinloch." Turner noted in his diary under 10 September, "The General seems quite feeble but does not complain of pain. He thinks himself better. God grant that this truly good man may recover." [52]

A few days after Ewell reached Dunblane, his brothers joined him. Ben and William found Dick "slowly convalescing and in fair spirits." Ben had been colonel of the Thirty-second Virginia earlier in the war and would soon become Joe Johnston's chief of staff. William started the war as chaplain of the Eighteenth Virginia, but he had recently transferred to the Fifty-eighth Virginia, a regiment in Dick's division. [53] The two brothers entertained the patient with conversation and novels, while Campbell Brown read him letters from Lizinka, Hattie, and Rebecca Ewell. [54]

With his family and friends at his side, Ewell's days at Dunblane passed peacefully. His health improved steadily. After just two weeks, three of the six ligatures applied to his arteries fell away and the others showed signs of following suit. Ewell still remained weak, though, and any movement of his leg caused him great pain. But he did not grumble. Indeed his patience and thoughtfulness toward others earned him the family's abiding love and respect. "He impressed us all as not only heroic and strong but as having the nicest consideration for others," wrote one of the ladies. "Though so ill, he was one day overheard reproving his future stepson for carelessly throwing away some waste paper that 'might give trouble to the ladies of the family.'"[55]

The sound of artillery fire reverberating from Antietam Creek, thirty miles away, shattered the plantation's tranquility on 17 September. Ewell seemed unusually excited by the noise and fidgeted in his bed. When asked why, he replied that "he could not listen to the sounds of the battle without fearing the loss of General Jackson, believing his preservation important and necessary to the success of the Confederate cause."[56] For the rest of the day Ewell fretted about Jackson's safety; by evening he would have cause to worry about his own.

CHAPTER 18

A Funeral and a Promotion

The sound of distant cannonfire from Antietam battlefield had not yet subsided on 17 September 1862 when a neighbor, George Belt, brought the Dunblane residents news that Union cavalry was in the area searching for General Ewell. "By George, Dick must be taken away from here!" Ben Ewell exclaimed. Someone suggested that General Ewell's escort defend the house, but Ben disagreed. "Oh, no!" he answered, "It would not do to risk a battle here." The general had to be taken across the mountains without delay.[1]

At first Ewell objected. He was still weak, and any movement to his stump pained him greatly. But the prospect of being taken prisoner was more distressing than the discomfort of traveling, and at length he consented. Throughout the night the house hummed with activity as soldiers and servants prepared for an early departure. They struck tents at dawn. After a hasty breakfast the general and his party headed west, up the slope of Bull Run Mountain. Eleanor Ewell remembered the departure: "The General was lifted again from bed to litter, and borne from the house in the same roundabout way by which he entered it. The men moved quickly with grave faces, realizing the importance of this new journey. There was no time for final leave-takings. Only my mother followed the litter a few steps from the door and silently pressed the hand that lay on the sheet." [2]

As the general was leaving, Dr. Jesse Ewell gave him a straight, short sword encased in a black leather scabbard. It had belonged to their grandfather Jesse Ewell, who had worn it in the American Revolution. The general accepted the cherished gift with thanks. He carried it with him for the rest of the war.[3]

With that the men scattered. General Ewell and his entourage headed up the mountain, Ben rode toward Richmond, and Dr. Ewell started on his daily medical rounds. William Stoddert remained inside the house until the general was gone, for he did not wish to see which way his brother went. When asked why, the honest chaplain remarked, "Oh, when I go from here I may have questions asked me, and I can say truly, 'I don't know.'" After the other soldiers were out of sight, he, too, departed, traveling by a road different from that taken by his brother. For the first time in two weeks Dunblane was quiet, even dull. "We missed the clever table talk of Colonel Ben Ewell and the Parson," wrote one of the women. "We missed the lighthearted sallies of Captain Brown, a great favorite with children as well as elders. We missed all these pleasant things, but worst of all we missed the man whose fortitude and patient endurance had drawn our hearts to him."[4]

On leaving Dunblane Dick Ewell's entourage struck the Mountain Road and followed that shady and secluded byway south along the lower slope of Bull Run Mountain to Hopewell Gap. There the party crossed the ridge and headed for Edward Turner's home, Kinloch.[5] A headquarters guard of twelve men carried the general in a litter on their shoulders by turns, four at a time, while someone walked at the wounded man's side with an umbrella to shade his face. As the litter neared the mountain summit, a woman cried out from a house, "Is it a dead man that you are taking away?" Gamely the supposed corpse replied, "Not dead yet." When the party reached the top of the mountain, a private named Fox went back to Dunblane to retrieve some forgotten gear. Ominously, he never returned. The others pressed on, reaching Kinloch in time for dinner.[6]

The journey over the mountain fatigued Ewell considerably, but there was no time to rest. At 10:00 P.M. a messenger brought news that Union cavalry was at Thoroughfare Gap, having come from the direction of Dunblane. Fox's failure to return added credence to the report. Ewell became visibly anxious, as well he might. Capture, in his feeble condition, would be tantamount to death. Despite the danger to his health, he determined to push on at first light.[7]

In the morning Ewell's attendants carried him west to Salem in an effort to outdistance their pursuers, unaware that the Federals had lost the scent and had turned north toward Aldie. At Salem the Confederates turned left and passed through Rixeyville. They stopped for the night at the home of an eccentric inventor named Ruhl outside town, then pushed on to Culpeper Court House. Boarding a train there, Ewell traveled to Charlottesville, where for several days he was the guest of Capt. Thomas L. Farish.

The journey from Dunblane to Charlottesville nearly did the general in. At some point the femur of his truncated limb poked through the stump, causing the wound to slough. Doctors had to remove another inch of bone.[8] When Ewell was again well enough to travel, he took the Virginia Central Railroad to Millborough Springs, a resort tucked away in the Allegheny Mountains thirty miles southwest of Staunton. Braced by the cool mountain air and fortified by the spring's healing waters, he began the slow road to recovery.[9]

Family members flocked to the injured man's side. William Stoddert came from Dunblane; Lizzie Ewell took the train from Richmond, while Lizinka and her daughter, Hattie, rushed up from Alabama. Before leaving Alabama, Lizinka wrote to the general, assuring him of her continued affection. "Dear Richard while I sympathize in your terrible suffering & loss it is only womanly to remember that one of its consequences will be to oblige you to remain at home & make me more necessary to you & another is that whereas I thought before you ought to marry & could very well marry a younger woman, now I will suit you better than any one else, if only because I will love you better."[10]

Tom Turner was the last member of Ewell's party to appear at Millborough Springs. Turner had stayed with the army after Ewell's wounding, briefly serving as a volunteer on Jeb Stuart's staff. The adventuresome aide joined Ewell at Millborough Springs only after learning that Hattie was there. Some whispered that the young couple was in love.[11]

By November Ewell was well enough to go to Richmond. Dr. Francis W. Hancock and Benjamin Ewell came to Millborough to take the general away. Hancock had been the chief medical officer of Ewell's division earlier in the year, but he had been forced to resign his post after injuring his leg in the Valley. He then took charge of Stock House Hospital in Hanover County. By year's end he had transferred to General Hospital #18 in Richmond.[12]

Ewell traveled to the capital on the Virginia Central Railroad, arriving around 17 November 1862. Rather than place the general in a hospital, Hancock kindly invited him to stay at his house at 306 East Main Street. He and his wife did everything in their power to make Ewell's stay pleasant, even going so far as to provide a room for Lizinka and Hattie.[13]

Lizinka became the "guardian" of her fiancé's "hearth and spirits." Visitors who came to see the general invariably found her "watching over him with sleepless vigilance, and cheering him up by hopeful and recreative converse."[14] Under her care the patient became stronger. By the end of the year he was taking short walks on crutches. But then came a setback. On Christmas Day 1862 he fell on a patch of icy pavement, knocking a piece of bone off the stump of his leg and reopening his wound. The accident set his recovery back at least two months.[15]

Ewell's stubbornness in refusing help from others contributed to the accident. Hancock warned Ben that if the general did not change his ways, another mishap might occur. "It is strange how an indisposition to have people stirring around you or helping you in case of sickness, even when unable to help one's self, runs in families," Ben told his daughter. "It is worse than folly though to carry it to the extreme your Uncle Dick does. If he does not exhibit more discretion," he asserted, "it will be proper to have a good and respectable wet nurse who is in the habit of having her own way" take charge of him.[16]

For the rest of the winter Ewell remained bedridden waiting for his leg to heal. While this would be trying for anyone, it was especially hard for a man of Ewell's nervous, active disposition. Company helped pass the time. Maj. Gen. Gustavus W. Smith visited in January 1863, and Lt. Gen. E. Kirby Smith dropped by a couple of weeks later. Ewell's most notable visitor, though, was Maj. Gen. Sterling Price. Ewell greatly admired the western general. When he learned that Price was in Richmond, he invited the general to come see him. Price accepted, and the two men had an agreeable meeting in Ewell's sickroom. A person present at the meeting long remembered "the hearty interchange of affection and respect" between the two men.[17]

Constance Cary came to see Ewell several times during his convalescence. Early in 1863 the Richmond belle received permission to visit Washington, D.C. Brig. Gen. Alexander Hays personally accompanied her back to Confederate lines. When Hays mentioned that he and Ewell had been friends in the Old Army, Cary informed him that Ewell had lost his leg and asked if Hays had any message for him. "Give my best love to good old Dick," replied the Union general with a laugh, "and tell him I wish it had been his head."[18]

While Ewell was convalescing in Richmond, his religious faith became noticeably stronger. Some traced his spiritual renewal to an episode in the Shenandoah Valley Campaign involving Stonewall Jackson. According to Judith McGuire, who supposedly got the story from Ewell himself, Ewell walked over to Jackson's tent the night before a battle. He was about to go inside, when the sound of Jackson praying aloud for guidance caused him to pause. Ewell later remarked "that he had never before heard a prayer so devout and beautiful; he then, for the first time, felt the desire to be a Christian. He retired to his tent quietly, without disturbing General J., feeling assured that all would be well."[19]

The Reverend Moses Drury Hoge played a more direct role in Ewell's spiritual resurgence. A close friend of the family, Hoge took an active interest in Ewell's spiritual welfare and visited him frequently during his convalescence. He persuaded Ewell to stop swearing and more than any other clergyman seems to have led Ewell to Christ.[20]

The most immediate effect of Ewell's renewed faith was a change in his language. After accepting Christ, Ewell gave up swearing. During his years in the Old

Stonewall Jackson had a major influence on Ewell's religious transformation.
Having personally witnessed the efficacy of Jackson's prayers, Ewell is said to have remarked,
"If this is religion, I must have it." (John William Jones, Christ in the Camp*)*

Army, he had developed that vice into an art. A man who met Ewell in the 1850s wrote that he "could swear the scalp off an Apache." Even as late as 1862 he was said to curse "in a style that defies description." But at Hoge's and Lizinka's gentle urging Ewell bridled his tongue. Campbell Brown claimed that he only heard his chief swear twice, "once to a stupid courier, and once to a man who was riding his horse cruelly," and aide James Power Smith affirmed that he never once heard the general utter an oath. On the contrary, wrote Smith, he knew Ewell to be "a Christian gentleman, reverent, devout, and free from the habit of profanity."[21]

Ewell's troops believed that to be the case. "It was generally understood in the army that General Ewell never swore after he became a Christian," the Reverend W. M. Dame told Hattie after the war, "and we had a greatly added respect for his character on this account, for we knew that aforetimes he did not confine himself to the dull neutralities of undecorated speech, and it took a strong manhood, backed by the grace of God to overcome that fixed habit." The only exception, as far as Dame knew, was when General Ewell dropped a burning coal on his bare foot. On that occasion, Dame admitted, Ewell did let a single expletive slip. Even so, the minister did not find fault. "I am sure the recording angel considered the circumstances and gave him credit, and a good deal of it, for restraining himself to *one*."[22]

Ewell exchanged several letters with Jubal Early during his convalescence. Early had taken command of Ewell's division after his wounding. On the surface the two men seemed very much alike, both being rather gruff with a sense of humor. In other respects they were quite different. Early was ambitious, critical, and outspoken to the point of insubordination. Under certain circumstances he could be devious and malevolent. Ewell, on the other hand, was a modest, charitable man who hesitated to impose his views on others even when he knew that he was right. Unlike Early, he was without guile.

John Cheves Haskell knew both men well. He described Ewell as "a queer character, very eccentric, but upright, brave and devoted. He had no very high talent but did all that a brave man of moderate capacity could. Early, who was his subordinate and successor, was as queer and a brave man of more ability than Ewell, but not near so good a soldier." Although Ewell's judgment and military instincts were superior to Early's, he lacked confidence in himself and often sought the advice of others whose judgment was inferior to his own. Early, on the other hand, exuded self-confidence. He had a stronger personality than Ewell and expressed his views forcefully. As time went on, Ewell came to rely heavily—perhaps too heavily—on his judgment.[23]

James A. Walker (Library of Congress)

Twice Early wrote to Ewell describing the performance of the division at Sharpsburg. In both letters he complained that he and Col. James A. Walker had been passed over for promotion. Ewell promised to speak to President Davis on Early's behalf. A few days later Early received his promotion. Ewell was lying in bed when the news arrived. Unable to rise, he expressed his satisfaction by enthusiastically waving an object about his head. He wrote to Early congratulating him "on your long-merited, and long delayed promotion. My only regret," he said, "is that I had nothing to do with it except talking." [24]

As a major general Early continued to press for Walker's advancement. On 23 January 1863 he again wrote to Ewell urging him to put in a good word for the colonel. Ewell wrote to the adjutant and inspector general later that week recommending that Walker be made a brigadier general. He urged Arnold Elzey to do likewise. It was one of the few times that Ewell had ventured to recommend a subordinate, a fact that he took care to point out in his letter. [25]

Isaac Trimble also sought Ewell's recommendation. Trimble was a splendid combat officer, but he was headstrong and undisciplined. He was also excessively ambitious. After the march to Bristoe Station on 26 August 1862, he had volunteered to push his fagged troops several miles farther in order to capture the Union army supply depot at Manassas Junction. Jackson pronounced the achievement the most brilliant he had witnessed during the war, and on 22 September he recommended that Trimble be bumped up to major general.

Unaware of Jackson's actions or perhaps hoping to augment them, Trimble wrote to Ewell late in the year brazenly asking that his former chief recommend him for promotion. The letter accompanied his report of the Seven Days Campaign. "I beg you to pardon any allusion to my own conduct," he added with a flourish of ill-disguised flattery, "in saying that I *do covet* your favorable opinion so far, as to be gratified with a recommendation for promotion from *you*." A promotion would be a matter of simple justice, he explained. After all, Dick Taylor had been promoted to major general based on a single battle. It was only fair that he, Trimble, be recognized for services on *two* fields: Cross Keys and Gaines's Mill. "You are the only one cognizant of the part I took in them," he told Ewell, "& from you alone can I expect or care for any notice that I may desire, & whether promoted or not I desire for my children any favorable notice I may deserve from my *immediate commander*."

Trimble's battle reports frequently contained criticisms of superiors, but his report of Gaines's Mill contained nothing but praise for Ewell—a transparent effort by Trimble to ingratiate himself with his former chief. Ewell took no action on Trimble's behalf, but the Marylander got his promotion anyhow. He was appointed major general on 23 December 1862 on the strength of Jackson's recommendation and was assigned to command Stonewall's former division. [26]

Advancement seemed to be on every officer's mind that winter. In a letter written to Ewell in March 1863, Robert Rodes weighed his chances for promotion to major general. One vacancy remained open—the command of D. H. Hill's old division—but as Rodes saw it, that slot would probably go to Brig. Gen. Cadmus M. Wilcox. "As he is a West Point man he will beat me almost to a certainty," wrote Rodes. "I would prefer being beaten by a baboon but will submit to it quietly, unless they place [him] in command of this Div."

Rodes hoped that the War Department would assign Ewell command of D. H. Hill's division, presuming that Ewell was not promoted. "The whole Division I doubt not would be delighted to have you as their commander," Rodes assured his former chief. "Do not then hesitate to avail yourself of every means of procuring this result, and be assured that I will be personally gratified to be under your command again. . . . Between you and others spoken of in connection with the position, Genls. Jackson and Lee would not hesitate a moment in deciding in your favor, and believing that, I should be annoyed to find even myself baulking their wishes." 27

As spring approached, Ewell began to ponder his future in the army. His leg was healing, albeit slowly. The Christmas mishap had retarded his recovery, and it was mid-February before he was able to sit up. March brought improvement. By the end of the month his stump had nearly healed, and he was able to take short rides in a carriage. Ewell still tired easily, though, and was unable to use a wooden leg, much less ride a horse. He estimated that it would be another two months before he could take the field. He hoped that the war would be over by then, but clearly that was not going to happen. And as long as there was fighting to do, Ewell wanted to be part of it. "I don't want to see the carnage & shocking sights of another field of battle," he told Early, "tho I prefer being in the field to any where else so long as the war is going on." 28

Where would he go? Early now commanded his division. Even though "Old Jube" courteously offered to relinquish command to Ewell "when you get your leg spliced," this was clearly out of the question. Ewell professed not to care what his next assignment was. "When I am fit for duty they may do what they please with me," he told Early with something of a martyr's tone. "I won[']t ask for any particular duty or station, but let them do as they see proper with me." For a while it looked as though he might be sent to Tennessee. Joe Johnston was looking for someone to command Confederate forces in the eastern part of the state, and Ewell seemed a likely candidate for the job. The former dragoon did not feel up to an independent command, however, and he said as much to Ben, who was now Johnston's chief of staff. Perhaps for that reason Johnston did not offer it to him.29

What Ewell really wanted was to return to the Army of Northern Virginia. Forgetting his vow not to lobby for any particular position, he wrote Jackson in early April informing him that he would soon be well enough to return to duty. He requested assignment to the Second Corps, hoping perhaps to get D. H. Hill's division, which had been without a permanent commander since January. "I have offered my services to resume duty in the field professing my willingness to take a small division in view of my short comings in the way of legs," he later told Beauregard.

Jackson was gratified by Ewell's desire to return to the corps. Writing through his adjutant, Lt. Col. Charles J. Faulkner, Jackson told Ewell that he wanted him back, but he urged his fellow Virginian not to return until his limb had healed. In a personal postscript Faulkner added, "I know of no event that would confer more pleasure upon the 2d corps than your return to the service. As a Brigadier General remarked a few days ago hundreds of gallant soldiers would compete for the honor of carrying you in an appropriate chair from post to post, if your disabled limb did not permit you to resume your seat in the saddle." [30]

That day was fast approaching, but meanwhile time wore heavily on Ewell's hands. On 6 March, at Jackson's request, Ewell wrote his report of the battle of Cedar Mountain, in which he took pains to commend both Early and Walker. He had written the report some time earlier but had misplaced it and had to draft another at the last minute. "It is hastily drawn up and is very barren," he explained to Early in almost apologetic tones, "merely giving the shortest possible notice of events. You may find it worth your time to read over my report & make any correction you may see fit." [31]

Ewell was well enough to get about on crutches, but except for sitting on a court of inquiry, he lived "an idle life." He gradually resumed riding—first in a carriage, then on horseback—and occasionally he dined out. On 2 April a mob composed principally of women rioted in Richmond to protest the scarcity of food. Jefferson Davis had to bring in troops to disperse the rioters. A month later Maj. Gen. George Stoneman led Union horsemen in a raid through central Virginia. Again troops were summoned to defend the city. So far as is known, Ewell did not take an active part in either disturbance. [32]

Stoneman's Raid took place in conjunction with the Army of the Potomac's 1863 spring offensive. On 30 April the Federals crossed the Rappahannock River above Fredericksburg and engaged Lee at Chancellorsville. Lee defeated the Northern host but lost Jackson, who died on 10 May after accidentally being shot by his own men.

Stonewall's corpse arrived in Richmond on 11 May. The next day a horse-drawn hearse bore his casket through the streets of Richmond to the capitol. Ewell, Longstreet, Elzey, Garnett, and George Pickett acted as honorary pallbearers. "I never saw human faces show such grief—almost despair," Hattie recalled as she watched the officers file past.[33] Jackson's casket lay in state for the remainder of the day before starting for Lexington on 13 May. According to later accounts Ewell accompanied Jackson's corpse from Richmond to Lexington, but contemporary sources do not bear that out.[34]

Jackson's death prompted Lee to reorganize the Army of Northern Virginia's infantry into three corps. Longstreet retained command of the First Corps. As for the other two, Lee recommended that Ewell take over Jackson's Second Corps and A. P. Hill head the newly created Third Corps. "The former is an honest, brave soldier, who has always done his duty well," Lee wrote Jefferson Davis. "The latter I think upon the whole is the best soldier of his grade with me. . . . I believe the efficiency of the corps would be promoted by being commanded by lt genls, & I do not know where to get better men than those I have named." Davis approved Lee's suggestion. On 23 May 1863 Adj. Gen. Samuel Cooper announced Ewell's and Hill's promotions to lieutenant general. The order placed Ewell's name before Hill's. Ewell thus became the third-ranking officer in the army, after Lee and Longstreet.[35]

Few questioned Ewell's selection to command the Second Corps. He was the ranking major general in the army, his record as a division commander had been close to flawless, and he was well liked and respected in the army. Moreover, he had been a member of the Second Corps and had been wounded in combat. Jackson's deathbed wish that Ewell succeed him in command of the corps clinched his claim.[36]

The soldiers of the Second Corps widely hailed Ewell's appointment. An officer from Trimble's old brigade testified that Ewell "was Jackson's first lieutenant and ranked next to him in popularity," while a sergeant in the Louisiana Brigade wrote that Ewell "was the choice of all the soldiers as well as the officers." "Ewell is the man of all others to put in [Jackson's] place," agreed a captain in the Stonewall Brigade, "though no man can fill it." Maj. Henry McDaniel of Georgia thought the new corps commander would fill Jackson's shoes just fine. "Ewell is considered as Jackson's equal, even in dash, and by many persons as his superior in ability," he wrote. "I am satisfied that he will sustain himself and the reputation of the army."[37]

Ewell accepted the appointment without comment and prepared to join his command. He should have waited a few more months. Although he was able to hobble about on his false leg and could ride a horse for short periods of time, his health was still fragile.[38] But with the army ready to embark on a new campaign, he could not delay. Ewell summoned members of his staff and prepared to travel to Fredericksburg. After being sidelined for nine months, he was going back into action.

CHAPTER 19

The Idol of His Corps

Before returning to the army, Dick Ewell took Lizinka as his wife. He had loved his attractive cousin since his teenage years when she had visited his family at Stony Lonesome. He had proposed to her then, it was rumored, but she had rejected his suit and married another. After that Ewell never had a serious relationship with any woman. It looked as if he would live out his life a bachelor. Lizinka's first husband, Percy Brown, died in 1844, however, and some years later she opened correspondence with Ewell, who by then was a captain in the dragoons. The two fell in love a few years later during Lizinka's visit to the Confederate army, and on 1 December 1861 he again asked for her hand in marriage. This time she accepted. The couple set no date for the ceremony, and Lizinka went to reside with relatives in Alabama. After Groveton she rushed back to Virginia to care for her injured fiancé and for eight months patiently nursed him to health.

As he improved, Ewell gave serious thought to their union. Should he defer marriage until the war ended? he asked Ben, or having secured Lizinka's approval, plunge into matrimony at once? Ben replied that women were uncertain creatures. Therefore all men "proposing to envelop themselves in the noose . . . ought to go in without delay, & have the knot tied." He gave this advice, he told his daughter, because he feared that if Dick did not marry right away, he might "fall back on some of his old habits—hard swearing, and drinking." The answer so pleased the general, Ben recalled, that "in an unusual fit of generosity he insisted on my taking his shawl, and various other articles of clothing, and among others his saddle, and after a delicate hint on the subject," a coat.[1]

Dick and Lizinka put off the nuptials until spring to give the general time to recover from his injury. On 23 May 1863 he was promoted to lieutenant general, and two days later he received orders to "proceed without delay" to Fredericksburg. The issue could not be put off any longer. On 26 May the Reverend Charles Minnigerode performed the wedding at St. Paul's Episcopal Church in

Richmond. President Davis and his wife were among the guests. The general undoubtedly donned his best uniform for the occasion; his bride wore a gray satin dress. For Ewell the wedding had been a long time coming—almost thirty years. As he later remarked to Brig. Gen. William N. Pendleton, he had "served as long as Jacob for his wife."[2]

The marriage posed a potential problem. As a ranking officer in the Confederate army, Ewell's property was subject to seizure by the U.S. government. That made little difference while he was a bachelor, for he had little property of his own. Lizinka, however, had vast holdings in Tennessee, Missouri, and Mississippi, some of which were already under Federal control. The U.S. government might use the marriage as a pretext to confiscate her property. To prevent this the couple signed a prenuptial agreement that excluded Ewell from any claim to his wife's property. A court later recognized the settlement for what it was and in 1872 declared it null and void.[3]

Ewell traveled to Hamilton's Crossing, south of Fredericksburg, by train on 29 May, accompanied by Lizinka, Hattie, and Lizzie. Much of the old Valley Army turned out to greet him. As he stepped from the train, the soldiers gave "an enthusiastic welcome" of three cheers. Ewell reviewed the troops with Lee and Longstreet before establishing his headquarters at Thomas Yerby's house, "Belvoir," less than a mile from the railhead.[4]

Yerby hosted a banquet in the general's honor. Guests included representatives from the areas's finest families. The men dressed in military attire; the ladies wore skirts of silk, lawn, and muslin. Yerby spared no expense to feed his company. On the tables were platters of turkey, ham, chicken, and mutton. From Norfolk came fresh oysters complemented by side dishes of fruit, biscuits, and cake. Beverages included wine, mint juleps, punch, and coffee. While the older folks conversed quietly among themselves, younger guests such as Brig. Gen. Fitz Lee passed the hours in dancing and romance. The excitement lasted through the night and concluded with a breakfast feast at 9:00 the next morning.[5]

Once the festivities ended, it was time to get down to work. For Ewell the first order of business was to assemble a staff. At Lee's suggestion he invited the former members of Stonewall Jackson's staff to stay on. Who knew the workings of the corps better than they? To those men he added a few officers from his own military family and one or two aides new to both groups. The resulting staff was as follows:

Col. Stapleton Crutchfield, Chief of Artillery
Col. Abner Smead, Assistant Adjutant and Inspector General

Lt. Col. Charles J. Faulkner, Assistant Adjutant General
Maj. William Allan, Chief Ordnance Officer
Maj. Benjamin H. Greene, Assistant Adjutant and Inspector General
Maj. Alexander Pendleton, Assistant Adjutant General
Maj. Wells J. Hawks, Chief Commissary Officer
Maj. John A. Harman, Chief Quartermaster
Capt. Henry B. Richardson, Chief Engineer
Capt. Campbell Brown, Assistant Adjutant General
Capt. Richard E. Wilbourn, Chief Signal Officer
Lt. Thomas T. Turner, Aide-de-camp
Surgeon Hunter McGuire, Chief Medical Officer
Jedediah Hotchkiss, Topographical Engineer

Lt. Col. Charles J. Faulkner, a gray-haired man of fifty-seven summers, became chief of staff. Within three weeks he resigned from the army, and the younger and more efficient Sandie Pendleton took his place. Col. John E. Johnson, Lt. Elliott Johnston, and Lt. Robert W. B. Elliott served with Ewell as volunteer aides-de-camp. The Reverend Beverley Tucker Lacy, who had held the position of head-quarters chaplain under Jackson, continued in that capacity under Ewell.[6]

The general was pleased with his staff, and they were pleased with him. "We have our wishes gratified here in having Gen. Ewell to command the old army of Gen. Jackson," Jed Hotchkiss told his wife; "as much of the ardor as could possibly be transferred to any man has been transferred by this Corps to Gen. Ewell." Col. Clement A. Evans of the Thirty-first Georgia confirmed Hotchkiss's statement. "The old confidence in Jackson, has found a new birth in our faith in Ewell," he wrote. "Always a favorite with his division, he is now the idol of his corps."[7]

On 30 May Lee formally reorganized the Army of Northern Virginia into three corps, each comprised of three divisions.[8] Robert Rodes, Jubal Early, and Edward Johnson commanded the three divisions in Ewell's corps. Ewell knew Rodes and Early well. Rodes had commanded a regiment in Ewell's brigade in 1861, and Early had commanded a brigade in his division. Both were brave and efficient officers. Ewell knew Johnson too, but not as well. "Old Allegheny" had graduated from West Point in 1838, two years before Ewell. After serving in the Seminole and Mexican Wars, he became colonel of the Twelfth Virginia Infantry. In May 1862 he was shot in the ankle leading his troops at the battle of McDowell. Since then the rough old soldier had been laid up at Richmond, courting the ladies and waiting for his foot to mend. It did, albeit imperfectly, and in May 1863 he

Edward Johnson (Library of Congress)

returned to the army sporting a cane and a major general's commission. Jackson's division, the most famous in the army, would now be his.

Col. Stapleton Crutchfield was the corps' chief of artillery. Each army corps received five battalions of artillery. Three were attached directly to infantry divisions; the remaining two served as a corps reserve. In the Second Corps Lt. Col.

Hilary P. Jones led the battalion assigned to Early's division, Lt. Col. R. Snowden Andrews commanded Johnson's batteries, and Lt. Col. Thomas H. Carter had charge of the guns assigned to Rodes. Col. J. Thompson Brown and Lt. Col. William Nelson commanded the corps' two reserve battalions. Crutchfield had been seriously wounded at Chancellorsville and had not yet returned to duty. In his absence Colonel Brown acted as the corps' chief of artillery.[9]

Ewell formally took command of the Second Corps on 1 June 1863. That day, at his Mine Road headquarters, Lee disclosed his plan to invade Pennsylvania. He would shift the army to Culpeper Court House, then march into Maryland and Pennsylvania via the Shenandoah Valley, gathering supplies as he went. Ewell's corps would lead the way.[10] Lee probably selected Ewell for this assignment because of his familiarity with the Shenandoah Valley, but he did so with misgivings. Ewell was an excellent officer, but he lacked decision and had an uncertain temper that caused him to be optimistic one moment and pessimistic the next. No one knew this better than Ewell himself. He admitted to Lizinka that he was "provoked excessively with myself at times at my depression of spirits & dismal way of looking at every thing, present & future & may be next day considering the same things as all 'Couleur de rose.'" Lee spoke to Ewell privately about his concerns. Whether his lieutenant would be able to change his behavior remained to be seen.[11]

While Ewell's state of mind was a source of concern to Lee, his physical health was not. On 31 May Lee wrote that his new lieutenant general "looks very well & is very stout of heart." Sandie Pendleton agreed. He told his mother that General Ewell's "health is pretty good now, & he seems quite pleased to get back into the field. He manages his leg very well & walks only with a stick, & mounts his horse quiet easily from the ground." A North Carolina soldier noted that, despite the artificial leg, the general "rides very well."[12] Others held an opposite view. Jed Hotchkiss thought his new chief "looked feebly," and Fredericksburg resident D. H. Gordon noted that Ewell mounted his horse "with great difficulty." Thomas Carter wrote that Ewell seemed "pale and anaemic." Henry Wingfield, a soldier in the Fifty-eighth Virginia, stated flatly that the returning general looked "quite badly."[13]

Spiritually Ewell was as fit as ever. The Sunday after his return to the army he joined Lee, A. P. Hill, William Pendleton, and "a crowd of lesser lights" in attending a worship service conducted by the Reverend Mr. Lacy. Five days later Pendleton (himself a minister) and Bishop John Johns met with Ewell to discuss ways to better proclaim the gospel to the soldiers. They found Ewell receptive to their ideas. As Johns later reported to the Virginia Council, "The interview assured me the more that the good providence and grace of God had prepared the way most invitingly for the extension of the Gospel in the army."[14]

Ewell met with Lee and Longstreet on 2 June to receive his orders for the campaign. Longstreet's corps began leaving Fredericksburg for Culpeper the next day. Ewell was right behind him. Rodes's division broke camp on 4 June, followed by Early and Johnson. Hill was to remain at Fredericksburg until Longstreet and Ewell were well on their way, then hurry after them.[15]

To reach Culpeper, Ewell's divisions marched southwest to Spotsylvania Court House, turned north, and crossed the Orange Plank Road at Verdiersville. From there they continued north, crossing the Rapidan River at Somerville Ford.[16] Ewell himself took a shortcut to Verdiersville, riding directly west over the Orange Plank Road. This reduced his travel and enabled him to see the Chancellorsville battlefield. "I gave Gen. Ewell an account of the fight as we went along," remembered Hotchkiss, "pointing out to him the localities of incidents as we passed—he was much interested & asked many questions—spoke of the fine positions of the enemy & was surprised that they had not held them longer." The night before he left Yerby's, Ewell drafted a will naming Lizinka as his sole beneficiary. Dr. McGuire and Tom Turner signed the document as witnesses.[17]

On 6 June Ewell proceeded to within one-half mile of Raccoon Ford. The next day, after morning prayers by Lacy, Ewell and his staff forded the river and rode upstream to Somerville Ford, where they found Early's troops in the process of crossing. "The troops soon recognized Gen. Ewell & began to cheer him as had been their habit with Gen. Jackson," wrote Hotchkiss, "thus transferring to him the ardor they felt for their old commander. He took off his cap & rode rapidly along the line."[18]

Ewell continued forward at a rapid gait and reached Culpeper Court House at 10:00 A.M., a good ride for a man with an amputated limb. Sandie Pendleton was duly impressed. "The more I see of Gen. Ewell the more I am pleased with him," the young staffer confided to his mother. "He resembles Gen Jackson very much in some points of his character, particularly his utter disregard of his own personal comforts & his inflexibility of purpose. Yesterday he rode some 20 miles on horse-back, often at full speed & exhibited no signs of fatigue last night. He is so thoroughly honest, too," Pendleton continued, "and has only one desire, to conquer the Yankees. I look for great things from him, and am glad to say that our troops have for him a good deal of the same feeling they had towards General Jackson, which must increase very much when they find on trial that he is so good a man."[19]

Ewell made his headquarters at the Cooper house, a deserted building northeast of town on the Rixeyville Road. Rodes's men camped a couple of miles beyond the house; Early and Johnson halted south of the town. The next day the latter two divisions shuffled through Culpeper and took position on the Sperryville Road. Lee gave Ewell a choice of starting his march on 9 June or 10 June. Ewell chose the later date, no doubt wishing to give his men an extra day's rest before making them climb the Blue Ridge.[20]

Jeb Stuart meanwhile staged a cavalry review for Lee and his generals at John Minor Botts's house near Brandy Station. Ewell attended the impressive display and as a former dragoon undoubtedly enjoyed it.[21] The cavalry spectacle that followed was not so pleasant. On 9 June three Union cavalry divisions, supported by a small force of infantry, crossed the Rappahannock River and surprised Stuart's troopers near Brandy Station. Lee ordered Ewell to support Stuart. The commanding general wished to conceal the presence of his infantry from Hooker, however, and directed Ewell to commit his troops only if it was absolutely necessary. In the meantime he was to keep his men out of sight west of Fleetwood Hill.

Rodes reached Brandy Station first. Anticipating Ewell's orders, he had marched toward the field of battle at the first sound of fighting. Ewell halted Rodes's division near the Botts house. He then rode with its commander to the Barbour house, three-quarters of a mile north of the station, to monitor the progress of the fight. Lee joined them there. The battle swayed back and forth in the valley below. At one point it looked as though Union cavalry might sweep past the Barbour house and capture the generals. Rather than surrender, Ewell suggested that they barricade themselves inside the house and defend it to the last. The battle shifted, though, and the danger passed. In the evening the Federals retreated across the river.[22]

The Union probe did not delay the Confederate offensive. Ewell began his march to Pennsylvania on 10 June as scheduled. His initial objective was Winchester, then occupied by Maj. Gen. Robert H. Milroy, a blustering Indiana lawyer with a reputation for bullying civilians. Ewell's sources represented, correctly, that Milroy had between 6,000 and 8,000 men at Winchester and that the town was strongly fortified. Another 1,800 Federals, under Col. Andrew T. McReynolds, occupied Berryville, ten miles east. Ewell would have to dispose of both forces before he could cross the Potomac in safety. While the Second Corps subdued Milroy and McReynolds and entered Maryland, Longstreet would move east of the Blue Ridge, screening Ewell's march. Hill would slip behind Longstreet and follow Ewell down the Valley.[23]

Ewell's corps streamed toward the Valley in two columns. Johnson and Early marched via Sperryville and Little Washington to Gaines's Cross Roads, then moved north through Chester Gap, camping between Front Royal and Cedarville. Rodes reached Gaines's Cross Roads by way of Newby's Cross Roads a few miles farther north. Ewell remained at Culpeper Court House until 11 June, then rode to Gaines's Cross Roads. There he met with Early and Johnson to discuss his plan for capturing Winchester. In anticipation of the coming conflict with Milroy, Ewell issued a general order to the corps reminding it "that discipline & obedience to orders are the means to secure success." He asked the troops "to join with him in asking that Divine aid which was the reliance of our lamented and illustrious chief," the reference of course being to Jackson.[24]

Ewell overtook Rodes the next morning between Flint Hill and Sandy Hook. Rodes climbed into Ewell's carriage and rode with him through Chester Gap to Front Royal. On the way Ewell outlined the plan of campaign to Rodes as he had done with Early and Johnson the night before. North of Front Royal the two forks of the Shenandoah River met. Ewell had ordered a pontoon bridge to meet his corps at the river in case it had flooded past fording. Engineers had delivered the bridge a day early and had thoughtlessly parked it at the water's edge. Had Union informants been looking for evidence of Ewell's approach, they need not have looked very far.[25]

The bridge was not needed. The Shenandoah was low, enabling Ewell's men to wade through the water. Rodes crossed first and proceeded to Cedarville, followed by Johnson. Early's division camped at the rear of the column, straddling the river.[26] Brig. Gen. Albert G. Jenkins camped at Crooked Run, north of the Shenandoah's confluence. Lee had directed Jenkins's 1,600-man cavalry brigade to report to Ewell. It would help him subdue Union forces in the Valley while Brig. Gen. John D. Imboden's cavalry brigade broke the B&O Railroad at various points between Cumberland and Martinsburg, thus preventing reinforcements from reaching Milroy.[27]

At Cedarville Ewell reviewed his strategy with Early, Rodes, and Jenkins. Johnson and Early would assail Milroy at Winchester. Jenkins and Rodes meanwhile would swing east, drive McReynolds from Berryville, and advance on Martinsburg, cutting off Milroy's retreat. Once the Confederates had disposed of the Federals in the lower Valley, Rodes and Jenkins would cross the Potomac River into Maryland to begin gathering supplies for the army. Early and Johnson would follow.[28] The success of the plan depended on coordination and speed. If Milroy got wind of the Confederates' approach, he could mount a stiff defense of Winchester, thereby detaining the Confederate advance down the Valley long enough for the Army of the Potomac to interfere with Lee's advance into Pennsylvania. On the other hand, if the Union general evacuated Winchester and fled to Maryland, he could contest the Confederate army's crossing of the Potomac River. Ewell had to subdue Milroy—and quickly.

By 4:30 A.M., 13 June, Ewell had his divisions marching toward their assigned objectives. Johnson advanced down the Front Royal Road toward Winchester, preceded by a small body of cavalry. At Opequon Creek the horsemen encountered Milroy's pickets and sent them scampering back toward the town. Ewell rode with Johnson at the head of the column. He had given Old Allegheny his orders, and now it was time to step aside. "You are the operator now," he told his stiff-legged subordinate, "I am only a looker on." [29]

Johnson shook out a line of skirmishers and pushed ahead. Two miles outside town, near Buffalo Lick, a Union battery opened fire on the Confederates from a point near the Millwood Road. Carpenter's battery drove off the enemy guns only to draw the fire of a dozen long-range Union cannon closer to the town. One shot struck a stone wall in front of the battery, endangering the Second Virginia Infantry Regiment nearby. Ewell ordered the regiment's colonel to move his troops to a place of safety. A private stepped from the ranks and called the general's attention to a hollow in front of the wall. Ewell saw at once that it was an ideal spot. "He thanked the soldier warmly, complimented his judgment, & made the change at once," remembered Campbell Brown. Although they endured a heavy shelling, not one soldier in the regiment was hurt. Johnson placed the rest of his division in line of battle astride the Front Royal Road, outside the range of Milroy's guns.[30]

Ewell rode over to the Valley Turnpike to check on Early. As ordered, Old Jube had left the Front Royal Road at Nineveh and angled northwest, striking the turnpike at Newtown. A few miles farther on, at Kernstown, the Baltimore Light Artillery dueled with two Union guns posted on Pritchard's Knob, a solitary knoll adjacent to the road. Federal infantry supported the guns and occupied a ridge farther to the left. Gordon's brigade seized the ridge, while Hays flanked the guns on the plain below. At dark the Federals fell back to Bowers Hill on the southern edge of town. Early followed them as far as Abraham's Creek.

Ewell reached the turnpike in time to see Gordon's attack, which he declared to be one of the finest movements he had ever witnessed. He stayed with Early for several hours before returning to his headquarters on the Front Royal Road. By then a heavy rain was falling. Unable to pitch his tent in the downpour, Ewell spent the night under his carriage. Before going to sleep he notified Lee that he had driven Milroy back into the city's defenses, which were stronger than expected.[31]

Milroy's fortifications were indeed formidable. On a range of hills north and west of town the Union general had built a chain of forts armed with twenty-four rifled guns, six of heavy caliber. The Confederates had driven Milroy into his defenses easily enough; driving him out, they realized, would be more difficult. "Consequently," wrote one, "we all began to feel as if we had caught the elephant, but could not tell what to do with it."[32]

The key to the Union defenses was Fort Milroy, also known as the Flagstaff Fort because a large garrison flag flew over it. Two thousand feet west of this fort stood Flint Ridge. The ridge overlooked the fort. Once in Southern hands the ridge would render the fort untenable. Reports indicated that Flint Ridge was undefended, but they were wrong. Ewell viewed the position through his binoculars early on 14 June and discovered that Milroy's forces not only occupied the ridge but had constructed on it a small, open work known as the West Fort. In order to capture the town, he would first have to capture the West Fort.[33]

Ewell rode over to the Valley Pike at 9:00 A.M. to discuss the matter with Early. When he got there, he found that Milroy had abandoned Bowers Hill and that Gordon's brigade was in possession of it. Ewell and Early climbed the hill to get a better look at Milroy's defenses. What they saw encouraged them. The West Fort held perhaps one battery. If the Confederates attacked suddenly and without warning, they could overrun it. The terrain favored such an attack. West of the fort and parallel to Milroy's main line of defense was Little North Mountain. The mountain offered excellent positions for artillery and would screen the approach of Confederates moving to attack the work. Early proposed attacking the West Fort from Little North Mountain, and Ewell concurred.[34]

Early left Gordon's brigade, the First Maryland Battalion, and two batteries south of Winchester to occupy Milroy's attention, then led the rest of his division to Little North Mountain by a concealed route. Jones's artillery battalion accompanied him. While Early moved into position to attack the West Fort, Ewell distracted Milroy with a series of noisy demonstrations south and east of town. At 11:00 A.M., as soon as he was convinced that Milroy was not planning any sorties, Ewell had Johnson place his division between the Millwood Pike and the Berryville Road. While Old Allegheny skirmished with Federals there, elements of Gordon's brigade infiltrated Winchester's southern suburbs. Ewell withdrew Gordon's men when it appeared that Milroy might shell the town. Camp gossip

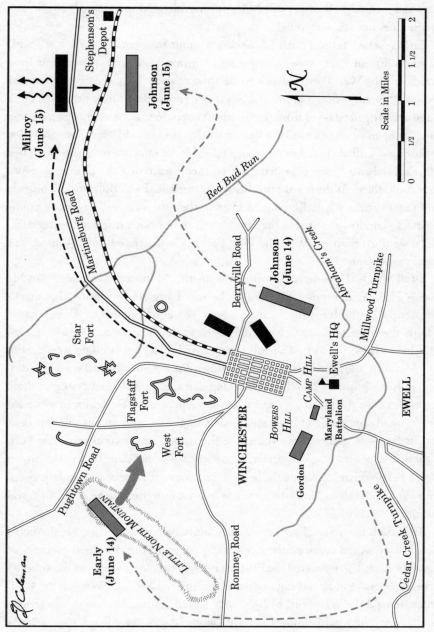

Second Winchester

later had it that Ewell demanded Milroy's surrender and was refused, but the evidence does not support this.[35]

Early reached Little North Mountain without incident. At 6:00 P.M., with darkness just an hour away, twenty guns of Brown's and Jones's battalions fired rapidly on the West Fort. Milroy's artillery, taken entirely by surprise, responded feebly. After forty-five minutes the Southern guns ceased their fire and Hays's Louisiana Brigade dashed from the woods. It swept forward irresistibly across 200 yards of open fields, tore apart a line of abatis, and bounded over the fort walls, capturing six rifled guns. Union troops rallied in an effort to retake the fort, but Hays turned two of the captured guns on them, scattering the bluecoats before they could form. As the sun dipped below the horizon, Extra Billy Smith's brigade and Jones's artillery battalion joined Hays in the fort, securing it against a counterattack. Union guns fired at the captured work in noisy protest long after dark, but it signified nothing. With the West Fort in Confederate hands, Winchester's capture was assured.[36]

Ewell watched the attack from a hill on the Millwood Turnpike, possibly Camp Hill. At one point he thought he saw Early riding among the attacking troops. "Hurrah for the Louisiana boys!" he cried excitedly. "There's Early; I hope the old fellow won't be hurt." As he spoke, a spent ball struck him on the chest, staggering him. The ball left a nasty bruise, but nothing worse. Still, Dr. McGuire thought Ewell should lie down for a while. To make sure he did, McGuire took Ewell's crutches, remarking that the general "had better let those sticks alone for the present." As much as he respected McGuire, Ewell was temperamentally incapable of lying still during a fight. Within seconds he was back on his feet—or rather foot—cheering the troops on. Beyond the West Fort, Union cavalry and wagons seemed to be leaving Winchester by the Pughtown Road. Fearing that Milroy might be trying to carry off some of his artillery, Ewell ordered Maj. Harry Gilmor to gather as many cavalrymen as he could find and cut the Federals off.[37]

After dark Early sent Ewell a dispatch announcing his success. He predicted that Milroy would evacuate the city during the night but promised to attack at dawn anyhow. Ewell ordered the First Maryland Battalion to support the attack.[38] Like Early, though, he did not expect the enemy to be there. Now that the Confederates held the West Fort, Milroy's only logical course of action was to retreat. In that event he would almost certainly use the Martinsburg Road, just as Banks had done in 1862. Ewell ordered Johnson to take three brigades and several guns to a point on the Martinsburg Road two and one-half miles from town. If Milroy attempted to escape during the night, Johnson would be in position to intercept him; if he chose to remain at Winchester, Johnson would be in position to support Early's attack in the morning.[39]

Milroy attempted to flee, as Ewell had predicted. When Johnson reached the Martinsburg Road that night, he found the Union army strung out along the road in full retreat. Parallel to the road ran the Winchester and Potomac Railroad. Johnson's men filed in the railroad cut at Stephenson's Depot and awaited attack. Milroy obliged them, hurling his regiments against the Confederate line in a series of desperate assaults. When these failed, he attempted to execute a double envelopment of Johnson's flanks. He met defeat when Johnson skillfully shuffled reinforcements to the endangered points. Demoralized and confused, some 2,500 Union soldiers threw down their arms and surrendered. Others sought refuge in nearby woods and fields only to be scooped up in the morning.[40]

Ewell heard the fighting at Stephenson's Depot and guessed its meaning. Still, he could not be certain that Milroy was involved, or if he was, that he had committed his entire force. The most direct route for Early's division to reach Stephenson's Depot was through Winchester. With dawn just hours away, Ewell decided to attack the town as planned. If Milroy was still there, fine; if not, Early could push on and join Johnson.

Early's division entered Winchester at first light. Gordon's brigade and the First Maryland Battalion came in from the south; Hays, Smith, and Hoke, from the west. Not a shot was fired. Eager Confederates raced toward a large U.S. flag that still flew defiantly over Fort Milroy and hauled it down. Ewell saw the flag descend from his point of observation on the Millwood Road. Certain now that the Federals had abandoned the town, he directed Gordon to secure the public property in Winchester and ordered Early to pursue Milroy. That done, he sat down and penned a brief dispatch to General Lee, apprising him of Early's success and vowing to push on after the Federals.[41]

The full magnitude of the Confederate victory did not become apparent until later in the day when Milroy's men returned to Winchester as prisoners of war. Ewell herded them inside the main fort until arrangements could be made to send them to Richmond. Milroy was not among the captives. To Ewell's chagrin the Union commander had eluded Johnson at Stephenson's Depot and fled toward Harpers Ferry. Ewell notified Rodes of Milroy's escape and expressed the hope that Jenkins's cavalry could intercept him. He even dispatched a small body of horsemen from Winchester in an effort to overtake the obnoxious Union general, but in vain: Milroy got away.[42]

Rodes meanwhile had crossed the Potomac and occupied Williamsport, Maryland. On 13 June, while the rest of the corps closed in on Milroy at Winchester, he had hurried north to attack McReynolds's brigade at Berryville. McReynolds evacuated the town just before Rodes arrived and marched to Winchester, where he shared Milroy's fate. Rather than pursue him, Rodes set a course for Martinsburg, which he reached late on 14 June. The small Federal garrison there fled at his approach, abandoning five cannon, 400 rounds of artillery ammunition, and 6,000 bushels of grain. Rodes chased the enemy across the Potomac River and on 15 June crossed three brigades into Maryland.[43]

By the end of the day no organized body of Federal troops remained in the Shenandoah Valley. Ewell had driven Milroy and his troops out of the state. In doing so he had captured more than 4,000 prisoners, twenty-three guns, 300 horses, and an abundance of quartermaster and commissary stores. More remarkable, he had done it all in just four days and at a cost of only 269 casualties. Few Confederate victories had been so decisive or so complete.[44]

Ewell announced the victory to the corps in a general order. He asked the men and officers of his command "to unite with him in returning thanks to our Heavenly Father for the signal success which has crowned the valor of this command." As had been his predecessor's custom, Ewell directed chaplains to "hold religious services in the respective regiments at such times as may be most convenient." The significance of the order was not lost on the troops. Said one soldier, "John, have you noticed how Gen. Ewell seems to be aping Gen. Jackson?" "How?" asked the other. "Why, since Jackson's death Ewell always has God in his dispatches."[45]

Ewell gave Hays's Brigade credit for the victory. He praised the Louisianians in the presence of Capt. William J. Seymour of Hays's staff and told a brigade chaplain that "next to God he was indebted to them for the almost bloodless victory he achieved over Milroy." In recognition of the brigade's gallantry, he sent the captured garrison flag back to Richmond with an escort of men selected from Hays's and Gordon's brigades and designated the range of hills west of town "Louisiana Ridge." Ewell honored Early for his part in the victory, placing him in command of the Department of Winchester with authority to dispose of all captured men and stores.[46]

Ewell made sure that the troops shared in the booty. "General Ewell said that heretofore the Quarter Masters and Commissaries had reaped the benefit of such things," wrote one contented Reb, "but this time it should not be so. While we were resting a day or two those supplies, including candy, nuts, tobacco, cigars, canned goods, etc. were issued to the troops." Another soldier did not remember the distribution of goods as being so orderly. "Our soldiers were just turned loose

& told to go [to] it," he wrote the folks at home. "I have as many nice clothing as I want, Sugar & coffee, rice & Everything else we wanted." A third soldier wrote that "Gen Ewel[l] had all the eatibles [*sic*] captured at Winchester divided amongst the men, such as candies, cigars, &c, which gave great satisfaction. . . . They did not get much apiece," he admitted, "but they liked the principle." Not even medical supplies were exempt. The Army of Northern Virginia's medical director reported to the surgeon general that "the Second Corps, who were in advance of the army and fought the battle, appropriated 'the spoils.' A large quantity of medical and hospital supplies must have fallen into our hands," he added sourly, "but Medical Director McGuire and his medical officers left behind them only the odds and ends."[47]

The license to plunder extended only to captured military and sutler stores. Ewell made it clear that he would not tolerate the plunder of private homes and businesses. He appealed to officers and soldiers alike to assist him in repressing such lawless acts, lest discipline suffer and the corps "become, like our enemies, a band of robbers, without the spirit to win victories."[48]

Ewell presided at the raising of the Confederate flag over Fort Milroy, which he rechristened "Fort Jackson." Patriotic women of Winchester had manufactured the banner from two Union flags that had flown over the fort. The 6:00 P.M. ceremony featured a thirteen-gun salute, after which the ladies gave Ewell three cheers.

"Thank you, ladies," he replied, "now call on General Early for a speech."

"Speech from General Early," cried the delighted women. For once the outspoken bachelor had nothing to say. Removing his hat, he stammered, "Ladies, I never could muster courage to *address one lady*, much less such a crowd as this."[49]

After the ceremony the generals accepted an invitation to have tea at the home of Mary Lee, one of the town's most ardent secessionists. They took tea in the yard, where Mrs. Lee had prepared a beautiful table. Ewell listened with interest to the ladies' accounts of the 14 June fighting, as seen from the Union lines, and informed them that "Mr. Milroy" had escaped to Harpers Ferry with about 200 men. Mrs. Lee found the general enchanting. "I was charmed with him," she confided to her diary; "he is rather abrupt in his manners but is enthusiastic & quick." At his hostess's invitation, Ewell made his headquarters at the house. He remained there throughout the evening, writing and receiving dispatches. One of the dispatches was from Milroy. It requested Ewell to treat his prisoners in a civilized manner. Before reaching Ewell, the message had gone through his former chief of staff, John M. Jones, who now commanded a brigade in Johnson's division. Jones viewed the dispatch as a ruse to enable the bearer to enter Winchester and ascertain the size of the Confederate force there. He sent the Union officer back to his own lines with no reply.[50]

The victory at Winchester marked the apogee of Ewell's military career. Skillfully planned and flawlessly executed, it had been brilliant in every respect. It was "one of the most perfect pieces of work the Army of Northern Virginia ever did," thought artilleryman Robert Stiles. Gunner William White claimed that it "equalled any movement made during the war." The Richmond *Examiner* went even further, stating with forgivable hyperbole, "Whether in perfection of the plan, the resolution of it's [*sic*] execution, the rapidity of it's completion or the magnificence of the result, [the victory] will stand comparison with any chapter in the history of any leader of any country or age."[51]

Soldiers in both armies saw Jackson's spirit in the rapid movements and swift attacks. A Union colonel captured at Winchester declared that the Confederates had purposely lied in saying that Jackson was dead—"that there was no officer in either army that could have executed that movement but 'Old Jack.'" Maj. Henry Kyd Douglas remarked, "The movement of Ewell was quick, skillful and effective—in fact, Jacksonian." The fact that Ewell's victory occurred at the same place where Jackson had routed Banks in 1862 added flavor to the comparison. "Ewell won his right to Jackson's mantle at Jackson's game on Jackson's ground," claimed William Blackford. "This success will give the corps more confidence in Ewell." Even such a staunch Jackson proponent as Sandie Pendleton was impressed. "Gen. Ewell is a grand officer," he told his mother, "& the more I see of him the more I like him."[52]

High accolades these and justly earned, but with them came the expectation of continued success. Having hailed Ewell as a "reincarnate Jackson," the Southern people expected him to continue winning victories, as they imagined Jackson would have if he were still alive. (They conveniently forgot, as historians still do, that even Stonewall sometimes failed.) Competing with Jackson's record was a daunting prospect; competing with his memory was a hopeless one. By creating expectations that he could not realistically fulfill, Ewell's greatest success would also prove to be his greatest misfortune.

CHAPTER 20

High Times in Pennsylvania

Pennsylvania! To Confederates weary of fighting on Southern soil the name had a magical ring. It meant a countryside unspoiled by war: luxuriant fields of wheat and corn, and orchards heavy with fruit. More than that it meant possible independence. A victory north of the Mason-Dixon Line would demoralize the North, encourage foreign intervention, and possibly result in a peace settlement predicated on Southern independence. The stakes were enormous, and if the campaigns of the past year were any indication of things to come, the South held the upper hand. Expiring Union enlistments following the battle of Chancellorsville had reduced the Army of the Potomac to fewer than 100,000 men, while the Army of Northern Virginia's numbers remained stable at approximately 75,000. If the South had ever been in position to strike a decisive blow, it was now.

The Second Corps led the army's advance into Pennsylvania. One day after defeating Milroy, Edward Johnson and Jubal Early began marching toward the Potomac. Robert Rodes was already there, having occupied Williamsport, Maryland, on 15 June.[1] The Confederates would not cross the river in force for a few days; meanwhile, they did everything in their power to cripple Union supply lines. Rodes put his men to work damaging the C&O Canal near Williamsport, and Johnson's men did similar service at Shepherdstown, Virginia, ten miles downstream. Confederate cavalry wreaked even greater havoc on the B&O Railroad. At Lee's orders John Imboden advanced down the South Branch of the Potomac River, destroying bridges and depots as far west as Cumberland, Maryland. Ewell ordered Maj. Harry Gilmor to destroy the Monocacy River bridge, south of Frederick, Maryland, but Gilmor found the structure so strongly guarded that he drew off without an attack.[2]

The Confederates were as industrious in collecting supplies for themselves as they were in denying them to the enemy. Food was a major concern to Robert E. Lee in June 1863. Once he crossed the Potomac, his supply lines with the South would be cut and his army would have to live off the land—a disturbing proposition for any commander. In anticipation of that event, Lee ordered Ewell to scour the Maryland countryside for food and other supplies needed by the army. Leather was a particularly valuable commodity, since a large number of men had no shoes. As soon as Rodes occupied Williamsport, he sent Jenkins's cavalry on a raid to Chambersburg, Pennsylvania, to seize supplies there before frightened residents could whisk them away. Jenkins pushed across Maryland's narrow neck and briefly occupied the town, but he relinquished it at the first sign of confrontation. As a result, Rodes noted with disgust, "most of the property in that place which would have been of service to the troops, such as boots, hats, leather, &c., was removed or concealed before it was reoccupied." It was Jenkins's second failure in less than a week, leading both Rodes and Ewell to question his capacity for command.[3]

Ewell lingered at Winchester until 16 June 1863, then moved up to Bunker Hill, a town slightly closer to the Potomac. Before leaving Winchester, he told Mary Lee and her friends that the great struggle of the war lay ahead and asked them to remember him in their prayers.[4]

At Bunker Hill, Ewell received authority from Robert E. Lee to push Rodes's division forward to Hagerstown, Maryland. He was to let on that the purpose of the movement was to invest Harpers Ferry, as Jackson had done in 1862. Milroy held the town with 8,000 men, a plum well worth picking if only Lee had the time. But he did not. Hooker had discovered the Army of Northern Virginia's departure from Fredericksburg and was marching north in an effort to interpose himself between the Confederates and Washington. If Lee was to reach Pennsylvania without interference from the Army of the Potomac, he had to keep moving. He therefore ordered Ewell to ignore Harpers Ferry and concentrate on collecting supplies for the army. "Repress marauding," he admonished his lieutenant. "Take what is necessary for the army, and give citizens of Maryland Confederate money or certificates. Do not expose yourself. Keep your own scouts."[5]

Ewell met with Rodes at Williamsport on 18 June. The next morning Rodes broke camp and headed for Hagerstown. When he reached the town, he turned south, as if headed toward Harpers Ferry. Johnson crossed the Potomac and marched to Sharpsburg, adding to the impression that Harpers Ferry was Lee's target. Early moved to Shepherdstown, where he found his progress blocked by the flooded waters of the Potomac River. Ewell's divisions remained in these positions for two days gathering supplies, waiting for Longstreet and Hill to catch up with them.[6]

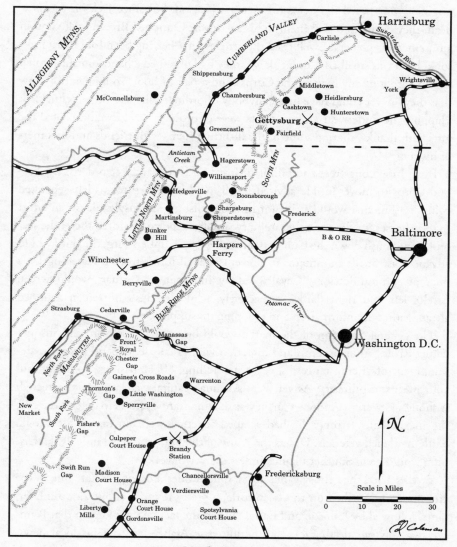

Gettysburg Campaign

Although his corps was stationary, Ewell was not. Between 19 and 21 June the forty-six-year-old cripple tirelessly shuttled back and forth between his far-flung divisions in a flurry of activity that would have tired a healthy man half his age. On one of his journeys a group of women presented him with a hat, two pair of buckskin gauntlets, a box of underwear, and a pair of boots. The ladies had originally purchased the items for General Jackson, but since Jackson was now dead, they decided to give them to his successor. Campbell Brown looked on in amusement as General Ewell tried the articles on. "Having been told that [Jackson's] head was small and his feet large, they had obtained a handsome hat which would hardly fit any man in the Corps" and a pair of boots so long and narrow that they "never could have fitted anybody of ordinary shape," Brown chuckled. Happily, the underwear and gauntlets were of ordinary size. Ewell accepted the gifts with thanks, sharing some of the ill-fitting items with friends and members of his staff.[7]

By 21 June Longstreet and Hill had closed on Ewell, and Lee ordered the Second Corps to move on. He advised Ewell to advance in three widely separated columns. The first would strike for McConnellsburg, Pennsylvania, in an effort to seize horses, cattle, and other military supplies reportedly stored there; the second would push down the Cumberland Valley to Chambersburg; the third would advance east of the mountains to prevent Federal forces from threatening Lee's lines of communications. Cavalry led by Imboden and Stuart would screen Ewell's left and right flanks, respectively, while Jenkins's horsemen galloped ahead, gathering information and scooping up supplies.

The general direction of the march would be northeast, toward the Susquehanna River. "Your progress and direction will, of course, depend upon the development of circumstances," Lee wrote, adding, "If Harrisburg comes within your means, capture it." As yet, Pennsylvania's capital was largely unprotected. Although Governor Andrew Curtin was making frantic efforts to defend the city, the inexperienced troops he had scraped together were no match for Ewell's battle-hardened veterans. Unless the Army of the Potomac acted quickly, Harrisburg would be in Southern hands in less than two weeks.[8]

Ewell started for Pennsylvania on 22 June. Rodes crossed the state line in the afternoon and pushed on to Greencastle, a pretty town of about 2,000 inhabitants, followed by Johnson and Early. "When the fact became known that Pennsylvania was our destination," an enthusiastic Alabamian told his local newspaper, "a shout of joy ran along the line, and when our troops crossed the line it was with a proud and defiant step, conscious that wherever Ewell leads we can follow."[9]

At that time Ewell was still several miles to the rear. On 22 June he left Ferry Hill and rode to Sharpsburg, where bloody fighting had occurred nine months earlier. He may have stopped to look at the battlefield, but if so, he did not stay long. By night he was at Beaver Creek, three miles beyond Boonsborough. Rodes and Early joined him there. Ewell read them Lee's instructions and parceled out assignments. Rodes would follow Jenkins down the Cumberland Valley toward Harrisburg; Early would cross South Mountain and proceed toward the Susquehanna on Rodes's right, while Johnson would send one brigade to McConnellsburg and follow Rodes with the rest of his division.

The meeting ended late in the evening. The next morning Ewell and Rodes rode north, escorted by members of the First Battalion Maryland Cavalry. At Hagerstown the generals stopped to rest at a hotel while the Marylanders waited outside. Before they left, a young lieutenant dashed up to the building, announced that he carried important dispatches for the general, and demanded to know where he was. His haughty attitude did not play well with Ewell's escort, one of whom replied dryly, "I expect the old gentleman has gone a fishing. I saw him an hour ago, digging worms for bait!" The response drew a howl of laughter from everyone present, except, of course, the upstart lieutenant.[10]

From Hagerstown Ewell made his way north via Middleburg, Pennsylvania, to Rodes's camp at Greencastle. The Confederates' reception grew noticeably colder as they crossed into Pennsylvania. "It is like a renewal of Mexican times to enter a captured town," Ewell told Lizzie. "The people look as sour as vinegar & I have no doubt would gladly send us all to kingdom come if they could." It had not been so in Maryland, at least not to such an extent. Some residents there, in fact, had welcomed Ewell with open arms—or at least had threatened to. The general's bulging eyes must have twinkled when a group of Maryland ladies sent back word that if he paid them a visit they would give "me no quarter in their delight at meeting me. What a pity a Bachelor could not have such an offer," he sighed.[11]

Rodes demanded large amounts of food, leather items, pistols, lead, tin, and other articles from the Greencastle City Council. Even Jed Hotchkiss put in an order, requisitioning two maps of the county. The council deemed Rodes's demands so excessive that it did not even try to satisfy them, whereupon the invaders searched the town themselves. They turned up a few saddles, bridles, and other leather goods, but little else.[12]

On 24 June Ewell's column split. Early crossed South Mountain and pushed eastward on Ewell's right flank. George Steuart's brigade set out to capture supplies reportedly stockpiled at McConnellsburg, while the rest of Johnson's division followed Rodes down the Cumberland Valley to Chambersburg, relieving Jenkins, who pushed on to Shippensburg.[13] Imboden and Stuart never appeared. Imboden had halted at the Potomac River, while Stuart—using the latitude granted him by Lee—rode eastward, around the Army of the Potomac. Ewell consequently had to forge through enemy territory with both of his flanks unprotected.

Nevertheless the march through Pennsylvania went without a hitch. "Our march under Ewell had been admirably conducted," Ed Moore of the Rockbridge Artillery later reflected. "We were always on the road at an early hour, and, without hurry or the usual halts caused by our troops crowding one another, we made good distances each day and were in camp by sunset." One Southerner remarked that he and his comrades took "breakfast in Virginia, whiskey in Maryland, and supper in Pennsylvania"—an exaggeration surely, but not an egregious one. The Richmond *Whig* proffered a tongue-in-cheek explanation for the Second Corps' swift gait: its commander had an artificial leg waiting for him in Philadelphia. Despite the rapid pace, straggling was negligible. The men had never been in finer trim or in higher spirits. "There was no demonstration, but a quiet undercurrent of confidence that they were there to conquer," Moore observed. The horses, fattened on Northern grain, seemed to catch the spirit. They carried their heads higher and pulled their loads with firmer steps.[14]

The Confederates' march took them through some of the North's richest farmland. Soldiers accustomed to musty hardtack and dried beef now feasted on fresh bread, fruit, and vegetables. "It is like a hole full of blubber to a Greenlander," Ewell told Hotchkiss, joking that "we will all get fat here." What Ewell's men did not eat, they sent back to supply depots in Winchester. They left nothing behind. Hill and Longstreet, following in Ewell's wake, found every house and store closed and every field and farm stripped clean. "No chance of getting anything while Ewell's corps is ahead," concluded one officer.[15]

Conduct toward Northern citizens was exemplary, largely because Lee insisted on it. Before the army entered Pennsylvania, he issued General Orders #72 outlining procedures for collecting supplies in enemy territory. The order strictly forbade looting. Ewell had the order read to the troops, then added an even stronger one of his own, threatening swift and severe punishment to any soldier caught taking private property. As a result, instances of private plundering were few. "It is wonderful how well our hungry, foot sore, ragged men behave in this land of plenty," Ewell told Lizzie, "better than at home." Sandie Pendleton thought the army's restraint particularly remarkable considering the depredations committed by Northern troops in Virginia. "Rather a pleasant feeling to know that you have a country at your mercy and are magnanimous," he mused with satisfaction. "The Yankees must feel rascally after their behavior in our country."[16]

Cherries apparently fell outside the ban. Southern Pennsylvania abounded in cherry trees, and the Second Corps stripped them clean. Ewell ate as much fruit as the next man. Unable to pick the cherries because of his disability, he had others climb the trees for him. One teenager assigned this duty watched in amazement as the general devoured branchful after branchful of the fruit, marveling that "so small a man could hold so many cherries." [17]

Shoes and boots were also fair game. Footwear was optional during the summer in Virginia, where most of the roads were dirt, but Pennsylvania's stone turnpikes made it a necessity. Ewell therefore consented when one of his barefooted soldiers asked permission to plunder a well-shod Northern civilian. The soldier walked up to a boy about his size surrounded by several girls and ordered him to take off his boots. The Northerner protested but quickly relinquished them when the Southerner's rifle, "old Bal," seconded the demand. The young warrior pulled on the boots and resumed his march to the enthusiastic shouts of his comrades, leaving the erstwhile owner to be consoled by his fair companions. [18]

Well fed and in some cases well shod, Ewell's veterans pressed on eagerly toward the Susquehanna. Rodes's fast-stepping division entered Chambersburg on 24 June led by a band blaring "The Bonnie Blue Flag." Jacob Hoke, a Chambersburg merchant, watched the Confederates file through town. At 10:30 A.M. he noticed a carriage stop in front of the Franklin Hotel. A "thin, sallow-faced man, with strongly-marked Southern features" stepped out. The man had lost a leg, and he had to use a crutch to get around. His "head and physiognomy . . . strongly indicated culture, refinement and genius," thought Hoke. Hobbling inside, the stranger took possession of the hotel's front parlor and ran a headquarters flag out an upstairs window. Dick Ewell had arrived. [19]

His first order of business was to secure the town. Ewell put Col. Cullen A. Battle of the Third Alabama in charge of Chambersburg and made Col. Edward Willis of the Twelfth Georgia its provost marshal. Alcohol posed the biggest threat to army discipline. Ewell strictly prohibited the sale of liquor to his soldiers and posted guards at all houses containing spirits. On the principle that it was easier to prevent trouble than to stop it, he sent a squad of soldiers to destroy whiskey stockpiled at a local distillery. The soldiers set aside a few barrels for the medical department, which had established a hospital in the local school. The Franklin Hotel provided sheets and mattresses for the establishment. [20]

Once Chambersburg was secure, Ewell summoned town leaders to the National Bank, where his staff presented a list of demands for supplies. The quartermaster called for 5,000 suits of clothing, including hats, shoes, and boots; 100 saddles and bridles; 10,000 pounds of leather; and 5,000 bushels of grain. The chief ordnance officer demanded 6,000 pounds of lead; 10,000 pounds of harness leather; fifty boxes of tin; and 1,000 curry combs and brushes. The chief commissary officer then called for 50,000 pounds of bread, 500 barrels of flour, 100,000 pounds of hard bread, and lesser amounts of vinegar, beans, coffee, dried fruit, sauerkraut, and sugar. Except for the grain, all supplies were to be delivered to the courthouse by 3:00 P.M.

The burghers were stunned. The town was unable to supply such vast quantities of food and material, they protested, and even if it could, it would require days, not hours, to deliver them. The Confederate officers were unyielding: the town must do the best it could. Jacob Hoke was the only merchant left in town. In obedience to Ewell's orders, he made out a list of the goods in his store and submitted it to authorities. It was the only such report that they received. Ewell declared the town leaders' efforts insufficient and at 3:00 P.M. gave his officers permission to take what they needed by force. Hoke alone was exempt. Because he had complied with Ewell's orders and submitted an inventory of goods in his store, the general ordered his business to be spared.[21]

While officers in the commissary, quartermaster, and ordnance departments searched stores for military supplies, Ewell's staff bought items for loved ones back home. Jed Hotchkiss picked up calico, wool, cotton, gloves, and other items for his wife, and Campbell Brown bought china buttons, calico dress patterns, soaps, and spices for his mother and sister. Sandie Pendleton and John Johnson made similar purchases for their families.[22]

Ewell did not take part in the shopping spree. As soon as he had established a provost guard in Chambersburg, he set up headquarters at a mill three miles outside town and began planning the next phase of the march. Early and Rodes joined him there. Ewell directed Rodes to continue down the Cumberland Valley as far as Carlisle, less than a dozen miles from Harrisburg. Johnson would follow him. Early was to break the Northern Central Railroad at York, then move up to Wrightsville and destroy the Susquehanna River bridge, thereby severing the Army of the Potomac's direct rail connection with Harrisburg. He would then rejoin the corps at Carlisle in time to participate in the assault on the Pennsylvania capital. Lizzie's mother's family lived at York, a town directly in Early's path. Ewell promised his niece he would let the family off easy for her sake, joking that he would not take "more than a few forks & spoons & trifles. . . . No house-burning or anything of that sort."[23]

On 26 June, with A. P. Hill and Longstreet marching rapidly toward Pennsylvania, Ewell ordered Rodes and Johnson to push on to Shippensburg, the next settlement in the Cumberland Valley. Confederate staff officers combed the town for military supplies, while Jenkins's cavalry scoured the countryside for horses. Ewell secured lodging at a farmhouse beyond the village. While he was there, the owner complained that soldiers were stealing two barrels of flour and some hams he had hidden in the barn. Ewell ordered the men to pay the farmer for the food or return it immediately.[24]

The Confederates reached Carlisle the next day. Three of Rodes's brigades took possession of the U.S. barracks, while a fourth pitched its tents on the grounds of Dickinson College. Johnson bivouacked nearby. Jenkins's cavalry pushed on to within a few miles of the Susquehanna. As they had done in previous towns, the Confederates requisitioned military supplies and searched every store. If there was one thing Southern soldiers did better than fight, it was forage. During Ewell's weeklong sojourn in the Cumberland Valley, he garnered 5,000 barrels of flour, nearly 3,000 head of cattle, large numbers of horses, and vast quantities of ordnance and medical stores.[25]

Ewell made his headquarters at Carlisle Barracks, in the same building he had once occupied as a second lieutenant of dragoons. The setting brought back fond memories, and he spoke at length of his experiences there. A report that soldiers were ransacking the barracks interrupted Ewell's reverie. Tom Turner was among the looters. He had grabbed two buffalo robes and was vying with a tenacious old lady for possession of a fox-skin robe when Ewell put a stop to the plunder.[26]

Ewell had hardly settled into his new quarters when a delegation of ministers called on him to ask if they might open their churches the following day, Sunday.

"Certainly," chirped the general. "I wish myself to attend Church."

The ministers thanked Ewell and departed, but they shortly reappeared with an additional request. Would the general object if they offered a prayer for President Lincoln?

"Not at all," Ewell replied. "I know of no man who is more in need of your prayers."

The clergymen silently withdrew.[27]

The Northern ministers preached to a largely Southern audience. Campbell Brown attended morning services at the town's Lutheran church. Sandie Pendleton, Hunter McGuire, and others visited the Presbyterian church. Jed Hotchkiss noted that many ministers offered prayers for the safety of the United States and for their friends in the Northern army. Some added prayers for "the strangers that were among them" and "for the dear ones *we* had left at home." The voices of Northern citizens and Southern soldiers alike joined in a fervent "amen" when the ministers offered prayers for peace.[28]

Unlike other towns in the Cumberland Valley, Carlisle had many citizens sympathetic to the South, some of whom Ewell remembered from his Old Army days. After church he sent Campbell Brown and Benjamin Greene to look in on one of them, a Mrs. Biddle. The officers were to see if she or any of her friends needed anything or wished to have a guard posted at their house. Ewell suggested that his young colleagues become acquainted with the woman's daughter, a girl in her twenties.[29]

A headache kept the general from making the social rounds himself, but he rallied long enough in the afternoon to participate in the raising of the "Stainless Banner." Tailors in the Southern ranks fashioned the new Confederate flag out of Union banners found at the post, modeling it after that of the Thirty-second North Carolina Regiment. As military bands played "The Bonnie Blue Flag" and "Dixie," Confederate soldiers unfurled the national emblem to the breeze. The generals did their part, delivering speech after speech from a nearby balcony. Ewell opened the ceremony with a few lisping remarks. He then turned the rostrum over to his more polished subordinates and retired to his sickbed.

Robert Rodes, Junius Daniel, and Isaac Trimble each took a turn at speaking. The generals had shared a keg of strong lager beer before the ceremony, and as the alcohol took effect, their remarks became increasingly incoherent. The crowds did not seem to notice, however, and continued to call for additional speakers. Benjamin Greene obligingly stepped forward. Like the generals who had preceded him, Greene had imbibed several drinks that morning and was in high spirits. He stepped out on the balcony with aplomb, acknowledged the ovations of the crowd with a casual wave of the hand, then launched into an rambling, unintelligible discourse. "A friend presently pulled him back by the coat-tail," remembered Brown, "& he disappeared for a few minutes, but returned to the charge & was making a worse exhibition than before, when pulled down a second time & put to bed." With Greene's abrupt exit the ceremony ended and the crowds dispersed. One soldier, reflecting on the disappointing performance of the officers, concluded "that heroism and oratory do not always go hand in hand."[30]

Trimble had rejoined the army after being sidelined for ten months by a wound he had received at Second Manassas. After his recovery the War Department had placed him in command of the Valley District. When the Army of Northern Virginia crossed the Potomac River, Trimble asked to tag along. Lee explained that he had no troops for Trimble save the few men belonging to Trimble's own Valley District, but the old man was not deterred. He confidently asserted that he could recruit a division of troops from the ranks of his native Marylanders.

Lee had no delusions that Trimble could raise a regiment north of the Potomac, much less a division, but he agreed to let him come along. Trimble joined Lee in Maryland and promptly made a nuisance of himself. After just two days

Lee sent him on to Ewell. Trimble caught up with his former commander at Carlisle on 28 June, the same day, by coincidence, that Ewell developed a headache. Within hours he was nagging Ewell to push on to Harrisburg. He offered to capture the city himself with just one brigade and four guns, if his former commander would let him try. For the next three days he pestered Ewell with chimerical proposals and gratuitous advice, just as he had pestered Lee.[31]

Ewell meanwhile was taking practical steps to capture the city. On 29 June Jenkins advanced to Harrisburg's outer works, west of the Susquehanna River, and traded artillery shells with the city's defenders. Ewell ordered Rodes to march to Jenkins's support and sent his chief engineer, Capt. Henry Richardson, forward to reconnoiter Harrisburg's fortifications. By the time Rodes cleared the right bank of the river of Yankees, Early would be up and Ewell would be in position to throw his entire corps against the city.[32]

Ewell was just starting for Harrisburg on 29 June when he received a dispatch from Lee that stopped him in his tracks. The Army of the Potomac, Lee wrote, had crossed the Potomac River and was moving north. He directed Ewell to unite with Hill and Longstreet at Chambersburg. Although it was well past noon, Ewell ordered Johnson's division, the corps wagon train, and two battalions of reserve artillery to start for Chambersburg. Rodes and Early would follow. Lee countermanded his order, however, and that night instructed Ewell to cross the mountains and join forces with Early near Heidlersburg. From there he was to march toward a thriving crossroads town called Gettysburg.[33]

CHAPTER 21

Gettysburg

Gettysburg, Pennsylvania, was a town of 2,400 inhabitants in 1863. Low, rocky ridges adjoined the town, which stood in the center of a lush agricultural valley. Though not large, Gettysburg was important regionally. It was the legislative seat of Adams County, it had a rail line that connected it with Baltimore and other important eastern cities, and it boasted a college and a Lutheran seminary. What made Gettysburg important from a military standpoint, however, was the system of roads that radiated from it to all points of the compass. Whoever controlled the town and its roads controlled south-central Pennsylvania.[1]

Toward Gettysburg Dick Ewell directed his corps on 30 June 1863. He did not do so gladly. He had set his heart on capturing Harrisburg, only to see that prize slip from his grasp. Not since those unhappy days at Conrad's Store in May 1862 had he been so frustrated. Jed Hotchkiss visited his chief late that night and found him on the warpath. "The Gen. was quite testy," Hotchkiss scribbled in his diary, "hard to please, because disappointed and had every one flying around. I got up in the night to answer questions & made him a map."[2]

Whether he liked them or not, orders were orders, and Ewell set about executing them. He told Robert Rodes to take his division across South Mountain to Heidlersburg and directed Jubal Early to join him there. Edward Johnson had started for Chambersburg with the corps wagon train the previous night and would cross the mountain at Cashtown Pass. Albert Jenkins, commanding Ewell's cavalry, was to continue shelling Harrisburg's defenses one more day and then fall back to Carlisle, following the infantry south.[3]

Ewell accompanied Rodes's division across South Mountain. En route to Heidlersburg he stopped at Papertown to examine the paper mill from which the town took its name. He paused again briefly at "a terrified Old Dutchmans" who lived at the summit of South Mountain. At one point Ewell received a false report that a strong Federal force blocked his path, compelling him to put out a line of skirmishers. Otherwise the march went well.[4]

At Heidlersburg Ewell received a dispatch from General Lee ordering him to proceed to either Cashtown or Gettysburg, as circumstances required, and a note from A. P. Hill informing him that the Third Corps was at Cashtown.[5] He also heard rumors that the Army of the Potomac's Eleventh Corps was at Gettysburg. His years as a dragoon had taught him to mistrust such reports. When Capt. Frank Bond appeared with a company of cavalry, Ewell sent him toward Gettysburg with instructions "to attack with vigor whatever opposition I might encounter, force them back, and learn if infantry or artillery were in our front"—a tall order for a company of 100 men. Bond did not encounter any organized body of Union troops, but he did capture three Pennsylvania soldiers who had slipped away from the army to visit their homes. From them Ewell may have learned something about the location of the Army of the Potomac and that George Meade had replaced "Fighting Joe" Hooker as its commander.[6]

Ewell met with Rodes, Early, and Trimble that night and informed them that the Eleventh Corps was reported (wrongly) to be at Gettysburg. He then produced Lee's order directing him to march to Gettysburg or Cashtown according to circumstances. He read the order several times, criticizing its "indefinite phraseology." As a subordinate of Stonewall Jackson, he had been taught to obey orders, not to interpret them. Discretionary orders like those issued by Lee made him uncomfortable. What did the phrase "according to circumstances" mean anyway? he asked. Rodes and Early supposedly offered unsatisfactory replies, at which point Trimble spoke up. He had been with Lee earlier in the week, he explained, and it was the commanding general's plan to attack the enemy's advance in overwhelming force and throw it back in confusion on the main body. The presence of the Eleventh Corps at Gettysburg was the circumstance required to do this, he argued. They should march there without delay. Ewell deferred his decision until morning, perhaps wishing to hear the results of Bond's reconnaissance before making a decision. "Why can't a Commanding General have some one on his staff who can write an intelligible order?" he grumbled.[7]

Bond's report was negative, and Ewell determined to join Hill at Cashtown. He ordered Rodes to march there via Middletown (Biglerville), while Early pursued a more southerly route by way of Hunterstown and Mummasburg.[8] It was a safe decision. Various roads crossed the route, permitting the corps to quickly redirect its march to Gettysburg if circumstances demanded it.

Robert E. Rodes (Library of Congress)

Ewell continued to accompany Rodes's division, which made Middletown around 10:00 A.M. Before reaching the town, Ewell received a dispatch from Hill. The Third Corps had encountered Union cavalry at Gettysburg, Hill announced, and was marching to that point. Ewell promptly moved to support him. He directed Rodes to turn south toward Gettysburg on the Middletown Road and ordered Early to proceed to Gettysburg by way of the Heidlersburg (Harrisburg) Road. Campbell Brown took notice of Ewell's change of direction to Lee at Cashtown. Col. John E. Johnson, a volunteer aide, carried a similar message to Hill.[9]

Three miles south of Middletown, artillery fire broke the morning quiet. Hill had engaged the enemy at Gettysburg. Rodes left the road and led his troops south along the crest of Oak Ridge to a point directly opposite the right flank of the Union army's First Corps, which was confronting Hill west of town. Ewell saw at once that Oak Hill, at the south end of the ridge, was an excellent position from which to make an attack. While Rodes brought his brigades into position, Ewell posted Lt. Col. Thomas H. Carter's battalion of artillery along the nose of the ridge, where it opened with "fine effect" on the Union line stretched across McPherson's Ridge.[10]

Rodes deployed his division in two lines. The brigades of Brig. Gen. Alfred Iverson, Col. Edward A. O'Neal, and Brig. Gen. George Doles comprised the first line. Iverson held the crest of Oak Ridge, Doles's brigade stretched across the plain to Iverson's left, and O'Neal occupied the hillside between the two. Brig. Gens. Junius Daniel and Stephen D. Ramseur held the second line. Daniel's North Carolinians stood 200 yards behind Iverson and to his right. Ramseur's men were on Daniel's left, in rear of Iverson.

No sooner had Rodes completed his arrangements than troops of the Union First Corps, which had hitherto confronted Hill, turned north with the apparent intention of attacking. At the same time Maj. Gen. Oliver O. Howard's Eleventh Corps issued from the town, turning Rodes's left flank. As Doles sidled left to engage Howard's troops east of the Carlisle Road, a dangerous gap formed between his brigade and O'Neal's Alabamians to its right.[11]

Ewell was watching this ominous development from Oak Hill when he received a dispatch from Lee admonishing him to avoid a general engagement if he found the enemy to be in "very heavy force." The two sides were then involved in a furious artillery exchange. Hill was engaged with the enemy, and Rodes was about to be. Under the circumstances, Ewell considered the order obsolete. "It was too late to avoid an engagement without abandoning the position already taken up," he later explained, "and I determined to push the attack vigorously."[12]

The initial attack, though vigorous, was a disaster. O'Neal's brigade went in with only three regiments and at an angle different from that indicated by Rodes. Instead of leading his troops in the attack, O'Neal remained in the rear with the Fifth Alabama, a reserve regiment. His brigade was repulsed. As O'Neal fell back, he exposed Iverson's men to the fire of Union soldiers posted behind a stone wall. Iverson was pinned down. Daniel, pushing past Iverson on the right, successfully attacked Federal forces posted in a railroad cut, but in doing so he incurred heavy casualties. Rodes's attack was in trouble.[13]

Matters went from bad to worse. On the far left, Brig. Gen. Francis Barlow's division threatened to turn Doles's left flank. Ewell had no troops to prevent this except Early's division, which was due to appear at any moment. Tom Turner and

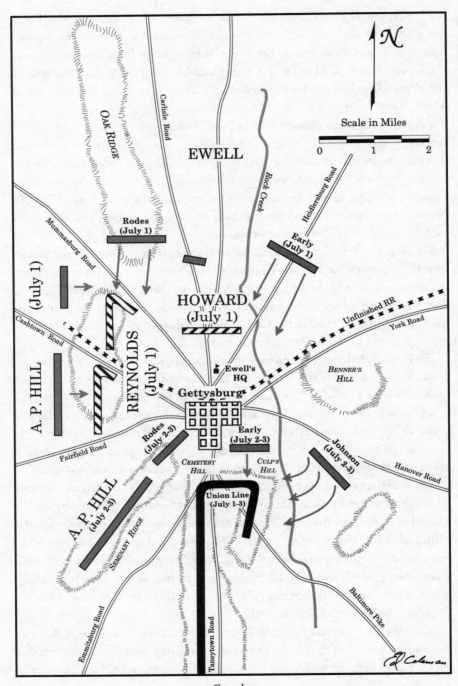

Gettysburg

Campbell Brown galloped off to find Early and hurry him forward, while Ewell monitored the developing threat to Doles's flank.[14]

Early arrived in the nick of time. At 3:30 P.M. his division appeared on the Heidlersburg Road, opposite the right flank of the Union troops now threatening Doles's line. Col. Hilary P. Jones's artillery battalion rolled onto a low rise to the left of the road and furiously shelled the Eleventh Corps' line. At the same time Gordon's infantry crossed Rock Creek and hit the enemy from the northeast. The startled Federals put up a short, stubborn fight, then broke for town. Hays's and Hoke's brigades (the latter commanded by Col. Isaac Avery) meanwhile advanced east of the Heidlersburg Road and charged a second Federal line. Hays fought his way into Gettysburg, capturing two guns and a large number of prisoners, while Avery wheeled left to face Cemetery Hill, one-half mile south of town.[15]

Early's attack supported the final stage of Rodes's offensive. On the left, Doles took advantage of collapsing Union resistance in his front to order his troops forward; in the center, Ramseur advanced to support Iverson and O'Neal, slamming into the Federal line near Oak Hill with "irresistible force"; on the right, Daniel negotiated the railroad cut and joined Maj. Gen. William Dorsey Pender in driving back Union troops along the Cashtown Road.[16]

Ewell orchestrated the victorious advance of his troops from a point on Oak Hill not far from Fry's battery. As his divisions surged toward town, he observed a body of Federal infantry move into the gap between Doles and Ramseur. Unless stopped, they would turn the Georgian's right flank. Doles did not observe the threat, and Ewell could not warn him of it, since he was by himself at the time and could not mount his horse without assistance. Fortunately Doles's rightmost regiments saw their peril and changed front in time, pouring a destructive fire into the Northern ranks. In exuberant overstatement, Ewell later told some of Rodes's men that he believed not more than twenty-five Federals escaped. "It was a pleasure to watch the play of the General's countenance when he was relating the incident," wrote one listener. "The wonderful sparkle and flash of those great brown eyes was enchanting."[17]

Pressured in front and on the flanks, the Union line crumbled. Soldiers of the First and Eleventh Corps fell back in disorder toward Cemetery Ridge, where their officers tried to rally them. Rodes overtook hundreds of the fugitives, and Early captured many more. Altogether more than 5,000 Union soldiers and three guns fell into Confederate hands.[18]

Ewell rode down the hill to the left in an effort to find Early. As he passed Capt. William P. Carter's battery near the McLean barn, a shell fragment struck his sorrel mare in the head. The general pitched violently to the ground.[19] Fortunately he was not hurt. Assisted by Maj. J. Coleman Alderson of Rodes's staff and the men of Carter's battery, Ewell mounted a new horse and continued to the left under a heavy artillery fire. If the tumble dazed him, he did not show it.[20]

Ewell encountered John Gordon, fresh from his recent victory over the Eleventh Corps, in a field north of town. Gordon eagerly urged Ewell to press forward and capture Cemetery Hill, an eminence just south of town on which the Federals seemed to be rallying. As they were talking, Maj. Henry K. Douglas of Edward Johnson's staff appeared. Douglas reported Johnson's division to be just a few miles outside town. It would be ready to attack as soon as it arrived. Gordon snatched at the news. If his brigade joined forces with Johnson, he argued, they could take Cemetery Hill before dark. Ewell said nothing. To Douglas he appeared "unusually grave and silent." Lee had ordered Ewell to avoid a general engagement until the entire army had arrived. Although he had felt it necessary to disregard those instructions when confronted by Union forces on Oak Hill, there was no justification for doing so now. He told Douglas to have Johnson halt when he reached the front and wait for orders, adding, " *Gen. Lee is still at Cashtown, six miles in rear.* He directed me to come to Gettysburg, and I have done so. I do not feel like going further or making an attack without orders from him." Ewell's seeming lack of aggression disappointed those around him. "Oh, for the presence and inspiration of Old Jack for just one hour!" muttered Sandie Pendleton.[21]

Ewell left Gordon and rode into town, probably by way of Carlisle Street. He sent Col. Abner Smead of his staff ahead to find Early and ask his advice on where to put Johnson's division when it arrived. As Ewell entered Gettysburg, Capt. James Power Smith joined him. Smith had just been with Lee and brought the welcome news that the commanding general was on Seminary Ridge, just outside town.[22] As if to confirm his statement, Maj. Walter H. Taylor soon appeared with a message from Lee. The commanding general had watched the Union retreat from Seminary Ridge and thought it only necessary to press the enemy to secure possession of Cemetery Hill. He ordered Ewell to attack the hill, if he "could do so to advantage." Ewell sent Taylor back to Lee with a message regarding the prisoners he had captured. "General Ewell did not express any objection, or indicate the existence of any impediment, to the execution of the order conveyed to him," remembered Taylor, "but left the impression upon my mind that it would be executed."[23]

Ewell had every intention of executing the order. Only Lee's injunction against bringing on a general engagement had deterred him from pressing the attack before, and now that order no longer seemed to be in effect. With a lighter heart Ewell nudged his horse forward through the crowds of milling soldiers and entered the town square. The success of the past hour made him exultant. When Brig. Gen. Harry Hays urged him to press on and seize Cemetery Hill, Ewell laughed and asked the Louisianian if his men never got enough fighting. Hays replied sharply that his only concern was to prevent the needless slaughter of his men in a future attack. Ewell refused to be hurried, however. He had sent for Early and Rodes, and he would not order an attack until he had consulted them.[24]

Ewell waited for his division commanders under a shade tree in the town square. While there, he received reports from various units in his command, issued orders for the posting of troops, gave directions concerning the distribution of ammunition, and made provisions for the large number of prisoners who had fallen into his hands. A young officer, perhaps knowing the general's fondness for Madeira, offered him a bottle of wine that he had found in a cellar. Ewell wisely declined it. Instead he chatted with Union prisoners, most of whom freely admitted that they had been whipped. Among the prisoners was Col. Henry A. Morrow of the Twenty-fourth Michigan Infantry, a regiment in the famed Iron Brigade. When Morrow told Ewell about the heavy losses his regiment had incurred, the Confederate chastised him for sacrificing his troops rather than surrendering. "General Ewell, the 24th Mich. came here to fight, not surrender," Morrow snapped.[25]

Meanwhile precious minutes passed. "It was a moment of most critical importance," James P. Smith later reflected, "more evidently critical to us now, than it would seem to any one then. But even then, some of us who had served on Jackson's staff, sat in a group in our saddles, and one said sadly, 'Jackson is not here.' Our corps commander, General Ewell, as true a Confederate soldier as ever went into battle, was simply waiting for orders, when every moment of the time could not be balanced with gold." Actually Ewell was not waiting for orders so much as for Early and Rodes, who arrived shortly. They reported that their troops had advanced beyond the town to the foot of Cemetery Hill and urged Ewell to attack the hill immediately, provided Lee could support his right. Ewell concurred. Turning to Smith, he said, "Captain, you have lately been with General Lee; perhaps you can find him again. Please tell him what Generals Early and Rodes wish to say!"[26]

While awaiting Smith's return, Ewell and Early rode south on Baltimore Street to get a better view of Cemetery Hill. Federal sharpshooters concealed in buildings at the foot of the hill quickly drove them back to cover, but not before they had glimpsed their objective.[27] What they saw was not altogether encouraging. At least one brigade of infantry seemed to be standing firm on the hillcrest, its position strengthened by stone walls and at least forty pieces of artillery. Brig. Gen.

John Buford's cavalry division guarded the western approaches to the hill. What Union forces lay beyond it was anybody's guess.[28]

Ewell's corps labored under several disadvantages. Johnson's division, marching via Cashtown, was still a few miles away. Of the two divisions at hand, Rodes had suffered 2,500 losses on Oak Hill that afternoon. His troops were tired and disorganized. Early had taken fewer than 500 casualties in the day's fighting, but only three of his four brigades were immediately available for an attack, and they were embarrassed by thousands of Union prisoners who had fallen into their hands. In order to attack Cemetery Hill, Ewell would have to maneuver around Gettysburg, then form his divisions beyond it or make his attack east of the town. In either case his troops would be within easy range of the Union artillery on the hill. Confederate gunners, on the other hand, had no position from which they could shell Cemetery Hill to advantage.[29]

Despite these difficulties, Ewell determined to pursue his advantage and attack the hill.[30] Before he could do so, however, Smith brought the distressing news that Lee had no troops available to support the attack. Lee urged Ewell to carry Cemetery Hill with the Second Corps alone, if possible, but in the same breath he reiterated his earlier order that Ewell avoid a general engagement until the entire army was present. Lee's message left Ewell baffled and frustrated. As he scanned the hill with its growing line of infantry and impressive array of guns, he realized that it would be impossible to take the position without becoming entangled with the enemy, if indeed he could take it at all.[31]

Fortunately there was an alternative. To the left of Cemetery Hill and commanding it stood a wooded eminence known as Culp's Hill. By seizing Culp's Hill, Ewell might compel the Union army to abandon Cemetery Hill without a fight. Moreover, seizing Culp's Hill would probably not entail a general engagement, something that Lee wished to avoid. Ewell accordingly canceled his plans to attack Cemetery Hill and determined to take Culp's Hill once Johnson's division reached the field.[32]

Isaac Trimble accompanied Ewell for much of the afternoon. Once the Federals had fallen back to Cemetery Hill, Trimble recalled, General Ewell "moved about uneasily, a good deal excited, and seemed to me to be undecided what to do next." Trimble had made a brief reconnaissance of the area. He announced that Culp's Hill commanded Cemetery Hill and recommended that Ewell seize it without delay. Ewell preferred to wait for Johnson's division before making the attempt. When Trimble continued to badger him about it, the Virginian's patience gave out. "When I need advice from a junior officer, I generally ask it," he snapped. Stung by the insult, Trimble stalked away in anger, never to bother Ewell again.[33]

Fast developing events seemed to justify Ewell's decision to wait for Johnson's division. Now or earlier Brig. Gen. William "Extra Billy" Smith reported a mixed Union force of considerable size advancing on the York Pike, threatening the Confederate army's left flank and rear. The report seemed incredible, but in the absence of Stuart's cavalry, who could say? Early ordered Gordon to reinforce Smith on the York Road.[34]

Ewell thought the matter important enough to investigate in person. Accompanied by Early and Rodes, he followed Gordon's brigade down the York Pike to a point whence he could see well down the road. The generals disagreed as to the truth of the report. Early later claimed that he placed no confidence in it, though Rodes, he said, was inclined to believe it. Ewell did not know what to think. As they discussed the matter, a dark line of skirmishers appeared in the distance. "There they come now!" cried Rodes. Ewell, too, thought that the distant figures looked like Federals, but Early vehemently disagreed. If they were Federals, he argued, Gordon would be firing on them. Ewell sent Tom Turner and Early's nephew Lt. Robert D. Early to investigate. As it turned out, Old Jube was right. (This was invariably the case in stories told by Early.) The men the generals had seen were Confederate skirmishers sent out by Smith earlier in the day. Although there seemed to be no immediate danger on the York Road, Ewell left Gordon's and Smith's brigades where they were. Rumors of Union troops in that sector would haunt him for another twenty-four hours.[35]

Having investigated matters on the left flank, Ewell again turned his attention to Culp's Hill. Had the Federals occupied it, and if so, how many troops did they have there? Ewell sent Turner and Robert Early to the top of the hill to find out. Meanwhile he rode with Jubal Early back into town. There they met Johnson, who had ridden to Gettysburg ahead of his division in order to get his instructions and reconnoiter the field. The bronzed old soldier struck Maj. John W. Daniel of Early's staff as "a 'rough-and-ready' looking soldier." The heavy staff he carried as a result of his crippled ankle seemed to the impressionable adjutant "as combative as an Irishman's shillalah [sic]."[36]

Johnson informed Ewell that his division was just a mile outside town, but that it would not arrive for an hour because a wagon train blocked its path. Ewell was in a hurry. If Culp's Hill was unoccupied, it would not stay that way for long. Turning to Early, he proposed that his division occupy Culp's Hill immediately and that Johnson's division fill the gap between him and Rodes when it came up.

Early bridled at the suggestion. He growled "that his command had been doing all the hard marching and fighting and was not in condition to make the move." The remark provoked "a tart reply" from Johnson and led to an exchange of words. In the end Ewell knuckled under to Early. He ordered his irascible lieutenant to go into camp and directed Johnson to bring his division to town and await further orders. It was an unfortunate decision.[37]

Johnson's division reached town just before sunset and halted near the college.[38] By then Turner and Robert Early had returned from Culp's Hill. The Iron Brigade occupied the west slope of the hill, but somehow in the growing darkness the two staff officers had failed to see it. They told Ewell that the hill was as yet free of Union troops. Rodes and Early were present when the officers made their report. Ewell turned to Rodes and asked him what he thought of sending Johnson's division up the hill that night. Rodes replied that Johnson's men were tired and that "he did not think it would result in anything one way or the other." Early took just the opposite view. When Ewell put the question to him, he replied bluntly, "If you do not go up there tonight, it will cost you 10,000 lives to get up there tomorrow." Ewell agreed and ordered Johnson to seize the hill if he still found it unoccupied. He detailed Turner and Robert Early to act as Johnson's guides.[39]

After sunset, when the fighting had subsided, Lee met with Ewell at a house outside town.[40] He wished to know about the condition of the Second Corps and the position of the enemy. Most important, he wanted to know what Ewell and his officers might accomplish the next day. Rodes was present when Lee arrived, and Ewell sent a rider after Early. Apparently he did not summon Johnson, who had just arrived at Gettysburg and was busy putting his division into line in front of Culp's Hill.

Lee wished to strike the enemy first thing in the morning and was looking for options. Could Johnson's division attack the Union right? Before Ewell could answer, Early spoke up. The ground was steeper and more rugged in front of Cemetery Hill than at other points of the line and thus more difficult to assail. Moreover, the Federals seemed to have concentrated the larger part of their force there. It would be better, he insisted, to throw Longstreet's corps against the Union left. Ewell and Rodes agreed.

Lee saw the reason in this and suggested that since the Second Corps could do nothing on the left, it might be best to draw it around to the right to support Longstreet. Again Early spoke up. Although the ground in front of Cemetery Hill did not favor an attack, he argued, it was well suited to defense. Abandoning the town after the success there on 1 July would demoralize the troops and require leaving behind many seriously wounded soldiers, not to mention lots of captured weapons. The Second Corps, he insisted, should remain where it was. Ewell and Rodes supported Early's position and added arguments of their own. Finding the generals opposed to his plan, Lee reluctantly agreed to leave the Second Corps where it was and to use Longstreet's corps to attack the Union army's left flank. Ewell was to make a diversion in Longstreet's favor, turning it into a real attack if the Union troops in his front showed any sign of weakness.[41]

The conference ended, and Ewell returned to his headquarters inside a barn near the junction of Carlisle Street and the Heidlersburg Road.[42] The mood there was buoyant. The Second Corps had whipped the enemy badly, and staff officers believed that it would thrash them even worse tomorrow. Even Sandie Pendleton seemed happy, remarking that "we finished the 11th Federal corps which we had beaten at Chancellorsville."[43]

Next to Ewell's headquarters stood the John Crawford house. The general and a few members of his staff wandered over to the building to beg a cup of tea. They found the ladies of the house caring for wounded Northern soldiers. When one of the women tearfully described the death of a young patient, Ewell said with more truth than tact, "Madam, we become hardened to such things in war." Such comments only stiffened the women's resentment toward the Southerners. Ewell and his staff got "plain fare, but no welcome," one unwilling hostess recalled, though she grudgingly admitted that many of the Confederate officers "were handsome and intelligent, and all polite and accommodating." The officers tried to strike up a conversation with the ladies, but their remarks met with stony silence. Someone then questioned them about the war. "We then very warmly expressed our feelings," remembered one woman, "and told them they were unwelcome guests." They must not have been too unwelcome, however, for Ewell got permission to return for tea the next morning. In return he posted a guard over the house and told the women to notify him if they needed anything.[44]

Meanwhile Lee had examined Cemetery Ridge and decided to draw his entire army around to the right, where the ground was more favorable to an attack. Col. Charles Marshall brought Ewell orders to evacuate Gettysburg and slide his corps southward. Ewell still opposed the idea. At 10 P.M., after discussing the matter with Early, he rode with Marshall to Lee's headquarters to persuade him to keep the Second Corps in town. Ewell predicated his argument on the belief that Johnson had seized, or would soon seize, Culp's Hill. With the hill in their possession, the Confederates could pry the Federals out of their strong position on

Cemetery Hill. Lee must have been skeptical when Ewell told him the enemy had not yet occupied Culp's Hill, but in the end he decided to let the Second Corps stay where it was.[45]

Ewell returned to his headquarters after midnight. Despite the lateness of the hour, he sent Tom Turner galloping to Johnson with orders to occupy Culp's Hill if he had not already done so.[46] Turner returned with bad news: the hill was in Union hands. Johnson had delayed his advance until he heard from Ewell. By then Union troops had seized the ground. To make matters worse, Confederate skirmishers on the Hanover Road had captured a Union courier. On him was a dispatch indicating that the Twelfth Corps was at Gettysburg and that the Fifth Corps would be there by dawn.[47]

Turner's report blasted Ewell's plans. He assumed that Johnson had seized Culp's Hill hours ago, and he had gotten Lee to change his plan of attack based on that assumption. Now to his embarrassment he learned that Union forces, rather than his own, occupied the summit. It would have been best to shift around to the right, as Lee had suggested, but Ewell sadly realized that that was no longer feasible. "Day was now breaking," he later wrote, "and it was too late for any change of place." Like it or not, he had no choice but to fight it out where he was.[48]

Ewell expected Longstreet's attack to begin early on 2 July, and he had his corps ready at dawn to support it. "Old Pete" was not ready to go at that hour, though, and Lee ordered Ewell to delay his attack until Longstreet's guns opened on the right. Ewell forwarded the message to Johnson and continued to wait. With the sun an hour high and the troops on the right still showing no sign of an attack, Ewell became impatient. He sent Campbell Brown to Lee to report that his corps was ready and waiting to go forward. Lee replied that Longstreet's corps was not yet in position. He ordered Ewell to await Longstreet's attack and when it occurred, "to make a simultaneous demonstration upon the enemy's right, to be converted into a real attack should opportunity offer."[49]

Ewell sat down on a ramp outside his headquarters to eat a snack. He was tired from lack of sleep, disappointed over his failure to take Culp's Hill, and impatient for Longstreet to attack. He was less than gracious, then, when a Union surgeon appeared asking for flour to feed a body of wounded Union prisoners. How many men were there? Ewell demanded. The man was not sure exactly but thought 2,000 rations ought to suffice. Ewell replied irritably that "it was a queer way of doing business, wanting bread to feed people and not knowing how many there were to feed," but he promised to send the flour. It never arrived. Years later the surgeon wrote that Ewell's "bearing toward me was that of a great superiority, giving the impression that it was to him a great condescension to enter into conversation with an ordinary Yank. I never saw him afterwards," he added, "and am unable to say whether the two days following knocked any of the nonsense out of him or not."[50]

Lee meanwhile was growing impatient. Although it was well past dawn, Longstreet still did not have his corps in position to advance. With the morning slipping away, Lee sent Maj. Charles S. Venable to question Ewell about the possibility of attacking on the left. If that was not feasible, Lee again proposed to draw the Second Corps around to the right and attack the Federals there. Ewell had opposed the plan the previous night, and he opposed it still. A daylight attack against either Culp's Hill or Cemetery Hill would be costly and of doubtful success. As for shifting his position, that simply was not practical. The Federals would easily detect any movement on his part and counter it using their shorter, interior lines. Ewell undoubtedly explained all of this to Venable as they rode together from point to point along the Second Corps front.[51]

When the officers returned from their ride at 9 A.M., they found Lee waiting for them. The commanding general had viewed Culp's Hill and Cemetery Hill from the almshouse cupola that morning, and he must have known that the odds of a successful attack there were slim. If he still entertained thoughts of drawing the Second Corps around to the right, Ewell dissuaded him from doing so, for his orders regarding the Second Corps remained unchanged. Lee left Ewell and returned to Seminary Ridge. Soon after, he notified Ewell that Longstreet's attack had been pushed back to 4 P.M.[52]

Ewell took breakfast with Early and Rodes at the Crawford house, then rode the lines with Early looking for suitable artillery positions. He found just two: Seminary Ridge, where Capt. Willis J. Dance had already posted his battalion, and Benner's Hill, south of the Hanover Road. Neither position was ideal. Seminary Ridge was more than a mile from the Union line, and Benner's Hill offered Confederate artillerists who occupied it little cover while exposing them to fire from Union guns on Cemetery Hill.[53]

Ewell also spent time that morning concentrating his infantry brigades for an attack on the heights. Smith and Gordon of Early's division picketed the York Road. Walker's Stonewall Brigade of Johnson's division watched the Hanover Road, a little farther south. Ewell had Early move Gordon back to town, leaving Smith to hold the York Road alone. He then ordered Albert Jenkins's cavalry to replace Walker's brigade on the left, freeing Walker to rejoin Johnson. By a strange twist of fate, a Union artillery round wounded Jenkins as he attempted to obey this order, and his brigade never reached its destination. As a result Walker continued to hold his position on the Hanover Road and was unable to join John-son's attack on Culp's Hill, a circumstance that may have had a significant impact on the outcome of the battle.[54]

Nothing is known of Ewell's activities on the afternoon of 2 July. Having been up all night conferring with Lee and trying to arrange an attack on Culp's Hill, he probably slept. At 4 P.M. Confederate guns on Seminary Ridge opened fire on Union soldiers in the Peach Orchard and on southern Cemetery Ridge. Ewell's artillery added its weight to the bombardment. Three rifled batteries of Dance's battalion shelled the Federal line from a point near the Lutheran Seminary. At the same time Snowden Andrews's battalion, commanded by Maj. Joseph W. Latimer and aided by Capt. Archibald Graham's battery, unlimbered on Benner's Hill and blasted the Federals from close range on the left.

Ewell's guns had the advantage of a converging fire; but otherwise their position was inferior, and they suffered badly. A soldier in the Chesapeake Artillery described Benner's Hill as "simply a hell infernal. Our position was well calcu-lated to drive confidence from the stoutest heart," he recalled. "We were directly opposed by some of the finest batteries in the regular service of the enemy, which batteries, moreover, held a position to which ours was but a molehill. Our shells ricochetted over them, whilst theirs plunged into the devoted battalion, carrying death and destruction everywhere."[55]

Latimer maintained the unequal contest for more than an hour before order-ing his guns away. He kept four pieces on the ridge to cover the advance of John-son's infantry. As the young artillerist sat on his horse calmly directing the fire of the guns, a shell burst over his head, inflicting a mortal wound. With his death Ewell lost his favorite and perhaps best artillery officer. "Major Latimer served with me from March, 1862, to the second battle of Manassas," he noted in his re-port. "I was particularly struck at Winchester, May 25, 1862, his first warm en-gagement, by his coolness, self-possession, and bravery under a very heavy ar-tillery fire, showing when most needed the full possession of all his faculties. Though not twenty-one when he fell, his soldierly qualities had impressed me as deeply as those of any officer in my command."[56]

Before Latimer's guns stopped firing, Longstreet assaulted Meade's left. Unable to see the southern end of the battlefield, Ewell had members of his staff climb a ladder into the cupola of the Roman Catholic church and call down to him the progress of Longstreet's fight. (Ewell's wooden leg kept him from going up him-self.) "Things are going splendidly," they reported, "we are driving them back everywhere." The news prompted Ewell to convert his demonstration into a gen-eral attack, as provided for in Lee's orders. Johnson's division would attack first,

Joseph W. Latimer (National Archives)

since it had the farthest distance to go and the most difficult terrain to cross. Once Johnson had engaged Union troops at Culp's Hill, Early and Rodes would go forward. The attack would be *en echelon* from left to right by divisions. Almost as an afterthought, Ewell sent a message to Brig. Gen. James H. Lane, commanding Hill's leftmost division, urging him to participate in the assault. Nothing came of the suggestion. If Hill and Ewell had any contact that afternoon, there is no evidence of it.[57]

Ewell watched the attack from a point on Early's front, near the center of his three-mile-long line. At 7 P.M. Johnson's division marched down the western slope of Benner's Hill, waded Rock Creek, and struck the Union line on Culp's

Hill. Ewell's former chief of staff, John M. Jones, took a bullet in the thigh while leading his brigade up the hill's east slope. Neither his troops nor Brig. Gen. Francis R. T. Nicholls's, on his left, could dent the Federal line on the main hill, but farther down the line, on the lower crest, "Maryland" Steuart captured some Federal entrenchments just 500 yards from Meade's lifeline, the Baltimore Pike. In the darkness Johnson probably did not know what he had gained; even had he known, the absence of Walker's brigade left him too weak to exploit the opportunity.[58]

Early's division likewise achieved some success. As soon as Johnson became engaged, Early ordered Hays and Avery to storm Cemetery Hill. The two brigades, together numbering just more than 2,000 men, swept up the dusky slope under a blaze of fire, overcame Howard's infantry, and momentarily found themselves among the Union batteries. It was Second Winchester all over again. It only remained for Rodes to secure the prize that Early's boys had won. But Rodes was not there. At the moment that he should have been charging up the west slope of Cemetery Hill, his division was still trying to clear the town. The only troops available to support Hays and Avery were Gordon's six regiments, which occupied Hays's former position near the base of the hill. But Early refused to order the brigade forward. Without Rodes's support, he deemed sending Gordon's troops to the crest a "useless sacrifice" and instead used them to cover the retreat.[59]

Old Jube was furious and rightly so. Riding to Ewell's headquarters, he complained bitterly about Rodes's failure to support his attack. The two generals visited Rodes at his headquarters to find out what had gone wrong. Rodes blamed his tardy advance on the number of Union guns in his front and on Lane's reluctance to support him on the right, but to Ewell the truth was all too clear: Rodes had failed to prepare his division properly for the attack.[60]

In contrast to the good humor that had prevailed the previous night, the mood at Second Corps headquarters the evening of 2 July was decidedly dour. Cemetery Hill had been in the Confederates' grasp (or so they thought), and they had let it slip away. The only thing they had to show for the day's work was the possession of a few hundred yards of Union trenches on the lower crest of Culp's Hill. Success had been no greater on the Confederate right, where Longstreet had battered the Union army's Third Corps but failed to break the main Union line. Despite the lack of success, Lee determined to renew the offensive in the morning. "The general plan was unchanged," he wrote. "Longstreet . . . was ordered to attack the next morning, and General Ewell was directed to assail the enemy's right at the same time."[61]

For Ewell an attack on Culp's Hill offered the only prospect of success. Johnson had made some gains there on 2 July, and if reinforced, he might be able to carry the hill. When some of his officers disagreed, Ewell supposedly replied with an oath "that he knew it could be done, and that the assault should be renewed." The only other alternative was an attack on Cemetery Hill, which, if made in broad daylight, would be nothing short of suicide. Ewell issued Johnson the necessary orders and during the night sent him Daniel's and O'Neal's brigades of Rodes's division and two regiments of Smith's brigade from Early's, doubling the size of his attack force. Jeb Stuart's cavalry had finally appeared and guarded Johnson's left flank, freeing Walker to take part also. In all, Johnson would have seven brigades available to attack Culp's Hill, three-quarters of the force later employed by Longstreet and Hill to assault Cemetery Ridge.[62]

Ewell planned to attack at dawn, but the Federals struck first. At 4:30 A.M. twenty-six Union guns opened on Johnson's position. When the firing let up, Jones, Nicholls, and Steuart surged forward. Thirty minutes after Johnson made his assault, Ewell received notice that Longstreet's attack had been put off until 10 A.M. Too late to disengage, he had no choice but to battle the enemy alone. With luck, perhaps he could sustain his attack until Longstreet pitched in.[63]

For almost six hours Ewell's veterans shed their blood on the rocky slopes of Culp's Hill. At 8 A.M. O'Neal's brigade went in, supported by Johnson's division. Walker and Daniel attacked around 10:00 A.M. By then it was obvious that Johnson could not take the hill, but Ewell ordered the attacks anyway. His goal was probably to draw attention away from Longstreet, whose assault was scheduled to begin any minute. If so, the attacks were in vain, for Longstreet was again delayed. Ewell had sacrificed his men to no purpose.[64] Johnson stubbornly maintained his position until 11 A.M., when he learned that a strong body of Union infantry was attempting to turn his left flank. He fell back 300 yards to a point near Rock Creek, a position he held for the rest of the day. "No further assault was made," he reported, "all had been done that it was possible to do."[65]

Ewell's activities on the morning of 3 July are as obscure as his movements the previous afternoon. As all the action was taking place in front of Johnson's division, he likely spent the morning there. Once Johnson's attack had expended itself, he rode into town with Maj. Henry B. Richardson, his chief engineer, to seek other possible points of attack. There had been considerable skirmishing on Early's and Rodes's fronts that morning. As Ewell and Richardson passed beyond the left of Hays's line to get a better look at Cemetery Hill, soldiers warned them to go no farther. Union sharpshooters armed with Whitworth rifles and telegraphic sights commanded the area, they claimed, and would pick them off. Ewell scoffed at the notion. The enemy was "fully fifteen hundred yards distant," he declared, "that they could not possibly shoot with accuracy at that distance & that he would run the risk of being hit." The two officers had not gone twenty paces when a bullet struck Richardson, seriously injuring him. Ewell saw to Richardson's safety, then confided to one of his aides that he too had been hit. The man helped him down from his horse and asked where he had been struck. "Here," replied the general, pointing to his wooden leg. "I'll trouble you to hand me my other leg." Thus fitted, he remounted his horse and returned to the front.[66] Ewell later used the incident to demonstrate the advantage of a prosthesis. "Suppose that ball had struck you," he later chirped to Gordon, "we would have had the trouble of carrying you off the field, sir. You see how much better fixed for a fight I am than you are. It don't hurt a bit to be shot in a wooden leg."[67]

Longstreet finally made his attack at 1 P.M., eight hours behind schedule. As usual, Confederate artillery opened the contest. One hundred and fifty guns, including some Second Corps batteries on Seminary Ridge and Benner's Hill, pelted the Union line along its entire length. Union artillerists bravely accepted the challenge. For an hour the ground around Gettysburg trembled as if caught in an earthquake. Then, as if by agreement, the guns fell silent. The men in both armies held their breath as 12,000 Confederates in Longstreet's and Hill's corps deployed for an attack on Cemetery Ridge.

Ewell viewed the attack from Seminary Ridge and prepared to support it if the Southern troops succeeded in breaking the Union line. "Longstreet, & A P Hill are advancing in splendid style," he informed Early, "if you see an opportunity, strike." But the Union troops on Cemetery Hill never weakened their lines. Thirty minutes after receiving Ewell's message, Early heard that the Confederates had been defeated. Pickett's Charge, as it became known, had failed.[68]

Meanwhile, beyond Ewell's left, Union and Confederate cavalry engaged one another in battle east of Gettysburg. Hearing that a mounted fight was in progress, Capt. Frank A. Bond slipped out of town with Company A, First Maryland Cavalry, in hopes of seeing some action. Ewell had appointed Bond provost marshal for the town, and when he discovered that the cavalryman had left, he sent orders for him to return at once. "The way that old gentleman pitched into me when I got back was a caution!" the refractory officer remembered in later years. "He had lost a leg, taken a wife, and joined the Church the previous year, and didn't swear then, but he was sufficiently emphatic without it."[69]

At sunset Lee held a meeting with several of his generals at his Cashtown Road headquarters. Three days of bitter fighting had failed to yield victory, leaving Lee no alternative but to return to Virginia. In preparation for the retreat, he ordered Ewell to withdraw his corps to Seminary Ridge, thus straightening and contracting the Southern line. The army would hold its ground on 4 July and retreat after dark if Meade did not attack.

Ewell withdrew his corps as ordered. Rodes and Johnson took up new positions on the ridge crest near the seminary, while Early formed in the low ground behind them, astride the Cashtown Road. Ewell made his headquarters on the ridge with Johnson and Rodes.[70] His new line stretched across the battleground of 1 July, and his men pitched their tents among broken fences, trampled crops, and swollen corpses. Artilleryman Robert Stiles noticed that some of the lifeless bodies had actually burst as a result of the "foul gases and vapors" that built up within them. "The odors were nauseating," he remembered, "and so deadly that in a short time we all sickened and were lying with our mouths close to the ground, most of us vomiting profusely."[71]

The Confederate army entrenched in anticipation of a Union attack, but Meade kept his distance. Although a few Federal regiments occupied the town, the Union army as a whole spent the day in its former position, its bands playing patriotic tunes in honor of Independence Day. Lee meanwhile sent his ambulances and a portion of his wagon train back through Cashtown Pass under charge of John Imboden. Heavy rains muddied the roads and retarded the Confederates' progress. At dark the infantry began its retreat. Hill's corps left first, followed by Longstreet, then Ewell. The Second Corps commander personally supervised the rear guard. The sun was several hours high before he left the ridge and joined the long line of men and wagons heading west.[72]

Many Southern soldiers refused to admit that Gettysburg had been a defeat. Those who did probably agreed with Campbell Brown, who "felt that the *position* & not the *enemy* had out done us." The army had incurred more than 20,000 casualties in three days of fighting, but like an injured animal, it was no less dangerous for that. If Meade was rash enough to risk another battle, Lee would be more than happy to oblige him. The Army of Northern Virginia may have suffered a setback, but in its own eyes, at least, it was far from defeated.[73]

★ ★ ★ CHAPTER 22 ★ ★ ★

The Natural Condition of Man

At the end of the war, when he was in prison and had ample time to reflect on the events of the preceding four years, Ewell told a fellow officer that "it took a dozen blunders to lose Gettysburg, and he had committed a good many of them."[1] Things had started well enough. When notified on 1 July that the enemy was at Gettysburg, Ewell had brought Rodes's and Early's divisions to the right place at the right time. As a result the Federal line had crumbled, and the Confederates rounded up 5,000 prisoners. But then things began to unravel. Critics claimed that Ewell should have followed up his success and seized Cemetery Hill, as Jackson surely would have done had he been alive. Even Lee indulged in such wishful thinking.[2]

Such criticism failed to take into account the strength of the Union position and ignored the obstacles in Ewell's path. The Union army had an estimated 12,000 soldiers on Cemetery Hill that afternoon. Sixteen hundred of these men belonged to Col. Orland Smith's brigade, which had not yet been engaged. The rest were fragments of the First and Eleventh Corps that had fought and been defeated. Although many Federal regiments had been badly mauled and were incapable of further combat, others remained in condition to resist a Confederate advance. They would have been supported by the Twelfth Corps, whose 9,000 men and four batteries were nearing the battlefield when the Union line collapsed. In addition to the infantry, Brig. Gen. John Buford had two brigades of cavalry and one battery of horse artillery south of Cemetery Hill, near the Peach Orchard.

Artillery was the key to Cemetery Hill's defense. Together the First and Eleventh Corps had no fewer than forty guns on the hill ready to meet Ewell's attack. These cannon commanded the open ground south and west of town and could have broken any line of battle sent against them. The answer, of course, was to silence the guns, but that was out of the question. The ground offered few favorable positions for Ewell's artillery.[3]

Robert E. Lee (Library of Congress)

To make the attack, Ewell had available two brigades of Early's division, together numbering roughly 2,500 men, and whatever troops Rodes could have
contributed. The latter would have been few, for Rodes had suffered 2,500 casualties, and his division as a whole was in no condition to press the attack. Rodes's
and Early's men were tired after their long march to the battlefield and burdened

with the 5,000 prisoners that had fallen into their hands. Under these circumstances Ewell's decision to await the arrival of Johnson's division seems prudent, even wise.[4]

Lee's orders played an important role in Ewell's decision not to attack Cemetery Hill. While on Oak Hill, Ewell received instructions from Lee not to risk a general engagement until the rest of the army arrived. After Ewell had entered the town, he received permission from Lee to attack the hill if he could do so to advantage, but in the same breath Lee reiterated his earlier order to avoid entanglement with the enemy. Faced with these seemingly contradictory orders and finding that he could expect no help from A. P. Hill, Ewell waived an attack on Cemetery Hill and determined to seize Culp's Hill instead. The capture of Culp's Hill by Johnson's division would effectively turn the Federal position and render an attack on Cemetery Hill unnecessary. It was a sensible solution to a thorny problem; unfortunately, it did not work.

Ewell's mistake on 1 July was not that he failed to attack Cemetery Hill, but that he did not take Culp's Hill. According to one contemporary source, he urged Early to do so, but his headstrong lieutenant balked at the suggestion and Ewell backed down. Instead he reverted to his original plan of having Johnson's division seize the hill. Mistakenly believing that Johnson was already in possession of the hill or soon would be, Ewell successfully argued to keep his corps on the left rather than drawing it around to the right, as Lee advocated. While he cannot be criticized for this counsel, he can be faulted for failing to communicate clearly with Johnson and for not knowing the state of affairs on his front.

The second of July was Ewell's worst day. He had orders to support Longstreet's attack, but his critics, including Longstreet himself, argued that he attacked too late.[5] Longstreet based his accusation on the false assumption that Ewell had orders to attack in conjunction with the First Corps. Such was not the case. Lee had ordered Ewell to make a demonstration in favor of Longstreet and to convert that demonstration into an attack if he saw a favorable opportunity for success. During the day an infantry assault on the heights was clearly impractical. Lines of Federal artillery frowned down on Early's and Rodes's divisions and easily could have broken up any assault. (An attack made in the full light of day, insisted Harry Hays, "could have been nothing else than horrible slaughter.") Ewell therefore limited himself to an artillery demonstration until sunset.[6]

Johnson was not as vulnerable to Federal artillery as Rodes and Early and could have attacked at an earlier hour, but he would have had to do so alone. Ewell naturally preferred a simultaneous assault by his entire corps. That being the case, he had no choice but to postpone his advance until dusk. Had he attacked just one hour earlier, he would have found the Federal trenches fully manned. Early and Rodes, advancing across open ground, would have taken a beating from the Federal guns on Cemetery Hill.[7] As it was, Early overran the Federal position on Cemetery Hill with amazingly few casualties, and Johnson was able to seize a portion of the Union trench line on Culp's Hill recently abandoned by the Twelfth Corps. Ewell's timing could not have been better, though admittedly his good fortune was as much a matter of luck as design.

A second criticism leveled at Ewell's 2 July performance was that he committed his troops piecemeal. Johnson, Early, and Rodes had each attacked at different times. Early disputed this. He and Johnson had attacked simultaneously, he argued; Rodes had not attacked at all. Although Ewell had instructed Rodes to support Early's attack, Rodes did not have his troops in position to assault the hill when the time came. This was Rodes's fault, but as his superior, Ewell, too, must shoulder part of the blame.[8]

A lack of coordination between the Second and Third Corps also contributed to the attack's lack of success. As army commander, Lee was responsible for coordinating the movements of his corps. When he did not do so, Hill or Ewell should have taken the initiative in the matter. Neither did. Just before going forward, Ewell called on James Lane, commander of Pender's division, to support his attack, but in vain. Ewell's negligence on 2 July is all the more remarkable because he was a conscientious officer. Perhaps he was suffering from fatigue resulting from a lack of sleep; on the other hand, the lack of information about his activities that afternoon suggests that he may have been napping at least part of the time. Whatever the cause—too little sleep or too much—he slipped.

He had no better success on 3 July. Ordered to support Longstreet's attack, Ewell engaged the enemy at dawn. When notified that Longstreet had been delayed, he struggled manfully to sustain his attack until the First Corps could pitch in. If Ewell can be faulted on 3 July, it must be for attacking too long and too vigorously. Once he learned that Longstreet's attack had been substantially delayed, Ewell probably should have broken off Johnson's attack. As it was, Old Allegheny sustained heavy casualties to no purpose.

Criticism of Ewell's performance at Gettysburg began on the battlefield and grew steadily in the years after the war. He heard the criticism and undoubtedly was stung by it, but he did not say a word publicly in his own defense. "He had, as I know, the means of vindicating himself," wrote Early, "but the unselfishness of his character induced him to trust rather to time for his vindication than to incur the risk of a discussion that might in the slightest degree injure the cause in which he was enlisted."[9] Among acquaintances, though, Ewell was not so reticent. "Yes; I know I have been blamed by many for not having pressed my advantage the first day at Gettysburg," he told a group of friends after the war. "But, then, I cannot see why I should be censured. General Lee came upon the ground before I could have possibly done anything, and after surveying the enemy's position, he did not deem it advisable to attack until re-enforced. Had I taken Johnson's fine division with me there would have been no second day at Gettysburg; but it reached me too late."[10]

Ewell's tepid performance at Gettysburg mirrored the actions of his division commanders. Although Ewell praised Rodes, Early, and Johnson collectively for their "wise counsel, skillful handling of their commands, and prompt obedience to orders," he could not have been very pleased with them.[11] Rodes had done the worst. His opening attack on 1 July had been disjointed, and when the Confederates finally took the town, he showed no inclination to push on and take Culp's Hill. On 2 July Rodes did not have his division in position to attack Cemetery Hill, and when called to task for this, he tried to deflect responsibility for his failure onto his subordinate, Stephen D. Ramseur. Ewell generously passed over Rodes's failure with the comment that "Major-General Rodes did not advance, for reasons given in . . . his report," though in private, wrote Campbell Brown, he "always thought Rodes fairly censurable. . . . Ewell & Early both thought Rodes had been too slow."[12]

Early had fought well. He had handled his troops skillfully both in the opening engagement and on 2 July. His decision to post both Gordon's and Smith's brigades on the York Pike, however, compounded by his stubborn refusal to seize Culp's Hill on 1 July when ordered to do so by Ewell, may have cost the Confederates the battle. Early's arguments against shifting the Second Corps from left to right that night were as obstinate as they were wrong. In retrospect one might also question his decision not to send forward Gordon's brigade to support Hays and Avery at Cemetery Hill on 2 July. Old Jube continued to be at once Ewell's greatest asset and his greatest liability.

Johnson's performance is harder to gauge. He failed to occupy Culp's Hill promptly when he reached Gettysburg, but it is hard to determine whether he or Ewell was at fault. According to Campbell Brown, Ewell held Johnson responsible for the mix-up, though Ewell typically refrained from any official criticism of his subordinate.[13] When Johnson did strike, he struck hard. He stubbornly maintained his 3 July attacks on Culp's Hill for fully six hours against a superior foe posted in a strong position. Future battles would confirm what Gettysburg promised: Johnson was a fighter.

It was almost noon, 5 July, before the last of Ewell's troops left Seminary Ridge and started down the Fairfield Road toward South Mountain. Lee visited Ewell in the morning and expressed his determination to fight the Army of the Potomac if it attempted to interfere with the retreat. The Federals kept their distance until late in the afternoon when Confederate wagons became snarled at Fairfield, a village near the eastern foot of the mountain. Seeing an opportunity to discomfit the enemy, a Union battery unlimbered and fired a few rounds into Ewell's column. One shot struck within a few feet of Lee, Longstreet, and Ewell as they conferred on a knoll about a mile from the guns. Ewell was still full of fight and begged the commanding general to let him turn back and attack the enemy. Lee appreciated his lieutenant's eagerness to fight, but it was not the proper time. "No, no, General Ewell, we must let those people alone for the present—we will try them again some other time," he replied. The Union demonstration did little harm and in fact accomplished much good, for it prompted frightened Confederate teamsters to clear the road. The Second Corps continued its march to the base of the mountain, where it spent the night.[14]

Lee's original plan called for Hill to relieve Ewell as the army's rear guard on 6 July. However, Lee sent Hill by a different route that day, leaving Ewell to bring up the rear again. For the second day in a row wagons blocked the roads, preventing Ewell from marching until noon. When his corps finally got under way, Early took the lead and Rodes brought up the rear. Union infantry briefly challenged the Confederates, but Rodes easily pushed them back. By nightfall the corps had passed safely through Monterey Gap and camped around Waynesboro.[15]

During the day Ewell sent Hotchkiss across the mountain to ask Lee about the route he was to take. Hotchkiss informed the commanding general that the Federals were again threatening the rear of the column. "If those people keep coming on turn back & thresh them soundly," Lee snapped. Hotchkiss carried the message to Ewell, who received it gladly. "By the blessing of Providence I will do it," he piped. Although it was late in the day, he sent Rodes back to smite his pursuers, but nothing came of it; the Federals had halted at the top of the mountain.[16]

As they crossed South Mountain, the Confederates passed the charred remains of wagons that had belonged to the Second Corps train. Ewell had sent much of the corps' baggage and captured property back to Virginia on the night of 3 July under the charge of his capable quartermaster, Maj. John A. Harman. In parting, he told Harman "to get that train safely across the Potomac or he wanted to see his face no more." Brig. Gen. Judson Kilpatrick's Union cavalry division attacked the train and burned several of the wagons as they passed through Monterey Gap. Ewell was mortified, thinking that he had lost much of his train. In fact, Kilpatrick had destroyed fewer than forty wagons.[17]

At Hagerstown the Confederates learned that Federal cavalry had wrecked their pontoon bridge across the Potomac. The water was high. Until it subsided or until the engineers rebuilt the bridge, the Army of Northern Virginia was trapped with its back to the river. It had no choice but to stand its ground until the bridge went up or the water went down.[18]

Ewell posted his corps north and northeast of Hagerstown. He made his own headquarters two miles out of town on the Greencastle Road. For the next two days Lee examined the countryside, looking for a suitable line of defense. Ewell accompanied him. Meanwhile the Army of the Potomac cautiously closed in. On 10 July it crossed South Mountain and advanced to Antietam Creek. The Confederates retreated across the stream and assumed a new defensive line that covered both Williamsport and the pontoon site at Falling Waters, four miles downriver. As at Gettysburg, Ewell held the left of this new line; Hill, the center; and Longstreet, the right. Lee admonished Ewell to strengthen his line and to do everything else within his power to ensure success. "You are aware of the importance of a victory to us on this occasion," he wrote, "for which I rely under God to the valour of our troops & the skill & fortitude of our officers. Let every man exert himself to the utmost."[19]

The troops set to work with a will to fortify their new position. Some of the men had lost heart when they discovered the Potomac was past fording, but as the breastworks took shape, their confidence returned. "Their spirit was never better than at this time," Ewell wrote, "and the wish was universal that the enemy would attack." Capt. William J. Seymour agreed. "We were all very anxious to have the Yankees attack us, for our position was a very strong one and we felt perfectly confident that we could defend it successfully."[20]

George Meade apparently held the same view, for he refrained from attacking. Despite his caution, battle seemed imminent. For two days the armies skirmished with one another while Meade looked for weaknesses in the Confederate line. But rain made accurate observations difficult. At one point Meade seemed to be massing his troops for an assault on the Confederate center, prompting Ewell to reinforce Hill. The Federals probed Hill's line but did not attack. Even so, Lee felt it wise to retreat. He did not relish the thought of fighting with a river to his back, and each day the forces arrayed against him grew stronger. Therefore when engineers completed the pontoon bridge at Falling Waters and reported that the water had fallen enough to permit the army to ford the Potomac at Williamsport, he ordered a retreat. The crossing began on the night of 13 July and was completed the next day. The First and Third Corps crossed the pontoon bridge at Falling Waters, while the Second Corps breasted shoulder-high water at Williamsport.[21]

By the Army of Northern Virginia's standards the crossing was chaotic. The Second Corps marched to the river by way of the Williamsport Turnpike. It was a dark and stormy night. Ewell planned to send both his infantry and artillery through the water at Williamsport, then ferry over his ammunition chests. When he reached the river, however, he found everything in confusion. The approaches were steep and slippery, there were no ferryboats, and no one seemed to be in charge. At the advice of the army's chief quartermaster, Col. James L. Corley, Ewell sent his artillery and ambulance train across the pontoon bridge at Falling Waters, escorted by Hays's brigade. The rest of the corps held their cartridge boxes and rifles over their heads and plunged into the Potomac's rushing waters.[22]

The Second Corps crossed at fords on either side of the Conococheague River. In order to reach the upper ford, Rodes first had to cross the Conococheague by wading through an aqueduct of the C&O Canal, an operation, he wrote, "not only involving great hardship, but . . . great danger." The crossing began at midnight and was completed by 8 A.M. Ewell did not lose a man in the perilous undertaking, though he left behind one caisson and necessarily lost a great deal of ammunition. Union troops skirmished briefly with Ramseur's brigade, which Ewell had left as a rear guard, but otherwise they did not interfere with his retreat. Matters took on a more serious aspect at Falling Waters, where Union cavalry attacked Heth's division and mortally wounded Brig. Gen. J. Johnston Pettigrew.[23]

The Second Corps rested for one day, then started for Darkesville, eighteen miles up the Shenandoah Valley. It remained there until 22 July. Longstreet and Hill bivouacked at Bunker Hill, three miles away.[24] Lee hoped that the Army of the Potomac would follow him up the Valley, but Meade instead chose to cross the Potomac east of the Blue Ridge. Anticipating that his adversary might attempt to get between him and Richmond, Lee reduced his baggage and marched to Culpeper Court House.[25] Longstreet snaked through Manassas and Chester Gaps near Front Royal on 20 July followed by Hill. Lee ordered Ewell to remain in the Valley a day or two longer, until the Confederates could evacuate their sick and wounded, then start for Culpeper.

Ewell made good use of the time by having Johnson tear up the B&O Railroad tracks west of Martinsburg. While engaged in this work, Johnson reported a Union force commanded by Brig. Gen. Benjamin F. Kelley camped near Hedgesville, at the eastern foot of North Mountain. He estimated Kelley's force at 10,000 men. If the Confederates moved quickly, they could bag the whole crowd. Ewell gave the necessary orders. Rodes hastened north to support Johnson near Martinsburg, and Early slipped across North Mountain in an effort to get behind the enemy. A local resident alerted Kelley to his peril, however, and he retreated before the trap snapped shut.[26]

Ewell's unsuccessful lunge at Kelley threw him out of position, and he had to hurry back up the Valley to catch up with Lee. Rodes and Johnson made Winchester on 22 July. The next day they pushed on to Front Royal, where they found Union troops trying to force their way through Manassas Gap. A. P. Hill had left Brig. Gen. Ambrose R. Wright's brigade to hold the gap. When Ewell arrived, he found the Georgians stubbornly contesting the enemy's advance. He sent Maj. Eugene Blackford ahead with 250 sharpshooters to check the enemy and deployed Rodes's division on a mountain spur to the rear.[27]

Ewell feared the Federals might try to capture the pontoon bridge at Front Royal. He ordered Johnson to guard the bridge and sent word to Early, at Winchester, to start immediately for Front Royal. If Ewell could not reach Front Royal that night, Ewell directed him to cross the North Fork of the Shenandoah at Strasburg. The bridge would meet him there. But again Meade was cautious. Although he had five of the army's seven corps at Manassas Gap, he did not try to force his way through the pass. It was probably a wise decision. Rodes held a strong position, and it would have required hundreds, if not thousands, of Union lives to drive him from it. Ewell held the enemy in check until dark, then marched up the Page Valley to Thornton's Gap, where he crossed the Blue Ridge on 27 July. Early crossed at Fisher's Gap, having come by way of Strasburg and New Market. By 29 July Ewell had reunited his corps at Madison Court House.[28]

It did not remain there long. Two days later the Union army shifted its base to Warrenton and pushed cavalry across the Rappahannock River. Fearing the move presaged an attempt by Meade to trap him between the forks of the Rappahannock and Rapidan Rivers or perhaps signaled a march by the Union army to Fredericksburg, Lee fell back to Orange Court House. He ordered the Second Corps to join him there. Ewell reached Orange late on 1 August after a severe march in sweltering temperatures. In the Twenty-first Virginia 50 percent of the men fell out of ranks, overcome by the sun's scorching rays. Several men in Daniel's brigade died of sunstroke. Without hesitation Dodson Ramseur declared it to be the hardest march he had ever experienced.[29] As an officer, of course, Ewell was able to ride to Orange. After his amputation he preferred to ride small horses because they were easier to mount. In the weeks after Gettysburg he was even seen riding a mule.[30]

Ewell held a line on the Confederate left stretching from Liberty Mills to Mt. Pisgah Church. His corps needed rest badly, and at Orange it got it. Meade halted his advance at Culpeper and for several weeks both armies enjoyed a period of repose. Ewell needed the rest as much as any. The two-month campaign had taken its toll. Although a correspondent for the Richmond *Whig* reported the general "in fine health and spirits," the truth was less rosy. A soldier who chanced to meet Ewell described him as having a slim and stooping figure with gray hair and beard and a wrinkled face. "He looks feeble," the man added, "& walks on crutches." The *Whig*'s assurances to the contrary, Ewell was a broken man. How much longer he could fulfill his responsibilities remained to be seen.[31]

Although it erred about Ewell's health, the *Whig* correctly assessed his high spirits. The reason was Lizinka. As soon as the army reached Orange, the impatient bride rushed up from Charlottesville to be at her husband's side. Her presence did him a world of good. She "has really made the old fellow look young again," Hotchkiss told his wife, "has taken away much of his former roughness of manner, in short, in his case, as in all other men's it is true that marriage is the natural condition of man, the one in which there is the fullest development of his whole nature and the greatest amount of earthly bliss."

Ewell would have agreed. The general adored his wife, and he made no secret of it. "Old Ewell is worse in love than any eighteen year old that you ever saw," chuckled Col. James Conner. Staff officers cast knowing glances or grinned outright as each night the "bald, bad man" mounted his horse and rode off to Orange Court House to be with his wife. Curious soldiers wishing to see the woman who had captured their commander's heart stared into the carriage and cheered lustily as it passed. The demonstration so embarrassed Ewell that he waited until dark to return to camp.[32]

Ewell eventually brought Lizinka, Hattie, and Lizzie to his headquarters at the Shaw house, one-half mile from Orange Court House. The large building stood on a breezy hill that offered a splendid view of the countryside. Out of courtesy for the owner or simply because it was more comfortable to camp outside on hot summer days, the general and his staff pitched their tents in the yard rather than occupying the house.[33]

Romance flourished around headquarters that summer and not just for Ewell. Sandie Pendleton was courting Kate Corbin of Caroline County, and in August he paid her a visit. When he returned to camp a few days later, he was engaged.[34] Lizzie and Hattie entertained a string of suitors. The *Vindicator*'s gossipy columnist reported that the girls were "the objects of considerable attention from the officers around them," a statement that Ewell's aide Lt. James P. Smith found all too true. Smith had a crush on Lizzie Ewell, but she had so many beaux, he complained, that he had "to commence the day before, and steal a march to get a word to her ears." When the future minister finally got Lizzie alone, he presented her with a religious tract in which he had boldly signed himself her "devoted" admirer. "Pretty rapid for him don't you think so?" she laughed to a friend.[35]

Edward Johnson was more forthright in his affections. The bluff forty-seven-year-old general had raised more than a few eyebrows in Richmond the previous year by cornering young ladies at parties and professing his love for them in thunderous tones. Apparently he did the same thing at Orange. Smith noted that Johnson was hanging around Ewell's headquarters, flirting with the ladies and "making himself agre[e]able or odious as the taste of one may determine."[36]

Ewell took his wife and the two younger ladies to picnics on Clark's Mountain, hosted dances for them at his headquarters, and accompanied them on visits to various brigade camps.[37] George Steuart's camp was particularly interesting. A stickler for neatness, Steuart had his troops sweep the forest floor with brooms made from twigs until only hard dirt remained. Ewell praised the camp and joked that "he was coming to play marbles on the smooth, hard floor."

When they were not policing the camp, Steuart had his men working at various home industries designed to aid the Southern cause. He organized wheelwrights to repair broken wagons, employed cobblers to make shoes, and put tailors to work mending torn and tattered clothing. His adjutant, Capt. George Williamson, enthusiastically seconded his efforts. One day, while riding with Ewell, Williamson pointed to a large pile of tin scraps that he thought might be used to repair broken canteens and other articles. When he suggested sending a wagon to collect them, Ewell heartily agreed. "Yes, a very good idea, Captain Williamson," he lisped, "Mrs. Ewell's bath tub wants mending." Williamson did not pursue the matter further.[38]

Ewell's response to Williamson clearly indicated that his mind was on Lizinka rather than on his corps. Dr. McGuire noted his commander's growing negligence toward his duties and thought that Lizinka should leave. Even Jed Hotchkiss, devoted family man that he was, had to admit that McGuire was right. Lizinka was hurting her husband's efficiency even as she was helping his spirits.

Criticism of Ewell came from other quarters as well. In a public statement that fall, the Council of Protestant Chaplains denounced Confederate officers who engaged in parties, picnics, and other pleasurable outings that were denied to the men in the ranks. The pronouncement angered Ewell. When Father James B.

Sheeran stopped by headquarters, Ewell asked Sheeran's opinion on the subject, hoping to find an ally in the Catholic priest. He was disappointed. Sheeran replied that such social events were not sinful in and of themselves, but that under the present circumstances they had a demoralizing effect on the troops. "How do you think our soldiers must feel, confined in their camp, and living on such rations as they now get whilst they see their officers riding about the country, gallanting ladies, indulging in luxuries and at the same time neglecting their business?" he asked pointedly. "I tell you, General, these parties had better be stopped or they will do much injury to your men. It is not the time for them." It was good advice, and Ewell would have done well to heed it. Unfortunately, he did not.[39]

Morale in the army was low after Gettysburg. The men were willing to endure long marches, short rations, and heavy casualties so long as victory crowned their efforts, but Gettysburg had been a defeat. In the weeks and months after the battle, many soldiers deserted the ranks and simply went home. On 26 July Lee issued a general order urging the absentees to return to the army, and got President Davis to offer a full pardon to those who complied. The measures had little effect. To stop the hemorrhaging of his army Lee ultimately had to resort to punishment.[40]

In August some thirty soldiers of Johnson's division deserted the army and set out for their homes in North Carolina. Guards challenged them at the James River. A scuffle ensued, and one of the guards was killed. Ten deserters were later rounded up and publicly executed by firing squad. Such displays revolted the soldiers, but whether they deterred others from deserting is hard to say. Thomas Boatright did not think so, because soldiers were hardened to such sights. John Casler thought their only effect was to make deserters go into Union lines. John Robson wrote that "as a terror to evil disposed person, and as a warning example to others, these public executions must be regarded very much as failures." Apparently most soldiers agreed with him.[41]

Military reviews helped foster esprit de corps among the soldiers. Between 26 August and 2 September Ewell held five separate reviews that collectively took in every brigade of his corps. A number of women attended the events, much to the delight of the troops. "We had quite a number of Orange and Madison beauties to grace the field," wrote a soldier in the Stonewall Brigade. "After the review we were requested to give them a rebel charge. . . . The ladies be it said stood their ground firmly, never flinching and I think they wished the gallants of the Brigade to capture them. As for my part I had a splendid [beauty] in view but she threw such a shower of smiles etc, as compelled me to retire."[42]

On 9 September, following the brigade reviews, Ewell held a grand review of the entire Second Corps in a field just east of Orange. His divisions stood in three lines, each stretching for about a mile. Early held the front line; Johnson, the second; and Rodes, the third. Each line formed 200 yards behind the one ahead of it. The three divisions comprised 16,000 men. One-quarter mile in front of Early's division stood a reviewing stand, over which Ewell's headquarters flag floated gaily in the breeze. Lizinka was there, her face beaming with delight. Hattie stood at her side. "Mrs. Ewell is a handsome and agreeable looking lady," wrote one man in the ranks, "and the general's daughter is almost a beauty." Another soldier was not so charitable. "The young lady was rather pretty," he admitted, "but the Madam was not so. She had two long curls, one on each side hanging down on her neck. She is about 45, I suppose."

Once all the troops had assembled, Ewell and his generals galloped onto the field, followed by a cloud of staff officers. "Never having seen General Ewell before, my eyes were riveted upon him," wrote one soldier. "He is a tall, slim individual, with extremely sharp features, and his Frenchified moustache and whiskers, make him look the warrior that he is; but the most remarkable feature about him is his restless eyes, which were constantly wandering over the field."

Lee appeared at noon and joined Ewell and his officers in front of the reviewing stand. A bugle called the troops to order. Lee and his staff rode to the right of Early's division and with bands playing started down the long line. Ewell and his division commanders rode behind the commanding general. As the officers passed, each brigade dipped its flags and presented arms in a military salute. When they reached the end of Early's line, the generals wheeled about and rode to the right of Johnson's division, reviewing it and Rodes's division in the same manner as they had Early's. A six-mile ride brought the officers back to the reviewing stand, where they stood as the brigades passed in review. After the last unit had marched past, the corps saluted as a body, raised three cheers for General Lee, and returned to its camps. In the opinion of participants and spectators alike, the military display was the event of the season, "the grandest review of the times." Two days later Hill's corps took the spotlight, and Ewell and his officers looked on. "It was a fine sight," admitted Sandie Pendleton, "but not near so good a show as we made."[43]

Pomp and pageantry could not hide the fact that things were not going well for the South. In August 1863 Maj. Gen. Ambrose E. Burnside advanced toward Knoxville, and Maj. Gen. William S. Rosecrans maneuvered Lt. Gen. Braxton

Bragg's Confederates out of Chattanooga, reestablishing Union control over the upper Tennessee River Valley. Farther west, Maj. Gens. Ulysses S. Grant and Nathaniel P. Banks captured Vicksburg, Mississippi, and Port Hudson, Louisiana, removing the final obstacles to Union navigation of the Mississippi River. Time was running out for the South.

In response to these reverses, President Jefferson Davis proclaimed 21 August a day of fasting and prayer. The Army of Northern Virginia responded enthusiastically. Throughout Orange County soldiers gathered for prayer. At Second Corps headquarters the Reverend Beverley Tucker Lacy preached to a congregation of 1,500 soldiers that included Generals Lee, Ewell, Rodes, and Johnson.[44] The high attendance was symptomatic of the religious revival that was sweeping the army. "The converts were so numerous," asserted John Worsham, "that they were numbered not by tens and hundreds but by thousands." Bishop John Johns and a host of other clergy flocked to the army to reap the harvest of souls. Lizinka hoped that her husband might offer himself for confirmation during Johns's September visit, but he was not yet ready to make such a commitment.[45]

Prayers preceded action. Confederate leaders wished to take the offensive before Union armies in the West converged on Bragg or drove into the Deep South. The question was not whether they should attack, but where. In late August Lee traveled to Richmond to discuss this question with President Davis and his advisers. Two weeks of earnest discussion resulted in the decision to send Longstreet's corps to Tennessee to reinforce Bragg.

Old Pete departed for Georgia the second week in September.[46] No sooner had he gone than the Army of the Potomac shook off its lethargy and crossed the Rappahannock River, pushing Stuart's cavalry back to the Rapidan. To meet the Union advance, Ewell concentrated his corps between Somerville and Germanna Fords. He took up residence at Morton's Hall, a house equidistant to Somerville and Raccoon Fords. At least one ill-clad Confederate looked forward to the Union army's advance with eagerness. "It is getting cold," he explained, "and we stand in need of blankets and overcoats."[47]

The Confederates expected Meade to attack, but the Union commander again disappointed them. On 19–20 September Bragg and Longstreet defeated Rosecrans's army at Chickamauga. Instead of taking advantage of Longstreet's absence to attack Lee, Meade sent the Eleventh and Twelfth Corps to reinforce Rosecrans. Lee promptly took the offensive in order to prevent Meade from detaching additional troops. On 3 October he met with Ewell, Hill, and Early on Clark's Mountain and announced his intention to turn Meade's right flank. He had sent scouts across the river to gain information about the exact location of Meade's army; the movement would begin as soon as they returned. Ewell readied his corps for action and sent Lizinka and Hattie back to Charlottesville. The past two months had been something of a vacation for the general, but it was now time to get back to work. For the next few weeks, war would again take center stage.[48]

CHAPTER 23

Autumn of Discontent

The Army of Northern Virginia quietly left its entrenchments on the night of 8 October 1863 and headed toward Madison Court House, the appointed staging area for Gen. Robert E. Lee's fall offensive. Lee intended to use much the same strategy he had employed against John Pope in 1862, engaging the enemy's attention along the Rapidan with part of his army while knifing toward the enemy's rear with the balance of it. Lee had hoped to pin Pope between the forks of the Rappahannock and Rapidan Rivers, but Pope had eluded that trap. Perhaps Meade would not be so fortunate.[1]

With Longstreet's corps absent in Georgia, Lee had only 48,000 men to bring against Meade's army. Ewell commanded more than 18,000 of those troops, complemented by eighty-one guns.[2] The Second Corps crossed the Rapidan River on 9 October at Peyton's and Barnett's Fords and proceeded to Madison Court House, where it joined A. P. Hill's troops. From there the Confederates marched north in an effort to turn the Union army's right flank and cut it off from the Rappahannock River. They moved in two arcs, Ewell on the inside, Hill on the outside. Lee accompanied Ewell's column. To avoid detection by Union signalmen, the marching columns shunned bare hilltops and large fields in favor of low, wooded terrain. The roads that Ewell's men followed, when they existed at all, were rough and made muddy by recent rains. As a result, the march was slow.[3]

Meade detected the danger to his flank and withdrew north of the Rappahannock. Lee responded by ordering yet another flank march. The Confederates again moved in a double arc, Ewell again taking the inside track.[4] Skirting Culpeper, the Second Corps headed north toward Fauquier White Sulphur Springs, a popular resort prior to the war. A bridge crossed the Rappahannock River one mile from the Springs. When a brigade of Union cavalry tried to keep the Confederates from crossing, Col. Thomas Carter brought forward sixteen guns and cleared the way. Stuart's cavalry clattered over the span and scooped up

300 prisoners. Rodes and Johnson crossed the river in Stuart's wake and bivouacked at the resort ruins, firmly establishing Confederate control over the bridge. Early remained south of the river to protect the corps wagon train.[5]

Ewell reached Warrenton at 9:00 A.M. on 13 October.[6] On the way he came upon Father Sheeran wrapped in a gray U.S. Army blanket.

"Why, Father, were you in the battle yesterday?" queried the general.

"Why do you ask?" replied Sheeran.

"I see you have a Yankee blanket and I thought you captured it."

"I was at the battle, General, but I captured nothing. Some of *your good boys* stole my overcoat, so I have to wear my blanket." Ewell and his staff roared with laughter at the reply.[7]

The Second Corps waited at Warrenton for Hill's troops to catch up. The Army of the Potomac was just a few miles ahead, and Lee wanted to have the two corps within easy supporting distance of each other. When the Third Corps arrived late that afternoon, it had to halt to distribute rations. The Second Corps remained where it was. Ewell took advantage of the pause in operations to visit friends in Warrenton. The women there showered him with hugs and kisses. In the evening a distant relative, Mrs. Tyler, fed the general and his staff a splendid dinner, replete with champagne and Madeira. It was a pleasant day indeed.[8]

While the Confederates rested, the Army of the Potomac retreated toward Washington along the Orange and Alexandria Railroad. Stuart kept tabs on its movements. Toward evening he found himself trapped between two enemy corps near Auburn. Maj. Gen. William H. French's Third Corps was east of him, and Maj. Gen. Gouverneur K. Warren's Second Corps was west of him. Detection might mean annihilation. It was already dark. Stuart wisely hid his command in a patch of woods and sent scouts through the Union lines to warn Lee of his predicament. Lee got the message at 1:00 A.M. on 14 October and ordered Ewell to march to Stuart's assistance. Rodes and Johnson approached Auburn from the northwest along the Dumfries Road. Early, supported by Fitz Lee's cavalry brigade, came in from the west on Double Poplar Road.[9]

At sunrise Ewell attacked. He was riding at the head of Rodes's column when his troops struck. Union bullets whistled past his ears. Junius Daniel's First North Carolina Infantry drove in the opposing skirmish line and captured the regiment that supported it, but a Union counterattack pushed the Tarheels back. Rodes sent forward the rest of Daniel's brigade, and at 10:00 A.M. Carter's artillery added its weight to the attack. By then Stuart was out of danger. As soon as the guns opened fire, the cavalryman came out of hiding and attacked Warren's rear. Before the Union general could recover from his surprise, Stuart had made good his escape.[10]

Warren fell back to Catlett's Station. Rather than pursue him, Lee directed Ewell north to Greenwich to rendezvous with Hill. The fighting at Auburn had delayed Ewell by more than four hours. When he reached the village, he found Hill's corps already passing through. Rather than wait for him to clear the road, Ewell turned his corps to the right and marched by fields and farm roads toward Bristoe Station. His route of march took him within sight of Stony Lonesome, but by then a battle was in progress and he could not stop.[11]

Bristoe Station was A. P. Hill's fight. Advancing eastward Hill encountered Sykes's Fifth Corps at Broad Run. He instantly deployed Heth's division into a line of battle and prepared to attack. Before Heth went forward, Warren appeared on his right flank, marching up the Orange and Alexandria Railroad. Without pausing to reconnoiter, Hill wheeled right and attacked him. The Confederates did not stand a chance. Warren posted his corps behind the railroad embankment, and as Heth's men swept down the slope, the bluecoats mowed them down. The Southerners fell back in disorder, abandoning five guns of Maj. David G. McIntosh's artillery battalion.[12] Ewell viewed the fighting with Lee and Brig. Gen. William N. Pendleton, then rode alone to speak with Hill, whom he found several hundred yards west of McIntosh's position. Hill suggested that the Second Corps advance perpendicular to the railroad and "sweep down on the enemy's flank." Ewell agreed to try.[13]

Early's division reached the battlefield first. Ewell put it in on Hill's right and deployed Johnson's men behind. As Early was bringing forward the rest of his division, John Gordon crossed Kettle Run with his brigade and pursued a body of Union cavalry toward Brentsville. Early sent staff officers to look for him. He meanwhile formed his remaining brigades perpendicular to the railroad, opposite Warren's left flank, and prepared to advance. But time had run out. Growing darkness and a dense pine thicket in his front prevented Early from attacking.[14]

By the next morning the Federals were gone. Warren had continued toward Washington after dark, leaving the field to the Confederates. Early reconnoitered with one regiment as far as Bull Run. Finding the enemy in force there, he returned to Bristoe, leaving Stuart to watch the enemy. On his way back Early picked up some 170 Union stragglers. Soldiers in Ewell's escort scooped up 74 more. The rest of the army remained in camp, cooking rations and gathering the dead and wounded. It rained much of the day.[15]

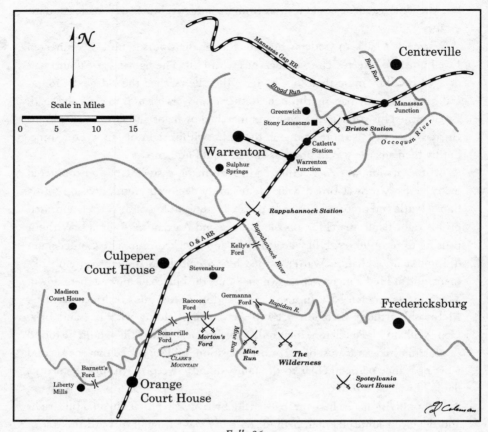

Fall 1863

Lee, Hill, and Ewell rode over the battlefield, now covered with slain Confederates. Half a century later, William W. Chamberlaine remembered the disappointed look on Lee's face. Strangely, he also remembered Ewell's smooth pate. "He was quite bald on top of his head, with gray hair on the back," recalled Chamberlaine. "His cap covered the top of his head, but left a bald place in the shape of a quarter moon. It was so noticeable that in my mind's eye I can see it now, forty-nine years after." [16]

With the Army of the Potomac safely behind Bull Run, Lee chose to withdraw. Meade's position was too strong to attack, and Lee could not readily outflank it. When faced with a similar situation a year earlier, Lee had opted to invade Maryland; but the season was too far advanced, and his force was too small to do that now. Lee could not stay where he was. The Federals had destroyed the Orange and Alexandria Railroad bridge over the Rappahannock River. Without that bridge, he could not feed his army in that destitute country. Retreat was the only option.[17]

To hinder the Army of the Potomac from immediately reoccupying the Rappahannock River line, Lee destroyed the railroad between Manassas and Rappahannock Station. Early tore up the tracks between Broad Run and Kettle Run, Rodes took the section between Kettle Run and Catlett's Station, and Johnson had responsibility for the portion between Catlett's Station and Warrenton Junction. The Third Corps extended the destruction all the way to the Rappahannock. Louis Leon of Rodes's division explained the process. "The way we tear up railroads is this: we take the cross-ties and make a square of them as high as your head. We place the rails on the cross-ties, then set it afire and the rails bend double." Railroad trestles, too, were destroyed. Even the stone abutments that supported them were not spared.[18]

Destroying the railroad took just two days' time. On 17 October the work was completed, and the army started for the Rappahannock. It retreated along the railroad through country ravaged by three years of war. "The whole way from Manassas to this point is one unbroken scene of desolation," wrote William Pendleton from Rappahannock Station. "Not a house left standing! Not a living thing save a few partridges and other small birds! No horse or cow, no hog or sheep, no dog or cat,—of course, no man woman, or child!" Walter Taylor had not thought such widespread destruction possible. "'Tis desolation made desolate indeed," he lamented. "As far as the eye can reach on every side, there is one vast, barren wilderness; not a fence, not an acre cultivated, not a living object visible; and but for here and there a standing chimney, on the ruins of what was once a handsome and happy home, one would imagine that man was never here and that the country was an entirely new one and without any virtue save its vast extent."[19]

Ewell lamented the desolation more than most, for this was his homeland; the blackened chimneys and barren fields belonged to his friends and neighbors. Stony Lonesome fared better than most houses in the region. On 29 June, prior to the campaign, a neighbor informed the general that the property "is pretty much statu[s] quo. The house standing, the fence tho' in bad order not burned. . . . The movable furniture is safe here and elsewhere, the stock principally saved except the sheep." Union soldiers had vandalized the property, however, and had taken many belongings, including the books of Thomas Ewell's "fine and well chosen" library and several letters written by Thomas Jefferson. Dick Ewell salvaged what little he could. Before leaving Stony Lonesome, the family had buried the china. The general unearthed the dishes after the battle and carried them away with what little furniture remained. There was nothing else to save.[20]

The Confederates crossed the Rappahannock River on 19 October and went into camp near Brandy Station, bringing the campaign to a close. Although Lee had not accomplished all he had wished, the offensive had not been entirely void of good results. Walter Taylor noted that the army had "taken about fifteen hundred prisoners, forced the enemy back to Alexandria and Centreville without any general battle, and gained from him, for a time at least, a large portion of our State." Ewell agreed that the campaign was worth the effort. The army had not gained much by it, but neither had it lost much. Responding to criticisms of his brother Ben, he said, "If inaction without chance of doing anything is as hazardous as action with the chances of great results, the choice is plain. The enemy would collect his strength untill there would be as much loss [doing nothing] as in taking the risk. We took the chances & are as well off as before the move."[21]

Others were not as philosophical. Most soldiers felt that the Army of Northern Virginia should have accomplished more. Hill received most of the blame, but Ewell got his share, too. Sandie Pendleton, who had been Ewell's biggest supporter in June, had become his most caustic critic. In a letter home Pendleton accused Hill of "disgraceful & culpable blundering" and said his own chief displayed "a want of promptness & decisive action," though he failed to give any examples. "What we shall do this winter I don't know," he moaned. "Gen. Lee must miss Gens. Longstreet & Jackson sadly; for Hill is a fool & a woeful blunderer . . . while Gen. Ewell, tho' he has quick military perceptions & is a splendid executive officer, lacks decision, and is too irresolute for so large & independent a command as he has."[22]

Once the army was safely across the Rappahannock, Lee and Ewell spent two days examining the river defenses. On 20 October they rode downstream to Kelly's Ford; the next day they changed direction and headed to Wellford's Ford. As they rode, they discussed Joe Johnston's and Gustavus Smith's actions on the Peninsula and Jackson's maneuvering along the Rappahannock in August 1862.[23]

The troops meanwhile entrenched. With cold weather just around the corner, many began constructing winter quarters.[24] Ewell initially established his headquarters at the house of Fred W. Brown near Brandy Station. He found the building damp, however, and soon moved to Mrs. Taylor's house, two miles south of Stevensburg. That was no better, and within a week Ewell moved back to Brandy Station. This time he stayed at the house of a Colonel Thom, which Sandie

Pendleton described as "a fine old mansion in quite good preservation, barring some panes of glass."[25]

Just days after the Confederates crossed the river, Ewell gave Pendleton permission to visit Kate Corbin in Caroline County. The couple were engaged to be married on 25 November. Ewell suggested that Pendleton bring his bride back to Brandy Station after the wedding to spend the winter. The haughty adjutant declined his offer, however, believing that "ladies should have maids, & decent cooks also," something Kate would not have at the Thom house.[26]

Pendleton scheduled his wedding for late November in the belief that the fall campaign would then be over. That was not the case. As soon as the Confederates withdrew behind the Rappahannock River, Meade rebuilt the Orange and Alexandria Railroad and began advancing southward.[27] Lee was determined to hold the Rappahannock line. Because the land on the left bank of the river dominated the right bank at several fords, he could not prevent the Union army from crossing. He decided instead to maintain a pontoon bridge at Rappahannock Station. If the Federals crossed the river, Lee could quickly pass troops over the span and strike at Meade's line of communications. If Meade divided his army in order to guard the bridge, Lee could attack and defeat the Federals piecemeal.

The success of the plan hinged on the Confederates holding the bridge. To do so, they constructed a bridgehead north of the Rappahannock. The line had its flanks anchored on the river and boasted two small redoubts that sheltered Capt. Charles A. Green's Louisiana Guard Artillery. Other batteries supported the line from hills immediately south of the river.

Early and Johnson took turns manning the bridgehead. Harry Hays's Louisiana Brigade occupied the works on 7 November when the Union army suddenly appeared and drove in its pickets. Early notified Lee and Ewell of this development and brought forward the rest of his division to support Hays. Rodes likewise reported Federals advancing in force on Kelly's Ford, four miles downriver. Lee ordered Maj. Gen. Richard H. Anderson's division to support Early at Rappahannock Station and sent Johnson to reinforce Rodes at Kelly's Ford. He then joined Early at Rappahannock Station, freeing Ewell to supervise affairs at Kelly's Ford.[28]

Dodson Ramseur's brigade had responsibility for Kelly's Ford that day. The Second North Carolina Infantry picketed the ford, supported by the Thirteenth North Carolina and Capt. John L. Massie's Fluvanna Artillery. Because the terrain on the left bank of the river dominated the right bank, Ramseur could not prevent the Federals from crossing the river if they were determined to do so.

His job was to contest the crossing long enough to allow Rodes to form a line of battle farther back from the river.[29]

At noon French's Third Corps drove in Ramseur's skirmishers at the ford. Ramseur advanced the Thirteenth North Carolina to support the Second, but Union artillery fire scattered the regiment as it approached the river. Massie bravely returned their fire, but enemy cannon quickly silenced his guns. Union infantry meanwhile waded across the river above the ford and slipped behind Ramseur's men, compelling more than 300 to surrender. The others quickly abandoned the ford. French pushed a division across the river to hold the ford and started construction of a pontoon bridge.[30]

Rodes posted his division in a line of battle a mile back from the ford and awaited reinforcements. Johnson came up after dark and extended Rodes's line to the right. To their delight, soldiers in the Stonewall Brigade found that their battle line ran directly through Rodes's camp. Rodes's men "had left everything belonging to them in their shanties except their arms," remembered John Casler with a grin. "We remained there about one hour, and plundered their camp thoroughly."[31]

As Johnson marched to Kelly's Ford, matters took a decided turn for the worse at Rappahannock Station. After driving Hays's skirmishers back to the works, Maj. Gen. John Sedgwick brought up cannon and began shelling the bridgehead. Confederate artillerists responded, but their long-range practice was so ineffective that Lee ordered all guns south of the river to cease firing. At 4:00 P.M. Brig. Gen. Robert F. Hoke's brigade arrived, and Early sent three of its regiments across the river to support Hays. He held Gordon's and Pegram's brigades in reserve south of the river.[32]

The Federals shelled the bridgehead throughout the afternoon but otherwise showed no disposition to fight, leading Lee and Early to conclude that the movement was merely a demonstration to cover French's crossing at Kelly's Ford. They were wrong. At dusk two Sixth Corps brigades using bayonets overran the works. Once inside, they swept the pontoon bridge with deadly fire. Hays was among the few defenders who escaped. As the general was in the act of surrendering, his horse bolted, drawing a flurry of lead. With nothing to lose, Hays spurred his horse across the bridge to safety.[33]

The Confederates lost approximately 1,700 men and four guns at Rappahannock Station. When added to Rodes's casualties at Kelly's Ford, their losses topped 2,000. Union casualties, by contrast, totaled just 370.[34] Southerners naturally sought explanations for the defeat. Lee thought that his officers had improperly posted their pickets. Early, on the other hand, blamed the disaster on defective engineering, too few pontoon bridges, and a lack of sufficient artillery support south of the river. Ewell disagreed with Early about the necessity for more artillery, arguing that "the darkness and nature of the ground" made even the guns that were present "of but little use in the final attack," but Early may have been right about the inferior quality of the works. At Rappahannock Station, Maj. Henry Richardson's absence was keenly felt.[35]

The bridgehead was the key to Lee's defensive strategy, and its collapse placed the entire army in jeopardy. If Meade moved quickly, he might pin the outnumbered and overextended Confederate army against the Rapidan River just as Lee had tried to pin him against the Rappahannock one month earlier. Ewell knew this. When he got the news, he purportedly exclaimed, "Then it's time we were out of this!" Lee apparently felt the same way. Within hours of the battle, he had his army marching for the Rapidan.[36] It crossed the river on 10 November. After four weeks of marching and fighting, the Army of Northern Virginia was back where it started.

Hill and Ewell became scapegoats for the campaign's failure. It seemed like a logical conclusion. Under Longstreet and Jackson the army had triumphed; under Hill and Ewell it had faltered. But was Ewell to blame? From a distance of more than 130 years, it is hard to find fault with his performance at Bristoe Station. The only charge that might be leveled against him is that he did not get his troops into position quickly enough to attack Warren on 14 October. But that appears to have been more the fault of Early and Gordon than of Ewell. Nor was he in any way to blame for the reverse at Rappahannock Station. Lee and Early commanded at the bridgehead; Ewell was at Kelly's Ford. Few soldiers knew that, however. As far as they were concerned, the Second Corps had been trounced, and Ewell was to blame.[37]

Sandie Pendleton continued to be Ewell's harshest critic. The defeats at Bristoe Station and Rappahannock Station, coming on the heels of Gettysburg, convinced him that his chief was not fit to command the corps. He felt sickened and disgraced by the outcome of the campaign, he told his mother, as did everyone in the command. "Oh, how each day is proving the inestimable value of General Jackson to us," he grumbled, though he failed to say how Jackson's presence might have changed the outcome. As the month progressed, Pendleton's bitterness increased. On 25 November he wrote to his sister complaining about his "superannuated chieftain." He claimed that Ewell was not up to command physically and criticized him for "doting so foolishly upon his unattractive spouse. Gen. Early is far superior to him as a commander," he concluded, "more energetic and a good disciplinarian, and withal more agreeable as an associate."[38]

Pendleton's comments suggest that his criticism of Ewell stemmed from personal rather than professional reasons. He obviously disliked Lizinka, who ruled the general's staff with the same iron hand with which she ruled the general. As chief of staff, Pendleton found this intolerable, and he vented his anger toward Lizinka by criticizing her husband.

To Pendleton's chagrin, Lizinka and Hattie returned to the army as soon as it recrossed the Rapidan. Ewell picked up the women at Orange Court House on 9 November and drove them back to Morton's Hall the following day. The Mortons occupied one end of the house, and Ewell's staff shared a room at the other end, leaving Lizinka and Hattie two rooms upstairs. Hattie found the staff "in possession of their usual health and spirits. Col Pendleton is as noisy as ever," she wrote, "Major Green[e] as obliging; Capt Smith as good; Mr Lacy as complimentary and flowery and fond of good eating, and Capt Turner as frisky." The only bad news, she told Lizzie, was that Smith intended to resign from the staff and devote himself to the ministry. "Don't you think it is a pity?" she asked. "I think it is a great mistake on his part and I am sorry for it because I think his influence is so good—so much better than Mr. Lacy's." [39]

Ewell encouraged Lizinka to come to Morton's Hall believing that the fighting had ended for the year. He was wrong. After driving the Confederates back beyond the Rapidan River, the Army of the Potomac advanced to Brandy Station and pushed its pickets all the way to the Rapidan. With the prospect of more action ahead, Lee canceled the leaves of all officers, including Pendleton, who was scheduled to marry Kate Corbin at the end of the month. The lovesick young man informed his fiancée of the bad news, adding "if 'hope deferred maketh the heart sick,' then my poor organ is well nigh until death.'" [40]

The new campaign also struck Ewell at a bad time. An ill-contrived wooden leg had ulcerated his stump, temporarily incapacitating him for field command. Lee suggested that he turn the corps over to Early and go to the rear, but Ewell demurred. It went against the grain for him to take himself out of action with a battle pending. After examining the general's leg, Dr. Samuel B. Morrison wrote out a certificate stating that Ewell would be fit to return to duty in ten days. In Ewell's opinion that was too long. He insisted that Morrison cross out "ten" and write "a few days" instead. That way he could return to action if anything developed. Lee, however, insisted that Ewell go to the rear. On 15 November he formally relieved his subordinate of command and put Early in charge, adding tersely that "Genl. Ewell was doing no good for himself or the country" by remaining with the army. Obviously Lee did not want Ewell around. [41]

Ewell relinquished command to Early on Sunday, 15 November, and was preparing to go to Charlottesville, when artillery fire erupted at Raccoon Ford. At Sandie Pendleton's suggestion, Ewell sent the headquarters wagons to the rear. Ewell's staff then reported to Early, while Ewell remained at Morton's Hall waiting for news. The commotion, however, was nothing more than a reconnaissance by Union cavalry. Within an hour the firing died away and things returned to normal.[42]

Ewell departed for Charlottesville the next morning "after much hesitation." Lizinka, Hattie, Campbell Brown, Tom Turner, and Dr. McGuire went with him. McGuire attended to Ewell, Campbell attended to his mother, and Turner attended to Hattie. As the party was leaving, some of the staff stepped outside to bid them good-bye. Lizinka knew that Pendleton and the others were glad to see her go and said as much.[43]

Ewell had the abscess on his leg treated at Charlottesville and received a new wooden leg. According to one source, he got the prosthesis from Dr. T. A. Lefar, who was in charge of the South Carolina Hospital in Charlottesville. A less reliable source insisted that a Maryland chaplain smuggled the leg into the South inside a crate of Bibles. Whatever the source, the new leg was not much better than the old one. Col. James Conner flatly proclaimed it to be "as poor a concern as ever I saw." Even so, Ewell's stump healed rapidly. He notified Early that he intended to return in a week. Until then, he jokingly admonished his subordinate "not to spoil his staff by letting them have too much baggage."[44]

Meanwhile the Federals embarked on a new campaign. On 26 November Meade crossed the Rapidan beyond Lee's right flank in an effort to turn the Confederates out of their strong position. Lee faced his army east to meet the threat. Johnson beat back assaults by two Union corps at Payne's Farm on 27 November, after which Lee withdrew to a strong position behind Mine Run and invited Meade to attack him there.[45]

Ewell rushed back to the army as soon as he heard that the Union army had crossed the river. He reached the front on the evening of 29 November to find the armies confronting one another across Mine Run. Instead of receiving Ewell warmly, Lee was angry that he had returned and "told him he ought not to have come back here." The commanding general refused to restore him to command while the campaign was in progress. It must have been painfully obvious to Ewell, if it had not been before, that Lee did not want him in command. The crestfallen general took up lodging with Early and waited for the fighting to end.[46]

For two more days the armies glowered at one another from the protection of their fortified positions. When Meade refused to attack the strong Confederate works behind Mine Run, Lee seized the initiative and attempted to turn Meade's left flank. His adversary, however, retreated over the Rapidan River before he could carry out his plan. Lee pursued Meade toward Germanna Ford but succeeded in picking up only a few hundred stragglers. Once again the Army of the Potomac had escaped.[47]

The Confederates returned to their camps and prepared for winter. With the fighting over, Ewell again applied for command of his corps. Lee initially ignored the request. Early generously offered to turn the command over to Ewell anyway, but Ewell declined taking it until Lee formally authorized him to do so. Ewell was a sensitive man, and Lee's hostile attitude puzzled and depressed him. As he sat at the Morton's house awaiting orders, he asked one of Early's staff if he ever wished himself dead, adding that "he sometimes thought it would save him a great deal of trouble."[48]

Finally, on 4 December, Lee sent Ewell orders to resume command of the corps. The order contained so much flattery that Campbell Brown thought that it would end with Lee refusing to restore Ewell to command. On the contrary, it told Ewell to take charge of the corps as soon as he felt able. He resumed his duties the next day.[49]

Despite Lee's kind words, Ewell must have known that he had lost the commanding general's confidence. Why Lee lost faith in him is not clear. He may have felt that Ewell was no longer up to the physical demands of an active campaign, or maybe, like Pendleton, he felt that his subordinate lacked decision. Perhaps he simply preferred that Early command the corps. Whatever the reason, Lee wanted Ewell out. It was not in Lee's character, however, simply to relieve a subordinate whom he found wanting. Instead he searched for a tactful way to shift Ewell to a command of less responsibility. That would take time. Until then, Ewell found himself back in command of the Second Corps. Between his questionable health and Lee's ill favor, though, his future in the army seemed anything but secure.

CHAPTER 24

Petticoat Government

Things had not gone well for the Army of Northern Virginia in the fall of 1863, but the Army of Tennessee had fared even worse. Lt. Gen. Braxton Bragg, commanding the western army, had defeated Maj. Gen. William S. Rosecrans's Union Army of the Cumberland at Chickamauga Creek, Georgia, in September, but he had failed to follow up his victory aggressively, enabling Rosecrans to entrench at Chattanooga, Tennessee. Although the acerbic Confederate leader promptly invested the city, his officers had lost faith in him and clamored for his removal. Jefferson Davis went to Tennessee to look into the matter, but his visit solved nothing. For the time being, Bragg remained in command.

Meanwhile President Lincoln placed Maj. Gen. Ulysses S. Grant in command of the newly created Division of the Mississippi, embracing the territory between the Mississippi River and the Appalachian Mountains. In a matter of weeks Grant broke Bragg's stranglehold on Chattanooga, replaced Rosecrans with Maj. Gen. George H. Thomas, and reinforced Thomas with 17,000 men from Maj. Gen. William T. Sherman's Army of the Tennessee. He then attacked Bragg's seemingly impregnable position on Missionary Ridge, carried it, and drove the demoralized Confederate army back to Dalton, Georgia.[1]

Davis now realized that Bragg had to go, but there was no one in the Army of Tennessee capable of replacing him. An outsider had to be brought in, but who? Davis suggested that Lee take over, but the Virginian demurred, saying that it would do no good to send him west unless he went there permanently. In that event, he argued, Davis would have to appoint someone to lead the Army of Northern Virginia. Ewell was next in line for the command, but in Lee's opinion Ewell's health was "too feeble to undergo the fatigue and labor incident to the position." Still uncertain about what to do, Davis summoned Lee to Richmond on 9 December 1863. Lee left immediately, not knowing whether he would ever return to the Army of Northern Virginia.[2]

For the next twelve days Ewell had command of the army. Less than a week after he took charge, Brig. Gen. William W. Averell led Union cavalry on a raid up the South Branch of the Potomac River. A second Union force, estimated at between 3,000 and 5,000 men, moved up the Shenandoah Valley toward Columbia Bridge. The enemy's movements must have reminded Ewell of Frémont's and Banks's strategy in 1862. Lee monitored the situation from Richmond. He ordered his chief of staff, Lt. Col. Walter Taylor, to send one or two brigades of cavalry to the Valley and infantry in like strength to Staunton. Fitzhugh Lee was already on his way to Staunton with two cavalry brigades, and Ewell sent a brigade of infantry from A. P. Hill's corps to reinforce him. Two days later Union cavalry entered Woodstock, a day's march north of New Market.

With the situation taking on a more serious aspect, Ewell sent Jubal Early to the Shenandoah Valley to coordinate the movement of Confederate forces there. Early reached Staunton on 16 December. By then Averell had broken the Virginia and Tennessee Railroad at Salem and was retreating northward. Early tried to cut him off, but Averell evaded his trap. He returned to Union lines safely, having destroyed the Salem depot, a significant section of railroad, five bridges, and several storehouses.[3]

Lee returned to the Army of Northern Virginia just before Christmas. After much discussion, President Davis selected Gen. Joseph E. Johnston to replace Bragg in Tennessee. Interestingly, Johnston had recommended Ewell as a possible candidate for the Tennessee command. Davis and Lee opposed the idea, however, on the grounds that Ewell was not suited for it physically or otherwise.[4] It was perhaps just as well, for misfortune seemed to dog the army and those associated with it.

James Longstreet had certainly found that to be the case. Lee had sent Longstreet's corps to Tennessee in September to reinforce Bragg. Bragg had then dispatched Longstreet to Knoxville in an effort to drive Maj. Gen. Ambrose Burnside out of East Tennessee. The expedition ended in failure, and on 30 December Longstreet asked to be relieved of command. Adj. Gen. Samuel Cooper notified Lee of Longstreet's request. He suggested that Ewell and Longstreet swap commands, but Lee rejected the idea, "believing that each corps would be more effective as at present organized." In the end Longstreet withdrew his request and retained command of the First Corps.[5]

Ewell would have welcomed transfer to Tennessee, for he had become disillusioned with the Army of Northern Virginia. Lee had lost confidence in him, and his subordinates whispered criticisms behind his back. By contrast, Joe Johnston was his friend and had a high regard for his ability. Ewell was therefore disappointed when he learned that the swap with Longstreet had fallen through. It galled him even more to learn that his health might have been a factor in the decision. "I am sorry I was not sent to East Tennessee," he complained to Ben. "My health was plenty good enough."[6] Health could be a precarious thing, though. In the first week of January 1864 Ewell's new gray mare slipped on the frozen earth and rolled over on him, leaving him lying bruised on the ground. For the second time in less than two months, he had to relinquish command of the Second Corps.[7]

Ewell's accident occurred just as the Confederate Congress was considering his confirmation to the rank of lieutenant general. Secretary of War James A. Seddon asked the general if he felt up to the demands of the position. Ewell referred the matter to Lee, knowing full well that the commanding general might use it to deprive him of his corps. "I am more interested in our success than in my own rank," he wrote to Lee, "and should it be thought best to promote another, I can assure you and his Excellency, the President, that my utmost exertions will be given in any capacity required."[8] Lee read over the correspondence and replied to Ewell as follows:

General:

I have received your letter of the 15th, transmitting a communication to you from the Secretary of War, with your reply. I am glad to hear that you now experience no inconvenience from your injury, and hope you may continue to feel none.

Your answer to the Secretary is such as I would expect from a true soldier and patriot as yourself. But I cannot take upon myself to decide in this matter. You are the proper person, on consultation with your medical advisors. I do not know how much ought to be attributed to long absence from the field, general debility, or the result of your injury, but I was in constant fear during the last campaign that you would sink under your duties or destroy yourself. In either event injury might have resulted. I last spring asked for your appointment provided you were able to take the field. You now know from experience what you have to undergo, and can best judge of your ability to endure it. I fear we cannot anticipate less labor than formerly.

Wishing you every happiness, and that you may be able to serve the country to the last,

I am, very truly, yours,
R. E. Lee
General.

Ewell sent both Lee's letter and his own to Secretary Seddon. Although he was willing to step aside if Lee wished to replace him, he did not think his health should weigh in the decision. "I have the authority of my Medical Director, Dr. H. McGuire for saying that my physical health is better than since the war commenced," Ewell asserted in his letter to Seddon, "& with the exceptions incident to my injury, I feel as capable of exertion as at any time for years. I feel it my duty however to say that I think the question involved in your letter should be decided by higher authority than my own. I can only answer to that of physical health." Lee offered no objections to Ewell's promotion, and on 2 February 1864 the Confederate Congress confirmed his appointment to lieutenant general.[9]

Although Ewell did not consider his health an issue, Lee did. Toward the end of January Davis asked Lee to recommend an officer to take charge of Confederate forces in West Virginia. Davis threw out Ewell's name as a possible candidate, but Lee thought Ewell's uncertain health disqualified him for the position.[10] While Ewell's health undoubtedly influenced Lee's decision, he was probably more concerned about his lieutenant's ability to exercise independent command.

Lee was not the only one who doubted Ewell's ability; by the winter of 1863–64 few seemed to have much faith in him. A soldier in the Second Virginia Infantry repeated a rumor that the Second Corps chief was going to resign in favor of Longstreet. "I hope it may be so," he wrote. "Never had much confidence in Gen. Ewell." During the Mine Run Campaign there had been talk that Brig. Gen. William N. Pendleton would replace Ewell as commander of the Second Corps. In February 1864 word spread that Lee intended to replace both Hill and Ewell. "The truth is, we want a new cut, shuffle and deal in Lieutenant Generals," wrote one South Carolina officer. "Ewell's great physical sufferings have impaired his efficiency; he seems to lack decision. . . . A. P. Hill has not risen to the requirements of a corps commander." Although rumors of a new cut were untrue, the fact that they existed at all indicated that the army wanted confidence in its corps commanders. Victory alone would restore its faith.[11]

Anticipating that Meade would attempt another offensive before cold weather set in, the Army of Northern Virginia delayed going into winter quarters until late December. Ewell guarded the lower stretch of the Rapidan River, from Clark's Mountain to Mountain Run. Hill extended the Confederate line upriver as far as Liberty Mills.[12] A few weeks after the army began its winter watch, Lee rode with Ewell along the river to examine possible artillery positions. Jubal Early and John Pegram tagged along. At Somerville Ford the group stopped and gazed across the river at a hill that divided the Federal camps. Pointing toward the enemy tents, Lee asked sharply, "What is there to prevent our cutting off and destroying the people in these nearer camps on this side of that hill, before those back yonder on the other side could get to them to help them?"

"This infernal river," snapped Early, "how are you going to cross that without giving warning?"

"Ford it, sir; ford it!"

"What are you going to do with your pneumonia patients?" Early asked sarcastically. Ewell and Pegram sided with Early as to the impracticality of fording the river at that time of year, and Lee did not pursue the matter. "I have never thought he seriously entertained such a purpose," wrote an officer in the party, "but he was evidently smarting under the slap in the face he had received [at Rappahannock Station], and he panted for some opportunity to return the blow." [13]

Lee almost got his chance in early February 1864 when Brig. Gen. Alexander Hays led his Union division across Morton's Ford. The crossing caught the Confederates between watches. As a result, only the Richmond Howitzers and a few infantry pickets stood between Hays and the Confederate works overlooking the ford. The Howitzers fired on the Federals, sounding the alarm. Ewell heard the cannon fire at his Morton's Hall headquarters, two miles away, and hurried over to investigate.[14]

"What on earth is the matter here?" he demanded. Before anyone could answer, he saw Union soldiers pouring across the river. "Aha, I see," he said. "Boys, keep them back ten minutes and I'll have men enough here to eat them up—without salt!" Putting his spurs to his horse, he disappeared down the road.[15]

Ewell had infantry on the scene within minutes. Pegram's brigade arrived first and filed into the trenches immediately confronting the Federals. Gordon's brigade arrived later in the day and took position on Pegram's left, near Dr. Morton's house. Just as Gordon's men appeared, the Federals started up the hill. For a few tense moments it was uncertain which side would reach the trenches first. When one of Gordon's colonels failed to move as rapidly as he should have, Ewell impatiently ordered artilleryman Robert Stiles to put the regiment into the works.

"Do you really mean that, General?" the startled lieutenant asked.

"Of course I do!" Ewell exclaimed.

Stiles took charge of the regiment and within seconds had it in its assigned position. According to Stiles, Ewell had previously urged his advancement, but he had refused it, arguing that he knew too little of tactics. Ewell reminded Stiles of this as the young officer returned to his battery. "Do you still insist, sir, that you don't know tactics enough to justify your being promoted?"[16]

Once Gordon's brigade had possession of the works, Ewell advanced a skirmish line and drove the Federals from the Morton house and its dependencies. The

Confederates did not hold the house long. Hays reinforced his line, and as night set in, the Federals retook the main house. That night, as Ewell rode along the picket line, he supposedly encountered two Union officers on horseback. He captured one, but the other got away. The captured officer said he was an aide to Hays and identified his general as the man who got away. The information upset Ewell, who was an old friend of Hays. Had he known who it was, said Ewell, "he would have knocked him down with his leg." [17]

While the fighting was going on at Morton's Ford, artillery fire erupted upstream at Raccoon Ford. Col. Clement A. Evans commanded Early's division that day and dispatched the Louisiana Brigade to the scene. The firing was a demonstration in favor of Hays, and it quickly died away; but Ewell did not forget Evans's prompt response. A few weeks later he recommended Evans's promotion to brigadier general. [18]

By evening Rodes's division had started arriving at Morton's Ford to reinforce Evans. The Federals' tepid performance to that point suggested that the crossing was nothing more than a reconnaissance-in-force. If so, they would be gone by morning. Ewell ordered Evans, Brig. Gen. George Doles, and Brig. Gen. Stephen D. Ramseur to watch them closely throughout the night and pitch into them if they retreated. If the Federals stood their ground, Ewell would attack them in the morning. [19] Despite these orders, Hays and his men escaped across the river that night, bringing the engagement to an end. They had suffered 255 casualties in the one-day affair; Ewell reported a loss of approximately 50 men. [20]

Ewell was nevertheless satisfied with the outcome. He believed that his swift and decisive action had prevented the Federals from seizing the Confederate earthworks behind the ford. "Had I not been here," he crowed to Ben, "there might have been a disaster the other day . . . but being on the spot as it were, I was able to give the necessary directions before the enemy had got a foothold." [21] Ewell overestimated his accomplishment, however. The purpose of Hays's demonstration was not to capture the Confederate works behind the ford but to hold Lee's army on the Rapidan while Maj. Gen. Benjamin F. Butler attacked Richmond from the east. The plan fell through when Butler failed to advance as planned. [22]

If Ewell was pleased with his performance at Morton's Ford, Ramseur was not. "Oh! for the spirit of Jackson," he complained to a friend. We "ought to have captured & killed the entire batch. I would have done so—had my plan been adopted by Lt. Genl. Ewell." [23] Ramseur did not say what his plan was. Since the Confederates did not have a sufficient force at hand to attack until sunset, it must have involved a night attack. Night attacks were rarely attempted in the Civil War because they rarely succeeded. There is no reason to believe one would have worked in this case. Ewell was wise to withhold his attack until dawn, though in this instance the Federals managed to escape.

At Morton's Ford, as in every battle that he fought, Ewell had exposed himself to the enemy's fire. Lizinka scolded him about it, and when he protested, she asked Father Sheeran to act as judge between them. Was a general justified in carelessly exposing himself on the battlefield? she asked. Sheeran promptly answered, "No mam! I think he is not. A general is the soul of the army, and his fall always causes despondency and sometimes greater disaster to his command. A general in my opinion should keep himself as far as possible out of danger, but in such a position as to see or hear of the movements in battle, but," he added, "there may arise circumstances which would require even a general to expose himself to every danger." Lizinka took Sheeran's answer as a confirmation of her views and, turning to her husband, said, "There now, General, you see that the Father is just of my opinion."

Sheeran liked the Ewells, particularly Lizinka, whom he described as "a lady of more than ordinary intellectual powers, well educated and for one of her sex remarkably well posted on military and political matters." He noted that she was "a rigid Episcopalian, somewhat fond of discussing religious subjects, but very respectful when speaking of Catholic dogmas." [24]

At one time Lizinka considered going to Maryland to live out the war with Rebecca Ewell, but in the end she decided to remain in Virginia. In December 1863 she and Hattie returned to Morton's Hall. [25] The ladies found few of the staff present. Elliott Johnston had resigned because of chronic health concerns resulting from the loss of a leg at Sharpsburg. James Power Smith had accepted an appointment as inspector of Brig. Gen. Cullen Battle's Alabama brigade. Sandie Pendleton, Jed Hotchkiss, and Hunter McGuire had accompanied Jubal Early to the Shenandoah Valley. Pendleton returned to Morton's Hall briefly at the end of December, then proceeded to Moss Neck for his wedding to Kate Corbin. He did not return to the army until the middle of February. McGuire, too, came back to Morton's Hall after just a few weeks, but Hotchkiss stayed west of the Blue Ridge for the remainder of the winter. [26]

The Reverend Beverley Tucker Lacy shared a room with Ewell at Morton's Hall, but when the ladies arrived, he moved to Orange Court House—to be closer to the army hospitals, he said, but perhaps also to be away from Lizinka. Benjamin Greene was in Richmond when Lizinka and Hattie returned, and Campbell Brown was sick, leaving Tom Turner to act as Ewell's assistant adjutant general. Paperwork did not suit Turner's adventuresome spirit, however. As soon as Brown returned to duty, Turner got leave to go to Fauquier County, where he probably joined Mosby's Rangers as he had done the previous winter. He did not stay away long. By mid-January he was back at Morton's Hall attending to his duties and successfully courting Hattie. The couple announced their engagement later that winter.[27]

No sooner did Lizinka return to Morton's Hall than she commenced meddling in military affairs. Col. James Conner, who was then serving as a judge on the Second Corps military court, thought her conduct "very seriously injured old Ewell, and the very cleverness, which would at other times render her agreeable, has only tended to make her more unpopular. She manages everything," he complained, "from the General's affairs down to the courier's, who carries his dispatches. All say they are under petticoat government." Robert Rodes knew how bossy Lizinka could be. One day he pulled Lacy aside and asked sarcastically who was in charge of the corps that day, General Ewell, Mrs. Ewell, or Sandie Pendleton, and expressed the hope that Pendleton was.[28] Rodes's remark, though made in jest, reveals the damage that Lizinka was doing to her husband's reputation.

Sandie Pendleton resented Lizinka's interference more keenly than anyone. As chief of staff it was his job to manage corps headquarters, but when Lizinka was present, she took that job on herself, usurping Pendleton's authority. As a result Pendleton disliked her intensely. Lizinka reciprocated the feeling. In December Ewell recommended Pendleton's promotion to brigadier general. Lizinka tried to block the move. She reminded her husband that Pendleton had criticized him behind his back. Further, she accused the young man of betraying Ewell by volunteering to accompany Early to the Valley. If anyone deserved promotion, she argued, it was Campbell or her future son-in-law, Tom Turner.

Ewell disagreed. "Do you think I would recommend or not because a man liked or disliked me ir-respective of his merits?" he asked reproachfully. "The connection I cannot see. If he is likely to make a good Brig. Genl. & to whip the Yankees I would recommend him if he were my worst enemy." Pendleton was an energetic officer, he asserted. "I directed on Saturday Campbell & Turner to reconnoitre the country in a certain direction. They would be ready Monday. Monday they would be ready Tuesday because they had found on Monday they had no money & I didn't send them. Pendleton was sent as far, on more troublesome duty, was ready at once & returned promptly doing his duty well. Which is the best friend?"[29] The letter says a great deal about Pendleton's character, but it says even more about Ewell's.

Although Ewell recommended Pendleton's promotion solely on the basis of merit, some members of his staff suspected another motive. At that time there was a bill before the Confederate Congress that, if passed, would have expanded the size of the general staff and increased the rank of corps chiefs of staff to full colonel. By promoting Pendleton to brigadier general, the officers whispered, Ewell would clear the way for Campbell Brown to become chief of staff, thus bumping him up two notches, from major to colonel. Brown's promotion, in turn, would create a vacancy in the position of junior assistant adjutant general, a position Turner seemed in line to fill. Col. James Conner and other members of Ewell's staff were sitting around the campfire one evening speculating on Brown's chances for promotion, when Turner spoke up.

"Old Ewell told me he had never exposed Campbell [to enemy fire] but once," he carped, "and then was so miserable until he came back, that he did not know what to do: 'If anything had happened to him, I could never have looked at his Mother again, sir,'" Turner said, imitating his chief. "Hang him, he never thinks of my Mother, I suppose, for he pops me around, no matter how hot the fire is."

After Turner left the group, another officer chimed in. "Well, Turner is safe, but I am in a tight place. Campbell Brown hangs on to his Mother's petticoats, and Turner is engaged to the little Brown girl, and she will prize him up, but I have to fight against the pair." Conner found it amusing that an entire staff could be set to trembling by "the manoeuvering of two women, and one fond, foolish old man." In the end all the political maneuvering and idle speculation came to naught, for President Davis vetoed the staff bill, and Pendleton declined promotion in favor of remaining on Ewell's staff.[30]

For Ewell the winter of 1863–64 passed pleasantly. He regularly went riding with Lizinka in his carriage; he entertained guests and attended parties hosted by other officers; and in the evenings, after his work was completed, he played whist with his staff.[31] Looking back on this winter from inside the damp stone walls of a prison cell eighteen months later, Ewell could say, "There was as little exterior charm about Morton's Hall to attract as possible, yet I was as contented there, except the war, as I could be & removing that deep tragedy I would be at a loss to combine more of what is essential to my happiness than were collected there."[32]

His troops remembered the winter less fondly. Food and clothing shortages made the winter of 1863–64 the hardest the army had yet endured. The food shortage became so great that in January commissary officers had to cut soldiers' rations to less than a quarter-pound of meat daily.[33] Officers suffered as well. Unlike enlisted men, who received rations, officers had to pay for food out of their salaries. In September 1863 Early had complained to Brig. Gen. Robert H. Chilton, the army's inspector general, that his officers had not been paid for months. To survive, they had to beg food from their men, a situation that bred

Ewell made his headquarters at Morton's Hall during the winter of 1863–64.
He later wrote, "There was as little exterior charm about Morton's Hall to attract, as
possible, yet I was as contented there, except the war, as I could be." (Donald C. Pfanz)

contempt toward the officers and eroded army discipline. Ewell and Early suggested that officers be allowed to run a tab with army commissaries until they received their wages. It was a good idea, but Commissary Gen. Lucius Northrup opposed it. And so the officers went hungry.[34]

Many soldiers, unwilling to bear the hardships, simply left. Desertion was particularly acute in the Louisiana Brigade, which lacked not only food but also shoes and warm clothing. Ewell tried to channel additional clothing to the brigade, but it did little good. In the meantime, Lee directed that he move the Louisianians to a point farther from the front so that it would be more difficult for deserters to go over to the enemy.[35]

Morale was better elsewhere in the army. When North Carolina politician and editor William W. Holden induced many North Carolina troops to desert by calling for a negotiated peace, the troops of Rodes's division passed a resolution declaring themselves "*in for the war*" without condition." Other divisions followed suit, though admittedly in some regiments the vote was rigged.[36] To buoy troop morale and gain political capital for himself, North Carolina governor Zebulon B. Vance visited the army in March 1864 and met with men from his state.

Ewell was present when Vance spoke to the First North Carolina Infantry of Steuart's brigade and again when he addressed Junius Daniel's brigade. "General Stewart [*sic*] has been with him nearly all the time since he came," one Tarheel wrote, "and a number of other Generals have been to hear him every time he spoke. Gen'l Lee has heard him twice, and I understand that old Gen'l Ewell has nearly shaken his wooden leg to pieces laughing at his jokes."[37]

As spring approached, Lee traveled to Richmond to confer with Davis. Ewell commanded the army in his absence, though as in December he commanded more in name than in fact. Lee's staff remained at Orange to carry out the day-to-day administration of the army and kept Lee apprised of army matters via telegraph.[38]

Union cavalry became active during Lee's absence. Late in February 1864 Brig. Gen. George A. Custer made a diversionary raid toward Charlottesville. At the same time Brig. Gen. Judson Kilpatrick dashed south in an effort to free Union prisoners being held in Richmond. Ewell dispatched infantry by rail to Charlottesville to head off Custer and sent Hampton's cavalry after Kilpatrick. The Confederates turned back both Union columns.[39]

Lee returned to Orange Court House on 29 February 1864, while the Kilpatrick Raid was in progress, but went back to Richmond less than two weeks later for another round of talks with President Davis and his advisers. The man on the Confederate leaders' minds was Ulysses S. Grant. On 12 March President Lincoln appointed Grant general in chief of the U.S. Army with the rank of lieutenant general. Grant would make his headquarters with the Army of the Potomac and personally guide its movements in the coming campaign. Grant was no stranger to Ewell. They had attended West Point together for one year and had crossed paths in the Old Army. Still there is no reason to believe the fantastic statement of an early Grant biographer that in 1861 Ewell had pointed to Grant as the man Confederates should fear more than any other.[40]

In the coming campaign Grant would bring almost 120,000 soldiers into the field against Lee. The Army of Northern Virginia could muster barely half that number, of which approximately 15,500 belonged to the Second Corps. To augment the South's waning strength, the Confederate Congress on 17 February 1864 passed a bill expanding the draft to include men as young as seventeen and as old as fifty. Other laws limited exemptions from military service and barred the use of substitutes.[41] These measures brought a few additional men into the ranks but hardly enough to offset the North's huge superiority in numbers.

That was not lost on the Confederate soldiers. Although they remained as confident as ever, they realized that hard work lay ahead. Privately Ewell predicted that the coming campaign would be the most desperate of the war. The cost in lives would be high. "Everything indicates that in less than 48 hours we may have the bloodiest battle of the war on this very ground," Hotchkiss wrote his wife on 1 May, "& the fresh green shores of the Rapidan [will] be stained by the life blood of thousands."[42] The timing and location of Hotchkiss's prediction were slightly off, but his estimate of the carnage was not. Within three weeks nearly 60,000 Americans would spill their blood on Virginia soil.

CHAPTER 25

Strike the Enemy Wherever I Find Him

On 2 May 1864 Gen. Robert E. Lee met with his corps and division commanders on the summit of Clark's Mountain in Orange County, Virginia. Ewell was there; so, too, were A. P. Hill, Longstreet, Anderson, Early, Rodes, and several others. It may well have been the greatest collection of Confederate military leaders to assemble during the war. Below them, stretched out like a carpet across Culpeper County, stood the tents of the Army of the Potomac. As the generals gazed upon the scene, Lee predicted that the Union army would shortly cross the Rapidan River beyond his right flank, at either Germanna or Ely's Fords. He admonished Lt. Benjamin L. Wynn, the officer in charge of the signal station on the mountain, to keep close watch on the Union camps and ordered his generals to prepare their commands for immediate action. The long winter encampment was just about over.[1]

The 1864 Campaign opened two days later. On the evening of 3 May, Wynn reported unusual activity in the enemy camps, indicative of a general movement. Lee alerted Ewell of this development and ordered him to be ready to march at dawn. Daylight confirmed Wynn's suspicions. The Army of the Potomac was marching toward Germanna Ford, as Lee had predicted. Southern cavalry posted downriver corroborated this information. By noon Lee had the Army of Northern Virginia in motion to meet the enemy.[2]

The Confederate army marched east along two main roads. The Second Corps used the Orange Turnpike, a crushed stone road that ran from Orange to Fredericksburg. Hill used the Orange Plank Road, approximately three miles south of the turnpike. The Plank Road was not as straight as the turnpike; consequently Hill had farther to march than Ewell. To prevent Ewell from getting too far ahead, Lee directed him to regulate his march by Hill's. Longstreet's First Corps started the day near Gordonsville and was one day's march behind.[3]

While Lee concentrated his army to meet Grant's advance, he could not overlook the possibility that his opponent might try to cross the Rapidan at the very points the Confederates had just abandoned. To guard against that possibility, Dick Anderson's division continued to man the Rapidan defenses above Newman's Ford. Dodson Ramseur guarded the crossings below Newman's Ford with ten Second Corps regiments. Anderson and Ramseur had orders to hold their ground until they were satisfied the Federals had left, then to rejoin their corps with all haste.[4]

The Confederate columns wended eastward to Mine Run, the muddy stream where they had held the Army of the Potomac at bay the previous year. It was a strong position, and Lee intended to defend it again if the Federals advanced in that direction. But as the day progressed, Southern cavalry reported that Grant was moving toward Fredericksburg. Lee pushed after him in hopes of attacking his rear. The Confederate soldiers sensed Lee's purpose and cheered as they shuffled past the previous year's defenses. "Mars Bob is going for them this time!" they said knowingly.[5]

East of Mine Run the Army of Northern Virginia entered the Wilderness, a region of dense woods and few clearings. Decades of iron mining had stripped the virgin timber from the land and left a second-growth forest of blackjack oak, pine, and chinquapin, rarely exceeding thirty feet in height. Undergrowth flourished among the stunted trees, making it difficult for troops to maneuver, much less fight. As Joe Hooker had discovered in 1863, it was an area where enemy troops might appear unexpectedly and where panic might take hold in an instant. The Wilderness furnished Lee with an ideal battlefield, for it largely neutralized Grant's superiority in cavalry, artillery, and infantry. But attacking Grant in the Wilderness had its risks. Lee would have to engage Grant initially without the benefit of Longstreet's, Anderson's, and Ramseur's commands, thus giving his adversary as much as a three-to-one advantage. Once Lee's missing troops arrived, Grant's margin of superiority would narrow to two-to-one.

The Second Corps left its camps along the Rapidan at noon on 4 May and bivouacked that night around Locust Grove, roughly halfway between Mine Run and the Union army's position at Wilderness Tavern.[6] Ewell rode with Johnson's division and at night slept with the brigade of his former adjutant, Brig. Gen. John M. Jones. Hill halted for the night at Verdiersville, a hamlet four miles southwest of Ewell on the Orange Plank Road. Longstreet camped at Brock's Bridge, just inside the Orange County line.[7]

When the day ended, Lee was still uncertain about Grant's intentions. He might move east toward Fredericksburg, as Hooker had done the previous spring;

west toward Mine Run, as Meade had done that fall; or south toward Spotsylvania Court House. Lee had to be ready for each contingency. That evening he directed Ewell to have his corps ready to march at dawn. If the Federals moved down the river toward Fredericksburg, Ewell was to push after them; but if Grant turned west toward Locust Grove, Ewell was to fall back to the entrenched line at Mine Run. In either event Lee wished to bring Grant to battle as soon as possible.[8]

The Confederates broke camp early on 5 May. Lt. Robert Stiles found Ewell crouched over a fire in the woods. The general was alone except for a single courier, who held his crutches and assisted him to mount. Stiles noted that the general seemed more thin and pale than usual, but otherwise "bright-eyed and alert." Nearby stood Ewell's old gray horse, Rifle. Stiles fancied a strange resemblance between the flea-bitten animal and its owner. It seemed to him that neither had slept or eaten. Ewell had rested a few hours that night, but by 3:30 A.M., when Jed Hotchkiss came looking for him, he had already ridden to the front. It is little wonder that both the general and his horse looked somewhat worn.

Ewell thought highly of Stiles and occasionally called him "My child," though the burly, bearded, twenty-seven-year-old officer had anything but a childlike appearance. Ewell invited Stiles to take coffee with him, and Stiles eagerly accepted. "He was a great cook," recounted the artilleryman. "I remember on one occasion, later in the war, I met him in the outer defenses of Richmond, and he told me someone had sent him a turkey leg which he was going to 'devil;' that he was strong on that particular dish; that his staff would be away, and I must come around that evening and share it with him. I willingly accepted on both occasions, and on both greatly enjoyed a chat with the General and the unaccustomed treat." Now as they quietly sipped coffee in the deep woods, Stiles asked Ewell if he objected to revealing his orders. It was a brazen request for a lieutenant to make of a general, but Ewell took no offense. "No, sir; none at all," he piped, "just the orders I like — to go right down the [turnpike] and strike the enemy wherever I find him." In accordance with Lee's instructions, Ewell planned to bring the enemy to battle as soon as possible.[9]

His corps started forward at early light. Jones's brigade took the lead, marching slowly so as not to outdistance Hill's men on the Orange Plank Road. To the left, the Culpeper Mine Road branched off the turnpike and headed in the direction of Germanna Ford. Ewell sent Maj. William H. H. Cowles's First North Carolina Cavalry Regiment down the road to protect his flank and reconnoiter toward the ford while the infantry continued forward on the pike.

At 8:00 A.M. Ewell dispatched Campbell Brown to notify Lee of his position.

Brown informed Lee that Ewell had encountered only a small Union picket and that he would continue down the pike until he encountered the enemy in force. Hill had engaged a regiment of Union cavalry at Parker's Store a short while before. Though he was steadily pressing it back, Lee feared that Ewell might get too far ahead, exposing himself to attack before Hill could catch up. Lee accordingly reiterated his orders for Ewell to regulate his march by Hill, whose progress he could accurately judge by the sound of firing at the head of Hill's column. "If the enemy advanced & showed a willingness to fight," Lee told Brown, "he did not want a general engagement brought on till Longstreet cd. come up. . . . He preferred falling back to our old position at Mine Run. Above all," he cautioned, "Gen. E. was not to get his troops entangled, so as to be unable to disengage them, in case the enemy were in force."[10]

By the time Brown returned to the Orange Turnpike, Ewell had encountered the enemy at a clearing known as Saunders Field. Ewell had reached the field at 11:00 A.M. and observed a Union column passing across his front in the distance, apparently heading for the Orange Plank Road. Recognizing the danger of his advanced position, he prudently halted his march and sent Sandie Pendleton to Lee for instructions. Like Brown, Pendleton brought back orders for Ewell to avoid a general engagement until the next day, by which time Longstreet and his men would be up.[11]

Ewell was willing to wait for Longstreet before starting the fight, but Grant might not be so obliging. Anticipating a Union attack, Ewell deployed Rodes's and Johnson's divisions into line of battle astride the turnpike. Rodes's brigades fanned out south of the road. Johnson's troops took position north of it. Jones's brigade screened the deployment. In accordance with Lee's orders, Ewell admonished his subordinates "not to allow themselves to become involved, but to fall back slowly if pressed."[12]

Ewell had not yet completed his arrangements when at 1:00 P.M. Maj. Gen. Gouverneur K. Warren's Union Fifth Corps attacked. Warren struck on both sides of the turnpike. North of the road his troops engaged Johnson's division in a brief hand-to-hand struggle and were repulsed. The Confederates captured two smoothbore cannon and herded hundreds of Union soldiers to the rear as prisoners. Among the captives were soldiers of the 146th New York Volunteers, a Zouave regiment whose colorful uniforms excited much interest among Johnson's tattered veterans. Ewell was less interested in the regiment's uniforms than its motivation. As one of its officers passed toward the rear, he asked, "What makes your boys fight so? Your regiment fought like hell!"[13]

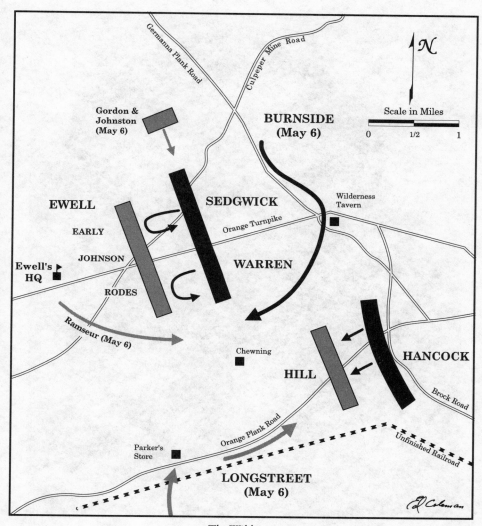

The Wilderness

South of the road Warren achieved greater success. His attack struck Jones's brigade and threw it back in confusion on Rodes's line. Jones was talking with Ewell, Early, and Rodes beside the turnpike when the fighting began. Mounting his horse, Jones rode to the front, where a Union bullet found him. As his troops fled to the rear, they piled through the line of Brig. Gen. Cullen A. Battle's brigade and threw it into disorder. The confusion increased when one of Jones's

John M. Jones. Jones was Ewell's chief of staff in 1862 and later died leading a brigade in the Wilderness. (Library of Congress)

officers, remembering Ewell's earlier instructions, shouted, "Fall back to Mine Run." Two of Battle's brigades obeyed the unfortunate order and marched to the rear, while the others fell back fighting. Battle's retreat uncovered the flank of Doles's brigade, to its right, and it too gave ground.

By 2:00 P.M. the entire right wing of the Second Corps seemed on the verge of collapse.[14] Ewell and Early did their best to stop the panic. Unfurling Early's headquarters flag beside the turnpike, they tried to rally Jones's and Battle's men as they passed to the rear. A few soldiers heeded their cries, but not enough to stem the rising tide of disaster. Fortunately Early's division was at hand. At the first sign of disaster, Old Jube sent a staff officer pounding down the turnpike to bring up Gordon's brigade, which was then approaching the field. Gordon found Ewell and Early sitting on their horses in the center of the turnpike. In a few words they explained the situation and ordered him to check the enemy's advance south of the road. Gordon saluted and turned to rejoin his brigade. As he did so, Ewell shouted after him, "General Gordon, the fate of the day depends on you, sir." Gordon replied, "These men will save it, sir."

As Gordon prepared to attack, a cannonball tore off the head of a man in the ranks. Unruffled, Gordon completed his arrangements, then addressed his men in ringing tones. "Georgians! I have never asked you to follow me in vain. Follow me now! Forward! March!" With a cheer, the brigade plunged into the woods and hit the Federals with irresistible force. Ewell looked on approvingly. "Isn't that magnificent!" he exclaimed. "It ought to make Gordon a Major General."

Ewell and Early matched Gordon's poise under pressure. An officer who observed them in this crisis noted that they "were as cool and calm as if conducting a plain matter of business, and there was as little excitement as I ever saw under fire on a battlefield. They both had 'well defined ideas' as to how they would 'save the day' and had a part in doing it, which they discharged in fine military fashion. I noticed them both closely through the conflict and never saw two men less affected by stirring and critical events." [15]

Gordon struck the Federals just as their attack was losing momentum and drove them back. Rodes's brigades rallied and joined the assault, screaming the rebel yell. Panic gripped Warren's men. They fell back in disorder across Saunders Field, enabling Ewell to reestablish his line at the field's western edge. Mindful of Lee's instructions to avoid a general engagement, he did not press his advantage. [16]

Ewell kept in close communication with Lee throughout the day. Just before Warren's attack, he had sent Brown to inform Lee that he would retire to Mine Run if attacked, as Lee had directed. Lee seemed bewildered. He told Brown that he and Pendleton had misunderstood him. He only wished the Second Corps to fall back if it was unable to hold its ground. Brown returned to Ewell with that clarification. By then the Confederates had defeated Warren and were strengthening their position on the ridge. Ewell sent the staff officer back to Lee with the message that "he could hold his ground with ease against any force so far developed," a confident statement in light of his narrow escape earlier in the day. [17]

Stafford's, Walker's, and Steuart's brigades of Johnson's division now held the ground north of the turnpike. Battle's, Doles's, and Daniel's brigades of Rodes's division held the ground south of it. Early's division remained in reserve near the turnpike, except for Gordon's brigade, which was next to Daniel on the right end of the line. Ewell sent Jones's brigade to the rear to re-form and eventually posted it in reserve along the turnpike. As events would show, it had lost its ability to fight. While Ewell's infantry dug in along the ridge, Armistead Long sought positions for the corps artillery. The wooded countryside was not conducive to the use of ordnance, but Long nonetheless found positions for some guns of Nelson's battalion along the turnpike and in the woods north of it. For the time being, the rest of the corps' artillery remained parked at Locust Grove near the corps' field hospitals.[18]

Following Warren's attack, both sides threw up breastworks and hurried forward reinforcements. As additional troops reached the front, fighting spilled over into the woods surrounding Saunders Field. The Second and Third Corps had not yet linked up, and both of Ewell's flanks dangled dangerously. Unsure where the enemy might next appear, Ewell wisely kept Early's division in hand and awaited developments. He did not have to wait long. At 3:00 P.M. Maj. Gen. Horatio G. Wright's Union Sixth Corps division appeared on the Culpeper Mine Road, opposite Stafford's brigade on Ewell's left flank. The Confederate commander received timely warning of the threat and promptly dispatched Hays's brigade to meet it. Hays and Stafford repulsed Wright's attack, then counterattacked and were themselves repulsed. In the confused fighting, Stafford was flanked by the Federals. As the lion-hearted Louisianian tried to withdraw his brigade from its perilous position, a Union bullet struck him in the right shoulder and traveled down his spine. He died three days later in a Richmond hospital.[19]

While Wright's attack was still in progress, Ewell committed his final reserves, sending Pegram's brigade to reinforce his embattled left flank. Pegram had only two of his five regiments with him; the other three had been left with Ramseur at the Rapidan River. His small force reached the left at 4:00 P.M. and immediately began entrenching. By dark it had constructed a stout breastwork between three and four feet high. Brig. Gen. Truman Seymour's Sixth Corps brigade attacked Pegram's works at sunset in an effort to turn Ewell's left flank, but the Confederates repulsed it with great slaughter. Pegram took a serious wound to the knee and had to turn command over to Col. John S. Hoffman of the Thirty-first Virginia. Otherwise the brigade suffered few casualties. With Seymour's repulse, the 5 May fighting on the Orange Turnpike ended.[20]

While Ewell successfully battled Warren and Sedgwick on the Orange Turnpike, Lee and Hill had been engaged in a separate contest three miles south on the Orange Plank Road. Grant learned that Hill was advancing on the Plank Road early in the day and had sent Maj. Gen. George W. Getty's Sixth Corps division to meet it. He later reinforced Getty with Maj. Gen. Winfield Hancock's Second Corps. Hancock and Getty attacked Hill at 4:00 P.M. and hammered at him for the next four hours. In some of the hardest fighting of the war, Hill beat back the Federal assaults and held his ground until dark. When Ewell heard of his success, he sent Hill a note of congratulations.[21]

Lee began planning for 6 May even before the 5 May fighting had ended. At 6:00 P.M. he ordered Ewell to send his wounded soldiers to the rear, replenish his ammunition, and prepare for action early in the morning. If Ewell found that Grant had weakened his force on the turnpike to reinforce Hancock, he was to advance his left flank and cut Grant off from Germanna Ford. If such an attack was impracticable, he was to remain on the defensive and send reinforcements to Hill. Lee reiterated the message an hour later, adding, "The attack on General Hill is still raging. Be ready to act as early as possible in the morning." In reply Ewell announced that he intended to attack Sedgwick in the morning with Johnson's division, supported by Ramseur, whose troops had just reached the battlefield. If the Federals attacked him instead, he was ready for that, too. "I am entrenched along my whole line and can hold it," he confidently asserted.[22]

Ewell spent the night preparing for the coming day's battle. He had two objectives. First, he had to concentrate a sufficient force on his left flank to carry the Federal position in front of him if he found the Federals had significantly weakened their force there. Second, he needed to strengthen his position so that, if necessary, he could detach troops to the Orange Plank Road. To accomplish the first objective, he shifted Gordon's brigade from the right of his line to the left and put Ramseur's troops in position north of the turnpike. Three of the regiments Ramseur brought to the battlefield belonged to Johnson's division; three others had been drawn from Pegram's brigade of Early's division. These six regiments returned to their original commands. Ramseur's own four regiments took position behind Early's left, where they could lead an assault on the Union right or reinforce Lee on the Orange Plank Road, as circumstances required. Thus by the morning of 6 May, Ewell had consolidated the brigades of his various divisions and had massed sixteen regiments—perhaps 5,000 men—on the left half of the line that had not been there before: Gordon's six, Ramseur's four, Pegram's three, and the three recently returned to Johnson.[23]

To accomplish the second objective—strengthening his position—Ewell relied principally on artillery. His infantry had entrenched well on 5 May, and he was confident that he could repel any attack made directly against his line. His flanks were another matter. Both ends of his line still dangled, inviting attack. He was particularly vulnerable on his right, where the removal of Gordon's brigade had left a mile-wide gap between his corps and Hill's troops on the Orange Plank Road. If the Federals penetrated that gap, they might divide the Confederate army and destroy it. Lee would probably fill the hole once Longstreet and Anderson arrived; until then Ewell had Braxton's artillery battalion cover the interval. He placed additional guns along Rodes's line and in positions near his left flank. Searching for positions the next morning, Col. J. Thompson Brown was killed by a Union sharpshooter.[24]

Ewell snatched a few hours of sleep at Locust Grove, but by 3:00 A.M. he was back at work. At the first blush of dawn, his skirmishers crept forward to test the strength of Sedgwick's line. Grant had ordered a 5:00 A.M. attack, but Ewell's reconnaissance beat him to the punch by a quarter of an hour, prompting Sedgwick to remark that "Ewell's watch must be fifteen minutes ahead of his." Finding the Federals still in force to their front, the Confederates fell back to their own works, closely pursued by Sedgwick's men. The Sixth Corps attacks fell heaviest on Pegram's (now Hoffman's) brigade, but there as elsewhere the Confederates repulsed them "with great slaughter." Warren, seeing the futility of attacking Ewell's position, limited his participation to skirmishing and some distant artillery fire.[25]

The morning attacks by Sedgwick and Warren clearly demonstrated that Grant had not appreciably weakened his force on the Orange Turnpike; consequently Ewell abandoned his plan to attack Sedgwick and prepared to send Ramseur's brigade to Lee. Before he could do so, he received information that a large Federal force was slowly making its way toward the gap on his right flank. Ewell ordered Ramseur to drive it back. Ramseur reached the gap ahead of the Federals—later identified as two divisions of Burnside's Ninth Corps—and extended his skirmish line to the right, in order to overlap the Federal line. Once his skirmishers were in position, Ramseur gave the order to charge. They not only succeeded in driving Burnside's skirmishers but pushed back the Union general's main line a distance later estimated by Ramseur as "fully half a mile." The Federals made no effort to retake the ground.[26]

About the time Burnside appeared in the gap, John Gordon discovered that his brigade overlapped Sedgwick's right flank. The Federals had posted videttes in front, but the line itself appeared to be unsupported. Four hundred yards beyond Sedgwick's flank was a field in which Gordon could form his brigade at right angles to the Union line.[27] Gordon sent his aide, Capt. Thomas G. Jones, to urge Ewell and Early to attack the Federal flank immediately using Gordon's brigade and one or two others.

Jones galloped off on his mission at 8:00 A.M., the same time Ramseur was engaging Burnside south of the turnpike. Jones rode along the lines until he spotted Ewell emerging from a patch of woods. As the general rode into the clearing, an officer dashed over and warned him to avoid a certain spot that had been the target of Union sharpshooters all morning. Perhaps remembering the episode at Gettysburg that resulted in Capt. Henry Richardson's injury, Ewell wisely chose an alternate route.[28]

Jones caught up with Ewell and was making his report when Early appeared. Old Jube had disobeyed an order of Ewell's just before the campaign opened, compelling Ewell to place him under arrest, but he had lost none of his pepper.[29] "Gen. Early questioned me very sharply," Jones remembered, "and called Gen. Ewell's attention to reports they had received about the flank movements of the enemy towards our left. He said that the information received, satisfied him that a heavy body of the enemy's troops . . . were in the woods, in supporting distance of the flank, and that the probabilities were our flank might be attacked."

Early had good reason to urge caution, for Federal troops were then attacking Ewell's front and attempting to turn his right. Moreover, Confederate scouts near the river reported Federals near Germanna Ford advancing upriver with the possible intention of turning Ewell's left flank. Since Ramseur had not yet identified the troops on his front as belonging to Burnside, Ewell feared the force operating on his northern flank might be the Ninth Corps. An attack by Gordon on Sedgwick's flank might expose the Confederates to a crushing counterattack by Burnside. Even had Ewell wished to attack, he had no troops available to do so. His men had their hands full with Warren and Sedgwick. His only disposable reserve—Ramseur's brigade—had gone to the right. An attack at that time simply was not possible.[30]

Early sent Jones back to Gordon with instructions to wait until he and Ewell could "come over to the left and see what could be done." Jones had gone only a short distance when he met Gordon riding toward the turnpike. He told his chief about Early's objections and led him to the generals. For the next twenty minutes, while Jones kept a respectful distance, Gordon pleaded his case to Ewell and Early. He had ridden well beyond Sedgwick's right that morning, he argued, and had seen no evidence of Union supports on that flank. Ewell seemed disposed to believe Gordon, but Early continued to oppose the attack as unsafe. Unsure of what to do, Ewell decided to investigate the matter personally.[31]

Before he could do so, Lee summoned him to a conference. Fighting on the Plank Road had been particularly heavy that day. At 5:00 A.M. Hancock had attacked Hill's corps and routed it. The timely arrival of Longstreet's corps had

John B. Gordon (Library of Congress)

checked Hancock's progress. The Confederates thereafter had discovered an unfinished railroad bed perpendicular to Hancock's left flank. Lee planned to use the railroad to attack Hancock's flank, and he wished Ewell to support the attack, if possible, with some sort of diversion on the Orange Turnpike. Ewell informed Lee about Gordon's proposed attack and promised to do what he could.[32]

Before he could think about attacking Sedgwick, though, he had to secure his own flanks. Although Warren's and Sedgwick's attacks had ceased by noon, scouts still reported Union infantry advancing from Germanna Ford toward Locust Grove, a move that would ultimately put them on Ewell's left and rear. Ewell ordered Doles's brigade to the left to combat this threat. No sooner did the Georgians leave their trenches south of the turnpike, though, than the Federals advanced, compelling them to return. Ewell's other brigades likewise found themselves pinned to their works. Fortunately, Brig. Gen. Robert D. Johnston's brigade appeared. Johnston had been on guard duty at Hanover Junction, thirty-five miles south of Fredericksburg, on 4 May when he received orders to rejoin the corps. A two-day march brought his brigade to the battlefield about noon, 6 May. Ewell sent it to the left in lieu of Doles's brigade to guard the roads leading to Early's rear.[33]

Johnston's appearance prompted renewed calls by Gordon to attack Sedgwick's flank.[34] He found Ewell more agreeable to the idea now, for many of the obstacles to the enterprise were gone. Warren and Sedgwick had ceased their attacks on Ewell's front; Hill's corps had closed the dangerous interval on Ewell's right flank; Burnside's Ninth Corps was now positively identified to be south of the turnpike rather than hovering near Germanna Ford; and the mysterious force that seemed headed for Locust Grove had withdrawn. Only one obstacle remained: a lack of troops with which to make the attack. Johnston's arrival increased the potential strike force from one brigade to two, but that still was too little for a daylight attack. Over Gordon's objections Ewell decided to postpone the offensive until sunset, when growing darkness would conceal the small size of the attacking force, create panic among the Union troops, and enable the Confederates to retreat without serious loss if anything went wrong.[35]

Ewell personally examined the left flank late in the afternoon and gave final approval for the attack. At sunset Gordon charged through the dark woods, taking the Federals completely by surprise. In less than an hour he routed two Union brigades and captured 600 prisoners, including two generals.[36] But then things began to go wrong. Johnston's brigade, which was supporting Gordon, lost contact with him and strayed to the left, completely missing its target. Hoffman's brigade had orders to attack once Gordon's troops had cleared the trenches in its front, but in the shadowy thickets it lost its cohesion and wound up shooting at Gordon's men instead of the enemy. Even Gordon's own regiments experienced confusion in the dense woods. The attack sputtered to a halt after dark, having achieved local success but nothing more.[37]

To his death Gordon believed that Ewell and Early had squandered an opportunity for a great victory. Had they permitted him to attack just one hour earlier, he insisted, he could have captured much of Sedgwick's Sixth Corps and brought disaster upon the entire right wing of the Federal army. Early took the opposite view. He claimed the growing darkness actually helped the attack by creating panic among Sedgwick's troops and preventing them from accurately assessing the diminutive size of Gordon's force.[38] Both men had a point. The same darkness that gave the attack its initial success by creating panic in the Union ranks doomed it to failure by creating confusion in the Confederate ranks. Yet it was the attack's weakness rather than its timing that ultimately limited its success. Ewell had only two brigades to commit to the attack. Such a slender force simply could not have routed one-third of the Union army.

Gordon's criticism notwithstanding, Ewell's performance in the Wilderness had been good and at times superb. By the skillful use of his reserves, he had protected his flanks, repulsed every attack directed against him, and made a successful assault of his own, all without supervision from Lee. He suffered just 1,125 casualties while inflicting fully five times that number on his enemies. Included in the latter figure were more than 1,000 Union prisoners, including Brig. Gens. Alexander Shaler and Truman Seymour, whom Gordon had captured in his attack. These two unfortunate officers spent the night of 6 May at Ewell's Locust Grove headquarters before heading to Richmond and Libby Prison.[39]

Ewell's twilight attack compelled Grant to throw the Army of the Potomac's right flank back across the Germanna Plank Road. Confederate skirmishers crept forward to locate the enemy's new position on 7 May, drawing an angry response from Warren's troops along the turnpike. Farther to the right, Ramseur drove away some Ninth Corps troops he encountered in the woods. Otherwise the day was quiet, save the constant crackle of skirmish fire and the occasional discharge of artillery.[40]

Grant's withdrawal gave Ewell's men an opportunity to bury the dead and assist the wounded. The number of Federal corpses in front of the Confederate works was appalling. "The burial parties from two divisions reported interring over 1,100 of the enemy," Ewell reported. "The third and largest made no report. When we moved probably one-third or more were still unburied of those who were within reach of our lines." Other accounts seem to corroborate these figures. Lt. McHenry Howard placed the number of Union dead buried by Johnson's division alone at 582, while Jed Hotchkiss estimated the total number of interments for all three divisions to be in the neighborhood of 1,500. Material gains were no less impressive. Lt. Col. William Allan, the Second Corps chief of ordnance, reported collecting 9,000 stand of small arms from the battlefield plus two cannon captured from Warren on 5 May.[41]

While the soldiers cleaned the battlefield of its human and material debris, the generals spent the day planning their next move. In the morning Ewell met with Lee on the Orange Plank Road, and in the afternoon Lee repaid the visit by coming to see Ewell on the Orange Turnpike. By then Confederate scouting parties reported that Grant had taken up his bridges at Germanna Ford.[42] Barring future attacks against Lee's entrenched position in the Wilderness, which seemed unlikely, that meant that the Union commander was either going to Fredericksburg or to Spotsylvania Court House. A move to Fredericksburg could be the first step in a general retreat, or it might simply indicate that Grant was shifting his line of advance from the Orange and Alexandria Railroad to the Richmond, Fredericksburg, and Potomac Railroad. A march toward Spotsylvania, on the other hand, could mean but one thing: Grant was continuing his drive toward Richmond.

Lee had to be ready for a move by the Federals toward either place. He was particularly concerned that Grant might beat him to Spotsylvania Court House, for whoever controlled the roads near the village held the inside track to Richmond. Once he determined that Grant was leaving his front, Lee directed Longstreet's corps, now commanded by Anderson, to move toward Spotsylvania. Ewell's corps would follow Anderson, leaving Hill to bring up the rear.[43] The movement began after dark on 7 May. As the soldiers left their trenches and tramped south, rumors spread that Grant was in full retreat, and a shout of joy ran along Anderson's line. Hill's men took up the cheer and enthusiastically passed it on to the farthest end of Ewell's line. It had hardly died when a second, then a third wave of cheers swept down the lines. "The effect was beyond expression," wrote a South Carolinian in the Third Corps. "It seemed to fill every heart with new life, to inspire every nerve with might never known before."[44]

Ironically, not two miles away, Union soldiers were also cheering. After two days of bloody stalemate with Lee in the Wilderness, most soldiers in the Army of the Potomac expected Grant to retreat across the Rappahannock River as his predecessors had done. Instead they found themselves marching away from the river toward Spotsylvania. Though it might mean several more costly battles, Grant was going to fight Lee to the end. For the Army of the Potomac there would be no more retreat.[45]

CHAPTER 26

Struggle for the Muleshoe

Maj. Gen. Richard H. Anderson was perhaps the least assuming officer to command a corps in the Army of Northern Virginia. Polite and reserved with thoughtful eyes and a neat, scholarly appearance, he seemed better suited to teach a college physics course than to lead troops in battle. But in this case looks were deceiving, for the forty-three-year-old South Carolinian was an able and experienced general. Like Ewell, Anderson had graduated from West Point and had put his training to use on the frontier as a captain of dragoons. When the Civil War began, he became major of the First South Carolina Infantry and in just fifteen months rose to command a division in the Army of Northern Virginia. He had served in that capacity until 7 May 1864, when Lee selected him to fill temporarily the place of James Longstreet, who had been wounded in the Wilderness. With Anderson's new assignment came orders to march Longstreet's First Corps to Spotsylvania Court House. He reached Spotsylvania early on 8 May, chased away a Union cavalry division there, and held the village for the rest of the day against repeated assaults by Gouverneur K. Warren's Fifth Union Army Corps. Anderson had passed his first test as a corps commander with flying colors.[1]

Dick Ewell followed Anderson to Spotsylvania. His corps had already started southward on 8 May when Ewell received orders from Lee to march to Anderson's assistance. At Lee's suggestion Ewell marched to Parker's Store on the Orange Plank Road, thence south to Shady Grove Church. Lee met him there. After a short halt to rest the troops, the two generals rode together to Spotsylvania, seven miles away, where Anderson continued to parry Warren's blows.[2]

For Ewell's troops the march to Spotsylvania was among the most distressing of the war. Most of the men had gotten little or no sleep the night before, and as they stumbled along the dry, dusty roads, many collapsed from exhaustion. Intense heat and thick dust added to their rigors. To make matters worse, the burning woods choked the soldiers with suffocating smoke.[3]

Ewell made several command changes during the march. In the morning, before reaching Shady Grove Church, he received a dispatch from Lee stating that A. P. Hill was ill and assigning Jubal Early to temporary command of the Third Corps. Lee wanted John Gordon to command Early's division in that officer's absence, but in order to put Gordon in charge, he had to sidestep Harry Hays, whose commission as a brigadier general predated Gordon's. To accomplish that, Lee transferred Hays's brigade to Johnson's division, consolidating it with Stafford's brigade, which had lacked suitable leadership since its commander's demise on 5 May. To make good the loss of Hays's brigade, Lee ordered Ewell to transfer Johnston's brigade from Rodes's division to Early's (now Gordon's). With this organizational sleight of hand, Lee deftly managed to place Gordon in command of Early's division, find a commander for Stafford's brigade, and equalize the size of Ewell's three divisions.[4]

Lee and Ewell reached Spotsylvania at 5:00 P.M. By then Anderson was in trouble. Sedgwick's Sixth Corps had joined Warren, and by sunset it was threatening to turn Anderson's right flank near the Brock Road. But, as in the Wilderness, Ewell beat Sedgwick to the punch. Rodes rushed into battle in the nick of time and pushed the Federals back one-half mile to a line of earthworks. He then retired and entrenched, extending Anderson's line to the right.[5]

Ewell watched Rodes's advance from a point near the front. The First North Carolina Infantry color-bearer had just fallen, and the regiment's colonel called for a volunteer to carry the flag into battle. A young boy in tattered clothes stepped forward and grasped the blood-stained banner. Ewell, who had witnessed the death of the previous color-bearer, inquired as to the boy's identity and said he would "gladly approve any recommendation that might be made for his promotion." Unfortunately the boy was taken captive four days later and never received the reward.[6]

Johnson followed Rodes to the battlefield and took position behind him. Ewell ordered Lt. McHenry Howard of George Steuart's staff to bring up Jones's brigade as quickly as possible. Howard did so and reported back to Ewell, who was then speaking with Johnson. To Howard's dismay, Ewell denied having told him to move Jones's brigade. Johnson began to upbraid the lieutenant when Ewell suddenly recalled having given the order. "I was greatly relieved," wrote Howard, "for my word might have availed little against General Ewell's."[7]

Brig. Gen. James A. Walker also received a scolding for moving troops without orders. When Walker's Stonewall Brigade reached the front that evening, Ewell posted three of its regiments on a hill, halting the others in soggy ground. Walker saw no reason why his troops should stand in ankle-deep mud and ordered the two regiments back to a drier position without Ewell's consent, a decision that led to a "sharp altercation" between the two officers.[8]

Ewell had a more cordial interview with Col. W. Cooper Talley of the First Pennsylvania Reserves. Talley was captured on 8 May while commanding a brigade in Warren's Fifth Corps and was taken back to Ewell. The general complimented the Reserves and remarked that he had once been stationed at Carlisle Barracks. When Talley told him that two of his companies came from the Carlisle area, Ewell asked if any of the soldiers knew Judge Graham. Talley replied that Graham's son was a captain in the brigade. This delighted the general to such an extent that he offered to parole Talley then and there, an offer that Talley politely declined. It was just as well he did, for a few days later Sheridan's cavalry recaptured him and returned him to his command.[9]

After dark, the firing at Laurel Hill tapered off, and the Confederates dug in. Rodes took position on Anderson's right, and Johnson formed on the right of Rodes. Gordon's troops remained in reserve near Spotsylvania Court House. The Confederate line followed a low ridge that crossed the Brock Road and angled northeast, toward the Landrum house. Before reaching the house, the line deflected sharply to the right toward Spotsylvania Court House, resulting in a large bulge that the troops promptly dubbed the Muleshoe Salient. Within the Muleshoe were two smaller salients, known respectively as Heth's and Doles's Salients after the generals who defended them. Salients are inherently weak defensive features, subjecting their defenders to a convergent and sometimes enfilading fire. Moreover, a break on any part of the line instantly places attacking forces on the flank or rear of the salient's other defenders. In short, salients are like bubbles waiting to burst, and at Spotsylvania the Confederates had three of them.[10]

Lee saw this as he rode along the Muleshoe on 9 May, and he was not happy about it. "This is a wretched line," he complained. "I do not see how it can be held!" Ewell agreed but urged him to hold it anyway. Otherwise, he argued, the Federals would seize the ridge and post artillery there that could command the Confederate line. Lee reluctantly agreed to let Ewell stay where he was, but only after engineers assured him that the Muleshoe could be held if properly supported by artillery. It was an unfortunate decision.[11]

To make the Muleshoe as secure as possible, Ewell fortified it with two battalions of artillery and had his troops entrench. The men had become proficient at such work. Within hours they constructed a four-foot-high logwork backed by a two-foot-deep ditch that enabled them to stand without exposing themselves to the enemy's fire. Once they completed the main line, the soldiers added headlogs to the top of the works, constructed traverses at right angles to the main line, and cut down trees and brush in front. Just in case the Federals breached the outer line, Ewell began constructing two reserve lines, one across the center of the Muleshoe and the other behind Doles's Salient.[12]

Throughout 9 May Union infantry probed the Confederate defenses looking for weaknesses. For a while it looked like the fighting might escalate into full-scale combat. At 9:00 A.M. Lee warned Ewell that several lines of Union infantry were advancing toward his position. Ewell ordered Gordon to support Rodes and Johnson, but the alarm proved groundless. Later in the day Ewell proposed making an attack with Johnson's division, supported by Anderson. Nothing came of the plan.[13]

Hancock's Second Corps crossed the Po River just before dark. On 10 May it pushed south of the Shady Grove Road in an effort to turn Lee's left flank. At the same time Warren resumed his attacks on Anderson's line west of the Brock Road. Ewell's front, by contrast, remained comparatively quiet. In the morning Ewell withdrew Gordon's division from the Muleshoe, where it was exposed to Union artillery fire, and sent it to the Brock Road to support Kershaw and Rodes, who seemed in danger of attack. If the Federals struck there, as seemed probable, Ewell planned to swing Johnson's division around and take them in flank.[14]

Grant was planning an attack, but at a point different from the one Ewell anticipated. In the afternoon Col. Emory Upton received permission to attack the Muleshoe with twelve Sixth Corps regiments—the equivalent of a full division. He chose Doles's Salient as his point of attack. Upton chased Doles's skirmishers back to their works and deployed his troops in a pine woods 200 yards from the Confederate line. This alarmed Ewell, who ordered Doles to reestablish his skirmish line at any cost.[15]

Doles was in the process of obeying Ewell's order when the storm broke. Just before 6:00 P.M. three Union batteries opened on Doles's Salient and fired furiously for ten minutes. Upton's men then charged the works, overwhelming Doles's men and capturing four guns from the battery of Capt. Benjamin H. Smith Jr. Ewell was with Doles at the time of the attack and narrowly escaped capture.[16]

Within minutes Upton had carried the outer and reserve trench lines and penetrated 300 yards into the Muleshoe Salient. He had smashed Doles's brigade and turned the flanks of Daniel and Walker, who were on either side of Doles. Lee and Ewell rallied the Confederate troops and helped bring up reinforcements. Ewell appeared first on Junius Daniel's front. Daniel had skillfully turned his brigade at right angles to the works to meet the Union attack. As his men braced for the shock, Ewell dashed up. Halting in the rear of the Forty-fifth

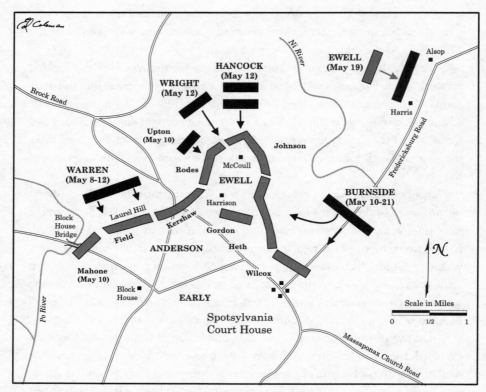

Spotsylvania Court House

North Carolina, he shouted, "Don't run boys; I will have enough men here in five minutes to eat up every d——d one of them." A man in the ranks remembered that as Ewell spoke, "His eyes were almost green." Heartened by Ewell's announcement, Daniel's men held their ground, pouring volley after volley into the charging Federal lines and stopping their progress down the west face of the Muleshoe Salient.[17]

Cullen Battle's brigade stopped the Federals' forward advance, while Daniel clawed at their right flank. At one point Ewell ordered part of Daniel's brigade to charge, but the Federals were too strong. The attackers fell back bloodied and battered. Ewell galloped among the troops, rallying stragglers and leading them back to the front. By his side rode a boy not more than twelve years old. Could it have been the Pueblo, Friday? Whoever it was, he fought with the courage of a veteran. "I may live to be a hundred years of age," wrote one man who saw him, "but I will never forget that little boy—his pony rearing up and pawing in the direction of the enemy, and the gallant little soldier firing his tiny pocket pistol as earnestly as Murat heading a charge." [18]

While Daniel worried Upton's right flank, other Confederate brigades pitched into Upton's left. The Stonewall Brigade had been thrown into some confusion by the Union general's sudden breakthrough, but Walker steadied his troops and led them back into battle against Upton's left flank. Other units rushed to his assistance. From the tip of the Muleshoe came Jones's brigade, now led by Col. William A. Witcher of the Twenty-first Virginia. Witcher's men joined Walker's on the firing line and, with help from Steuart's brigade, thwarted Upton's advance in that direction. Some of Steuart's troops hazarded a charge, but a "withering fire" stopped them in their tracks. [19]

The Confederates had contained Upton, but they were unable to expel him from the works. The Federals still clung tenaciously to the outer line. It fell to John Gordon to drive them out. As soon as Upton attacked, Ewell had ordered Gordon to hurry his division to support Rodes. Robert D. Johnston led Gordon's advance. The brigadier found Ewell in a state of feverish excitement near the front, anxiously tugging at his moustache with both hands. When Ewell saw him, he shouted, "Charge them, Gen'l! D'n em charge em!"

"All right, Gen'l," replied the younger officer, "but wait until my men get in position." Johnston formed his brigade less than 200 yards from Upton's line and charged. With the help of Evans and Daniel, he broke Upton's hold on the salient. [20] Ewell may have helped lead the charge. "The excitement of the advance as they leaped the second line of works & charged the enemy . . . was beyond anything I have ever felt," wrote Campbell Brown. "I shouted till I was hoarse." [21]

By nightfall the fighting was over. The Confederates had retaken the works and inflicted 1,000 casualties on Upton's command. Ewell calculated his own losses at approximately 650, more than half of whom had been captured. Like most officers, Ewell tended to exaggerate enemy casualties and to minimize his own. He surely did in this case. Brig. Gen. Marsena R. Patrick, the Army of the Potomac's provost marshal, noted that Upton captured precisely 37 Confederate officers and 913 enlisted men. Patrick was a meticulous man, and his figures cannot be doubted. Given the stubborn nature of the contest, it is hard to imagine that Ewell suffered fewer than 1,500 casualties in the 10 May battle. [22]

Ewell and his staff had been in the thick of the fighting from start to finish. Campbell Brown astonished himself, if not others, by his coolness under fire. Despite the dangerous circumstances, only one member of the staff was injured: Tom Turner was shot through one leg and broke the shin bone of the other while helping to recapture Smith's battery from the Federals. Ewell praised the aide's "bravery and dash" in his report of the battle and told acquaintances that "he was behaving beautifully when wounded." [23]

Upton's attack had revealed the Muleshoe's weakness, particularly in the area of Doles's Salient. Anticipating that Grant would renew his assault there in the morning, Lee ordered Ewell to strengthen the recaptured works and to distribute a new supply of ammunition to the troops. Ewell's men worked throughout the night, digging a ditch outside the works and adding a barrier of felled trees in front. Lee visited Doles's Salient early on 11 May to inspect their work and to be on hand in case Grant struck again. Skirmish fire alone disturbed the morning's quiet, however. For the time being, Grant withheld his blow. [24]

Toward evening Anderson and Early reported Union troops leaving their fronts. At the same time Confederate cavalry hovering on Grant's left reported a concentration of Union supply wagons and ambulances on the Fredericksburg Road. Obviously Grant was moving, but where? Some reports indicated that he was sliding around Lee's right flank; others, that he was moving toward Lee's left. Still others suggested that he was retreating toward Fredericksburg. As Lee sifted through the contradictory reports at Ewell's headquarters at the Harrison House, he remarked that his greatest difficulty was "to distinguish the true from the false reports which come from the scouts." In the future that task would be immeasurably more difficult. That very day Jeb Stuart was mortally wounded in fighting at Yellow Tavern, near Richmond. [25]

In Stuart's absence Lee could only guess at Grant's next move. If the Union general was moving, as reports seemed to indicate, the Army of Northern Virginia had to be ready to pursue him at a moment's notice. Lee ordered Ewell to evacuate the Muleshoe that night and concentrate his corps near the village. During the day a storm blew in. Believing his men would be more comfortable in their present location than at a new bivouac, Ewell asked Lee to let his infantry remain at the Muleshoe until morning. Lee agreed. [26]

His decision did not pertain to the artillery. Just before dark, Page's and Nelson's battalions, which supported Johnson, left the front and headed for the village. Hardaway's battalion, which supported Rodes, was about to follow when its commander ran into Brig. Gen. Armistead L. Long, Ewell's chief of artillery. Long told Hardaway that "he did not intend for the guns to be brought out until the troops left." Hardaway sent word to his battery commanders to remain at the front until the infantry had left. Two of Cutshaw's batteries that supported Rodes also stayed put.

Page's and Nelson's guns continued to the rear. Grant had not yet seriously attacked Johnson, and there was nothing to suggest that he intended to do so. Lee and Ewell were therefore willing to risk the withdrawal of the guns that supported him. Rodes's division, by contrast, had skirmished for three days and had been the target of Upton's 10 May attack. Confederate leaders were understandably more reluctant to remove Rodes's artillery support than they were Johnson's. Perhaps that is why Long directed Hardaway's and Cutshaw's guns to remain at the front while permitting Page and Nelson to go to the rear.

Terrain may have affected the decision. Hardaway's and Cutshaw's guns occupied relatively open ground and had easy access to the rear. Because they could withdraw the guns quickly when orders came to move, the Confederate generals may have felt that they could afford to leave them at the front until morning. The ground held by Page and Nelson, on the other hand, was wooded and offered no convenient avenues of withdrawal. It would take considerably more effort to remove them from the salient. To save time, Lee and Ewell decided to start the guns off that night.[27]

Ed Johnson was not notified of his superiors' decision. He only learned of it later that night after Page and Nelson had already started for the rear. He must have been uneasy to see the guns leave, for without them his position was indefensible.[28]

The removal of the guns made no difference if Grant was retreating, as Lee supposed, but he was not. Instead of falling back to Fredericksburg, Grant was moving his troops into position to assault the Muleshoe Salient. Johnson first became aware of his danger that night, when officers on picket duty reported the enemy massing in their front. They believed the Federals would attack in the morning. Johnson agreed. Sometime before midnight he sent his adjutant, Maj. Robert W. Hunter, to inform Ewell of this development and to request the immediate return of his artillery. Ewell was not swayed by Johnson's warning. He told Hunter that "General Lee had positive information that the enemy was moving to turn his right flank, and had been so informed by the most reliable scouts, and that it was necessary for the artillery to move accordingly."

Hunter delivered Ewell's response to Johnson, who then returned with him to the Harrison House to speak to Ewell personally. The two men found the general "lying down, and apparently very uneasy." After some discussion Johnson persuaded Ewell that an attack was imminent. Ewell sent Johnson's adjutant Maj. Henry K. Douglas to Long with orders to return the guns at once. Ewell usually took the precaution of sending important messages by two riders. That way if something happened to one, the message would still get through. He apparently failed to do so in this instance. If so, it was a costly oversight.[29]

Secure in the belief that the guns would be back in position by dawn, Ewell lay down and tried to sleep. Although he sent his message to Long around 1:00 A.M. on 12 May, Douglas did not deliver it until 3:30. By then dawn was just twenty minutes away. Long passed the order on to Page, whose troops were soundly sleeping in their tents. Page roused his men. Within minutes they were galloping back to the muddy gunpits they had left a few hours earlier. For some reason Nelson's battalion remained in camp and did not return to the front.[30]

Ewell meanwhile notified Lee of the expected attack and took steps to support Johnson with Gordon's division. Gordon's largest brigade—Evans's—was already at the McCoull House directly in rear of Johnson's line. Hoffman's and Johnston's brigades were one-quarter mile farther back, at the Harrison House. In response to Johnson's plea for reinforcements, Gordon sent Hoffman's brigade forward. At dawn Evans's and Hoffman's troops filed into the secondary-line trenches that Rodes had constructed immediately in rear of Doles's Salient. From there they peered into the foggy darkness and anxiously awaited the anticipated assault.[31]

A distant shout "like the roaring of a tempestuous sea" announced the dawn attack. At 4:35 A.M. Hancock's Second Corps, 20,000 strong, broke out of the woods in front of the Muleshoe and rolled like a tidal wave toward Johnson's line. "Look out, boys! We will have blood for supper!" cried one Confederate as the blue wave crashed on his line. Jones's brigade broke first. Never one of Ewell's best units, the brigade had been nearly worthless since its leader's death on 5 May. As the Federals struck the tip of the salient, Jones's men panicked and ran for the rear, leaving a hole in the center of the line. Like water bursting through a crack in a dam, Hancock's troops poured through the breach and spread left and right, taking Johnson's remaining brigades in flank and rear. Three thousand Confederates threw down their rifles in surrender. The Muleshoe's fragile bubble had burst.[32]

Among those captured in the assault were Generals Johnson and Steuart. Johnson was hobbling up and down the line encouraging his men when the Federals surged over the works. Unable to escape and unwilling to surrender, he struck at enemy soldiers with his cane until they finally subdued him. Johnson's artillery also fell into Union hands. Page's battalion reached the front just as the bluecoats swept over the works. The guns hardly got off a shot before Hancock's men took possession of them. Farther to the left, Northern troops overpowered Cutshaw's two batteries. Altogether, twenty Confederate guns fell into Hancock's hands.[33]

Ewell faced the greatest crisis of his career. Hancock had broken his line, captured nearly one-quarter of his force, and now threatened to divide and destroy the rest of Lee's army. The news was not all bad, however. On the right, Lane's brigade had stopped the Union penetration down the east face of the salient. On the left, Junius Daniel successfully beat back Union efforts to expand down the salient's west face.[34]

Ewell was at the Harrison House when the Federals struck. At the first sound of fighting he galloped to the front. Near the McCoull House he encountered John Gordon, whose division Lee had posted in the center of the Muleshoe for just such an emergency. At the first indication of trouble, Gordon led Robert D. Johnston's small brigade toward the front. In the foggy woods below the McCoull House, he ran headlong into a strong Union column that enfiladed it from the right. A bullet tore across Johnston's scalp, and his overmatched brigade tumbled to the rear with heavy casualties.[35]

Though disastrous in its immediate consequences, Johnston's attack bought the Confederates the time necessary to organize resistance to Hancock's assault. Back near the McCoull House, Ewell fired off dispatches to Anderson and perhaps to Early asking for help. He notified Lee of the disaster and recommended that every pioneer in the army be put to work constructing a new line across the base of the Muleshoe Salient. Having sent his own staff to other parts of the field, Ewell borrowed a staff officer from Gordon. Ewell explained his orders poorly, and when he finished speaking, the officer asked for clarification. "General Ewell was so incensed at this insinuation of lack of perspicuity," remembered Gordon, "that he turned away abruptly, without a word of explanation, simply throwing up his hand and blowing away the young officer with a sort of 'whoo-oo-oot.' There is no way to spell out this indignant and resounding puff," he chuckled, "but even in the fierce battle that was raging there was a roar of laughter from the other members of my staff as the droll and doughty warrior rushed away to another part of the field."[36]

Gordon meanwhile discovered that the Federals overlapped his right. He accordingly withdrew his remaining regiments to the fields surrounding the Harrison House and prepared to attack the enemy. Lee and Ewell joined him there. Lee attempted to lead the division into combat, but Gordon's men forced him to the rear. Gordon then led his troops in what he termed a "headlong & resistless charge" that "carried everything before it." His men recaptured several hundred yards of breastworks on the eastern face of the salient and stubbornly held them against Federal attacks for the rest of the day.[37]

One by one, other Confederate brigades waded into action. From Rodes's division came Ramseur's brigade, one of the finest in the army. Ewell personally led it into the McCoull House clearing. Once there, Ramseur formed a line of battle and charged Doles's secondary trench line, now held by the Federals. "For a moment," wrote one of Daniel's men, "it seemed to me our brigade ceased firing and held its breath as these men went forward, apparently into the very jaws of death." Ramseur's horse collapsed under him, and a bullet struck the general in the arm in the early stages of the attack; but his brigade did not falter. With Ewell and Rodes looking on, it carried both the secondary and outer lines of works.[38]

By 6:00 A.M. the fighting at the salient had reached a bloody impasse. Gordon had secured the eastern face of the Muleshoe, and Rodes had retaken part of its western face; but the Federals still firmly held the apex. To break the logjam, Grant ordered Maj. Gen. Horatio Wright's Sixth Corps to support Hancock's attack. Wright's assault focused on a slight turn in the Southern works thereafter known as the Bloody Angle.[39]

Confederate reinforcements were headed toward the same point. About 6:00 A.M. Brig. Gen. Abner Perrin appeared in the salient. Perrin commanded an Alabama brigade in Brig. Gen. William Mahone's Third Corps division. To that time he had been guarding Block House Bridge on the Po River, at the far left end of the Confederate line.[40] Perrin found Ewell, Rodes, and Gordon "engaged in an earnest and animated discussion" at the McCoull House. "Things looked desperate, and there was a considerable show of excitement," in the opinion of one Alabamian. "Perrin was looking from one to the other as if at a loss for his orders. Gordon was talking rapidly and literally foaming at the mouth."

While the generals discussed what to do, Perrin's men lay down to avoid the bullets zipping around them. The sight of soldiers lying on the ground struck Ewell as cowardly, and he exclaimed, "Oh, boys, for God's sake don't lie down— it don't look well in a soldier to lie down in the presence of the enemy." Springing to his feet, a soldier explained that he and his comrades had been ordered to lie down. "Oh, well, if you were ordered to lie down that's all right," Ewell replied. "No, General, I don't want to do anything that looks badly in a soldier," the man insisted. Ewell assured him that it was all right to lie down if that was the order. "I suppose the gallant old fellow realized at once that in excitement, he had 'talked through his hat,'" the soldier recalled. "The rest of the boys well knowing they were at their proper duty had all remained as they were, and were smiling at the situation."[41]

In a moment Perrin's troops were back on their feet and following their commander toward the Bloody Angle. The secondary line behind Doles's Salient extended to that point. As Perrin's horse leaped over the inner works, its rider fell mortally wounded. Many of Perrin's men fell at his side from a deadly cross fire emanating from the woods to their right. The brigade dissolved and as a unit saw no further fighting that day.[42]

The Confederates in the Muleshoe fought without additional reinforcements until about 8:00 A.M., when Brig. Gen. Nathaniel H. Harris's Mississippians reached the field.[43] Like Perrin, Harris belonged to Mahone's division. As his brigade double-quicked up the salient, Union artillery opened on it with a galling fire. Rodes directed Harris to recapture the breastworks on Ramseur's right. Union soldiers there were raking the North Carolinians' flank. As Harris's men charged into the maelstrom, Corp. Arthur T. Watts saw Lee and Ewell standing beside a battery. Both men exhibited "considerable anxiety," he thought. Another soldier remembered seeing Ewell leaning on his crutch behind an unfinished earthwork some 400 yards from the front—a reference to Gordon's reserve line. Started three days earlier, the trenches had never been completed.[44]

Harris got off to a bad start. Rodes had detailed a member of his staff to guide the Mississippian to the correct part of the line, but as they got close to the fighting, the man became frightened and fled, leaving the brigade to stumble blindly into the fray. As a result, it came in too far to the left and partly overlapped Ramseur's position. Harris had to slide his men to the right, driving the enemy from the works as he moved, until he had gained a sufficient front. In the process he lost a third of his brigade. As his casualties mounted, he sent Lt. Col. Abram M. Feltus of the Sixteenth Mississippi to Ewell for reinforcements. While Feltus was addressing Ewell, a bullet pierced his heart, and he fell dead at the general's feet.[45]

Whether Feltus had a chance to relay Harris's message to Ewell before he died is not known. Even if he did not, the roar of musketry must have convinced Ewell that more troops were needed at the front. At 10:00 A.M., an hour after Harris went into battle, Ewell ordered Brig. Gen. Samuel McGowan to extend Harris's beleaguered line to the right. McGowan's South Carolinians sprang eagerly to the task, but like Harris's brigade, they angled too far to the left and came in behind the troops that had preceded them. McGowan was wounded in the charge, and Col. Joseph Brown took command of the brigade. With Harris's help, Brown shifted his troops to the right. In the process he recaptured several traverses and extended the Confederate line a short distance east of the Bloody Angle.[46]

For the next seventeen hours the fighting raged around the Bloody Angle with an intensity and duration never before seen in America. Opposing soldiers fired at close range, beat one another with clubbed muskets, and jabbed each other with bayonets. Despite a daylong downpour that dampened ammunition, Union musketry felled a twenty-two-inch oak tree that stood behind the angle. The bodies of dead soldiers had to be cleared from the traverses or piled in heaps to make room for the living. Water in the trenches ran red with blood. "The question became, pretty plainly, whether one was willing to meet death, not merely to run the chances of it," wrote a South Carolinian.[47]

Union artillery added to the carnage. "Guns were run up close to the parapet, and double charges of canister played their part in the bloody work," remembered Horace Porter of Grant's staff. "The fence-rails and logs in the breastworks were shattered into splinters, and trees over a foot and a half in diameter were cut completely in two by the incessant musketry fire. . . . We had not only shot down an army, but also a forest." For the first time in the campaign, mortars lobbed shells into the Confederate works. A correspondent for the Richmond *Whig* estimated that Union artillery fired an average of 30 shots a minute over the course of the day. In the early stages of the battle, Junius Daniel counted as many as 100 discharges per minute.[48]

The constant crash of artillery affected even a seasoned veteran like Ewell. Col. J. Catlett Gibson of the Forty-ninth Virginia encountered the general writing orders at his portable field desk just behind the front. Union shells, noted Gibson, "were falling fast and furious all around. Ewell was wearing an artificial leg in the place of the natural one he lost near Sudley's Mills. . . . He had become very nervous and every time a shell exploded near him he would hop his good leg up and curse with the vehemence of an old trooper and the unction of a new church member."[49]

Ewell remained at the Muleshoe throughout the day funneling reinforcements into the fight, rallying soldiers of broken units, and seeing to it that troops in the trenches had sufficient ammunition.[50] Early in the conflict an officer in the Louisiana Brigade saw Lee and Ewell rallying the survivors of Johnson's brigade. He observed a strong contrast in the demeanor of the two officers. "Gen. Lee was calm, collected and dignified," he remembered. "He quietly exhorted the men not to forget their manhood and their duty, but to return to the field and strike one more blow for the glorious cause in which they were enlisted." Ewell, on the other hand, was "greatly excited and, in a towering passion, hurled a terrible volley of oaths at the stragglers from the front, stigmatizing them as cowards, etc. It is hardly necessary to say Gen. Lee's course was by far the more effective of the two." The officer commented that Ewell had been known for swearing early in the war but had given up the habit when he married and joined the church. Nevertheless, "the excitement of this occasion was too much for his religious scruples, and he swore with all of his old time vehemence and volubility."[51]

A Georgian also noted the contrast between Lee's and Ewell's conduct. "Gen Lee, in the calmest and kindest manner, said: 'Boys, do not run away, go back, go back, your comrades need you in the trenches.' Gen. Ewell, forgetting himself in the excitement of the moment, said: 'Yes, G-d d—n you, run, run; the Yankees will catch you; that's right; go as fast as you can.'" The soldier added, "All that Gen. Lee addressed at once halted and returned to the assistance of their comrades. All that Gen. Ewell so angrily reproached continued their flight to the rear." [52]

At one point Ewell lost his head and began beating some of the fleeing soldiers over the back with his sword. Lee reined in his enraged lieutenant, saying sharply, "General Ewell, you must restrain yourself; how can you expect to control these men when you have lost control of yourself? If you cannot repress your excitement, you had better retire." Then "in the quietest manner," Lee "moved among the men, and through their officers reformed the broken ranks." Ewell's behavior on this occasion undoubtedly was the source of a statement made by Lee to his secretary, William Allan, after the war that on 12 May he "found Ewell perfectly prostrated by the misfortune of the morning, and too much overwhelmed to be efficient." [53]

Because of Ewell's efforts, or perhaps in spite of them, at least 600 men of Johnson's division rallied to the colors and went to work on a new defensive line constructed across the base of the Muleshoe Salient. Lee's chief engineer laid out the line during the day, but Ewell did not begin entrenching until after dark, perhaps for fear of exposing the workers to Union artillery. The digging continued well into the night. The troops fully realized the gravity of the situation and worked with a will, encouraged by Lee and Ewell, who walked up and down the works telling them that the fate of the army depended on the line's being completed by dawn. "I knew by the way they acted that it was a critical time," wrote Pvt. John Casler. [54]

While Johnson's men entrenched, Ewell ordered Maj. R. M. C. Page to collect whatever troops remained in his command and retrieve four brass guns that he had lost earlier in the day, but which Confederate troops supposedly had recaptured. Page returned an hour later to report his failure. Upon Ewell's questioning, Page admitted that he had not personally conducted the search but had delegated the duty to "a reliable and intelligent sergeant." Ewell had no patience with lazy officers. With ill-disguised disgust, he snarled, "Well sir the sergt. had better be made the Major and you the sergeant." Stung by the general's rebuke, Page personally led thirty men back to the front to continue searching for the guns. He never found them. [55]

Sometime after midnight Johnson's men finished the new line, and Ewell ordered the troops at the front to fall back. By dawn, 13 May, the evacuation was complete. Lee and Ewell were up much of the night preparing the troops for attacks they feared might come in the morning. To Lt. Robert Stiles, Ewell "seemed busy and apprehensive," as certainly he was.[56] Stiles might also have added "tired," for Ewell had not slept much the preceding night, or the entire week for that matter. Grant did not attack when morning came. Instead he strengthened his hold on the Muleshoe's outer line by having his pioneers reverse some of the logworks to face south.

For the next four days the Army of the Potomac was unusually quiet. Union soldiers probed Ewell's new line on the thirteenth but chose not to attack it. When the morning passed without an assault, Ewell returned the troops he had borrowed from Anderson and Early to their proper corps. He made an effort to thank those Second Corps units, such as the Sixth Louisiana, that had fought particularly well. He singled out Dodson Ramseur for special praise, calling him the hero of the day. Meeting some of Hoffman's troops, Ewell pulled out a Northern paper that described the Confederates' tenacity in the fight and read it to them. "But, boys, you ought to hear what General Lee says about you," he added with a smile. The soldiers clamored for Ewell to tell them, but the general just laughed and said it would make them too vain. "He never told us," wrote one proud Virginian, "but we felt sure it was something good, and, if possible, we were more willing than ever to do just what Marse Robert wanted done."[57]

Ewell did not get an opportunity to thank Harris's brigade or any of the other First or Third Corps units that had come to his relief, but he did not forget their services. Seven months after the battle, Ewell wrote Harris a letter complimenting his brigade's conduct in the battle. Yet when he wrote his report of the campaign in March 1865, he hardly mentioned Harris's and McGowan's brigades and passed over Perrin altogether. Some accused Ewell of purposely downplaying the contributions of units outside his own corps, but the oversight was surely unintentional. Ewell never hesitated to praise those who deserved it.[58]

For six days rains soaked the battlefield, turning unpaved roads into mud and effectively slowing military operations to a crawl. Even so, Ewell worried about an attack on his line. Throughout the week he slept in the trenches with his troops. Except for Pendleton, he did not ask his staff to share that hardship but allowed them to stay at a house in the rear. Hotchkiss, noting this circumstance to his wife, commented that the general was "very kind."[59]

The rain did not halt Grant's movements entirely. After dark on 13 May, he shifted Warren's corps from the far right, opposite Anderson, to the far left, beyond the Fredericksburg Road. Lee became aware of the movement early the next day. Although he did not understand the purpose of the action at first, he correctly surmised that Grant was sliding to the left. He inquired if the Federals still occupied Ewell's front and was assured that they did. When Warren later pushed the Confederates off Myers's Hill, east of the Fredericksburg Road, Lee ordered Maj. Gen. Charles W. Field's division of Anderson's corps to Spotsylvania Court House. Hancock followed Warren across the Fredericksburg Road that night, prompting Anderson to send Kershaw's division after Field at midnight, 16 May.[60]

With the departure of Anderson's two divisions, Ewell held the Confederate left. It was a worrisome position. Since the annihilation of Johnson's division on 12 May, he had only two divisions in his corps. Even after Ewell put every available man on the line, there was still a mile-wide gap between his left flank and the Po River. If the Federals exploited that gap, he had no troops in reserve to stop them. Ewell therefore was understandably anxious when scouts reported Maj. Gen. John Gibbon's division of the Union Second Corps moving toward the Po River on 16 May. Gibbon's objective was to retrieve several hundred wounded Union soldiers inadvertently left at a field hospital when Hancock's corps had abandoned the area the previous day. He hastily loaded the patients onto ambulances and started back toward the Fredericksburg Road, happy to have accomplished his mission without provoking a fight.[61]

On 17 May the rains that had plagued the Army of the Potomac's movements ceased, and Grant resumed offensive operations. Finding that Lee had shifted Anderson's division toward the Telegraph Road, Grant sent Hancock's and Wright's corps back to the Muleshoe Salient after dark to strike Ewell on 18 May. Grant would have roughly 22,000 men to assault approximately 6,000 defenders.[62]

The dawn attack found Ewell's veterans ready and waiting behind their breastworks. They had been there for five days. In that time they had added abatis more than 100 yards deep in front of their works. When the Federals reached the obstruction, they had to cut their way through. As they did so, twenty-nine Confederate cannon blasted them at close range with shot, spherical case, and canister. "Vainly do they endeavor to press forward," a Confederate artillerist wrote of the struggling bluecoats, "again and again, we break them, and their officers uselessly dash up and down their lines, endeavoring to hurl them upon our works. . . . They are but food for our gun-powder."[63]

When the smoke cleared, the Federals were fleeing in confusion. Their officers rallied them and twice more essayed to carry the line, but Southern guns again "drove them crippled & shattered from the field." Ewell's infantry joined the action, but they were not needed; Long's artillery was able to throw back the assailants without help. In the brief fight, the Confederates suffered fewer than 30 casualties while inflicting more than 500 on the foe.[64] It was a vivid demonstration of what massed artillery could accomplish and served as a reminder of what might have happened on 12 May had Ewell's guns been in place just ten minutes earlier.

Hancock and Wright remained near the Muleshoe Salient for the rest of 18 May. After dark they retraced their steps and once again took up positions east of the Fredericksburg Road. When Lee discovered they had left Ewell's front, he ordered his subordinate to shift his corps to the right end of the line. Later he had second thoughts. Before Ewell moved to the right, Lee ordered him to undertake a reconnaissance to locate Grant's right flank. Ewell persuaded Lee to convert the movement into a reconnaissance-in-force utilizing his entire corps.[65]

Ewell erroneously believed that the Federals still held the north face of the Muleshoe Salient. As a result, he made a long and needless detour by way of the Brock Road before swinging north and east toward the Fredericksburg Road. He took six guns of Braxton's battalion with him; but after two or three miles the rain-soaked roads became impassable for artillery, and Ewell sent them back. Although he was criticized for this, the decision was sound. The guns could not have crossed the swollen Ny River. Even if they had, they would have been of little use in the wooded terrain where he later fought. Had they continued with the column, they probably would have been abandoned and captured in the subsequent retreat.[66]

Ewell approached the Fredericksburg Road late on the afternoon of 19 May. When Federal troops appeared at Harris Farm, Ewell deployed his corps into line of battle to meet them. Rodes's division took the right; Gordon's, the left. The Union troops belonged to Brig. Gen. Robert O. Tyler's brigade, comprised of heavy artillery regiments recently converted to infantry and sent down from Washington, D.C. Some of Tyler's green regiments counted more than 2,000 muskets; taken altogether, they outnumbered Ewell's depleted corps by one-third.[67]

Ramseur's brigade led Ewell's march and was the first unit to encounter the "Heavies." Although the rest of the corps was not yet up, Ramseur asked for permission to attack, believing that further delay might be disastrous. His veterans plowed into Tyler's men and shoved them toward the road. As Union reinforcements came on the scene, though, Ramseur had to give ground. He fell back 200 yards, where the remaining brigades of Rodes's division shouldered in beside him on the firing line.

Gordon deployed on Rodes's left. Like Ramseur he enjoyed initial success but had to fall back in the face of Union counterattacks. A panic ensued, and the retreat nearly became a rout. As Gordon retired, he uncovered Rodes's left flank, and Rodes's brigades also began to peel away. Fortunately Hoffman's brigade stood firm. With the help of Daniel and Ramseur, it was able to keep the Federals at bay until dark. Lee could hear the escalating battle from his position near the courthouse. Fearing that Ewell might be in over his head, he ordered Early to make a demonstration in Ewell's favor. Hampton's cavalry had accompanied Ewell on the march. As darkness fell, two guns of his horse artillery also weighed in with a few shots.[68]

Ewell helped Hoffman's men beat back the Federal attack. At one point in the battle his sorrel mare was killed, and the general took a nasty fall. Nearby troops helped roll the dead horse off him and persuaded the shaken general to go to the rear. It was the third and last horse Ewell lost in the war. In each instance the animal was a sorrel mare.[69]

Besides these few facts, little is known about Ewell's personal involvement in the fight. Maj. William Allan spoke with Robert E. Lee about it after the war. According to Allan, Lee told him that Ewell had "lost all presence of mind" at Harris Farm, "and Lee found him prostrate on the ground, and declaring he cd not get Rodes div. out. (Rodes being heavily engaged with the enemy.) He (Lee) told him to order Rodes back, and that if he could not get him out, he (Lee) could." This is damning testimony, to be sure. There is only one problem with it: Lee was not there. If Ewell did, in fact, lose his head during the fight, no credible evidence of it has yet come to light.[70]

At 10:00 P.M. the fighting at Harris Farm ceased and the Confederates withdrew unmolested to their line at the base of the Muleshoe Salient. Ewell, perhaps shaken from his fall, managed the retreat poorly. Four hundred and seventy-two of his men were inadvertently left behind and captured by the Federals. The rest of the corps trickled back to its position in dribs and drabs. While the slipshod nature of the retreat can be attributed to the weariness of troops, the poor condition of the roads, and the difficulty of marching through heavy woods at night, it also reflected a lack of effective leadership.[71]

Ewell had accomplished his mission of locating Grant's right flank, but at considerable cost. He reported losing 900 men in the fight, roughly one-sixth of his remaining troops. That he had inflicted nearly 1,500 casualties on the Federals did not matter. By 1864 the South simply could not afford to swap casualties with the North for anything less than a clear-cut victory.[72]

The fighting at Harris Farm marked the last major combat at Spotsylvania. The next night Grant broke the stalemate by sending Hancock's Second Corps to Milford Station, well south of the Confederate lines. Lee had no choice but to head him off. On 21 May the battle-weary Confederates took to the road again, their destination now being Hanover Junction. How many casualties they left is uncertain, but if the Second Corps is any indication, the number was shockingly high. The corps had started the campaign with 15,500 men. It fielded fewer than half that number when it left Spotsylvania on 21 May. Casualties among general officers had been particularly high. Of the sixteen generals under Ewell's command on 4 May, Jones, Stafford, Perrin, and Daniel had been killed; Pegram, Walker, Johnston, Ramseur, and Hays had been wounded; and Edward Johnson and George Steuart had been captured. Losses among field officers were proportionately high. Winfield Hancock exaggerated only slightly when he reported that Ewell's corps after 12 May "was almost destroyed."[73]

Bad as his losses were, Ewell felt that he had dealt an even heavier blow to the enemy. In his report he bragged that the number of Union dead at Spotsylvania had been "immense" and that their casualties "must have exceeded ours in the proportion of at least 6 to 1, taking all the engagements together."[74] That was wishful thinking. Ewell's corps alone had suffered at least 8,000 casualties since 5 May, while the total loss to the Union army in that same period was less than 37,000. Yet many in the Army of Northern Virginia shared Ewell's optimism. Despite the terrific carnage, many Confederates (including Ewell) felt that the Union army's new general in chief had taken his best shot and had failed.[75] Maybe so, but Grant was not willing to concede defeat; if he had failed to crush the Army of Northern Virginia at Spotsylvania, he would shift ground and try again elsewhere. The eighteen-day-old campaign—already the bloodiest in American history—would go on.

CHAPTER 27

I Am Unwilling to Be Idle at This Crisis

At dawn on 21 May 1864 Robert E. Lee learned that the Federals were again shifting southward. He ordered Dick Ewell to leave the Muleshoe and place the Second Corps on the Army of Northern Virginia's right flank, south of the Po River. Ewell did so, establishing his headquarters first at Stanard's and then at Beasley's Gate. As the day progressed it became clear that Grant was doing more than simply shifting position; he was marching toward Bowling Green in an effort to get between the Army of Northern Virginia and Richmond. In response, recalled Hotchkiss, Lee ordered the army to leave Spotsylvania Court House and hasten south "as hard as we could." The race for Hanover Junction was on.[1]

Lee accompanied Ewell down the Telegraph Road.[2] Hoke's brigade arrived from Petersburg and fell in behind the Second Corps, acting as its rear guard. When Ewell stopped to rest, the North Carolinians gathered around him. He told them that Grant had incurred heavy losses up to that point and stressed the importance of beating the Federals to Hanover Junction. In the summer heat the men perspired freely, including Ewell, who sweltered in a thick winter shirt. At 11:00 P.M. he and his corps slumped down to sleep at Dickinson's Mill, having plodded more than twenty miles. Three hours later they continued on their way, arriving at Hanover Junction at 1:00 P.M., 22 May, ahead of Anderson and Hill and well ahead of Grant.[3]

Lee established a defensive line below the North Anna River, covering Hanover Junction and the Virginia Central Railroad. Ewell held the right end of the line, from the Telegraph Road to Cedar Farm Bridge. On 23 May Warren's corps began crossing the river at Jericho Ford, opposite the Confederate left. Lee ordered A. P. Hill to throw Warren back across the river, but Hill committed only one division and was beaten back. The same day, Hancock overran a Confederate redoubt north of the river and seized control of the Chesterfield Bridge.[4]

The Army of the Potomac now had two toeholds south of the river: Hancock at the Chesterfield Bridge and Warren at Jericho Ford. Five miles separated them. Lee continued to hold Ox Ford, between Hancock and Warren. He refused his flanks to create a line shaped like an inverted "V," thus dividing the Union army and placing himself in a position to destroy one part or the other. It was a brilliant plan, but it failed because Lee was ill and unable to exercise effective command. Had Ewell possessed more boldness and independence, he might have initiated an attack on his own responsibility. As it was, Grant discovered his peril in time and entrenched. By the end of the day the danger was past; the Army of Northern Virginia had squandered its best and perhaps last chance to cripple the enemy.[5]

For two days the two armies confronted one another, each side unwilling to attack. Grant broke the stalemate on 26 May by retreating across the North Anna and recrossing downriver. Ewell had predicted as much in a letter written earlier that day to Lizinka on the first anniversary of their marriage. "We are still in juxtaposition with the Yankees," he informed her, "mutually watching, they entrenched so strongly as to make it impossible to attack any part of their lines on this flank, while they are equally afraid to . . . come against us. This will probably continue untill they take advantage of darkness to past [sic] across our flank when we will be forced to move back again to get in their front. We are getting too near Richmond for this to continue much more & one side or the other will have to change tactics & go at it 'hammer & tongs.'"[6]

That day was just around the corner. On 27 May Grant crossed the Pamunkey River at Hanovertown and Nelson's Ferry, compelling Lee to abandon the North Anna River line. The two sides clashed briefly at Totopotomoy Creek, then slid south to Cold Harbor. For three days they fought inconclusively around the village. Finally Grant lost his patience and attacked the entrenched Confederate line. In the brief, bloody struggle that followed, he lost more than 5,500 casualties.[7]

Ewell did not participate in the fighting around Cold Harbor. On 26 May he fell ill with diarrhea, and by the next morning he felt so poorly that he relinquished command of the Second Corps to Early. Ewell had enjoyed "capital health" up to that time. Despite sleeping in the trenches at Spotsylvania, subsisting on a diet of salt meat and few vegetables, and doing an immense amount of work, he had never felt better. Hard campaigning seemed to agree with him.[8] But the long hours and bad diet finally took their toll. Ewell began feeling sick while at North Anna River. When the army abandoned that line and marched toward Totopotomoy Creek, he had set aside his responsibilities and followed it south in an ambulance. He stopped at the Satterwhite house on 27 May and after resting there continued on to Mechanicsville. For two days he lay in his tent while his troops sparred with the enemy, just three miles away.[9]

Lee of course knew that Ewell was sick. On 29 May he sent his subordinate a note of condolence. In it he urged Ewell to "proceed to some place where you can enjoy that repose and proper care of yourself which I trust will speedily repair the injury you have sustained from your late arduous services." To drive home his point, he issued a special order assigning Early temporary command of the corps. The directive formally granted Ewell permission "to retire from the field that he may have the benefit of rest and medical treatment." Alarm gripped Ewell as he read the order. He anticipated that Lee might use his illness as an excuse to remove him from command, and the order confirmed his fears. He instantly sent a note to Lee assuring him that he was on the mend and would be fit for duty in two days. To head off objections that he was returning to duty too soon, he enclosed a certificate signed by Dr. McGuire attesting to his improvement.[10]

As Ewell anticipated, Lee blocked his return. The commanding general wrote on 31 May to congratulate him on his improving health, but he refused to restore him to command. "Your troops are now in line of battle under Gen Early & I do not think any change at the present time would be beneficial," he explained. "I advise you therefore as soon as you can move with safety to retire until the coming battle is over & endeavor to recuperate your health & restore your strength for future service. To report for duty now would be I fear to expose your life & health with out corresponding advantage."[11]

In his tactful way Lee was asking Ewell to step aside. Ewell had fought with the army far too long, however, simply to fold his tent and slip silently into the night. He met with Lee that evening in an effort to persuade Lee to let him return to duty. The commanding general refused to yield. The next day Ewell wrote to Lee's adjutant, Col. Walter Taylor, asking for a copy of the order that removed him from command. "The only authority I have is S.O. [134] of the 29th Ulto. which contemplates my temporary absence caused by sickness. This now having reported for duty does not cover the case." Lee brushed aside that technicality. Through Taylor, he stated that the special order was the only one yet issued regarding Ewell's removal. If a subsequent order was issued, Ewell would get a copy of it. Until then he was at liberty to leave the army under the authority of the existing order.[12]

Ewell continued to press his point. Lee had objected to his return for two reasons: first, that he had not sufficiently recovered his health and would endanger himself and perhaps the safety of his corps by reporting for duty too soon, and second, that it would be dangerous to change commanders in the immediate presence of the enemy. Ewell addressed each point in turn. As for his health, he wrote, "The opinion of my medical attendant, Dr. McGuire, and that of myself, is that I am as able for duty to-day as at any time since the campaign commenced." As for the danger of switching commanders in the middle of a campaign, Ewell made it clear that he was prepared to wait. "I am unwilling to be idle at this crisis," he told Taylor, "and, with the permission of the commanding general, I would prefer to remain with this army until circumstances may admit of my being replaced in command of my corps." [13]

Lee replied promptly to Ewell's letter. After again expressing pleasure at his lieutenant's rapid recovery, he reiterated his reluctance to change commanders in the middle of a campaign. The Confederate Congress had just passed a law permitting army commanders to accord temporary promotions to officers in the event of an emergency. Lee had taken advantage of that law to place Early in temporary command of the Second Corps. "Under the recent bill," he wrote Ewell, "Early is assigned to the command of your Corps for the present & Ramseur to the command of Early's division. They are in line of battle & from the firing I now hear may be engaged. It would be impossible for me to make changes at this time without great risk and hazard."

The argument did not hold water. In the past month alone, Lee had shuffled corps assignments no less than four times: Anderson for Longstreet, Early for Hill, Hill for Early, and now Early for Ewell. In each case the change had been made under difficult circumstances, and in each case it had gone smoothly. He would never have offered such an objection had Jackson or Longstreet made a similar request. Clearly, he did not want Ewell to return. Ewell must have recognized this, but he refused to yield gracefully. Instead he remained with the army for another week so as "to place the question of health beyond a doubt." [14]

On 4 June Lee formally announced Early's temporary promotion to lieutenant general and assigned him command of the Second Corps. Ewell was powerless to stop him. "I have neither influence nor intrigue," he had admitted to Lizinka, "& at the earliest moment possible will have to give way to those that [do]." That moment had arrived, and Ewell had no choice but to step down. The change in commanders provoked a mixed response among Ewell's staff. According to Campbell Brown, everybody was "disgusted" by the change, including Sandie Pendleton, who "declared before four or five that it was outrageous treatment." Others, such as William Allan and Hunter McGuire, quietly approved of Ewell's ouster. "Every body was uncomfortable for the Gen.," wrote Allan, "& yet we all felt that his removal was inevitable & indeed was proper." Ewell alone affected to be unconcerned by the loss of command, telling Lizinka that "I only care about it on your account . . . knowing how ambitious you are." In a weak attempt at humor, he told his wife that she had only herself to blame if she was disappointed: "You should have thought of this before we were married."[15]

Early denied any responsibility for Ewell's removal. The day after Lee announced his appointment to corps command, Early wrote to Ewell denying that he had anything to do with the decision "directly or indirectly either by procurement or suggestion." He insisted that the arrangement was just temporary "until there is such a pause in our operations as to result in such a state of things as to permit a change of commanders without inconvenience." He further affirmed that "I would have been gratified if you had remained in command all the time. I shall be so when you return." Although Early may have been sincere, some members of Ewell's staff did not believe him. Campbell Brown, for one, thought Early felt guilty and therefore avoided looking him in the face. "He looks at me like a sheep-stealing dog, out of the corner of his eye," wrote Brown, "very different from his usual manner." Two men in the Signal Corps applied to be relieved from their headquarters duties to protest the change. Although Ewell never accused Early of plotting his removal, it is significant that the two erstwhile friends never corresponded after that.[16]

Ewell found himself a general without a command. In an earlier conversation, Lee had proposed assigning Ewell to manage the Richmond defenses, a sedentary position better suited to a man of Ewell's feeble health. Ewell had declined the offer, considering it "merely a polite way of being laid on the shelf." He was a combat officer and had no use for a desk job.[17]

In a final effort to return to the army, Ewell secured an audience with Jefferson Davis on 7 June. The purpose of the visit was not to plead for his corps but to ask Davis to place him in command of his old division, now commanded by Ramseur. Davis explained that Ewell's high rank forbade such an arrangement. Ewell thereupon offered to resign his commission so that Davis could appoint him a major general. But Davis would not do it. He needed Ewell at the head of his corps, he said. He urged Ewell to speak with Lee again about being reinstated to his former position.

Ewell secured an interview with the commanding general the next morning. He opened the conversation by assuring Lee that he had not come to plead for his corps. Instead he wished to resign and be assigned to some lower duty. There was no call for that, Lee insisted. When the present campaign was over, he intended to restore him to command of his corps.

"But, General," protested Ewell, "I am in as good health now as I ever was. I was up yesterday 3 a.m. to 1 a.m., not fatigued or unwell, have worked as hard as anyone on the campaign. I was sick a little at Hanover Junction, but the instant we moved or the necessity arose for increased exertion beyond my powers, I went on sick report and was cured by two days' rest."

"I have been constantly uneasy about you since last fall," answered Lee. "You will go on exerting yourself and I have been dreading every moment to hear that you have killed yourself by your exertions without good."

"My stump does not show the slightest injury," the one-legged general insisted, "is perfectly well and so far from impairing my health or injuring my powers of recuperation the doctor tells me the reverse is rather the case. I certainly never recovered so easily from so severe an attack. The injury last fall was as purely accidental as if it had been cut by a knife. I think highly of Early. If I thought you preferred him for other than mere physical reasons, which I feel to be erroneous, I would not say a word, but I know my own endurance."

"I do not prefer Early to you except I think him stronger. I am unable to perform the duties of Corps Commander, which requires great labor."

"Did I not perform them all?" asked Ewell.

"Perfectly well," answered Lee, "but remember how tired you were. You would sleep on the ground, liable to take cold."

"But I never did," Ewell reminded him. "I was without dyspepsia for the first time for years so long. I am better for riding all day—twelve hours."

"I am glad to hear you give such an account of yourself," said Lee, "but I cannot but have my fears. I feel friendly to you, but the public interests are paramount to everything else. My own impression and that acquired from others makes me think that it is possible at any moment you may give way and in the most critical operations confusion might occur and disaster. Such are my fears, and it is my duty to avoid all risks. A few days may end all this and see you in command. You are now free from anxiety."

"These last few days are the most anxious I have spent," replied Ewell despondently.

"It is due Early and the Corps that he receive the appointment just as Anderson has," said Lee, referring to Dick Anderson's recent promotion.

Ewell did not seem to hear him. He was still dwelling on Lee's earlier statement that the fighting might end in a few days, enabling him to resume command. "I don't want to command the Corps as a peace officer," he objected, "but there is no doubt that since the 4th of May the Corps has been on the most desperate work at times—always acquitting themselves to your expressed satisfaction, and undoubtedly inflicting more than our share of loss on the enemy."

Lee was tiring of the conversation. "Your best plan is to recover your health," he said.

"It is recovered," replied the dejected lieutenant. "But I will go somewhere to be out of the way."

"You are not in the way, but you had better take care of yourself."

Ewell rose from his chair. His last attempt to salvage his command—and his self-respect—had failed.[18]

Lee had determined as early as 29 May that Ewell should not return to the army. Initially he denied him command on the basis of his health. When Ewell produced evidence that he had fully recovered, Lee abruptly changed tactics and insisted that it would be too hazardous to change commanders in the middle of active operations. But Ewell called his bluff by remaining with the army. As the armies entrenched, Lee reverted to his previous argument that Ewell was too feeble to undergo the rigors of a grueling campaign. Ewell knew better. He stubbornly argued that his health was better than it had been for some time. Lee thereupon changed tactics again, arguing that Early deserved a chance at higher command. This inferred that Ewell had not measured up to his responsibilities as corps commander. When Ewell challenged that statement by pointing to the corps' record since the opening of the campaign, Lee abruptly ended the dialogue and insisted that Ewell go to the rear. It was a sad denouement for the gallant old soldier.

Why was Ewell removed? The answer, of course, is that Lee had lost confidence in him. His mistrust dated back to Gettysburg. In a private conversation with Lee, Isaac Trimble had complained that Ewell had not been sufficiently aggressive on the first day of fighting. Lee apparently agreed. Thenceforth his dissatisfaction with Ewell grew steadily. Although it is difficult in retrospect to hold Ewell responsible for the disasters at either Bristoe Station or Rappahannock Station, Lee seems to have done so. When Ewell asked to be reinstated to command during the Mine Run Campaign following a brief leave of absence, Lee bluntly told him "no." The Second Corps leader's conduct off the field that winter further damaged his reputation. Military duties took a back seat to squiring Lizinka around camp or to hosting social events at Morton's Hall. It was obvious to anyone who saw them together that the strong-willed wife had her "fond, foolish" husband under her thumb.

Ewell's performance had improved in 1864. In the Wilderness he fought splendidly, but even then Lee had a negative impression of his conduct. He was not with Ewell during the two-day battle. Consequently he did not see the skillful way his lieutenant had maneuvered his corps. When Lee finally did visit the Orange Turnpike on 7 May, John Gordon took him aside and complained that Ewell and Early had squandered an opportunity to crush the Federal army on 6 May by not attacking Sedgwick's flank early that day. Circumstances made an attack at that hour impracticable, but Lee did not know that. Gordon's comments probably convinced Lee that Ewell had been too cautious.[19]

Spotsylvania confirmed Lee in his opinion that Ewell was not fit to command a corps. Ewell had brought his troops to the battlefield in good time on 8 May and had successfully repulsed major Federal attacks on 10, 12, and 18 May, albeit at a high cost to his corps. Yet Lee saw much to criticize in his lieutenant's conduct. He remembered Ewell's unfortunate advice to hold the Muleshoe on 9 May; he was dissatisfied with Rodes's imperfect fortifications on 10 May; he was offended by Ewell's unprofessional conduct in rallying Johnson's troops on 12 May; and he blamed Ewell for being lured into a full-scale battle at Harris Farm on 19 May.

Lee was not the only one dissatisfied with Ewell's performance at Spotsylvania. At some time in the two-week battle—probably after Harris Farm—Robert Rodes purportedly protested to Lee about Ewell's remaining in command of the corps.[20] What prompted Rodes to take such unusual action is unknown, but coming on the heels of Gordon's criticisms a few days before, it proved decisive. From that time on, Lee sought an opportunity to remove Ewell.

Rank may have been another consideration in Lee's decision. With Longstreet's demise, Ewell became the army's ranking corps commander. If Lee was wounded or fell ill, Ewell would command the army. This was by no means a remote possibility. Several times in the Wilderness and at Spotsylvania Lee had been under fire, and at North Anna River he had been ill. As the campaign ground on and military crises became more frequent, the chance of Lee becoming disabled increased. For the good of the army, he had to consider who would succeed him. He was determined that it should not be Ewell.[21]

Finally, there was Jubal Early to consider. Lee liked the irascible and outspoken general and had confidence in his ability. Early had led the Second Corps capably at Mine Run and handled the Third Corps well at Spotsylvania. Lee had seriously considered appointing him to succeed the wounded Longstreet, but in the end he chose Anderson because of that officer's former association with the First Corps. One way or another, though, Lee was determined to find a spot for Early. The simplest way was to get rid of Ewell.[22]

While Lee wished to remove Ewell, he did not wish to disgrace him. To the end he maintained—disingenuously—that he had removed Ewell strictly for reasons of health and that he would restore him to corps command as soon as he had recovered. But Lee had other plans for him. On 12 June he recommended to Adj. Gen. Samuel Cooper that Ewell be placed in charge of Richmond's defenses. Even then he maintained that the arrangement was temporary, as he "proposed to replace him in command of his corps after the present occasion for extraordinary exertion shall have passed." Such a statement allowed Ewell to leave the army with a measure of dignity. At the same time, it left the door open for Lee to reappoint Ewell if Early did not pan out. Cooper complied with Lee's request. On 15 June he ordered Ewell to take command of the Department of Richmond.[23]

Many soldiers expressed sorrow at Ewell's leaving. A week before the general's reassignment, David P. Woodruff wrote, "I dont know what disposition has been made on Genl Ewell. His physical condition unfitted him for the command I suppose. I think highly of the old fellow though. His gallantry and bravery are unquestioned." Artilleryman William S. White echoed Woodruff's remarks, saying, "Few men in this war have made such a brilliant name or have been held in higher estimation for sterling worth than Richard S. Ewell; but, gallant old warhorse, his many wounds are proving too severe for him, and he is no longer able to bear the privations of an active campaign." Years later Gen. E. Porter Alexander wrote that "no man in the army, in any corps, but loved & still loves the name & memory of good old Ewell or that did not see him leave with regret."[24]

No one regretted Ewell's departure more than Ewell himself. For three years the army had been his home, his life. The thought of sitting behind a desk in Richmond while his comrades struggled against the enemy galled him. If only he could join them! But there seemed little chance of that. The Army of Northern Virginia stood between Grant and Richmond, leaving Ewell little more than a backseat spectator. The general sorrowfully packed his few belongings and rode south to Richmond. His days of fighting the Yankees, it seemed, were at an end.

CHAPTER 28

The Department of Richmond

From the beginning of the war, the capture of Richmond had been a primary objective of Union armies in the East. In addition to being the political capital of the Confederacy, the city was a major industrial, transportation, and commercial center and a symbol of Southern resistance. Primary responsibility for defending Richmond fell to the Army of Northern Virginia, but the army was often far away. Its commander could not always give proper attention to the city's defense. A separate force was needed to provide for the internal security of Richmond, to guard its prisons, to construct its defenses, and to protect it from Union cavalry raids.

To accomplish these and other tasks, the War Department in 1861 created the Department of Henrico. Sixty-year-old Brig. Gen. John H. Winder initially commanded the department, but the job proved to be too big for the aging general. In April 1863 the War Department transferred responsibility for defending the city to Maj. Gen. Arnold Elzey. It called Elzey's command the Department of Richmond. Winder continued to run the Department of Henrico, though his duties were limited to the administration of Confederate prisons and to keeping order in the city.

Maj. Gen. Robert Ransom succeeded Elzey in command of the Department of Richmond in April 1864. When Ransom transferred to the Shenandoah Valley a month later, the War Department assigned Ewell the job. Winder left Richmond about the same time, and the War Department took advantage of this circumstance to abolish the Department of Henrico and assimilate it into Ewell's Department of Richmond.

Ewell complained that his new command came without troops, but that was not exactly so. On paper, at least, the department had more than 6,000 men, though the actual number fell considerably short of that.[1] It was the quality of his command, however, rather than its thin numbers that bothered Ewell most. Inexperienced heavy artillery battalions, undisciplined reserve units, and irregular local defense troops comprised the majority of the soldiers in his department. What a difference from the days when he had proudly led Stonewall Jackson's corps!

When Ewell reached Richmond on 13 June 1864, he found himself not only without quality troops but without a proper staff. Ransom had taken most of the department staff with him to the Shenandoah Valley, while Ewell's own staff had remained with the Second Corps and now served under Jubal Early. Ewell promptly took steps to remedy the deficiency. Writing to Adj. Gen. Samuel Cooper, he requested that his stepson, Maj. Campbell Brown, be ordered to report to him as assistant adjutant and inspector general.[2] His aide Lt. Harper Carroll likewise joined him, and Tom Turner reported for duty as soon as he recovered from the injuries he had received at Spotsylvania. In the coming weeks at least nine other officers joined his staff. Most had previously served under either Ransom or Winder. By the end of the summer Ewell's military family looked like this:

Maj. James W. Pegram, Assistant Adjutant General
Maj. Legh R. Page, Assistant Adjutant General
Maj. Theodore O. Chestney, Inspector General
Maj. Campbell Brown, Inspector General
Maj. Isaac Carrington, Provost Marshal
Maj. Harry H. Selden, Quartermaster
Maj. Thomas P. Turner, Aide-de-camp and Commandant of Libby Prison
Capt. Francis T. Forbes, Acting Chief Commissary Officer
Capt. John H. Parkhill, Post Quartermaster
Capt. James Ker, Chief Ordnance Officer
Capt. Thomas T. Turner, Aide-de-camp
Lt. Harper Carroll, Aide-de-camp[3]

Ewell had hardly settled into his new duties at Richmond when Joe Johnston requested his transfer to the Army of Tennessee. On 14 June Lt. Gen. Leonidas Polk was killed in the fighting outside Atlanta. Johnston suggested that Ewell replace him. Jefferson Davis referred the matter to Lee, who consented to spare Ewell if Johnston wanted him. "My own opinion is that Genl E's health is unequal to his duties," he added, "but he does not agree with me. Johnston knows & likes him, & I do the same."[4] In the end Ewell did not get the assignment, which went instead to Maj. Gen. Alexander P. Stewart. Ewell did not know that he was being considered for the position until Stewart was appointed. It was a bitter blow, for Ewell admired Johnston and wished to serve under him. Had he known of the vacancy sooner, he told Ben, he would have tendered his resignation and telegraphed Johnston at once to ask for the command. "Had I have thought [Johnston] wanted my services, [I] would have gone in spite of every thing," he told Ben. "I would be a Captain under him if he were Col. of a reg,t. He was my only hope of regaining command."[5]

Meanwhile the war in Virginia entered its next phase. In June 1864 Maj. Gen. David Hunter marched up the Shenandoah Valley, crossed the Blue Ridge near Lexington, and headed for Lynchburg with 18,000 Union soldiers. Lee could not afford to have Hunter in his rear, and he dispatched Early with the Second Corps to drive him back. Early defeated Hunter at Lynchburg and chased him west across the mountains.

Grant meanwhile continued his relentless drive toward Richmond. Unable to break Lee's lines at Totopotomoy Creek or at Cold Harbor, he boldly crossed the James River and laid siege to Petersburg, twenty miles south of Richmond. For the next nine months he extended his lines around the city, methodically cutting every wagon road and railroad that led into it from the south until he ultimately choked the city into submission. To do this he had at his disposal Meade's Army of the Potomac and Maj. Gen. Benjamin F. Butler's Army of the James. In May Butler had landed with some 40,000 men at Bermuda Hundred, a broad neck of land situated between the James and Appomattox Rivers, but once there, he had allowed Gen. P. G. T. Beauregard to contain him with a much smaller Confederate force. Butler had been there ever since.

Grant planned to threaten Lee simultaneously on three fronts: Petersburg, Richmond, and Bermuda Hundred. Because Lee did not have a sufficient number of men to defend all three sectors at once, he would have to shift troops rapidly from one threatened point to the next. He reasoned that if he could eliminate one of the fronts, his job would be that much easier. Richmond was the obvious choice. A single pontoon bridge at Deep Bottom, eight miles below Richmond, was the only link between Union troops north of the James and those at Bermuda Hundred. Lee urged Ewell to attack the bridgehead and destroy it. That was easier said than done, however, for the position was strongly defended and supported by gunboats anchored in the James River. After a close examination of the ground, Ewell reported an assault there to be inadvisable.[6]

An attack on Union shipping in the James River offered greater promise. The James was Grant's lifeline. If the Confederates could disrupt river traffic, it would greatly embarrass his operations. Ewell proposed to hinder Union navigation by posting a battery of heavy guns at Wilcox's Landing and by seeding the river with

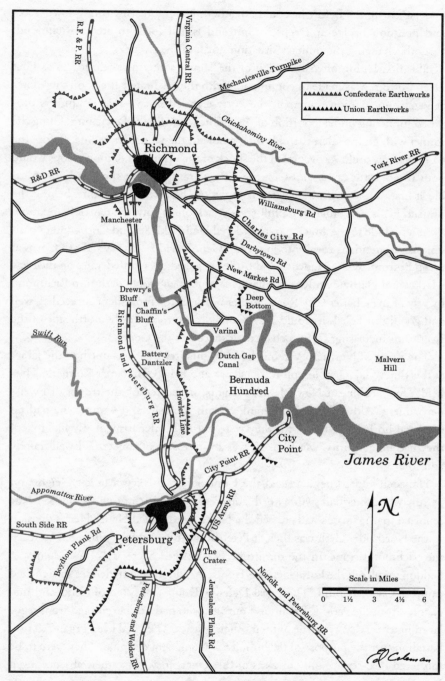

Richmond and Petersburg

underwater mines. Before he could do either, the Union army threw down a second pontoon bridge at Deep Bottom and issued forth to attack Richmond, abruptly changing the military situation north of the river.[7]

This first Union offensive north of the James, sometimes referred to as First Deep Bottom, was made in conjunction with the celebrated attack on the Crater at Petersburg. Union miners in the Forty-eighth Pennsylvania Volunteers proposed tunneling under a portion of the Confederate line at Petersburg, filling the tunnel with gunpowder, then blowing a hole in the Confederate line. Before the Confederates could recover from the shock of the explosion, Union troops would pour through the crater and seize the town. Grant thought the idea impracticable at first, but as the mine neared completion, he threw his support behind the project. He issued orders for a full-scale attack on 30 July, the day of detonation.

As a prelude to the attack, Grant ordered Hancock's Second Corps and two divisions of Sheridan's cavalry to join Maj. Gen. David B. Birney's Tenth Corps at Deep Bottom. While Hancock and Birney engaged the Confederates on the New Market and Darbytown Roads, Sheridan's horsemen would dash into Richmond by way of the Charles City Road, farther north. If the movement succeeded, well and good; if it failed, it would draw Confederate troops to the north side of the river, thus increasing Grant's chances of success at the Crater.[8]

The Army of Northern Virginia had two infantry divisions north of the James at this time: Maj. Gen. Joseph B. Kershaw's and Brig. Gen. James Conner's. They held a forward line at New Market Heights, supported by the troops of Ewell's department. Although Ewell outranked both Kershaw and Conner, he had no direct authority over them, for they were not in his department. By like token, they had no authority over him. "It was a mixed sort of concern," Ewell frankly admitted.[9]

Hancock and Birney engaged the Confederates at New Market Heights on 27 July while Sheridan swung north and west toward Richmond. When Kershaw reported that Hancock had crossed the James, Lee hurried Henry Heth's division to the Northside. Heth was then at Petersburg. It would take him a day to reach the Richmond front. In the meantime Ewell urged Secretary of War James A. Seddon to call out the Local Defense Troops to hold the Confederates' entrenched camp at Chaffin's Bluff. The Local Defense Troops consisted of clerks and mechanics from the various Richmond bureaus who had been exempted from regular military service by virtue of their official duties. They had been organized into battalions for the purpose of defending the Confederate capital. They were to be mustered into service only in cases of dire emergency, since their absence, even for a short time, caused "serious derangement and confusion" in the departments from which they were drawn. Seddon reminded Ewell of this. Ewell took the hint and for the moment withdrew his request.[10]

As the morning passed and Hancock and Birney failed to press their attacks, Ewell became suspicious. He directed Brig. Gen. Martin W. Gary's cavalry brigade to feel the Union right. Gary encountered Sheridan's cavalry on the Charles City Road and drove it back in "great disorder" toward New Market Heights. Ewell joined Gary on the Charles City Road on 28 July. What he saw there convinced him that the capital was still in danger and prompted him to make yet another appeal for the local troops. This time Seddon consented to release the troops. He dragged his feet to such an extent, however, that they did not reach the front until late on 29 July, fully two days after Ewell's initial request. By then the crisis had passed. Ewell informed Seddon that the Local Defense Troops could return to their normal duties.[11]

Although he had approved Ewell's request for the local troops, Seddon again took occasion to remind the general that the Local Defense Troops were not to be used "for ordinary service, but only for an emergency involving the safety and actual defense of the city." He admonished Ewell not to ask for them again "unless under such pressing need as their organization contemplates." In reply Ewell stated that the recent Union movement had in fact been a genuine emergency. The Union army had sufficient force to take Richmond but had simply been too timid to do so. "The enemy were within ten miles of our lines," he wrote, "and we cannot trust always to his want of enterprise."[12] The conflict over the use of the Local Defense Troops remained a sore point for the rest of the war. For Ewell it was a no-win situation. If he called for the local troops at the first sign of danger, he risked incurring the wrath of Seddon and other government officials. On the other hand, if he delayed summoning them until the city was in actual peril, as the secretary insisted, they would arrive too late to do any good. It was a problem that afforded no easy solution.

Grant meanwhile abandoned his effort to capture Richmond from the Northside. Finding that Lee had shifted a considerable part of his army across the James to meet the threat to Richmond, he recalled Hancock's and Sheridan's forces to Petersburg to take part in the attack on the Crater. The sudden disappearance of these troops puzzled and worried Ewell. "The movements of the Yankees are incomprehensible on any grounds I can give," he told Lizinka on 30 July, "and I have a half sort of feeling with something of the ludicrous [sic] as well as serious, that they are about to try some previously unheard of plan of taking Richmond, by balloons or underwater, or that they may suddenly appear in some quarter impossible under every rule that usually governs troops. Why did Sheridan cross or why did he go back," he mused, "or whether he went back or if he did not go back, where is he, are all questions equally hard to answer." [13]

The day Ewell wrote this letter Grant sprang the mine at Petersburg, blowing a 170-foot-wide hole in the Confederate line. Federal troops rushed into the smoking crater but failed to take the high ground beyond it. In a morning of desperate fighting, Lee restored his line. Another Federal plan that promised success ended in failure.[14]

For the next few months the Richmond front remained quiet. The Federals withdrew from the Northside, except for Birney, who kept a division at Deep Bottom to protect the pontoon bridges. Lee wished to dislodge Birney's force, but the strength of the Union position made a direct attack out of the question. Lt. Col. John C. Pemberton, commanding Ewell's heavy artillery, suggested dropping mortar shells on the bridgehead and its supporting gunboats. Unfortunately, Ewell had only two mortars large enough to do the job and no sling carts with which to transport them. Until the Ordnance Department could remedy those deficiencies, he had no choice but to leave Birney alone.[15]

While Ewell watched over a quiescent front, Jubal Early was creating a stir in the North. After defeating Hunter at Lynchburg, Old Jube led the Second Corps down the Shenandoah Valley and across the Potomac River to the outskirts of Washington. Grant hurried the Sixth and Nineteenth Corps up the Potomac River in time to defend the city. Early wisely refrained from an attack and withdrew to Winchester. After a cautious pursuit, the Federals attacked Ramseur's division on 20 July at Stephenson's Depot. The Confederates fled, disgracing themselves and their gallant young leader. Ramseur was mortified. When he sent Ewell his report of Spotsylvania three weeks later, he asked his former commander to stand up for him against his Richmond critics. Rodes, too, wrote to Ewell on Ramseur's behalf. This was ironic, since both men had been critical of Ewell.[16]

Notwithstanding Ramseur's defeat at Stephenson's Depot, Early's Valley Campaign had been relatively successful. With a single corps he had threatened Washington and tied down two Union corps that otherwise would have been free to support Grant at Petersburg. In August Lee determined to up the ante by sending Fitz Lee's and Joseph Kershaw's divisions to reinforce Early.

Fitz Lee's departure left Wade Hampton the ranking Confederate cavalry commander at Petersburg. On 12 August Robert E. Lee formally appointed the South Carolinian to be the Army of Northern Virginia's chief of cavalry. One of Hampton's first acts was to urge the creation of a Bureau of Cavalry that would oversee "the care, direction, and organization of the cavalry arm of the service." Lee endorsed Hampton's proposal and recommended Ewell as "the officer best qualified by experience and information and service for the position of chief. Besides possessing great merit," wrote Lee, "he has great claims." However, Ewell did not want the job. After twenty-five years in the saddle, he had no desire to sit in an office.[17]

Thus far the Union navy had played only a minor role in the campaign. Its ironclads were able to sail up the James River only as far as Trent's Reach, a short distance above Deep Bottom. Beyond that they came under fire from Battery Dantzler, a Confederate fort that anchored the northern end of the Howlett Line, the Confederate earthworks that stretched across Bermuda Hundred. Battery Dantzler stood on the outside of an oxbow in the river. Between the two ends of the oxbow was a narrow neck of land known as Dutch Gap. Ben Butler realized that if he could cut a canal across Dutch Gap, Union gunboats could bypass Battery Dantzler's guns and enfilade Confederate lines both north and south of the river. Digging began on 10 August 1864.[18]

The Confederates detected the work at once. Maj. Gen. George E. Pickett, at Bermuda Hundred, reported Union occupation of Dutch Gap on 10 August, and within two days Lee learned that the Union army had started digging a canal there. Realizing the danger that the canal would pose to the integrity of the Howlett Line, Lee urged Ewell to attack it. As at Deep Bottom, the presence of Union gunboats prevented Ewell from making a direct assault on the position. Instead he constructed a fortified battery on nearby Signal Hill, whence Confederate guns might effectively shell the canal. There was little more he could do.[19]

Grant meanwhile learned that Lee had dispatched Fitz Lee's and Kershaw's divisions to reinforce Early. In order to prevent Lee from sending any more troops to the Valley, Grant ordered Hancock and Birney to attack the Confederates at Deep Bottom. At the same time, Union cavalry would drive toward Richmond on the Darbytown and Charles City Roads. The fighting took place the week of 13 August. Boils on his stump and under his arms kept Ewell out of the battle, at least in its initial phases. The Confederates held their ground without him. After several days of inconclusive fighting, Grant abandoned the movement and ordered Hancock and the cavalry back to Petersburg. Another Northside offensive had come to naught.[20]

Grant's strategy at Petersburg was taking on a familiar pattern: a right jab toward Richmond followed by a left hook at Petersburg. So far Lee had ably parried his opponent's blows, but he could not keep it up forever. "Without some increase in strength," he warned Seddon on 23 August, "I cannot see how we can escape the natural consequences of the enemy's numerical superiority."[21] The secretary sympathized, but he had no more troops to give: four years of war had bled the South white.

Events that fall foreshadowed the Confederacy's decline. On 2 September Maj. Gen. William T. Sherman captured Atlanta, Georgia. The news struck the South like a thunderbolt. Next to Richmond, Atlanta was its most strategic point. The Confederacy had fought tooth and nail to save it, but like Nashville and New Orleans it had fallen to Federal arms. Would Richmond be next? Developments in Virginia suggested that it might. In August Grant seized the Weldon Railroad, one of the last remaining supply routes into Petersburg. Over in the Valley, Sheridan drubbed Early at Winchester, then won an even more decisive victory at Fisher's Hill. The South's fortunes had reached a new low.

Robert Rodes and Sandie Pendleton died defending the Valley, Rodes at Winchester and Pendleton at Fisher's Hill. Both men had spoken unkindly of Ewell, but he bore them no malice. In a note to Pendleton's father, Ewell expressed the admiration that the Second Corps had felt toward his son. "I know the men of my old Corps said it is not Ewell but Sandie who commands the second corps," he wrote, "but I never felt a pang of jealousy." He then quoted from his May 1864 report in which he had praised the young man's "great gallantry, his coolness and clearness of judgment under every trial, his soldier-like and cheerful performance of every duty." His praise was genuine. To members of his own family, Ewell confided that Sandie had been "the most promising young man" in the army.[22]

Even as Ewell grieved the loss of one staff officer, he welcomed the arrival of another. On 26 September Benjamin Ewell reported for duty as his brother's assistant adjutant general. Ben was an experienced hand at such work, having served on Joe Johnston's staff since November 1862. When Johnston lost his job as commander of the Army of Tennessee to General John B. Hood on 17 July, Ben found himself out of a job. Dick happened to need an assistant adjutant general, and he arranged for Ben's transfer to the Department of Richmond.[23]

Ben's arrival coincided with Grant's third and most serious Northside offensive. When the Union commander learned of Sheridan's success in the Valley, he stepped up his attacks against Petersburg. Butler urged him to attack Richmond as well, scouts having reported that the city's defenses were thinly manned. Grant agreed, knowing that Butler's attack would serve as a useful diversion to Meade even if it failed.[24]

Butler's information about Richmond's vulnerability was all too true. Detachments to Petersburg and to the Valley that fall had diminished the Confederate force north of the James River to just 8,600 men. Of that number, 2,900 belonged

Benjamin S. Ewell, the general's older brother (Donald C. Pfanz)

to the Army of Northern Virginia and took orders from Brig. Gen. John Gregg. Gregg's men held a forward line of works that stretched from New Market Heights to Signal Hill, a line judged by Ewell to be "naturally strong but not worked sufficiently to help the defence." The rest of the Confederate force—mostly second-rate troops from Ewell's department—manned the Intermediate Line closer to the city. Against this meager force Butler could throw more than 26,000 men.[25]

Butler relied on strength and speed for success. His army was divided into two corps of infantry and one division of cavalry. Birney's Tenth Corps crossed the James at Deep Bottom and stormed Gregg's position at New Market Heights. Simultaneously, Maj. Gen. Edward O. C. Ord's Eighteenth Corps threw a pontoon bridge across the river at Aiken's Landing, more than a mile upriver from Birney, and advanced toward Richmond on the Varina Road. Once Ord and Birney were in motion, Brig. Gen. August V. Kautz's cavalry crossed behind Birney, to the right, and dashed toward the capital via the Darbytown Road.[26]

Butler's movement commenced after dark on 28 September. Ewell learned that Union troops were crossing the river in force at 4:00 the next morning and immediately passed this information on to Lee. Realizing the gravity of the situation, Lee ordered Maj. Gen. Charles Field's division from Petersburg to Chaffin's Bluff and telegraphed Seddon to mobilize Richmond's Local Defense Troops. It would be hours before these troops reached the front. Until then, Lee encouraged Ewell to "take the field with all you have. Encourage the men to fight boldly."[27]

Ewell's Confederates would have to fight boldly and then some, for the Federals outnumbered them three to one. To make matters worse, Ewell mistakenly judged Ord's goal to be Signal Hill. He accordingly massed much of his available force at that point. Gregg, on the other hand, had concentrated his brigades at New Market Heights to meet Birney's advance from the direction of Deep Bottom. Between Signal Hill and New Market Heights was a two-mile-wide gap. Ord's corps, advancing up the Varina Road, penetrated the gap and drove straight toward Richmond.[28]

In Ord's path stood the Exterior and Intermediate Lines and Ewell's entrenched camp at Chaffin's Bluff. Forts and batteries buttressed the Confederate works, most notably Fort Harrison, whose heavy guns commanded the Varina Road. From Fort Harrison entrenched lines ran north to the Mill Road and southwest to the Osborne Turnpike, each roughly a mile distant. Forts Gilmer and Gregg acted as twin sentinels on the Mill Road. Forts Hoke and Maury stood ready to challenge any Federal advance up the Osborne Turnpike.

Fort Harrison was the key to Richmond's defenses. Lt. John H. Guerrant's Goochland Artillery operated nine guns in and around the fort, supported by some 200 Tennessee and Georgia riflemen. As Ord's lead division approached the fort, Guerrant's artillerymen jerked their lanyards. To their dismay, four of the guns did not fire. The other five guns blasted the oncoming blue lines with shell and rounds of double-canister. Nearly 600 Northerners fell in the charge. The others swept over the fort's walls, capturing Guerrant's guns and some 50 Southern defenders. By 6:00 A.M. the fort was in Butler's hands.[29]

Ewell notified his superiors that Fort Harrison had fallen, then rode to the front to rally its scattered defenders. "What in the h—— are you running for?" he demanded of one group of fugitives. Without breaking stride, a soldier shouted back the standard punch line, "Because we can't fly."[30]

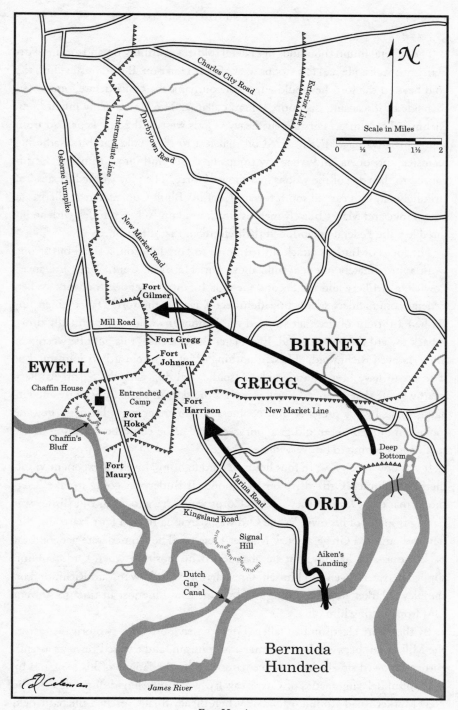

Fort Harrison

The general found thousands of Federal soldiers swarming on and around Fort Harrison's walls. He had few troops west of Fort Harrison. If Ord pushed into the void beyond the fort, he would effectively outflank the Confederate forts on either side of it, causing the entire line to collapse. The Union army might be in Richmond by sunset. Fortunately, heavy woods west of the fort kept Ord from seeing his advantage. Ewell seized on that fact to try a bold gambit. Gathering teamsters, prisoners, and what few troops he could find into a thin line, he advanced to the edge of the woods in a show of force. The ploy worked. Instead of striking west, Ord turned south toward Chaffin's Bluff. Confederate artillerists at Forts Hoke and Maury bravely met his attack head on. When Ord fell with an injured leg, the Federals abandoned their efforts in that direction.[31]

The focus of Butler's attack shifted north to Fort Johnson, a small but strong work approximately one-half mile above Fort Harrison. Capt. Willis J. Dance's Powhatan Artillery and the Second Georgia Infantry defended the work. When Federal commanders sent a brigade directly against the fort, Dance's men unleashed a torrent of fire that stopped the Union line cold and eventually drove it back toward the Varina Road. Ewell later claimed that "this fight between 7 & 8. A.M. saved Richmond." He said nothing of his own role at Fort Johnson, but it seems to have been considerable. A soldier fighting with the Salem Artillery nearby wrote that "General Ewell was with the skirmish line, constantly encouraging them by his presence and coolness. I remember very distinctly how he looked, mounted on an old gray horse, as mad as he could be, shouting to the men, and seeming to be everywhere at once."[32]

It was now 10:00 A.M. In four hours of hard fighting, Ewell's inexperienced soldiers had blunted Ord's drive on Richmond. If Butler was going to take Richmond that day, David Birney's Tenth Corps would have to do it. But Birney was having troubles of his own. While Ord was marching toward Fort Harrison, Birney had attacked Gregg at New Market Heights. The Confederate general beat back the assault handily, but he abandoned his position when Ord's column slipped between Ewell and himself. Gregg hastily withdrew toward Richmond on the New Market Road, reaching the Intermediate Line just in time to prevent Ord from cutting him off.

By then Fort Harrison had fallen. Gregg wisely posted his two brigades across the Mill Road, between Forts Gilmer and Johnson, and awaited Birney's assault. Birney followed slowly, his advance hampered by the fatigue of his men and by the skillful delaying tactics of Gary's cavalry, which Ewell had dispatched to the New Market Road around 9:30 A.M. When Birney finally reached the battlefield early that afternoon, he sent his divisions against Fort Gilmer one at a time and was defeated piecemeal.[33]

U.S. Colored Troops comprised a large portion of Birney's command. A battalion of these men, advancing farther than their comrades, reached Fort Gilmer's moat, only to have explosive shells rolled down on them by Confederate defenders from the parapet. Those not killed quickly surrendered. "It was an ugly affair all through," wrote Lt. Col. Moxley Sorrel. It soon got even uglier. As the black troops climbed out of the ditch, the Confederates ruthlessly murdered some of them. Ewell was "horrified" when Col. John McAnerney brought news of the slaughter. "Co'l tell your men, they must be patient and prudent[.] These negroes are now Federal soldiers, and we must treat them as such." McAnerney raced back to the fort with the general's orders. The killing stopped.[34]

With Birney's repulse at Fort Gilmer, Butler's hopes for capturing Richmond vanished. Even before Birney ended his assaults, Confederate reinforcements from Petersburg began deploying in the trenches. Lee told Ewell not to delay his attack. "It will take time for troops from here to reach north side," he telegraphed that morning. "Don't wait for them; endeavor to retake the salient at once." Attacking with the small force at hand was clearly impracticable, however, and Ewell wisely ignored Lee's aggressive order until additional troops arrived. At 3:00 P.M. he informed Lee, "We will take the offensive as soon as troops come up."[35]

Lee reached the Northside in the afternoon and personally took charge. He saw at once that the Federals were too strong to attack with the troops then available and postponed his assault until the next day. The delay allowed Butler to strengthen his hold on Fort Harrison. When Lee attacked it the next afternoon with two divisions of Anderson's corps, he was repulsed.[36]

In the rush of events, Ewell's heroic efforts in saving Richmond on 29 September went largely unnoticed. When city newspapers mentioned the general at all, it was to criticize him for being taken by surprise, a charge that Ewell hotly denied.[37] In contrast to the armchair generals in Richmond, those who fought under Ewell had nothing but praise for him. General Ewell commanded in person, recalled one butternut soldier, "and by his cool courage and presence wherever the fight was hottest, contributed as much to the victory gained as any one man could have done." Ewell personally regarded the battle of Fort Harrison as his greatest accomplishment of the war, contending that "it was in the enemy's power not only to have taken that place but Richmond."[38]

At least one prominent historian has agreed with this assessment. In his book

Richmond Redeemed: The Siege of Petersburg, Richard J. Sommers wrote that "the purely tactical nature" of the situation on 29 September brought forth Ewell's best military qualities. "Such qualities had shown before, in those halcyon days ere the II Corps had ever heard of Cemetery Hill: at First and Second Winchester, at First Stephenson's Depot, at Cedar Mountain, at Strasburg, and above all at Cross Keys. Yet great as were his accomplishments then," asserted Sommers, "they do not equal his achievement this day. Acting in the face of imminent disaster to forge and sustain a continuous line from Fort Gilmer to the James that bade fair to contain the Federal breakthrough and save Richmond was the greatest contribution Ewell ever rendered to the Confederate cause."[39]

Ewell had saved Richmond, but neither he nor Lee could retake Fort Harrison. With that dominating bastion now firmly in Union hands, the Confederates had no choice but to construct a new line of works to its west. Ewell and Anderson accompanied Lee as he examined the proposed line on 30 September. As they rode along, Ewell's horse stumbled and rolled over onto its rider in what Col. Moxley Sorrel termed "an awful cropper." Sorrel was sure that the general's head and neck were broken, but Ewell was lucky. He emerged from the accident without serious injury, though his face was "scratched, bruised, torn and bloody." Lee sent him to Richmond for treatment and ordered him to stay there until he had recovered. Before the day ended, however, Ewell was back at the front, as hard at work as ever. Staff officers smiled at his "painfully comical" appearance. Wrapped tightly in bandages from his shoulders up, he resembled a mummy more than a lieutenant general. But he was no less efficient for that. "Quite indifferent . . . to such mishaps," wrote Sorrel, "he was sharp about his work and lisping out directions as usual."[40]

Butler's 29 September attacks succeeded in capturing not only Fort Harrison but also three miles of the Exterior Line that stood between the fort and the Darbytown Road. An attempt by Lee to recapture a portion of that line on 7 October failed, forcing the Confederates to construct a new line closer to Richmond.[41] Slaves provided labor for this task, but when the work proceeded more slowly than expected, Ewell employed 150 U.S. Colored Troops confined in Richmond prisons to assist them.

These were Ben Butler's men. When that Union general heard that Ewell was making them dig trenches, he was outraged, all the more because he had been told the black soldiers were exposed to Union artillery fire. In retaliation Butler ordered a like number of Confederate prisoners to be put to work at Dutch Gap Canal, which was under constant bombardment from Confederate guns. Butler's actions angered Lee. To show Butler that he would not be intimidated, the Confederate commander shelled the canal more furiously than before and ordered 100 Union prisoners to be held at a point then under fire from Union guns. This situation did not last long. Neither Grant nor Lee favored this type of warfare. When Lee wrote, explaining that the impressment of black prisoners had been done without his knowledge and had been stopped, Grant ordered Butler to cease his reprisals. So the matter ended.[42]

James Longstreet returned to duty on 19 October 1864. He had been shot through the neck in the Wilderness in May, but he had recovered and was now ready to resume command of the First Corps. Longstreet's troops defended Richmond and Bermuda Hundred, and Lee put him in charge of both fronts. Ewell supported Longstreet north of the James River. As his subordinate in rank, Ewell took orders from Longstreet, something he had not done while Anderson commanded the corps.[43]

Less than two weeks after Longstreet took command, Butler made another jab at Richmond by way of the Williamsburg Road, an effort that Longstreet easily repelled. For the next two months the Richmond front was quiet. Just before Christmas, Union troops seemed to be massing for yet another attack near Fort Harrison. Recent detachments had cut Longstreet's force in front of Richmond to half of its earlier strength, prompting Seddon to call out the Local Defense Troops to augment Ewell's force.[44]

Postmaster General John H. Reagan hit the roof. In recent months dozens of his employees had been pulled from their clerical duties in order to fight Yankees. So many were absent, he complained, that his department could no longer carry out its duties. He insisted that Ewell return the employees to their jobs immediately. Ewell replied that he had no authority to do so; the secretary of war alone could dismiss them from duty. Ewell advised Reagan to apply to Seddon for return of the workers. He further suggested that Reagan consider employing women to do the duties of the missing clerks. The suggestion enraged Reagan, who took his complaint directly to President Davis. Davis spoke to Lee about the matter, who in turn consulted Longstreet. In the end the clerks returned to their jobs. Although their loss was of minor importance to Ewell, the fact that the president, two cabinet officers, and three top generals had become embroiled in a dispute involving no more than a handful of soldiers (and poor ones at that) was a clear indication of just how desperate the Confederates were for men.[45]

Apart from occasional squabbles with Reagan, Ewell enjoyed a pleasant winter. As cold temperatures set in, he left the Chaffin farm and made his headquar-

*Ewell made his headquarters at the Chaffin farm, outside Richmond,
for much of the latter half of 1864 (Harper's Weekly)*

ters in Richmond, living with his family and staff a few blocks from the capital.
He took Lizinka for rides in his buggy when weather permitted. On Sundays they
probably attended worship services at nearby St. Paul's Church, where Ewell had
been confirmed on 2 October 1864 by the Right Reverend John Johns.[46]

The general became a familiar sight in Richmond. City residents grew accustomed to "the spectacle of a worn and mutilated man looking prematurely old,
mounted on a white horse that had often snuffed the battle with defiance, but was
now scarcely more than a halting, crippled skeleton," remembered newspaperman Edward Pollard. "Sometimes the veteran drove through the streets in a dilapidated sulky. It was a sorrowful picture," he recalled, "but a nearer view disclosed a man remarkable even in the ruin of health and constitution, whose gray
eye was as sharp and fierce as ever, and whose precise conversation showed that
the vigour of his mind was as yet untouched."[47]

Ewell traveled short distances on foot, despite his wooden leg. One day he was
hobbling through the city when a major stopped him and asked if his leg hurt
him. Ewell thought the fellow was being pert until he looked down and saw that
he, too, had a wooden leg. He answered, "Yes does yours hurt you[?]" to which
the man replied, "no I have gotten accustomed to mine."

One day Ewell was talking in public with another one-legged veteran, Col. Duff Green. Both officers were "homely" and poorly attired. As they chatted, an older citizen walked up to them and, noting their disabilities, offered them jobs at his Georgia factory. When Green introduced himself and General Ewell, the man offered his apologies, saying, "Well gentlemen I beg your pardon but you looked like common folks mightily."[48]

Ewell's common appearance fooled even his own men. One day while riding to the front in an ambulance, he encountered Pvt. John W. Stott and two fellow soldiers of the Nineteenth Virginia Heavy Artillery Battalion resting by the road. Stott asked him for a ride, and Ewell consented. Only after he climbed in did Stott recognize the driver as General Ewell. A peculiar dialogue followed.

"To what command do you belong?" Stott began.

"I belong all around here generally," replied the driver evasively.

"You present a very striking resemblance to General Ewell," Stott remarked.

"How do you know it is not him?"

"I would not expect to see him riding in an ambulance."

"Does General Ewell never ride in an ambulance?"

"Probably he does," answered the artilleryman, "but I would think [it] strange to see him alone and driving himself."

"Nevertheless he does do such things," the older man replied, giving the horses a smart stroke with his switch.

Lt. Col. John C. Pemberton had commanded the heavy artillery battalions in the department that fall, but recently he had been reassigned to duty as an ordnance inspector. Ewell expressed the opinion that Pemberton was an able officer and that he had been unfairly maligned for the loss of Vicksburg. He also spoke earnestly about Joe Johnston, lamenting that his friend had been removed from command just when his country needed him most. Ewell then asked Stott how the men "would like to have Gen. Lee for commander-in-chief and mentioned during the conversation nearly all our leading officers. He hardly ever expressed a decided opinion upon any subject," Stott recalled, "only seeming desirous of getting mine, and that of the troops. His whole conversation was uttered in the kindest manner possible, and he never spoke ill of any one. I believe him to be a true christian gentleman."

In what seemed a short time, the ambulance reached its destination. Stott thanked Ewell for the ride and hopped out of the vehicle. Only then did his benefactor drop his transparent disguise and admit that he was in fact General Ewell, which Stott of course had known for some time.[49]

For Stott and the other soldiers in the Department of Richmond, the winter of

1864–65 brought hardship. Rations were short, and fuel was difficult to find. Health and morale suffered.[50] Ill tidings from the South added to the soldiers' misery. After capturing Atlanta in the fall of 1864, Sherman had marched across Georgia to the Atlantic Ocean, destroying everything in his path. Savannah surrendered in December, followed by Wilmington, North Carolina, and Charleston, South Carolina. The South suddenly found itself cut off from the rest of the world. The only hope, it seemed, was in negotiation. In February Jefferson Davis sent emissaries to a peace conference at Hampton Roads, Virginia, but the talks faltered on the issue of Southern independence. Lincoln would not agree to that, and Davis would accept nothing less. The two delegations parted, having achieved nothing. Generals rather than politicians would have to settle the issue.

The failure of the Hampton Roads Conference embittered Ewell and demoralized his troops. By then most of the soldiers had concluded that the cause was hopeless. Quietly they began to discuss among themselves what they would do if the South surrendered. Some vowed to fight to the death. Others threatened to become bushwhackers. Still others privately determined to desert before the collapse occurred. Each night soldiers slipped away from the picket line and gave themselves up as prisoners to the Union army. Others left camp on wood-cutting details and never returned.[51]

Desertion among the Local Defense Troops posted at Chaffin's Bluff was particularly high. Many men in those units felt that the Confederate government had "despotically invaded" their rights by compelling them to serve at the front for extended periods, and they used this to justify their going over to the enemy. In order to make it more difficult for them to desert, Confederate officers clamped down on fraternization, prohibited wood-cutting details downriver, and kept up a sporadic skirmish fire throughout the night.[52] Ewell went a step further. William L. Nuckolls of the Twenty-fifth Virginia recalled that the general made his troops shell the enemy when he thought the two sides were becoming too friendly. Such tactics limited the army's hemorrhage, but they could not stanch it altogether. By spring Ewell's department had lost hundreds of men.[53]

Ewell became increasingly critical of the Confederate government during the final months of the war. Vigorous action was necessary to save the South, he felt, and the politicians simply were not doing enough. In a letter to an unknown correspondent Ben expressed his brother's views. "Reasoning from what has happened," Ben wrote, "he cannot escape the conclusion that [Richmond's] capture is highly probably [sic] if not inevitable unless wisdom prevails in our councils, & energetic action in the administration of our affairs." Drastic measures alone could save the South. "No one feels more attached to his State than my brother," wrote Ben. "He took part in this contest because she made herself one of the parties, & for no other reason. No one would regret more to see her further desecrated, & almost blotted out from among the nations of the earth. His feelings & judgment [are] . . . that she ought to be preserved, & defended, but he is also convinced that something besides talk is necessary to accomplish this." [54]

The Confederate government did take some positive steps that winter. In February 1865 it appointed Lee commander in chief over all Confederate armies, a position comparable to Grant's in the North. At the same time President Davis appointed John C. Breckinridge as secretary of war in place of James A. Seddon and reinstated Joe Johnston in command of the Army of Tennessee. These moves collectively strengthened the South's military leadership, but alone they could not change the course of the war. If the Confederacy was to survive, it had to have more men. The South had fought against superior numbers all along, but in recent months the manpower shortage had reached critical proportions. Lee had lost more than 30,000 men in the 1864 Overland Campaign. Though Grant had lost many more, he was able to replenish his losses, whereas Lee could not. The subsequent fighting around Petersburg coupled with detachments of force to North Carolina and the Shenandoah Valley diminished Lee's numbers to the point where he found it impossible to cover Petersburg, Bermuda Hundred, and Richmond adequately.

Grant realized this and stepped up the pressure. In February 1865 he sent Maj. Gen. David M. Gregg's cavalry division to intercept a Confederate wagon train moving to Petersburg on the Boydton Plank Road. The movement underscored Lee's need for additional Confederate troops to protect his right. Ewell offered to hold the Richmond front with nothing more than Local Defense Troops, convalescents and attendants from the city hospitals, and Virginia Military Institute cadets. That would free Longstreet's two divisions north of the James to go to Petersburg. Lee, however, thought the measure too risky. While praising Ewell as "a brave old soldier, ready to attempt anything," he felt it unsafe to entrust the capital's safety to his lieutenant's pseudo-soldiers. [55]

Instead the Confederate government adopted a measure that, in its own way, was more dangerous still: it determined to arm the slaves. Ewell had privately advocated the enlistment of black troops as early as 1861, but the Confederate Congress refused to even consider the measure until 1865, when it became a military necessity. On 18 February the House of Representatives voted by a narrow margin to authorize President Davis to requisition a quota of slaves from each state to serve as soldiers. The Senate, however, defeated the measure by a single vote.

The Virginia state legislature thereupon took matters into its own hands and enacted a bill authorizing the enlistment of slaves within its borders starting on 13 March.[56]

The bill passed the Virginia legislature due largely to Lee's influence. The general regarded the use of black troops as essential. "If we do not get these men," he told Ewell, "they will soon be in arms against us, and perhaps relieving white Federal soldiers from guard duty in Richmond."[57] Lee knew that Ewell supported the measure and assigned him the task of organizing the first (and only) black companies to enlist into Confederate military service. Ewell delegated the task to Majs. James W. Pegram and Thomas P. Turner of his staff.[58] The two officers went to work immediately. On 11 March, two days before the act officially went into effect, they placed a notice in Richmond newspapers announcing a rendezvous for black volunteers at Smith's factory in the city.[59]

Richmond leaders actively opposed arming the slaves and did everything in their power to prevent it. They refused to let their own slaves enlist and tried to prevent others from doing so. Blacks who did enlist were scorned and abused. "Some of the bl[ac]k soldiers were whipped," Ewell remembered angrily, "they were hooted at & treated generally in a way to nullify the law."[60] Lee urged his lieutenant to build support among white citizens who favored the statute and to do everything in his power to prevent those opposed to the measure from demoralizing the black soldiers. "Harshness and contemptuous or offensive language or conduct to them must be forbidden," he warned, "and they should be made to forget as soon as possible that they were regarded as menials."[61]

In the end Pegram and Turner organized just two black companies, one comprised of workers from Winder Hospital and the other of workers from Jackson Hospital. Each hospital also raised one white company. The four companies formed a single battalion led by Dr. Chambliss of Winder Hospital. "We had dress parade several times on the Capitol grounds," remembered one of the white soldiers, "and the city papers praised our manual of arms and drill." Unfortunately for the South, the black troops never got beyond drilling. Richmond fell three weeks later, and the companies dissolved in the chaos surrounding the city's last hours.[62]

That time was fast approaching. On 2 March 1865 Maj. Gen. Philip Sheridan attacked Early's small army at Waynesborough and scattered it. Having destroyed the last vestige of organized Confederate resistance in the Shenandoah Valley, Sheridan rode east to unite with Grant at Petersburg. His route brought him within twenty miles of Richmond. Confederate authorities feared he might attack the capital from the north while Butler assailed it from the east, but Sheridan by-passed the city and continued to Petersburg. For a few more days Richmond was safe.

The threat of attack by Sheridan prompted Ewell to tap the last available source of white manpower in Richmond: its old men. When he learned that the Union cavalry had crossed the mountains and was heading toward Richmond, Ewell wrote to Surgeon General Samuel P. Moore inquiring about the ability of men between the ages of fifty and sixty to bear arms. Moore replied that while some men of that age might be able to shoulder a rifle, most could not. "The service proposed for this class may be considered 'extraordinary,'" he concluded. "It is for others to decide whether the necessity justifies the extraordinary demand." Ewell determined that it did. Four days later he asked the Virginia general assembly to authorize the enrollment of men fifty years and older who were capable of bearing arms. "The danger is imminent," he warned, "and calls for the most energetic action in strengthening the force which now holds our lines."[63]

The end was near, and Ewell knew it. Although duty required him to fight the Federals to the last, he had no wish to endanger his family. Around February he quietly sent Lizinka and Harriot north, out of harm's way. Mother and daughter traveled first to "Clydesdale," the King George County home of Dr. Richard Stuart. They stayed there for ten days waiting for a dark, rainy night to cross the Potomac River into Maryland. A U.S. steamship bore down on their rowboat halfway across, but the women and their escorts avoided detection. Before dawn they landed safely at Port Tobacco. From there the women traveled to Washington, D.C., and then to St. Louis, Missouri, where they found refuge with Tasker Gantt.[64] They left Richmond none too soon. Spring came early that year. As the roads began to dry, Grant set his army in motion against Lee's right flank. The final campaign of the war had begun.

CHAPTER 29

The Jig Is Up!

Grant launched his 1865 campaign at the earliest opportunity. In late March he ordered George Meade to capture Five Forks, a critical road intersection southwest of Petersburg. Just three miles north of Five Forks was the South Side Railroad, Lee's last direct supply route with the west. With the railroad in Union hands, the Confederate commander would have no choice but to abandon Petersburg and Richmond and move into the open, where he would be easy prey for Grant's large and well-equipped army. Grant selected his scrappy thirty-four-year-old chief of cavalry, Maj. Gen. Philip H. Sheridan, to lead the operation. On the twenty-ninth Sheridan drove Confederate horsemen out of Dinwiddie Court House, and two days later, with the assistance of the Fifth Corps, he overwhelmed George Pickett's infantry and Fitz Lee's cavalry at Five Forks. The South Side Railroad now lay within the Union army's grasp.

The Army of Northern Virginia faced a crisis. Sheridan's smashing victory at Five Forks not only secured the Union a foothold on the South Side Railroad, it also severed Pickett's and Fitz Lee's commands from the rest of the Army of Northern Virginia. In a desperate attempt to shore up his broken right flank, Robert E. Lee sent three brigades of Anderson's corps to defend the railroad and ordered Longstreet to bring Field's division to Petersburg. Longstreet left Richmond on the night of 1 April, turning command of the Northside defenses over to Ewell. Ewell rode to the front to speak with Longstreet before he departed, but he arrived too late. Old Pete had already started south.[1]

Longstreet left Ewell with approximately 5,000 men to defend ten miles of earthworks. Martin Gary's cavalry brigade held the far left of Ewell's line, covering the eastern approaches to Richmond; Joseph Kershaw's veteran division occupied the center, near Fort Gilmer; and Custis Lee's division held the right, near Chaffin's Bluff. To fill the void left by Field's departure, Ewell called out the Virginia Military Institute cadets, three battalions of convalescent troops culled from the city's military hospitals, and the Local Defense Troops—a ragtag force that altogether may have added another 2,000 rifles to his thin ranks.[2]

Grant followed his victory at Five Forks with a general assault on Petersburg. The 2 April attack shattered the Confederate line, compelling Lee to evacuate the city. Ewell got word of the impending evacuation at 10:00 A.M. He immediately returned to Richmond, where at 3:00 P.M. he received positive orders to evacuate the city after dark. Sunset was less than four hours away. In the meantime there was much to do. Transportation had to be rounded up, excess property destroyed, artillery started to the rear, and rations issued to the troops—all in such a manner so as not to alert the enemy or alarm the populace.[3]

Ewell issued the necessary orders, then took a train to Petersburg to confer with Lee concerning details of the evacuation. As Ewell was leaving the meeting, the commanding general insisted that he take with him a dinner of two cold sweet potatoes, an act reminiscent of Francis Marion's offer to a British officer during the American Revolution. Ewell was fond of sweet potatoes, and he accepted the gift with relish. By evening he was back in the capital.[4]

Ewell successfully concealed his preparations from the enemy, but he could not keep the news from the city's populace. As rumors of the evacuation spread, anxious crowds began to gather in the streets. Officially the government said nothing—it did not have to. The removal of state documents from government offices, the shipment of the Confederacy's gold reserves to Danville, and the departure of the president and other high officials proclaimed Richmond's fate more plainly than any formal announcement could have done. Some citizens followed their leaders' example and fled the doomed city; others secured their houses and prepared for the worst.[5]

It was not long in coming. As darkness fell over Richmond, fear exploded into violence. Vandals smashed windows and looted stores in the business district, joined in their frenzy by army deserters, slaves, and destitute citizens. Ewell had foreseen such an event months earlier and had appealed to the city council to establish a volunteer police force to keep order during the evacuation. Only one man had volunteered. Richmond now paid the price for its leaders' neglect. In an effort to curb the escalating violence, the city council sent out parties of men to destroy liquor supplies. "This was done," noted historian Benson J. Lossing, "and, by midnight, hundreds of barrels of spirituous liquors were flowing in the gutters, where it was gathered up in vessels by some stragglers of the retreating army, and rough citizens, and produced the very calamity the authorities were trying to avert."[6]

The rioting raged throughout the night. When police could not quell the disturbance, municipal officials appealed to Ewell for help. The only troops the general had available were a few convalescent troops from the city's hospitals. He promptly dispatched this force to repress the rioters, but it was inadequate to the task. Ewell thereupon sent all his available staff and couriers out "to scour the streets, so as to intimidate the mob by a show of force." At the same time, he sent orders to Kershaw, who was approaching Richmond from the southeast, to hurry his leading regiment into town.[7]

Fires added to the nightmare. Weeks earlier Lee had ordered Ewell to remove public cotton and tobacco stores from the city. What could not be removed was prepared for destruction should evacuation of the capital become necessary. Ewell personally visited the tobacco warehouses with councilman and warehouse owner James A. Scott to determine if the buildings could be burned without endangering the city. Scott believed that they could. Ewell accordingly gave his provost marshal, Maj. Isaac H. Carrington, orders to prepare the buildings for destruction. The Ordnance Department offered to furnish Ewell turpentine to mix with the tobacco to ensure that it burned, but he declined the offer for fear of setting fire to the city.[8]

That had been more than a month earlier. Now that the evacuation of Richmond had become necessary, Ewell prepared to set fire to the warehouses. A delegation of citizens sent by Mayor Joseph Mayo implored Secretary of War John C. Breckinridge to rescind the order. Its plea fell on deaf ears. According to one source, the secretary told the committee *"that he didn't care a d—n if every house in Richmond was consumed, the warehouse[s] must be burned."*[9] Ewell had received a similar response from Breckinridge when he had protested the burning order earlier.

Ewell issued the distasteful order just before dawn. In all, he set fire to four warehouses: the public warehouse and Shockoe Warehouse, located at opposite ends of the canal basin; Mayo's Warehouse, at the foot of Mayo's Bridge; and Dibrell's Warehouse, on Cary Street, one block from Libby Prison. A fresh breeze from the south quickly spread the flames to adjacent buildings. By morning the entire business district was ablaze.[10]

Meanwhile Ewell's troops had left their trenches outside the city and started toward Amelia Court House, forty miles away, to unite with the Army of Northern Virginia. Ewell had orders to cross the James River at and above Drewry's Bluff and proceed west on the Genito Road. His wagon train and artillery were to go to Amelia by way of Powhatan Court House (Meadeville). The movement was scheduled to begin at 8:00 P.M., the artillery moving first, followed by the infantry and the cavalry. Once the entire corps had crossed the James River, Ewell was to burn the bridges and press on to Amelia with all haste.[11]

That was clear enough, as far as it went, but many questions remained. What were the conditions of the roads? Were boats available above Richmond with which to ferry wagons and artillery across the James? Was there anyone familiar with the area between Richmond and Amelia Court House who could act as a guide? Lee sent his chief engineer, Brig. Gen. Walter H. Stevens, to assist Ewell in the retreat and to provide guides, but many problems remained unsolved. Despite having had a full winter to prepare for it, the evacuation of Petersburg and Richmond seems to have taken the Confederate army by surprise.[12]

Custis Lee's division left its trenches at 10:00 P.M. His two brigades, totaling 2,700 men, crossed Wilton Bridge, two miles above Chaffin's, and headed west out Genito Road. Because most of his division had never fought outside Richmond's defenses, Lee had accumulated little in the way of transportation. When Ewell issued orders to march, Lee found himself short of wagons. His soldiers scoured Richmond and farms outside the city, impressing into service every wheeled vehicle they could find, but they still had to leave much behind.[13]

Kershaw's division comprised the other half of Ewell's corps. Kershaw had been placed under Ewell's command on 1 April when Longstreet accompanied Field to Petersburg. After dark, Kershaw's men left their camps near Fort Gilmer and headed for Mayo's Bridge in Richmond. Kershaw sent Capt. Charles S. Dwight ahead to get orders from Ewell. Dwight found the capital in chaos. Throngs of people crowded the streets, plundering stores and lapping up liquor from the gutters. Demented or drunk individuals shrieked and howled. "It was pandemonium indeed," Dwight remembered, "Bedlam broke loose."[14]

The South Carolinian nudged his horse through the crowds to the War Department, where he found Ewell and Breckinridge seated on horseback. Dwight remarked on the different appearance of the two men. "Breckenridge [*sic*] as he sat on his fine horse was simply magnificent; his noble face bright and cheerful, giving no sign of the anguish that wrung his heart. . . . He spoke strongly and calmly, giving his orders and his advice to Gen. Ewell and others around him." Ewell's appearance, by contrast, was anything but inspiring. "He looked the wreck that he was," wrote Dwight. "His thin, narrow face looked wizen and worn, and twitched nervously, as did his arms and hands. I had seen him at his best—here was his worst. . . . The old hero looked worn and shaken at this heart-breaking crisis." Dwight tried to reach Ewell through the surging crowds, but he could not. Fortunately he recognized Campbell Brown among the throng. From

Brown, Dwight received orders for Kershaw to march for Amelia Court House by the most direct route.[15]

Impatient for Dwight's return, Kershaw rode into the city to speak with Ewell himself. Ewell directed him to hurry his leading regiment into town to disperse the rioters and head with the rest of his division for Mayo's Bridge. In order to reach the bridge, Kershaw's men had to cross the James River and Kanawha Canal. As they approached the waterway, a burning barge drifted under the canal bridge and set it on fire. Only quick work by Confederate engineers saved the structure. Although the fire appears to have been an accident, Ewell viewed it as a deliberate attempt by Union sympathizers to embarrass his retreat and ordered Capt. Clement Sulivane to post a 200-man guard at the bridge. "The first one that puts a torch to this bridge except by my orders I wish shot down," he snapped.[16]

It was then about 7:00 A.M. As Kershaw's last regiments hurried over the bridge, Ewell crossed the river to speak with General Stevens in Manchester. Lt. Moses P. Handy studied Ewell's features as the men talked. Like most observers, he found the general's appearance anything but prepossessing. "He sat with his old black hat pulled over his brows," wrote Handy, "rising in a peak at the top, with firmly compressed lips and a keen little eye glancing from point to point with the greatest rapidity. He rode upon his old gray horse, wearing a faded cloak, and carrying in his hand a stout walking-stick. His manner of speaking was short, and indeed rather rude, although the latter was, of course, unintentional."[17]

At Stevens's direction, Confederate engineers prepared Mayo's Bridge and two railroad bridges farther upstream for destruction. He and Ewell were discussing arrangements for detonating the bridges when a terrific explosion split the air. A second explosion followed. The Confederate navy was blowing up its ironclads below the city. Kershaw's troops, already on edge, quickened their pace.[18]

Martin Gary's cavalry brought up Kershaw's rear. Gary had orders to hold the picket line outside Richmond until 2:00 A.M., then gather his command and head for Mayo's Bridge. The sun was an hour high when the horsemen trotted into town and clattered across the bridge. As the last company crossed, Gary tipped his hat to Sulivane and called out, "All over, good-bye; blow her to h-ll." Sulivane followed Gary across the river, calmly setting fire to the bridge as he went. In a matter of seconds the structure burst into flames. Union cavalry dashed into town in a desperate effort to save the bridge, but they were too late.[19]

The growing breeze whipped the flames into other sections of the city. Trede-gar Iron Works escaped destruction, but the arsenal did not. As flames entered the building, the stockpiled shells began to explode. "No one could tell how many burst a minute," wrote one terrified woman, "but every one was like the crash of thunder." Firefighters looked on helplessly; vandals had cut the fire hose.[20]

Ewell viewed the growing inferno with Kershaw from a hill above Manchester. The sight incensed him. "I recommended the Sec'y of War not to have the tobacco in the city fired," he growled. "If I could have had my way, it would never have been done." His bitterness toward the Kentuckian did not quickly subside. A week later, in discussing the fires, he told a Union surgeon, "I acted under orders, but regret that those orders did not include Breckinridge, who should have been thrown into the hottest of the flames."[21]

Ewell argued that he had made every effort consistent with duty to prevent the disaster. He had protested to Breckinridge and possibly to Davis against burning the tobacco and, when overruled, had consulted with the warehouse owners as to the safest method for its destruction. When the offensive order came, he had no choice but to obey. "He was a soldier under orders," he defiantly told a Federal officer one week later, "and under like circumstances he'd have set the world on fire."[22]

He told a different story in his official report. There he blamed the conflagration on the rioters, who at 3:00 A.M. had "set fire to some buildings on Cary street, and began to plunder the city." He eventually got the mob under control, but in the meantime it burned many buildings that he directed should be spared. "The arsenal was thus destroyed," he wrote, "and a party of men went to burn the Tredegar Works, but were deterred by General Anderson arming his operatives and declaring his intention to resist." After retreating across the river to Manchester, Ewell and Kershaw saw a mill above the Danville depot burst into flames. The mill was far removed from the warehouses and caught fire after the army had crossed the James. Rumor had it that vandals had threatened to burn another mill in town but desisted when the owner agreed to let them loot the place. "If correct, it affords exact proof of what I am firmly convinced is the case," wrote Ewell, "that the burning of Richmond was the work of incendiaries, and might have been prevented by the citizens."[23]

The general stressed this point to relatives. In a letter to Lizinka, he described how a mob composed of blacks, women, and Jews had rampaged through the city, plundering both the public and the private stores. "They burned the Arsenal, cut the fire hose & set fire to the bridge thereby endangering the capture of Breckinridge & all North of the James. The tobacco was burned by the order of the govt.," he admitted, "but had the mob not interfered this would have been all. I was exceedingly averse to burning anything, but you know it was even contemplated to destroy the Capitol but Houdin's statue prevented it."[24]

Ewell reiterated these points to Rebecca. "I am abused for burning Richmond," he complained. "It was burned by the mob. There were no troops to keep order. I had told the principal citisens [*sic*] months before, what would happen and urged them to form a constabulary force, to keep order, but they would not. . . . The fire hose was cut and the arsenal burned by the mob. I had taken every precaution possible, & the people must blame themselves."[25] In fact Ewell had done everything in his power to prevent the destruction of Richmond consistent with his duty as an officer. However, he was fooling himself if he believed that the warehouse fires that had been set at his orders had not contributed to the general conflagration.

Northern newspapers certainly did not hold him guiltless. One correspondent described his "wickedness" in setting fires; another characterized him as a "drunken brute." Such comments cut deep. "Gen. Ewell always protested bitterly against the injustice done him in public opinion in the matter of the burning of Richmond," Campbell Brown recalled in later years. He was so hurt by the suggestion that he "would willingly injure any citizen of Virginia . . . [and] so distressed at the orders to burn cotton & tobacco, and so reluctant even to prepare for such a step, that I cannot bear the idea of his being blamed for it. I know how shocked we both were, when from Manchester Heights, we saw the Mills on fire. I knew the noble soul, the tender heart, the courage to suffer & be silent under wrong accusation from patriotic motives in which no man could have surpassed Gen. Ewell."[26]

Perhaps no single event troubled Ewell so much as the accusation that he had wantonly destroyed Richmond. "I have this matter very deeply at heart," he confessed to his niece two months after the event. "I repeatedly see myself blamed. I rather fell short of than exceeded my instructions." The issue would not go away. In 1871 a group of Richmond citizens, led by tobacco owners, sued for damages they had incurred in the fire. A judge ultimately dismissed the suit, but not before it caused Ewell considerable worry.[27]

On 3 April 1865, however, more pressing matters engaged the general's attention. With a tug of the reins, he rode with his staff toward Amelia Court House. Ben had resigned from the army three weeks earlier on account of failing health and had remained in Richmond with Lizzie. When the war ended, he returned to Williamsburg to resume teaching at the College of William and Mary.[28] Failing health also prevented Friday from joining the retreat. The mischievous Pueblo had become sick the previous fall and was admitted to Jackson Hospital. When the Confederacy collapsed, he accompanied a doctor to North Carolina and was never heard from again.[29]

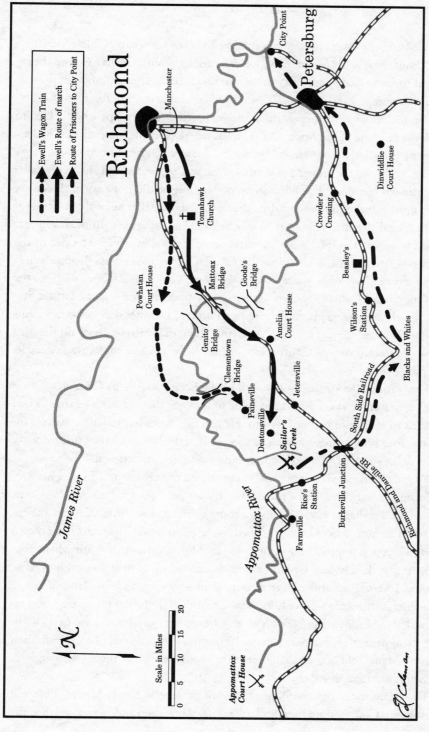

Richmond to City Point

Ewell and the others rode south, joining Kershaw's division as it left Manchester. About three miles out of town, Kershaw fell in behind Custis Lee, and the reunited corps headed southwest out Genito Road. It marched throughout the day, finally stopping near Tomahawk Church, fifteen miles outside Richmond.[30]

The fourth of April began in a drizzle. Ewell led his corps toward Genito Bridge, a crossing of the Appomattox River, where Confederate engineers had reportedly prepared a pontoon bridge for his passage. During the morning, however, a local resident brought news that there was no bridge and the river was as much as ten feet deep. Ewell may have cursed, but he did not despair. He knew there must be other bridges nearby. After notifying Lee that he could not cross at Genito, he dispatched engineers to seek alternate crossing sites. In the meantime he led his corps toward Goode's Bridge, seven miles downriver. The rest of the army was crossing there. If nothing better offered, he would cross there as well.[31]

He did not have to go quite that far. Between Genito and Goode's Bridge the Richmond and Danville Railroad crossed the Appomattox River at Mattoax Station. Ewell's engineers planked the railroad bridge, and after dark his weary corps crossed. It rested for just a few hours. Before dawn the corps was back on the road tramping toward Amelia Court House, where Robert E. Lee anxiously awaited its arrival.[32]

The commander in chief was vexed. He had come to Amelia Court House expecting to find rations for his army, only to discover that the supplies that he had ordered to meet him had not arrived. He had no choice but to halt at Amelia for twenty-four hours while foraging parties scoured the barren countryside for food. "The delay was fatal," he later wrote, "and could not be retrieved."[33]

An attack on Ewell's supply train exacerbated the problem. To speed his subordinate's march, Lee had ordered Ewell's wagons to travel to Amelia Court House via Powhatan Court House, a route different from that taken by the infantry. The unprotected train crossed the Appomattox River at Clementown Bridge and was approaching Amelia Court House early on 5 April when Brig. Gen. Henry E. Davies's Union cavalry descended on it near Paineville. Davies burned 200 wagons and captured more than 600 men and five cannon before Confederate horsemen drove him away. Consumed in the flames were 20,000 rations designed for Custis Lee's division, whose men would now have to do without. To appease their hunger, some of Lee's artillerists stole ears of corn from their horses. Many soldiers, denied even that, wandered from their commands in search of food, never to return.[34]

The army spent the morning of 5 April at Amelia Court House. Before it moved out, Commodore John R. Tucker's naval battalion and Maj. Frank Smith's artillery battalion joined Custis Lee's division, adding to the odd recipe of that general's already diverse command. "Infantry, cavalry, light and heavy artillery and sailors, we had thus in our small division all the elements of a complete army and navy, and with the Richmond Locals and Defences some material for civil government besides," commented one officer. Ewell would need every new man he could get, for his overworked troops were falling out of the ranks at an alarming rate. "The Genl says it is needless to carry men along who would be worthless," Robert E. Lee's adjutant informed Ewell, "but that every able bodied man must be kept in ranks." [35]

Lee intended to follow the line of the Richmond and Danville Railroad to North Carolina. There he would join forces with Joe Johnston and attack Sherman. The unscheduled delay at Amelia Court House spoiled his plans, however. Just a few miles beyond Amelia, at Jetersville, Lee found Sheridan's cavalry blocking his path. The Confederate commander considered attacking Sheridan in an effort to reopen the Danville Road, but he changed his mind when he learned that Union infantry was nearby. Instead he struck for Farmville in a desperate attempt to bypass the Federal forces in his path. Longstreet led the march, followed by Anderson, Ewell, and the army's wagon train. John Gordon, now commanding the Second Corps, followed the wagons and acted as rear guard. The Confederate column marched through the night. Inevitably, it became extended. By dawn on 6 April, Longstreet had reached Rice's Station on the South Side Railroad, while Ewell's corps was still back at Amelia Springs, ten miles to the rear. In a night of stop-and-go marching, Ewell's men had scarcely covered seven miles.[36]

The army was on its last legs. Soldiers with empty stomachs and blistered feet fell out of the ranks by the hundreds, unwilling or unable to go on. No one tried to stop them. Famished soldiers shot at chickens and pigs from the roadside, unhindered by their officers. One group of hungry men slaughtered a small ox that wandered too close to the road and devoured it raw with Ewell's blessing. "It was, perhaps, the only instance in my experience during the war," wrote McHenry Howard, "when the plea of military, or rather of human, necessity imperatively overruled all consideration due to private property and military discipline." [37]

At 8:00 A.M. on 6 April, Union cavalry appeared to the south, swarming like bees around Ewell's left flank. Simultaneously, Union infantry began pressing Gordon from the rear. Ewell threw out flankers and kept moving. Ahead, Anderson had halted his corps in order to repulse an attack by Sheridan's cavalry at a country intersection known locally as Holt's Corner. Unaware that Anderson had stopped, Longstreet kept on, creating a dangerous gap in the column. Anderson resumed his march once Ewell came up, but it was too late. Sheridan pushed two mounted divisions into the gap between him and Longstreet, effectively cutting the Confederate column in two.

The magnitude of the crisis was not immediately evident. At first Ewell knew only that the Federals had burned some wagons on the road ahead. To avoid the congestion, he ordered the wagon train in his rear to turn onto the Jamestown Road, closer to the Appomattox River. Ewell kept his corps at Holt's Corner until the train had passed. With Gordon approaching, he then led his troops across a marshy tributary of the Appomattox River known as Little Sailor's Creek. He had no sooner crossed the creek than he encountered Fitz Lee, who brought news that Sheridan held the road ahead in force. Ewell galloped ahead to speak with Anderson. The South Carolinian confirmed that two Federal divisions stood in his path. The Confederates were trapped. Anderson and Ewell had two choices: they could unite forces and try to break through the Union barrier, or they could try to escape by slipping through the woods to the north. Anderson opted to attack. Ewell doubted that such an attack could succeed, but he deferred to Anderson's judgment.[38]

Ewell ordered Custis Lee to support Anderson's attack. Before Lee had gone more than a few hundred yards, however, he had to face about to meet a threat from the opposite direction.[39] When Ewell ordered the wagons to detour onto the Jamestown Road, Gordon had followed them, exposing Ewell's rear to attack. Whether Ewell meant for Gordon to follow the wagon train is unclear, but the evidence suggests that he did not. Ewell's closest companion, Campbell Brown, later wrote that by turning off after the trains, Gordon had left Ewell's rear "accidentally exposed," a statement supported by Joseph Kershaw. In his report of the battle, Kershaw asserted that he "was not informed that Gordon would follow the wagon train as he did, and was therefore surprised on arriving at Sailor's Creek to find that my rear was menaced." These statements imply that Ewell intended for Gordon to continue in his rear rather than follow the wagon train down the Jamestown Road. But if that was the case, who was to protect the wagons? Ewell said nothing on this score, and historians since have not offered a satisfactory answer to this thorny question.[40]

Ewell and Anderson had to act quickly. The Federals stood on either side of them and might advance at any time. The Confederates' only chance was to beat them to the punch. Anderson volunteered to clear the road in front if Ewell would hold back the Union forces in their rear. Ewell agreed and returned to Little Sailor's Creek to prepare his troops for the battle. He formed his corps on a pine-covered ridge approximately 300 yards west of the stream. Custis Lee's division held the left of the line, and Kershaw's the right. Commodore Tucker's Naval Battalion stood near the road, behind Lee's right flank. Brig. Gen. Benjamin G. Humphreys's brigade skirmished with the enemy east of the creek until Ewell had completed his arrangements, then joined the rest of Kershaw's division on the ridge.[41]

Across Sailor's Creek, Maj. Gen. Horatio G. Wright's Sixth Corps was preparing to attack. Brig. Gen. Truman Seymour's division came into line first. Seymour had been captured by Ewell in the Wilderness, but on this day he would have his revenge. As Seymour deployed perpendicular to the road, Brig. Gen. Frank Wheaton wheeled into line on his left. Together their two divisions numbered 10,000 men, a force roughly twice Ewell's. In tone and morale the difference between the two bodies was greater still. The coming contest had all the makings of a crushing Union victory.[42]

Artillery opened the battle. As opposing infantrymen glared at one another across the valley, Union gun crews galloped forward and unlimbered in the fields around the James Hillsman House, within 800 yards of the Confederate line. For half an hour they raked the butternut line with impunity. Ewell's men could only hug the ground and endure, for they had no guns with which to reply. "The expression of the men's faces indicated clearly enough its effect upon them," remembered Maj. Robert Stiles, himself an artillerist. "They did not appear to be hopelessly demoralized, but they did look blanched and haggard and awestruck."[43]

Ewell seemed unfazed by the lethal bombardment. After meeting with Kershaw on the ridge, he rode down to the creek to hurry the rear of his corps across. Encountering an ordnance officer, he gave orders for the wagons in the hollow to double up, saying, "If they don't get away from here, they will all be captured." Moments later the Union guns unleashed their fire. As one anxious soldier hurried past, he overheard Ewell say casually to another officer, "Tomatoes are very good; I wish I had some." The incongruous remark had a strangely calming effect on the eavesdropper, who found himself laughing in spite of his peril.[44]

At 6:00 P.M. the Union artillery ceased firing. Wright's men formed ranks and swept down the hill and through the swollen, marshy creek. Once across, they redressed their lines and started forward again. Kershaw held his fire until the enemy got within fifty yards, then delivered a withering blast that sent the attackers scampering to the rear. On Custis Lee's front the Confederates repulsed the Union attack and countercharged, driving the enemy back across the stream.[45]

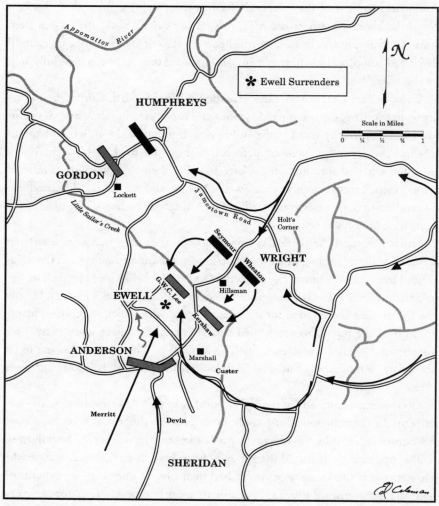

Sailor's Creek

Ewell saw none of this. Before Wright's infantry started forward, he rode back up the road to witness the effect of Anderson's attack on Sheridan. Anderson's men were just starting forward as Ewell arrived. Five minutes later they came racing back across the field in disorder. "Anderson was badly whipped," Ewell later confided to his wife. Before the South Carolinian could rally his men, Sheridan counterattacked. Union horsemen charged among the discouraged Confederates, slashing left and right with their sabers. Hundreds of Anderson's men threw down their arms in surrender. The rest fled into the nearby woods in an effort to elude their pursuers. Anderson was among those who escaped.[46]

Wright meanwhile renewed his attacks on Ewell's corps. Taking advantage of his greater numbers, he extended his line until he overlapped Ewell on both flanks. When he saw Union troops curling around his right, Kershaw ordered his division to fall back toward the road. Only then did he discover Sheridan's cavalry in his rear. Kershaw directed the men and officers nearest to him to scatter, but it was too late. The Union encirclement was complete. With one exception, the general and his entire staff gave themselves up as prisoners of war.[47]

On the other side of the road Custis Lee fought on, unaware of Kershaw's surrender. At one point the battle degenerated into a savage hand-to-hand conflict. "I saw numbers of men kill each other with bayonets and the butts of muskets," wrote Stiles, "and even bite each others' throats and ears and noses, rolling on the ground like wild beasts." Only at sunset, after discovering that Kershaw had yielded and that his own command was completely surrounded, did Lee order his division to lay down its arms. Ewell's corps ceased to exist. Of the 3,000-odd men that he took into the fight, the Virginian conservatively estimated that he lost 150 killed or wounded and 2,800 captured. Annihilation was complete.[48]

Ewell surrendered with his corps. As soon as he saw that Anderson's attack had failed, he returned to his own corps "to see if it were yet too late to try the other plan of escape." He rode through the fields north of the road, looking for some route by which he might yet extricate his command. "On riding past my left," he wrote, "I came suddenly upon a strong line of the enemy's skirmishers advancing upon my left rear. This closed the only avenue of escape, as shells and even bullets were crossing each other from front and rear over my troops, and my right was completely enveloped."[49]

Ewell and his staff surrendered to a cavalry officer who came in on the same road that Anderson had gone out on—another indication, if any were needed, that the Confederates were beset on all sides.[50] Custer himself soon appeared. Ewell entreated the Union general to cease his attacks. "At my request," wrote Ewell, "he sent a messenger to General G. W. C. Lee, who was nearest, with a note from me telling him he was surrounded, General Anderson's attack had failed, I had surrendered, and he had better do so too, to prevent useless loss of life." Before the messenger got through, both Custis Lee and Kershaw had surrendered.[51]

For Ewell the war was over. He was a prisoner in enemy hands, subject to mercy or harsh treatment as his captors might see fit. Never again would he lead

The surrender of Ewell's corps at Sailor's Creek on 6 April 1865 (Library of Congress)

troops in battle. Like the sun that was then setting in the western sky, his military career had run its course; its lingering rays would not see the final conflict.[52]

By Ewell's own admission his captors treated him with every courtesy. After his surrender he was taken to the headquarters of General Wright, whom he had known at West Point. Many years had passed since then, but Wright had not forgotten him. "I am glad to see you Ewell," he remarked as the prisoner dismounted. Ewell was not so cordial. "I'll be blank-blanked if I'm glad to see you, Wright," he replied. But this was mere bluster. In no time, the two generals were chatting like old friends.

the last of Ewells Corps april 6

Ewell told Wright that he had not intended to fight the Sixth Corps. He had assumed that Sheridan's cavalry was nipping at his rear, and by the time he found out the truth, it was too late to avoid a battle. As the Confederate line collapsed, he and his staff had purposely ridden toward Wright's line in the hope of surrendering to him rather than to Sheridan. "I'll be blank-blanked if we will surrender to Sheridan's cavalry," he had told his staff. "We will find the infantry skirmish line and surrender to them." As Ewell was telling this story, another Union officer joined the group. Ewell's face probably reddened when Wright introduced the newcomer as Sheridan himself.[53]

The Union officers complimented Ewell for putting up a good fight, but they saved their highest praise for Maj. Robert Stiles, whose heavy artillery battalion had fought like tigers. Ewell called Stiles over and complimented him in front of the group. Privately he told Lizinka that "Stiles distinguished himself." Ewell was no less complimentary of Custis Lee and Joseph Kershaw. In his report of the battle, written in December 1865, he commented that "the discipline preserved in camp and on the march by General G. W. C. Lee, and the manner in which he handled his troops in action, fully justified the request I had made for his promotion. General Kershaw, who had only been a few days under my command, behaved with his usual coolness and judgment."[54]

Wright invited Ewell to dine with him. Afterward they joined other officers in front of Sheridan's tent, reminiscing about West Point and discussing the prospect of the present campaign. Ewell did not join fully in the conversation. He seemed despondent, thought one observer. Much of the time he stared at the ground, as if trying to avoid attention. A Confederate soldier wrote that "'Fighting Dick Ewell' looked like an old eagle with one of his wings clipped."[55]

When Ewell did speak, his words dripped with bitterness. He claimed that the South had been doomed the day the Union army crossed the James River and laid siege to Petersburg. Government authorities should have opened peace negotiations then, while they could still claim concessions. Instead they had held out for independence. Now that "the cause was lost," Ewell said, "they had no right to claim anything." "For every man that was killed after this somebody would be responsible," he snarled, "and it would be little better than murder. He could not tell what General Lee would do, but he hoped that he would at once surrender his army." Ewell concluded his tirade by urging Sheridan to demand the surrender of Lee's army in order to prevent further loss of life.[56]

Ewell's words had more effect than he expected. Among the officers gathered around the fire that evening was Dr. Smith, a relative of the general's who was a surgeon in the Union army. Ewell's comments impressed Smith, and when the surgeon encountered General Grant the next day, he told him what Ewell had said. Smith's statement, together with favorable reports from Sheridan, prompted Grant to send Lee a dispatch on 7 April proposing the Confederate army's surrender. It was the first in a series of letters between the two commanders that would lead to the Army of Northern Virginia's capitulation two days later.[57]

By then Ewell was miles away. On the morning of 7 April 1865, after breakfasting with Wright, he and the other Confederate prisoners started for Grant's headquarters at Burkeville Junction.[58] Besides Ewell, the Union army had captured seven Confederate generals at Sailor's Creek: Joseph Kershaw, Custis Lee, Montgomery D. Corse, Dudley M. DuBose, Eppa Hunton, Seth M. Barton, and

James P. Simms. Ewell left his horse Rifle with Wright's staff and rode with the other Confederate generals in an ambulance at the head of the 5,000-man column. A cold rain drenched the prisoners. By the time they reached Burkeville, they were "a sorry company of tired and hungry and dejected men."[59]

At Burkeville Junction, Grant's military secretary passed out hot whiskey punch to Ewell and thirty other Confederate officers and built a bonfire to warm them. To one observer the Southerners seemed "sullen, quiet, [and] defiantly submissive in their defeat." Grant was not there, but Ewell took the opportunity to scribble him a note, explaining that he had set fire to Richmond's warehouses by order, not by choice. With the end of the war at hand, he may have anticipated that he would be tried for burning the city and wanted to make his innocence a matter of record. That night Ewell and the other Confederate generals were secured in a village house. A Union cook kindly served them some bean soup, the only meal that many of them had eaten since morning.[60]

On 8 April the Confederate prisoners proceeded down the South Side Railroad to a station called Blacks and Whites. It was "a weary, doleful, mournful march," one remembered. Ewell happened to know some of the Union officers guarding the column, and he struck up a conversation with them. According to Hunton, he "seemed bent on making himself popular" with his captors. He told them that the South was as guilty as the North when it came to devastating enemy property and admitted that the Confederate government had treated Union prisoners cruelly. Hunton took Ewell to task for the remarks. "I was very indignant with General Ewell," he later wrote. "He was thoroughly whipped and seemed to be dreadfully demoralized."[61]

Col. Benjamin F. Taylor of Maryland commanded the Union brigade that guarded the Confederates. In the evening Taylor invited Ewell, Hunton, and another Southern officer to dinner. "Gen. Ewell was far from unpleasant," he recalled. "I was much with him, and rode in his ambulance as often as I could spare the time. He spoke readily and interestingly of the battles in which we had played our parts, eulogized the 1st Md., C.S.A., and related their heroic action at Winchester and Port Republic. At times he was taciturn and sometimes fiery." Ewell's temper flared twice in Taylor's presence: once as he described Longstreet's failure to head off Sheridan near Richmond in March 1865, and once when Taylor showed Ewell an article from the New York *Herald* denouncing his so-called wickedness for setting fire to Richmond.[62]

On 9 April Taylor led his prisoners east to Wilson's Station.[63] The Union army had established a field hospital there, and as the Confederate officers gathered around their fires, Dr. William H. Reed wandered over. "Finding that strangers were welcome," he wrote, "I sat by their fire talking of their campaign, of the prospects of General Lee's escape, and of the general crisis of the war, which all frankly admitted was at hand. Ewell appeared infirm and prematurely old," he noted. "A cripple, he moved feebly on crutches, and had the air of a tired, worn-out, disappointed man. He took the best view of his capture; said his men would not fight, and that the war was near its close. The days of old Stonewall Jackson were over, he said; but he believed that even with his inspiration, nothing more could have been done."

On 10 April the Confederate prisoners split up. Sick and lame soldiers boarded a train bound for City Point; enlisted men in good health remained at Wilson's Station awaiting rations. Ewell and the other 800 officers in the column continued down the South Side Railroad toward Ford's Station.[64] En route, a messenger brought news that Robert E. Lee had surrendered the Army of Northern Virginia to Grant. Ewell and Custis Lee doubted the report, but when Brig. Gen. Henry W. Benham later arrived bearing the terms of the surrender, they could deny it no longer. Custis Lee hung his head in despair, while Ewell threw up his arms and exclaimed, "The jig is up!" By the terms of the surrender, the Confederates who capitulated at Appomattox were paroled and allowed to return to their homes. Ewell hoped to obtain the same terms for the soldiers who had surrendered with him at Sailor's Creek, and he lost no time petitioning Union authorities to that end. But his request was denied. While the rest of Lee's army started for home to begin rebuilding their lives, Ewell's men headed for Northern prisons.[65]

The Confederate officers traveled less than five miles on 10 April, perhaps so as not to get too far ahead of the enlisted men who had lingered at Wilson's. The officers stopped for the night at Beasley's, a house roughly two miles west of Ford's Station. Brig. Gen. Orlando B. Willcox had his headquarters in the building and invited Ewell to be his guest. Like Wright and Sheridan, he found the Confederate bitter toward the South's political leaders, whom he held responsible for its defeat. "He is very indignant at Jeff Davis & the 'Confederate Congress' & throws all the blame on them," Willcox wrote his wife, adding, "I think U S Grant had something to do with the matter!"[66]

A muddy march on 11 April brought the Confederate prisoners to Crowder's Crossing, ten miles east of Petersburg.[67] There Custis Lee learned that his mother was near death at Richmond. With the permission of Union authorities, he was released to be at her side. Only after he arrived at the capital did he discover that the story was a hoax concocted by friends in the Union army to keep him out of prison. The ploy worked. Although Lee immediately turned himself in to the provost marshal's office in Richmond, he was permitted to go home and did not have to spend any time in prison.[68]

His fellow officers were not so fortunate. On 12 April they passed through Petersburg and pushed on to City Point, where the provost marshal formally registered them as prisoners.[69] Grant returned to City Point that day, but Ewell did not see him. Instead, he and Brig. Gen. Rufus Barringer spent the evening with Brig. Gen. and Mrs. Charles H. T. Collis, who occupied a house in the riverside village. Septima Collis was an accomplished cook. She prepared her Southern guests a splendid feast that included raw oysters, green-turtle soup, James River shad, and a beef filet. For beverages she offered her guests whiskey, brandy, and cups of piping hot coffee. Mrs. Collis remembered Barringer as a charming and appreciative guest. Ewell, on the other hand, appeared "irritable, disappointed, and disposed to be out of humor with every thing and everybody." At one point he chided Mrs. Collis, who was a Southerner by birth, for espousing the Union cause. In reply she said "that I had only followed the example of many other Southrons, —I had 'gone with my State,' mine being the state of matrimony." The clever riposte caused Ewell to smile in spite of himself, defusing what might have been an unpleasant conversation.[70]

On the thirteenth, Ewell boarded the USS *Cossack* and started with other Confederate prisoners for Washington, D.C.[71] The passage up the choppy waters of the Chesapeake Bay was particularly hard on Eppa Hunton, who was already suffering from chronic diarrhea and fistula. According to Hunton, Ewell had $500 or $600 of gold that he used to improve his own accommodations aboard the ship, but he refused to crack his purse to assist anyone else. "He knew I was sick," complained the younger officer. "I had to lie down on the floor where the Yankee guard had spit their tobacco juice, and eat the rations, sick as I was. General Ewell went to the table and slept in a bed, and never offered to help me at all. This was the more remarkable because he and I had known each other almost from my boyhood." Ewell's thoughtlessness toward Hunton during the voyage may account in some measure for the bitter comments that Hunton later made about him in his memoirs.[72]

The *Cossack* anchored off Point Lookout for a few hours on 14 April before proceeding to Washington. It was a beautiful day, and from the deck of the ship the prisoners got a splendid view of Mount Vernon, Fort Washington, and other landmarks along the river. The ship reached the capital about 3:00 P.M.[73] Waiting for it was Montgomery Blair, the former postmaster general of the United

States. Blair was a friend of Ewell's cousin, Tasker Gantt, and his wife was an acquaintance of Lizinka's. Gantt had notified Blair that Ewell would be arriving in Washington that day and asked his friend to give Ewell some money that Lizinka had sent. Blair was waiting at the dock when Ewell came "limping" off the vessel. "He looked like a game cock," the Northerner remembered.[74]

When Blair reached the pier, he found hundreds of people there. Many were simply curious to see the Confederate prisoners; others came to jeer and abuse them. "There was especially noticeable one rough, rowdyish fellow who used some bitter threats about us," remembered one butternut soldier, "and who, in his heroic rage, shaking his brawny fist in the direction of Gen. Ewell . . . swore that he should never leave that town alive." A man who had braved as many dangers as Ewell was hardly intimidated by a thug, but his guards were not taking any chances. As soon as he hobbled off the ship, they hustled him into a carriage and drove him to the provost marshal's office on Pennsylvania Avenue. The other prisoners followed on foot, shadowed by an angry crowd that grew larger every minute.[75]

Blair rode ahead of the crowd and was at the provost marshal's office when Ewell arrived. He handed the Virginian a note from Gantt and gave him the money that Lizinka had sent.[76] Maj. Gen. Christopher C. Augur was present and likewise offered Ewell money. As Ewell chatted with Blair and Augur, Rebecca Ewell appeared. Ewell's oldest sister had been living in Washington since 1862. When she learned that Dick would be passing through the city, she rushed to the provost marshal's office to bring him clothing and refreshments. Surprisingly, he seemed annoyed to see her. Perhaps he feared that she might be harmed by the mob, or it may just have been another outgrowth of the demoralized behavior that he displayed that entire week. Whatever the reason, he did not welcome his sister as warmly as one might expect after a four-year separation.[77]

Union authorities sent Ewell and the other Confederate generals to Fort Warren in Boston Harbor; officers below the rank of general went to Johnson's Island on Lake Erie. Through Augur's influence, Campbell Brown received permission to accompany Ewell to Fort Warren despite his lesser rank. Tom Turner was not accorded that privilege and had to go to Johnson's Island with the other prisoners of his status. As it turned out, he got the better of the bargain.[78]

It was 7:30 P.M. when the train carrying the Confederate generals left Washington. Less than three hours later, actor John Wilkes Booth shot President Lincoln at Ford's Theater. Ewell and the other generals learned of the assassination the next morning while they were on the Jersey ferry. Interestingly, they got the news from Maj. Gen. Benjamin F. Butler, who happened to be a fellow passenger. Ewell instantly grasped the consequences of the act and threw his hands up in despair. "My God!" he cried, "I am sorry for that; it is the worst thing that could happen to the South." Enraged Northerners on board the ship threatened to throw the Confederate generals overboard, but to his credit Butler discouraged them from doing so. It was a prelude of things to come.[79]

The train reached New York City at 6:00 A.M., 15 April. G. B. Russell was in charge of the guard. He treated his prisoners to breakfast near the Twenty-seventh Street depot, then put them on a train to Boston. Outside the restaurant the excitement was "immense." At 7:22 A.M. President Lincoln died from his wound. As news of his death raced over the telegraph wires to cities throughout the North, people reacted with grief and rage. The Confederate generals mourned, too, more perhaps for themselves and their countrymen than for the president. Ewell reportedly wept.[80]

News of the president's death put the North in an ugly, vengeful mood. Recognizing this, Russell endeavored to get his prisoners to Fort Warren as quickly as possible. As soon as they had finished eating, he hurried them to the train depot. En route to Boston the train had to pass through New Haven and Hartford, Connecticut, and Springfield, Massachusetts. "At every depot an effort was made to raise a mob to hang us," remembered Eppa Hunton. "One man jumped on the train, and rode sixty miles, just to jump out at every station and cry 'Hang them.'" The fellow was finally arrested at Springfield, but others took his place. At one station the crowd cried out, "Three groans for Ewell," and picked up stones to hurl at the general's car. Thinking quickly, the conductor announced that the train was carrying blockade runners rather than Confederate generals. Before the mob realized that they had been duped, the train pulled out of the station. Russell thought that "if a crowd could have gotten hold of our prisoners, there would be a small chance for them." Ewell later wrote Lizinka about his adventures, commenting that he "could hardly have believed that after the murder of so popular a Prest. that a party of Con. Genls. would be treated with such forbearance." He was speaking, of course, about the guards who escorted him to Fort Warren, not the seething crowds that he encountered along the way. Those people wanted his head.[81]

Russell wisely telegraphed military authorities in Boston, asking them to have an armed guard waiting at the station when the train arrived. Forty soldiers and six coaches were sent. When the train reached Boston at 5:00 P.M., the officer in charge hustled his prisoners into the vehicles and drove them through the city at full speed. At the city dock, they boarded a waiting steamer that carried them across the harbor to Fort Warren. The generals reached the fort at 6:30 P.M. after a windy passage. As they left the ship, they took turns clasping Russell's hand. The trip to Fort Warren had been fraught with peril, but he had brought them through safely.[82]

That evening the Union officers at Fort Warren formally admitted the new prisoners and conducted them to their cells. After two weeks of danger and fatigue, the Confederate generals faced the prospect of prolonged confinement and boredom. How long they would be kept at Fort Warren was anyone's guess. With the mood of the country being what it was, it might be months—even years.[83]

CHAPTER 30

Fort Warren

Fort Warren was thirty-one years old in 1865. Built of granite, the five-sided structure stood guard over Boston Harbor from its perch on George's Island, a rounded parcel of land five miles from the city. From its grassy parapet one could look east over the boundless green ocean, south toward Weymouth, north toward Massachusetts Bay, or west toward Bunker Hill and the city of Boston. This beautiful yet isolated spot would be Dick Ewell's home for the next ninety-five days.[1]

Ewell and the other prisoners spent the larger part of each day locked inside the fort's stone casemates, some of which had been converted into prison cells. It was not a pleasant existence. The casemates were cold and damp. The barred windows and bolted doors admitted but little ventilation or light into the dark and gloomy environment. Fires helped illuminate the rooms and dispel the dampness. Each casemate was equipped with a cooking grate and anthracite coal, which the inmates used to keep a fire going day and night.[2]

Conversation helped brighten the otherwise cheerless cells. Confederate officers shared two adjoining casemates. There were as many as sixteen officers in these rooms along with Ewell: Commodore John R. Tucker of Virginia; Gens. Edward Johnson, John R. Jones, Eppa Hunton, Seth M. Barton, and Montgomery D. Corse of Virginia; Henry R. Jackson, Dudley M. DuBose, George W. Gordon, and James P. Simms of Georgia; Thomas B. Smith and John W. Frazer of Tennessee; William L. Cabell of Arkansas; Joseph B. Kershaw of South Carolina; and John S. Marmaduke of Missouri.[3]

DuBose was "always pleasant and jovial"; Jackson, by contrast, was pessimistic and always feared the worst. The twenty-nine-year-old Gordon was "quite young . . . sprightly, honest & aspiring," with a "pleasant face & temper," compared with Smith, who was described as a "stupid, well-meaning, good-natured" chap with handsome features and a romantic mien.[4] Kershaw was intelligent, handsome, and sociable—the beau ideal of the Southern gentleman. Ed Johnson was the same rough, uncouth character that he had always been and always would be. Ewell's cellmates "were as kind as possible" to him except in one matter: many of them smoked tobacco, which was "as bad as poison to him."[5]

Because of post regulations, Campbell Brown and Ewell initially were assigned to different parts of the fort. The two men saw each other from a distance during their daily walks on the parade ground and were permitted to exchange written correspondence, but otherwise they could not communicate. This, of course, was not at all what General Augur had intended when he allowed Brown to accompany Ewell to Fort Warren. After about three weeks Ewell succeeded in getting his stepson transferred to his own casemate, where he proved useful to the general as a helper and companion.[6]

Ewell had hoped that he, Brown, and the other Confederates captured at Sailor's Creek would be paroled like their comrades who had surrendered at Appomattox Court House. Robert E. Lee, in fact, wrote to Grant suggesting that very thing on 25 April 1865. "I see no benefit that will result by retaining them in prison; but, on the contrary, think good may be accomplished by returning them to their homes. Indeed, if all now held as prisoners of war were liberated in the same manner I think it would be advantageous. Should there, however, be objections to this course," he added, "I would ask that exceptions be made in favor of the invalid officers and men, and that they be allowed to return to their homes on parole. I call your attention particularly to General Ewell."[7]

Unfortunately, Federal authorities did not grant the request. In the wake of President Lincoln's assassination, the nation was in no mood to be generous to Confederate prisoners, especially toward those who had been leaders of the rebellion. Ewell knew exactly where to place the blame for his confinement. "I thought we were entitled to [the] terms off [sic] Lee's men," he told Lizinka on 20 April, "but I suppose must thank Boothe for that & numberless future woes."[8]

Ewell abhorred Lincoln's assassination and foresaw the disastrous consequences it would have for the Confederacy. In its anger, the North held the South as a whole responsible for the act, not just Booth and his accomplices. Ewell's train trip to Fort Warren had been proof of that. He thought it imperative that the Northern people know that true Southerners repudiated the murder. To that end he called his fellow prisoners together to draft a resolution to General Grant. Eppa Hunton later wrote that he opposed the resolution with all his might. "I asked them if they thought it becoming for thirteen gentlemen who were thought worthy to wear the stars of general officers of the Confederate Army to declare to the world that they were not assassins. By great exertions, and the efforts of several who came to my aid, the resolution was defeated." Not content merely to criticize the measure, Hunton proceeded to abuse its author. "I asked General Ewell where the leg he lost at second Manassas was buried; that I wished to pay honor to that leg, for I had none to pay to the rest of his body. He replied that he didn't know where it was."[9]

Hunton boldly penned these words in a private autobiography written for his family. Subsequent developments show that his opposition to the document—if, in fact, he did oppose it—did not prevent Ewell from sending it. The letter, written on 16 April and signed by Ewell, read as follows:

GENERAL: You will appreciate, I am sure, the sentiment which prompts me to drop you these lines. Of all the misfortunes which could befall the Southern people, or any Southern man, by far the greatest, in my judgment, would be the prevalence of the idea that they could entertain any other than feelings of unqualified abhorrence and indignation for the assassination of the President of the United States, and the attempt to assassinate the Secretary of State. No language can adequately express the shock produced upon myself, in common with all the other general officers confined here with me, by the occurrence of this appalling crime, and by the seeming tendency in the public mind to connect the South and Southern men with it. Need we say that we are not assassins, nor the allies of assassins, be they from the North or from the South, and that coming as we do from most of the States of the South we would be ashamed of our own people, were we not assured that they will reprobate this crime. Under the circumstances I could not refrain from some expression of my feelings. I thus utter them to a soldier who will comprehend them.

He concluded by listing the officers in his cell, all of whom, he claimed, "heartily concur with me in what I have said." Interestingly, Hunton's name appeared on the list.[10]

During the three months that Ewell was a prisoner there, Fort Warren was manned by troops of the First Battalion, Massachusetts Heavy Artillery. Its commander was Maj. Harvey A. Allen, a North Carolina native who had attended West Point with Ewell. The guards maintained firm discipline, as was their duty, but they treated their prisoners with courtesy and respect, granting them every indulgence that the strict regulations would allow.[11]

The prisoners' day began at 7:00 A.M. with breakfast, which usually consisted of toast and butter complimented by coffee or tea. Sometime before noon the guards unbolted the cell doors and permitted the Confederate officers to take a morning walk. This was the highlight of the prisoners' day. Because Fort Warren stood in the harbor, the summer temperatures remained delightfully mild. "I would say it is the most delicious summer temperament I ever felt," Ewell wrote Lizinka.[12] Initially, the post commander restricted the prisoners to the parade ground, where they could enjoy neither the sea breezes nor the view, but by mid-May he changed the rules to permit the officers to walk along the fort's grassy parapet. Ewell was pleased by the change, which he likened to moving "from cellar to roof." "We have a better walk & a more extensive prospect than was given us before & enjoy it prodigiously," he told Rebecca. "We can go during the day, on the ramparts—quite an improvement."[13]

Confederate vice-president Alexander Stephens was also a prisoner at the fort. From his cell across the compound, he could see the officers taking their exercise on the parapet. He noticed that Ewell was hobbling about on crutches and wondered aloud why he did not use a wooden leg. A Federal officer who happened to be with Stephens told him that the general had said that before ordering the leg he wanted to first see if the authorities intended to hang him. If they did, he did not wish to go to the expense. Stephens smiled. "Ewell has a sense of humour," he thought. After perhaps a half-hour of exercise, the prisoners returned to their cells to await dinner, which was delivered at 3:00 P.M. Three hours later they took their evening walk. Promptly at 9:30 P.M. bugles or drums sounded lights out. It was a routine that seldom changed while Ewell was there.[14]

Ewell messed with six or seven other officers, including his stepson, Campbell Brown. "I have large undeveloped talents for cooking," the younger officer asserted, "and expect to astonish the mess." Apparently he did, for two weeks later Ewell informed Campbell's mother that her son "was cook last week & acquitted himself so well that the mutton chop story didn't make much impression. They wont let me cook," he added ruefully.[15] The variety of food was rather narrow, consisting of meat and bread occasionally supplemented with baked beans or grits. Vegetables had to be purchased separately. Campbell Brown, who had lived on army rations for the past four years, thought the meals were "of good quality & quantity." Alexander Stephens, on the other hand, was used to dining on better fare. He considered the amount of food meager and the quality horrendous.[16]

Prisoners who did not like government rations were at liberty to purchase food from the post sutler, A. J. Hall. Upon registering at the fort, they had turned their money over to the post authorities, who established an account in their name with Hall. When a prisoner made a purchase from the sutler, the price of the item was deducted from his account. Prices were not cheap, of course, since Hall had a monopoly on the market, but they may have seemed reasonable by Confederate standards. Prisoners could buy the food already prepared or cook it themselves. Ewell knew much about cooking from his years on the frontier and preferred to prepare his meals himself. "I have improved my fare by getting my beef raw, which I cook a la Navajoe," he informed Lizinka. Perhaps the worst thing about buying from the sutler was that the prisoners were never sure they would get what they ordered. Ewell complained that prisoners "are not allowed to visit [the] Sutler's Store & when we give an order for articles we are furnished with such as suit his convenience. I have been trying to buy a small earthenware tea pot ever since I have been here," but after three weeks he still had not gotten it.[17]

As dissatisfaction with the post sutler grew, the generals began to rely more heavily on articles sent to them by relatives and friends. Ewell regularly sent his sister Rebecca detailed instructions of what to send. His 8 May letter was typical. "We have two months supply of tea," he informed her. "It is not worth while to send such luxuries as canned fruits being expensive & bulky. In a month we use about 8 lbs of coffee, 12 to 16 of sugar[,] 12 of butter. A sapsago cheese would be good relish, a bottle of Anchovy sauce, [ditto] of *best* olive oil for table, some mustard, about 12 lbs candles, 1/2 lb honey soap. You could send a few needles & buttons. I wish also you would send a bible of something about the same print as the prayerbook. . . . The items I mention are suggestive," he told her. "You might see some things of the kind that I know nothing of. Corn starch or something of the kind as we get no vegetables might be useful. No fish or cheese is wanted, except sapsago cheese. We buy potatoes & onions. . . . A bottle of tomatoe catchup would add to our diet—a little Cayenne pepper."[18]

As a result of these dietary supplements, Ewell and the officers in his mess fared well—so well in fact that the press took notice. "The Boston papers make mention of Major-General [sic] Ewell's epicurean tastes as exhibited during his late imprisonment at Fort Warren," the Newman, Georgia, *Herald* reported in September. "We guess the gallant General always lived pretty well at his own headquarters. We spent a night with him last December (he is an old personal friend of more than twenty years standing.) and he set before us turkey and a bowl of apple tod[d]y, which General Custis Lee . . . pronounced excellent."[19]

Although he enjoyed a hearty diet at Fort Warren, Ewell's health was not the best. Twenty-three hours a day in a cramped, smoke-filled casemate, shut off from sunlight and fresh air, was not conducive to health in an able-bodied individual, much less to a man in Ewell's crippled condition. He no sooner reached the fort than he began to suffer from neuralgia, a nervous condition characterized by severe headaches and localized swelling about the eyes. (In one instance the swelling became so bad that he could hardly see out of one eye—"a la Prize fighter," he told Lizzie.) His health improved by the end of May and continued fair until July, when he suffered a fall. Although the incident alarmed his wife, Ewell suffered little from it. More serious, if less dramatic, was a bout of diarrhea he contracted in the middle of the month that laid him up for three days and added to his general debilitation.[20]

Tedium rather than sickness was the general's greatest enemy at Fort Warren. Conversation with fellow prisoners helped relieve the monotony, but it generally centered around the war, a topic that Ewell preferred to forget. For him the late conflict had been "a horrid dream," he told Lizinka, and he saw little point in rehashing it. He had greater interest in agriculture and politics. Fertilizer seemed to be his favorite topic. "It would amuse you to hear grave discourses on the mines of wealth hidden in 'Stony Lonesome', and to be brought out by judiciously applied guano," Campbell Brown wrote his mother. In a letter written on 27 May, Ewell advised Rebecca to "try to get an agent to look at Stony Lonesome & if possible have grass, guano & love dust sowed there this fall. There was a good deal of love dust as well as . . . lime put on the ground in winter of 61," he reminded her.[21]

Even in confinement Ewell's "mania for farming" remained as strong as ever. To gratify his agricultural instincts, he asked Rebecca to send him some geraniums. He set them in an embrasure both "as a defence against bad odors, tobacco &c. and [for] a little amusement." The first shipment of plants reached him in mid-June, but they were not very fresh. Ewell split the plants with his stepson. While the general fussed and fretted over his plants, Brown used what he termed a "Bo Peep" strategy, leaving his alone. Neither scheme was very successful, and by 25 June every plant had died. Undaunted, the two men sent off for a second lot. Ewell did not have any greater success with the second batch than he had with the first, though Campbell's new plant did well. "I expect to hear him boast of superior skill without duly crediting the superior condition of the plant when received," Ewell told the boy's mother. "However he has the merit of letting it alone more than I have." In horticulture both men took a backseat to Ed Johnson. Ewell informed Hattie that the general "shows his sentimental tastes by adorning his window there with a potato-vine, a geranium and an onion!"[22]

Chess, cards, and reading also helped to while away the long summer hours.[23] Prisoners could check books out of the post library or purchase them from the sutler. In both cases the selection was limited, consisting mostly of novels. After a while Ewell and Brown began getting their books through a mail-order catalog or from family members. Brown, in particular, could not get enough of them. At any given time he might be reading half a dozen different books. Although most of the prisoners read strictly for entertainment, some of the younger ones tried to improve their minds. Brown, for instance, sought to teach himself Spanish.

Gordon studied French. Hunton pondered the law. They were the exceptions, however. Most of the officers frittered away their time waiting for the mails or reading novels.[24]

Ewell seems to have belonged to the latter group. In his letters to Lizinka, he mentioned reading just two books, both popular novels: Anne Brontë's *Tenant of Wildfell Hall* and Charlotte M. Yonge's *Clever Women of the Family*. That he read so little might have been due to poor lighting in the casemates. His sister Elizabeth, fearing he might hurt his eyes, offered to send him a set of reading glasses, but Ewell declined them. "I am very much obliged for the offer in regard to the spectacles," he told her, "but my eyes are pretty fair still & I have no trouble in reading yet. I take a good deal of care of them—avoid reading after meals, put cold water in them &c." Although Stonewall Jackson had been dead for more than two years, his quaint remedies lived on.[25]

Newspapers were the most popular reading material in the fort. At 10:30 A.M. each day a ship arrived at George's Island bringing a variety of newspapers. Ewell personally subscribed to the New York *Tribune*, which he considered the least biased of the lot, but he had access to many other papers, principally those published in Boston or New York.[26]

Sometimes the newspapers contained unpleasant surprises. On more than one occasion he found himself quoted—or rather misquoted—by the press. There was a medical convention in Boston that summer and on 7 June hundreds of doctors visited the fort. "Before the guard could stop them," wrote Ewell, "they crowded into the prisoners rooms like bees & some of them asked me in regard to action in bringing on the war. I told them I was absent in Arizona in 60, & had to come in sick in the Spring of 61, that I was quite unwell in a secluded part of Va & found the war suddenly inaugurated, that on one side I had a handsome position, good pay & some means saved from long years service. All this I forfeited by going South," he had told them, "but that I had to fight with or against my state & did what the people of Mass. would have done & which I should have done at forfeit of my head. They agreed somewhat with my views & I saw myself published in the Boston papers as hurrying in from Arizona to take part in the war & many other like absurdities, the greatest being that I did not regret being taken p[r]isone[r]!"[27]

Still more aggravating to Ewell was the publication of a fictitious letter attributed to him and published in the 21 April 1865 edition of the *National Intelligencer*. In it he supposedly pleaded with Lee to surrender his army. Campbell Brown clipped the article and sent it to his mother. "You can see it is not his style," the young man wrote, "being both unmilitary and bombastic."[28] Even more annoying was the publication of a private letter that Ewell had written to Joseph Lewis, a soldier with whom he had served twenty-five years earlier at Fort Scott. Ewell had explained to Lewis the reasons that impelled him to leave the U.S. Army in 1861 and take up arms with the Confederacy. The letter was meant for Lewis's eyes only, but Lewis had it published in the St. Paul, Minnesota, *Pioneer*. Within days newspapers around the country had reprinted it. People had no right to publish his letters without his permission, Ewell indignantly told Lizinka. "Never since being here have I written a word for publication." [29]

With that single disagreeable exception, sending and receiving letters was Ewell's "greatest pleasure" in prison. Initially at least, Major Allen allowed the prisoners to send just two letters a week. Prison authorities carefully examined each one before it left the fort. Happily, Allen placed no restrictions on the number of letters prisoners could receive, provided that they were of reasonable length. Ewell received regular letters from members of his family as well as correspondence from friends and strangers. Some of the letters made him laugh. One from his sister Elizabeth informed him that he had many admirers in Georgetown, including a lady who said she wanted to kiss his feet! On another occasion a female correspondent who had seen his daguerreotype wrote to him to ask if he were as handsome as his picture represented. "When one remembers that that kind of likeness never flatters," he told Lizzie, "it is almost enough to make me vain." [30]

His favorite letter came from Mabel L. Appleton, the three-year-old daughter of acting post commander Maj. John W. M. Appleton. While visiting the fort one day, the little girl wandered over to the parapet where the generals were taking their daily walk. She was an instant hit with the prisoners, who later sent her a box of candy. In reply they received the following note of thanks, undoubtedly penned by her mother: "Miss Mabel Lander Appleton desires to acknowledge the receipt of the box of dulces which Gen. Ewell and her other friends have sent her. She fully appreciates this sweet kind of admiration, and is duly grateful—while it lasts!" Another letter from Mabel arrived a few days later containing her ferrotype, a lock of hair, and a remedy for sore canary feet! Ewell asked both Lizzie and Rebecca to send him something nice to give the child, suggesting perhaps a book or an orange. [31]

Although the little girl did not know it, she had a rival for the generals' attentions in Miss Salter. The young lady's mother was a sister of Col. Joseph C. Ives of the Confederate army. Although she had never met the prisoners, Mrs. Salter sent them a variety of gifts. "She is the most perserveringly kind person to strangers I ever saw," Ewell told his wife. But it was Mrs. Salter's daughter who

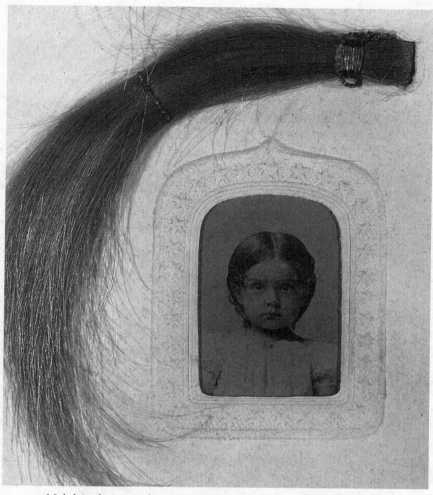

Mabel Appleton met the general while he was imprisoned at Fort Warren.
The little girl's family gave the general this photograph of Mabel and a lock of her hair.
(Filson Club Historical Society)

stole the generals' hearts. One day they received a letter from the child addressed to her "dear Rebel friends." It informed them that on Thursday she would be sailing on the bay and that she would wave a handkerchief at them as she passed the fort. "And oh, if I could only take you all aboard and carry you with me to liberty, how happy I would be," she concluded. The letter delighted the generals. When the appointed day arrived, they took turns watching the harbor. "Toward the close of the afternoon," recalled Eppa Hunton, "we spied a vessel coming, and when opposite to us we saw the little handkerchief fluttering in the hands of the dear little child. We gave her as fine a 'Rebel yell' as ever was heard. Each one of us took a copy of the letter." [32]

The society of the other prisoners, an abundance of books and newspapers, frequent letters from family and friends, and friendly communications from people like the Salters and the Appletons made the months of confinement at Fort Warren bearable. "In fact I feel ashamed sometimes at receiving so much commisseration [sic]," Ewell confessed to Lizinka, "when in fact as far as exteriors are concerned we are very well off." [33] No matter how comfortable they were, though, the Confederate officers were still prisoners and might continue to be so for some time. In the wake of the Lincoln assassination, the North was in no mood for clemency. Until the passions aroused by that despicable act subsided, all they could do was wait.

The Civil War ended while Dick Ewell was in prison. The end came quickly. Lee surrendered to Grant at Appomattox Court House on 9 April 1865, Joe Johnston surrendered to Sherman on 26 April, and E. Kirby Smith surrendered to Maj. Gen. Edward Canby one month after that. With Smith's capitulation the last Confederate army in the field was eliminated. Reconstruction of the South could begin in earnest.

Even before the last Confederate army had surrendered, the officers imprisoned at Fort Warren began applying for pardons. Ewell made a special appeal for the release of Brig. Gens. William L. Cabell of Arkansas and John S. Marmaduke of Missouri. Both men had commanded troops west of the Mississippi River, where the war still lingered. Ewell urged Federal authorities to free them so that they could return to their home states and convince the Confederate troops there to lay down their arms. [34]

Campbell Brown made a similar plea for himself. In a letter to Montgomery Blair dated 14 May, he admitted that the Confederacy was finished. He asked Blair if it would be better for him to take the oath at once or to wait until it was offered to the general officers with whom he was imprisoned. Within the week he made up his own mind on the subject. On 17 May he told his sister that he did not wish to leave Fort Warren as long as General Ewell was there. He asked her to have Tasker Gantt arrange it so that he would not be released before his stepfather. "I am a great help to the Gen'l," he wrote, "of course he will say I am of no use as he always has done in such cases. I have told him nothing of my wishes in this regard, and want it quietly settled before he hears anything of it. I think it important to him, he should have me with him, and I am in earnest about it." [35]

Ewell would have objected to Brown's comments had he known of them, for he felt that he could take care of himself. If anything, he asserted, it might benefit *Brown* to stay with *him*. "The fact is it is a great advantage to him to have to exercise forbearance & patience," he told the boy's mother, "& I fear he will miss me to his disadvantage when he gets out. . . . Probably he will be married some of these days & may find the use of preparatory trials," he added humorously.[36]

No one at Fort Warren, except Brown, wanted to stay there any longer than necessary. The prisoners admitted that the South was defeated. If the government was not willing to issue them pardons, they were prepared to take the oath of allegiance. Certainly Ewell was. He told Lizinka that he did not have the "slightest objection" to taking the oath; after all, what good would it do to resist? Now that the war was over, he believed it the duty of every citizen to support the U.S. government regardless of previous loyalties. "I would not support in [the] future a man who, whatever might have been his course during secession, provided of course it had been honest, who should not be a thoroughly patriotic citizen of the country. I am sick of halfway men." [37]

For Ewell and the other officers imprisoned at Fort Warren, the question was not whether to take the oath, but whether they would get the chance. As the general told his wife, "There has been much confusion & more talk in this debating club on the question of not what to do but *how*, as every one is perfectly willing like Capt Allen's Company of Regulars in the old Army; 'to swear to anything the Captain pleases.'" Each day the prisoners anxiously scanned the newspapers looking for some clue as to the conditions under which they might be permitted to take the oath. "As each successive paper has a different version of what they will be," Ewell remarked, "the spirits of some of the party rise & fall in proportion. One who is habitually persuaded of the certainty of the more dire events said the other day that there was nothing left but to 'die gracefully'. It is curious to see how the same prognostic of some ignorant 'penny-a-liner' will be interpreted by one man as altogether favorable & another as shutting out all hope." [38]

Two days after writing this letter, Ewell and his colleagues got their answer. On 29 May President Andrew Johnson issued an amnesty proclamation in which he ordered the release of all individuals then imprisoned by military authorities. The proclamation threw the Confederate prisoners into a "state of excitement." For more than a week they waited anxiously for the proclamation to take effect. On 9 June it was finally announced that all those under the rank of major were to be paroled and released under the late order.[39] Brig. Gen. Henry Jackson, the same man who just a few days before had gloomily announced that there was nothing to do but "die gracefully," was also released at this time. "Gen. Jackson's release took his breath away," remembered Brown. "He could hardly believe it, and it was actually painful to see the amazed look upon his face, and his slowness to comprehend it, quick and bright as he generally is." [40]

Jackson was the exception. Ewell and the other general officers at the fort were not released. Tacked on to Johnson's 29 May amnesty proclamation was a list of fourteen classes of individuals who were excepted from the benefits of the general amnesty. People belonging to those classes had to apply for amnesty on an individual basis. In a letter to Johnson, Ewell acknowledged that he failed to qualify for the general amnesty on three counts: he had been a general officer, he was currently being held as a prisoner of war, and he had been educated at the U.S. Military Academy. People ill disposed toward him might have added three other counts: he had resigned his commission in the U.S. Army in 1861 to avoid putting down the rebellion; as the officer in charge of the Department of Richmond, he was responsible for the mistreatment of Union soldiers confined in Richmond prisons; and by his 1863 marriage to Lizinka he now possessed property in excess of $20,000. [41]

Campbell Brown remained a prisoner too. He failed to qualify for the general amnesty on two counts: he was a prisoner of war, and his personal wealth exceeded $20,000. Brown attributed his prolonged confinement to President Johnson's personal animosity toward his mother. The release of Gen. Henry Jackson "& my continued detention convince me of personal malignity in your case," Brown wrote his mother. Ironically, his own influence rather than the president's probably kept him behind bars. Gantt apparently had taken his cousin at his word three weeks earlier when Brown directed him to see to it that he was not released prior to General Ewell. Now that request was coming back to haunt him. [42]

Ewell received permission from the attorney general to take the oath of allegiance as prescribed in the 29 May proclamation. He wasted no time doing so. On 16 June he sent Johnson a signed copy of the oath with a letter listing the reasons that he was not eligible for general amnesty. "This oath," he wrote, "is the strongest proof I can give of my wish to become a loyal citizen and, as far as in me lies, to do my duty to the country." [43] Ewell meant what he said. Privately he told his wife that he was "heartily anxious to become a law-abiding member of the community, if allowed & would be the best one to be found, either to put down guerillas or stop the mouths of demagogue talkers of sedition, the worse of the two, provided the govt. establishes such an office. I am willing to take either Amnesty or Allegiance, as I have seen nothing yet that one with these views should object to." [44]

Ewell had numerous individuals working behind the scenes for his freedom, many of whom were people of influence in the government. His strongest advocate remained Montgomery Blair, but he also received support from Generals Grant and Sherman. David Meriwether, the former governor of the New Mexico Territory and a member of the Kentucky state legislature, was also in his corner. Meriwether had accompanied Ewell on more than one excursion in the Southwest prior to the war. Now that Ewell was in prison, he offered to do everything in his power to effect the general's release. "It would give me great pleasure to see you once more, and talk over our many long tramps together in former days; I often think of them and you and would like to go over them again with my old travelling companion."[45]

Ewell urged Meriwether and his other Northern friends to exert themselves on Lizinka's behalf rather than his own. His wife was then under house arrest in Missouri. She and Hattie had left Richmond early in 1865 and fled to St. Louis, where they turned themselves in to the local provost marshal. The authorities gave them three choices: they could be deported to Southern lines, suffer imprisonment in a St. Louis jail, or apply for amnesty and have their property restored to them. The women chose the latter course.[46]

Lizinka remained under house arrest at Tasker Gantt's until 23 March 1865, when a telegram arrived from President Lincoln permitting her to take the amnesty oath. She did so on the twenty-fifth.[47] Curiously, Hattie was not permitted to take the amnesty oath; instead she was required to take the more stringent ironclad oath in which she had to vow to uphold the Constitution and to swear that she had never taken up arms against the United States or voluntarily aided the rebellion in any way. This put the girl in a difficult position. In her heart she knew that she had assisted the Confederacy, but if she refused to take the oath, the authorities would deport her. Faced with that unpleasant alternative, she signed. "She was sometimes terribly distressed about it," Lizinka confided to a friend, "said she felt perjured, etc. I persuaded her to do it."[48]

After taking the amnesty oath, Lizinka traveled to Maury County, Tennessee, to check on her farm, which she had been told was "a wreck." She reached Nashville on 3 April 1865 and immediately set about laying claim to her property in the city. This created waves with the various squatters who occupied the lots. On 5 April she was hauled into U.S. circuit court and forced to take the amnesty oath for a second time. As a result of the hearing, the judge ordered the proceedings against her to be dismissed and decreed that her property be restored to her upon her paying $560 in court fees.[49]

Having cleared that legal hurdle, Lizinka returned to the task at hand: getting

Lizinka's house in Nashville, Tennessee (Harper's Monthly Magazine)

control of her property. She found her Nashville house occupied by Andrew Johnson's family. With more boldness than tact, she hastily inspected the premises, then wrote a note to Mrs. Johnson pertly asking permission to use "one or two rooms in my own house." Mrs. Johnson took offense at the request and made no reply. For Lizinka, it would be a costly mistake.[50]

While Lizinka was in Tennessee, national events passed with dizzying speed. On 3 April the Union army occupied Richmond, on 9 April Lee surrendered the Army of Northern Virginia, and on 14 April John W. Booth assassinated President Lincoln. Overnight the North's buoyant mood turned sour and vengeful. Lizinka was staying in Mrs. Thomas Washington's house in Nashville when she learned of the president's assassination. The next morning Union soldiers left a note at the house saying that Lincoln had been murdered by the occupants' "rebel friends." It warned the Washingtons that if they did not display some sign of mourning at the house—and soon—mobs would destroy it.[51]

About this same time Lizinka learned that Richard and Campbell had been captured and sent to Fort Warren. This, together with the ugly mood then pervading the nation, prompted her to write President Johnson urging him to free her husband and son. She suggested that once Dick and Campbell were free, the family might leave the country for a few years and travel in Europe. If she wrote this in the belief that Johnson would favor such a course, she was mistaken. According to Montgomery Blair, the letter impressed the president "very unfavorably."[52]

Meanwhile Lizinka continued to stir up trouble by trying to take legal possession of her Tennessee property. On 21 April Horace H. Harrison, U.S. district attorney for the Middle District of Tennessee, informed Johnson that Lizinka had filed an application in court to have the proceedings against her dismissed based on President Lincoln's amnesty proclamation and on the fact that she had taken the oath of allegiance. "I have no sort of confidence in her sincerity," wrote Harrison, though he admitted he could not prove her disloyalty or "resist a decree dismissing proceedings." Nevertheless, he insisted, "I will not consent to a decree directing the Marshal to put her in possession."

Harrison's message, together with Lizinka's note to Mrs. Johnson and other actions, convinced Johnson that she was unrepentant. On 21 April he ordered her to be placed under arrest and sent back to St. Louis, at the same time suspending restoration of her property.[53] Unaware of Johnson's role in the matter, Lizinka penned the president a letter as soon as she got back to St. Louis. Only after several weeks had passed and she received no reply did it occur to her that Johnson himself had ordered her arrest.[54] Montgomery Blair confirmed that fact in subsequent conversations with the president. Johnson liked Mrs. Ewell, Blair insisted, but he resented "the want of national feeling he thinks he finds in her letters." The president had also been annoyed to learn that Lizinka had returned to Nashville and was "demanding rents from the negroes who had built Shanties on some vacant lands" that she owned in the city (a charge that Lizinka denied). Convinced that Lizinka was unrepentant, Johnson ordered her arrest. Blair tried to persuade him to release Lizinka, Dick, and Campbell, but he would not budge. For the time being, all three members of the family would have to remain in confinement.[55]

Lizinka kept a low profile and desisted from any further appeals to Johnson. "Having done mischief instead of good by my appeal to the supposed friendship of the President I shall keep quiet & make no further useless efforts," she wrote her husband. But as weeks passed without any new developments, Lizinka grew anxious. The cause of her arrest, she told her husband, was "a mystery & is beginning to have on my mind the evil effect of a ghost-story—some thing unseen & dreadful because you cannot get hold of it. I have been so careful & quiet; not even visiting the kindest people for fear of giving offense or getting into trouble that I feel injured & indignant as well as mortified & provoked."[56]

Lizinka's imprisonment provoked the general even more than it did Lizinka herself. Ewell told an acquaintance that he felt "a thousand times worse on her account than on my own," and he urged Meriwether and other powerful friends to exert their energies on her behalf.[57] He feared for his wife's property as much as he did for her liberty. Ewell anticipated the government might use Lizinka's marriage to him as a pretense for seizing her land. "He seemed to be possessed with the idea that the property of his wife 'Mrs. Brown,' would be confiscated," recalled Eppa Hunton. "It was very large."[58] The impasse continued for almost two months. On 19 June Lizinka finally broke her silence and wrote to Maj. Gen. John Pope, who commanded the Department of Missouri, requesting permission to go east. Pope forwarded her request to the secretary of war, who gave her leave to travel to Washington or any other place in the North except Tennessee. Obviously Johnson had not forgotten the stir Lizinka had caused the last time she was there.[59]

Lizinka and Hattie arrived in Baltimore within a week. While there, they stayed at the home of their cousin William Reynolds, who lived at 131 North Fayette Street. Lizinka secured an interview with President Johnson on 28 June. She had three objectives: obtain paroles for her husband and son, get permission to visit them at Fort Warren, and have her property in Nashville and St. Louis restored to her.[60] In a tense, three-hour meeting, Johnson agreed to pardon Lizinka and Campbell and to restore Lizinka's property if she returned in three days with a written petition to that effect. He would not consent to freeing the general.

The interview left Lizinka confused. "The Prest.'s promises are large but vague," she observed in a letter to her husband. "He gave me to understand that he would sign my 'pardon' & C's but not yours. One thing is puzzling—if a special amnesty from Mr. Lincoln is not binding or effective—why should one from Mr. J. be so? However, it is egregious folly to complain of the form if the end is obtained," she concluded, "but the truth is I am so disappointed at being refused your release, that the proffer to give binding force to an act of Mr. Lincoln's so kindly done by him two months ago seems like mockery."[61]

Lizinka had to take what she could get, and on 1 July she returned to the White House, petition in hand. Johnson thereupon recognized Lincoln's pardon and directed that Lizinka be "permitted to return to Nashville, Tennessee, free from arrest, or other detention by Military Authorities, and to take possession of her property, as decreed by the U.S. District Court for the Dist. of Middle Tennessee."[62]

The order covered Lizinka and her property but did not address Dick's and Campbell's imprisonment. As long as members of her family remained in prison,

Lizinka had no intention of relaxing her efforts. After delivering her petition to the White House, she called on Grant and Blair to enlist their continued support in freeing her husband and son. Hattie recalled that General Grant was "exceedingly polite" to her mother and "said he would do all in his power to help his old friend Ewell." Blair, who had already gone out of his way for the family, was also "very kind."[63]

While in Washington, Lizinka received permission to visit her husband and son at Fort Warren. The long-awaited reunion took place on or about 9 July. Lizinka rejoiced to see Dick and Campbell, but her husband's feeble appearance alarmed her. To make matters worse, Campbell hinted that he was considering taking a bride. Lizinka was about to lose her daughter to marriage; now she had to face the possibility of losing her son as well.[64]

Faced with these various concerns, her composure snapped. Returning to Wakefield, Rhode Island, where she was temporarily staying with the Reynolds family, she sat down and wrote Andrew Johnson an impassioned letter imploring the release of Dick and Campbell. "I have seen my husband & son haggard from three months confinement in stone cells & the former debilitated & almost helpless from injury to his leg and the effects of poor diet & imprisonment," she complained. With a stroke of his pen, Johnson could free them. "Will you write it?" she asked. "Or are your professions of kind feeling towards me merely air — intended to deceive one too miserable & insignificant to be worthy of such artifice from such a man. . . . I am afraid to write more," she concluded. "I could not write less, but if Richard dies in Ft. War[r]en how I will hate you, wicked as it is to hate anyone."[65]

She had no sooner mailed this letter than she received a telegram from Johnson urging her to return to Washington to discuss the release of her husband and son. He had sent the dispatch to her Baltimore address a week earlier, and it had only now caught up with her. Lizinka's gloom instantly vanished; again she was joyful and exuberant. She started at once for Washington, but not before taking a moment to write Dick and Campbell of the good news. "Probably—almost certainly—I am required to give bond & security for the good behaviour of you both," she laughed, "& *won't* you have to walk straight & give an account of yourselves every evening. I don't know which to pity most," she wrote her husband, "you with your wild Indian tastes [or] C. with his love of fun [and] adventure. Both will have to toe the mark when I am your jailor."[66]

Lizinka had her final meeting with the president on 17 July. Although Johnson had received her ill-timed letter by then, he took no offense at it. He permitted her to return to Nashville to take possession of her property, in accordance with

Lincoln's order of 23 March, and authorized General Ewell's release on the condition that he take the oath of allegiance and post a $10,000 bond. Ewell filled those requirements on 19 July and left Fort Warren later that day accompanied by his stepson. The other Confederate officers remained in prison, but before the week was over, they too would be released.[67]

Lizinka may have hand-carried the order that resulted in Dick's and Campbell's release. In any case, she was present at Fort Warren when her husband and son gained their freedom. As the family was leaving the fort, a Union soldier took her aside and told her that the garrison was delighted at the general's release. Another Union soldier, unaware of Ewell's aversion to tobacco, thrust a couple of cigars into his hand and wished him well. At the Frémont House in Boston, where the family took lodging that night, a chambermaid confided to Lizinka that the entire hotel staff was pleased that the general was finally free.[68]

What a difference three months had made! In April, Northern mobs enraged by President Lincoln's assassination had sought Ewell's life. Now Boston citizens treated the general and his family like honored guests. Nor were they an isolated case. All across the nation a spirit of reconciliation was afoot. War's heated passions had started to subside; its wounds, though deep, had started to heal.

CHAPTER 31

Cotton Fever

Dick Ewell was starting over. For a quarter-century he had been under arms. In that time he had participated in two major mounted expeditions, fought in two wars, and risen in grade from a lieutenant to a lieutenant general. Three times he had been wounded; once he had almost died. Five horses had been shot from under him. Through it all he never faltered in his duty; he had been faithful to the last. But his days in the army were behind him now; at age forty-eight he had to find a new career. His first inclination was to return to Stony Lonesome and take up farming, but a visit there quickly dispelled that notion. The farm had never been very productive, and four years of war had left it more desolate than ever. Sadly Ewell concluded that he must seek his fortune elsewhere.[1]

The general turned his attention south to the James River Valley. In August 1865, while he and his wife took up temporary residence in Warrenton, Virginia, Campbell Brown traveled from Goochland to Gloucester looking for a suitable place for the family to settle. Lizinka fancied a residence near Richmond, but Campbell warned her that the city had become a "disagreeable and dangerous" place to live. He recommended a house in Williamsburg, but Lizinka rejected the colonial capital and its marshy environs as being too unhealthy. "I had rather be buried underground than in a sickly place above it," she insisted. Westover, in Charles City County, was a more attractive prospect. The plantation had an excellent wheat crop and boasted one of the finest houses in Virginia. It was equidistant to Richmond and Williamsburg, and its situation on the James River provided easy access to New York, Baltimore, and other ports along the East Coast. Of all the places in Virginia that the Ewells considered, it came closest to filling their needs.[2]

In the end, however, the Ewells chose to live in Tennessee. Lizinka owned considerable property in the state, and it would be easier to manage it if she was nearby. More important, her children intended to reside in that part of the country, and Lizinka would rarely see them if she lived in the East. Although the general preferred settling in Virginia, a mother's love won out: the Ewells were going to Tennessee.[3]

Before they did so, Lizinka had some business to take care of. In confirming President Lincoln's pardon in June, President Johnson had directed Attorney General James Speed to permit Lizinka "to take possession of her property, as decreed by the U.S. District Court for the Dist. of Middle Tennessee." The catch was that the U.S. district's court's decree referenced just a few of Lizinka's tracts, and the least valuable ones at that. It said nothing, for instance, about her house in Nashville or her farm in Maury County. Consequently, Johnson's order had no bearing on those properties. Until the president issued new orders, the Freedman's Bureau continued to treat them as confiscated properties. It leased Lizinka's Maury County farm to a carpetbagger named Northrup and rented her Nashville house to Tennessee's Unionist governor, William G. "Parson" Brownlow. In a separate action, the U.S. Attorney's Office took steps to freeze Lizinka's assets in St. Louis as well. Lizinka's land and money were the Ewells' primary source of income. Until she was free to use those assets, the family found itself short of cash.[4]

Lizinka took her case directly to the president. On 5 September 1865 she went to the White House and secured Johnson's help in recovering her property. Johnson had recently issued an order to the Freedman's Bureau directing it to release the lands of Southerners who had taken the amnesty oath. Lizinka had done so; consequently, she would receive title to her Tennessee lands within a matter of days. As for her assets in Missouri, Johnson told Lizinka that he would direct the attorney general to cease all legal proceedings against her property there on condition that she pay the court fees, which amounted to slightly more than $400. Lizinka did so, and on 15 September the district attorney dropped his suit. After almost six months of legal wrangling, Lizinka had finally regained control of her property.[5]

General Ewell meanwhile was fighting a legal battle of his own. In order to secure his parole, he had had to agree to post a $10,000 bond, report weekly in writing to the secretary of war, and remain in Virginia. Such conditions had not been required of the other Confederate officers confined with him at Fort Warren. When Ewell learned of the discrepancy, he asked the War Department to adjust the terms of his parole so as to bring them in line with those of the others.[6]

Like his wife, the general started at the top. In August he traveled to Washington for interviews with President Johnson, Attorney General Speed, and Montgomery Blair. While in the capital, a group of Confederate sympathizers invited him to dinner. Ewell reputedly scorned their offer, saying that he "did not care to consort with those who pretended to be friends with the South, but could not make up their minds to fight for her during the war." The story may well be true. Ewell had no patience for those who sought to prolong the animosity between North and South, particularly individuals who had been too cowardly to take up arms when it counted. From a more practical standpoint, it would have been imprudent for him to be seen associating with political dissidents at a time when he was seeking favors from the government.[7]

Following his trip to Washington, Ewell wrote letters to President Johnson, the War Department, and Maj. Gen. Winfield S. Hancock, who commanded the military department in which he resided.[8] His persistence paid off. On 7 October the War Department granted him permission to change his place of residence from Virginia to Tennessee, and a week later it adjusted the terms of his parole to match those of the other generals confined with him at Fort Warren. The way was now clear for him to go to Tennessee.[9]

The Ewells left Virginia around the third week in October 1865. On the way west they stopped in Baltimore to attend Hattie's wedding to Tom Turner. The ceremony had been scheduled for September, but Hattie had come down with a serious case of diphtheria, compelling them to postpone it. The nuptials were performed by a Catholic priest at the Reynolds house. Like most parents, Lizinka gave away her daughter with a heavy heart. Hattie had been more than a daughter to her; she had been her best friend and constant companion. Parting was difficult.[10] After the wedding General Ewell traveled to Philadelphia to purchase a new prosthesis and consult with specialists about his neuralgia. George Meade had his headquarters in the city. When he learned that Ewell was in town, he arranged a meeting. As one might imagine, their conversation focused on Gettysburg.[11]

The Ewells reached Tennessee in late October. They had hoped to move into Lizinka's Spring Hill farm right away, but they found it still occupied by Northrup. The Freedman's Bureau had leased him the property until 1 February 1866. Although Lizinka now had title to the property, Northrup's agreement with the Freedman's Bureau remained valid. If the Ewells wished to occupy the farm before then, they would have to pay Northrup to break the lease. Compensating a carpetbagger for the right to live in her own house was distasteful to say the least, but there was no helping it. Lizinka wrote Northrup a check for $1,554.[12]

By December Northrup had moved out of Spring Hill, and the Ewells were able to start rebuilding their lives. The Maury County farm stood thirty-two miles south of Nashville at the point where the Nashville and Decatur Railroad crossed the Spring Hill Turnpike. Sometimes referred to as "Maury Farm" or

Harriot ("Hattie") Brown Turner, Lizinka's daughter (Harper's Monthly Magazine)

"Sutherland," the property encompassed 3,290 acres of "splendid cotton land." [13] Like Stony Lonesome, it had felt the hand of war. George Thomas's troops had camped on the plantation in 1862, and opposing armies had marched through the area several times since then. The soldiers had spared the house and many of its dependencies, but they had driven off livestock, torn up fences, cut down large amounts of timber, and destroyed the farm's cotton gin and cisterns. Ewell realized he would have to start pretty much from scratch. "There is no fencing hardly

Thomas T. Turner, Ewell's adventuresome aide-de-camp and husband of his stepdaughter, Harriot Brown (St. Louis Post-Dispatch)

& scarcely any improvements of any kind," he complained to his brother, "it is like opening an entirely new farm." [14]

Ewell wasted no time pitching in. His first priority was to put a crop in the field, so that the farm could start earning revenue. That meant buying mules and seed, hiring laborers, and splitting rails. By mid-January 1866 he had five plows in operation and had started fencing the field closest to the stable. [15] Problems dogged his early efforts. Cutworms damaged his corn, his cotton crop came up badly, and his cotton press broke down. When his brother William accidentally left a gate open, two of Ewell's finest lambs wandered into the orchard and were devoured by hogs. Worst of all, the bottom fell out of the cotton market. In one week cotton prices plummeted from forty-five cents to just twenty-five cents per pound. On the other hand, the price of corn and pork, which Ewell needed to feed his workers, remained high. Campbell Brown summed up the situation in a letter to Jed Hotchkiss: "We are making great efforts & small progress," he wrote in March, "consoled and cheered only by the equal or greater failures of our neighbors. We shall not make a fortune—will be lucky if we don't ruin ourselves." Ewell expressed even greater discouragement. "I cant say I am getting on very well or am very well contented," he confessed to Hotchkiss. "I sometimes feel like envying those that 'Sleep the sleep that knows no waking.'"[16]

Finding reliable workers was Ewell's toughest problem. "Labor of every kind is scarce & high," he told his sister Elizabeth, "there is so much to be done that every one is behind & one owes high wages and personal obligations for what is done." Black farmhands were the least expensive source of labor, but they required constant supervision to keep them at their work. "I am as usual fretting my soul away because of the darkies who wont see that 12.50 [a month] & rations are any particular reasons for working hard," Ewell complained to Lizzie. "In fact they think they are conferring a favor on us." European immigrants made better workers, Ewell felt, but they were also more expensive, the price of male farmhands running as high as $15 a month. Moreover, he would have to pay a $5 commission for each immigrant that he hired and fund their passage from New York City to Nashville. He decided to stick with his black hands.[17]

Despite a rocky start, Spring Hill prospered. In 1870 the farm produced 2,100 bushels of winter wheat, 3,000 bushels of corn, 2,000 bushels of barley, 200 bushels of Irish potatoes, 50 bushels of sweet potatoes, 300 tons of hay, and 70 bales of cotton. These figures do not include produce grown in the farm's orchard, vegetable garden, and vineyard. In 1869 General Ewell harvested 30 bushels of grapes from the vineyard, most of which undoubtedly went toward providing wine for his table.[18]

Spring Hill was first and foremost a stock farm, however. Starting in 1867 Lizinka established a dairy farm using Ayrshire, Jersey, and Durham cattle. That same year she purchased two Alderneys in Baltimore and had them shipped to Spring Hill at a cost of $1,000. They were the first cattle of that kind to be introduced into Tennessee. Each animal was marked with the Ewells' brand—a capital *E* on its right side.[19] By 1870 Lizinka's herds had grown to 12 oxen, 70 milch cows, and 150 other cattle. Her reputation as a dairy expert grew apace. In 1871

Spring Hill, Lizinka's Tennessee farm, where Ewell lived and died
following the Civil War (Donald C. Pfanz)

she submitted an article to the *Columbia Herald* titled "Dairying in Tennessee." Ironically, she submitted the article just as she was planning to get out of the business. Dairy farming had become "unremunerative & burdensome" to her, she complained, bringing in just $800 a year, a sum barely sufficient to pay the wages of a Scottish couple whom she had hired to run the enterprise.[20]

General Ewell managed the farm's mules and sheep. He purchased mules to work Spring Hill's fields in January 1866 and later that year started raising them for profit. Mules were in short supply in the South, and when Ewell had an opportunity to buy 250 from a relative, he jumped at the chance. He bred the animals and sold them for $125 to $150 apiece to customers such as James Longstreet, Gen. Carter L. Stevenson, and Adm. Raphael Semmes.[21] For Ewell, mules were a sideline. Sheep were his specialty. Of the 900 sheep in his herd, Cotswolds and Southdowns dominated. Ewell sheared their wool for sale to dry goods dealers and sold lambs to other farmers. Either way he turned a handsome profit.[22]

Twenty-two horses, forty-three hogs, some chickens, and a few goats rounded out the Ewells' livestock. Among the last-named animals were two cashmere goats and a feisty Angora buck. One day Ewell encountered the Angora coming toward him on a farm path. As in the initial meeting between Robin Hood and Little John, both parties stubbornly refused to yield to the other. When Ewell tried to push the buck aside, the animal caught the general between the legs with his horns and threw him flat onto his back. The goat tried to gore Ewell while he was down, but the general held him at bay by poking him in the nose with his wooden leg until a farmhand came and drove the animal away.[23]

Whether they were dealing in goats, cattle, horses, or sheep, the Ewells bought only top-quality stock. "We must have the best herd West of the Alleghenies—if we breed at all," Lizinka once declared. She was referring to cattle at the time, but she might just as well have said the same thing about any of their livestock. The family's postwar correspondence is sprinkled with references to "full-blooded" pigs, "pedigree" bulls, "high grade" sheep, and "thorobred" cattle. As a result of this commitment to quality, they soon turned Spring Hill into one of the finest stock farms in the country.[24]

The 1870 census placed the value of Spring Hill at $80,000. Not counted in this figure was $2,500 worth of machinery and $16,350 in livestock. The farm then had 3,800 acres. Of these, 2,000 were wooded and 1,800 were improved. Spring Hill's annual production, including the sale of crops, timber, wool, dairy products, and animals for slaughter, was valued at $28,580. It was by far the largest farm in its district and one of the largest in the state.[25]

In addition to the Ewells and the Browns, the 1870 census showed five other people living at Spring Hill: a gardener named Saxton Lawrence, a twenty-four-year-old farmhand named William M. McLean, and three abandoned children named Cross. The children belonged to a former employee who had run off with his wife in September 1866. Dick's and Lizinka's aunt, Rebecca Hubbard, lived with her husband, Maj. David Hubbard, on a twenty-acre farm nearby.[26]

Not appearing on the census, at least in the Ewell household, were Spring Hill's many farmhands. The number of workers the Ewells employed on an average day is unknown, but there must have been at least a dozen, for the general estimated that he annually spent $10,000 on them in wages and board. By 1867 the expense of maintaining a workforce led him to question the profitability of hiring hands at all. "It is evident that if one wishes to farm profitably to any extent," he told Campbell, "it must be by grazing or else by planting on shares." Ewell did, in fact, lease portions of Spring Hill to sharecroppers, but it is unclear for how long or to what extent he tried this experiment.[27]

The 1870 census gives a good picture of the farming operations at Spring Hill, but it by no means provides a complete assessment of the Ewells' total wealth. In addition to the Maury County farm, Lizinka owned a large house and half a dozen lots in Nashville; seven properties in central Tennessee; three tracts in northwest Tennessee; three plantations in Mississippi; two lots in Washington, D.C.; and one lot in St. Louis. Altogether the 1870 census valued her real estate holdings at $175,000 and her personal property at $55,000.[28]

The general's assets were modest by comparison. His father, Thomas Ewell, had owned a large tract of land in Grayson County, Kentucky, that was passed down to his children after his death. Campbell Brown estimated the property's value at between $15,000 and $20,000 in 1872. Dick Ewell took an interest in the place but seldom, if ever, visited it. His family may have rented the property, but no evidence has been found to support that supposition. In addition to his share of the Kentucky land, the general had four properties in Maury County. On 2 February 1867 he purchased a 47.5-acre tract along Flat Creek from Robert H. Harrison for $500. He must have disposed of it at some point, for there is no mention of it in his will. Later that same month he bought a second tract from a man named Thompson. This piece of land, located six miles southeast of Spring Hill, encompassed 102.5 acres.[29]

His final land purchases took place in 1869. On 15 October he successfully bid on 252 acres of rolling land that were offered at a public auction. The property, which he called "the Barrancas," stood adjacent to the Nashville and Decatur Railroad, three miles below Spring Hill. It bordered Lizinka's "Deshon" tract. The property contained a modest whitewashed house, a well, and a spring-house—all in need of repair. He later acquired eight acres adjoining the Barrancas from a man named McCormick, increasing the size of the tract to 260 acres. Ewell sowed cotton, wheat, and barley there in 1870, and the next year he rented it to a man who harvested wheat and tended his sheep. After the general died, Benjamin and Elizabeth Ewell sold the tract for $6,500.[30]

Land was the Ewells' greatest economic asset, but it was not their only one. They also had money invested in gold, stocks, and bonds.[31] In addition Lizinka leased many of her properties and loaned large sums of money at interest.[32] Curiously, family members kept their finances strictly separate from one another. General Ewell, Lizinka, and Campbell each had their own land, money, and investments, and under no circumstances did they mix accounts. Occasionally family members might loan money to one another free of interest, but they never gave it away. Full and prompt repayment was always expected. On one occasion Campbell made the mistake of suggesting that his mother give him part of the Spring Hill farm. Lizinka became livid. The very notion of *giving* away her land, even to her son, was anathema to her. She comforted herself with the thought that his proposition was either a "bad joke" or that Campbell had written the letter while suffering from a mild fit of insanity. She would be happy to sell him the land at a fair price, but give it away? Never![33]

General Ewell personally supervised the work at Spring Hill. Each day he was up and working before sunrise, regardless of the weather or time of year. It was a rigorous schedule for a crippled man approaching his fiftieth birthday, and Ewell's health suffered. His neuralgic attacks, which had declined after his release from Fort Warren, picked up again in 1866 and were more savage than before. He complained of feeling "stretchy & nervous," and on some mornings he could only open one eye. His dyspepsia also continued to nag him. Although less painful than the neuralgia, it was no less annoying. He drank tea and ate a concoction of oatmeal gruel to alleviate his discomfort, but whatever relief such home remedies may have afforded was at best temporary.[34]

The best remedy, his family thought, was a vacation. For some time Lizinka had been after the general to take her to St. Louis. Hattie lived at a dairy farm called "Marietta," just outside the city, and Lizinka wished to see her. While there, the Ewells could check on some property Lizinka had in the city and visit Tasker Gantt. The Ewells left Spring Hill in May 1866, after they had put in the spring crops and sheared the winter wool off the sheep. For the general it was an unpleasant trip. He no sooner reached St. Louis than he suffered a severe attack of neuralgia. For several days he was laid up in his room at the Southern Hotel. Lizinka went without him to Marietta and spent several delightful days with her daughter. Hattie was then three months pregnant. When she gave birth to a little girl later that year, she christened it Lizinka in honor of her mother. To the family the child became known as Lily.[35]

After leaving St. Louis the Ewells traveled to New Orleans, Louisiana, where the general visited Dick Taylor and other former officers in the army. "How well I remember our chat!" wrote Taylor. "How he talked of his plans and hopes and happiness, and of his great lot of books, which he was afraid he would never be able to read through. The while 'my wife, Mrs. Brown,' sat by, handsome as a picture, smiling on her General, as well she might, so noble a gentleman. . . . His last years were made happy by her companionship," Taylor reflected, "and comfortable by the wealth she had brought him. Dear Dick Ewell! Virginia never bred a truer gentleman, a braver soldier, nor an odder, more lovable fellow."[36]

In July, little more than a month after they returned from New Orleans, the Ewells took a pleasure trip to Capon Springs, West Virginia. Illness again marred the trip. Lizinka felt sick as she boarded the train in Nashville, and by the time she reached Louisville, Kentucky, she was suffering from a full-blown bilious attack—"the most severe . . . I have had for years." Despite his wife's illness, the

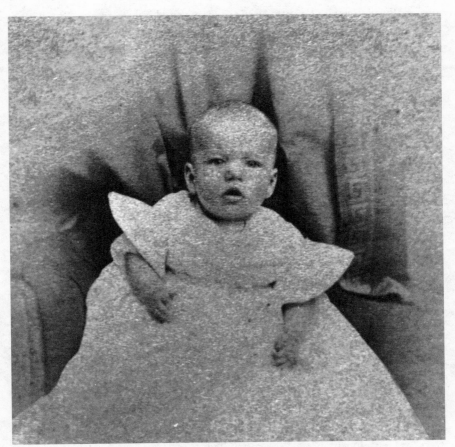

Lizinka C. ("Lily") Turner, the oldest of Lizinka's fourteen grandchildren
(Tennessee State Library and Archives)

general had "quite a levee." In the brief time that he was in Louisville, he entertained Gens. E. Kirby Smith and Don Carlos Buell and a stream of other visitors. On the day he departed, he jotted in his pocket diary, "I have left my home of affections." [37] Was he referring to the many friends he had in Louisville or was he perhaps thinking of some young lady he had courted while stationed there in 1845? On that intriguing question the record is silent.

From Louisville the Ewells traveled by train to Winchester, Virginia. There they took a carriage to Capon Springs, a popular mountain resort in the Allegheny Mountains. They reached the springs around 22 July 1866 and remained there for one week. The weather was fine and the society pleasant. Everywhere he turned, Ewell met with an enthusiastic welcome and kind treatment. "R.d has not been in such spirits since the surrender," Lizinka told Campbell. At the springs he ran into several old friends from Baltimore, among them Majors Harry Gilmor and William W. Goldsborough. Also present was a Union surgeon who had married a Winchester girl. Ewell went fishing with him. When the other Southern guests expressed astonishment that he had associated with a Northerner, "he told them we must make all the friends we can from the north—we'll need them all in the coming trials."[38]

The Ewells left Capon Springs and traveled to Baltimore to spend a week with the Reynolds family. While Lizinka shopped and visited friends, Dick journeyed to northern Virginia to see Rebecca, who was then living near Stony Lonesome. It was their last meeting. Rebecca died of bilious diphtheria one year later in Williamsburg and was laid to rest beside her mother in an unmarked grave in the William and Mary faculty cemetery. Next to Ben, Dick was closer to Rebecca than any member of his family. Her death distressed him greatly.[39]

After a week in Baltimore the Ewells traveled to Williamsburg to see Ben before heading west to the mountain resort of Bath Alum Springs. Lizzie accompanied them. Everywhere the general went, he received red-carpet treatment, and not by Confederate sympathizers only. On the voyage down the Chesapeake Bay toward Williamsburg, the ship's captain gave General Ewell a free ticket and his best stateroom, even though the ship's owner was a Union man. "Consideration is shewn [sic] him everywhere," Lizinka wrote her son. Lizzie, too, found that traveling with a celebrity had its advantages. When they reached Bath Alum Springs, her connections made her the center of attention. "It is very pleasant to travel as Genl. Ewell's niece," she concluded.

Bath Alum Springs was thirty miles southwest of Staunton, Virginia, deep in the Allegheny Mountains. The place brought back bittersweet memories for the general, who had spent several weeks at nearby Millborough Springs after his amputation. He had been in pain then, but he was in even greater pain now. Before reaching Bath Alum Springs, he had caught a cold that triggered a new wave of neuralgic attacks. The episodes lasted from morning until night and were fiercely intense—more painful even than the loss of his leg had been. Opium alone brought relief. Because of his injury, the general rarely left his room at Bath Alum Springs. When he did, it was to sup with Joe Johnston and his wife, with whom he and Lizinka shared a table in the hotel dining room.[40]

The Ewells returned to Tennessee by late August. In their absence Campbell had undertaken major repairs to Spring Hill. He tackled the main house first. In an effort to make the building more comfortable for his mother, he hung wall-

Susan Polk Brown, 1866 (Tennessee State Library and Archives)

paper, painted the exterior, and constructed new hearths. Turning his attention to adjoining dependencies, he whitewashed the smokehouse, dug a six-foot-deep cistern, and constructed a new kitchen and stables. At the same time, he managed to sell a crop of wheat, put in a supply of hay and oats, purchase large numbers of cattle and sheep, buy a cider mill, hire a blacksmith, and drill for oil. Campbell Brown was a busy man.[41]

Brown had strong incentive for wanting to get Spring Hill in top condition: he intended to bring his bride there. After returning to Tennessee, he had started courting Susan Polk, the daughter of Brig. Gen. Lucius E. Polk. In April 1866 he proposed marriage to her. Unfortunately he did so without first consulting his mother, an oversight that briefly cast a shadow over their relationship. General Ewell effected a reconciliation, however, and the wedding ceremony took place on 12 September 1866 following the Ewells' return from the East. The Browns honeymooned at Niagara Falls, after which Campbell enrolled in the University of Virginia School of Law. When he and Susie returned to Tennessee in the summer of 1867, they were expecting a child. Susie gave birth on 1 August to a boy, whom she named Lucius after her father.[42]

Lizzie Ewell got married the following year. In May 1867 she announced her engagement to Beverly Scott, a young man from Prince Edward County, Virginia. The couple exchanged vows at Spring Hill on 12 December. Surprisingly, Benjamin Ewell did not attend the ceremony. He claimed that he could not break free from his duties at the college, but privately he admitted that he could not bear to see his daughter married. After the wedding, Lizzie moved to her husband's house in Prince Edward County. She missed her father, though, and after a year she prevailed on her husband to settle in Williamsburg, where Scott took over management of Benjamin Ewell's farm. Not long after, Lizzie gave birth to a son. General Ewell blushed as he read the news: the child's name was Richard Stoddert Ewell Scott.[43]

Dick Ewell's postwar career falls naturally into two periods: the years between 1866 and 1868, when he actively managed Lizinka's Spring Hill plantation in Tennessee, and the years from 1869 to 1871, when he devoted much of his time to managing Melrose and Tarpley plantations in Mississippi. Lizinka and her children had inherited Melrose from James Percy Brown in 1844. The Bolivar County property consisted of approximately 1,500 acres of swampy cotton land tucked inside a bend of the Mississippi River. At one time it had been quite valuable, but in recent years it had suffered from damage and neglect. By 1869 its value had dropped to just $10 per acre.[44]

Charles I. Field managed the family's Mississippi holdings. His assessment of Melrose was anything but cheery. The levee was collapsing, he informed Lizinka in 1865, the fencing was rotten, and the fields were flooded and required ditching. In short, he concluded, the place was "almost an entire wreck." Campbell Brown wished to dispose of the property. Rather than sell it at a loss, he determined to first improve it, then sell it or lease it at a profit.[45] Family responsibilities and a budding legal career in Tennessee, however, prevented him from making any improvements to the property until 1869.

Meanwhile General Ewell rented Tarpley, a 412-acre plantation just a few miles downriver from Melrose in Washington County. He learned about the property from Capt. William F. Randolph, who had commanded his cavalry escort during the war. Randolph seems to have taken over management of Melrose upon Field's death in 1867. In December 1868 he informed Ewell that a man named Robert M. Carter was offering to lease Tarpley at $8 per acre. Randolph predicted that the land could produce as much as one bale of cotton per acre. With cotton prices then ranging between 13 and 20 cents a pound, Ewell stood to make as much as $30,000.[46]

Of course expenses would eat up most of that amount. In addition to renting the land, Ewell would have to pay, feed, and clothe four dozen farmhands; hire a full-time manager; buy and feed mules and oxen; and maintain a cotton gin and other equipment. Even under ideal circumstances, he could not expect to clear more than $10,000 on his investment, and circumstances were seldom ideal. Bad weather, a broken levee, infestation by boll weevils, or a shortage of laborers at picking season could ruin all or part of a crop, leaving its owner deeply in debt. In short, cotton was a risky business, promising a handsome profit to those who could avoid its perils but bringing financial ruin to those who could not.[47]

Ewell was a gambler when it came to finances, though, and in December 1868 he signed an agreement with Carter to rent Tarpley for the coming calendar year. He engaged Randolph to manage the property for him. According to the terms of their agreement, Randolph would hire the hands, oversee the day-to-day work on the plantation, keep accounts, and generally look out for Ewell's interests. In return Ewell agreed to split the profits equally with Randolph up to $6,000. If profits exceeded that amount, Ewell would get two-thirds of the balance, and Randolph one-third.[48]

Ewell kept close tabs on his investment. In January, June, and November 1869 he made trips to Mississippi to check on the property, staying for weeks and months at a time. He had lost a fortune at the Patagonia Mine back in the 1850s because others had mismanaged his investment, and he was not about to let that happen at Tarpley.[49] Perhaps because of his close oversight, Tarpley produced a bumper crop in 1869. Randolph boasted that they had the best cotton in the county and optimistically predicted that they would harvest a minimum of 400 bales.[50] But at the height of the picking season, bad weather set in. Violent rains lashed the countryside in December, interrupting the harvest. Ewell tried to coax his black laborers into the fields, but they refused to go. For two weeks he watched as rain drenched the countryside and his cotton rotted on the stalks. "My prospects at Tarpley are considerably darker than a month since," he wrote Lizinka discouragingly. "For the month [of] Decr. there have been incessant & violent rains allowing . . . but two days picking & then the darkies stopped work.

We have lost fully 100 bales dropped & rotting on the ground while there are nearly that number still unpicked."

Ewell had shipped 110 bales to market when the rain commenced. One hundred more had been picked and were ready to be ginned. "The profit rests with those in the field," he wrote, "& I fear there is but little hope of getting the most of that out. The negroes are all drunk & spending what money they have in trinkets whiskey & horses. . . . As for any hope of raising cotton after the next few years with negro labor as now organized, I think it hopeless. Here the only good weather for 4 weeks they spend in drinking although we are losing hundreds of dollars by their neglect." The experience prompted Ewell to look again into hiring immigrants (Chinese and Scandinavian laborers) to work his fields, but as before he found the costs of transporting them prohibitive. Like it or not, he would have to stick with the workers he had.[51]

Because of the pickers' refusal to work in the rain, Ewell was able to harvest only 300 of the 400 bales grown at Tarpley that year. He was disappointed, but not daunted. Even at just 300 bales he had made enough profit to persuade him to lease the land for a second year. But Randolph beat him to the punch. When Ewell approached Robert Carter about leasing Tarpley again in 1870, he discovered his erstwhile manager had already leased the land for himself. Ewell consequently found himself without either a plantation or a manager.[52]

Undeterred, he looked for a new place to plant his cotton. This time, however, he wanted to buy the land, not simply rent it. Campbell Brown was astonished. He had been pouring thousands of dollars into Melrose to improve the property in hopes of selling it. The idea that someone else would willingly put themselves in that same fix struck him as crazy. "For what on earth he wishes a permanent investment in a country, which he never visits without cursing it, I can't imagine," Brown wrote to his mother, "or why he is willing to change a safe investment for a risky one, unless for the excitement, which is wearing him out as it is, & would wear out anybody. But it is of no use for you or me to argue that our position here is different. We are but 'throwing the helve after the hatchet,' he is buying a hatchet & helve to try his luck with. In other words," he concluded, "we have the land & must lose it or use it. He wants to buy, in order to use it or lose it."

Before Ewell purchased land, however, Tarpley again became available. Randolph was unable to raise enough money to rent the place, leaving the door open for Ewell to take it for a second year. The general jumped at the chance and again hired Randolph to manage the plantation for him. Brown continued to disapprove. His stepfather had been lucky to break even in 1869, he insisted, and he would almost certainly lose money if he was foolish enough to plant cotton again in 1870. "Gen'l. won't believe his success at Tarpley was almost a miracle," he told his mother, "but *I will*."[53]

Lizinka meanwhile was becoming increasingly dissatisfied with Spring Hill. The rural neighborhood offered nothing in the way of society, and despite Campbell's improvements two years earlier, the farmhouse remained old and drafty. Lizinka pressed the general to buy her a more comfortable house somewhere else—in Nashville perhaps, or maybe Virginia—but he refused. For three years he had worked tirelessly to rebuild Spring Hill, and now that the farm was finally turning a profit, he was not about to sell it and start over someplace else.[54] Since the general refused to leave Spring Hill, Lizinka determined to remodel the house. Early in 1869 she drew up plans to enlarge the farmhouse and alter some of its existing rooms. She sought the general's advice on the project, but he refused to have anything to do with it. "R. wont say a word," Lizinka complained to Campbell, "and I have to decide every-thing for myself but I'll do it—& do it vigorously too."[55]

Construction on the house began in December 1869. The job got off to a bad start when the contractor accidentally destroyed a railroad car full of supplies. After that, workers installed two ugly oriole windows in the garret against Lizinka's expressed wishes, failed to finish the basement, and used the wrong type of wood on the porch and in several of the new rooms. "I have been disappointed in almost every particular," Lizinka sadly admitted. It was the timing of the job rather than the poor workmanship that distressed her most, however. Hattie was pregnant, and in a few weeks she was expected to arrive at Spring Hill to deliver her baby. With half a dozen workers hammering nails, sawing boards, and plastering walls, there was no way Lizinka would be able to make her daughter comfortable.[56]

In addition to overseeing construction of the house, Lizinka had to manage the farming operations at Spring Hill and send men, mules, and supplies to General Ewell in Mississippi to keep Tarpley and Melrose running. The stress of these responsibilities finally became too much for her. On 19 December she wrote to her husband a dispirited letter urging him to come home as soon as he had concluded his business in Mississippi. General Ewell had intended to return to Spring Hill in time for Christmas, but "important pecuniary interests" made it necessary for him stay in Mississippi into the new year. He was then supervising the work at Melrose. Once Campbell sent someone down to relieve him there, he told Lizinka, he planned to return to Tarpley for a few days, then take a quick business trip to New Orleans. "Just now Melrose is all that keeps me down here," he told her.[57]

The letter touched off an angry response. Lizinka's first husband had frequently neglected her on the pretense of taking care of Melrose, and now General Ewell seemed to be doing the same. It was one thing to be looking after his own interests at Tarpley, but Melrose did not even belong to him! In a series of wild, disjointed missives Lizinka accused her husband of neglecting Spring Hill in favor of Melrose and of leaving her in the "singularly uncomfortable & unladylike position" of having to take care of the Tennessee farm herself. "[I] hope you will make enough money at Tarpley to pay you for all the pain & mortification your absence has caused me," she wrote reproachfully. "I *wonder* sometimes whether I'm taken now for a lady or a washerwoman. I have tried to write amiably but I cannot. My feelings are too bitter & my mortification too great." [58]

Lizinka's anger peaked on 3 January 1870 when a worker who had just returned from Melrose innocently told her that the general seemed happier there than at Spring Hill. "If that is so there is no more to be said," she wrote in anguish, "tho the taste is another incomprehensible thing to me, but of one thing you may be certain & I can't stand this kind of life & rather than undergo another five weeks similar to the last I'd sell Melrose at $5⁰⁰ an acre or give it away. . . . If it is possible you like to stay at Melrose you can stay & leave me here to attend to business seldom expected from any woman however narrow the circumstances of the family, but I won't wear myself out at it any more." She then laid down an ultimatum: "If you choose to stay at Melrose & let business here go to the dogs do so, but I'll stay here now until Hattie's visit is over & then if you decide to stay away months at a time I'll just go somewhere else, where I can have quiet & rest. . . . I won't stay here. O how I hate it." [59]

Ewell had departed for New Orleans by the time Lizinka's letters reached Tarpley, and he did not get them until his return a few days later. He started for Tennessee without delay, arriving sometime near the middle of the month. Hattie reached Spring Hill about the same time. On 23 January 1870 she gave birth to a daughter whom she named Anne Lucas Turner. The family called her Nancy. [60] Ewell stayed at Spring Hill just long enough to assuage his wife's injured feelings, then returned to Mississippi to complete his business. After that, he continued on to Mobile, Alabama, to sell some mules to Adm. Raphael Semmes, and to New Orleans to take advantage of the "vapor baths," which he hoped might soothe his neuralgia. [61]

While in the Crescent City, Ewell attended worship services at Trinity Church, where Bishop Leonidas Polk had once presided. He shared a pew with Gens.

Cadmus Wilcox and James Longstreet. Longstreet had allied himself with the Republican Party after the war and was consequently scorned by most Southerners. As Ewell slid in beside Longstreet, he felt the eyes of the congregation upon him. "I thought I could see a good many scowling glances thrown at me in church," he told his wife, "taking me I suppose for a Northern officer." After the service Ewell called on some female acquaintances in the city. The women expressed astonishment that he had associated with Longstreet, though after some discussion they acknowledged that the principles that the general advocated were now being adopted by others. Longstreet had simply been the first. "The fact is," wrote Ewell, "most people seem to want to quarrel with some one & dont know with whom. . . . All in talking of Longstreet regret that people took the course they did in tabooing him & I believe if it were to go over again they would not follow the same plan as regards him." [62]

On his way back to Tennessee, Ewell stopped at Melrose to see Campbell. Melrose's farmhouse was under repair, and Brown was staying at the home of Maj. Gen. Carter L. Stevenson. Ewell and Stevenson were old friends, having known each other since their days at West Point. Though a Virginian, Stevenson had moved to Mississippi after the war and rented a 200-acre plantation known as "Salona." Like Tarpley, Salona had been carved from Robert Carter's "Woodstock" estate. For the next two years Stevenson and Ewell would be neighbors and business associates. Stevenson provided Ewell farmhands for Melrose and Tarpley, and Ewell provided Stevenson mules for Salona. [63]

Ewell exchanged greetings with his old friend, then rode with Campbell to Melrose. The young man had cleared 350 acres and was ready to begin cultivation. He initially put in 30 acres of corn, 50 acres of cotton, and 2 acres of sorghum. As the year progressed, he cleared additional acreage and planted as much as 400 acres of cotton and 150 acres of corn. He might have put in even more could he have found laborers to do the work. [64] Restoring Melrose to a productive plantation was not without cost. More than once General and Mrs. Ewell had to advance him money to keep the place going. They did so without complaint, the general even going so far as to sell some stock he had in the B&O Railroad to raise the necessary funds. He also loaned money to Stevenson and to Maj. Asher W. Garber, the former commander of the Staunton Artillery. [65]

Ewell spent much of 1870 in Mississippi overseeing work at Tarpley and Melrose. To make up for his prolonged absences from Spring Hill, he took his wife on a summer trip to New York. The couple stopped briefly in Louisville, Kentucky, where Ewell visited with Philip St. George Cooke, his commander in the

Old Army, then continued east to New York City and Niagara Falls. They returned to Spring Hill in August.[66]

Ewell returned to Mississippi in time to supervise the cotton harvest. He stopped first at Melrose, then continued downriver to Tarpley. The cotton at both plantations looked splendid. At Tarpley the hands had already picked 100 bales and ginned 38. Within two weeks that amount would double. Barring bad weather, Ewell foresaw no difficulty in clearing 300 bales that season. He wrote Lizinka optimistically that it was "A Promising Land, if not the Land of Promise."[67]

Promises are easily broken, though, and so it was in this case. At the height of the picking season, Ewell's cotton gin broke down, forcing him to stop ginning until he could get parts to fix it. Once the machine was back in order, he had to run it twenty-four hours a day to make up for lost time. To add to his troubles, his workers began acting up. Once the cotton blossomed, it was necessary to pick it promptly or it would rot on the stalks. The field hands understood this. They not only demanded higher wages during harvest season but also delighted in not coming to work just when the cotton crop was at its peak. It was enough to drive a man crazy.[68]

Then there was the problem of finding a good manager. William Randolph had started the year as Ewell's manager, but at some point he left Tarpley to watch over Woodstock. Ewell was not sorry to see him go. Randolph knew cotton, but he was lazy and had no head for bookkeeping. Moreover, he was officious, meddlesome, and a bore. Ewell was well rid of him. Nevertheless his departure left the general in a bind. For a while he depended on a fellow named Jackson. Unlike Randolph, Jackson was energetic and a good accountant, but he was also a tyrant. If left in charge, he would drive off all of the general's workers. Ewell could ill afford that, especially during the harvest season. He consequently stayed at Tarpley himself until he found someone more reliable to take over management of the farm.[69]

Tarpley had no house. When Ewell was there, he slept under canvas on the banks of the Mississippi River with a black worker named Charley. Campbell Brown described the setting for his mother. "His tent is quite comfortable & commands a beautiful view of the river. Being in a bend where the river runs directly *North*, the sun *rises* across it from him, & the sunrise I saw there was one of the finest I ever looked at. His goose that Charley is stuffing, & his turkeys are in large boxes near the tent-door—a piece of beef hangs to a tree near by." For Ewell it was an idyllic existence—or would have been were it not for Randolph. Each day the former cavalryman came over from Woodstock. He stayed at Tarpley for hours, offering gratuitous advice and making a nuisance of himself generally. Ewell found his presence intolerable, but he was too polite to tell him to leave.[70]

Ewell remained at Tarpley until the picking season ended. Remembering Lizinka's violent reaction the previous winter, he assured her that he would not stay away any longer than necessary. "I will if the weather continues good, finish I think, picking in two weeks," he wrote her in November 1870. "I dont want to lose anything by the worthlessness of others & am willing to put up with an inconvenience. But if you are worried by more than you can attend to, I am willing to give up any or all. I think I see daylight beginning."[71]

Lizinka was more tolerant of her husband's absence in 1870 than she had been in 1869. "It seems to do him so much good to go down there & turn savage for awhile that I cannot object to it," she wrote Campbell from Spring Hill, "tho' I think this place suffers very much from it." Even when he was at Spring Hill, the general could not keep his mind off Tarpley, an indication to Lizinka of "the obstinate if not incurable nature of his cotton fever."[72]

Ewell's preoccupation with Tarpley was less a matter of taste than of finance. He had a small fortune tied up in the plantation, and if he had a bad crop, he stood to lose heavily. He therefore felt it necessary to manage the plantation himself until he could find a trustworthy person to do it for him. Hugh Reynolds filled the bill. Hugh was the son of Ewell's Baltimore friend and kinsman, William Reynolds. At the Ewells' invitation, Hugh had come to work at Spring Hill late in 1869. Though young, he impressed his relatives as "amazingly steady and industrious," and in 1870 Campbell Brown hired him to manage Melrose. Brown moved to Melrose later that year, freeing Reynolds to manage Tarpley, which General Ewell had just leased for a third consecutive year. Hugh was hardworking and reliable and unlike Randolph could be depended on to do a good job. As a result, Ewell made just one trip to Tarpley in 1871.[73]

Under Reynolds's capable management, Tarpley produced its third successful crop in as many years. Ewell's hands picked approximately 250 bales of cotton in 1871, bringing him a profit of $3,600. Reynolds got one-third of that amount, leaving Ewell just $2,400. It was a small return, thought Brown, considering that his stepfather had invested more than $8,000 in the property. Actually Ewell was fortunate to have done that well. During the year a broken levee had temporarily flooded half of his fields, an infestation of cotton worm had damaged a portion of his crop, and a hailstorm had killed many of his plants. He was lucky he had not lost his shirt.[74]

As 1871 came to an end, Ewell had to decide whether to renew his lease on

Tarpley, buy a plantation of his own, or get out of the cotton business altogether. His thoughts on the matter changed from day to day, but in the end he chose to get out. It was a difficult decision and for a time threw him into depression. Although he did not particularly like planting cotton, the high-stakes nature of the business had an addictive effect on him that Lizinka likened to gambling. She believed her husband would never be happy until he owned a cotton plantation of his own, and she may have been right. "Cotton fever" was in his blood.[75]

CHAPTER 32

Peace

As 1872 dawned, Dick Ewell could look back on his brief career in agriculture with satisfaction. He had taken Lizinka's dilapidated Tennessee farm and in just three years had made it a premier stock farm. Turning his attention to cotton, he had then leased a plantation in Mississippi and made a profit there for three consecutive years despite recurrent floods, broken cotton gins, and obdurate field hands. It was a record of which he could be justly proud.[1]

Farming left him little time for other pursuits. Nevertheless, Ewell participated in a modest way in a few local and civic organizations. He was president of the Columbia Female Academy's board of trustees, a communicant at St. Peter's Episcopal Church in Columbia, and president of the Maury County Agricultural Society.[2]

The Columbia Female Academy was Lizinka's creation. Highly educated herself, she wished to do something to raise the standard of female education in her neighborhood. When the local girls' school came on the market in December 1871, she snapped it up. William Stoddert agreed to teach one of the classes, and Campbell Brown accepted a position on the board of trustees. Although General Ewell believed that "a flock of sheep would pay better than [a flock] of girls & be easier managed," he too agreed to serve on the board.[3]

Veterans' organizations took only a small amount of Ewell's time. He was a member of the Memphis Chapter of the Confederate Historical and Relief Association, served as a vice-president in the Lee Memorial Association, and financially supported several charitable Southern causes.[4] The Lee Memorial Association was formed in 1870 for the purpose of erecting a suitable monument to Gen. Robert E. Lee, who had died in October of that year. Ewell gladly accepted a position on the committee. Although he felt that Lee had been wrong in transferring him from the Army of Northern Virginia in 1864, he did not hold a grudge. On the contrary, he had offered to donate $500 to Washington College in 1868 on the condition that the money be used to augment Lee's salary. (Lee was president of the institution at that time.) The gesture had elicited the following response from his former commander:

Washington College, Lexington, Va, March 3, 1868.
My Dear General:

I have just seen a letter from Genl Lill[e]y stating that you had given $500 to the Endowment of Washington College, with the condition that it be applied to increasing my salary. This generous donation on your part was not necessary to convince me of the lively interest you retained for the Institutions of your native state, or of your friendly consideration for myself, & I fully appreciate the kind motives which prompted you thus to appropriate it. But when I tell you that I already receive a larger amount from the College than my services are worth, you will see the propriety of my not consenting that it should be increased.

The great want of the College is more extensive buildings, suitable libraries, cabinets, philosophical & chemical apparatus, &c. &c. A liberal endowment will enable it to enlarge the means of its usefulness, to afford facilities of education to worthy young men who might not otherwise obtain one, & as we must look to the rising generation for the restoration of the Country, it can do more good in this way than in any other.

I thought it right to make you this explanation. I hope now that your care & toils are over, that your health, under the pleasing influences of your present life, has been greatly improved. For my own part I much enjoy the charms of civil life, & find too late that I have wasted the best years of my existence.

I beg that you will remember me most kindly to Mrs. Ewell, Mrs. Turner, & Major Brown, and believe me truly your friend
R E Lee.[5]

Lee suffered a fatal heart attack two and one-half years later. Hearing the news, Ewell remarked to Campbell Brown, "The greatest man in America lies dying in Lexington today." Lee died on 12 October 1870. While the South mourned his passing, the Lee Memorial Association set about raising funds to erect a monument over his grave. Ewell was put in charge of collecting money from Confederate veterans living in Tennessee. He hoped to get an average of one dollar from each Confederate veteran in the state, but he fell far short of that goal. Few Tennessee veterans had served in the Army of Northern Virginia, and those who did had little money to spare. At least one suspicious Reb refused to contribute because he believed that the project was a clever fund-raising ploy for Washington College. In spite of the Volunteer State's poor showing, the association raised sufficient funds to commission sculptor Edward Valentine to create a recumbent statue of the general.[6]

After the war Ewell received numerous requests for information from people writing histories of the Civil War. The first appeal came from Lee himself. On 31 July 1865 Lee sent letters to his generals asking them to submit to him copies of reports covering the final year of the war. He wished to use the reports to write a history of the Army of Northern Virginia. At that point Ewell had been out of prison for less than a month. It would be another five months before he finally got around to writing his report of Sailor's Creek. By then Lee had accepted the position as president of Washington College and had set the project aside.[7]

Other individuals also asked for information. Edward Pollard, author and former editor of the Richmond *Examiner*, wrote to Ewell asking for biographical data and other information for his book, *Lee and His Lieutenants*; J. William Jones requested material about Stonewall Jackson for his book *Lee Memorial*; historian Benson Lossing asked for facts about the burning of Richmond for his upcoming history of the Civil War; and Jed Hotchkiss wrote to Ewell asking him to endorse his book *Battle Fields of Virginia*. At one point Ewell considered writing an article himself. Henry B. Dawson was publishing a series of papers titled "The Conflicts of the War" for *The Historical Magazine*, and he asked the general to pen an account of the 1861 skirmish at Fairfax Court House. Ewell put a few words to paper, but if he ever submitted the article, it was never printed.[8]

Family and business kept Ewell too busy to dwell on events of the past. By 1872 he was the patriarch of a rapidly growing family. Hattie had four girls, and Campbell had three boys—all six years of age or younger. (Hattie and Campbell would have seven more children between them.)[9] Like Lizzie, Campbell named one of his sons Richard Ewell. The general protested, of course, but privately he was delighted. "It was long before he ceased to complain of the injustice done the boy," Campbell told Lizzie in later years, "but he was very fond of him. So it was with your child. He insisted it should have been named after your Father, but he was always apparently fond of it, and spoke of it affectionately."[10]

Ewell doted on the children, particularly the older ones. He took the boys on horseback rides around Spring Hill and squired the girls about in a carriage, stopping every now and then so that they could hop out and collect cotton balls from the fields. Nothing distressed him more than to see the children suffer. Hattie's oldest daughter, Lily, once misbehaved during a visit to Spring Hill and received a spanking from her mother in an upstairs room of the house. General Ewell heard the child crying. Not knowing the cause, he insisted that Lizinka go upstairs to see that the girl was all right. (He undoubtedly would have gone himself, but the loss of his leg made it difficult for him to climb the stairs.) On another occasion Lily playfully struck Ewell on the face with a stick. Hattie threatened to spank her, but the general intervened on Lily's behalf, telling Hattie that "if I punished her on his account he would be very much hurt & that she had done nothing wrong." The children appreciated the general's love and returned it with interest. But Lily had one question: "If General Ewell likes her what makes him say D——— old Dutch to her?" [11]

With a growing family, a successful farm, a good reputation, and a sizable fortune, Ewell looked forward to a bright future in 1872. If he had one concern, it was his health. In recent months his neuralgic attacks had stepped up, and he complained of pain in his leg. His headaches were becoming more frequent, and he tired more easily than before. He also seemed to be getting thinner, if that was possible. In short, the years were catching up with him. [12]

Typically, Ewell refused to slow down. He continued to work long hours on the farm and went outside in all kinds of weather. On 22 December 1871 he rode with Tom Turner to Hamilton Place to deliver Christmas presents to Susie Brown. The mercury in the thermometer registered ten degrees above zero. "I think the day they came down here was the coldest I have felt this season," Susie informed her husband. "The Genl. seemed to be suffering very much." Ewell shook off the chill, though, and ten days later ventured out again, this time to pay his New Year's respects to Susie's mother and other ladies in the area. A friend who accompanied him on the excursion thought that the general "enjoyed the pleasure thus afforded him as much as any young man in full health and unmaimed would have done." Undoubtedly he did. Age may have made inroads on Ewell's health, but it had not dulled his social inclinations one whit. [13]

But the general's time was running out. In the first week of January 1872 the weather turned "damp, raw & unpleasant," spreading sickness across the land. At Spring Hill, where both the Turner and the Brown families (minus Campbell) happened to be visiting, five people fell ill with fevers: Lucius Brown, Julia Turner, Susie Brown, a young relative named George Campbell, and the Ewells' shepherd, James Monroe. [14]

The general came next. On Monday, 8 January, he took a ride around the farm and became chilled. He wrapped himself in blankets and lay in front of the fire until tea time, then retired to his bedroom on the first floor of the house. By the end of the day his air passages had become inflamed and he was running a temperature. A physician who examined Ewell that evening diagnosed the illness as "catarrhal fever." When the doctor returned the next morning, he changed his diagnosis to pneumonia of the right lung. This put a more serious aspect on the illness, but he assured the family that there was nothing to worry about: the case was mild. With rest and proper care the patient would soon recover.[15]

In fact Ewell did rebound quickly. On Tuesday he showed significant improvement, and by Wednesday he was feeling so much better that he threw open his windows to admit fresh air into the room. That was a fatal mistake. The cold air rekindled his disease and checked his recovery. By Thursday morning he was in worse shape than before. For the first time, family members began to fear that he might not recover. Lizinka and William kept vigil by his bedside that night and in the morning summoned Dr. Maddin, a pneumonia specialist from Nashville. The general's condition continued to decline. His breathing became labored. By Friday night, wrote Hattie, "he was taken with violent pain in the liver which ascended to the lungs." To those sitting nervously by his bedside, "he seemed in imminent danger of death."[16]

Dr. Maddin and the other physicians offered no hope. In contrast to the rosy prognosis given earlier, they now predicted General Ewell's speedy demise. They told family members on Saturday, 13 January, that he had just twenty hours to live.[17] Sensing that the disease might prove fatal, Ewell dictated a codicil to his will. In the original document, he had directed that his entire estate go to his wife and her heirs. He had written that on 4 June 1863, one week after his marriage, at a time when most of Lizinka's property was in Union hands. Now that the war was over and his wife had regained title to her property, she had no need of his money; consequently, Ewell decided to disperse it to members of his own family.

In his codicil he directed that his brother Ben and his nephew Richard Ewell Scott each receive $3,000, and that his sister Elizabeth and his brother William receive $2,000 apiece. He set aside smaller sums to repay the kindness of those who had befriended him and his family. Fifteen hundred dollars went to the family of his late Uncle William Stoddert, which had raised Tom Ewell back in the 1830s, and $1,000 went to the grandson of his cousin Dr. Jesse Ewell, whose family had cared for him after his amputation in 1862. Finally, the general stipulated that Campbell's son Ewell get his shotgun and that $500 of his estate go toward erecting a monument over his mother's grave in Williamsburg, Virginia. For some reason this last provision was never carried out.[18]

The general did not die as quickly as anticipated. In fact he rallied so strongly on Sunday, 14 January, that by the beginning of the week the doctors began to entertain hopes that he might pull through. Throughout the ordeal Lizinka and William remained faithfully at his side, tending to his every need. Lizinka's devotion ultimately cost her her life. On Monday, the very day that the general was exhibiting signs of recovery, she came down with his disease. She felt nauseous and, as the day progressed, complained of pains in her side and shoulders. Concerned family members put her to bed in an upstairs room and assigned a relative, Nannie Campbell, to take care of her. Ewell's seventy-three-year-old aunt, Rebecca Hubbard, and Hattie's eight-week-old baby, Harriot, fell ill about the same time. By mid-month as many as eight people at Spring Hill were sick.[19]

Death stalked the household. Susie Brown and little Harriot seemed on the verge of death, but both rallied. Instead, Lizinka was the first to perish. For five days she held her own, battling what doctors diagnosed as a case of "well developed acute pneumonia." She began to lose ground on Saturday, 20 January. That day she began experiencing pains to the liver, much as her husband had done eight days before. Doctors cupped her to ease her pain, but relief was fleeting. By midnight, 21 January, she was noticeably worse.

At no time was the bond of love between General Ewell and his wife stronger than in those final days. Rather than complaining of their own illnesses, each constantly inquired about the welfare of the other. "Not a fear, not a selfish motive, not a trace of any of the baser part of humanity appeared in either," Campbell Brown asserted. For both, the thought of dying was not half as distressing as the prospect of surviving the other. "Oh Hattie!" Lizinka once exclaimed to her daughter, "if I can only last as long as he does!" But she did not. The infection spread to her vital organs, and she sank rapidly. Her faith alone remained strong. She wanted to live, she said, but she was resigned to death if it was God's will. Over and over she prayed, "Not *my* will but Thine be done."[20]

Campbell reached Spring Hill on 22 January 1872. He had been at Melrose when he received a letter from Lizinka informing him of the sickness that had gripped the household and urging him to return home at once. He arrived twelve days later to find his mother on her deathbed and his wife and stepfather gravely ill. He went first to his mother, whose condition seemed most dire. Lizinka had given up hope of ever seeing her son again, and her face visibly brightened when he entered the room. She revived so much, in fact, that doctors who examined her at 11:00 A.M. thought she might make it through the day. But she was not as strong as she appeared. As soon as the doctors completed their examination, she suffered a relapse. Hattie was caring for her own sick child down the hall when she learned that her mother was failing. "I had barely time to reach her bedside from the next room when she breathed out her pure life, quietly & easily without a struggle," she wrote. "Her last words were 'God is very merciful.'"[21]

News of Lizinka's death spread quickly. The Tuesday edition of the Nashville *Republican Banner* carried the story, adding ominously "that General Ewell was not expected to live until this morning." Campbell Brown wired a brief but urgent message to Elizabeth Ewell: "Mr[s]. Ewell is dead. Tell Colonel Ewell to come to his brother immediately." [22]

The family did not immediately tell General Ewell of his wife's death for fear that the news would kill him. Not until the following night, when it appeared that he was failing, did they break the news to him. "He was dreadfully agitated," remembered William, "called for her picture to be hung around his neck, which he put over his heart, & seemed for a time to be dying himself." [23]

Attendants prepared Lizinka's body for burial. On Wednesday morning, 24 January, a train carried the casket to Nashville for interment in the city cemetery. Lizinka was buried in the Campbell family plot with her parents, her brother George, and her son Percy, who had died in 1853 at age ten. Before she was taken away, Ewell demanded to see her one last time. As her body was brought into the room, attendants lifted the general up so that he could behold her face. He gazed silently at her lifeless features, then whispered, "It is all right," and fell back onto his pillow. Although too weak to show much emotion, he expressed the wish that her funeral might be delayed for a day or two so that they might be buried together. In this he was disappointed. Lizinka was interred later that day. [24]

Death came quickly after that. William, an ordained minister in the Presbyterian Church, sat with his brother throughout the day. No one else was admitted into the room, the doctors deeming it "absolutely necessary" that the patient should not be disturbed. In spite of his feeble condition, Ewell's mind remained sharp. He asked William to tell Ben that he had always looked up to him as a father, and to tell Elizabeth that he had intended to write her once he got well. Mostly, though, he talked about his own approaching death. The day Ewell had fallen ill, he had been wearing a pair of surplus U.S. Army pantaloons. The blue trousers were thinner than the pants he normally wore, a circumstance that he believed had contributed to his illness. "After all my fighting against the United States so long," he remarked, "it is strange that an old pair of infantry pantaloons should kill me at last."

Like Lizinka, he faced death with Christian resignation. That his faith remained strong was no thanks to Tasker Gantt, who in recent months had sent him agnostic books designed to turn his heart from God. In the end, though, Ewell rejected his cousin's sophistry. Speaking to Tom Turner earlier that day, he remarked, "Captain, those books of Gantt's are all stuff. I don't know how it all is, but the mercy of God is greater than the mercy of men." He maintained that simple belief to the last. Writing the day of his brother's death, William affirmed that "he had died in the full hope of the Gospel." [25]

Ewell seemed particularly concerned about the disposition of Lizinka's property. In her will Lizinka had left him half of her estate, bequeathing the rest to Campbell and Hattie. Ewell, by like token, had directed that most of his estate go to her. With Lizinka's death, however, Ewell's brothers and sisters became his legal heirs. As such they could lay claim to the property that he had inherited from her estate. Lizinka would not have approved of that, and neither did he. In the most emphatic manner possible, Ewell told William that no member of his family should have anything to do with Lizinka's estate. Instead, his share of her property was to go to Campbell and Hattie, where it belonged. His brothers and sister abided by his wishes. [26]

As for funeral arrangements, he said that he wanted a simple ceremony in which "his comrades and friends, if they desired, might show their respect in a plain and unostentatious way." He did not want a monument over his grave, just a headstone stating that he had been a lieutenant general in the Confederate army. Above all, he insisted that nothing disrespectful to the United States government be inscribed upon his tomb. [27]

Campbell returned from Lizinka's funeral that evening accompanied by the Reverend Dr. George Beckett, the Ewells' minister at St. Peter's Episcopal Church in Columbia, Tennessee. Two of the general's friends, Col. George W. Polk and Major Yeatman, also came along. At 8:30 P.M. Hattie led the group into General Ewell's room for one last communion service. Ewell noticed the sorrow in his stepdaughter's eyes. How much like her mother she looked! "Poor thing," he said, then he asked her if she thought he would make it through the night. Hattie saw no point in giving him false hope. Quietly she answered, "No, general." "I would rather die," he answered, "but am willing to live if it is God's will." Beckett administered the sacrament. When the ceremony was over, Hattie bent down to kiss the dying man, but he turned away. "I understood his feeling & stopped," she later wrote, "& that was the last time I ever saw him." [28]

Nine o'clock passed, then ten. Midnight came, bringing with it a new day: 25 January 1872. In two weeks General Ewell would be fifty-five years old. His breathing was harder now. As the hours passed, he complained frequently about fatigue and oppression to his lungs. At times his voice failed him, and he had to make his wishes known by signs. The end was near. [29]

Campbell Brown, Colonel Polk, and Ewell's physician, Dr. James L. Hardin, stood vigil in the room. Sometime after midnight William Stoddert and Tom

Turner joined the deathwatch. At one o'clock the general's mind, which had been remarkably clear throughout his illness, grew clouded. He became lightheaded and mumbled incoherently—not about some distant scene of battle, but about his brother Ben. After a few minutes he closed his eyes and drifted off to sleep. His breathing became softer, and at 1:30 A.M. it ceased altogether. The warrior was at rest.[30]

News of General Ewell's death spread quickly across the land. The day after his demise, the Nashville *Republican Banner* published a story titled "EWELL: Death of a Great Confederate Commander." The Nashville *Union and American*, with less care for accuracy, ran an obituary with headline "Gen. Robert Stoddard Ewell." Newspapers in New York, Richmond, and elsewhere picked up the story of Ewell's death and modified it to suit the tastes of their readers. Southern papers naturally focused on the general's career as a Confederate officer. Northern papers cited his request that nothing critical of the United States be inscribed on his tomb as evidence that he had repented of his rebellion against the national government.[31]

Northern and Southern newspapers alike praised Ewell for his valor and unimpeachable character. The article in the Memphis *Daily Appeal* was typical. "His fame and deeds are inscribed upon every page of the history of the South through the four year's war," it asserted. "His honesty of purpose was attested by heroic self-devotion; his valor, by his wounds; his genius for war, by brilliant achievements. . . . His last words attest his devotion to his country, and his tombstone will attest the fact, however ardent his affection for the South, it was finally measured, when the clangor of arms was silenced, by an undying patriotism that compassed a continent." Five hundred miles away, D. H. Hill extolled Ewell's character in his newspaper, *The Southern Home*. "There was no purer patriot in the South, no more devoted friend, no more exemplary citizen," his article concluded. "All his rare gifts and accomplishments were sanctified by a living piety, which influenced every thought and act. Truly a prince and a great man has fallen in our beloved South."[32]

Gen. Joseph E. Johnston wrote Benjamin Ewell five days after the general's death. "I have learned from the newspapers with much sorrow, of the death of my friend your brother Genl. Ewell," Johnson began. "I was prepared for the intelligence when it came, for it had been announced a few days before, that he was suffering under a severe attack of Newmonia [*sic*]. And it seemed to me unlikely that a constitution so impaired as his had been by wounds and the exposure of military service, could bear up under such a complaint. If he had been otherwise unknown to me, I should have been interested in him as your brother," he

The Ewells' tomb in the Old City Cemetery, Nashville, Tennessee (Donald C. Pfanz)

continued. "But association with him in camp and in the field, had enabled me to appreciate his high military qualities, and estimable professional ones. Of all my comrades in the war, there is none but yourself whose death I should have regretted more." [33]

General Ewell was buried on 26 January. A special railroad car carrying his body and some six dozen relatives and friends arrived in Nashville shortly after 10:00 A.M. The coffin was placed in a hearse and carried to Christ Church, followed by a procession of twenty-two carriages. The funeral service was scheduled to take place at 11:00 A.M., but crowds thronged the church long before the appointed hour. Many mourners, unable to secure a place inside the building, had to stand outside.

Ewell's friend the Right Reverend Bishop C. T. Quintard conducted the funeral service, assisted by the church rector, the Reverend William Graham. The pallbearers included some of Nashville's most distinguished citizens: Governor John C. Brown, Col. Thomas Claiborne, and Gens. Lucius E. Polk, Robert D. Lilley, Bushrod R. Johnson, E. Kirby Smith, Samuel R. Anderson, William B. Bate, and William H. Jackson. When the service concluded, Ewell's body was carried to the Nashville City Cemetery and buried beside that of his wife.[34] In accordance with his wishes, the inscription on his tomb stated just the essential facts of his existence:

RICHARD STODDERT EWELL
Third Son of
DR. THOMAS & ELIZABETH STODDERT
EWELL
was Born at Georgetown D.C.
Feb. 8, 1817,
& died at Spring Hill Tenn.
Jan. 25, 1872.

A shorter inscription on the reverse side of the tomb added simply that he had been a lieutenant general in the Confederate army. Lizinka's inscription was chiseled beside her husband's and was likewise brief. Other than those few words, the tombstone was blank. It contained no verses of heavenly or human inspiration or any discussion of its occupants' virtues and attainments—just a solitary word wreathed in laurel: "Peace."

The Right Arm of Jackson

In going to war in 1861, Ewell had risked everything for the South. He did so not because he agreed with its principles or from any hope of gain or advancement. Like most soldiers who fought in the Civil War, he simply followed his state. Once he had made that decision, he never looked back. Frustration was his greatest enemy in those early days. Ewell was a born fighter, yet in the first year of the war he saw very little action. At First Manassas and, later, on the upper Rappahannock and at Conrad's Store he found himself on the sidelines, little more than a spectator to the great events unfolding around him. He chafed and he fumed, all the while impatiently awaiting the day when he would have an opportunity to strike a blow for the Confederacy.

That day came on 23 May 1862, when Ewell's division stormed into Front Royal at the head of Jackson's Army of the Valley. The attack routed the Union First Maryland Regiment and set the stage for Nathaniel Banks's retreat from Winchester. From then until his wounding at Groveton, Ewell would be, to use D. H. Hill's phrase, "the right arm of Stonewall Jackson."[1] As Jackson's lieutenant, Ewell helped expel Banks from the Shenandoah Valley, drove the Pennsylvania Bucktails from the fence at Harrisonburg, parried Frémont's feeble attacks at Cross Keys, and turned the tide of battle at Port Republic. Jackson got the credit for these triumphs, and rightfully so, but Ewell's division did the lion's share of the fighting. As Jubal Early later observed, Jackson's victories in the Valley "would all be shorn of half their proportions if Ewell's name was blotted from the record. Jackson never made a demand upon his energy, courage, or skill that was not promptly honored."[2]

Ewell added to his laurels in the Seven Days battles outside Richmond and at Cedar Mountain. He led Jackson's flank march around Pope's rear and skillfully held back Hooker's division at Bristoe Station, enabling Jackson to destroy Pope's base of supply at Manassas Junction. Ewell's record up to the time he was wounded at Groveton was spotless. He was arguably the Army of Northern Virginia's best division commander up to that point. The fact that Jackson never had any serious complaint about Ewell and later recommended him to command the Second Corps speaks more eloquently of his abilities than praise in any formal report could have done.

Ewell did not perform as well under Lee. After the war, individuals surmised that the loss of his leg, his marriage to Lizinka, his formal acceptance of Christianity, or some combination of the three had impaired his fighting spirit. No one would have suggested such a thing in June 1863. At Second Winchester Ewell swept Robert Milroy from the Shenandoah Valley, then boldly led his corps to the outskirts of Harrisburg, Pennsylvania, the farthest north any Confederate general would get during the war. Jackson himself could not have done better.

But disappointment followed. At Gettysburg on 1 July, Ewell routed two corps of the Union army and garnered some 5,000 Federal prisoners. His decision not to attack Cemetery Hill, however, gave the Union army a good position from which to fight over the next two days. Although in retrospect the decision was probably correct and conformed to Lee's orders, Ewell was criticized for it thereafter.

Critics then and later accused Ewell of being indecisive, but no one has offered any credible evidence to back up such a claim. Faced with the dilemma of dislodging the Federals from Cemetery Hill without disobeying Lee's orders to avoid a general engagement, Ewell elected to maneuver the enemy from this strong position by having Johnson's division occupy Culp's Hill. Unfortunately, the plan failed because the Federals manned the hill before Johnson could do so. The decision seemed logical at the time, and he stuck by it. He did not waffle; he was not indecisive. In later years, as the Confederate defeat at Gettysburg took on greater significance, so, too, did Ewell's failure to take Cemetery Hill. Some Southerners, seeking explanations for why they lost the war, pointed to Gettysburg and blamed Ewell. Sadly, that has been his legacy ever since.

After Gettysburg the army's confidence in Ewell plummeted. The defeats at Bristoe Station and Rappahannock Station, though not Ewell's fault, seemed to confirm the soldiers' suspicions that he was not fit to command the corps. Ewell's fawning behavior toward his wife that fall added to that impression. It led the general to neglect his duties and made him look foolish in the eyes of his subordinates. That he had lost Lee's confidence became painfully obvious at Mine Run, when Lee adamantly refused to restore him to command until the battle was over. The writing was on the wall: unless Ewell could regain Lee's confidence, and quickly, his days in the Army of Northern Virginia were numbered.

The battle of the Wilderness should have redeemed Ewell's reputation. On 5 May 1864 he was at his best, shifting troops from one threatened sector to another with an experienced hand, and on 6 May he successfully turned Grant's right flank. Ewell successfully beat off the attacks of two Federal corps (three if one counts Burnside's feeble efforts on 6 May) and in the process inflicted many times more casualties on the Federals than he himself sustained. But ironically the battle only confirmed Lee's lack of confidence in him. John Gordon's slanted claims that Ewell missed a golden opportunity to roll up the Federal flank on 6 May convinced Lee that Ewell should have done more.

Spotsylvania sealed Ewell's fate with the army. In two weeks of desperate fighting, the Second Corps took a beating, losing roughly half its numbers. Ewell was alternately at his best and worst in the battle. He successfully rallied his troops after Upton's 10 May attack, but he lost his temper after the Federal breakthrough at the East Angle on 12 May and conducted a sloppy battle in the 19 May fighting at Harris Farm. When he became sick a few days later, Lee had him transferred to the Department of Richmond and turned the Second Corps over to Jubal Early.

To go from commanding Stonewall Jackson's corps to leading a ragtag collection of heavy artillery battalions, reserve units, and local defense troops was a heavy blow to Ewell, and he was understandably bitter. He swallowed his pride, however, and continued to serve the Confederacy to the best of his ability. The coming months tested his resourcefulness. As odds against the South increased, Lee drew defenders from the Richmond front to defend Petersburg, setting the stage for the Union breakthrough at Fort Harrison on 29 September 1864. Ewell rose to the occasion. In what was perhaps the greatest feat of his career, he held back the Army of the James with a handful of mostly third-rate troops, saving Richmond from capture. Had Jackson been in charge rather than Ewell, historians would have touted the battle as a military masterpiece. But Ewell was in command, not Jackson, and in the rush of events the episode was forgotten. Historians have all but ignored it since.

Appropriately, Ewell rejoined the Army of Northern Virginia for the final act of the war in Virginia. When Grant pierced Lee's lines at Petersburg on 2 April 1865, Lee ordered Ewell to evacuate Richmond and join him at Amelia Court House. Four days later, as the army trudged toward Appomattox, Philip Sheridan's cavalry penetrated a gap in the Confederate column, separating Ewell's and Dick Anderson's corps from the rest of the Confederate army. As ranking officer on the field, Ewell had three choices: he could surrender, he could try to cut his way through Sheridan's force, or he could attempt to escape by roads to the north.

Escaping the Federals, he must have reasoned, would be all but impossible, given the impaired condition of his command. Fighting Sheridan's men offered but little better chance of success.

In the end Ewell left the decision to Anderson, who opted to try and cut his way out. This was not a shirking of responsibility on his part, as some have argued, but rather deferring to the judgment of an officer who, by virtue of better information, was better equipped to make a difficult decision. Anderson's corps rather than Ewell's would have to make the attack. Who could better gauge the probable success of the venture than Anderson himself? But Anderson judged wrongly. The attack failed to crack Sheridan's lines, and by nightfall Ewell and his corps were prisoners of war. It was Ewell's last battle, and the only one as a commander that he ever lost.

Despite an enviable record, Ewell was not regarded as a successful commander. Col. Thomas H. Carter wrote that as an executive officer, Ewell was "unsurpassed," but the general opinion of his contemporaries was that he lacked the decision necessary for corps command. The reason for this is not clear. Perhaps it was because he had the misfortune of being Stonewall Jackson's successor, or maybe it was because he happened to command the Second Corps at a time when the tide of war was inevitably turning against the South. Whatever the reason, historians have written Ewell off as a failure. His record does not bear that out. While he was not in the same class as Lee or Jackson, he was as good as any other general in the Army of Northern Virginia and was considerably better than most.[3] Good or bad, he gave his all for the Confederacy. No man could have done more.

Ewell Family Genealogy

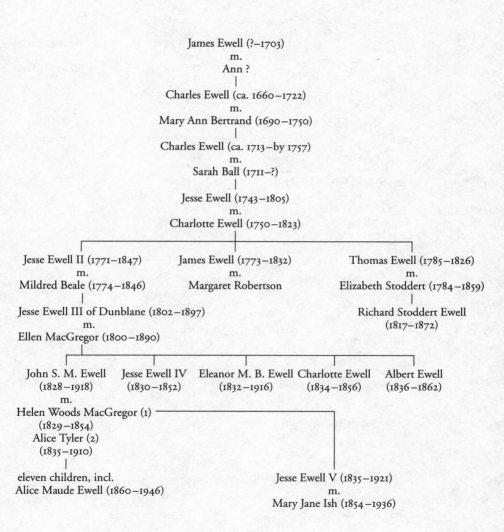

James Ewell (?–1703)
m.
Ann ?
|
Charles Ewell (ca. 1660–1722)
m.
Mary Ann Bertrand (1690–1750)
|
Charles Ewell (ca. 1713–by 1757)
m.
Sarah Ball (1711–?)
|
Jesse Ewell (1743–1805)
m.
Charlotte Ewell (1750–1823)

Jesse Ewell II (1771–1847)
m.
Mildred Beale (1774–1846)
|
Jesse Ewell III of Dunblane (1802–1897)
m.
Ellen MacGregor (1800–1890)

James Ewell (1773–1832)
m.
Margaret Robertson

Thomas Ewell (1785–1826)
m.
Elizabeth Stoddert (1784–1859)
|
Richard Stoddert Ewell
(1817–1872)

John S. M. Ewell
(1828–1918)
m.
Helen Woods MacGregor (1)
(1829–1854)
Alice Tyler (2)
(1835–1910)
|
eleven children, incl.
Alice Maude Ewell (1860–1946)

Jesse Ewell IV
(1830–1852)

Eleanor M. B. Ewell
(1832–1916)

Charlotte Ewell
(1834–1856)

Albert Ewell
(1836–1862)

Jesse Ewell V (1835–1921)
m.
Mary Jane Ish (1854–1936)

Stoddert Family Genealogy

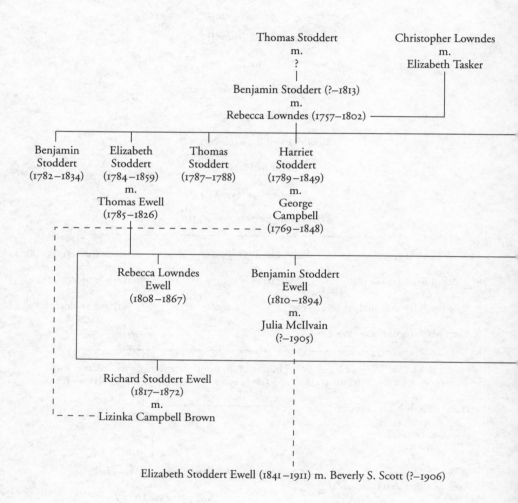

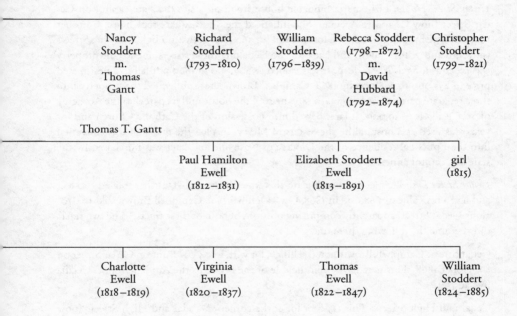

Nancy Stoddert m. Thomas Gantt

Richard Stoddert (1793–1810)

William Stoddert (1796–1839)

Rebecca Stoddert (1798–1872) m. David Hubbard (1792–1874)

Christopher Stoddert (1799–1821)

Thomas T. Gantt

Paul Hamilton Ewell (1812–1831)

Elizabeth Stoddert Ewell (1813–1891)

girl (1815)

Charlotte Ewell (1818–1819)

Virginia Ewell (1820–1837)

Thomas Ewell (1822–1847)

William Stoddert (1824–1885)

Lizinka's Landholdings

Lizinka's landholdings were extensive and spread out over a large area. Her property came from three main sources: her father, George Campbell; her brother, George Campbell Jr.; and her first husband, James Percy Brown. Below is a brief description of each property.

Nashville Lots

Cedar Street House: Lizinka's fashionable house stood opposite the state capitol on Cedar Street (now Charlotte Avenue). She inherited the 8,100-square-foot house from her brother. The building stood on a lot that ran for 360 feet, between High and Vine Streets (now 6th and 7th Avenues), and back for 180 feet along those streets. Hence the property was twice as long as it was deep. It was valued at $69,000 in 1860 but fell to an estimated price of $55,000 to $58,000 by 1868. Campbell Brown later subdivided the property into three separate parcels (see below). In 1868 he sold the house and its parcel to the Academy of St. Cecilia for $39,000. It later passed into possession of the Catholic Church and for years was used as a hospital by the Sisters of Mercy. In 1894 the mansion was converted into the Episcopal residence of the Diocese of Nashville and later was purchased by the state as a capitol annex.[1]

Cedar Street Lots: Lizinka had two lots on this street (#110 and #122) that totaled 360 feet and had a tax value of $68,000 in 1868. On 8 October 1868 Campbell Brown sold 104′10″ along Cedar Street, apparently comprising portions of both of these tracts.[2] The two tracts thus became the following three tracts:

Cedar Street: Campbell Brown noted selling a lot with a 104′10″ front on Cedar Street on 8 October 1868. This may have been the sale of the house to the Academy of St. Cecilia (see above).[3]

Cedar and High Streets: This 113-foot lot at the corner of Cedar and High Streets (now Charlotte and 6th Avenues) was valued at $18,000 in 1872.[4]

Cedar and Vine Streets: This lot had a 144′4.5″ front at the corner of Cedar and Vine (now Charlotte and 7th Avenues) and was worth $16,000 in 1872.[5]

Cherry and Gay Streets: George Campbell Sr. willed Lizinka Lot 108, at the northwest corner of Cherry (now 4th Avenue) and Gay Streets. The lot had a 128-foot front and was worth $2,000. It contained what a Freedman's Bureau official described as "Two small & indifferent brick dwellings." It was known as Lot #58 and was valued at $10,300 in 1863 when the U.S. government seized it. Campbell Brown valued the property at between

$12,500 and $15,000 in 1865. In 1868 a portion of the property was cut off to make Gay Street. This gave it a front of 118'4". In 1872 it was valued at $9,165.[6]

South Cherry Street: This lot, part of College Lot #28, had a 38-foot front and was valued at $1,000 in 1872.[7]

North College Street: Lizinka had half-ownership in this property, which was then occupied by the Second National Bank. In 1872 this 32-foot lot was valued at $10,000.[8]

South College Street: This property, inherited from Lizinka's father, had a frontage of 123'5" and was known as Lot #43. It stood somewhere between Church Street and Broadway. Two small houses stood on the site. Lizinka rented the property until her death. Campbell Brown estimated its value at $18,000 in 1868, and it was valued at $18,512.50 in 1872.[9]

Colonnade Building: Lizinka had a 50 percent ownership in this building, located at the corner of Cherry Street (now 4th Avenue) and Dendrick Street.[10]

Glenoak: This house stood two and one-half miles outside Nashville. In 1865 it was valued at $12,500. Campbell Brown advised his mother to sell the dilapidated house in 1865, but after getting his law degree, he fixed up the house and moved into it himself. It was here that he wrote his Civil War memoir. Lizinka offered to sell the property to Campbell for $8,000 in 1868. Apparently he took her up on this offer, then turned around and tried to sell the property for $11,000. The house is still standing.[11]

Vine Street: This lot was located north of Cedar Street (now Charlotte Avenue) and on the west side of Vine Street (now 7th Avenue). It had a 78'10.5" front. At the end of the war it was assessed at $9,400 and was called Lot #133. There was a small frame or log building on the property—the third door north of Cedar Street—that stood immediately opposite the state capitol building. The building was then occupied by black tenants, who paid rent. The value of the property dropped to $8,000 in 1868 and to $5,000 in 1869. By 1872 it was valued at just $3,943.75.[12]

Maury County, Tennessee, Tracts

Deshon Tract: Sometimes spelled "Dechon," this property comprised 145 acres and stood between the Nashville and Decatur Railroad and the Franklin Pike, about eight miles north of Columbia. A Freedman's Bureau official described it as having good land but poor cabins and enclosures. It was worth $2,000 when Lizinka received it from her father. In 1872 the property was listed at 140 acres and had a value of $5,000.[13]

Spring Hill: Also known as Maury farm or Sutherland, this plantation, thirty-two miles from Nashville, was the Ewells' principal residence after the Civil War. The property encompassed 3,018.25 acres in 1872 and was valued at $128,235.68. Like the Deshon tract, it stood on the Nashville and Decatur Railroad.[14]

Central and Western Tennessee Tracts

Cheatham County: Lizinka owned 50 acres of land here worth $500 in 1872.[15]

Giles County: George W. Campbell purchased 5,000 acres along Richland Creek in 1804. By the time of his death, the size of the property had increased to 6,000 acres. Campbell willed the property to his son, George Jr., and Lizinka in turn inherited it upon George's death. It had a value of $210,000 in 1854. Lizinka sold 775 acres of this in July 1854, but when one of the buyers defaulted on the payment, she sued and got part of the land back in 1865. After that she authorized her uncle David Hubbard to sell the land, which he apparently did prior to 1872, since it does not appear in her will.[16]

Humphreys County: This property, located west of Nashville, was estimated at 50 acres and was worth just $50 in 1872.[17]

Lincoln County: From her father Lizinka received 640 acres of land in Lincoln County valued at $10,000. She apparently disposed of this land prior to 1872, for it does not appear in her will.[18]

Marion County: This tract, also called the Old Rodgers Place, stood in the Sequatchie Valley, near Jasper, Tennessee. The property encompassed 400 acres of swampy, unhealthy ground. In 1872 it had a value of $4,000.[19]

Perry County: This 75-acre tract was worth just $75 in 1872.[20]

Northwest Tennessee Tracts

Dyer County: George W. Campbell Sr. willed Lizinka 1,841 acres near Dyersburg worth $5,000. In 1867 Lizinka put the land's value at $2.50 per acre. This property does not appear in Lizinka's will.[21]

Lake County: This property comprised 400 acres and was worth $400 in 1872.[22]

Obion County: Lizinka had two lots here totaling 2,628 acres. It was hilly land on the Obion River, with rich soil that was good for tobacco. George W. Campbell Sr. willed the property to his son, who in turn passed it on to Lizinka. It was worth $20,000 upon the death of George W. Campbell Sr. It is not listed in Lizinka's will, suggesting that she sold it prior to her death.[23]

Mississippi Tracts

Bogue Phalaya: This tract, originally owned by James Percy Brown, consisted of 1,200 or more acres of wild land in Bolivar County and was worth perhaps $10 per acre. Lizinka inherited the land and leased it for five years at a time to people who grew cotton on it.[24]

DeSoto County: Nothing is known about this property, which is mentioned in passing along with several others in an 1869 letter from Lizinka to Campbell.[25]

Melrose: This 1,492-acre tract stood in Bolivar County at a bend in the Mississippi River, not far from the town of Greenville. Lizinka received the property from her first husband and sold half of it in 1854 for $70,000 to a man named Yerger. At the end of the Civil War the property was dilapidated and required extensive repairs. Campbell Brown eventually brought it up to par. The family sold 320 acres of the tract on 24 April 1869 to J. T. Newly, but they got the land back on 5 January 1871 when he defaulted on the payments. The property included a house, a smokehouse, three cisterns, seven single cabins, and two double cabins. It was located on swampy ground and suffered from floods and erosion. Nevertheless it was good cotton land, worth about $30,000 in 1871.[26]

Other Lots

Missouri: Lizinka and Tasker Gantt jointly owned a lot at Third and Chestnut Streets in St. Louis.[27]

Washington, D.C.: Lizinka owned two lots in the city. The first fronted 22nd Street and was on the second square south of Pennsylvania Avenue, near the equestrian statue of George Washington. It was 4,592 square feet in area. The second lot stood on Third Street between F and G Streets, northeast of city hall. It totaled 2,084 square feet. These lots went by the designations of Square 55, Lot 16, and Square 530, Lot 13. The 3rd Street property was sold for $1,148 in 1867. The 22nd Street lot was sold in 1871 for an undetermined sum.[28]

Ewell Cemetery Plots at Williamsburg

Prior to the Civil War Benjamin Ewell was president of the College of William and Mary in Williamsburg, Virginia, and lived with his mother at the President's House. When Elizabeth Ewell Sr. died, the college faculty voted to establish a cemetery on college grounds. Excerpts from an 18 January 1859 meeting read as follows:

> Resolved, That the portion of the College land in the rear of the President's garden . . . be set apart as a burying ground for the Professors of the College, their families & the students, and be called the College Cemetery.

> Resolved, That Mr. Ewell be allowed to transfer the remains of his father and of such other members of his family as he may think proper to College Cemetery.

Today nine people are buried in the small graveyard: Benjamin Ewell, his mother, his sister Rebecca, his daughter Lizzie, his son-in-law Beverly S. Scott, Professor Lucien Minor, a woman named Matilda Southall, and two students. With the exception of Ewell and Minor, all of the graves are unmarked. The graveyard stands behind the Wren Building on the old campus, adjacent to Old Dominion Hall. A brick wall encloses it. The graves are situated as shown:

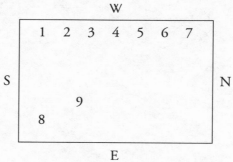

1. George Turner (student)
2. Beverly S. Scott
3. Elizabeth Ewell Scott
4. Benjamin Stoddert Ewell
5. Elizabeth Stoddert Ewell
6. Rebecca Lowndes Ewell
7. Matilda Southall
8. Lucien Minor
9. ? Snead (student)

Additional information on the cemetery may be found under the heading "Buildings and Grounds—College Cemetery," in the subject file at the College Archives, Swem Library, College of William and Mary.

Ewell's Staff

Following is a list of sixty-eight men who served on Ewell's staff. It includes their positions and the years that they served under him. Compiled service records for most of these individuals appear in Record Group 109, microcopy 331, at the National Archives in Washington, D.C.

Allan, William	Capt. and OO, 1863–1865
Barbour, James	Maj. and AAG, 1862
Barksdale, William	VADC, 1862
Brown, George C.	1st Lt. and ADC, 1862
	Capt. and AAG, 1862–63
	Maj. and AAG, 1863–64
	Maj. and AIG, 1864–65
Brown, John T.	Col. and CA, 1863
Carrington, Isaac	Maj. and PM, Dept. of Richmond, 1864–65
	Maj. and Commander, Post of Richmond, 1865
Carroll, Robert G. H.	1st Lt. and Acting ADC, 1864
	1st Lt. and ADC, 1864
Chestney, Theodore O.	Maj. and AAG, 1864–65
Christy, George W.	Capt. and OO, 1862
Clarke, William H.	1st Lt. and OO, 1865
Conner, James	Col. and JMC, 1863–64
Courtney, Alfred R.	Maj. and CA, 1862
Elhart, Adolph E.	Capt. and Paymaster, 1863–64
Elliott, Robert W. B.	VADC, 1863
Ewell, Benjamin S.	Col. and AAG, 1864–65
Faulkner, Charles J.	Lt. Col. and AAG, 1863
Forbes, Francis T.	Capt. and Acting CS, 1864–65
	Maj. and CS, 1865
Garber, A. M.	Capt. and Acting QM, 1863
	Capt. and AQM, 1863–64
Greene, Benjamin H.	VADC, 1861–62
	Maj. and CS, 1862
	Maj. and AIG, 1863–64
	Maj. and Acting EO, 1864
Griswold, Joseph G.	Acting AAG, 1861–62
Hancock, Francis W.	MD, 1861–62

Harman, John A.	Maj. and QM, 1863–64
Hawks, Wells J.	Maj. and CS, 1863–64
Heaton, Henry	VADC, 1862
Hinrichs, Oscar	1st Lt. and EO, 1862
Hotchkiss, Jedediah	Topographical Engineer, 1863–64
Howard, Charles	Maj. and CS, 1864
Hudnut, Edgar A.	Clerk, 1861
Jackson, James	Col. and JMC, 1863
Johnson, John E.	1st Lt. and VADC, 1863
Johnston, Elliott	1st Lt. and VADC, 1862–63
Jones, John M.	Lt. Col. and AAG, 1862
Ker, James	Capt. and OO, 1864–65
King, M.	VADC, 1861
Koerner, P. W. Oscar	1st Lt. and EO, 1864–65
Lacy, Beverley T.	Chaplain, 1863–64
Lee, Fitzhugh	Capt. and AAG, 1861
Lee, Richard H.	Col. and JMC, 1863–64
Lock, John J.	Capt. and ACS, 1863–64
McGuire, Hunter	MD, 1863–64
Mason, Robert F.	VADC, 1861
	Capt. and AQM, 1861
	Capt. and QM, 1861
Meade, Richard K.	Lt. and AIG, 1864
Nelson, Hugh M.	1st Lt. and ADC, 1862
Old, William W.	Capt. and VADC, 1864
Page, Legh R.	Maj. and AAG, 1864
	Maj. and AIG, 1864
Parkhill, John H.	Maj. and QM, 1864–65
Pegram, James W.	Maj. and AAG, 1864
	Maj. and AIG, 1864–65
Pendleton, Alexander S.	Lt. Col. and AAG, 1863–64
Randolph, James I.	1st Lt. and EO, 1862
Rhodes, Charles H.	Capt. and AQM, 1861
Richardson, Henry B.	1st Lt. and EO, 1862
	Capt. and EO, 1863
Robinson, Powhatan	Capt. and EO, 1862
Rogers, John D.	Maj. and QM, 1864
Selden, Harry H.	Maj. and QM, 1864–65
Smead, Abner	Lt. Col. and AIG, 1863–64
Smith, James P.	1st Lt. and ADC, 1863
	Capt. and AAG, 1863
Snodgrass, Charles E.	Maj. and QM, 1862
Stoddert, William	VADC, 1862

Taliaferro, John	2nd Lt. and ADC, 1861 (cadet)
	Cadet and Acting ADC, 1864
Taliaferro, Thomas S.	Capt. and PM, Military Court, 1863–64
	Capt. and Acting JAMC, 1864
Thornton, William W.	Capt. and ACS, 1862
Turner, Thomas P.	Maj., Commandant of Libby Prison, 1864–65
Turner, Thomas T.	VADC, 1861
	1st Lt. and ADC, 1862–64
Tyler, Charles H.	Capt. and AAG, 1861
Walton, Thomas	Maj. and AAG, 1864–65
Wilbourn, Richard E.	Capt. and SO, 1863–64
Wilson, Daniel A., Jr.	Capt. and JAMC, 1863
	Col. and JMC, 1863–64
Wilson, John P., Jr.	VADC, 1862

Abbreviations

AAG	Assistant Adjutant General
ACS	Assistant Commissary of Subsistence
ADC	Aide-de-Camp
AIG	Assistant Adjutant and Inspector General
AQM	Assistant Quartermaster
CA	Chief of Artillery
CS	Commissary of Subsistence
EO	Engineer Officer
JAMC	Judge Advocate, Military Court
JMC	Judge on Military Court
MD	Medical Director
OO	Ordnance Officer
PM	Provost Marshal
QM	Quartermaster
SO	Signal Officer
VADC	Volunteer Aide-de-Camp

Campbell Family Genealogy

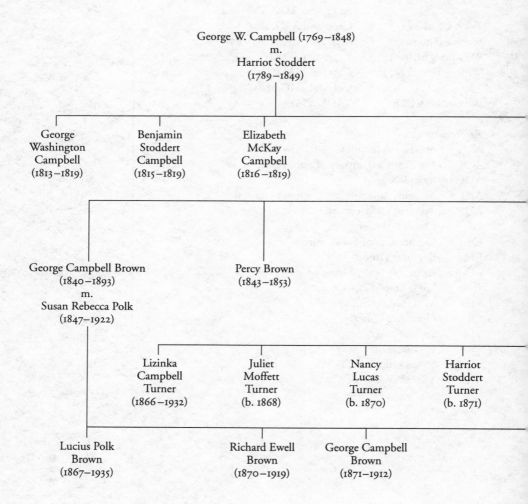

George W. Campbell (1769–1848)
m.
Harriot Stoddert
(1789–1849)

George Washington Campbell (1813–1819)

Benjamin Stoddert Campbell (1815–1819)

Elizabeth McKay Campbell (1816–1819)

George Campbell Brown (1840–1893)
m.
Susan Rebecca Polk (1847–1922)

Percy Brown (1843–1853)

Lizinka Campbell Turner (1866–1932)

Juliet Moffett Turner (b. 1868)

Nancy Lucas Turner (b. 1870)

Harriot Stoddert Turner (b. 1871)

Lucius Polk Brown (1867–1935)

Richard Ewell Brown (1870–1919)

George Campbell Brown (1871–1912)

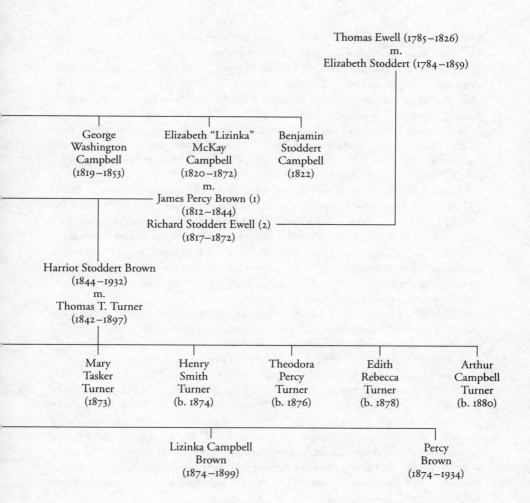

The Ewell-at-Manassas Controversy

Ewell's inaction at First Manassas was a subject of debate in 1861, but it was soon forgotten in the escalating whirlwind of events. The subject was revived in November 1884 when an article critical of Ewell appeared in *Century Magazine* under Gen. P. G. T. Beauregard's name. (An abridged version of this article appears in *Battles and Leaders*, 1:196–227.) Actually the article was not written by Beauregard but by two "New York friends" with the general's permission. It unfairly criticized Ewell for failing to advance on the morning of 21 July when he learned through Brig. Gen. David R. Jones that he had been ordered to do so. The authors contrasted Ewell's behavior at Manassas with that of the French General Desaix, who at the Battle of Marengo marched to the sound of battle despite a lack of orders, thereby saving the day for Napoleon.

The article raised a storm of protest. Maj. Gen. Fitzhugh Lee, who had been on Ewell's staff in 1861, leaped to his former chief's defense. Lee pointed out that Ewell did in fact advance as soon as he received Jones's message. He demanded that Beauregard retract the statement and make a public apology. Realizing that he had gotten himself into a fix by permitting his friends to pen an article under his name, Beauregard wrote to his former chief of staff, Col. Alfred Roman, for advice. Roman reviewed the offending article, compared it with the known facts, and concluded that Beauregard was wrong. He suggested that the general retract the statement in some way.[1]

Meanwhile other friends of General Ewell added their voices to the hue and cry. Capt. George Harrison wrote an article in the *Southern Historical Society Papers* showing conclusively through military correspondence that Ewell had acted properly under the circumstances and was innocent of any blame.[2] Joe Johnston and Campbell Brown contributed similar articles to *Century Magazine* (both reprinted in *Battles and Leaders*, 1:240–61). These public rebukes only stiffened Beauregard's pride. Rather than apologize to Ewell's defenders, he instead published a book on the campaign, *A Commentary on the Campaign and Battle of Manassas of July, 1861*, in which he lambasted Johnston and attempted to sustain the criticisms of Ewell made by his two friends. All the while he protested his friendship and admiration for Ewell. Beauregard's *Commentary*, published in 1891, was the last shot fired in this unnecessary and unseemly literary skirmish. Johnston and Beauregard died shortly thereafter. Lee, Brown, and Harrison, having done their duty by General Ewell, moved on to more profitable pursuits.

A Chronology of Events on 24 May 1862

The time frame set forth in the text for the events of 24 May 1862 is an approximation based on times noted on various dispatches found in the *Official Records*. The chronology of that day is perplexing in large measure because of what Ewell himself wrote of it. In his notes on the campaign, Ewell recalled hearing Jackson's guns on the Valley Turnpike at noon. He wrote that he had ordered his troops to march to Winchester soon thereafter, reaching the outskirts of the city "about dusk."[1] Clearly these times are too early. Ewell clouded the issue further by stating in his report of the battle that he commenced his march to Winchester at 5:00 P.M.

The first two statements are simply the result of poor memory and are easily disproved. Jackson's attack on Banks did not begin until 3:30 P.M.; Ewell could not have heard it prior to that time. As for his claim that he reached Winchester "about dusk," Jackson sets the record straight. In his report of the battle, he stated that Ewell's division reached the town "as early as 10 o'clock in the night."[2] Col. George M. Beal of the Tenth Maine Infantry, which was picketing the Front Royal Road just outside Winchester that evening, confirmed Jackson's estimate, affirming that "the enemy made their appearance on the road about 10 o'clock p.m. 24th of May."[3]

Ewell's contention that he began his march at 5:00 P.M. is true but misleading. At 5:00 P.M. he received an order from Jackson, written at 4:00 P.M., ordering him to march to Winchester.[4] He started immediately but had not gone far when a second dispatch from Jackson, written at 4:30 P.M., arrested his march.[5] As Ewell anxiously awaited orders, the sound of battle on the turnpike shifted noticeably northward, indicating a Federal retreat to Winchester.

Around 6:45 P.M. Ewell started toward the town. He did this on his own initiative and in direct violation of Jackson's 4:30 dispatch, which had ordered him to stay put until further orders. Within minutes after resuming the march, Ewell's judgment was vindicated by the receipt of a 5:45 P.M. dispatch ordering him to march to Winchester.[6] (That it was Jackson's 5:45 order rather than his 4:00 P.M. order that Ewell received at this point, there can be no doubt. In his account of the Valley Campaign written after the war, Ewell noted that the order directing him to march to Winchester, which he received just minutes after initiating the march on his own, was written in Jackson's typical "laconic style." Only the 5:45 order fits this description.)

Ewell's force thus started for Winchester twice that afternoon: at 5:00 P.M. and at 6:45 P.M. This theory fits well with what is known about the detachment of Elzey's brigade to Jackson. Jackson ordered Ewell to send him Elzey's brigade at 4:30 P.M.[7] The dispatch took approximately one hour to deliver and probably reached Ewell around 5:30. By then,

Ewell's force was on the march, a fact stated by Ewell in his official report and alluded to by Jackson in his dispatch. Yet Ewell and others categorically stated that Elzey's brigade went to join Jackson before the march began. These contradictory pieces of evidence reconcile only if Ewell started his march at 5 P.M., halted, then restarted at a later time. Jackson ordered Ewell to resume his march to Winchester at 5:45 P.M. As he had moved somewhat farther north along the Turnpike by the time he sent this dispatch, it probably did not reach Ewell until nearly 7:00 P.M., just minutes after Ewell had ordered his troops forward by his own authority. Hence, Ewell's column must have resumed its march about 6:45 P.M. Campbell Brown remembered that the march from Nineveh to Winchester was slow because Jackson had ordered Ewell to keep apace with the rest of the army, marching parallel to him on the Valley Pike.[8] A slow pace of perhaps two miles an hour would have brought Ewell's column to the outskirts of Winchester at approximately 10:00 P.M., the time given by both Jackson and Beal.

It is possible, then, to reconstruct the chronology of Ewell's movements on 24 May as follows:

Noon   Jackson begins march from Nineveh to Middletown
3:30   Ewell hears Jackson's attack on Banks at Middletown
4:00   Jackson orders Ewell to march to Winchester
4:30   Jackson orders Ewell to send him Elzey's brigade and to halt advance on Winchester
5:00   Ewell begins march to Winchester in accordance with Jackson's 4:00 P.M. dispatch
5:30   Ewell halts march to Winchester and sends Elzey's brigade to the Valley Turnpike in accordance with Jackson's 4:30 order
5:45   Ewell writes to Jackson suggesting that he march to Newtown
5:45   Jackson orders Ewell to recommence march to Winchester
6:45   Ewell starts for Winchester on his own authority, notifying Jackson of what he has done
7:00   Ewell receives Jackson's 5:45 orders affirming his decision to go to Winchester
7:00   Jackson receives Ewell's 5:45 dispatch and orders him to march to Newtown
7:45   Ewell receives Jackson's order to march to Newtown but chooses to disregard it
8:00   Jackson receives notification that Ewell has continued march to Winchester
10:00   Ewell reaches outskirts of Winchester.

Auburn and Dunblane

Ewell was carried by litter from Sudley Springs to Auburn, Ariss Buckner's home, on 29 August 1862. His litter-bearers probably carried him west on Sudley Road (Route 234) to McGraw's Ridge Road/Gum Spring Road (Route 659), then north a distance of approximately three miles to a farm road that skirted Auburn as it headed west toward the Bull Run Mountains. Buckner owned a large estate of 1,500 acres and at least twenty-three slaves.[1] A large, two-story, square, brown stone house, built early in the twentieth century, now stands on the site of the Civil War house. To reach Auburn, drive north on Sanders Lane (Route 705) from Sudley Road a distance of 3.3 miles. The house stands on the right side of the road, just past a dairy farm and beyond the point where power lines cross the road. Immediately east of the house is a ridge once lined by slave cabins and covered with piles of stones pulled from nearby fields. According to local tradition, the Confederates used the abandoned slave dwellings on that ridge as their hospital, and Ewell's leg was amputated there rather than in the main house. The amputated limb, so the story goes, was buried beneath a pile of rocks.[2]

Campbell Brown, an eyewitness to the event, implies that the operation took place in the main house and says specifically that John Frame, Ewell's servant, buried the limb in a corner of the garden.[3] The main house stood directly beneath the current one. Being longer, it extended a short distance to the north of it. The large garden stood adjacent to the house, on its south side, and extended perhaps 200 feet, approximately to the fence that now encloses the dairy farm.[4]

A week or so after his amputation, Ewell was carried by litter from Auburn to Dunblane, the home of his cousin Dr. Jesse Ewell III.[5] Rather than follow established roads to Dunblane, which would have made the journey considerably longer, Ewell's attendants probably carried him westward along the aforementioned farm road (a trace of which can still be seen crossing Sanders Road today) to Logmill Road, and then by the Carolina Road to Ewell's Chapel.[6] To reach Dunblane, follow Sudley Road to the James Madison Highway (Route 15) and drive north 2.8 miles to Loudoun Drive (Route 615), which is on the left. Go 0.1 mile and turn left onto Largo Vista Drive (Route 1750). The site is 0.75 mile down the road on the left, out of sight of the road. According to E. R. Conner III, the house burned in 1911 and was rebuilt.[7] The more recent structure still stands. Both Dunblane and the site of Auburn are private property. Please respect the owners' privacy.

As you leave Dunblane to return to Route 15 on Largo Vista Drive, Edge Hill plantation stood on the left 0.3 mile down the road. Edge Hill was the home of Jesse Ewell's eldest son, John Smith Magruder Ewell. The house has long since been destroyed, but two dependencies still exist (though just barely), as does the Ewell family cemetery.

At the junction of Largo Vista Drive and Loudoun Drive stood Ewell Chapel, where General Ewell's guard camped during his stay at Dunblane. The chapel was torn down a few years ago, and now a modern house occupies the site. As you turn right onto Loudoun Drive to return to Route 15, there is a weathered white clapboard house on the right side of the road that was once the home of Alice Maude Ewell, Jesse Ewell III's granddaughter, who authored *A Virginia Scene*, a quaint and informative book about the Ewell clan.

When Was Ewell Shot?

It is widely believed that Dick Ewell was shot in his wooden leg during the first day's fighting at Gettysburg. The basis for this belief is the colorful but unreliable memoir of John Gordon. Gordon recalled accompanying Ewell through the streets of Gettysburg. Suddenly Union soldiers opened fire on them from fences and buildings in the town. "A number of Confederates were killed or wounded, and I heard the ominous thud of a Minié ball as it struck General Ewell at my side," wrote Gordon. "I quickly asked: 'Are you hurt, sir?' 'No, no,' he replied; 'I'm not hurt. But suppose that ball had struck you: we would have had the trouble of carrying you off the field, sir. You see how much better fixed for a fight I am than you are. It don't hurt a bit to be shot in a wooden leg.'"[1]

Other accounts corroborate Gordon's testimony. Jacob Hoke quotes a citizen of Gettysburg who witnessed Ewell ride out Baltimore Street with his staff on 1 July only to beat a hasty retreat when shot at by Federal troops. "Reaching a sheltered place near the court house, some of his attendants either pulled off the general's boot or examined a probable wound, which he had just received," wrote Hoke.[2]

Another civilian, Mary Johnston, elaborated on the episode to an even greater extent in an article written for *Confederate Veteran* magazine. According to Johnston, Ewell and Gordon were riding together down a road lined with stone fences. As they galloped along, Ewell commented nervously, "Wish old Jackson was here! Wish Marse Robert had Old Jackson! This is the watershed, General Gordon; yes, sir, this is the watershed of the war. If it still doesn't go right to-day—It seems to me that that wall there's got a suspicious look." Before Ewell could complete his sentence, a body of Federals rose up from behind the wall and fired a volley that perforated his leg.[3]

Johnston's account, obviously based on Gordon's memoirs and a hefty dose of hindsight, is clearly fictional. Hoke's account, by contrast, has the stamp of authenticity about it, although it errs in respect to the removal of the general's boot. There is no doubt that Ewell and his party came under fire from Federal soldiers on Baltimore Street that afternoon. John W. Daniel, Jubal Early, Isaac Trimble, and Campbell Brown, who accompanied Ewell in his reconnaissance, say as much. Significantly, none of them mention Ewell as being hit at this time, though Daniel recorded that a Federal bullet cut the stirrup leather of a lieutenant riding next to him.[4]

Evidence that Ewell was hit on 3 July comes from a statement made by Capt. William Seymour of Hays's staff. In his diary entry for that date, Seymour wrote that "Gen. Ewell, accompanied by Major Richardson, his Chief of Engineers, rode past our Brigade and started on a little reconnoitring tour on a road that entered the town where our left rested. We told him that it was dangerous to go out that road—that the enemy's sharpshooters commanded it with their long-ranged, telescopic sighted Whitworth rifles." Ewell would not listen. "The old General declared that they were fully fifteen hundred yards distant— that they could not possibly shoot with accuracy at that distance & that he would run the risk of being hit. He had not proceeded twenty paces when a ball perforated his wooden leg and Major Richardson was shot through the body."[5]

Campbell Brown's memoir confirms certain details of Seymour's account, although it mistakenly places the date of the incident on 2 July. Brown wrote, "About noon, as well as I remember, our former engineer officer, Capt. H. B. Richardson, was shot & seriously wounded while riding near Hays' line, being hit, they told me, from at least a quarter of a mile away."[6] Jed Hotchkiss wrote in his diary under 3 July that "Captain Richardson of the Engineer Corps was wounded yesterday." On the surface this seems to suggest that Richardson was wounded on the second day of the battle. Careful reading of the entry, however, indicates that Hotchkiss actually jotted the entry on 4 July. That would place the incident on 3 July.[7]

This makes sense as far as Gordon is concerned, too. On 1 July, at the time the Georgian claimed to be with Ewell in Gettysburg, he should have been—and probably was— leading his brigade out the York Pike. Two days later, however, his brigade was at Winebrenner's Run, not far from where Seymour noted that Ewell was shot. Ewell probably encountered Gordon as he returned from his reconnaissance and made the remark Gordon attributed to him at that time. Such a series of events seems far more likely than the 1 July episode mentioned by Gordon in his memoirs.

Ewell's Capture at Sailor's Creek

After the Battle of Little Sailor's Creek, there was a dispute in the Army of the Potomac as to who had captured General Ewell. Two units claimed the honor: the Fifth Wisconsin Infantry and Maj. Gen. George A. Custer's cavalry division. Custer's claim is by far the stronger of the two, being supported by the testimonies of Ewell and Campbell Brown as well as at least two of Sheridan's officers.[1]

The Fifth Wisconsin's claim has more supporters than that of Custer's division, though they are not as reliable. The Fifth Wisconsin's commander, Col. Thomas S. Allen, reported that Ewell surrendered unconditionally to Sgt. Angus Cameron. "Soon after," wrote Allen, "a squad of cavalry came up and claimed the prisoners and took possession of them. . . . The names of the six men who captured General Ewell are, Sergt. Angus Cameron, Corpl. Charles Roughan, Corpl. August Brocker, and Private H. W. True, Company I."[2] Allen's superiors, Col. Oliver Edwards and Bvt. Maj. Gen. Frank Wheaton, repeated this claim in their reports of the battle, Edwards likewise taking credit for the capture of Maj. Gen. Custis Lee.[3]

Bvt. Brig. Gen. William S. Truex, commanding a brigade in Seymour's division of the Sixth Corps, stated in his report of the battle that Ewell's adjutant, Maj. James Pegram, rode forward with a flag of truce and "surrendered Lieutenant-General Ewell and staff" to his brigade, though he stops short of saying that he actually captured the Confederate general. Bvt. Maj. H. W. Day, an adjutant on Truex's staff, supports that assertion, adding that the cavalry came up as the fighting was slackening and "seized Gen. Ewell and some others, who were then in charge of our infantry, and took them along . . . as trophies of war." Day does not appear to have been a witness to this encounter, however.[4]

An officer on General Wright's staff with the initials T.H.F. wrote in 1920 that a detachment of the Thirty-seventh Massachusetts Infantry, fighting near the road, encountered a party of mounted Confederate officers and demanded its surrender. Ewell identified himself and asked to surrender to a commissioned officer. When the officer ordered him to dismount, Ewell pointed out that he had only one leg and was strapped to his horse. The soldiers then sent Ewell and his staff as prisoners to General Wright's headquarters.[5] This article has several problems, the most prominent of which are its late date and the fact that it credits the capture of Ewell to the Thirty-seventh Massachusetts rather than the Fifth Wisconsin. The author was not present at the capture and probably got his information from stories circulating around Wright's headquarters at that time.

The place of Ewell's capture is also a matter of dispute. Several sources indicate that Ewell surrendered near the Swep Marshall House, on the crest of the hill south of the road. An early historian of the battle, W. A. Watson, made this claim, citing as his source a deceased judge who had resided in the area.[6] F. C. Robinson likewise had Ewell being captured at a cluster of buildings, though he does not identify them by name.[7] James A. Lawrence, a soldier in the 126th Ohio Infantry, by contrast, placed Ewell's capture in the "swampy bottom on the Hillman farm"—in other words, near the creek below the Hillsman house. This is certainly wrong.[8]

Contradicting these accounts is Ewell's own statement that he was "riding past my left" when he encountered the enemy forces closing in on him. This would place him on the north side of the road, near the left end of his line. Significantly, a map that appears in an 1888 letter written by Campbell Brown to Charles Venable also shows the location of Ewell's surrender north of the road. Taken together, these two pieces of evidence must be considered decisive.[9]

★ ★ ★

Notes

Abbreviations

BSE	Benjamin Stoddert Ewell
CB	Campbell Brown
CBM	Campbell Brown Memoirs, Brown-Ewell Papers, Manuscript Division, Tennessee State Library and Archives, Nashville.
CWM	Manuscript Department, College of William and Mary, Williamsburg, Va.
DU	Manuscript Department, William R. Perkins Library, Duke University, Durham, N.C.
EE	Elizabeth Stoddert Ewell Sr.
ELB	Richard Stoddert Ewell Letterbook, Manuscript Department, William R. Perkins Library, Duke University, Durham, N.C.
ESE	Elizabeth Stoddert Ewell Jr.
F	Frame(s)
FC	Brown-Ewell Family Papers, Manuscript Department, Filson Club, Louisville, Ky.
FRSP	Fredericksburg and Spotsylvania County Battlefields Memorial National Military Park, Fredericksburg, Va.
GWC	George Washington Campbell Papers, Manuscript Division, Library of Congress, Washington, D.C.
HB	Harriot Brown (Turner)
HP	Jedediah Hotchkiss Papers, Manuscript Division, Library of Congress, Washington, D.C.
LC	Richard Stoddert Ewell Papers, Manuscript Division, Library of Congress, Washington, D.C.
LCB	Lizinka Campbell Brown (Ewell)
LE	Elizabeth "Lizzie" Stoddert Ewell (Scott)
M	Microcopy
MHS	Maryland Historical Society, Baltimore
NA	National Archives, Washington, D.C.
OR	U.S. War Department. *The War of the Rebellion: A Compilation of the Official Records of the Union and Confederate Armies.* 128 vols. Washington, D.C.: U.S. Government Printing Office, 1880–1901.

PBE   Polk-Brown-Ewell Papers, Southern Historical Collection, University of North
           Carolina, Chapel Hill
R   Reel(s), Roll(s)
RG   Record Group
RLE   Rebecca Lowndes Ewell
RSE   Richard Stoddert Ewell
SHC   Southern Historical Collection, University of North Carolina, Chapel Hill
TN   Brown-Ewell Papers, Manuscript Division, Tennessee State Library and
           Archives, Nashville
TSLA   Manuscript Department, Tennessee State Library and Archives, Nashville
TTG   Thomas Tasker Gantt
TX   Jesse Ewell Papers, Manuscript Department, University of Texas, Austin
USAMHI   Manuscript Department, United States Army Military History Institute,
           Carlisle Barracks, Pa.
USMA   United States Military Academy Archives, West Point, N.Y.
UVA   Manuscript Department, University of Virginia, Charlottesville
VHS   Virginia Historical Society, Richmond
WHM   Washington Hands Memoir, Manuscript Department, University of Virginia,
           Charlottesville
WM   Benjamin Stoddert Ewell Papers, Manuscript Department, College of William
           and Mary, Williamsburg, Va.
WNP   William Nelson Pendleton Papers, Southern Historical Collection, University
           of North Carolina, Chapel Hill
WS   William Stoddert

Preface

1. Hunter McGuire to Jedediah Hotchkiss, 27 June 1896, R34, F170, HP.

Chapter 1

1. Richard Taylor, *Destruction*, 37.

2. Newspaper clipping in box 1, folder 15, PBE. This article was later republished in Williams, "High Private," 159.

3. Folders 22 and 23, WM; Harriot Stoddert Turner, "Ewells of Virginia," 1, CWM. According to one family tradition, the Ewell name was of English origin and was variously spelled Awell, Etwell, Yowell, Yewell, or Uel. Another tradition holds that the name was a corruption of the Welsh name Llewellen.

4. "Ewell Family History," 1, TX; Mrs. Nathaniel McGregor Ewell to author, 13 Jan. 1987, 22 June 1996. The names of the children were George, Mark, Patience, Ann, Solomon, Comfort, and Charles. There may have been an eighth child, James Jr., but he is not mentioned in his father's 1703 will. James Jr. may have died before his father.

5. Mrs. Nathaniel McGregor Ewell to author, 13 Jan. 1987; Hayden, *Virginia Genealogies*, 334. Hayden, following a family tradition prevalent at the turn of the century, states that Charles Ewell "came to Virginia under contract to build the State Capitol at Williamsburg, 1690." A letter written in 1958 from Mary R. M. Goodwin of the research department at Colo-

nial Williamsburg to Wendell Holt puts that myth to rest. Mrs. Goodwin wrote, "We have no information at all connecting your ancestor, Charles Ewell, with work on the capitol building in Williamsburg. . . . Hayden's statement is inaccurate. We have no way of knowing when Charles Ewell came to Virginia, but we do know that neither the capitol nor the city of Williamsburg was thought of until the Statehouse at Jamestown burned in 1698."

6. Biographical sketch of Thomas Ewell, folder 23, WM; miscellaneous notes, TX; "Ewell Family History," 2-3, TX; Hayden, *Virginia Genealogies*, 334; Jesse Ewell to ESE, 21 Oct. 1880, WM.

7. Miscellaneous notes, TX; Hayden, *Virginia Genealogies*, 335-38; 1885 advertisement for Bel Air, folder 21, WM. Bel Air has withstood the passage of time and is today one of the oldest buildings in Prince William County. According to its current owner, Dr. William E. S. Flory, Charles Ewell built the house on the stone foundation of a frontier fort constructed in 1673 by Governor William Berkeley. The house was described in an 1885 advertisement as an "architectural curiosity. . . . Its monster chimney, its numerous fire-places, its old-fashioned stairway, its dormer-windows, its thick stone and brick walls, and even the lumber and brick and nails used in its erection, are matters of remark among observing people" (folder 21, WM). Bel Air stands off Old Delaney Road, approximately five miles west of Dale City.

8. Hayden, *Virginia Genealogies*, 335-36, 341; Johnson and Malone, *Dictionary*, 4:498. Washington noted the arrival of the Prince William militia in Winchester on 6 May 1756, adding, "An hour later Colonel Ewel came to town." Craik also attended Gen. Edward Braddock following the latter's wounding at the battle of the Monongahela on 3 July 1755.

9. "Ewell Family History," 6-7, TX; Hayden, *Virginia Genealogies*, 338-39; Jesse Ewell to ESE, 30 Sept. 1880, folder 9, WM; *Provisional List*, 17, 23; Alice M. Ewell, "Life in Old Bel Air"; Harriot Stoddert Turner, "Ewells of Virginia," 11-12, CWM. Years later, while a lieutenant in the Old Army, Richard Ewell was best man at the Bel Air wedding of Lt. Robert Tansill and Fanny Weems. Tansill later became military governor of San Francisco. During the Civil War he was on the staff of Maj. Gen. William H. C. Whiting.

10. Hayden, *Virginia Genealogies*, 339, 349-52.

11. Ewell Family Bible Records, folder 23, WM; Ewell Family Bible Records, TX. Thomas was born on 22 May 1785 at Bel Air.

12. Various letters, Jesse Ewell to Thomas Ewell, WM; Johnson and Malone, *Dictionary*, 6:230; Henry S. Foote, *Bench and Bar*, 172; Thomas Ewell biographical sketch, folder 23, WM. Dr. George Graham was the great-grandfather of Varina Howell Davis, the wife of Jefferson Davis.

13. Thomas Ewell biographical sketch, folder 23, WM.

14. Ibid.; Johnson and Malone, *Dictionary*, 6:230-31; Chapman, "Benjamin Stoddert Ewell," 15, CWM; Harriot Stoddert Turner, "Ewells of Virginia," 14, CWM.

15. Johnson and Malone, *Dictionary*, 6:231; Thomas Ewell biographical sketch, folder 23, WM.

16. Ewell Family Bible Records, folder 23, WM; Eberlein and Hubbard, *Historic Houses*, 28; genealogical notes in folder 22, WM.

17. Harriot Stoddert Turner, "Ewells of Virginia," 18, CWM; miscellaneous note, folder 23, WM; 1795 plat of Georgetown, Library of Congress; Eberlein and Hubbard, *Historic Houses*, 22; Truett, *Guide*, 354; Ecker, *Old Georgetown*, 77. Thirty-fourth Street was then known as Frederick Street.

18. Thomas Ewell biographical sketch, folder 23, WM; Bryan, *National Capital*, 2:7; George R. Brown, *Washington*, 228; Harriot Stoddert Turner, "Ewells of Virginia," 18, CWM; Chapman, "Benjamin Stoddert Ewell," 28, CWM. The Ewell house stood on the west side of Pres-

ident's Square (now Lafayette Square) near Pennsylvania Avenue. It was described as a brick house "of the usual local design,—two stories high with a sloping roof pierced by dormer windows" and an attic (Bryan, *National Capital*, 2:7). The house's address at the time of the Civil War was No. 7, 16½ Street, but it later became 14 Jackson Place. The building was destroyed in 1930, and the Brookings Institute was built on the site.

19. Thomas Ewell biographical sketch, folder 23, WM; anonymous notes, folder 23, WM; Johnson and Malone, *Dictionary*, 6:231; Chapman, "Benjamin Stoddert Ewell," 28, CWM. The evidence of Thomas's alcoholism, though not conclusive, is convincing. The *Dictionary of American Biography* speaks of the "convivial habits which weakened his health." A biographical sketch in folder 23, WM, refers to Thomas's failure to learn the "habits of self control" and speaks of his "chequered life." Thomas's son Paul later made speeches against drinking, and his great-great-great-granddaughter Rebecca Paluzy told Anne W. Chapman that Thomas had suffered from both alcoholism and depression.

20. Miscellaneous notes, folders 22 and 23, WM; "Ewell Family History," 7, TX; BSE to Uncle William Stoddert, 7 Dec. 1834, WM; Mrs. Nathaniel McGregor Ewell to author, 28 May 1986; Johnson and Malone, *Dictionary*, 6:231; Prince William County, Va., Deed Book 34, 335–36; Agricultural Schedule, 1850 Census, Prince William County, Va. Thomas Ewell purchased the property, which stood on Kettle Run four miles west of Bristoe Station, from his cousin Solomon Ewell. Stony Lonesome appears on plate 45, no. 6, of the *Official Military Atlas*.

The property's acreage is difficult to ascertain. An 1820 agreement between Rebecca Stoddert and Thomas Ewell in the Thomas Ewell Papers, VHS, indicates that the tract had approximately 1,300 acres. Later census records indicate that the farm had decreased to 480 acres by 1850 (Agricultural Schedule, 1850 Census, Prince William County, Va., T-1132, R3, NA). By 1883, when William Stoddert acquired it, the tract consisted of just 414 acres (deed in folder 20, WM).

The house was destroyed early in the twentieth century. Conversations by the author with elderly local residents indicate its site is on the east side of Lonesome Road (Route 707), one-half mile north of Kettle Run. A modern dwelling stands adjacent to the site of the old house, of which no traces remain. Virginia Writers Program, *Prince William*, mistakes both the location of the house and the origin of its name.

21. In 1824 the Ewells acquired four ½-acre lots in the town of Centreville from Gordon, Eliza, and Robert Allison in exchange for 344 acres and 80 poles of land in Fairfax County. Adams, Mary, Main, and Francis Streets bordered the lots, which, taken together, formed a complete block near the center of town. Four Chimney House stood on lot 13, and a school-house—possibly the one later used by Mrs. Ewell and her daughters to teach—stood on lot 15. Four Chimney House was a white frame house with dark trim, 46 by 30 feet in size, two stories high, with a stone foundation and cellar. A kitchen and stable stood on the grounds.

After Thomas Ewell's death, the family was unable to maintain the home properly and it fell into disrepair. Rebecca described its condition to Ben in 1840: "The roof of the large house caught on fire sometime since, and the rain comes in and has necessarily done a great deal of damage to the walls and plastering while much of the underpinning has given way and the cellar is deluged with water. the porch is propped with rails the enclosure falling and burnt down. one of the small houses looks ready to tumble and the other ready to follow it" (RLE to BSE, June 1840, WM). Mrs. Ewell and her children sold the Centreville property to Alexander Spotswood Grigsby in 1846 for $600. The new owner apparently restored Four Chimney

House, which afterward became known as the Grigsby House. The structure received harsh treatment in the Civil War and fell into ruin by the turn of the century.

Four Chimney House stood near the intersection of modern Pickwick Road and Willoughby Newton Drive in Fairfax County. The recent construction of townhouses has destroyed any evidence of the structure, but as late as 1989 remains of the well could be seen just a few feet from the intersection. For more information on the house, see Eugenia B. Smith, *Centreville, Virginia*, 41–43. References to the purchase and sale of the Centreville lots are in Fairfax County's land records in Deed Book V2, 59–62, 72–75, and Deed Book L3, 317–19, 321–22. In addition, the following Ewell family correspondence contains references to the Centreville house: RSE to LCB, 20 Feb. 1862, LC; Thomas Ewell Jr. to EE, 7 Mar. 1840, WM; RLE to BSE, June 1840, WM; note dated 14 May 1846, folder 21, WM.

22. Harriot Stoddert Turner, "Ewells of Virginia," 19, CWM; George R. Brown, *Washington*, 303; Bryan, *National Capital*, 2:7 n. For twenty years cabinet officials leased the house. Its occupants included Smith Thompson, secretary of the navy under James Monroe; Samuel L. Southard, secretary of the navy under Monroe and John Q. Adams; John M. Berrien, attorney general under Andrew Jackson; and Levi Woodbury, secretary of the navy and secretary of the treasury under Martin Van Buren. Congressman (later Maj. Gen.) Daniel Sickles was living at the house in 1859 when he shot and killed Philip Barton Key. After the Civil War the house became the residence of President Ulysses S. Grant's vice-president, Schuyler Colfax.

23. 1830 Census Records, Prince William County, Va., R196, 66, NA. The Slave Schedule for the 1850 Census shows four slaves at Stony Lonesome. By 1860 there were just two. See Slave Schedule, 1850 Census, Prince William County, Va., R992, 783, and Slave Schedule, 1860 Census, Prince William County, Va., R1896, 92, NA.

24. Harriot Stoddert Turner, "Ewells of Virginia," 20–22, CWM. For other references to this loyal family servant, see ESE to RLE, May 1834, 11 Apr. 1838, folder 8, WM, and Gache, *A Frenchman, a Chaplain, a Rebel*, 81–82.

25. Thomas Ewell biographical sketch, folder 23, WM.

26. Johnson and Malone, *Dictionary*, 6:231; Ewell Family Bible Records, folder 23, WM; Chapman, "Benjamin Stoddert Ewell," 20, CWM. Thomas Ewell died on 1 May 1826 and was buried in the family garden at Centreville.

27. BSE to ESE, 6 Dec. 1892, WM.

28. Morton, *Robert Carter*, 37–38; McGrath, *Pillars*, 314–17; Powell, *Tercentenary History*, 4:31–32, 890–91; miscellaneous notes, folders 22, 23, and 24, WM. See Appendix B.

29. Johnson and Malone, *Dictionary*, 18:62–63; Ecker, *Old Georgetown*, 12, 32–35, 77–79; Powell, *Tercentenary History*, 4:17–18; Bryan, *National Capital*, 1:97, 123–24, 223, 330; Eberlein and Hubbard, *Historic Houses*, 22–28, 54, 144; miscellaneous notes, folder 23, WM. On Benjamin Stoddert's insolvency at the time of his death, see also RSE to LE, 11 May 1859, LC.

30. Miscellaneous notes, folders 21 and 23, WM; TTG to LCB, 16 July 1855, TN; ESE to BSE, 2 Apr. 1884, WM; Ewell Family Bible Records, folder 23, WM; Harriot Stoddert Turner, "Ewells of Virginia," 14–17, CWM; Wharton, *Social Life*, 38–41.

31. Harriot Stoddert Turner, "Ewells of Virginia," 20, CWM; ESE to BSE, 2 Apr. 1884, WM; Paul Ewell to BSE, 14 Feb. 1831, WM; Agriculture Schedule, 1850 Census, Prince William County, Va., T-1132, R3, 31, NA. The 1850 Agriculture Schedule shows 400 improved acres and 80 unimproved acres worth a total of $2,400—or just $5 an acre. At that time the farm had an annual yield of 30 bushels of wheat, 45 bushels of Indian corn, 30 bushels of Irish potatoes, and 50 tons of hay. Livestock included 4 horses, 6 milch cows, 2 oxen, 9 cattle, 20 sheep, and 5 swine, worth $300.

32. RSE to LCB, 20 Feb. 1862, LC; BSE to Paul Ewell, undated letter, folder 5, WM; EE to BSE, 16 May [1835?] and undated letter [ca. 1830], folder 7, WM; RSE to BSE, 29 Mar. 1840, LC; miscellaneous notes, folders 8 and 21, WM; Cullum, *Biographical Register*, 1:339.

33. Ewell Family Bible Records, folder 23, WM; Hamlin, *Old Bald Head*, 4; BSE to RLE, 10 Apr. 1830, WM; Paul Ewell to BSE, 14 Feb. 1831, WM; EE to BSE, 13 Mar. 1831, WM; RLE to BSE, 15 Mar. 1831, WM; EE to BSE, 17 Apr. [1831], WM; BSE to ESE, 6 Dec. 1892, WM; ESE to ?, undated letter, folder 42, PBE; Ewell family sketch, folder 22, WM; miscellaneous note, folder 23, WM; Chapman, "Benjamin Stoddert Ewell," 29 n., CWM. The Ewell family cemetery is located in a small field south of Centreville, near the junction of Mount Olive Road and Folkers Landing Road. Cedar trees and fieldstones mark the graveyard, but there are no headstones. Encroaching development threatens the site (1997). See Conley, *Cemeteries*, p. 122.

34. EE to BSE, 12 May 1832, WM; TTG to LCB, 29 June 1855, TN. For evidence of Ewell's eccentricity, see Hunton, *Autobiography*, 97; Haskell, *Memoirs*, 18; Munford, "Reminiscences," 523; Richard Taylor, *Destruction*, 78; and Hunter McGuire to Jedediah Hotchkiss, 27 June 1896, R34, F170, HP.

35. ESE to CB, 4 May 1885, FC; ESE to ?, undated letter, folder 42, PBE.

36. RLE to BSE, 15 May 1835, WM; Thomas Ewell Jr. to EE, 2 May 1841, WM; Hamlin, *Old Bald Head*, 6–7; BSE to Paul Ewell, 1 Apr. 1830, WM. The Ewells may have attended the Episcopal church in Brentsville (EE to BSE, 15 Mar. 1840, WM). For evidence that the book in question was a Bible, see RSE to RLE, 2 Mar. 1844, LC.

37. Harriot Stoddert Turner, "Ewells of Virginia," 26, CWM; BSE to RLE, 10 Apr. 1830, WM.

38. Detailed accounts of this incident are in EE to RLE, 12 Apr. 1835, WM, and in [ESE] to BSE, undated letter [Apr. 1835], folder 19, WM. A brief account of the episode appears in Harriot Stoddert Turner, "Ewells of Virginia," 26–27, CWM.

39. Harriot Stoddert Turner, "Ewells of Virginia," 27, CWM; EE to BSE, 17 Apr. [1831], 16 May [1835?], folder 7, WM; D. L. Ewell to RSE, 3 Sept. 1866, WM; miscellaneous note, folder 23, WM; ESE to BSE, 16 Sept. 1834, WM; ESE to LE, 16 July 1894, WM; ESE to ?, undated letter, folder 42, PBE. Plate 45, no. 6, of *Official Military Atlas* shows a Fitzhugh residence in Fauquier County, between Stony Lonesome and Warrenton. This may be where Richard attended school under Mr. Knox.

40. Uncle William Stoddert to BSE, 17 Nov. 1834, WM; BSE to Uncle William Stoddert, 7 Dec. 1834, WM; TTG to BSE, 11 Feb. 1835, WM; ESE to BSE, 16 Sept. 1834, WM.

41. EE to RLE, 12 Apr. 1835, WM; [ESE] to BSE, undated letter [Apr. 1835], folder 19, WM; TTG to BSE, 11 Feb. 1835, WM. The engineers administered the U.S. Military Academy at that time.

42. EE to RLE, undated letter and 10 Mar. 1836, folder 7, WM; U.S. Military Academy Application Papers, RG 94, M688, R103, application no. 66, NA; BSE to RLE, 22 May 1836, WM.

Chapter 2

1. *Regulations*, 2; RSE to RLE, 29 Aug. 1836, USMA; Cullum, *Biographical Register*, vol. 2. Richardson would graduate one year late because of an academic deficiency.

2. Ewell biographical sketch, box 84, folder 5, Yeatman-Polk Papers, TSLA; Boyd, *Reminiscences*, 22; RSE to LCB, 10 Feb. 1862, Museum of the Confederacy. David French Boyd is the

authority for the statement on the friendship of Ewell and Sherman. Boyd was a professor at the Louisiana Military Academy when Sherman was its superintendent. He probably derived his information from Sherman.

3. RSE to RLE, 29 Aug. 1836, USMA; Chapman, "Benjamin Stoddert Ewell," 20, CWM. Later that same year Tom Ewell was also mistaken for Dick, although he was five years Dick's junior.

4. Ambrose, *Duty, Honor, Country*, 39; Fleming, *West Point*, 38–40; Morrison, *"Best School,"* 69; *Regulations*, 17.

5. Special Orders 13 and Battalion Orders 52, Post Orders, 6:402, USMA; Battalion Orders 3 and 92, Post Orders, vol. 7, USMA.

6. RSE to RLE, 29 Aug. 1836, USMA.

7. Fleming, *West Point*, 46, 94; Battalion Orders 26 and 97, Post Orders, vol. 7, USMA; Battalion Orders 53, Post Orders, 6:403, USMA; *Regulations*, 29–30; Ambrose, *Duty, Honor, Country*, 152; Lloyd Lewis, *Sherman*, 52.

8. RSE to BSE, 16 Nov. 1836, USMA; *Southern Home* (Charlotte, N.C.), 5 Feb. 1872; "Register of Officers and Cadets," RG 404, ser. 299, Conduct Rolls, Class of 1840, 19, USMA. Campbell graduated twenty-seventh and stood near the bottom of his class in conduct.

9. Ambrose, *Duty, Honor, Country*, 154; "Statement of Cadet Accounts," RG 404, ser. 242, USMA.

10. Fleming, *West Point*, 47, 55, 92, 100–101; Morrison, *"Best School,"* 44, 81; Ambrose, *Duty, Honor, Country*, 51, 150, 163; *Regulations*, 31–36; O'Connor, *Thomas*, 65; "Official Register of Delinquencies, 1838–1842," RG 404, ser. 101/102, 88, USMA; U.S. Military Academy Academic Records, RG 404, ser. 299, USMA.

11. Morrison, *"Best School,"* 85–86; Ambrose, *Duty, Honor, Country*, 151; Fleming, *West Point*, 59; RSE to RLE, 6 May 1838, LC.

12. Ambrose, *Duty, Honor, Country*, 24–26, 166; Cleaves, *Rock of Chickamauga*, 12–13; Orders 167, Post Orders, 6:444, USMA; *Bulletin of the Dialectic Society*, 1840, USMA. A certificate testifying to Ewell's membership in the Dialectic Society is on file at USMA.

13. Anonymous notes, folder 21, WM; RSE to BSE, 16 Nov. 1836, USMA.

14. Morrison, *"Best School,"* 23; U.S. Military Academy Academic Records, 1840, RG 404, ser. 299, 6–7, USMA.

15. RSE to RLE, 6 May 1838, LC; Morrison, *"Best School,"* 4.

16. Ambrose, *Duty, Honor, Country*, 74–80, 90, 93–94, 131–33; Fleming, *West Point*, 31, 45, 62–64; Morrison, *"Best School,"* 87–88.

17. Ambrose, *Duty, Honor, Country*, 91–92; Morrison, *"Best School,"* 92; RSE to BSE, 16 Nov. 1836, USMA.

18. RSE to RLE, 29 Aug. 1836, USMA.

19. Order 162 and Special Orders 43, Post Orders, vol. 6, USMA; RSE to BSE, 16 Nov. 1836, USMA.

20. Special Orders 1, Post Orders, 6:486–87, USMA; Battalion Orders 2, Post Orders, 6:489, USMA; EE to BSE, 24 Jan. 1837, WM.

21. Battalion Orders 62 and Special Orders 63, Post Orders, 6:589, 591, 595, USMA; U.S. Military Academy Academic Records, 1837, RG 404, ser. 299, USMA.

22. Morrison, *"Best School,"* 69–70.

23. ESE to CB, 2 Mar. 1874, TN.

24. RSE to RLE, 29 Aug. 1836, USMA; RSE to RLE, 6 May 1838, LC; RSE to BSE, 16 Nov. 1836, USMA; RSE to EE, 3 Oct. 1839, in Hamlin, *Letters*, 26.

25. RSE to BSE, 16 Nov. 1836, USMA; RSE to EE, 3 Oct. 1839, in Hamlin, *Letters*, 26.

26. Morrison, *"Best School,"* 93; U.S. Military Academy Academic Records, 1838, RG 404, ser. 299, USMA.

27. RSE to RLE, 6 May 1838, LC; EE to BSE, 18 Sept. 1838, WM; RSE to BSE, 29 Mar. 1840, LC; RLE to BSE, May 1838, WM.

28. U.S. Military Academy Academic Records, 1839, RG 404, ser. 299, USMA; *Regulations*, 40; Morrison, *"Best School,"* 72; Battalion Orders 74, Post Orders, vol. 7, USMA; Battalion Orders 21, Post Orders, vol. 7, USMA; "Registers of Punishments, Oct. 1837–1900," RG 404, ser. 105, USMA.

29. Ambrose, *Duty, Honor, Country*, 163; RSE to BSE, 10 Jan. 1840, LC.

30. Fleming, *West Point*, 96–97; Ambrose, *Duty, Honor, Country*, 126; Morrison, *"Best School,"* 40; RSE to BSE, 10 Jan. 1840, LC.

31. RSE to BSE, 10 Jan., 29 Mar. 1840, LC; RSE to EE, 3 Oct. 1839, in Hamlin, *Letters*, 28–29.

32. Morrison, *"Best School,"* 93–94; *Regulations*, 12–14; RSE to BSE, 29 Mar. 1840, LC; U.S. Military Academy Academic Records, 1839, RG 404, ser. 299, USMA; "Adjutant's Office, June 29, 1839," Post Orders, vol. 7, USMA.

33. Ewell character sketch, folder 27, WM; Battalion Orders 52, Post Orders, vol. 7, USMA; Morrison, *"Best School,"* 72; Fleming, *West Point*, 100.

34. Fleming, *West Point*, 102–3; Order 50, Post Orders, vol. 7, USMA; Battalion Orders 61, Post Orders, vol. 7, USMA.

35. Quoted in Hamlin, *Old Bald Head*, 10. "Animal" was another name for a plebe.

36. Ambrose, *Duty, Honor, Country*, 135; Battalion Orders 68, Post Orders, vol. 7, USMA.

37. Note by Harriot Turner in folder 21, WM; excerpt from a speech by Henry Kyd Douglas to the R. E. Lee Camp of Confederate Veterans, quoted in folder 24, WM.

38. Ambrose, *Duty, Honor, Country*, 98; Morrison, *"Best School,"* 94; Special Orders 15, Post Orders, 8:40, USMA.

39. Morrison, *"Best School,"* 47, 96–97; Fleming, *West Point*, 111, 170; Ambrose, *Duty, Honor, Country*, 99–102; Library Circulation Records, U.S. Military Academy, 1836–41, USMA.

40. "Register of Officers and Cadets at U.S. Military Academy," 1840, USMA; "Adjutant's Office," Post Orders, 8:70–71, USMA.

41. RSE to EE, 3 Oct. 1839, in Hamlin, *Letters*, 27; RSE to BSE, 29 Mar. 1840, LC.

42. RSE to EE, 3 Oct. 1839, in Hamlin, *Letters*, 27; RSE to BSE, 29 Mar., 10 Jan. 1840, LC.

43. RSE to BSE, 10 Jan. 1840, LC.

44. Heitman, *Historical Register*, 1:410; Ambrose, *Duty, Honor, Country*, 166.

Chapter 3

1. RLE to BSE, June 1840, WM; Thomas Ewell Jr. to EE, 17 Jan. [1837], 9 Jan. 1840, WM; Ewell Family Bible Records, folder 23, WM.

2. ESE to BSE, 15 Jan. 1838, WM; EE to BSE, 10 Mar. 1838, 15 Mar. 1840, WM; RLE to BSE, June 1840, WM. In a postscript to a letter written about 1835, Dick signed his name Richard Stoddert. Thereafter he always used his surname (EE to BSE, 16 May [1835?], folder 7, WM).

3. Ulysses S. Grant, *Memoirs*, 1:42; Thomas Ewell Jr. to EE, 16 Aug. 1840, LC.

4. RSE to BSE, 21 Oct. 1840, LC; RSE to RLE, 12 Nov. 1840, LC.

5. Merrill, *Spurs to Glory*, 80–81.

6. Thomas Claiborne Reminiscences, folder 15, Claiborne Papers, SHC; RSE to BSE, 21 Oct. 1840, LC; RSE to RLE, 12 Nov. 1840, LC.

7. RSE to BSE, 21 Oct. 1840, LC; RSE to RLE, 12 Nov. 1840, LC.

8. RSE to RLE, 12 Nov. 1840, LC.

9. RSE to BSE, 2 Feb. 1841, LC. Fort Gibson was at the mouth of the Neosho River, thirty-five miles southeast of modern-day Tulsa (*Official Military Atlas*, plate 160).

10. Oliva, "Fort Scott," 2; Harry Myers, "Guardians," 8–9.

11. Regimental Orders 61, RG 94, M744, R1, F270, NA; *Official Military Atlas*, plate 160; RSE to BSE, 2 Feb. 1841, LC.

12. RSE to RLE, 13 Nov. 1841, LC.

13. William Eustis to "Dear Bob," 3 Dec. 1841, Johnston Papers, USMA.

14. RSE to RLE, 10 Apr. 1842, 3 Oct. 1845, LC; RSE to BSE, 2 Feb. 1841, LC. For Ewell's comments on his horses, see RSE to BSE, 18 Feb. 1844, LC.

15. RSE to RLE, 13 Nov. 1841, LC.

16. RSE to BSE, 1 Aug. 1844, LC.

17. RSE to RLE, 25 Oct. 1844, LC.

18. RSE to BSE, 2 Feb. 1841, LC.

19. RSE to RLE, 13 Nov. 1841, LC.

20. Hamlin, *Old Bald Head*, 13–14. In another letter written about this time, Tom grumbled, "Fortune does frown upon me in a very dirty manner, & Nature too has been unkind, for she has given me a large fleshy tongue which instead of uttering Christian words, produces a contemptible kind of noise between lisp & a mutter, & exposes me to more mortification than I would care for my enemy to be aware of. . . . Young Love a Cadet from Nashville, told me that I talked just like Richard—I wonder if R. has the same mass of a tongue." Apparently he did (Thomas Ewell Jr. to EE, undated letter [ca. Nov. 1841], folder 10, WM).

21. RSE to BSE, 13 Nov. 1841, LC; Hamlin, *Old Bald Head*, 195. Contrary to popular belief, there is no evidence of Ewell being widely known by this or any other nickname during the Civil War.

22. RSE to RLE, 2 Mar. 1844, LC; Benjamin S. Ewell, "Jackson and Ewell," 29.

23. RSE to RLE, 13 Nov. 1841, 2 Mar. 1844, LC; RSE to BSE, 18 Feb. 1844, LC.

24. BSE to LE, 28 Feb. 1863, WM.

25. William Eustis to "Dear Bob," 3 Dec. 1841, Johnston Papers, USMA; Heitman, *Historical Register*, 1:888.

26. Harry Myers, "Guardians," 10; RSE to RLE, 13 Nov. 1841, LC.

27. RSE to RLE, 10 Apr. 1842, LC.

28. Oliva, "Fort Scott," 2–3.

29. Ibid., 5; "Returns from U.S. Military Posts, 1800–1916," Fort Scott, Kans., Oct. 1842, RG 94, M617, R1138, NA.

30. Philip St. George Cooke, *Scenes and Adventures*, 236, 240–41. For evidence suggesting that Ewell contracted the disease at this time, see EE to BSE, 1 Jan. 1846, WM, and RLE to BSE, 31 Jan. 1846, WM.

31. Otis E. Young, "Dragoons," 45; Philip St. George Cooke, *Scenes and Adventures*, 240, 247, 263; Connelly, "Journal," 250–51.

32. Connelly, "Journal," 251–52.

33. RSE to BSE, 5 Nov. 1843, LC; Connelly, "Journal," 252.

34. Connelly, "Journal," 252.

35. Philip St. George Cooke, *Scenes and Adventures*, 273–77; RSE to BSE, 5 Nov. 1843, LC.

36. Philip St. George Cooke, *Scenes and Adventures*, 259.

37. Ibid., 278.

38. Connelly, "Journal," 253–54. Cooke got Ewell's middle initial wrong.

Chapter 4

1. RSE to BSE, 18 Feb. 1844, LC; RSE to RLE, 2 Mar. 1844, LC.

2. J. H. K. Burgwyn to Abraham R. Johnston, 23 Dec. 1840, Johnston Papers, USMA; J. B. Ewell to Martha M. Ewell, 19 Jan. 1846, TX.

3. Hamlin, *Old Bald Head*, 195–96; Williams, "High Private," 157.

4. RSE to RLE, 2 Mar. 1844, LC. Fanny Elssler was a famous ballet dancer of the period.

5. RSE to BSE, 18 Feb. 1844, LC; Regimental Orders 13, Post Returns, Fort Scott, Kans., May 1844, RG 94, M617, R1138, NA.

6. RSE to BSE, 1 Aug. 1844, LC; EE to BSE, 1 Jan. 1846, WM.

7. Ulysses S. Grant, *Memoirs*, 1:43–49; RSE to LCB, 28 May 1865, FC.

8. RSE to BSE, 1 Aug., 17 Oct. 1844, LC.

9. RSE to BSE, 1 Aug. 1844, LC.

10. RSE to RLE, 25 Oct. 1844, LC.

11. RSE to BSE, 5 Nov. 1843, 1 Aug., 17 Oct. 1844, LC.

12. RSE to BSE, 17 Oct. 1844, LC; RSE to RLE, 25 Oct. 1844, LC.

13. RSE to BSE, 28 Feb. 1845, LC; RSE to RLE, 14 Jan. 1845, LC.

14. RSE to RLE, 14 Jan., 3 Oct. 1845, LC.

15. RSE to BSE, 28 Feb. 1845, LC.

16. Regimental Returns, First Dragoons, Jan. 1846, RG 94, M744, R2, NA; EE to RLE, 16 June 1845, WM. Ewell had attended a "tea fight" at O'Fallon's with Colonel Kearny the previous October.

17. Gardner, "March of the 1st Dragoons," 247–51.

18. Ibid., 252–55; Carleton, *Prairie Logbooks*, 158–62.

19. Philip St. George Cooke, *Scenes and Adventures*, 291; Carleton, *Prairie Logbooks*, 172.

20. Carleton, *Prairie Logbooks*, 169.

21. Quoted in Merrill, *Spurs to Glory*, 41; Carleton, *Prairie Logbooks*, 178–79, 265.

22. Philip St. George Cooke, *Scenes and Adventures*, 313, 319; Carleton, *Prairie Logbooks*, 232–34, 237; Longworthy, *Scenery of the Plains*, 51–52.

23. Philip St. George Cooke, *Scenes and Adventures*, 335–38.

24. Ibid., 338, 431–32.

25. Post Returns, Fort Scott, Kans., Aug.–Sept. 1845, RG 94, M617, R1138, NA.

26. RSE to RLE, 3 Oct. 1845, LC.

27. Ibid.

28. Ibid.

29. Ibid.; Post Returns, Fort Scott, Kans., Nov. 1845, RG 94, M617, R1138, NA.

30. EE to BSE, 1 Jan. 1846, WM.

31. RSE to LE, 16 Aug. 1859, LC.

32. For Tom's education and career, see WS to EE, 1 Jan. 1837, WM; EE to BSE, 11 July 1837, 10 Mar. 1838, WM; Thomas Ewell Jr. to EE, 3 Dec. 1837, 18 Jan. 1838, 29 Sept. 1839, 30 Apr.

1842, WM; Thomas Ewell Jr. to BSE, 1 Sept. 1842, 1 Jan. 1846, WM; RLE to BSE, 15 Dec. 1845, WM. For biographical sketches of Tom Ewell, see folders 22 and 23, WM.

33. EE to BSE, 1 Jan. 1846, WM.

34. Ibid.; RLE to BSE, 31 Jan. 1846, WM.

35. EE to BSE, 11 July 1837, 10 Mar. 1838, WM; RLE to BSE, Aug. 1837, 15 Dec. 1845, 31 Jan. 1846, WM; ESE to BSE, Mar. 1851, WM; Harriot Stoddert Turner, "Ewells of Virginia," 16, CWM.

36. RLE to BSE, 31 Jan. 1846, WM; RSE to Adjutant General's Office, 24 Feb., 21 Mar. 1846, RG 94, M567, NA. Drs. Joseph C. Greenfield Jr., Marvin Rozear, and G. Ralph Corey of the Duke University Medical Center believe Ewell suffered from a vivax malaria (plasmodium vivax) infection. They base their theory on the debilitating and recurrent nature of Ewell's attacks and on the prevalence of the disease in the areas in which he served. For a summary of Ewell's medical history, see Welsh, *Medical Histories*, 63–66.

37. Heitman, *Historical Register*, 1:410; Cullum, *Biographical Register*, 1:602; Regimental Orders 26, RG 94, M617, R1138, NA. Notice of Ewell's promotion does not appear in Fort Scott's records until December 1845, a month after he had left the post.

38. RLE to BSE, 31 Jan. 1846, WM; Cullum, *Biographical Register*, 1:602; Hamlin, *Old Bald Head*, 34; Special Orders 31, RG 94, M744, R2, NA; Special Orders 42, RG 94, M744, R3, NA. Ewell was assigned to the Coast Survey by Special Orders 31, dated 14 April 1846, but he did not report for duty until 1 May at the expiration of his leave (RSE to Adjutant General's Office, 23 Mar. 1846, RG 94, M567, R314, NA). On assignment with the Coast Survey at the same time were Lts. Henry Prince, Edward O. C. Ord, and Roswell S. Ripley, all of whom later became generals in the Civil War. Whether Ewell served directly with any of them is unknown.

39. Singletary, *Mexican War*, 9, 13.

40. RSE to Roger Jones, 4 June 1846, RG 94, M567, R314, NA; RSE to Adjutant General's Office, RG 94, M567, R314, NA.

41. EE to BSE, 27 Oct. 1846, WM; RSE to Roger Jones, 4 June 1846, RG 94, M567, R314, NA.

42. EE to BSE, 27 Oct. 1846, WM.

43. RSE to Roger Jones, 23 Aug. 1846, RG 94, M567, R314, NA.

44. EE to BSE, 27 Oct. 1846, WM. Elizabeth quotes a letter from Dick.

Chapter 5

1. Hamlin, *Old Bald Head*, 5; Henry Hunt to BSE, 1 Dec. 1886, LC.

2. Singletary, *Mexican War*, 71; Thomas Ewell Jr. to BSE, 12 Feb. 1847, LC.

3. EE to BSE, 27 Oct. 1846, WM; Thomas Ewell Jr. to BSE, 12 Feb. 1847, LC; Hamlin, *Old Bald Head*, 35.

4. Singletary, *Mexican War*, 73–75.

5. Winfield Scott to BSE, 16 Dec. 1850, RG 107, 15W3, row 11, compartment 5, shelf A, box 59, NA.

6. Singletary, *Mexican War*, 78; Winfield Scott, *Memoirs*, 2:432.

7. RSE to BSE, 3 May 1847, LC; Harriot Stoddert Turner, "Ewells of Virginia," 28–29, CWM; Columbia *Beacon*, 28 May 1847; RSE to EE, 22 Apr. 1847, LC; Nashville *Republican Banner*, 26 Jan. 1872. Ewell's original 22 April letter has not been found. Cited here is a copy of the letter as transcribed by Mrs. Ewell.

8. RSE to EE, 22 Apr. 1847, LC. For other eyewitness accounts of Thomas Ewell's wounding and death, see the Columbia *Beacon*, 28 May 1847, and Lt. Thomas Claiborne's reminiscences in folder 15, Claiborne Papers, SHC. Ewell and Claiborne later exhumed Tom's body and shipped it back to Jackson, Tenn. (Ewell Family Bible Records, folder 23, WM; Nashville *Republican Banner*, 26 Jan. 1872).

9. Singletary, *Mexican War*, 82−83; RSE to BSE, 3 May 1847, LC.

10. Singletary, *Mexican War*, 85−87.

11. Ibid., 86−87.

12. RSE to BSE, 25 Nov. 1847, LC.

13. Ibid.

14. Ibid.; Singletary, *Mexican War*, 87−88.

15. Wilcox, *Mexican War*, 378−80; Ripley, *The War*, 2:269; *Message*, 309.

16. RSE to BSE, 25 Nov. 1847, LC.

17. Ibid.; RSE to EE, 1 Sept. 1847, LC; Ripley, *The War*, 2:269, 278−79; Harriot Stoddert Turner, "Ewells of Virginia," 27, CWM; *Message*, 313; extract of Harney's official report of the battle, in LC; Regimental Returns, First Dragoons, Company G, Aug. 1847, RG 94, M744, R2, NA.

18. RSE to EE, 1 Sept. 1847, LC.

19. Singletary, *Mexican War*, 94−97.

20. RSE to BSE, 25 Nov. 1847, LC. Ewell is quoted in EE to BSE, 5 Dec. 1848 [*sic*; 1847], WM.

21. Utley, *Frontiersmen in Blue*, 1; Wilcox, *Mexican War*, 483.

22. Quoted in EE to BSE, 5 Dec. 1848 [*sic*; 1847], WM.

23. Wilcox, *Mexican War*, 511, 710−11; RSE to LCB, 22 June 1865, TN; EE to BSE, 5 Mar. 1848, WM; *Constitution of the Aztec Society*, a pamphlet in LC; anonymous clipping in Campbell Brown scrapbook, box 20, folder 13, TN.

24. Wilcox, *Mexican War*, 511; Ewell letter quoted in [EE] to BSE, 14 May 1848, LC.

25. Regimental Returns, First Dragoons, Company G, Dec. 1847, RG 94, M744, R2, NA; Cullum, *Biographical Register*, 1:602; Heitman, *Historical Register*, 1:410.

26. Quoted in EE to BSE, 5 Dec. 1848 [*sic*; 1847], WM.

27. Quoted in EE to BSE, 5 Mar. 1848, WM.

28. EE to BSE, 5 Mar. 1848, WM; [EE] to BSE, 14 May 1848, LC. Dick's Aunt Harriot Campbell went so far as to solicit President Polk for a leave of absence on his behalf.

29. Singletary, *Mexican War*, 160; Ewell quoted in [EE] to BSE, 14 May 1848, LC.

30. TTG to BSE, 16 Aug. 1848, WM. Dr. Jack D. Welsh defines facial neuralgia as "paroxysmal pain that extends along the course of one or more nerves in the face" (Welsh, *Medical Histories*, 274).

31. WS to BSE, 6 Sept. 1848, WM.

32. Ibid.

33. RSE to BSE, 4 Apr. 1849, LC.

34. Regimental Returns, First Dragoons, Company G, Feb. 1849, and Company E, Apr. 1849, RG 94, M744, R2, NA; RSE to BSE, 18 Mar. 1849, LC.

35. For references to Schaumburgh, see RSE to BSE, 18 Feb., 13 Mar., 17 Oct. 1844, 28 Feb. 1845, 18 Mar. [1849], 4 Apr. 1849, LC.

36. RSE to BSE, 13 Mar. 1844, 4 Apr. 1849, LC.

37. RSE to BSE, 4 Apr. 1849, LC.

38. Ibid.; Heitman, *Historical Register*, 1:863. Jefferson Davis was instrumental in defeating Schaumburgh's confirmation. According to Campbell Brown, Ewell esteemed Davis thereafter

(Jefferson Davis to CB, 9 July 1885, Davis Association Papers, Rice University, and CB to Jefferson Davis, 23 July 1885, Davis Papers, Tulane University).

39. RSE to Lorenzo Thomas, 20 Apr. 1849, RG 94, M567, R404, F620, NA; RSE to LCB, 8 June, 11 [June] 1865, FC; Heitman, *Historical Register*, 1:751. Northrup joined the First Dragoons in 1833, became a first lieutenant in 1836, and was dropped from the rolls in January 1848. He was reinstated seven months later with his promotion to captain dating from 21 July. He remained in the U.S. Army until 1861, when he resigned to become commissary general of the Confederacy.

40. Heitman, *Historical Register*, 1:410; RSE to BSE, 18 Mar. 1849, LC. *Webster's New Collegiate Dictionary* defines a brevet as "a commission giving a military officer higher nominal rank than that for which he receives pay."

41. Ewell once critically derided Baltimore as "a stupid place where one is bored to death either with Presbyterianism or the Mexican war" (RSE to BSE, 4 Apr. 1849, LC).

42. RSE to E. D. Townsend, 2 Mar. 1850, RG 94, M567, R427, F549, NA.

43. Coffman, *Old Army*, 147.

44. Coulling, *Lee Girls*, 27–29; RSE to RLE, 25 Feb. 1850 (fragment), LC. Britannia was Mary Lee's cousin (Freeman, *Lee*, 1:105).

45. Harriot Stoddert Turner, "Ewells of Virginia," 29–30, CWM; Robertson, *A. P. Hill*, 19; Henry Hunt to BSE, 1 Dec. 1886, LC. Hunt claimed that he visited Ewell frequently.

46. EE to RLE, 7 Feb. 1850, WM; RSE to BSE, 7, 20 June 1849, LC.

47. Thomas Ewell Jr. to EE, 16 Aug. 1840, LC; TTG to BSE, 8 Mar. 1850, WM.

48. RSE to BSE, 4 Apr. 1849, LC; RSE to RLE, 25 Feb., 24 Apr. 1850, LC.

49. RSE to RLE, 27 May 1865, LC; Prince William County, Va., Deed Book 34, 335–36. See also RSE to RLE, 28 Jan. 1854, LC.

50. BSE to RLE, 12 July 1850, WM. Apparently Ewell visited his cousin Lizinka Campbell Brown while in Nashville (RSE to LE, 21 Dec. 1852, LC).

51. Peters, *Kit Carson*, 368–69; RSE to BSE, 10 Aug. 1850, LC.

52. Heth, *Memoirs*, 81–83; Ann Gantt to BSE, 4 Oct. 1850, WM.

53. Harvey L. Carter, *"Dear Old Kit,"* 128–29; Peters, *Kit Carson*, 369–70. For evidence of Ewell's friendship with Carson, see RSE to BSE, 25 Feb. 1854, LC.

54. Special Orders 40, Department of New Mexico, RG 393, pt. 1, entry 3172, NA.

Chapter 6

1. Cremony, *Life among the Apaches*, 38; Utley, *Frontiersmen in Blue*, 80–84.

2. Utley, *Frontiersmen in Blue*, 85; Special Orders 40, Department of New Mexico, RG 393, pt. 1, entry 3172, NA; Harvey L. Carter, *"Dear Old Kit,"* 129.

3. Post Return, Rayado, N.M., Oct. 1850, RG 94, M617, R1535, NA; Morrison, *"Best School,"* 21; Utley, *Frontiersmen in Blue*, 12, 43.

4. Post Return, Rayado, N.M., Oct. 1850, RG 94, M617, R1535, NA.

5. Utley, *Frontiersmen in Blue*, 29; RSE to W. A. Nichols, 1 Nov. 1853, RG 393, M1102, R6, F800, NA; RSE to Lafayette McLaws, 1 June 1851, RG 393, M1102, R3, F463–64, NA.

6. RSE to Lafayette McLaws, 2 Apr. 1851, RG 393, M1102, R3, F489, NA; RSE to Assistant Adjutant General, 25 July 1852, RG 393, M1102, R5, F49, NA.

7. RSE to J. C. McFerrar, 1 Apr. and 7 May 1852, RG 393, M1102, R5, F17 and F37, NA; RSE to W. A. Nichols, 21 Mar. 1854, RG 393, M1120, R3, F647, NA; Post Return, Rayado, N.M., July 1851, RG 94, M617, R1535, NA.

8. General Orders 44, Department of New Mexico, RG 393, pt. 1, entry 3172, NA.

9. RSE to Lafayette McLaws, 6 June 1851, RG 393, M1102, R3, F466–67, NA; Heitman, *Historical Register*, 1:1032; Utley, *Frontiersmen in Blue*, 42. Joseph H. Whittlesey became major of the Fifth U.S. Cavalry in 1861. He retired from military service in November 1863.

10. Utley, *Frontiersmen in Blue*, 86.

11. Post Return, Rayado, N.M., July 1851, RG 94, M617, R1535, NA; RSE to Don Carlos Buell, 12 and 17 July 1851, RG 393, M1102, R3, F473 and F478–79, NA.

12. General Orders #19 (25 July 1851) and #23 (4 Aug. 1851), Ninth Military Department, RG 393, NA; Post Return, Rayado, N.M., Aug. 1851, RG 94, M617, R1535, NA; RSE to Don Carlos Buell, 27 July 1851, RG 393, M1102, R3, F484, NA; L. M. Maxwell to RSE, 30 July 1851, RG 393, M1102, R4, F140, NA; Utley, *Frontiersmen in Blue*, 86; RSE to Lafayette McLaws, 1 May 1851, RG 393, M1102, R3, F461, NA.

13. Utley, *Frontiersmen in Blue*, 87; RSE to Don Carlos Buell, 5 Sept. 1851, RG 393, M1102, R4, F140, NA; Orders and General Orders, Department of New Mexico, 36:14, RG 393, pt. 1, entry 3170, NA. Fort Defiance stood just west of the Arizona–New Mexico border.

14. Post Return, Fort Defiance, N.M., Sept. to Nov. 1851, RG 94, M617, R301, NA; Special Orders 90 and 92, Department of New Mexico, letterbook 27, pp. 19–20, RG 393, pt. 1, entry 3172, NA; Frazer, *Forts and Supplies*, 69; U.S. Secretary of War, *Annual Report*, 1856–57, pp. 244–45. Sumner initially ordered Ewell to Galisteo, twenty-five miles south of Santa Fe. When forage there proved insufficient, Sumner ordered him to proceed instead to Los Lunas or Sabinal. Ewell chose Los Lunas.

15. RSE to J. C. McFerrar, 24 Feb. and 12 Apr. 1852, RG 393, M1102, R5, F9 and F32, NA; RSE to Assistant Adjutant General, 17 Sept. 1852, RG 393, M1102, R5, F56, NA; Frazer, *Forts and Supplies*, 82. For an example of a shortage of horses and mules, see RSE to W. A. Nichols, 4 Nov. 1853, RG 393, M1102, R6, F802, NA.

16. RSE to J. C. McFerrar, 7 May 1852, RG 393, M1102, R5, F39, NA; RSE to Samuel Cooper, 21 Aug. 1853, RG 94, M567, R480, F260–61, NA; RSE to BSE, 21 July 1852, LC.

17. RSE to Samuel Sturgis, 24 May 1853, RG 94, M567, R480, F199–201, NA; RSE to Samuel Cooper, 21 Aug. 1853, RG 94, M567, R480, F260–61, NA. In a letter written in July 1856, on the eve of Company G's transfer to Arizona, Ewell expounded on the importance of gardens and other such endeavors to troop morale. "One of the Lieuts of my Comp'y the other day was asked why he did not make a fuss about the orders changing our station &c, but he said that all he cared about was seeing how the sweet potatoes would turn out. This looks silly but is in reality a key to Army life," Ewell explained. "Unless one drinks or gambles it is necessary to keep from absolute stagnation that interest should be taken in something. Promotion & the profession dont answer . . . & hence it is necessary to get up some outside humbug to take interest in & not to let yourself know that it is humbug" (RSE to ?, 28 July [1856], PBE).

18. RSE to BSE, 21 July, 23 Dec. 1852, LC; RSE to RLE, 28 Jan. 1854, LC. Whether the money was a gift to Elizabeth or part of some financial arrangement is not clear.

19. RSE to BSE, 23 Dec. 1852, LC; RSE to ESE, 5 Mar. 1856, LC.

20. RSE to BSE, 21 July 1852, 26 Mar. 1856, LC. For evidence of Ewell's quest for financial independence, see RSE to RLE, 28 Jan. 1854, LC.

21. RSE to BSE, 25 Feb. 1854, LC.

22. RSE to BSE, 26 Mar. 1856, LC.

23. RSE to RLE, 1 July 1855, LC; RSE to BSE, 25 Feb. 1854, LC.

24. Post Returns, Los Lunas, N.M., Jan. 1852–Dec. 1853, RG 94, M617, R648, NA; Heit-

man, *Historical Register*, 1:722, 1045; RSE to BSE, 21 July 1852, LC. Moore graduated fourteenth in the class of 1851. He became a captain in the regiment in April 1861, then transferred to the First U.S. Cavalry in August. He died on 16 January 1862.

25. RSE to BSE, 23 Dec. 1852, LC; RSE to Roger Jones, 1 Aug. 1852, RG 94, M567, R462, F296, NA.

26. RSE to BSE, 21 July 1852, LC.

27. RSE to BSE, 21 July, 23 Dec. 1852, LC; Heitman, *Historical Register*, 1:880–81; Boatner, *Civil War Dictionary*, 746. During the Civil War Shepherd fought for the Union army. He became colonel of the Fifteenth U.S. Infantry in January 1863, was brevetted brigadier general on 13 March 1865 for gallant and meritorious service at the battle of Stones River, and retired from military service in 1870.

28. RSE to Samuel Sturgis, 18 Jan. 1853, RG 393, M1102, R6, F714–15, NA. Sturgis later commanded a division in the Army of the Potomac.

29. RSE to Samuel Sturgis, 14 Aug. 1853, RG 393, M1102, R6, F751, NA.

30. RSE to W. A. Nichols, 22 Apr. 1854, RG 393, M1120, R3, F651, NA; Serven, "Sonoita Creek," 47.

31. RSE to W. A. Nichols, 16 Jan. 1854, RG 393, M1120, R3, F639, NA; RSE to RLE, 28 Jan. 1854, LC; Opher and Opher, "Mescalero Apache History," 6.

32. Utley, *Frontiersmen in Blue*, 148; Utley, *Indian Frontier*, 48; Post Returns, Los Lunas, N.M., June–July 1854, RG 94, M617, R648, NA. The post returns show Ewell on detached service from 1 June to 24 July 1854. This suggests that he may have taken part in expeditions against the Utes and Jicarillas.

33. Utley, *Frontiersmen in Blue*, 90; Dobyns, *Mescalero Apache People*, 40; Opher and Opher, "Mescalero Apache History," 5.

34. RSE to W. A. Nichols, 15 Oct. 1854, RG 393, M1120, R3, F670–71, NA.

35. U.S. Secretary of War, *Annual Report*, 1855–56, pp. 506–7; Utley, *Frontiersmen in Blue*, 148–49. For a slightly different estimate of the number of people in the Mescalero tribe, see Dobyns, *Mescalero Apache People*, 41.

36. Utley, *Frontiersmen in Blue*, 149; RSE to W. A. Nichols, 24 Dec. 1854, RG 393, M1120, R3, F703, NA, and 10 Feb. 1855, RG 393, M1120, R4, F402–5, NA; U.S. Secretary of War, *Annual Report*, 1855–56, p. 58; Sonnichsen, *Mescalero Apaches*, 75; Brooks and Reeve, *Forts and Forays*, 59–60.

37. RSE to W. A. Nichols, 10 Feb. 1855, RG 393, M1120, R4, F402–5, NA; Sonnichsen, *Mescalero Apaches*, 78–79; Brooks and Reeve, *Forts and Forays*, 61–63.

38. U.S. Secretary of War, *Annual Report*, 1855–56, pp. 57–58; Michael Steck to J. H. Eaton, 4 Feb. 1855, RG 393, M1120, R4, F400, NA.

39. U.S. Secretary of War, *Annual Report*, 1855–56, pp. 57–58; RSE to Samuel Sturgis, 25 Feb. 1855, RG 393, M1120, R4, F407–8, NA; RSE to Dr. Samuel Ringgold, 29 Mar. 1855, Ringgold Papers, MHS.

40. Opher and Opher, "Mescalero Apache History," 7; U.S. Secretary of War, *Annual Report*, 1855–56, pp. 506–7; Special Orders 46, Department of New Mexico, letterbook 27, p. 177, RG 393, pt. 1, entry 3172, NA; Utley, *Frontiersmen in Blue*, 151–52.

41. Utley, *Indian Frontier*, 50–51; Brooks and Reeve, *Forts and Forays*, 67–68.

42. Utley, *Frontiersmen in Blue*, 152; Post Returns, Los Lunas, N.M., Sept.–Dec. 1855, RG 94, M617, R648, NA; Special Orders 91, Department of New Mexico, letterbook 27, p. 204, RG 393, pt. 1, entry 3172, NA; RSE to Assistant Adjutant General, Headquarters of the Army, 21 Nov. 1855, RG 94, M567, R514, F642, NA. In the party were four soldiers implicated in a

mutiny at Taos that year. One of them, Pvt. Aaron Stephens, later escaped and joined abolitionist John Brown. He was captured during Brown's attack on Harpers Ferry in 1859 and was hanged (George R. Stammerjohan to author, 15 Mar. 1991).

43. Utley, *Frontiersmen in Blue*, 12; RSE to BSE, 25 Feb. 1854, LC.

44. George W. Lay to BSE, 19 Jan. 1855, LC; J. F. Lee to BSE, 8 Mar. 1855, WM. In a personal note to Ben written in 1850, Scott referred to Dick as a "gallant & energetic officer." He added that during most of the Mexico City campaign, Dick "although suffering with ague & fever, was never out of his saddle when an enterprise was to be undertaken or deeds of daring to be performed" (Winfield Scott to BSE, 16 Dec. 1850, RG 107, 1523, row 11, compartment 5, shelf A, box 59, NA).

Chapter 7

1. See the Stoddert family chart in Appendix B and Stoddert Family Bible Records, box 4, item 5, GWC. Hubbard had been wounded in the hip in the battle of New Orleans. After the War of 1812, he moved from Tennessee to Alabama and served in both houses of the state legislature. He held a seat in the Confederate States Congress between 1861 and 1863 and for the remainder of the war capably served as the Confederacy's first commissioner of Indian affairs (Thomas M. Owen, *History of Alabama*, 3:854).

2. George W. Campbell tombstone inscription, Old City Cemetery, Nashville, Tenn.; Jordan, "Diary," 155–56; George W. Campbell to James Madison, 26 Sept. 1814, GWC.

3. Jordan, "Diary," 155–56 n.; Wharton, *Social Life*, 193–94; Harriot S. Turner, "Recollections," 168; Marietta M. Andrews, *Scraps of Paper*, 109; Lizinka Ewell tombstone inscription, Old City Cemetery, Nashville, Tenn.; diary of George W. Campbell, 24 Feb. 1820, box 4, GWC; miscellaneous notes, folder 37, PBE; miscellaneous notes, box 84, folder 5, Yeatman-Polk Papers, TSLA. For other evidence of Lizinka's association with the royal couple, see LCB to CB, 12 Apr. 1862, TN.

4. RLE to BSE, 15 Mar. 1831, WM; EE to BSE, 24 July 1838, WM.

5. RLE to BSE, 15 May 1835, WM.

6. George W. Campbell tombstone inscription, Old City Cemetery, Nashville, Tenn.; miscellaneous papers, box 8, folder 5, Provine Papers, Tennessee Historical Society; Jordan, "Diary," 152–55.

7. BSE to RLE, 22 May 1836 and undated [ca. 1836], WM.

8. EE to RLE, 12 Apr. 1835, WM; EE to BSE, 24 Dec. 1836, WM; miscellaneous note, folder 37, PBE. Stories of the couple's past romance circulated freely during the Civil War (Richard Taylor, *Destruction*, 78; Hunton, *Autobiography*, 97; John B. Gordon, *Reminiscences*, 157; and *Southern Home* [Charlotte, N.C.], 5 Feb. 1872). An unsigned note in folder 23, WM, states that Ewell proposed to Lizinka but was refused.

9. Thomas Ewell Jr. to EE, 27 Apr. 1839, WM; RLE to BSE, 28 May 1842, WM; RSE to EE, 3 Oct. 1839, LC.

10. George W. Campbell, Percy Brown, and Harriot Turner tombstone inscriptions, Old City Cemetery, Nashville, Tenn.; Campbell Family Chart, folder 1, TN; TTG to LCB, 1 Sept. 1853, TN; miscellaneous notes, box 84, folder 5, Yeatman-Polk Papers, TSLA; miscellaneous notes, folder 37, PBE. George was born in 1840, Percy in 1843, and Harriot in 1844. For information on Lizinka's marriage and the death of her husband, Percy Brown, see EE to BSE, 11 Mar. 1850, WM.

11. RSE to RLE, 28 Jan. 1854, LC; notes on George W. Campbell's will by Campbell Brown, box 20, folder 5, TN; TTG to LCB, 1 Feb. 1854, TN; miscellaneous notes, box 20, folder 1, TN. The $500,000 figure is high. In the 1860 census Lizinka's real estate was valued at $152,000 and her personal estate at $75,926 (1860 census, 22nd District, Maury County, Tenn., R1264, p. 105, NA). Lizinka's Richland estate comprised approximately 6,000 acres. For a full listing of her landholdings, see Appendix C.

12. RSE to RLE, 28 Jan. 1854, LC.

13. RSE to RLE, 1 July 1855, LC.

14. TTG to LCB, 2 Nov., 26 Dec. 1855, TN.

15. TTG to LCB, 26 Dec. 1855, TN.

16. LCB to RSE, 24 Jan. 1856, PBE.

17. WS to RLE, 28 May 1856, WM.

18. LCB to RSE, 15 Nov. 1855, PBE; LCB to David Hubbard, 23 Dec. 1855, Hubbard Papers, TSLA. For other references to the Spring Hill farm offer, see LCB to RSE, 24 Nov. 1855, PBE, and [LCB] to [RSE], undated letter [ca. Nov. 1855], folder 44, PBE.

19. LCB to David Hubbard, 10 Jan., 23 Dec. 1855, Hubbard Papers, TSLA; LCB to RSE, 6 May 1857, PBE; W. R. Palmer to LCB, 23 Aug. 1858, TN; Graf and Haskins, *Papers of Andrew Johnson*, 3:620–21. The president declined to appoint Ewell, Lizinka wrote, "on account of the number of Pay masters from Virginia & the Superior services of Capt. [Thomas G.] Rhett." This explanation did not seem valid to her, since Buchanan later "appointed two civilians from Virginia Pay masters." "I think Buchanan has treated Dick & the rest of us shamefully," she later complained (Graf and Haskins, *Papers of Andrew Johnson*, 3:621; LCB to EE, undated letter, folder 1, WM).

20. TTG to LCB, 26 Dec. 1855, TN; RSE to ESE, 5 Mar. 1856, LC.

21. RSE to Assistant Adjutant General, Headquarters of the Army, 21 Nov. 1855, RG 94, M567, R514, F642, NA; RSE to Samuel Cooper, 3 Jan., 6 Feb., and 5 Mar. 1856, RG 94, M567, R536, F592, F629, and F721, NA; Rouse, "'Old Buck,'" 18–20; Cullum, *Biographical Register*, 1:399; Benjamin Ewell biographical sketch, folder 22, WM; BSE to RLE, 24 Nov. 1851, WM. For a detailed portrait of Benjamin Ewell's life, see Anne C. West, "Benjamin Stoddert Ewell: A Biography" (Ph.D. dissertation, College of William and Mary, 1984). Benjamin Ewell's plantation, "Ewell Hall," built ca. 1848, stands three and one-half miles west of Williamsburg on Richmond Road (Route 60). The large white frame house currently houses the administrative offices of Williamsburg Memorial Park (1987).

22. EE to BSE, 24 Jan. 1837, WM; EE to RLE, 16 June 1845, WM; RLE to BSE, 15 Dec. 1845, WM; miscellaneous notes, folder 23, WM; Hayden, *Virginia Genealogies*, 349; BSE to Uncle William Stoddert, 7 Dec. 1834, WM; William Stoddert biographical sketch, folder 22, WM.

23. TTG to LCB, 2 June 1856, TN.

24. Merrill, *Spurs to Glory*, 88–93.

25. WS to RLE, 28 May 1856, WM.

26. Frazer, *Mansfield*, 48–49; RSE to W. A. Nichols, 22 May 1856, RG 393, M1120, R5, F562, NA.

27. Orders 7, Department of New Mexico, letterbook 36, p. 359, RG 393, pt. 1, entry 3170, NA.

28. Frazer, *Forts and Supplies*, 94; Sacks, "Fort Buchanan," 215–16.

29. RSE to EE, 10 June 1857, LC; WS to RLE, 21 June 1859, WM; RSE to RLE, 19 May 1859, LC.

30. Browne, *Adventures*, 22; Pumpelly, *Pumpelly's Arizona*, 61–62; Eaton, "Frontier Life," 178; Joseph F. Park, "The Apaches," 140. For examples of the frequent violence, see Tucson *Weekly Arizonian*, 15 Sept., 20 Oct. 1859.

31. Utley, *Frontiersmen in Blue*, 82. Sylvanus Mowry, who claimed to "have investigated this subject with probably more care than any other person," believed the total number of Apache warriors did not exceed 2,000 (Mowry, *Arizona and Sonora*, 32).

32. RSE to LE, 16 May 1858, LC; Sacks, "Fort Buchanan," 215–16; Browne, *Adventures*, 142, 252; Pumpelly, *Pumpelly's Arizona*, 23; Frazer, *Forts and Supplies*, 122–23.

33. Frazer, *Forts and Supplies*, 123–24; Sacks, "Fort Buchanan," 217; Browne, *Adventures*, 144, 155.

34. Frazer, *Forts and Supplies*, 125; Enoch Steen to Department of New Mexico, 3 Mar. 1857, RG 393, M1120, R6, F1418–25, NA.

35. Enoch Steen to Department of New Mexico, 31 Jan. and 3 Mar. 1857, RG 393, M1120, R6, F1393–95 and F1418–25, NA; Post Returns, Calabasas Ranch, Nov.–Dec., 1856, RG 94, M617, R156, NA; RSE to Isaiah N. Moore, 3 Mar. 1857, RG 393, M1120, R6, F1428–29, NA.

36. Frazer, *Forts and Supplies*, 125–27; RSE to Isaiah N. Moore, 3 Mar. 1857, RG 393, M1120, R6, F1428–29, NA.

37. Enoch Steen to Department of New Mexico, 31 Jan. 1857, RG 393, M1120, R6, F1393–95, NA.

38. Enoch Steen to W. A. Nichols, 3 May 1857, RG 393, M1120, R6, F1522–23, NA; RSE to W. A. Nichols, 8 June 1857, RG 393, M1120, R6, F259–63, NA. Chapman later served as a captain of artillery in the Confederate army. Randal became colonel of the Twenty-eighth Texas Cavalry and commanded a brigade when he was slain on 30 April 1864 at Jenkins Ferry, Arkansas. Moore and Davis fought for the Union. Moore died as a lieutenant in January 1862, and Davis became colonel of the Eighth New York Cavalry. Davis is best remembered for safely leading Union cavalry out of Harpers Ferry during Stonewall Jackson's investment of the town in September 1862. He was killed nine months later at Brandy Station (Heitman, *Historical Register*, 1:296, 351, 357, 722, 814).

39. RSE to W. A. Nichols, 8 June 1857, RG 393, M1120, R6, F259–63, NA; Hammond, *John Van Deusen DuBois*, 20.

40. RSE to W. A. Nichols, 8 June and 9 Sept. 1857, RG 393, M1120, R6, F259–63 and F560–61, NA; RSE to EE, 10 June 1857, LC. Thomas Claiborne stated that during a skirmish in the Mogollon Mountains Ewell killed the old and famous Apache chief Cucheo Negro (Black Knife). He does not mention the time or place of the skirmish (Thomas Claiborne Reminiscences, folder 22, Claiborne Papers, SHC).

41. RSE to W. A. Nichols, 8 June 1857, RG 393, M1120, R6, F259–63, NA; Alexander McCook to L. W. O'Bannon, 7 July 1857, RG 393, M1120, R6, F266–67, NA. The highest-ranking member of the "Fighting McCooks," Alexander McCook would command the Twentieth Army Corps at Murfreesboro, Tullahoma, and Chickamauga (Warner, *Generals in Blue*, 294).

42. RSE to EE, 10 June 1857, LC.

43. Hart, *Old Forts*, 65. Lazelle later became colonel of the Sixteenth New York Cavalry (Heitman, *Historical Register*, 1:620).

44. Heitman, *Historical Register*, 1:230, 708; Warner, *Generals in Gray*, 193–94; Hammond, *John Van Deusen DuBois*, 21–22; Dixon Miles to Benjamin Bonneville, 13 July 1857, RG 393, M1120, R6, F327–41, NA; Utley, *Frontiersmen in Blue*, 155. Neither Bonneville, Miles, nor Lor-

ing particularly distinguished themselves in the Civil War. Bonneville, like many aging officers, was not equal to the rigors of the conflict and retired at its outset. Miles hung on but was repeatedly passed over for promotion. He died on 16 September 1862 in the unsuccessful defense of Harpers Ferry. Loring rose to become a major general in the Confederacy, serving first in the eastern then the western theater.

45. Dixon Miles to Benjamin Bonneville, 13 July 1857, RG 393, M1120, R6, F327–41, NA; J. S. Simonsen to W. A. Nichols, 1 July 1857, RG 393, M1120, R6, F1534–35, NA. Compare Hammond, *John Van Deusen DuBois*, 21.

46. Dixon Miles to Benjamin Bonneville, 13 July 1857, RG 393, M1120, R6, F327–41, NA.

47. Hammond, *John Van Deusen DuBois*, 21–24. DuBois later became a colonel and served the Union as a staff officer in the Civil War (Heitman, *Historical Register*, 1:385).

48. RSE to Dixon Miles, 13 July 1857, RG 393, M1120, R6, F315–18, NA; Dixon Miles to Benjamin Bonneville, 13 July 1857, RG 393, M1120, R6, F327–41, NA; U.S. Secretary of War, *Annual Report*, 1857–58, p. 137; Hammond, *John Van Deusen DuBois*, 25–26.

49. Hammond, *John Van Deusen DuBois*, 28; RSE to Dixon Miles, 13 July 1857, RG 393, M1120, R6, F315–18, NA.

50. Hammond, *John Van Deusen DuBois*, 28–29.

51. Ibid.; RSE to Dixon Miles, 13 July 1857, RG 393, M1120, R6, F315–18, NA; Dixon Miles to Benjamin Bonneville, 13 July 1857, RG 393, M1120, R6, F327–41, NA.

52. RSE to Dixon Miles, 13 July 1857, RG 393, M1120, R6, F315–18, NA; Dixon Miles to Benjamin Bonneville, 13 July 1857, RG 393, M1120, R6, F302–8, NA; Thomas Claiborne Reminiscences, folder 22, Claiborne Papers, SHC. Whipple attained the rank of brigadier general in the Civil War, serving as chief of staff to Gen. George H. Thomas. After the war he served on Gen. William T. Sherman's staff. Steen was a brigadier general for the South and served in the Trans-Mississippi theater. He died in battle at Kane Hill, Arkansas, in 1862. Lt. John Rogers Cooke of the Eighth Infantry, later a brigadier general in the Army of Northern Virginia, also served under Ewell in this expedition (Heitman, *Historical Register*, 1:324, 919; Warner, *Generals in Blue*, 555; Warner, *Generals in Gray*, 61).

53. Hammond, *John Van Deusen DuBois*, 30–31.

54. Ibid., 29–30; Dixon Miles to Benjamin Bonneville, 13 July 1857, RG 393, M1120, R6, F302–8 and 327–41, NA; U.S. Secretary of War, *Annual Report*, 1857–58, pp. 136–37. "Cols. Bonneville & Miles are *bragging* wonderfully of *their* exploits," DuBois wrote after his return to the depot. "One would imagine that they actually proposed & executed the plans . . . when both remained in rear & notoriously disapproved of Capt. Ewell's pushing on & thus forcing them to leave their beaten trail for home. Well, as they write the reports, everybody will believe that it was so & Ewell will receive no credit for his doing everything" (Hammond, *John Van Deusen DuBois*, 35).

55. Dixon Miles to Benjamin Bonneville, 13 July 1857, RG 393, M1120, R6, F327–41, NA; Hammond, *John Van Deusen DuBois*, 29–30; Utley, *Frontiersmen in Blue*, 154–57. Four Apache women were also killed in the attack. "Two of these women were killed by the Peublo [*sic*] Indians," wrote Miles, "one was . . . killed while fighting with a bow and arrow, the other I presume was accidentally shot for at a short distance only it is difficult to distinguish by dress the men from the women, so much are they alike" (Miles report in RG 393, M1120, R6, F307–8, NA). According to DuBois, one Apache warrior was captured in the battle. With Bonneville's consent the man was taken outside the camp by a Pueblo and shot to death, a base and cowardly act that the other officers deplored. Needless to say, this incident does not appear in official reports of the campaign.

Chapter 8

1. Hammond, *John Van Deusen DuBois*, 35; Frazer, *Forts and Supplies*, 128; RSE to Dixon Miles, 13 June 1857, RG 393, M1120, R6, F315–18, NA; Post Returns, Fort Buchanan, N.M., Aug. 1857, RG 94, M617, R156, NA; Post Orders 50, RG 94, M617, R156, NA; RSE to LE, 31 Oct. 1857, LC.

2. RSE to LE, 31 Oct. 1857, LC; Special Orders 104, RG 393, pt. 1, box 1, NA. Ewell was attending the trial of Bvt. Maj. William M. Gordon of the Third Infantry.

3. RSE to LE, 31 Oct. 1857, LC; HB to RSE, 11 Feb. 1856, PBE.

4. Faulk, *U.S. Camel Corps*, 125–27.

5. Frazer, *Forts and Supplies*, 128; Averell, *Ten Years in the Saddle*, 126; Special Orders 125 and 128, Department of New Mexico, pt. 1, box 1, RG 393, NA. Averell became a Union general in the Civil War. Chapman suffered from chronic illness and died in January 1859.

6. Tevis, *Arizona in the '50's*, 100; Sacks, "Fort Buchanan," 224; U.S. Secretary of War, *Annual Report*, 1859–60, p. 306. For the fort's location, see Hart, *Old Forts*, 37, and Bruce Grant, *American Forts*, 331.

7. Frazer, *Forts and Supplies*, 128, 136. A lengthy description of Fort Buchanan and the troops who served there is in Serven, "Sonoita Creek." The fort was located in Santa Cruz County near the present-day town of Sonoita. Samuel Heintzelman visited Fort Buchanan in September 1858 and like Johnston considered it "rather a straggling affair." A local newspaperman agreed. "The fort, as existing, was miserably planned," wrote the correspondent, "the buildings poor and built without judgment or discrimination" (North, *Samuel Peter Heintzelman*, 75, and Altshuler, *Latest from Arizona!*, 122). For other comments about the fort, see Pumpelly, *Pumpelly's Arizona*, 37.

8. RSE to LE, 8 Mar. 1858, LC.

9. RSE to LE, 16 May 1858, LC.

10. RSE to LE, 10 Aug. 1858, LC. Samuel Heintzelman visited the mine with Ewell on 3 September 1858. He recorded the outing in his diary: "I went down into the mine, near 50 feet deep in a bucket. The vein is near three feet wide and plenty of metal. It is a lead ore and said to contain near $100 per ton of silver." Further analysis showed that the mine was not nearly so rich. "The Patagonia lead ore yields but 39 oz [to] the ton," Heintzelman wrote on 16 September. "It is a great disappointment to the owners" (North, *Samuel Peter Heintzelman*, 74, 84).

11. RSE to LE, 21 Dec. 1858, Sept. 1859, LC.

12. RSE to LE, 16 May 1858, Sept. 1859, LC.

13. Edward Fitzgerald to W. A. Nichols, 8 May 1858, RG 393, M1120, R7, F540–41, NA; Enoch Steen to W. A. Nichols, 4 Jan. and 3 Mar. 1858, RG 393, M1120, R8, F222 and F272, NA; RSE to LE, 16 May 1858, LC.

14. Enoch Steen to W. A. Nichols, 3 Jan. 1858, RG 393, M1120, R8, F218–20, NA; RSE to LE, 16 May 1858, LC; Edward Fitzgerald to W. A. Nichols, 12 July and 12 Aug. 1858, RG 393, M1120, R7, F549–51 and F557, NA; Post Returns, Fort Buchanan, N.M., June–Aug. 1858, RG 94, M617, R156, NA; Heitman, *Historical Register*, 1:422.

15. Edward Fitzgerald to W. A. Nichols, 12 Aug. 1858, RG 393, M1120, R7, F557, NA; Heitman, *Historical Register*, 1:641; RSE to LE, 10 Aug. 1858, LC. Lord was an officer in the First U.S. Cavalry during the Civil War. For other references to him, see the Ferguson memoir, DU, and Tevis, *Arizona in the '50's*, 62.

16. RSE to LE, 28 Nov. 1858, LC. The doctor was Assistant Surgeon Bernard J. D. Irwin and the lieutenant was Richard S. C. Lord, although in a previous letter Ewell had described Lord

as being a married man. See Post Returns, Fort Buchanan, N.M., Nov. 1858, RG 94, M617, R156, NA.

17. Edward Fitzgerald to W. A. Nichols, 8 May 1858, RG 393, M1120, R7, F540–41, NA; Post Returns, Fort Buchanan, N.M., Aug.–Dec. 1858, RG 94, M617, R156, NA; RSE to LE, 14, 28 Nov. 1858, LC.

18. RSE to LE, 28 Nov. 1858, 16 Aug. 1859, LC; RSE to LCB, 27 Sept. 1865, PBE; Thomas H. Carter, "Letter of Colonel Thomas H. Carter," 7. For additional evidence of Ewell's cooking ability, see Robert Stiles, *Four Years*, 245.

19. RSE to LE, 16 Aug. 1859, LC. The author is indebted to Drs. Joseph C. Greenfield Jr., Marvin Rozear, and G. Ralph Corey of Duke University Medical Center for this modern analysis of Ewell's dyspepsia.

20. RSE to LE, 28 Nov. 1858, LC. Lizzie and her father were then preparing to move from Williamsburg to their plantation outside town. Ewell believed this would help Lizzie to lose weight. "When you move to the farm you need not be under so many apprehensions of plumpness," he wrote. "At a distance from market, with no students I have an idea the table will not be apt to produce gout. Probably none of you are good providers and when one bolts his food like Papa [Ben] he cares not a fig whether he is eating fish, flesh, or fowl. Does not know in fact."

21. Cremony, *Life among the Apaches*, 89; Mowry, *Arizona and Sonora*, 30; Enoch Steen to W. A. Nichols, 1 Jan. 1857, RG 393, M1120, R6, F1379–84, NA; RSE to LE, 14 Nov. 1858, LC.

22. RSE to Samuel Cooper, 2 Feb. 1859, RG 94, M567, R600, F118–19, NA; RSE to John Wilkins, 17 and 26 Jan. 1859, RG 393, M1120, R9, F329–30 and F336–37, NA; Sweeney, "Cochise," 432. See also RSE to John Wilkins, 2 Feb. 1859, RG 393, M1120, R9, F339, NA.

23. Tevis, *Arizona in the '50's*, 149; anonymous newspaper clipping in Campbell Brown scrapbook, box 20, folder 13, TN; Tucson *Weekly Arizonian*, 17 Nov. 1859; Sweeney, "Cochise," 432–36. The author of the Tucson article was James Tevis.

24. Bourke, *On the Border with Crook*, 118. For a detailed look at Cochise's deteriorating relationship with the U.S. government in 1859–60, see Sweeney, "Cochise."

25. Isaac Reeve to John Wilkins, 8 Sept. 1859, RG 393, M1120, R10, F454 and 468, NA; Sweeney, "Cochise," 438–39; Tucson *Weekly Arizonian*, 15 Sept. 1859. For a week-to-week account of Apache depredations and other newsworthy events in southern Arizona in 1859 and 1860, see Altshuler, *Latest from Arizona!*

26. Isaac Reeve to John Wilkins, 18 July 1859, RG 393, M1120, R10, F424–26, NA. With obvious frustration, Reeve outlined the problem to his superiors in Santa Fe: "Something ought be done to check and punish these Indians, but this post is just strong enough to be powerless for that end. . . . As to overtaking by the most vigorous pursuit any party, committing depredations at any considerable distance from the post, the thing is impossible. A few Indians driving off a number of animals, change from one to another as fast as those they ride become tired, and even if they kill some and abandon others, and get off with but few, they are still the gainers in the chase, and they are not therefore obliged, as we are, to spare their animals."

He went on to cite as an example a pursuit then in progress.

The animals taken from Arivaca were at least 60 miles from here by the shortest known route when taken and by the time the information reached here, they were at least one hundred miles from that place, computing their travel at the very moderate average of five miles per hour. It is highly probable that they have been divided into a dozen parties, each with plenty of spare animals to travel faster than dragoons can travel under any circumstances, and are at this hour farther from the troops than when the latter left the post last night. For any small party to pursue the trail far into the Indian country and demand the animals without the force to sustain such demand, would be worse than folly.

27. Mowry, *Arizona and Sonora*, 55–56.

28. Post Returns, Fort Buchanan, N.M., Mar. 1859, RG 94, M617, R156, NA; Heitman, *Historical Register*, 1:822. Reeve received two brevets in the Mexican War, went on to command the First U.S. Infantry during the Civil War, and was breveted brigadier general in 1865 after leaving active service.

29. RSE to John Wilkins, 4 Apr. 1859, RG 393, M1120, R9, F350, NA. Assistant Surgeon B. J. D. Irwin's February 1859 report provides a detailed analysis of sanitation and disease at Fort Buchanan at this time. His report is quoted at length in Serven, "Sonoita Creek," 28–33.

30. Ewell Family Bible Records, folder 23, WM; excerpts from the College of William and Mary faculty minutes for 18 Jan. 1859, pp. 236–37, CWM.

31. RSE to LE, 19 May 1859, LC.

32. Isaac Reeve to John Wilkins, 11 Aug. and 3 Oct. 1859, RG 393, M1120, R10, F451–52 and F487, NA; RSE to LE, 16 Aug. 1859, LC.

33. RSE to LE, 14 Nov. 1858, 16 Aug. 1859, LC; RSE to RLE, 27 Sept. 1859, LC.

34. RSE to LE, 19 May 1859, LC; Isaac Reeve to John Wilkins, 20 May 1859, RG 393, M1120, R10, F404–7, NA.

35. Isaac Reeve to John Wilkins, 18 July, 3 Aug., and 8 Sept. 1859, RG 393, M1120, R10, F424–25, F441–60, and F454 and 468, NA; Altshuler, *Latest from Arizona!*, 96–97, 114; RSE to LE, 14 Nov. 1858, LC. See also RSE to LE, 1 Aug. 1859, LC.

36. RSE to LE, 16 Aug. 1859, LC; RSE to RLE, 27 Sept. 1859, LC; Farish, *History of Arizona*, 2:292–93; Browne, *Adventures*, 203–10; North, *Samuel Peter Heintzelman*, 134.

37. RSE to LE, 31 Oct. 1857, LC; RSE to RLE, 10 Jan. 1860, LC.

38. Charles H. Tompkins to BSE, 14 Dec. 1885, LC; Tucson *Weekly Arizonian*, 6 Oct. 1859.

39. Sorrel, *Recollections*, 56–57.

40. RSE to LE, 26 Oct. 1859, LC; Tucson *Weekly Arizonian*, 27 Oct. 1859.

41. Acuna, "Ignacio Pesqueira," 146–53.

42. E. D. Townsend to Isaac Reeve, 10 Oct. 1859, RG 59, M179, R175, F101–2, NA; Isaac Reeve to John Wilkins, 6 Nov. 1859, RG 393, M1120, R10, F518–20, NA. Guaymas is 250 miles south of the border.

43. William Porter to RSE, 11 Nov. 1859, RG 59, M179, R175, F105–6, NA; RSE to Samuel Cooper, 30 Nov. 1859, RG 59, M179, R175, F109–10, NA. Porter became a commodore in 1862 and served with distinction in naval actions on the Mississippi and Tennessee Rivers during the Civil War. He was the son of Commodore David Porter, brother of Adm. David D. Porter, half-brother of Adm. David Farragut, and cousin of Gen. Fitz John Porter (Boatner, *Civil War Dictionary*, 662).

44. RSE to Samuel Cooper, 30 Nov. 1859, RG 59, M179, R175, F112–14, NA.

45. Isaac Reeve to John Wilkins, 27 Nov. 1859, RG 393, M1120, R10, F527–33, NA.

46. Post Returns, Fort Buchanan, N.M., Dec. 1859, RG 94, M617, R156, NA; Isaac Reeve to John Wilkins, 9 Dec. 1859, RG 393, M1120, R10, F554–55, NA; RSE to RLE, 10 Jan. 1860, LC; U.S. Secretary of War, *Annual Report*, 1860–61, pp. 200–201; John Walker to RSE, 16 Jan. 1860, RG 393, M1120, R11, F557, NA; Cullum, *Biographical Register*, 1:602; Columbia (Tenn.) *Herald*, 2 Feb. 1872; Altshuler, *Latest from Arizona!*, 25.

47. Altshuler, *Latest from Arizona!*, 102, 105; Serven, "Sonoita Creek," 34.

48. Tevis, *Arizona in the '50's*, 63. Tevis's memory played him false regarding the name of Ewell's servant. Her name was Hester (RSE to LE, Sept., 26 Oct. 1859, LC).

49. Tevis, *Arizona in the '50's*, 62–63. For additional information on Ewell's domestic arrangements at Fort Buchanan, see North, *Samuel Peter Heintzelman*, 75. For the difficulty of growing potatoes in that region, see Tucson *Weekly Arizonian*, 25 Sept. 1859. In 1856 Ewell had asked his sister Elizabeth to send him seed for cabbages, cauliflower, nutmeg melons, spinach, turnip-rutabagas, watermelons, and other plants (RSE to ESE, 15 Jan. 1856, LC).

50. Tevis, *Arizona in the '50's*, 73–75, 90–91.

51. Ibid., 63–64.

52. Ibid., 63–69.

53. RSE to John Wilkins, 17 Mar. and 10 Apr. 1860, RG 393, M1120, R11, F580–81 and F586–88, NA; Post Returns, Fort Buchanan, N.M., Mar. 1860, RG 94, M617, R156, NA; Browne, *Adventures*, 155; Tevis, *Arizona in the '50's*, 69–73; Forbes, *The Penningtons*, 13–21; Harriot Stoddert Turner, "Ewells of Virginia," 31, CWM; Altshuler, *Latest from Arizona!*, 47–52, 58, 62, 64–67, 69.

54. Bancroft, *History of Arizona*, 507 n.; Altshuler, *Latest from Arizona!*, 69–70. A correspondent who witnessed Ewell's arrival in Tucson with Mercedes wrote that "blessings were showered on his head for the active part he had taken in the rescue. It was doubtless a proud moment for him to which he will look back with satisfaction as long as he lives. He had not returned as a victorious chieftain with the laurels of victory encircling his brow, but he had restored peace and happiness to a despairing family, had snatched an humble captive from the hands of savages. . . . It was but one of many noble acts of an eventful career in which he had won the hearts of the people."

55. RSE to LE, 2 May 1860, LC. Ewell County was one of Arizona's four original counties, but the legislature changed its name in 1864 after Ewell joined the Confederacy. It comprised the land now encompassed by Pima and Santa Cruz Counties. Other Arizona landmarks named in Ewell's honor include Ewell Pass (now Apache Pass) in the Chiricahua Mountains, Ewell's Spring near the town of Dos Cabezas, and Old Baldy Peak near the site of Fort Buchanan (Barnes, *Arizona Place Names*, 29, 256, and Harriot Stoddert Turner, "Ewells of Virginia," 31, CWM). Compare Altshuler, *Latest from Arizona!*, 70 n.

The army honored Ewell by naming a fort after him on the south bank of the Nueces River in LaSalle County, Texas. Fort Ewell was occupied in May 1852 and was abandoned a year and a half later (Reynolds, "Early Texas Forts," 43–47).

56. Frazer, *Forts and Supplies*, 161; RSE to John Wilkins, 22 May 1860, RG 393, M1120, R11, F616–18, NA; Altshuler, *Latest from Arizona!*, 77, 84, 91; RSE to LE, 2 May 1860, LC. For Ewell's arguments on keeping Fort Buchanan, see Frazer, *Forts and Supplies*, 160–61.

57. RSE to LE, 22 Jan. 1861, LC. The court convened in El Paso to try Capt. William K. Van Bokkelen of the Quartermaster Department. Capt. John M. Jones of the Seventh Infantry was also on the board. He later served on Ewell's staff and commanded a brigade in the Second Corps.

58. Special Orders 6, RG 94, M619, R19, F165–67, NA. Fauntleroy later offered his services to the Confederacy but was turned down. Instead he accepted an appointment as brigadier general of Virginia state troops (Heitman, *Historical Register*, 1:415).

59. RSE to LE, 22 Jan. 1861, LC.

60. Ibid.; Orders 13, Adjutant General's Office, 21 Jan. 1861; Special Orders 6, RG 94, M619, R19, F165–67, NA; Williams, "High Private," 159; Harriot Stoddert Turner, "Ewells of Virginia," 31 n., CWM.

61. RSE to Adjutant General's Office, received 12 Mar. 1861, RG 94, M619, R19, F165–67, NA; RSE to LCB, 5 June 1865, PBE.

62. Williams, "High Private," 159; RSE to LCB, 11 [June?] 1865, FC; RSE to Lorenzo Thomas, 24 April 1861, RG 94, M619, R19, F199, NA. The secretary of war accepted Ewell's resignation on 7 May 1861.

63. RSE to LCB, 8 June, 11 [June?] 1865, FC; Williams, "High Private," 159; Harriot Stoddert Turner, "Ewells of Virginia," 31, CWM.

Chapter 9

1. *OR* 51(2):36–37. See also Robertson, *Proceedings*, 12–13, and Virginia Council Minutes, 26 Apr. 1861, letter #12, RG 109, M998, R2, NA.

2. RSE to John Pemberton, 1 May 1861, RG 109, M998, R2, F587, NA.

3. RSE to G. F. Harrison, 12 May 1861, RG 109, M998, R2, F1164–65, NA; RSE to Robert Garnett, 12 May 1861, RG 109, M998, R1, F476, NA; Robert Garnett to RSE, 13 May 1861, RG 109, M998, R1, F93, NA. As of 20 May seven companies were at Camp Ashland: the Chesterfield Centre Guards, Goochland Light Dragoons, Henrico Light Cavalry, Cumberland Light Dragoons, troops from Amelia and Hanover Counties, and one other.

4. RSE to John Pemberton, 5 and 10 May 1861, RG 109, M998, R2, F814 and F1065, NA; RSE to ?, 13 May 1861, RG 109, M998, R1, F477, NA.

5. RSE to Robert Garnett, 13 May 1861, RG 109, M998, R2, F1213–14, NA.

6. Corson, *My Dear Jennie*, 6–7; *Southern Generals*, 346.

7. Eggleston, *Rebel's Recollections*, 156–60. Eggleston claimed that Ewell offered him the position after he became a brigadier general, but in the same passage he mentions that he did not see Ewell from the time he left Ashland until 1864. Since Ewell was still a lieutenant colonel at the time he left Ashland, Eggleston's memory must be at fault.

8. *OR* 51(2):95; HB to "My dear Aunt," 16 June 1861, FC; Flournoy, *Calendar of Virginia State Papers*, 11:130.

9. *OR* 2:62.

10. William Smith, "Fairfax Courthouse," 1. Fairfax Station Road is now South Payne Street.

11. CB, "From Fairfax C.H. to Richmond," folder 20, PBE; Ewell manuscript fragment, folder 20, PBE; HB to "My dear Aunt," 16 June 1861, FC; William Smith, "Fairfax Courthouse," 1–2; *OR* 2:62.

12. CB, "From Fairfax C.H. to Richmond," folder 20, PBE; Ewell manuscript fragment, folder 20, PBE; *OR* 2:63. Apparently a few Confederate horsemen remained in town after the initial Union charge, but they did not stay long. "My cavalry, the few I succeeded in forming, disappeared at the first fire," wrote Ewell with some contempt, "an advantage over Inf. in being mounted" (HB to "My dear Aunt," 16 June 1861, FC).

13. CB, "From Fairfax C.H. to Richmond," folder 20, PBE; Ewell manuscript fragment, folder 20, PBE; William Smith, "Fairfax Courthouse," 5–6. The coat was found the next day on the porch of a family named Powell.

14. *OR* 2:50; William Smith, "Fairfax Courthouse," 5–6; HB to "My dear Aunt," 16 June 1861, FC; CB, "From Fairfax C.H. to Richmond," folder 20, PBE. Elsewhere Ewell estimated the number of men at about thirty (HB to "My dear Aunt," 16 June 1861, FC).

15. *OR* 2:63–64; CB, "From Fairfax C.H. to Richmond," folder 20, PBE; Ewell manuscript fragment, folder 20, PBE; HB to "My dear Aunt," 16 June 1861, FC. Sources do not agree as

to the time of Ewell's wounding. Extra Billy Smith claimed that Ewell was shot by the Federals during their initial rush through town. On the other hand, Campbell Brown, in a postwar account of the skirmish reviewed by Ewell, indicated that his kinsman was shot when the Federals first returned to town. Ewell stated in his report of the skirmish that he received his wound during the Federals' "last attack."

16. Ferguson memoir, 14, DU; CB, "From Fairfax C.H. to Richmond," folder 20, PBE. Campbell Brown stated that the man who inquired about Ewell's injury was Extra Billy Smith, but this seems unlikely.

17. *OR* 2:63; William Smith, "Fairfax Courthouse," 6.

18. *OR* 2:60–64; *Southern Generals*, 344–45; William Smith, "Fairfax Courthouse," 4–5; *OR* 2:63; CB, "From Fairfax C.H. to Richmond," folder 20, PBE.

19. Richmond *Daily Enquirer*, 7 June 1861; William Smith, "Fairfax Courthouse," 2; *OR* 2:61–63.

20. HB to "My dear Aunt," 16 June 1861, FC.

21. *OR* 2:61; HB to "My dear Aunt," 16 June 1861, FC. There may have been some basis to the rumor. Lt. Charles Tompkins, who led the charge through Fairfax Court House, reported that he had encountered 1,000 Confederates. The authorities may have taken him at his word. Following the skirmish, Brig. Gen. Irvin McDowell suspended scouting expeditions toward the Confederate lines and reported that Tompkins's ill-advised foray had "frustrated unintentionally, for the time, a more important movement." What that movement was, he did not say (William C. Davis, *Battle of Bull Run*, 33–34, and *OR* 2:61).

22. CBM; *OR* 2:934; RSE to Milledge Bonham, 21 June 1861, Bonham Papers, University of South Carolina; RSE to LCB, 10 Feb. 1862, Museum of the Confederacy. Three days after his advancement, Ewell signed a required oath of loyalty pledging to "bear true faith, and yield obedience to the Confederate States of America" and to "serve them honestly and faithfully against their enemies" (Ewell's compiled service record, RG 109, M331, R89, NA).

23. Samuel Melton to "My Dear Wife," 2 June 1861, Melton Papers, University of South Carolina; HB to "My dear Aunt," 16 June 1861, FC.

24. Jubal A. Early, *Autobiographical Sketch*, 4–5; Roman, *Beauregard*, 80.

25. *OR* 2:450; RSE to LE, 31 July 1861, LC; Jubal A. Early, *Autobiographical Sketch*, 6; *OR* 2:459–61; RSE to J. H. Balfour, 22 Oct. 1861, Early Papers, Library of Congress; Beauregard, "Bull Run," 199; *OR* 51(2):172; Jefferson Davis, *Rise and Fall*, 1:323. Bonham sent Ewell notice of the impending movement, but Ewell, in a private letter written that month, stated that "the troops at the Court-house fell back without warning me at the station." He added, "In the hurry of movements they forgot the most important orders sometimes."

26. CBM; CB to "My dear Aunt," 20 Aug. 1861, PBE; RSE to LE, 31 July 1861, LC; *OR* 2:467; William Miller Owen, *In Camp and Battle*, 26–27. Ewell regarded Rodes as both "an able man & efficient officer."

27. William Miller Owen, *In Camp and Battle*, 25–26; John B. Gordon, *Reminiscences*, 41–42. The young lady was Oceola Mason, daughter of Dr. J. Seddon Mason (Curtis, *From Bull Run to Chancellorsville*, 48).

28. *OR* 2:459; Jubal A. Early, *Autobiographical Sketch*, 7; William Miller Owen, *In Camp and Battle*, 26.

29. CBM.

30. John William Jones, "Gen. A. P. Hill," 234; CBM; RSE to RLE, 8 May 1865, LC; Richard Taylor, *Destruction*, 37; Sorrel, *Recollections*, 56–57. Other good descriptions of Ewell appear in Ledford, *Reminiscences*, 80, and the Richmond *Times-Dispatch*, 24 Dec. 1911. Ewell's oath of

allegiance, in LC, sets his height at five feet, eight inches, but this was after he lost his leg. In an 1865 letter to Rebecca, Ewell gives his height as five feet, ten and one-half inches, "supposing both legs present."

31. John S. Wise, *End of an Era*, 332; Fremantle, *Three Months*, 222; Haskell, *Memoirs*, 134; Ewell oath of allegiance, LC; Sorrel, *Recollections*, 56-57; Harriot Stoddert Turner, "Ewells of Virginia," 38, CWM; Alexander, "Tribute," 228; Lyman, *Meade's Headquarters*, 275; Dobbins, *Grandfather's Journal*, 68. A South Carolinian who saw Ewell at this time in the war thought him "undoubtedly the wildest looking man I ever saw" (Abbeville [S.C.] *Medium*, 15 Aug. 1895).

32. CBM.

33. Ibid.; Everard H. Smith, "Peter W. Hairston," 86.

34. William Miller Owen, *In Camp and Battle*, 30; Jubal A. Early, *Autobiographical Sketch*, 10-11.

35. CBM; Jubal A. Early, *Autobiographical Sketch*, 12-13.

36. *OR* 2:486-88; Roman, *Beauregard*, 1:98.

37. RSE to LE, 31 July 1861, LC; Ewell Manassas manuscript, FC; Beauregard, *Commentary*, 115; *OR* 51(2):186. A copy of this dispatch made from the original by Edgar A. Hudnut is in folder 8, PBE.

38. John B. Gordon, *Reminiscences*, 39.

39. RSE to LE, 31 July 1861, LC; Ewell Manassas manuscript, FC.

40. John B. Gordon, *Reminiscences*, 38. See also George F. Harrison, "Ewell at First Manassas," 357.

41. John B. Gordon, *Reminiscences*, 38; BSE to LE, 28 Feb. 1863, WM; HB note in folder 21, WM.

42. John B. Gordon, *Reminiscences*, 38-40.

43. *OR* 2:536; CB, "From Fairfax C.H. to Richmond," folder 20, PBE; RSE to LE, 31 July 1861, LC; Beauregard, *Commentary*, 114-16; Ewell Manassas manuscript, FC; CBM. Fitz Lee was the staff officer sent to Jones. Long after the war Lee claimed to have brought Jones's dispatch to Ewell; however, Ewell's official report of the battle and other sources indicate that Ewell received the dispatch from one of Jones's own men (Fitzhugh Lee to CB, 17 Dec. 1884, PBE).

44. CB, "From Fairfax C.H. to Richmond," folder 20, PBE; CBM. On Ewell's communication with Beauregard, see Alfred Roman to Beauregard, 29 Dec. 1884, Palmer Papers, Western Reserve Historical Society.

45. *OR* 51(2):207; Beauregard, *Commentary*, 115. Alexander Chisolm to P. G. T. Beauregard, 1 Aug. 1861, in Chisolm's compiled service record, RG 109, M331, R54, NA. Chisolm found Ewell "very uneasy" at the thought that he had not received Beauregard's earlier order to advance.

46. CBM.

47. RSE to Benson Lossing, 29 Apr. 1866, PBE; RSE to Joseph Johnston, 15 Aug. 1866, PBE; CB, "From Fairfax C.H. to Richmond," folder 20, PBE; Ewell Manassas manuscript, FC. In his battle report Ewell identified the officer who brought the order as Col. Terry; in a postwar letter he remembered it as being Col. Lucy. Neither officer has been identified.

48. George F. Harrison, "Ewell at First Manassas," 358; RSE to LE, 31 July 1861, LC; Fitzhugh Lee to CB, 17 Dec. 1884, PBE; *OR* 2:475.

49. CBM. See also George W. Booth, *Personal Reminiscences*, 14-15, and McKim, *Soldier's Recollections*, 34.

50. George F. Harrison, "Ewell at First Manassas," 358; CBM; CB to Henry Hunt, 27 Jan. 1885, Hunt Papers, Library of Congress.

51. Fitzhugh Lee to CB, 17 Dec. 1884, PBE.

52. Joseph E. Johnston, *Narrative*, 54; RSE to Joseph Johnston, 15 Aug. 1866, PBE.

53. Fitzhugh Lee to CB, 17 Dec. 1884, PBE; CB, "From Fairfax C.H. to Richmond," folder 20, PBE; CBM.

54. TTG to Henry Hunt, 19 May 1886, container 4, Hunt Papers, Library of Congress; Jefferson Davis to CB, 14 June 1886, TN; RSE to LE, 20 July 1862, LC. See also TTG to CB, 30 Apr. 1886, and CB to Jefferson Davis, 17 May 1886, both in Davis Papers, Tulane University.

55. Beauregard, *Commentary*, 115–18; *OR* 51(2):198–99; CBM.

56. J. Cutler Andrews, *South Reports*, 90–91; CBM.

57. Thomas H. Carter, "Letter of Colonel Thomas H. Carter," 6; HB to Jubal Early, 29 Mar. 1878, Early Papers, VHS.

58. Jubal A. Early, "Review," 259–60; HB to Jubal Early, 29 Mar. 1878, Early Papers, VHS; George F. Harrison, "Ewell at First Manassas," 356–59. Ewell's stepdaughter wrote in 1878, "I know how much he suffered from ignorant censure & unjust criticism. His sensitiveness made him feel bitterly the injustice & unkindness of his treatment at Manassas." See Appendix G for a review of the 1884 Ewell-at-Manassas controversy.

59. RSE to LE, 31 July 1861, LC.

Chapter 10

1. English Combatant, *Battle-Fields of the South*, 59.

2. CBM.

3. Ibid.; *OR* 5:778–79; CB to Rebecca Hubbard, 20 Aug. 1861, PBE.

4. Joseph E. Johnston, *Narrative*, 69; Richard Griffith to RSE, 10 Oct. 1861, vol. 3, Early Papers, Library of Congress; CBM.

5. CB to Rebecca Hubbard, 20 Aug. 1861, PBE. Some notes made by Ewell on commands and maneuvers are in ELB, 1–2.

6. CBM. For Connie Cary's account of her visit to the army, see Constance C. Harrison, "Virginia Scenes in '61," 160–66.

7. Joseph E. Johnston, *Narrative*, 77; Longstreet, *Manassas to Appomattox*, 60–61; Jubal A. Early, *Autobiographical Sketch*, 50; CBM. Early remembered the movement as having occurred on 15 October; Johnston and Longstreet place it four days later.

8. Shortly after the reorganization took place, John Gordon petitioned Ewell for permission to raise either a regiment or a battalion from unattached Alabama companies in the army. Ewell recognized Gordon's ability and gave his consent to the scheme, promising to give him two companies from the Sixth Alabama, if possible (RSE to John Gordon, 13 Sept. 1861, RG 109, M437, R23, item 11,041, NA).

9. Jubal A. Early, *Autobiographical Sketch*, 51; *OR* 5:913, 939; CBM; CB, "From Fairfax C.H. to Richmond," folder 20, PBE; Order 1, First Division, Beauregard's Corps, 5 Oct. 1861, Van Dorn Papers, Chicago Historical Society.

10. CB, "From Fairfax C.H. to Richmond," folder 20, PBE; Ewell's compiled service record, RG 109, M331, R89, NA; Kean, *Inside the Confederate Government*, 18; CBM; George Wise, *Campaigns*, 45.

11. CBM; RSE to LCB, 20 Feb. 1862, LC; Eugenia B. Smith, *Centreville, Virginia*, 41; RSE to LCB, undated [ca. Mar. 1862], LC.

12. CBM.

13. Ibid.; Ferguson memoir, 12–13, DU.

14. CBM; George Wise, *Campaigns*, 45.

15. CBM; RSE to LCB, undated letter fragment [ca. Jan. 1862], FC; Duncan, *Letters*, 25.

16. RSE to LCB, undated letter fragment [ca. Jan. 1862], FC.

17. Ibid.

18. RSE to LCB, undated [ca. Mar. 1862], LC.

19. RSE to LCB, 20, 21 Feb. 1862, LC.

20. RSE to LCB, 20, 21, 23 Feb. 1862, LC. For additional comments by Ewell on the administration's meddling in army affairs, see RSE to LCB, 16 Mar. 1862, LC; RSE to LCB, 5 Mar. 1862, Museum of the Confederacy.

21. RSE to LCB, 18, 21 Feb. 1862, LC; RSE to LCB, 5 Mar. 1862, Museum of the Confederacy.

22. RSE to LCB, 20, 21 Feb., 16 Mar. 1862, LC; RSE to LCB, 5 Mar. 1862, Museum of the Confederacy; RSE to LCB, 13 Apr. 1862, PBE.

23. RSE to LE, 20 July 1862, LC; CB to LCB, 6 June 1862, PBE. Rebecca Hubbard was Dick's and Lizinka's aunt.

24. Harriot S. Turner, "Recollections," 172; Durham, *Nashville*, 181, 195 n.; Graf and Haskins, *Papers of Andrew Johnson*, 5:409; RSE to LCB, 10 Feb. 1862, Museum of the Confederacy. Ewell suggested that Lizinka write the note, which is now in GWC. Both men had attended West Point with Ewell.

25. CB to LCB, 6 June 1862, PBE; LCB to Francis P. Blair, undated [1865], folder 44, PBE. The troops who entered Lizinka's house belonged to George Thomas's brigade.

26. RSE to LCB, 7 Mar. 1862, LC; RSE to LCB, 5 Mar. 1862, Museum of the Confederacy. See also RSE to LCB, 21 Feb. 1862, LC.

27. RSE to LCB, 20 Feb. 1862, LC.

28. Jubal A. Early, *Autobiographical Sketch*, 52; CB, "From Fairfax C.H. to Richmond," folder 20, PBE; Joseph E. Johnston, *Narrative*, 90, 95–96; Richmond *Whig*, 18 June 1863; Jubal Early to James Kemper, 9 Feb. 1862, Kemper Papers, UVA; Ewell's compiled service record, RG 109, M331, R89, NA. A. P. Hill assumed command of the Virginia brigade upon Ewell's promotion.

29. Jeb Stuart to wife, 24 Jan. 1862, Stuart Papers, VHS; Macon *Daily Telegraph*, 16 June 1862.

30. Richard Taylor, *Destruction*, 37. RSE to LCB, 13 Apr. 1862, PBE. Ewell's belief that Davis was prejudiced against him dated from 1849 when, as a U.S. senator from Mississippi, Davis had used his influence to have Lucius Northrup promoted over Ewell. Although Davis could be vindictive, there is nothing to suggest that he harbored any ill will toward Ewell.

31. Edward Reeve to wife, 21 Jan. 1862, Reeve Papers, SHC.

32. *OR* 5:1078–79; RSE to LCB, 23 Feb. 1862, LC; Evans, *Confederate Military History*, 2:68, 158–61; Houghton and Houghton, *Two Boys*, 53–54; Haskell, *Memoirs*, 18–19; Oates, *The War*, 142; Franklin M. Myers, *Comanches*, 39; miscellaneous note, folder 18, WM; Freeman, *Lee's Lieutenants*, 1:348.

33. Evans, *Confederate Military History*, 2:159–61; Houghton and Houghton, *Two Boys*, 53–54; Haskell, *Memoirs*, 18–19; Oates, *The War*, 142; Franklin M. Myers, *Comanches*, 39; miscellaneous note, folder 18, WM; Freeman, *Lee's Lieutenants*, 1:348.

34. Boyd, *Reminiscences*, 13; Freeman, *Lee's Lieutenants*, 1:349; Boatner, *Civil War Dictionary*, 827–28; Handerson, *Yankee in Gray*, 91; Franklin M. Myers, *Comanches*, 39; Alison Moore, *Louisiana Tigers*, 49–51; Terry L. Jones, *Lee's Tigers*, 64; Richard Taylor, *Destruction*, 40.

35. CBM. Lee's, Mason's, Rhodes's, Taliaferro's, and Tyler's compiled service records are in RG 109, M331, rolls 155, 165, 210, 241, and 253, respectively, NA.

36. Franklin M. Myers, *Comanches*, 39; the compiled service records of Barbour, Christy, Greene, Hancock, Jones, and Snodgrass are in RG 109, M331, rolls 15, 55, 111, 116, 144, and 233, respectively, NA; George Campbell Brown, "Notes," 256, 258, 261; Crute, *Confederate Staff Officers*, 57–58; CBM. Apparently Ewell first offered one of the adjutant positions to twenty-seven-year-old Samuel Wragg Ferguson, an officer who had served on Beauregard's staff in 1861. When Ferguson failed to report at the appointed time, Ewell apparently withdrew the offer. "I may & probably will place an older & more mature person in the place," he informed his fiancée; "I will not risk any younger Officer" (RSE to LCB, 13 Apr. 1862, PBE).

37. The compiled service records of Nelson and Turner are in RG 109, M331, rolls 186 and 252, respectively, NA; George Campbell Brown, "Notes," 256. Turner's father, Henry S. Turner, gathered intelligence for the Confederacy in Washington, D.C., in 1862 (*OR* 12[3]:849 and Henry Hunt to TTG, 27 Feb. 1875, Hunt Papers, Library of Congress). On Ewell's high opinion of Brown and his reasons for not appointing him assistant adjutant general at an earlier date, see RSE to LCB, 10 Feb. 1862, Museum of the Confederacy.

38. Brown's compiled service records are in RG 109, M331, R35, NA; RSE to LCB, undated [ca. Mar. 1862], LC; CB to LCB, 12 Apr. 1862, PBE; RSE to LCB, 13 Apr. 1862, PBE; George Campbell Brown, "Notes," 256.

39. RSE to LCB, 23 Feb., 16 Mar. 1862, LC; RSE to LCB, 13 Apr. 1862, PBE; [WS] to RLE, 22 Mar. 1862, folder 18, WM; CB to LCB, 12 Apr. 1862, PBE; Hayes, *War between the States*, 6. William Stoddert arrived around 8 March 1862.

40. Joseph E. Johnston, *Narrative*, 107–8.

41. RSE to LCB, 16 Mar. 1862, LC.

42. RSE to LCB, 7, 16 Mar. 1862, LC; McPherson, *Battle Cry*, 430.

43. RSE to LCB, 7 Mar. 1862, LC.

44. Jubal A. Early, *Autobiographical Sketch*, 56; Joseph E. Johnston, *Narrative*, 107–8.

45. RSE to RLE, 23 May [*sic*; Mar.] 1862, LC; CBM.

46. Richard Taylor, *Destruction*, 37–38.

47. Oates, *The War*, 89; CBM; Goldsborough, *Maryland Line*, 33–34.

48. Richard Taylor, *Destruction*, 39–40.

49. CBM; Fravel, "Jackson's Valley Campaign," 418.

50. CBM; Russell, *Mosby*, 107–8.

51. CBM. In his *Recollections* McHenry Howard states that Ewell's headquarters were at Brandy Station on 26 March, suggesting that Ewell may have moved into the Barbour house a few days prior to his engagement with Heintzelman. Compare RSE to RLE, 23 May [*sic*; Mar.] 1862, LC. The Barbour house stands 0.8 miles due north of Brandy Station and is today a dairy farm known as "Beauregard" (Howard, *Recollections*, 73).

52. Oates, *The War*, 90; Richard Taylor, *Destruction*, 38.

53. RSE to Johnston, 8 Apr. 1862, Ewell Papers, DU; Richard Taylor, *Destruction*, 38–39.

54. *OR* 12(3):32, 50, 80, 845, 849, 851; Beauregard, "Bull Run," 202–9; Freeman, *Lee*, 2:36. Approximate locations and numbers of troops for both sides may be found in G. F. R. Henderson, *Stonewall Jackson*, on the map facing 1:284.

55. *OR* 12(3):81; CBM.

56. CBM.

57. *OR* 12(3):847.

58. *OR* 12(3):845–46, 848, 851; RSE to Thomas Jackson, undated [14 Apr. 1862], in ELB, 4–5.

59. RSE to RLE, 2 Mar. 1844, LC.

60. RSE to Thomas Jackson, undated [14 Apr. 1862], in ELB, 3–4; *OR* 12(3):845–48, 852, 861.

61. *OR* 12(3):845–46, 848–49, 865; RSE to Thomas Jackson, two undated dispatches [both written 14 Apr. 1862], in ELB, 3–5.

62. *OR* 12(3):845–47; RSE to Thomas Jackson, two undated dispatches [both 14 Apr. 1862], in ELB, 3–5. Campbell Brown states that the couriers initially used Chester Gap, then Thornton's Gap, but there is no evidence to support this assertion (CBM).

63. John William Jones, *Personal Reminiscences*, 187; Dabney, *Life and Campaigns*, 337; Munford's address on the life of Elzey, 4, miscellany, box 3, Munford-Ellis Papers, DU; *OR* 12(3):850–51.

64. *OR* 12(3):850–51. On 16 April, the date Ewell applied for permission to attack McDowell, Brig. Gen. Rufus King's infantry division and Col. George D. Bayard's cavalry brigade were at Catlett's Station, and Brig. Gen. George A. McCall's infantry division was at Manassas Junction. Interestingly, Ewell made no mention of Abercrombie's brigade, which was still at Warrenton Junction (*OR* 12[3]:80).

65. *OR* 12(3):852, 858. Ewell received Johnston's dispatch on the night of 17 April.

66. *OR* 12(3):853, 858; Douglas, *I Rode with Stonewall*, 50–54; CBM.

67. *OR* 12(3):115, 854, 876–77; McKim, *Soldier's Recollections*, 82–83; CBM. Ewell initially left one regiment of infantry and some cavalry to picket the Rappahannock line. He later reduced that force to just three companies.

68. *OR* 12(3):860–61.

69. McKim, *Soldier's Recollections*, 82–83; Goldsborough, *Maryland Line*, 34–35; *OR* 12(3):853–54, 857–58; Isaac Seymour to William Seymour, 2 May 1862, Seymour Papers, University of Michigan.

70. *OR* 12(3):861; CBM.

71. *OR* 12(3):866–68, 871, 875. Lee planned to relieve the pressure on Richmond by taking the offensive against McDowell at Fredericksburg. In addition to the troops of Anderson and Field, he intended to send two other brigades to the town. That would have increased the total number of Confederate troops in the area to more than 15,000 men, exclusive of any troops that Ewell might bring. Both Lee and Ewell thought the troops in that sector should be placed under the leadership of a single officer (*OR* 12[3]:871, 876).

72. *OR* 12(3):868–71; Thomas Jackson to RSE, 26 Apr. 1862, Milligan Papers, MHS.

73. *OR* 12(3):871–72, 876–77; McMullen, *A Surgeon*, 25. The substance of the conversation is derived from Jackson's 29 April dispatch to Lee, Jackson's 3 May dispatch to Ewell, and Ewell's 30 April dispatch to Lee. For Ewell's preference for an attack on New Market, see *OR* 12(3):878.

Chapter 11

1. Oates, *The War*, 92–93; George W. Booth, *Personal Reminiscences*, 29–30; Goldsborough, *Maryland Line*, 35; McKim, *Soldier's Recollections*, 86.

2. CBM; Hotchkiss, *Make Me a Map*, 34–35; Franklin M. Myers, *Comanches*, 37. Ralph Hutton, in his book *History of Elkton*, 15, 18, claims that Ewell occupied the home of Dr. S. P. H. Miller, but he gives no authority for this statement.

3. Hotchkiss, *Make Me a Map*, 34–35; Tanner, *Stonewall in the Valley*, 185; *OR* 12(3):884.

4. Buck, *With the Old Confeds*, 28; Douglas, *I Rode with Stonewall*, 55. On Ewell's knowledge of Jackson's destination, see *OR* 12(3):876–77, 881.

5. Boyd, *Reminiscences*, 8–10; *OR* 12(3):876–77.

6. John William Jones, "Port Republic," 364–65.

7. George Edgar Sipe, "Civil War Recollections," 4, VHS.

8. W. M. Dame to HB, 24 Mar. 1890, folder 23, WM; Eggleston, *Rebel's Recollections*, 158–59; Munford, "Reminiscences," 523.

9. John William Jones, "Down the Valley," 187; Franklin M. Myers, *Comanches*, 37.

10. Hotchkiss, *Make Me a Map*, 34; CBM; *OR* 12(3):882.

11. CB to LCB, 9 May 1862, PBE.

12. *OR* 12(3):878.

13. *OR* 12(3):881, 884.

14. *OR* 12(3):140, 882–883, 12(1):458–60; Richard Taylor, *Destruction*, 47; CB to LCB, 9 May 1862, PBE; Wilson, *Borderland Confederate*, 12; Pendleton, "Official Report," 199.

15. Benjamin Hubert to Letitia Bailey, 2 May 1862, Hubert Papers, DU; *OR* 12(3):880–85. At Ewell's orders Branch placed two regiments of infantry and a small force of cavalry near Culpeper to watch the Rappahannock line, keeping the balance of his force at Gordonsville.

16. RSE to Robert Lee, 13 May 1862, folder 3, Heartt-Wilson Papers, SHC.

17. Franklin M. Myers, *Comanches*, 38; *OR* 12(3):885; Munford, "Reminiscences," 525–26. Fisher's Gap seems to have also gone by the names of Friters and Williams's Gaps.

18. Franklin M. Myers, *Comanches*, 38; *OR* 12(3):886. Myers anticipates Ashby's promotion. He was still a colonel at the time.

19. RSE's compiled service record, RG 109, M331, R89, NA; Harriot Stoddert Turner, "Ewells of Virginia," 35 n., CWM.

20. Munford, "Reminiscences," 526–27; RSE to Lawrence Branch, 12 May 1862, Branch Papers, UVA; RSE to Robert Lee, 13 May 1862, folder 3, Heartt-Wilson Papers, SHC.

21. Boyd, *Reminiscences*, 12.

22. *OR* 12(3):162.

23. RSE to Robert Lee, 13 May 1862, folder 3, Heartt-Wilson Papers, SHC; Munford, "Reminiscences," 526–27. No dispatch like that quoted by Munford has been found.

24. *OR* 12(3):889, 892–93; RSE to Lawrence Branch and Robert Lee, 13 May 1862, Branch Papers, UVA; RSE to Robert Lee, 13 May 1862, folder 3, Heartt-Wilson Papers, SHC.

25. Munford, "Reminiscences," 527.

26. *OR* 12(3):887–88.

27. RSE to Robert Lee, 13 May 1862, folder 3, Heartt-Wilson Papers, SHC.

28. RSE to Jeb Stuart, J. E. B. Stuart Papers, Huntington Library.

29. RSE to LE, 13 May 1862, LC.

30. *OR* 12(3):887–89.

31. *OR* 12(3):890–92. Ewell's original dispatches to Branch are in the Branch Papers, UVA.

32. Isaac Seymour to William Seymour, 2 May 1862, Seymour Papers, University of Michigan.

33. McKim, *Soldier's Recollections*, 87; CB to LCB, 17 June 1862, PBE; Robert Stiles, "Monument," 25. Campbell Brown wrote to his mother at the conclusion of the 1862 Valley Campaign: "You will hear no more however of rapid movements & forced marches, if the Army gets to be a large one, and the fighting that is done will be slower & more cautious. If we ever get rid of the immense wagon-train that now encumbers the Army of the Valley & retards its movements, & if Jackson's Division once gets its baggage reduced to the same degree of lightness & mobility as ours, using tent-flies which weigh only 15 pounds, instead of tents which weigh 90, we can move nearly as fast as ever, without anything like the same fuss & groaning over it." Jackson's immense train was the result of captures that he made during the campaign.

34. *OR* 12(3):199, 892. According to Robert L. Dabney, Jackson's chief of staff, the abandonment of New Market Gap by the Federals briefly led Ewell to believe that Banks's whole army had gone to Richmond. No evidence has been found to support that statement (Dabney, *Life and Campaigns*, 360).

35. *OR* 12(3):889, 893; RSE to Lawrence Branch, 16 May 1862 (two dispatches), Branch Papers, UVA; CBM.

36. *OR* 12(3):893; RSE to Thomas Jackson, 16 May 1862, West Papers, VHS.

37. *OR* 12(3):894–96; John M. Jones to Lawrence Branch, 17 May 1862, Branch Papers, UVA; McKim, *Soldier's Recollections*, 87; George W. Booth, *Personal Reminiscences*, 30–31.

Chapter 12

1. Hotchkiss, *Make Me a Map*, 46. Jackson's headquarters were at Castle Hill, just west of Mt. Solon.

2. Wayland, *Stonewall Jackson's Way*, 102; *OR* 12(3):888, 894–95.

3. *OR* 12(3):897.

4. Douglas, *I Rode with Stonewall*, 99.

5. *OR* 12(3):895, 897–98, 51(2):560; John M. Jones to Lawrence Branch, 18 May 1862, Branch Papers, UVA. Compare Dabney, *Life and Campaigns*, 364, and Tanner, *Stonewall in the Valley*, 198.

6. Richard Taylor, *Destruction*, 47; Hotchkiss, *Make Me a Map*, 46, 168; Dabney, *Life and Campaigns*, 359–60.

7. McKim, *Soldier's Recollections*, 87–88; John M. Jones to Lawrence Branch, 18 May 1862, Branch Papers, UVA.

8. Lawrence Branch to "Nannie," 18 May 1862, Branch Papers, UVA. Ewell's contradictory 16–17 May 1862 orders to Branch and the reasons behind them are in the Branch Papers.

9. *OR* 12(3):896–98. Why Johnston elected to send messages via courier, which required two or three days of travel, rather than using the telegraph is unknown.

10. Hotchkiss, *Make Me a Map*, 47.

11. Ibid., 168; Douglas, *I Rode with Stonewall*, 99.

12. *OR* 12(3):896–98.

13. Tanner, *Stonewall in the Valley*, 191, 201; Joseph Johnston to RSE, 18 May 1862, Jackson Papers, VHS. Robert Tanner skillfully reconstructs the sequence of events in *Stonewall in the Valley*, 201–2.

14. Franklin M. Myers, *Comanches*, 48–49.

15. Dabney, *Life and Campaigns*, 364; CB to LCB, 17 June 1862, PBE; CBM; CB, "From Fairfax C.H. to Richmond," folder 20, PBE.

16. *OR* 12(3):895–97. Dabney, *Life and Campaigns*, 364, claims Jackson never had any intention of making a direct attack on Strasburg, but Jackson's orders to Ewell suggest otherwise.

17. G. F. R. Henderson, *Stonewall Jackson*, 1:309–10; Allan, *History*, 146; Johnson and Buel, *Battles and Leaders*, 2:301; Douglas, *I Rode with Stonewall*, 58; Franklin M. Myers, *Comanches*, 49. Dabney, *Life and Campaigns*, 346, puts Jackson's strength at 16,000 men and 40 guns.

18. Wilson, *Borderland Confederate*, 15; *OR* 12(1):730. Munford had been ordered to Richmond to procure rifles for his command and did not return to the Valley until after the battle of Winchester.

19. *OR* 51(2):561, 12(3):598; McClendon, *Recollections*, 53.

20. Ewell's account of the Valley Campaign, folder 18, PBE.

21. *OR* 12(1):702–3, 733–34; Wilson, *Borderland Confederate*, 15.

22. *OR* 12(1):702. Accounts of the First Maryland's disaffection and subsequent restoration are chronicled in Evans, *Confederate Military History*, 2:68–70; John E. Howard to Mrs. Eugene Post, 17 June 1862, Civil War Collection, MHS; McKim, *Soldier's Recollections*, 86, 96–97; WHM, 46–47; George W. Booth, *Personal Reminiscences*, 31–32.

23. The first, second, and third roads correspond, respectively, to modern-day routes 522, 340, and 340/522.

24. Evans, *Confederate Military History*, 2:71; John E. Howard to Mrs. Eugene Post, 17 June 1862, Civil War Collection, MHS.

25. Evans, *Confederate Military History*, 2:72; John E. Howard to Mrs. Eugene Post, 17 June 1862, Civil War Collection, MHS; George W. Booth, *Personal Reminiscences*, 31–32.

26. *OR* 12(1):555–57, 702–3, 725, 778–79; WHM, 49–50; Evans, *Confederate Military History*, 2:71–72; McClendon, *Recollections*, 21. Crutchfield could discern "no apparent damage to the enemy" from the Confederate fire, though Bradley Johnson later remembered that Brockenbrough's battery silenced the Union guns.

27. Franklin M. Myers, *Comanches*, 51.

28. *OR* 12(1):556–57; 733–34, 778–79; Ewell account of the Valley Campaign, folder 18, PBE; Evans, *Confederate Military History*, 10:215; Oates, *The War*, 97; Richard Taylor, *Destruction*, 53–54.

29. Evans, *Confederate Military History*, 2:73; Donohoe, "Fight," 309; Franklin M. Myers, *Comanches*, 51; *OR* 12(1):734.

30. Dabney, *Life and Campaigns*, 369; Hotchkiss, *Make Me a Map*, 48; *OR* 12(1):779.

31. Evans, *Confederate Military History*, 2:73.

32. *OR* 12(1):703; Jedediah Hotchkiss to his wife, 26 May 1862, R4, F421–28, HP.

33. *OR* 12(1):778.

34. *OR* 12(1):546, 703; Tanner, *Stonewall in the Valley*, 215.

35. Hotchkiss, *Make Me a Map*, 48; McClendon, *Recollections*, 55; Richard Taylor, *Destruction*, 54.

36. George Campbell Brown, "Notes," 256.

37. Ibid., 255–56; Tanner, *Stonewall in the Valley*, 204; RSE to Samuel Cooper, 14 May 1862, in ELB; CBM; Hotchkiss, *Make Me a Map*, 30; Allan, *History*, 92; Johnson and Buel, *Battles and Leaders*, 2:301.

38. George W. Booth, *Personal Reminiscences*, 12–13, 19–20; Evans, *Confederate Military History*, 2:167–68; Boatner, *Civil War Dictionary*, 796; *OR* 12(3):895–97.

39. Munford, "Reminiscences," 528; *OR* 12(1):731, 734.

40. Munford, "Reminiscences," 528; Tanner, *Stonewall in the Valley*, 384 n. 63. Estimates of the number of companies under Ashby's command range from twenty-one to twenty-six.

41. Franklin M. Myers, *Comanches*, 51.

42. CBM.

43. *OR* 12(1):779; Hotchkiss, *Make Me a Map*, 48.

44. *OR* 12(1):703; unpublished draft of Ewell's report on Front Royal and Winchester, TN. Newtown now goes by the name of Stephens City.

45. Hotchkiss, *Make Me a Map*, 48; Allan, "Jackson in the Shenandoah," 246; *OR* 12(1):703. Jackson stated that Steuart "advised me of movements which indicated that Banks was preparing to leave Strasburg" and captured several prisoners, wagons, and ambulances (*OR* 12[1]:546).

46. Allan, "Jackson in the Shenandoah," 246.

47. *OR* 12(1):703; Tanner, *Stonewall in the Valley*, 221.

48. Ewell's account of the Valley Campaign, folder 18, PBE; *OR* 51(2):562.

49. *OR* 12(3):899.

50. *OR* 12(1):574, 703, 779; Ewell's account of the Valley Campaign, folder 18, PBE; draft of Ewell's report on First Winchester, TN.

51. Unpublished draft of Ewell's report on Front Royal and Winchester, TN; *OR* 12(3):899−900. Ewell's dispatch to Jackson has not been found.

52. *OR* 12(1):704, 12(3):900.

53. *OR* 12(3):899−900; CBM. The courier may have been Capt. Keith Boswell, Jackson's chief engineer. For an explanation as to the chronology presented in the text and how it was derived, see Appendix H.

54. *OR* 12(1):609, 704−5, 779; unpublished draft of Ewell's report on Front Royal and Winchester, TN; Ewell's account of the Valley Campaign, folder 18, PBE; Evans, *Confederate Military History*, 3:240.

55. Oates, *The War*, 97.

56. Franklin M. Myers, *Comanches*, 52−53; unpublished draft of Ewell's report on Front Royal and Winchester, TN; Ewell's account of the Valley Campaign, folder 18, PBE. Neither this dispatch nor any of the others that may have passed between Jackson and Ewell that night have been found.

57. *OR* 12(1):779. Ewell placed the time of the advance at 5:40 A.M., while Campbell Brown put it at 5:20 (CBM).

58. *Official Military Atlas*, plate 85, no. 2; CBM; Oates, *The War*, 98; McClendon, *Recollections*, 56; *OR* 12(1):794. Exit 80 of Interstate 81 now occupies the hill on which Ewell made his command post.

59. *OR* 12(1):779−80.

60. Ewell's account of the Valley Campaign, folder 18, PBE; unpublished draft of Ewell's report on Front Royal and Winchester, TN; CBM; *OR* 12(1):705, 779, 794; Oates, *The War*, 98−99; George Campbell Brown, "Notes," 256.

61. *OR* 12(1):794; Evans, *Confederate Military History*, 2:73−74.

62. Allan, "Jackson in the Shenandoah," 246−47; *OR* 12(1):779, 794; CBM.

63. CBM; CB, "Ewell's Division at Winchester," TN; Allan, "Jackson in the Shenandoah," 247; *OR* 12(1):794.

64. *OR* 12(1):726−27; CB, "Ewell's Division at Winchester," TN; Ewell's account of the Valley Campaign, folder 18, PBE; George Campbell Brown, "Notes," 257; CBM; Richard Taylor, *Destruction*, 59; McKim, *Soldier's Recollections*, 100−102.

65. George W. Booth, *Personal Reminiscences*, 34; Evans, *Confederate Military History*, 2:74−75; CB, "Ewell's Division at Winchester," TN.

66. *OR* 12(1):779, 794; McClendon, *Recollections*, 56−57; CBM.

67. *OR* 12(1):706−7; Jackson, *Memoirs*, 262.

68. *OR* 12(1):706−7, 709−10, 12(3):901; Jedediah Hotchkiss to wife, 26 May 1862, R4, F241−48, HP; Oates, *The War*, 99; CBM.

69. CBM.

70. CBM; *OR* 12(1):709−10; Lacy, *Memorials, Addresses, Sermons*, 52−53.

71. *OR* 12(1):551, 608−11; CBM; Evans, *Confederate Military History*, 2:75; Edward A. Moore, *Story of a Cannoneer*, 60; Howard, *Recollections*, 111.

72. *OR* 12(1):708, 719−24; Jedediah Hotchkiss to wife, 26 May 1862, R4, F421−23, HP; Hotchkiss, *Make Me a Map*, 48−49. Not included in this figure were an additional 20,000 pounds of bacon and 40,000 pounds of hardtack distributed directly to Ewell's men by division quartermaster Maj. Charles E. Snodgrass. Snodgrass's failure to report these stores elicited

a rebuke from Maj. Wells J. Hawks, the army's chief commissary officer. Hawks's protests were more a matter of principle than practicality; he already had far more captured supplies than he could transport.

73. *OR* 12(1):708, 780–81; Allan, *History*, III, 127.

Chapter 13

1. Munford, "Reminiscences," 527–28; *OR* 12(1):707, 730, 734, 12(3):271, 738; Franklin M. Myers, *Comanches*, 54–56.

2. *OR* 12(1):707.

3. Franklin M. Myers, *Comanches*, 56–57. The Federal force may have been the Fifth New York Cavalry, which Saxton had dispatched on a reconnaissance toward Halltown that morning.

4. Franklin M. Myers, *Comanches*, 58–59.

5. *OR* 12(1):708, 12(3):267, 294; Wilson, *Borderland Confederate*, 119–20; Evans, *Confederate Military History*, 2:76; Oates, *The War*, 100. Quartermaster John Harman estimated that the train was eight miles long (Tanner, *Stonewall in the Valley*, 271).

6. *OR* 12(1):707.

7. Franklin M. Myers, *Comanches*, 59; Evans, *Confederate Military History*, 2:75; Oates, *The War*, 99; Douglas, *I Rode with Stonewall*, 73.

8. Oates, *The War*, 99; CBM; *OR* 12(1):793; Ewell's account of the Valley Campaign, box 1, folder 20, PBE.

9. *OR* 12(1):649, 682–83, 12(3):259; Frémont's advance was at Cedar Creek, five miles from Strasburg. His main force was seven miles farther back at Cottontown (Gilmor, *Four Years*, 40).

10. WHM, 56; Capt. John E. Howard to Mrs. Eugene Post, 17 June 1862, Civil War Collection, MHS.

11. Tanner, *Stonewall in the Valley*, 354–55.

12. Richard Taylor, *Destruction*, 61; *OR* 12(3):904.

13. Oates, *The War*, 100; Wilson, *Borderland Confederate*, 20; *OR* 12(1):14; Richard Taylor, *Destruction*, 62, 66; Charles Wight Memoir, VHS.

14. Richard Taylor, *Destruction*, 64–65.

15. George W. Booth, *Personal Reminiscences*, 38–39; CBM; Richard Taylor, *Destruction*, 66–67; Oates, *The War*, 101; *OR* 12(1):14, 650, 711, 730–31; Hotchkiss diary, 1 June 1862, R1, HP; Wingfield, "Diary," 11; Wilson, *Borderland Confederate*, 20; Goldsborough, *Maryland Line*, 277; George Campbell Brown, "Notes," 257.

16. Munford, "Reminiscences," 528. Compare Oates, *The War*, 101.

17. Tanner, *Stonewall in the Valley*, 277; *OR* 12(1):731; Allan, *History*, 138; Dabney, *Life and Campaigns*, 398. Steuart had failed previously at Winchester and Round Hill. Ewell urged Jackson to place the Second and Sixth Virginia Cavalry under Ashby after the commanders of those regiments, Col. Thomas T. Munford and Lt. Col. Thomas Flournoy, complained to him of Steuart's incompetence.

18. Richard Taylor, *Destruction*, 69–70; Howard, *Recollections*, 119; Franklin M. Myers, *Comanches*, 60–61. The following night Jackson suffered a similar indignity at a stream just above New Market (Hotchkiss, *Make Me a Map*, 51).

19. *OR* 12(1):16, 679, 681, 711, 12(3):359, 905; Wingfield, "Diary," 11; Wilson, *Borderland Confederate*, 20; Douglas, *I Rode with Stonewall*, 82.

20. Franklin M. Myers, *Comanches*, 61.

21. *OR* 12(3):906; Hotchkiss diary, 6 June 1862, R1, HP; Richard Taylor, *Destruction*, 70; George W. Booth, *Personal Reminiscences*, 40; Munford, "Confederate Cavalry Officer's Reminiscence," 287.

22. *OR* 12(1):18, 652, 680, 12(3):365. Confederate sources place the number of Union prisoners at between forty and sixty (Capt. John E. Howard to Mrs. Eugene Post, 17 June 1862, Civil War Collection, MHS; George W. Booth, *Personal Reminiscences*, 40; Goldsborough, *Maryland Line*, 49; CB to LCB, 6 June 1862, PBE). According to Wilson, *Borderland Confederate*, 21, Ewell witnessed the attack and congratulated Ashby on his success, but this seems unlikely.

23. *OR* 12(1):18; Munford Ms., Miscellany, box 1, Munford-Ellis Papers, DU.

24. CB to LCB, 6 June 1862, PBE; Richard Taylor, *Destruction*, 71; Evans, *Confederate Military History*, 2:77; Charles Wight Memoir, VHS; Avirett, "Sketch," 290.

25. Goldsborough, *Maryland Line*, 50; Charles Wight Memoir, VHS; Dabney, *Life and Campaigns*, 399; RSE to John Esten Cooke, 10 Feb. 1864, Cooke Papers, VHS; Evans, *Confederate Military History*, 2:78.

26. Evans, *Confederate Military History*, 2:78–79; George Campbell Brown, "Notes," 257; Avirett, "Sketch," 290; George W. Booth, *Personal Reminiscences*, 41; Hewes, "Turner Ashby's Courage," 613. M. Warner Hewes recalled that the Federals stood behind a rail fence, facing the woods, at the edge of a 400-yard-wide clover field.

27. Evans, *Confederate Military History*, 2:78–79; Charles Wight Memoir, VHS; George Campbell Brown, "Notes," 257; Dabney, *Life and Campaigns*, 400; Avirett, "Sketch," 290; CB to LCB, 6 June 1862, PBE; CBM.

28. *OR* 12(1):788–89; RSE to John Esten Cooke, 10 Feb. 1864, Cooke Papers, Western Reserve Historical Society; Evans, *Confederate Military History*, 2:79; CBM.

29. Goldsborough, *Maryland Line*, 50; Johnson Ms., Miscellany, box 5, p. 134, Johnson Papers, DU; Evans, *Confederate Military History*, 2:79–80; WHM, 60–61; George W. Booth, *Personal Reminiscences*, 41.

30. George Campbell Brown, "Notes," 257; *OR* 12(1):18, 652, 783; Johnson Ms., Miscellany, box 5, p. 134, Johnson Papers, DU. In 1864 Ewell wrote that the Fifty-eighth Virginia and the First Maryland had lost sixty killed and wounded and that the "enemy's loss was much heavier" (RSE to John Esten Cooke, 10 Feb. 1864, Cooke Papers, Western Reserve Historical Society).

31. CBM.

32. *OR* 12(1):732; Munford, "Reminiscences," 529; CB, Notes on the battle of Harrisonburg, TN. See also Munford Ms., Miscellany, box 1, Munford-Ellis Papers, DU; CBM; Dabney, *Life and Campaigns*, 401.

33. CBM.

34. Munford, "Reminiscences," 529; Thomas Munford to Jedediah Hotchkiss, 19 Aug. 1896, R49, F242, HP.

Chapter 14

1. McClendon, *Recollections*, 64; CBM.

2. Goldsborough, *Maryland Line*, 54; Evans, *Confederate Military History*, 2:281. After the war the Marylanders were reinterred at Loudon Park Cemetery in Baltimore, Maryland.

3. *OR* 12(3):906; Dabney, *Life and Campaigns*, 410.

4. CB, "Harrisonburg & Ashby's Death," TN; *OR* 12(1):18, 781; Allan, *History*, 151; McKim, *Soldier's Recollections*, 109.

5. *OR* 12(1):698–99, 713.

6. Franklin M. Myers, *Comanches*, 65; CB, "Cross Keys," TN; Munford Ms., Miscellany, box 1, Munford-Ellis Papers, DU. Watts gained command of the Second Regiment when Munford took charge of the army's cavalry on 7 June.

7. *OR* 12(1):781.

8. *OR* 12(1):781, 795, 801–2; Richard Taylor, *Destruction*, 72–73; CB, "Cross Keys," TN; Evans, *Confederate Military History*, 3:256; RSE to John Esten Cooke, 10 Feb. 1864, Cooke Papers, Western Reserve Historical Society.

9. CBM; *OR* 12(1):781; Oates, *The War*, 102; McClendon, *Recollections*, 55.

10. CBM; *OR* 12(1):781, 782, 798–99; Goldsborough, *Maryland Line*, 50; Dabney, *Life and Campaigns*, 416. Canister is ineffective at ranges greater than 500 yards.

11. CBM; *OR* 12(1):19; Boyd, *Reminiscences*, 14; McKim, *Soldier's Recollections*, 113.

12. *OR* 12(1):782; Goldsborough, *Maryland Line*, 54; CB, "Cross Keys," TN; McKim, *Soldier's Recollections*, 115; WHM, 63; Boatner, *Civil War Dictionary*, 264–65, 796.

13. CBM.

14. McKim, *Soldier's Recollections*, 115.

15. Richard Taylor, *Destruction*, 72–73; Dabney, *Life and Campaigns*, 418; McGuire and Christian, *Confederate Cause*, 197; Lenoir Chambers, *Stonewall Jackson*, 1:578; James Hewes memoirs, 80–81, Palmer Papers, Western Reserve Historical Society.

16. *OR* 12(1):20, 781, 791–93, 795–96; Allan, *History*, 154–55 n.

17. CBM; *OR* 12(1):21.

18. Evans, *Confederate Military History*, 2:80–81. See also *OR* 12(1):782. Ewell later made the arrangement official, publishing it in General Orders 30.

19. Krick, *Conquering the Valley*, 255.

20. *OR* 12(1):666–68, 789–90, 796–97, 799, 801–2; Allan, *History*, 154–56 and n.; Dabney, *Life and Campaigns*, 418; RSE to John Esten Cooke, 10 Feb. 1864, Cooke Papers, Western Reserve Historical Society.

21. *OR* 12(1):768; RSE to John M. Patton, 12 May 1867, PBE; Krick, *Conquering the Valley*, 253.

22. *OR* 12(1):668, 770.

23. Hotchkiss, *Make Me a Map*, 131. At a later point in the battle, probably after Stahel's repulse but before Schenck's threatened attack, Ewell sent Campbell Brown to Jackson to report "things going on smoothly" (CBM).

24. Dabney, *Life and Campaigns*, 418; Richard Taylor, *Destruction*, 73.

25. Allan, *History*, 156; *OR* 12(1):797, 781–82; RSE to John Esten Cooke, 10 Feb. 1864, Cooke Papers, Western Reserve Historical Society. Compare CB, "Cross Keys," TN; Dabney, *Life and Campaigns*, 419.

26. Munford Ms., Miscellany, box 1, Munford-Ellis Papers, DU; Dabney, *Life and Campaigns*, 419; *OR* 12(1):786. Ewell selected Col. John Patton's brigade to be the rear guard. That night Patton rode to Port Republic to speak with Jackson. Stonewall gave Patton detailed instructions on how to conduct the rear guard action, adding, "*I'll be back to join you in the morning.*" For a discussion of this episode, see Krick, *Conquering the Valley*, 285. See also Dabney, *Life and Campaigns*, 420–21, and RSE to John M. Patton, 12 May 1867, PBE.

27. Munford Ms., Miscellany, box 1, Munford-Ellis Papers, DU; *OR* 12(1):797–98. Trimble's brigade numbered 1,348 men at the time of the battle, one-ninth that of Frémont's

available force. Ewell's decision not to attack the Union army that night may have been influenced to some degree by an order of battle found that day on a captured Union staff officer. The order indicated that Frémont had seven infantry brigades in addition to his cavalry (*OR* 12[1]:783).

28. *OR* 12(1):664–65, 783–84, 799; Munford, "Reminiscences," 530; Hotchkiss to wife, 15 June 1862, R4, HP. Trimble's report is in *OR* 12(1):795–99.

29. WHM, 63; Willie Walker Caldwell, "Life of Walker," 64, VHS; RSE to John M. Patton, 12 May 1867, PBE; *OR* 12(1):714.

30. Kern Papers, p. 5, SHC.

31. Dabney, *Life and Campaigns*, 419–20; Richard Taylor, *Destruction*, 74; *OR* 12(1):774.

32. Freeman, *Lee's Lieutenants*, 1:451; *OR* 12(1):728; Edward A. Moore, *Story of a Cannoneer*, 74. For descriptions of the battlefield, see Dabney, *Life and Campaigns*, 422; Allan, *History*, 158; and Richard Taylor, *Destruction*, 74. Of the six guns at the coaling, three belonged to Battery E, Fourth U.S. Artillery, commanded by Capt. Joseph C. Clark. The two remaining guns belonged to Battery H, First Ohio Artillery, commanded by Capt. James H. Huntington. Clark's guns were on the left; Huntington's, on the right (*OR* 12[1]:691–93, 696, 714, 729).

33. *OR* 12(1):786; Evans, *Confederate Military History*, 2:81; Goldsborough, *Maryland Line*, 57. The First Maryland Regiment was informally brigaded with Scott.

34. Campbell Brown stated that the Fifty-eighth Virginia numbered fewer than 200 men at the battle of Harrisonburg, where it lost fifty-three men. Col. William C. Scott reported that the Forty-fourth Virginia had "not more than 130 men" at Cross Keys. It lost four men there (*OR* 12[1]:783–84, 789–90; George Campbell Brown, "Notes," 257).

35. Charles Wight Memoir, VHS; *OR* 12(1):786, 790–91; Dabney, *Life and Campaigns*, 423; unpublished draft of Ewell's report on Cross Keys and Port Republic, TN. In a draft of his report on the battle, Ewell wrote that he "called for Volunteers from these two Regts to pull down some fences in the front. This was done under fire of Artillery & musketry, & I regret that the rapid course of events made it impossible to record their names. These fences were perpendicular to the enemy's line of advance, & a third much higher, I directed to be left as a cover, intending the two Regts to take post behind it." He deleted this passage from his final report.

36. CB to LCB, 17 June 1862, PBE; Charles Wight Memoir, VHS; N. Dixon Walker to Noah Walker, 10 Feb. 1863, Walker Papers, MHS.

37. *OR* 12(1):715, 763, 786; Edward A. Moore, *Story of a Cannoneer*, 75; CB, "Port Republic," TN. Davis, an ancestor of the author of this biography, was badly wounded in this effort. His gun was overrun and captured by the Fifth Ohio Volunteers.

38. Neese, *Three Years*, 75.

39. New Orleans *Daily Picayune*, 10 June 1866; *OR* 12(1):802–3; Evans, *Confederate Military History*, 10:217. A short time earlier Col. Henry Kelly of the Eighth Louisiana Infantry remembered seeing Ewell "on foot and cap in hand" leading reinforcements down the road (Kelly, *Port Republic*, 22).

40. Wingfield, "Diary," 12.

41. Richard Taylor, *Destruction*, 75; *OR* 12(1):698–700, 715, 741–42, 774, 786. After crossing the South River, Walker was ordered to follow the route taken by the Louisiana Brigade, but he lost Taylor's trail in the mountains. Ewell thereupon ordered him to reinforce the Forty-fourth and Fifty-eighth Virginia Regiments (unpublished draft of Ewell's report on the Battles of Cross Keys and Port Republic, TN).

42. LaBree, *Camp Fires*, 306; Krick, *Conquering the Valley*, 437. Krick's detailed book is by far the best source on Cross Keys and Port Republic.

43. Richard Taylor, *Destruction*, 76; Douglas, *I Rode with Stonewall*, 97.

44. *OR* 12(1):22–23, 714, 716, 766–67, 770–71, 798; Oates, *The War*, 104–5; Dabney, *Life and Campaigns*, 425; Boyd, *Reminiscences*, 14.

45. *OR* 12(1):715. At Cross Keys and Port Republic Jackson inflicted more than 1,900 casualties on the Federals. By contrast Jackson himself suffered roughly 1,260 losses, of whom 1,018 belonged to Ewell (Krick, *Conquering the Valley*, 507–12). Compare *OR* 12(1):690, 717–18, 784, 787; Allan, *History*, 162.

46. Wingfield, "Diary," 12. Wingfield may be mistaken about the death of Ewell's horse. The general did not submit a claim of reimbursement for the animal from the Confederate government.

47. Boyd, *Reminiscences*, 14–15; Douglas, *I Rode with Stonewall*, 97; Hotchkiss diary, 9 June 1862, R1, HP; CBM.

48. Munford, "Reminiscences," 530. An earlier, abbreviated version of this conversation is in Munford Ms., Miscellany, box 1, Munford-Ellis Papers, DU. In that account Munford remembered the conversation as having occurred the evening of 8 June outside Jackson's headquarters.

49. George W. Booth, *Personal Reminiscences*, 43.

50. Franklin M. Myers, *Comanches*, 68–69; *OR* 12(1):781–83.

51. McGuire and Christian, *Confederate Cause*, 209.

52. Richmond *Daily Enquirer*, 18 June 1862; John William Jones, "Reminiscences," 187.

53. Jackson, *Memoirs*, 287.

Chapter 15

1. *OR* 12(1):24–25, 32–34, 656, 685.

2. *OR* 12(1):659, 12(3):382, 391, 401, 409, 419.

3. *OR* 12(1):661.

4. *OR* 12(1):661.

5. *OR* 12(1):661, 12(3):913–14.

6. John William Jones, "'Stonewall' Jackson," 174. See also John William Jones, "Port Republic," 363–64; John William Jones, "Career," 84–85; CB to LCB, 3 July 1862, PBE; CBM.

7. Douglas, *I Rode with Stonewall*, 103.

8. In one account Dabney stated that the conversation took place at Mechum's River Station. He later remembered it as having taken place at Charlottesville (Hill, "Lee's Attacks," 348–49; Dabney, *Life and Campaigns*, 434–35).

9. CBM.

10. Jedediah Hotchkiss to G. F. R. Henderson, 31 Mar. 1896, HP; Chambers diary, 22 June 1862, North Carolina Department of Archives and History; Douglas, *I Rode with Stonewall*, 104; *OR* 11(3):612; CBM.

11. *OR* 11(2):490.

12. Dabney, *Life and Campaigns*, 440. Dabney identifies the two officers only as "commanders of divisions": hence Ewell, Whiting, or Winder. The quirky nature of the question and the speaker's knowledge of Jackson's habits strongly suggest that the quoted officer was Ewell, though this is not certain. According to "Extra Billy" Smith, Ewell once remarked "that Jackson could do the praying and he could do the swearing, and that the two together could whip the devil" (Richmond *Daily Whig*, 4 Sept. 1863).

13. Kearns diary, 26 June 1862, VHS; CBM; *OR* 11(2):553, 605, 882; George W. Booth, *Personal Reminiscences*, 44; Dabney, *Life and Campaigns*, 440; *Official Military Atlas*, plate 68,

no. 8; Worsham, *Jackson's Foot Cavalry*, 54; Richard Taylor, *Destruction*, 83; Miscellany, box 5, p. 141, Johnson Papers, DU; Dowdey, *Seven Days*, 177–78; Lenoir Chambers, *Stonewall Jackson*, 2:33.

14. *OR* 11(2):882; WHM, 68–69.

15. WHM, 67; CBM; Oates, *The War*, 114; *Official Military Atlas*, plate 63, no. 8; Dabney, *Life and Campaigns*, 442; Goldsborough, *Maryland Line*, 59; Miscellany, box 5, p. 141, Johnson Papers, DU; Freeman, *Lee*, 2:139–40.

16. *OR* 11(2):552–53, 605, 836–37; Freeman, *Lee*, 2:149–50; Sears, *To the Gates*, 223–24; CB, "Gaines' Mills," TN; Goldsborough, *Maryland Line*, 59; Dabney, *Life and Campaigns*, 443–44; WHM, 69; CBM.

17. Dabney, *Life and Campaigns*, 443–44; Miscellany, box 5, p. 141, Johnson Papers, DU.

18. *OR* 11(2):605; CB, "Gaines' Mills," TN.

19. Richard Taylor, *Destruction*, 83; *OR* 11(2):605, 614.

20. "Maj. Chatham Roberdeau Wheat," 427; Evans, *Confederate Military History*, 10:221; *OR* 11(2):605; CB, "Gaines' Mills," TN; Handerson, *Yankee in Gray*, 45–46; Terry L. Jones, *Lee's Tigers*, 103–5.

21. Lane, *"Dear Mother,"* 172; *OR* 11(2):614.

22. McClendon, *Recollections*, 77; *OR* 11(2):606; Oates, *The War*, 115.

23. CB, "Gaines' Mills," TN; CBM; *OR* 11(2):568, 595–96, 605–6; Howard, *Recollections*, 137; McClendon, *Recollections*, 77.

24. Address on the life of Elzey, Miscellany, box 3, pp. 15–16, Munford-Ellis Papers, DU.

25. Buck, *With the Old Confeds*, 42; CB to LCB, 3 July 1862, PBE; CB, "Gaines' Mills," TN; BSE to LE, 9 July 1862, WM; CBM. The Confederate government later reimbursed Ewell $200 for the loss of the horse (Ewell's compiled service record, RG 109, M331, R89, NA).

26. *OR* 11(2):606, 857; Kearns diary, 27 June 1862, VHS; CBM.

27. CBM; CB, "Gaines' Mills," TN. At Gaines's Mill, Elzey lost 246 men; Seymour, 174; and the Maryland Line, 8. Trimble suffered a loss of 400 men at Gaines's Mill and Malvern Hill, almost all of whom were lost at Gaines's Mill (*OR* 11[2]:974–75).

28. Buck, *With the Old Confeds*, 42; Worsham, *Jackson's Foot Cavalry*, 55; Edward A. Moore, *Story of a Cannoneer*, 83–84; *Southern Home* (Charlotte, N.C.), 5 Feb. 1872; *OR* 11(2):888.

29. Hotchkiss diary, 28 June 1862, R1, HP; CB, "Down the Peninsula," TN; *OR* 11(2):493–94, 515–16, 607, 617; Oates, *The War*, 122.

30. *OR* 11(2):494–95, 556–57; Freeman, *Lee*, 2:194–96.

31. Franklin M. Myers, *Comanches*, 78–79.

32. Jefferson Davis, *Rise and Fall*, 2:117; *OR* 11(2):494, 607; Miscellany, box 5, chap. 10, pp. 2–3, Johnson Papers, DU; Handerson, *Yankee in Gray*, 47; CBM.

33. WHM, 74–75; George W. Booth, *Personal Reminiscences*, 48; Franklin M. Myers, *Comanches*, 77–78; Richard Taylor, *Destruction*, 89; Miscellany, box 5, chap. 10, pp. 2–3, Johnson Papers, DU; CBM.

34. *OR* 11(2):607; 617–18; Richard Taylor, *Destruction*, 89; Mugler diary, p. 186, West Virginia University.

35. *OR* 11(2):494–95, 556–57; CB to LCB, 3 July 1862, PBE.

36. *OR* 11(2):494–95, 556–57; Freeman, *Lee*, 2:194–96.

37. CBM.

38. Jubal A. Early, *Autobiographical Sketch*, 77; William C. Davis, *Confederate General*, 2:89; CBM.

39. *OR* 11(2):627–29; Richard Taylor, *Destruction*, 91–92; Sears, *To the Gates*, 310.

40. *OR* 11(2):557–58, 607; Miscellany, box 5, chap. 10, pp. 3–4, 7–8, Johnson Papers, DU.

41. CBM.

42. Ibid.; Douglas, *I Rode with Stonewall*, 114.

43. *OR* 11(2):618; CBM; CB, "Some Comments on the Peninsula Campaign," TN; Freeman, *Lee's Lieutenants*, 1:599; Sears, *To the Gates*, 322−23.

44. *OR* 11(2):496, 607, 611−12, 627−29; Edward A. Moore, *Story of a Cannoneer*, 87; WHM, 75; Hale, "Recollections," 332−33; Jubal A. Early, *Autobiographical Sketch*, 78−82.

45. *OR* 11(2):729.

46. *OR* 11(2):728−29. The two regiments that Ewell led into battle have not been identified. Kershaw claimed they belonged to Ewell's division, but the only regiments in Ewell's division present were Bradley Johnson's First Maryland and the regiments in Early's brigade. None of those units took part in the attack.

47. Jubal A. Early, *Autobiographical Sketch*, 78−82; *OR* 11(2):629; CBM; Miscellany, box 5, chap. 10, pp. 7−8, Johnson Papers, DU.

48. Sears, *To the Gates*, 336; Franklin M. Myers, *Comanches*, 81. Myers claimed that Ewell and Whiting considered making a night attack, but this is improbable considering the events of that afternoon and the generals' subsequent conversation with Jackson.

49. McGuire and Christian, *Confederate Cause*, 197; Douglas, *I Rode with Stonewall*, 114; Dabney, *Life and Campaigns*, 473. Compare CBM. Lenoir Chambers, *Stonewall Jackson*, 2:84, quotes a dialogue between Jackson and Ewell at this meeting, mistakenly citing Dabney as his source. Ewell respected Jackson's judgment, but he was not taking any chances. After the meeting, he ordered thirty or forty captured ammunition wagons to be sent to safety across the White Oak Swamp.

50. Jubal A. Early, *Autobiographical Sketch*, 83−84; *OR* 11(2):815−16.

51. CBM; Sorrel, *Recollections*, 57.

52. Freeman, *Lee*, 2:225−26; Dabney, *Life and Campaigns*, 475−76.

53. Douglas, *I Rode with Stonewall*, 115−16.

54. George W. Booth, *Personal Reminiscences*, 54; Dabney, *Life and Campaigns*, 476; *OR* 11(2):607, 619.

55. CBM; CB to LCB, 25 Apr. 1867, TN; CB, "Down the Peninsula," TN; Freeman, *Lee*, 2:227−28. The officer in question may have been Col. James A. Walker of the Thirteenth Virginia. The troops blamed Jackson for the near-slaughter. Rumor had it that Stonewall had ordered the attack and that Longstreet had overruled him. Only after the war did Ewell learn that Lee had ordered the attack and that Jackson had talked him out of it (CBM).

56. CBM. Compare BSE to LE, 9 July 1862, WM.

57. Goldsborough, *Maryland Line*, 64; *OR* 11(2):497, 619, 622; Jubal A. Early, *Autobiographical Sketch*, 88.

58. *OR* 11(2):497; Freeman, *Lee's Lieutenants*, 1:667. As soon as the campaign ended, A. P. Hill began feuding with Longstreet, and D. H. Hill quarreled with Brig. Gen. Robert Toombs. In each instance a duel was narrowly averted.

Chapter 16

1. WHM, 77; *OR* 11(2):607, 619; CBM; *Official Military Atlas*, plate 100, no. 2; RSE to LE, 20 July 1862, LC.

2. Benjamin S. Ewell, "Jackson and Ewell," 30. For evidence of the troops' dissatisfaction with Jackson, see CB to LCB, 3 July 1862, PBE; Boyd, *Reminiscences*, 8−10; and Terry L. Jones, *Lee's Tigers*, 111.

3. Benjamin S. Ewell, "Jackson and Ewell," 30; Richard Taylor, *Destruction*, 38; RSE to LE, 13 May 1862, LC; Munford, "Reminiscences," 526; Judith W. McGuire, *Diary*, 215; Jackson, *Memoirs*, 287; Robert Stiles, *Four Years*, 245.

4. Dabney, *Life and Campaigns*, 486–87. Kyd Douglas, writing many years after Dabney, remembered that Jackson "wished General Lee to take command of the expedition, but said he was willing to serve in it under Longstreet or Ewell or one of the Hills" (Douglas, *I Rode with Stonewall*, 117).

5. OR 12(3):473–74, 915, 919; Hamlin, *Old Bald Head*, 117.

6. OR 12(3):915, 916; Henry A. Chambers, *Diary*, 44–45; Wingfield, "Diary," 14; Benjamin S. Ewell, "Jackson and Ewell," 32–33.

7. Terry L. Jones, *Lee's Tigers*, 111; Boatner, *Civil War Dictionary*, 827; Richard Taylor, *Destruction*, 93. The Louisiana Brigade was reorganized at this time. At Taylor's suggestion, the First Special Battalion ("Tigers") was disbanded and the Ninth Louisiana Regiment transferred out of the brigade. Their loss was made good by the addition of the Fifth and Fourteenth Regiments (George Campbell Brown, "Notes," 260).

8. CBM.

9. CBM; Houck, *Confederate Surgeon*, 47, 51–54. A photograph of Barbour appears on p. 64 of Houck's book. A picture of the house is on p. 65.

10. Houck, *Confederate Surgeon*, 47, 51–54; Lenoir Chambers, *Stonewall Jackson*, 2:101; OR 12(2):53; Dabney, *Life and Campaigns*, 491.

11. RSE to LE, 20 July 1862, LC.

12. OR 12(3):918, 964–65. Ewell's division counted 4,863 rifles on 31 July 1862.

13. CB, "Cedar Run Mountain," TN; CBM; Johnson, *University Memorial*, 215–16.

14. Hotchkiss, *Make Me a Map*, 65; Arthur Cummings to F. W. M. Holliday, 9 Aug. 1862, and RSE to F. W. M. Holliday, 26 Mar. 1863, Holliday Papers, DU.

15. OR 12(2):182, 214–15.

16. Frank Moore, *Rebellion Record*, 5:331–32; OR 12(2):226; Franklin M. Myers, *Comanches*, 88.

17. OR 12(2):189, 228–29; Howard, *Recollections*, 170.

18. CBM; Krick, *Cedar Mountain*, 86; OR 12(2):227, 235.

19. CBM.

20. *Land We Love* 5 (1868): 443–44.

21. Krick, *Cedar Mountain*, 140, 149.

22. CBM; Douglas, *I Rode with Stonewall*, 130; Worsham, *Jackson's Foot Cavalry*, 66; OR 12(2):184, 227.

23. OR 12(2):227.

24. Columbus (Ga.) *Daily Enquirer*, 23 Aug. 1862; OR 12(2):227; Diary Kept by a Confederate Artilleryman, 1861–January 1864, New York State Library.

25. RSE to LCB, 17 Aug. 1862, LC.

26. Krick, *Cedar Mountain*, 332; Evans, *Confederate Military History*, 3:313; Alexander Pendleton to RSE, 10 Aug. 1862, Pendleton Papers, Chicago Historical Society.

27. OR 12(2):184–85, 227; Hotchkiss, *Make Me a Map*, 67–68; Casler, *Four Years*, 104–5; Worsham, *Jackson's Foot Cavalry*, 68; McClendon, *Recollections*, 95; Jubal A. Early, *Autobiographical Sketch*, 101–2; Krick, *Cedar Mountain*, 350. At Pope's request, Jackson later extended the truce to 5:00 P.M.

28. OR 12(2):185; Franklin M. Myers, *Comanches*, 94; Alexander Pendleton to RSE, 11 Aug. 1862, Pendleton Papers, Chicago Historical Society.

29. Franklin M. Myers, *Comanches*, 94–95.

30. Jubal A. Early, *Autobiographical Sketch*, 102–3; CBM; Krick, *Cedar Mountain*, 368–69; *OR* 12(2):184–85, 228, 550. Ewell reported his casualties as follows: Artillery 8, Early 161, Trimble 18, and Forno 8. Returns taken the day after the battle showed Ewell with 5,027 officers and men present for duty (*OR* 12[3]:965).

31. RSE to LE, 14 Aug. 1862, LC.

32. RSE to LCB, 17 Aug. 1862, LC; Hotchkiss, *Make Me a Map*, 68; Longstreet, *Manassas to Appomattox*, 158; *OR* 12(2):546–51.

33. *OR* 12(2):641; Jubal A. Early, *Autobiographical Sketch*, 105; Trimble, "Report," 306.

34. CBM; John William Jones, "'Stonewall' Jackson," 152; John William Jones, "Reminiscences," 365. In a similar article written for *Confederate Veteran*, Jones identifies the speaker as Dr. James L. Jones (John William Jones, "'Stonewall' Jackson," 174).

35. RSE to LCB, 17 Aug. 1862, LC.

36. Goldsborough, *Maryland Line*, 64; George W. Booth, *Personal Reminiscences*, 54, 60; WHM, 77; McKim, *Soldier's Recollections*, 119–20; RSE to Bradley Johnson, 13 Aug. 1862, Johnson Papers, DU; Miscellany, box 5, chap. 10, p. 163, Johnson Papers, DU; *OR* 12(2):644; RSE to George W. Randolph, 13 Aug. 1862, Museum of the Confederacy. Johnson had served as a provost marshal in 1861. When he visited Ewell, he brought with him Lt. George W. Booth, who was also in need of a position. Johnson urged Ewell to appoint Booth to his staff, but Ewell declined because of Booth's extreme youth. "I bear no malice, however, against the old hero," wrote Booth in later years. "He was doubtless quite right in his judgment."

37. Wingfield, "Diary," 14; Trimble, "Report," 306; *OR* 12(2):641, 654, 704, 12(3):966; Jubal A. Early, *Autobiographical Sketch*, 106; CBM. David Holt, a soldier in the Sixteenth Mississippi Volunteers, relates a story that supposedly took place after Cedar Mountain in which Ewell hung a spy who brought him a false piece of information. Like many of Holt's tales, it contains as much fancy as fact and is therefore left out of the narrative (Cockrell and Ballard, *Mississippi Rebel*, 102–3).

38. *OR* 12(2):720.

39. *OR* 12(2):642, 705; CBM; Jubal A. Early, *Autobiographical Sketch*, 107.

40. Jubal A. Early, *Autobiographical Sketch*, 107; *OR* 12(2):705; Wingfield, "Diary," 15; CBM.

41. Jubal A. Early, *Autobiographical Sketch*, 108, 112.

42. *OR* 12(2):650, 706–7; CBM; Jubal A. Early, *Autobiographical Sketch*, xiii, 110–12.

43. Longstreet, *Manassas to Appomattox*, 165; King and Derby, *Camp-Fire Sketches*, 59; CBM.

44. *OR* 12(2):642; Trimble, "Report," 306; Hotchkiss, *Make Me a Map*, 71.

Chapter 17

1. *OR* 12(2):643, 650, 708; Taliaferro, "Jackson's Raid," 501–2; CBM.

2. *OR* 12(2):643; CBM. This mileage figure is an approximation based on Taliaferro, "Jackson's Raid," 502; Trimble, "Report," 306; and CBM.

3. Thomas, *Doles-Cook Brigade*, 218; *OR* 12(2):643, 650, 747; McClendon, *Recollections*, 101; Taliaferro, "Jackson's Raid," 502.

4. *OR* 12(2):650, 717, 747; Munford Ms., Miscellany, box 1, p. 13, Munford-Ellis Papers, DU.

5. Munford Ms., Miscellany, box 1, p. 13, Munford-Ellis Papers, DU; *OR* 12(2):717; McClendon, *Recollections*, 101; Oates, *The War*, 134; Taliaferro, "Jackson's Raid," 503.

6. McClendon, *Recollections*, 101–2; Oates, *The War*, 134; *OR* 12(2):650; CBM.

7. CBM. Brown says the house stood "in a field five or six hundred yards south of the station & on our side of the R.Rd," which is contradictory, since the area south of the station was not on the Confederate side of the tracks. He probably meant west rather than south. An 1863 map does show a ruin at that location (*Official Military Atlas*, plate 45, no. 7).

8. *OR* 12(2):554, 643; Trimble, "Report," 306; McClendon, *Recollections*, 103; Taliaferro, "Jackson's Raid," 503; Trimble's compiled service record, RG 109, M331, R250, NA.

9. *OR* 12(2):643, 708; Taliaferro, "Jackson's Raid," 504; McClendon, *Recollections*, 105.

10. *OR* 12(2):651, 708–9, 717; McClendon, *Recollections*, 104; Munford Ms., Miscellany, box 1, p. 13, Munford-Ellis Papers, DU. Two regiments, the Twelfth Georgia and the Fifteenth Alabama, reported to Trimble at Manassas Junction.

11. *OR* 12(2):708, 717.

12. *OR* 12(2):708–9.

13. *OR* 12(2):7, 35, 709, 718; CBM. After the battle Ewell bestowed "some high encomiums" on the Louisiana Brigade (Sheeran, *Confederate Chaplain*, 11).

14. *OR* 12(2):709; CBM.

15. CBM.

16. CBM.

17. CBM.

18. *OR* 12(2):710; *Proceedings*, pt. 2, p. 812.

19. *OR* 12(2):14, 35, 643–44, 710, 716, 734–35, 748; CBM; Munford Ms., Miscellany, box 1, p. 13, Munford-Ellis Papers, DU. Compare *OR* 12(2):14. Ewell lost 200 men at Bristoe Station; Hooker reported losing 300.

20. CBM; Taliaferro, "Jackson's Raid," 505; Sheeran, *Confederate Chaplain*, 11.

21. CBM; *Proceedings*, pt. 2, pp. 812–13, 816–17. Brown states that Early's brigade camped east of the junction and the other two brigades camped south of it. He does not mention the whereabouts of the fourth brigade. Early, on the other hand, states in his report that the brigades of Ewell's division camped separately north of the junction. He says his camp stood in a grassy field about halfway between the junction and Blackburn's Ford.

22. Lenoir Chambers, *Stonewall Jackson*, 2:148–49; Hennessy, *Return to Bull Run*, 136, 143–44.

23. CBM; *OR* 12(2):710–11. Brown remembered directing Trimble to Sudley Church, but Early's report clearly states that Trimble followed Early across Blackburn's Ford.

24. *OR* 12(2):649, 710–11; Jubal A. Early, *Autobiographical Sketch*, 119; CBM; McClendon, *Recollections*, 106; Oates, *The War*, 136; Hennessy, *Return to Bull Run*, 144.

25. Taliaferro, "Jackson's Raid," 507–8; CBM.

26. Taliaferro, "Jackson's Raid," 509; *OR* 12(2):656, 710; Jubal A. Early, *Autobiographical Sketch*, 120; *Proceedings*, pt. 2, p. 814.

27. William W. Blackford, *War Years*, 119–20; Taliaferro, "Jackson's Raid," 509. The house was probably the Brawners'. See Robert E. L. Krick's report on Ewell's wounding, on file at Manassas National Battlefield Park.

28. CBM; William W. Blackford, *War Years*, 120–21.

29. CBM; *OR* 12(2):377–78, 645, 710–11; Trimble, "Report," 307; *Official Military Atlas*, plate 22, no. 4; Taliaferro, "Jackson's Raid," 510; Hennessy, *Return to Bull Run*, 166–81.

30. Taliaferro, "Jackson's Raid," 510.

31. Hennessy, *Return to Bull Run*, 189–90.

32. *OR* 12(2):645; Taliaferro, "Jackson's Raid," 510–11; CBM. For an excellent analysis of the

circumstances surrounding Ewell's injury, see Robert E. L. Krick's report on Ewell's wounding, on file at Manassas National Battlefield Park.

33. Oates, *The War*, 141; CBM; *Medical and Surgical History*, 3(2):242; Evans, *Confederate Military History*, 8:596.

34. CBM.

35. Jubal A. Early, *Autobiographical Sketch*, 121; Harriot Stoddert Turner, "Ewells of Virginia," 34, CWM; *Proceedings*, pt. 2, p. 815. In a speech delivered after the war, Hunter McGuire recalled that to those inexperienced with such injuries, gunshot wounds to the knee often did not appear very serious. "The opening in the skin, by the resiliency of the tissue, may have contracted to less than half the size of the ball which made it: the joint may not be swollen, and only a drop or two of blood is trickling from the wound; the limb, perhaps, is not at all out of 'drawing,' and the idea of amputation is horrible, to an unprofessional or inexperienced observer. General Ewell's leg . . . presented this appearance" (Hunter McGuire, "Gun-shot Wounds of Joints," 261–62).

36. Hamberton Belton to RSE, 14 Nov. 1868, Manassas National Battlefield Park; CBM. Brown says that Ewell was taken first to a field hospital located near a gate, a few hundred yards from the front. This was probably somewhere on the elevation known as Stony Ridge. The "woods road" used by Ewell to go to Sudley Springs was probably Featherbed Road. The second hospital seems to have been an unidentified building associated with the Sudley community. Unfortunately Brown failed to provide specific names, leaving these matters open to conjecture.

37. *Medical and Surgical History*, 3(2):242; Hunter McGuire, "Gun-shot Wounds of Joints," 262.

38. Franklin M. Myers, *Comanches*, 103–4.

39. CBM; *Medical and Surgical History*, 3(2):242; John Esten Cooke, "Humors of the Camp," 565; Hunter McGuire, "Gun-shot Wounds of Joints," 262. According to Campbell Brown, "Dr. Robertson of La. opened the leg along the track of the ball, in order to show me that they were justified in taking it off—a Dr. Tanner of Ala. having objected to it—but it had been plainly a necessity" (CBM). There is no record of a surgeon named Tanner being associated with the Army of Northern Virginia. The physician in question was probably Isaac S. Turner (1818–1903), the surgeon of the Twenty-first North Carolina Infantry, a regiment in Ewell's division.

40. Andrew B. Booth, *Records of Louisiana Confederate Soldiers*, vol. 3, pt. 2, p. 350; Schildt, *Hunter Holmes McGuire*, 44; CBM; Alice M. Ewell, *Virginia Scene*, 62; *Medical and Surgical History*, 3(2):242. Harriot Turner erroneously claimed that Ewell's leg was amputated at the upper third of the femur, his leg being so thin that sufficient flaps of skin for covering the stump could not be had farther down (Harriot Stoddert Turner, "Ewells of Virginia," 34–35, CWM, and Harriot Turner note in folder 21, WM).

41. Ewell's wound was one of 1,194 recorded cases of primary amputation of the lower third of the femur for shot fracture. Of those cases, 973 survived, 927 died, and the outcome of 14 cases was not reported (Schildt, *Hunter Holmes McGuire*, 44).

42. CBM; McMullen, *A Surgeon*, 39.

43. Alice M. Ewell, *Virginia Scene*, 60, 62, 64; CBM. Harriot Turner later wrote that an outbreak of erysipelas at Auburn had prompted the move (Harriot Stoddert Turner, "Ewells of Virginia," 34–35, CWM). For additional information on Dunblane, see Appendix I.

44. Alice M. Ewell, *Virginia Scene*, 64–65. For the location of Ewell's Chapel, later known as Grace Episcopal Church, see Appendix I.

45. Alice M. Ewell, *Virginia Scene*, 62–63.

46. Ibid., 51–52; "Ewell Family History," 17–20, Genealogy folder, TX; BSE to Dr. Jesse Ewell, 9 Mar. 1872, in possession of Mrs. Nathaniel McGregor Ewell Jr. of Charlottesville, Va. Alice was Eleanor's daughter. Jesse Ewell V, later of Ruckersville, Va., was born on 30 July 1853 to John Smith Ewell of "Edge Hill" and his wife, Helen Woods McGregor.

47. Alice M. Ewell, *Virginia Scene*, 63.

48. Ibid., 64.

49. CBM.

50. Alice M. Ewell, *Virginia Scene*, 64–65; RSE to LCB, 27 May 1865, PBE. Little is known about John Frame, whom Eleanor Ewell described as an "elegant" man and "a very dignified personage."

51. Dr. Jesse Ewell of Dunblane to CB, 12 July 1873, TN; Maury County, Tenn., Records, R184, book F, pp. 414–16, TSLA.

52. Alice M. Ewell, *Virginia Scene*, 65; Ramey, *Years of Anguish*, 23.

53. Benjamin S. Ewell, "Jackson and Ewell," 30. Benjamin Ewell's compiled service record is in RG 109, M331, R89, NA. William Stoddert's compiled service record is in RG 109, M331, R237, NA.

54. CB to LCB, 18 Sept. 1862, PBE. The books were *My Novel*, by Edward B. Lytton, and *Debit and Credit*, by Gustav Freytag.

55. CB to LCB, 18 Sept. 1862, PBE; Alice M. Ewell, *Virginia Scene*, 67.

56. Benjamin S. Ewell, "Jackson and Ewell," 30.

Chapter 18

1. Alice M. Ewell, *Virginia Scene*, 65. For the date of Ewell's departure, see Ramey, *Years of Anguish*, 23.

2. Alice M. Ewell, *Virginia Scene*, 66.

3. Note in folder 23, WM; E. Dillon to CB, 27 Feb. 1870, TN; Harriot Stoddert Turner, "Ewells of Virginia," 11–12, CWM.

4. Alice M. Ewell, *Virginia Scene*, 66–67.

5. CBM. Brown does not mention the gap by name, saying only that it was the gap nearest to Dunblane. Hopewell Gap, just north of Thoroughfare Gap, is the most direct route between Dunblane and Kinloch (*Official Military Atlas*, plate 7, no. 1).

6. CBM; Harriot Stoddert Turner, "Ewells of Virginia," 35–36, CWM; Alice M. Ewell, *Virginia Scene*, 68; Ramey, *Years of Anguish*, 23. Although the author does not specifically say so, the remark was undoubtedly made by Ewell himself. For Kinloch's location, see Appendix I.

7. Alice M. Ewell, *Virginia Scene*, 67–69; CBM; Ramey, *Years of Anguish*, 23; Harriot Stoddert Turner, "Ewells of Virginia," 35–36, CWM; Richmond *Daily Whig*, 25 Sept. 1862. Two battalions of U.S. cavalry sent to capture Ewell searched Dunblane and other houses in the neighborhood less than twenty-four hours after he left.

8. Ramey, *Years of Anguish*, 23; *Southern Generals*, 350; *Medical and Surgical History*, 3(2):242; Hunter McGuire, "Gun-shot Wounds of Joints," 262.

9. CBM; RSE to LCB, 5 June 1865, PBE; Hotchkiss, *Make Me a Map*, 195; CBM. At Millborough Springs Ewell stayed at the home of Capt. Dickinson.

10. CBM; Constance C. Harrison, *Recollections*, 111; LCB to RSE, 21 Sept. 1862, box 6, folder 11, TN. Like many people, Lizinka had aged greatly as a result of the war. "The truth is I have

grown old very rapidly during the last six months," she confessed, "my eyesight is not good & my hair is turning grey, besides being thin & sallow, but you will care none the less for me on that account when anxiety had so much to do with it."

11. CBM.

12. Francis Hancock's compiled service record, RG 109, M331, R116, NA; George Campbell Brown, "Notes," 258.

13. Henry A. Chambers, *Diary*, 70; Hamlin, *Old Bald Head*, 130; BSE to LE, 5 Nov. 1862, WM; Richmond *Daily Whig*, 18 Nov. 1862. Hancock had offered Lizinka a room at his house as early as March 1862 (RSE to LCB, 5 Mar. 1862, Museum of the Confederacy).

14. Constance C. Harrison, *Recollections*, 110–11; Henry S. Foote, *Bench and Bar*, 171.

15. Hunter McGuire, "Gun-shot Wounds of Joints," 262; Richard Taylor, *Destruction*, 78; RSE to Jubal Early, 7 Jan. 1863, vol. 3, Early Papers, Library of Congress; BSE to LE, 10 Feb. 1863, LC.

16. BSE to LE, 22 Jan. 1863, LC.

17. RSE to Jubal Early, 26 Jan. 1863, Early Papers, VHS; LCB to Maj. David Hubbard, 4 Jan. 1863, PBE; Henry S. Foote, *Bench and Bar*, 171. Brewer had served on the staff of Maj. Gen. John C. Breckinridge (*Report of the Adjutant General of the State of Kentucky*, 2:416).

18. Constance C. Harrison, *Recollections*, 110–11.

19. RSE to LCB, 23 Feb. 1862, LC; Benjamin S. Ewell, "Jackson and Ewell," 26–33; Munford, "Reminiscences," 523; John William Jones, *Christ in the Camp*, 105–6; James Power Smith, "With Stonewall Jackson," 77; Pollard, *Lee and His Lieutenants*, 461; Judith W. McGuire, *Diary*, 215–16. Less reliable versions of this incident appear in Jackson, *Memoirs*; John William Jones, *Christ in the Camp*, 97; Robert Stiles, "Monument," 25; and "Stonewall Jackson at Prayer," 111–13. Benjamin Ewell refuted Echols's version of the story in "Jackson and Ewell," 29.

20. Benjamin S. Ewell, "Jackson and Ewell," 29; Hoge, *Moses Drury Hoge*, 167. Lizzie Ewell resided with the Hoge family in Richmond for much of the war.

21. Browne, *Adventures*, 156; Munford, "Reminiscences," 523; CB, "From Fairfax C.H. to Richmond," folder 20, PBE; James Power Smith, "With Stonewall Jackson," 77.

22. Rev. W. M. Dame to Harriot Turner, 24 Mar. 1890, WM.

23. Haskell, *Memoirs*, 13; Thomas H. Carter, "Letter of Colonel Thomas H. Carter," 5–6; Oates, *The War*, 90; Richard Taylor, *Destruction*, 37. For other references to Ewell's indecision, see TTG to LCB, 26 Dec. 1855, TN; Thomas Ewell Jr. to EE, 16 Aug. 1840, WM; WS to RLE, 28 May 1856, WM; and Richmond *Times-Dispatch*, 12 Nov. 1911.

24. RSE to Jubal Early, 7 Jan. 1863, LC; BSE to Jubal Early, 30 Jan. 1872, Benjamin Ewell Faculty File, box 1, "Biographical" file, CWM; RSE to Jubal Early, 26 Jan. 1863, Early Papers, VHS.

25. Jubal Early to RSE, 23 Jan. 1863, and RSE to Samuel Cooper, 28 Jan. 1863, both in James A. Walker's compiled service record, RG 109, M331, R257, NA.

26. Isaac Trimble to RSE, undated letter, vol. 4, Early Papers, Library of Congress; OR 12(2):614–19; Isaac Trimble's compiled service record, RG 109, M331, R250, NA.

27. Robert Rodes to RSE, 22 Mar. 1863, PBE.

28. Ibid.; BSE to LE, 10 Feb. 1863, LC; Susan Hoge to Mosby, 24 Feb. 1863, Hoge Family Papers, VHS; RSE to Jubal Early, 8 Mar. 1863, LC.

29. Jubal Early to RSE, 23 Jan. 1863, in James A. Walker's compiled service record, RG 109, M331, R257, NA; RSE to Jubal Early, 8 Mar. 1863, LC; BSE to LE, 9 Apr. 1863, WM. Despite Ewell's claim that he did not want the Tennessee command, he nevertheless became provoked when it was given to another (BSE to LE, 4 May 1863, WM).

30. RSE to P. G. T. Beauregard, 9 May 1863, in Ewell's compiled service record, RG 109, M331, R89, NA; Charles Faulkner to RSE, 20 Apr. 1863, PBE.

31. Charles Faulkner to RSE, 26 Feb. 1863, FC; RSE to Jubal Early, 8 Mar. 1863, LC; OR 12(2):226–28.

32. RSE to P. G. T. Beauregard, 9 May 1863, in Ewell's compiled service record, RG 109, M331, R89, NA; RSE to Jubal Early, 8 Mar. 1863, LC; Judith W. McGuire, *Diary*, 202–3, 210–11.

33. Judith W. McGuire, *Diary*, 211–12; Douglas, *I Rode with Stonewall*, 222; Casler, *Four Years*, 157; Marietta M. Andrews, *Scraps of Paper*, 109. For a detailed description of the procession and its participants, see the Richmond *Daily Enquirer*, 12 May 1863.

34. Couper, *One Hundred Years*, 191; captain of *The Marshall* to Jubal Early, undated letter, vol. 7, Early Papers, Library of Congress; Susan P. Lee, *Memoirs*, 270; Lexington *Gazette*, 20 May 1863; Lenoir Chambers, *Stonewall Jackson*, 2:153–54. The Virginia Military Institute museum has a small black and white ribbon supposedly worn by Ewell as a badge of mourning at the 15 May funeral. It may have been worn by him at Jackson's funeral procession in Richmond instead.

35. Dowdey and Manarin, *Wartime Papers*, 488–89; Samuel Cooper dispatch dated 23 May 1863, in Ewell's compiled service record, RG 109, M331, R89, NA.

36. Longstreet, "Lee's Invasion," 245; Borcke, *Memoirs*, 2:262; Wingfield, "Diary," 25; Crabtree and Patton, *"Journal,"* 413; Joseph Hilton to cousin, 15 May 1863, Hilton Papers, Georgia Historical Society; Nashville *Union and American*, 27 Jan. 1872; New York *Herald*, 8 Apr. 1865; Lynchburg (Va.) *Daily Republican*, 15 May 1863. Compare Everard H. Smith, "Peter W. Hairston," 77, and Hassler, *General to His Lady*, 237. Hunter McGuire, the chief medical officer of the Second Corps, seems to have been the source of this story. In an anonymous article in the 13 May 1863 Richmond *Daily Enquirer*, published three days after Jackson's death, McGuire wrote that Jackson "frequently expressed to his aid[e]s his wish that Major General Ewell should be ordered to the command of the corps; his confidence in General Ewell was very great, and the manner in which he spoke of him showed that he had duly considered the matter." McGuire was a close associate of Jackson's and was with him in his final days of life.

37. Terry L. Jones, *Lee's Tigers*, 156; Judith W. McGuire, *Diary*, 409; Oates, *The War*, 141; McDaniel, *With Unabated Trust*, 161.

38. Kean, *Inside the Confederate Government*, 64–65.

Chapter 19

1. BSE to LE, 28 Feb. 1863, WM. Dick later insisted that Ben took the coat without his consent.

2. OR 25(2):824–25; Weddell, *St. Paul's Church*, 1:206; Marietta M. Andrews, *Scraps of Paper*, 110; Bean, *Stonewall's Man*, 128. Records in the Stoddert Family Bible, box 4, item 5, GWC, indicate that the wedding occurred on 23 May 1863, but a letter written by Ewell to Lizinka on the first anniversary of their wedding confirms the 26 May date (RSE to LCB, 26 May 1864, FC).

3. Nashville Chancery Court Minutes, 13 June 1872, book 5, p. 396, TSLA. See also RSE to James Lyons, 25 May 1863, and reply in James Lyons to [RSE], undated, both in box 4, folder 5, Lyons Papers, VHS.

4. Hotchkiss diary, 29 May 1863, R1, HP; Isiah Fogleman diary, p. 26, BV 113, FRSP; Wingfield, "Diary," 26; Winchester *Evening Star*, 22 Mar. 1904; Sandie Pendleton to mother, folder

33A, WNP; Ardrey diary, 29 May 1863, Davidson College. See also Huntsville (Ala.) *Daily Confederate*, 10 June 1863.

5. Marietta M. Andrews, *Scraps of Paper*, 110–12.

6. *OR* 27(2):452; Charles Faulkner's compiled service record, RG 109, M331, R81, NA; Beverley Lacy to James Smith, 2 June 1863, Lacy Papers, VHS. Brown apparently was still a captain at this time, despite Ewell's efforts to get him promoted to major. See (George) Campbell Brown's compiled service record, RG 109, M331, R35, NA.

7. Robert G. Stephens Jr., *Clement Anselm Evans*; Jedediah Hotchkiss to wife, 31 May 1863, R4, HP.

8. *OR* 25(2):840.

9. *OR* 27(2):439.

10. Hotchkiss, *Make Me a Map*, 146; Walter H. Taylor, *Four Years*, 91.

11. RSE to LCB, 5 June 1865, PBE; William Allan manuscript, p. 8, Allan Papers, SHC.

12. Robert Lee to Mary Anna Randolph, 31 May 1863, Lee Family Papers, VHS; Sandie Pendleton to "My Dear Rose," 4 June 1863, folder 33B, WNP; Susan P. Lee, *Memoirs*, 276; F. M. Parker to wife, 31 May 1863, Parker Papers, North Carolina Department of Archives and History.

13. Winchester *Evening Star*, 22 Mar. 1904; Hotchkiss, *Make Me a Map*, 146; Thomas H. Carter, "Letter of Colonel Thomas H. Carter," 6; Wingfield, "Diary," 26.

14. Jedediah Hotchkiss to wife, 31 May 1863, R4, HP; Susan P. Lee, *Memoirs*, 293–94; John S. Wood, *Virginia Bishop*, 48.

15. Longstreet, "Lee's Invasion," 248–49; Longstreet, *Manassas to Appomattox*, 337; Hotchkiss diary, 4 June 1863, R1, HP; *OR* 27(2):499, 545; Seymour, *Memoirs*, 58; Wingfield, "Diary," 26.

16. *OR* 27(2):546. A map showing Ewell's route of march to and from Gettysburg appears in *Official Military Atlas*, plate 43, no. 7.

17. Hotchkiss diary, 5 June 1863, R1, HP; Ewell will, R184, book F, pp. 414–16, Maury County Records, TSLA.

18. Hotchkiss diary, 7 June 1863, R1, HP.

19. Sandie Pendleton to mother, 8 June 1863, folder 36, WNP.

20. Ibid.; Hotchkiss diary, 7, 9 June 1863, R1, HP; Seymour, *Memoirs*, 58; Wingfield, "Diary," 26; *OR* 27(2):546.

21. Susan P. Lee, *Memoirs*, 277; *OR* 27(3):48.

22. Hotchkiss diary, 9 June 1863, R1, HP; *OR* 27(2):439–40, 546; CBM.

23. *OR* 27(2):43, 93, 295, 440; Freeman, *Lee*, 3:33. Milroy reported having 9,000 men at Winchester, but only 6,900 effectives.

24. *OR* 27(2):440; Hotchkiss diary, 11 June 1863, R1, HP; a copy of Ewell's general order is in vol. 4, Early Papers, Library of Congress.

25. Hotchkiss diary, 12 June 1863, R1, HP; CBM.

26. Hotchkiss diary, 12 June 1863, R1, HP; *OR* 27(2):546; Jubal A. Early, *Autobiographical Sketch*, 239; Douglas, *I Rode with Stonewall*, 233; CB diary, 12 June 1863, box 3, PBE.

27. Hotchkiss diary, 12 June 1863, R1, HP; *OR* 27(2):546–47, 27(3):879; Goldsborough, *Maryland Line*, 93.

28. *OR* 27(2):546–47.

29. McKim, *Soldier's Recollections*, 145; Sheeran, *Confederate Chaplain*, 46; Hotchkiss diary, 13 June 1863, R1, HP.

30. *Official Military Atlas*, plate 43, no. 3; *OR* 27(2):44, 440, 500; CBM.

31. *OR* 27(2):45, 295; CBM; Hotchkiss diary, 13 June 1863, R1, HP.

32. *OR* 27(2):94; Richmond *Daily Enquirer,* 22 June 1863. According to Extra Billy Smith, Ewell expressed an aversion to the slaughter that would attend an attack on the Union works, then retired to his tent to pray for guidance (Richmond *Daily Whig,* 4 Sept. 1863).

33. *OR* 27(2):46, 440–41.

34. *OR* 27(2):440–41, 461; Jubal A. Early, *Autobiographical Sketch,* 240, 243–44; Seymour, *Memoirs,* 60; CBM.

35. Jubal A. Early, *Autobiographical Sketch,* 240, 243–44; *OR* 27(2):440–41, 461; Edmonston, *Dear Emma,* 411; Gilmor, *Four Years,* 179; Seymour, *Memoirs,* 60. Milroy replied that he would defend the town until "Hell froze over," according to William Seymour, an officer on Harry Hays's staff. Harry Gilmor insisted that Milroy threatened to burn the town if Ewell tried to take it by force. "Ewell replied that if he did he would raise the black flag and put the garrison to the sword without mercy," claimed the cavalryman. Highly dramatic testimony but, regrettably, all fiction. Neither Ewell, Milroy, nor any officer close to them mentioned any communication between the two generals during the battle.

36. Seymour, *Memoirs,* 61–62; *OR* 27(2):462–63; Jubal A. Early, *Autobiographical Sketch,* 248–49.

37. Hotchkiss diary, 14 June 1863, R1, HP; Grunder and Beck, *Winchester,* 40; Gilmor, *Four Years,* 89–91.

38. Jubal A. Early, *Autobiographical Sketch,* 249; Goldsborough, *Maryland Line,* 95.

39. *OR* 27(2):440–41, 500.

40. *OR* 27(2):441–42, 501–2.

41. John Gordon to wife, 21 June 1863, box 3, Gordon Papers, University of Georgia; Jubal A. Early, *Autobiographical Sketch,* 250; CB diary, 15 June 1863, box 3, PBE; Hotchkiss, *Make Me a Map,* 152; *OR* 27(3):890, 896.

42. *OR* 27(2):442; Gilmor, *Four Years,* 91–92. One Union soldier who returned to Winchester as a prisoner that day remembered Ewell watching them from his carriage as they entered the fort. Behind him, on horseback, was "a Colored French gentleman carrying his crutches," undoubtedly a reference to Ewell's domestic, John Frame (Grunder and Beck, *Winchester,* 52–53).

43. *OR* 27(2):442, 548–49. Ewell received a dispatch from Rodes on the evening of 16 June announcing that he was at Williamsport and that Jenkins was headed for Pennsylvania (Lee diary, p. 415, Handley Library).

44. *OR* 27(2):441–42, 450.

45. *OR* 27(3):894; *Southern Confederacy* (Atlanta, Ga.), 30 July 1863.

46. Seymour, *Memoirs,* 63; Sheeran, *Confederate Chaplain,* 46–47; Gilmor, *Four Years,* 90; Hardy, "Winchester," 114; John Gordon to wife, 21 June 1863, box 3, Gordon Papers, University of Georgia; *OR* 27(3):895; Jubal A. Early, *Autobiographical Sketch,* 251.

47. Parramore et al., *Before the Rebel Flag Fell,* 66; Terry L. Jones, *Lee's Tigers,* 163; Abram Schultz Miller, "Civil War Letters," 34–35, Handley Library; *OR* 27(3):916. Miller added, "I think that he will make himself equally as popular as Gen. Jackson was. At the same time he will make them do their duties. I think he is the right man to fill Gen. Jackson's place. He is a splendid fighter and was very popular with his old division. He managed the affairs about Winchester very well."

48. *OR* 27(3):895.

49. "Personne," *Marginalia,* 73; CBM; Hotchkiss, *Make Me a Map,* 153.

50. Lee diary, p. 415, Handley Library.

51. Robert Stiles, *Four Years,* 192; William S. White, "Diary," 189.

52. Seymour, *Memoirs,* 63; Douglas, *I Rode with Stonewall,* 234; Susan L. Blackford, *Letters,*

176–77; Sandie Pendleton to mother, 18 June 1863, folder 33B, WNP. For other comparisons to Jackson, see undated Richmond *Examiner* clipping in folder 21, WM; Chisolm, "Forward," 449; and William Pendleton to wife, 14 June 1863, WNP.

Chapter 20

1. Hoke, *Great Invasion*, 87; Gallagher, *Ramseur*, 69; Hotchkiss diary, 17 June 1863, R1, HP; Douglas, *I Rode with Stonewall*, 235.

2. OR 27(2):503, 27(3):547, 550, 905–6, 913; Gilmor, *Four Years*, 92–93; Goldsborough, *Maryland Line*, 177.

3. OR 27(2):442, 547, 551; Hoke, *Great Invasion*, 105; Hotchkiss diary, 16 June 1863, R1, HP. Jenkins's first error was his failure to seize Millwood on 12 June as Rodes had ordered.

4. Hotchkiss diary, 16 June 1863, R1, HP; Sandie Pendleton to mother, 16 June 1863, folder 36, WNP; OR 27(3):905; CB diary, 17 June 1863, folder 3, PBE; Lee diary, p. 418, Handley Library. Pendleton states that Ewell's camp was three miles north of Winchester, while a dispatch by Lee indicates that it was four miles north of town. Campbell Brown's diary says that Ewell's headquarters were at "Camp Stevens," four and one-half miles southeast of Martinsburg on the Williamsport Road. In all likelihood, these descriptions represent the same place.

5. OR 27(2):297, 27(3):900–901.

6. OR 27(2):296, 442–43, 503, 550–51, 27(3):905; Hotchkiss diary, 18–19 June 1863, R1, HP; Douglas, *I Rode with Stonewall*, 235; Casler, *Four Years*, 180.

7. Hotchkiss diary, 19–23 June 1863, R1, HP; CBM; CB diary, 19–23 June 1863, folder 3, PBE; OR 27(2):551. On 19 June Ewell rode from Williamsport to Leetown, Virginia, for a conference with Longstreet, whose corps had moved up to Charlestown. He slept that night at the Douglas home, "Ferry Hill," opposite Shepherdstown, and the next evening returned to speak to Rodes, whose headquarters were then at Hagerstown. He attended worship services with Rodes Sunday morning, 21 June, at the local Catholic church, visited an acquaintance in Hagerstown, and by evening was back at Ferry Hill.

8. OR 27(2):307, 503, 27(3):913–15; Coddington, *Gettysburg Campaign*. Lee's dispatch was dated 22 June 1863, but it seems to have been written one day earlier.

9. OR 27(2):551; Frank McCarthy to sister, 10 July 1863, McCarthy Papers, VHS; Mobile *Advertiser & Register*, 15 July 1863.

10. OR 27(2):551; Hotchkiss diary, 22, 24 June 1863, R1, HP; *Land We Love* 2 (1867): 471.

11. Hotchkiss diary, 24 June 1863, R1, HP; RSE to LE, 24 June 1863, LC.

12. Hoke, *Great Invasion*, 134–35.

13. Ibid., 135, 146; OR 27(2):443, 464–65, 503, 551; CB diary, 24 June 1863, folder 3, PBE; McKim, *Soldier's Recollections*, 193; Hotchkiss diary, 24 June 1863, R1, HP; Jubal A. Early, *Autobiographical Sketch*, 254. Steuart left Johnson's column at Greencastle on 24 June and rejoined it near Carlisle four days later.

14. Edward A. Moore, *Story of a Cannoneer*, 184–85; Shelby Foote, *Civil War*, 2:441–43; Lane, *"Dear Mother,"* 246; Abram Schultz Miller, "Civil War Letters," p. 37, Handley Library.

15. Hotchkiss to wife, 25 June 1863, R4, HP; CB diary, 23 June 1863, folder 3, PBE; Susan P. Lee, *Memoirs*, 280–81.

16. OR 27(3):912–13; Hoke, *Great Invasion*, 131; RSE to LE, 24 June 1863, LC; Susan P. Lee, *Memoirs*, 281.

17. John C. Early, "Southern Boy's Experience," 417. See also Thomas H. Carter, "Letter of Colonel Thomas H. Carter," 7.

18. *Land We Love* 3 (1867): 432–33.

19. Hoke, *Great Invasion,* 136.

20. Ibid., 137–38; Mobile *Advertiser & Register,* 15 July 1863; CBM.

21. Hoke, *Great Invasion,* 138–43.

22. Hotchkiss to wife, 25 June 1863, R4, HP; CBM; Sandie Pendleton to mother, 25 June 1863, folder 33B, WNP; Bean, *Stonewall's Man,* 135. Brown also carried a list of goods to be purchased for Gens. James Longstreet and Robert H. Chilton.

23. CBM; Hotchkiss diary, 24–25 June 1863, R1, HP; Jubal A. Early, *Autobiographical Sketch,* 255; *OR* 27(2):464–65; RSE to LE, 24 June 1863, LC.

24. *OR* 27(2):307, 443, 613; CB diary, 26 June 1863, folder 3, PBE; Hotchkiss diary, 26 June 1863, R1, HP; CBM.

25. Hotchkiss diary, 27 June 1863, R1, HP; Hotchkiss to wife, 28 June 1863, R4, HP; CBM; Clark, *Histories,* 2:233, 502; *OR* 27(2):336, 443, 551. Ewell's requisition on the citizens of Carlisle is on file at the Carlisle Barracks Collection at USAMHI.

26. Jedediah Hotchkiss to wife, 28 June 1863, R4, HP; Douglas, *I Rode with Stonewall,* 237; CBM. See also *OR* 27(2):551. When professors and students at Dickinson College complained to Ewell of depredations by Doles's Georgians, Ewell reestablished order on the campus and promised to protect its property (Carlisle *Evening Sentinel,* 21 June 1863).

27. Staunton *Vindicator,* 2 Oct. 1863. See also Douglas, *I Rode with Stonewall,* 237; Robert Stiles, *Four Years,* 206; and Hotchkiss to wife, 28 June 1863, R4, HP.

28. Bean, *Stonewall's Man,* 137; CB diary, 28 June 1863, folder 3, PBE; Jedediah Hotchkiss to wife, 28 June 1863, R4, HP. A bitterly Unionist woman in Carlisle wrote that Ewell "sent word to our ministers that he wished us to have church as usual, but none save Mr. Bliss & Mr. Phillips would gratify him. During church hours the old hypocrite sent around to have the houses searched but we were all too cute to be found even in church" (R. K. Hitner to Mrs. David Hastings, 6 July 1863, Carlisle Barracks Collection, USAMHI).

29. John C. Early, "Southern Boy's Experience," 416; Mobile *Advertiser & Register,* 15 July 1863; CBM.

30. Hotchkiss diary, 28 June 1863, R1, HP; Wellman, *Rebel Boast,* 119; Clark, *Histories,* 2:526; CBM; Green, *Recollections,* 174. According to a Carlisle resident, Ewell paid a visit to a Mrs. McClure, whom he had known many years before (R. K. Hitner to Mrs. David Hastings, 6 July 1863, Carlisle Barracks Collection, USAMHI).

31. *OR* 27(3):923; Isaac Trimble to John Bachelder, 8 Feb. 1883, Bachelder Papers, New Hampshire Historical Society; Charles Marshall to Jubal Early, 13 Mar. 1878, vol. 9, Early Papers, Library of Congress; Trimble, "Battle and Campaign of Gettysburg," 121. According to Trimble, Ewell accepted his offer to capture Harrisburg with this token force, and he was preparing to do so when Lee ordered Ewell to march to Gettysburg. Trimble's imagination frequently outdistanced the facts, as is the case here.

32. Hotchkiss diary, 29 June 1863, R1, HP; McKim, *Soldier's Recollections,* 167; *OR* 27(2):443; Coddington, *Gettysburg Campaign,* 188.

33. *OR* 27(2):443, 467, 27(3):943; Jubal A. Early, *Autobiographical Sketch,* 263.

Chapter 21

1. Coddington, *Gettysburg Campaign,* 265.

2. Hotchkiss diary, 29 June 1863, R1, HP.

3. *OR* 27(2):444, 468, 552; Jubal A. Early, *Autobiographical Sketch*, 264; CB diary, 24 June 1863, folder 3, PBE; Bond, "Company A," 78.

4. *OR* 27(2):552; Trimble, "Battle and Campaign of Gettysburg," 121–22; Grace, "Rodes's Division," 614–15; Hotchkiss diary, 30 June 1863, R1, HP; John C. Early, "Southern Boy's Experience," 417.

5. *OR* 27(2):317, 444.

6. Bond, "Company A," 78; Goldsborough, *Maryland Line*, 176–77; CB diary, 24 June 1863, folder 3, PBE. Bond later wrote that he rode all the way to Gettysburg without encountering any Union troops, but this cannot have been true, since Union cavalry held the town. The soldiers he captured may have belonged to Col. Thomas C. Devin's cavalry brigade.

7. Isaac Trimble to John Bachelder, 8 Feb. 1883, Bachelder Papers, New Hampshire Historical Society; Trimble, "Battle and Campaign of Gettysburg," 122.

8. *OR* 27(2):444, 468, 552. Trimble later wrote that he advised Ewell to march to Middletown, which was roughly equidistant from both Cashtown and Gettysburg, while awaiting positive orders from Lee. In an 1883 letter to John Bachelder he repeated this tale, adding that he offered the advice a couple of hours after the march began. By that time, however, Ewell was already at Middletown, or fast approaching it (Trimble, "Campaign and Battle of Gettysburg," 211, and Trimble, "Battle and Campaign of Gettysburg," 122; also Isaac Trimble to John Bachelder, 8 Feb. 1883, Bachelder Papers, New Hampshire Historical Society).

9. *OR* 27(2):444, 552, 607; CBM; Bond, "Company A," 79. Bond mistakenly states that Johnson, a Virginian, was from South Carolina.

10. *OR* 27(2):444, 552, 592–93; Trimble, "Campaign and Battle of Gettysburg," 211; Trimble, "Battle and Campaign of Gettysburg," 122; Isaac Trimble to John Bachelder, 8 Feb. 1883, Bachelder Papers, New Hampshire Historical Society; CBM. Trimble later claimed to have led Rodes's division to Oak Hill. Neither Ewell nor Rodes mentions him doing this, leading one to question the truth of the claim.

11. *OR* 27(2):444, 552; Trimble, "Battle and Campaign of Gettysburg," 122. Trimble wrote that Ewell ordered Doles onto the plain.

12. *OR* 27(2):444; CB note in box 2, folder 41, PBE.

13. *OR* 27(2):444–45, 552–54, 556–57, 579–80, 592–93; Green, *Recollections*, 175.

14. CBM; Pfanz, *Culp's Hill*, p. 38.

15. *OR* 27(2):445, 468–69; Hotchkiss diary, 1 July 1863, R1, HP; Jubal A. Early, *Autobiographical Sketch*, 268–69. Ewell supposedly claimed that at Gettysburg Gordon's brigade inflicted more casualties on the enemy in proportion to its own numbers than any other command during the war (Robert Stiles, *Four Years*, 210–11).

16. *OR* 27(2):444–45, 552–55; Walter H. Taylor, *Four Years*, 94.

17. *OR* 27(2):450, 582; Grace, "Rodes's Division," 615. The Union force seen by Ewell was probably the 157th New York Infantry.

18. *OR* 27(2):317–18, 445. Ewell placed the number of prisoners at 4,000.

19. Hotchkiss diary, 1 July 1863, R1, HP; Kathleen Georg [Harrison], "Blocher Farm Historical Report," 1979, Gettysburg National Military Park; CB, "Notes on Gettysburg," box 4, GWC. In a draft review of James Longstreet's book *Manassas to Appomattox* (R48, HP), Jed Hotchkiss, replying to disparaging remarks about Ewell made by Longstreet on p. 375, wrote that Ewell "was everywhere in the place of danger urging to action and by his presence stimulating the courage of the officers and men of his command notwithstanding the fact that the loss of his leg made it dangerous for him to be on a spirited horse as he always rode in the very presence of the hottest part of the engagement." Ewell later submitted a $1,200 claim for the

mare, his second and most expensive horse killed during the war (Ewell's compiled service record, RG 109, M331, R89, NA).

20. William Carter to John Daniel, 17 Mar. 1904, Daniel Papers, DU; James Smith to John Daniel, 15 July 1903, box 23, Daniel Papers, UVA; Maynard F. Stiles, "Maj. J. Coleman Alderson," 87.

21. Douglas, *I Rode with Stonewall*, 238–39; Douglas, "Lee and Ewell at Gettysburg," 87; Carrington, "First Day," 332–33. For an excellent appraisal of this quote and its impact on subsequent interpretations of the battle, see Carmichael, "Lost Cause Plea."

22. Jubal A. Early, "Review," 255; James Smith to CB, undated letter, vol. 4, Early Papers, Library of Congress.

23. Walter H. Taylor, *Four Years*, 95; OR 27(2):445.

24. Freeman, *Lee's Lieutenants*, 3:94 n.; Jubal A. Early, "Review," 255.

25. James Power Smith, "With Stonewall Jackson," 56–57; James Power Smith, "Lee at Gettysburg," 390; Isaac Trimble to John Bachelder, 8 Feb. 1883, Bachelder Papers, New Hampshire Historical Society; Gettysburg *Star and Sentinel*, 2 July 1913; OR 27(1):257, 272–73.

26. James Power Smith, "Lee at Gettysburg," 144; James Power Smith, "With Stonewall Jackson," 56–57; James Smith to CB, undated letter, vol. 4, Early Papers, Library of Congress.

27. CBM; Isaac Trimble to John Bachelder, 8 Feb. 1883, Bachelder Papers, New Hampshire Historical Society; Jubal A. Early, "Review," 255–56. The generals viewed Cemetery Hill from a point near High Street, where Baltimore Street begins its descent to the foot of Cemetery Hill.

28. Hunt, "First Day," 283; Pfanz, *Culp's Hill*, 54–58. The brigade was Col. Orland Smith's of the Eleventh Corps.

29. OR 27(2):445–46, 469–70, 554–55.

30. CBM; CB note in box 2, folder 41, PBE.

31. OR 27(2):317–18. James Power Smith, "With Stonewall Jackson," 56–57; James Power Smith, "Lee at Gettysburg," 391; James Smith to CB, undated letter, vol. 4, Early Papers, Library of Congress. Smith later remembered that Lee told him, "Please say to Gen. Ewell that Gen. Longstreet's people are not up yet, and I have no troops to advance on this point [Cemetery Ridge]. I will direct Gen. A. P. Hill to support Gen. Ewell. Tell Gen. Ewell he must do in his front what seems best, taking Cemetery Hill if he can: and I will do all we can to help him." Smith did not mention these details in his published accounts, and they seem contradictory. Lee promised to support Ewell with Hill's corps yet claimed he did not have any troops available to seize the ground on Ewell's right, precisely the spot where Ewell needed them. Hill, on the other hand, made it clear in his report that he had no intention of going farther, thinking it unwise to "push forward troops exhausted and necessarily disordered, probably to encounter fresh troops of the enemy" (OR 27[2]:607).

32. Thomas Turner, "Gettysburg," vol. 4, Early Papers, Library of Congress; OR 27(2):470.

33. Trimble, "Battle and Campaign of Gettysburg," 123–24; Isaac Trimble to John Bachelder, 8 Feb. 1883, Bachelder Papers, New Hampshire Historical Society. According to Lt. Randolph McKim, who was not present but who may have known Trimble after the war, Trimble pointed toward Culp's Hill and vowed to take it if Ewell would only give him a division. When Ewell refused, Trimble vowed to take the hill if given just a brigade. When Ewell refused to give him even one brigade, Trimble said, "Give me a good regiment and I will engage to take that hill." When Ewell still refused, Trimble threw down his sword in disgust and left, declaring "that he would not serve longer under such an officer!" (McKim, "Gettysburg Campaign," 273).

34. *OR* 27(2):445, 469–70; CBM; Jubal A. Early, "Review," 255; Jubal A. Early, *Autobiographical Sketch*, 269–70; CB to Henry Hunt, 6 May 1885, Hunt Papers, Library of Congress. The time of Smith's arrival is a matter of dispute. Early claimed that he received Smith's report before he encountered Ewell in town, but Campbell Brown wrote that Ewell was with Early at the time. Possibly Smith came twice. Ewell's report is vague as to the time of Smith's arrival, though it seems to indicate that he appeared later in the day.

35. Jubal A. Early, "Review," 256; *OR* 27(2):445.

36. Edward M. Daniel, *Speeches and Orations*, 81–82; *OR* 27(2):470; Thomas Turner, "Gettysburg," vol. 4, Early Papers, Library of Congress.

37. Charlottesville *Progress*, 22 Mar. 1904.

38. CB note in box 2, folder 41, PBE; R. W. Hunter to Jubal Early, 10 Oct. 1877, and James Walker to Jubal Early, 13 Oct. 1877, in vol. 9, Early Papers, Library of Congress.

39. Pfanz, *Culp's Hill*, 79–80; Thomas Turner, "Gettysburg," vol. 4, Early Papers, Library of Congress; CBM.

40. James Power Smith, "Lee at Gettysburg," 393–94; Jubal A. Early, "Review," 257; John C. Early, "Southern Boy's Experience," 421 n. On the time of the conference, see CB to Henry Hunt, 6 May 1885, Hunt Papers, Library of Congress. Tradition places the meeting at the John Blocher house, at the intersection of the Bendersville and Carlisle Roads. For a thorough discussion of this point, see Kathleen Georg [Harrison], "Blocher Farm Historical Report," Gettysburg National Military Park.

41. *OR* 27(2):446; Walter H. Taylor, "Memorandum," 83–84; John C. Early, "Southern Boy's Experience," 421 n.; Jubal A. Early, "Review," 271–74; James Power Smith, "Lee at Gettysburg," 393–94.

42. Jed Hotchkiss noted that Ewell slept at Spangler's, near the edge of town. In his map of the battlefield (*Official Military Atlas*, plate 43, no. 2), he shows the house on the Heidlersburg Road, near its junction with the Carlisle Road. This is in the vicinity of the John Crawford house, where the general took refreshment on both 1 and 2 July. The map that accompanied George Steuart's report of the battle and that appears on plate 28, no. 4, of the atlas places Ewell's headquarters at the same location. Campbell Brown's memoirs vaguely describe corps headquarters as having been "in rear of Gettysburg," though an 1878 memorandum that he wrote after he revisited the battlefield (box 4, GWC) indicates that Ewell had his headquarters at the Kentz house, "just by the almshouse."

Most accounts indicate Ewell stayed in a barn rather than a house. Jubal Early's aide, Maj. John W. Daniel, on p. 15 of his "Account of Gettysburg" (Daniel Papers, VHS) states that Ewell slept in a barn with Rodes and Early. Other evidence supports that assertion. In an undated letter to Campbell Brown in vol. 4 of the Early Papers, Library of Congress, James Power Smith states that Ewell stayed at a barn west of town. John Gordon, on p. 156 of his *Reminiscences*, said that he met with the general late that night in a red barn, and a Union surgeon who came to see Ewell the next morning likewise says he found the general sitting on the bridge to a barn (*National Tribune*, 20 Oct. 1898).

There is no contemporary evidence to support the traditions recorded in Freeman, *Lee's Lieutenants*, 3:94 n., that Ewell had his headquarters at either the Blocher House on the Carlisle Road, the Daniel Lady Barn on Benner's Hill, or the J. Lutz House adjacent to Rock Creek on the Hanover Road.

43. Bean, *Stonewall's Man*, 139.

44. Gettysburg *Star and Sentinel*, 2 July 1913; Anna M. Young, *Soldier of Indiana*, 2:121–22; "Reminiscences of the Gettysburg Battle," 59.

45. *OR* 27(2):446; Charles Marshall to Jubal Early, 15 Mar. 1876, Early Papers, VHS, and 13 Mar. 1878, vol. 9, Early Papers, Library of Congress; Thomas Turner, "Gettysburg," vol. 4, Early Papers, Library of Congress; CBM; Longstreet, *Manassas to Appomattox*, 360.

46. *OR* 27(2):446; Thomas Turner, "Gettysburg," vol. 4, Early Papers, Library of Congress; CBM; Longstreet, *Manassas to Appomattox*, 360.

47. *OR* 27(2):446; Thomas Turner, "Gettysburg," vol. 4, Early Papers, Library of Congress; R. W. Hunter to Jubal Early, 10 Oct. 1887, vol. 9, Early Papers, Library of Congress.

48. *OR* 27(2):446; CBM; Longstreet, *Manassas to Appomattox*, 360; Thomas Turner, "Gettysburg," vol. 4, Early Papers, Library of Congress; Eugene C. Gordon, "Controversy about Gettysburg," 465; John B. Gordon, *Reminiscences*, 156. In later years John Gordon claimed that he rode to Ewell's headquarters at 2:00 A.M., 2 July, to advocate a night attack on Culp's Hill before the Federals could fortify it. "There was a disposition to yield to my suggestions," he wrote, "but other counsels finally prevailed."

Like all of Gordon's stories, this one must be taken with caution. The Georgian felt compelled to offer his advice, he wrote, after "listening to the busy strokes of Union picks and shovels on the hills, to the rumble of artillery wheels and the tramp of fresh troops as they were hurried forward by Union commanders and placed in position." Such sounds could not have been heard by Gordon from his distant position on the York Pike.

49. CBM; *OR* 27(2):318–19, 446.

50. *National Tribune*, 20 Oct. 1898.

51. James Power Smith, "Lee at Gettysburg," 395; Longstreet, "Account of the Campaign," 76–77.

52. James Power Smith, "Lee at Gettysburg," 395; Freeman, *Lee*, 3:87, 92; Isaac Trimble to John Bachelder, 8 Feb. 1883, Bachelder Papers, New Hampshire Historical Society; *OR* 27(2):318–19, 470; Long, *Memoirs*, 281; Hotchkiss diary, 2 July 1863, R1, HP; CBM.

53. Alexander, *Military Memoirs*, 408–9; *OR* 27(2):504; Edward A. Moore, *Story of a Cannoneer*, 189.

54. Pfanz, *Culp's Hill*, 178; Shevchuk, "Wounding of Albert Jenkins," 61–63.

55. *OR* 27(2):604; Pfanz, *Culp's Hill*, 170; Goldsborough, *Maryland Line*, 324.

56. *OR* 27(2):446–47, 504; Seymour, *Memoirs*, 74. Actually, Latimer was just nineteen when he died.

57. *OR* 27(2):556, 666; Lt. Col. Henry S. Huidekoper letter, 23 Nov. 1916, Coco Collection, USAMHI.

58. CBM; *OR* 27(3):447, 504, 518–19; McKim, *Soldier's Recollections*, 199; Pfanz, *Culp's Hill*, 213.

59. *OR* 27(2):447, 470, 556; Jubal A. Early, "Review," 280; Terry L. Jones, *Lee's Tigers*, 172; John Daniel, "Account of Gettysburg," pp. 13–14, Daniel Papers, VHS; Pfanz, *Culp's Hill*, 235–83.

60. Thomas Turner, "Gettysburg," vol. 4, Early Papers, Library of Congress; *OR* 27(2):319.

61. Douglas, *I Rode with Stonewall*, 240; *OR* 27(2):320.

62. *OR* 27(2):447, 556; Coddington, *Gettysburg Campaign*, 466; Pfanz, *Culp's Hill*, 287; U.S. Congress, *Report of the Joint Committee on the Conduct of the War*, 5:416–17.

63. Coddington, *Gettysburg Campaign*, 469; *OR* 27(2):447–48, 504–5.

64. Pfanz, *Culp's Hill*, 292; *OR* 27(2):447–48, 511; WHM, 98–102; McKim, *Soldier's Recollections*, 188, 203–6; CBM.

65. *OR* 27(2):448, 505. The threat against Johnson's left may have been Brig. Gen. Thomas H. Neill's occupation of Wolf's Hill, a move that was essentially defensive in nature (Pfanz, *Culp's Hill*, 336–37).

66. Seymour, *Memoirs*, 79; CBM; Staunton *Spectator*, 28 July 1863. Ewell and Richardson probably rode out Liberty Street.

67. John B. Gordon, *Reminiscences*, 157. Decades after the war, Gordon claimed that Ewell fell on 1 July when he was hit. For a discussion of the date of Ewell's near-injury, see Appendix J.

68. *OR* 27(2):352, 456; John Daniel, "Account of Gettysburg," p. 16, Daniel Papers, VHS.

69. Bond, "Company A," 79.

70. Hotchkiss diary, 3 July 1863, R1, HP; Imboden, "Confederate Retreat," 420; *OR* 27(2):471; CBM.

71. Robert Stiles, *Four Years*, 219–20.

72. McKim, *Soldier's Recollections*, 189; Handerson, *Yankee in Gray*, 44; Jubal A. Early, *Autobiographical Sketch*, 276; Coddington, *Gettysburg Campaign*, 537–38; James Power Smith, "Lee at Gettysburg," 401; *OR* 27(2):452. Among those left behind was Ewell's chief engineer, Maj. Henry Richardson.

73. Coddington, *Gettysburg Campaign*, 536; CBM.

Chapter 22

1. Hunton, *Autobiography*, 98.

2. William Allan's notes on conversations with Robert E. Lee, vol. 3, folder 2, p. 21, Allan Papers, SHC; Robert E. Lee Jr., *Recollections*, 415; James Power Smith, "Lee at Gettysburg," 403.

3. Coddington, *Gettysburg Campaign*, 296–97; Pfanz, *Culp's Hill*, 52–58; Armistead Long to Jubal Early, 30 Mar. 1876, vol. 8, Early Papers, Library of Congress.

4. Coddington, *Gettysburg Campaign*, 317–21; Pfanz, *Culp's Hill*, 76–77; Edward M. Daniel, *Speeches and Orations*, 84–85; Hunt, "First Day," 284; Jubal A. Early, "Review," 253, 260; Alexander, *Fighting for the Confederacy*, 233; Armistead Long to Jubal Early, 30 Mar. 1876, vol. 8, Early Papers, Library of Congress. Col. Armistead Long of Lee's staff viewed Cemetery Hill at the height of the Federal rout. "I found Cemetery hill occupied by a considerable force," he wrote, "a part strongly posted behind a stone fence near its crest, and the rest on the reverse slope. In my opinion an attack at that time with the troops then at hand would have been hazardous and of very doubtful success." Early later concluded that Ewell was right. "The question of the propriety of the advance was submitted to Ewell's judgment, and he did not think it prudent to make the attempt until the arrival of Johnson; and I must confess that, though my opinion at the time was different, subsequent developments have satisfied me that his decision was right."

5. Alexander, *Military Memoirs*, 411; Long, *Memoirs*, 286; Longstreet, "Lee's Right Wing," 341; Longstreet "Account of the Campaign," 67.

6. *OR* 27(2):480; Jubal A. Early, "Review," 276–78.

7. Coddington, *Gettysburg Campaign*, 432.

8. Alexander, *Military Memoirs*, 410, 412; Walter H. Taylor, *Four Years*, 99; Jubal A. Early, "Review," 280.

9. Jubal A. Early, "Review," 265–66.

10. Philadelphia *Record*, 8 July 1900.

11. *OR* 27(2):452.

12. *OR* 27(2):447; CB to Henry Hunt, 7 May 1885, Hunt Papers, Library of Congress.

13. CBM. Walter Taylor, in his book *Four Years*, p. 96, wrote that in a conversation after the war, Johnson "assured me that there was no hinderance [*sic*] to his moving forward; but that,

after getting his command in line of battle, and before it became seriously engaged or had advanced any great distance, for some unexplained reason, he had received orders to halt." Jubal Early, in the *Southern Historical Society Papers*, surmised that Ewell had ordered Johnson to take Culp's Hill but later countermanded the order after Lee ordered him to draw the Second Corps around to the right (Jubal A. Early, "Review," 263).

14. *OR* 27(2):448, 558; CB diary, 5 July 1863, folder 3, PBE; John Daniel, "Account of Gettysburg," pp. 20–21, Daniel Papers, VHS; William S. White, "Diary," 211–12; Hotchkiss diary, 5 July 1862, R1, HP; Jubal A. Early, *Autobiographical Sketch*, 281.

15. Jubal A. Early, *Autobiographical Sketch*, 281; *OR* 27(2):448.

16. Hotchkiss diary, 6 July 1863, R1, HP.

17. Ibid., 4 July 1863; Fremantle, *Three Months*, 218, 222–24; John Daniel, "Account of Gettysburg," p. 23, Daniel Papers, VHS; Seymour, *Memoirs*, 80.

18. *OR* 27(2):309; Long, *Memoirs*, 297.

19. Jubal A. Early, *Autobiographical Sketch*, 281; Hotchkiss diary, 7–11 July 1863, R1, HP; CB diary, 7–9 July 1863, folder 3, PBE; *Official Military Atlas*, plate 42, no. 5; Robert Lee to RSE, 11 July 1863, Lee and Lee Papers, USAMHI.

20. CBM. *OR* 27(2):448; Seymour, *Memoirs*, 80. For similar expressions of confidence, see *OR* 27(2):558; McKim, *Soldier's Recollections*, 180–81; Howard, *Recollections*, 217; George W. Booth, *Personal Reminiscences*, 94–95.

21. *OR* 27(2):309–10; Hotchkiss diary, 12 July 1863, R1, HP; Howard, *Recollections*, 216; CB diary, 12 July 1863, folder 3, PBE; Jubal A. Early, *Autobiographical Sketch*, 282–83.

22. *OR* 27(2):323, 448–49.

23. *OR* 27(2):449, 457, 549, 558–59; Wingfield, "Diary," 28; Howard, *Recollections*, 217. Ewell elected to cross at those points rather than at the regular ford, a short distance downstream, because the water was not flowing so rapidly there (Jubal A. Early, *Autobiographical Sketch*, 283; Gallagher, *Ramseur*, 75).

24. *OR* 27(2):505, 560, 27(3):1006. Ewell initially made his headquarters at Big Spring, three miles from Martinsburg, but later moved to Darkesville (Hotchkiss diary, 15–16 July 1863, R1, HP).

25. Marshall, *Aide-de-Camp*, 246–47; Freeman, *Lee*, 3:144–45; Hotchkiss diary, 16–17 July 1863, R1, HP.

26. *OR* 27(2):362, 449, 505, 27(3):1026–27; Hotchkiss diary, 17, 20, 21 July 1863, R1, HP; Jubal A. Early, *Autobiographical Sketch*, 284; Seymour, *Memoirs*, 81.

27. *OR* 27(2):449–50, 560–61, 626–67.

28. *OR* 27(1):98, 27(2):560–61, 27(3):1035; Hotchkiss diary, 27, 29 July 1863, R1, HP; Handerson, *Yankee in Gray*, 65. For a map showing the campsites and routes of march of the Second Corps from 4 June to 1 Aug. 1863, see *Official Military Atlas*, plate 43, no. 7.

29. Longstreet, *Manassas to Appomattox*, 431–32; Freeman, *Lee*, 3:145; *OR* 27(2):324; Worsham, *Jackson's Foot Cavalry*, 110; Leon, *Diary*, 43; Gallagher, *Ramseur*, 75.

30. Richmond *Sentinel*, 15 Aug. 1863.

31. Worsham, *Jackson's Foot Cavalry*, 114; Richmond *Daily Whig*, 8 Aug. 1863; Achilles W. Hoge diary, 8 Aug. 1863, VHS.

32. Jed Hotchkiss to wife, 15, 30 Aug. 1863, R4, HP; James Conner, *Letters*, 114–15; Robert G. H. Carroll to Ella T. Carroll, 20 Sept. 1863, Carroll Papers, MHS; Staunton *Vindicator*, 2 Oct. 1863; Eugene Blackford to Mary, 4 Aug. 1863, book 33, Leigh Papers, USAMHI.

33. James Smith to sister, 22 Aug. 1863, Smith Papers, FRSP; Hotchkiss diary, 1, 8 Aug. 1863, R1, HP; Jedediah Hotchkiss to wife, 15 Aug. 1863, R4, HP; Achilles W. Hoge diary, 8 Aug. 1863, VHS; Sheeran, *Confederate Chaplain*, 56.

34. Sandie Pendleton to Rose, 24 Aug. 1863, folder 34B, WNP.

35. Staunton *Vindicator*, 2 Oct. 1863; LE to Bessie Hoge, 18 Aug. 1863, WM. Lizzie and Hattie playfully tagged Smith and other members of the staff with nicknames. Ben Greene was "The Vivacious," Smith was "Mr. Friskie," Tom Turner was "Troublesome Tom," and an angelic fourth officer earned the sobriquet "The Cherub."

36. Chesnut, *Mary Chesnut's Civil War*, 444–45; James Smith to sister, 22 Aug. 1863, Smith Papers, FRSP.

37. HB to LE, 12 Oct. 1863, WM; James Smith to sister, 22 Aug. 1863, Smith Papers, FRSP; LE to Bessie Hoge, 18 Aug. 1863, WM; Hotchkiss diary, 19, 31 Aug. 1863, R1, HP; Manson, "A. P. Hill's Signal Corps," 12.

38. Howard, *Recollections*, 224, 234–35, 251. For another instance of home industries in Ewell's corps, see Worsham, *Jackson's Foot Cavalry*, 111.

39. Sheeran, *Confederate Chaplain*, 54–55; Jedediah Hotchkiss to wife, 30 Aug. 1863, R4, HP.

40. Freeman, *Lee's Lieutenants*, 3:217–19.

41. Casler, *Four Years*, 188–90; Thomas Boatright to uncle, 9 Sept. 1863, Boatright Papers, SHC; Howard, *Recollections*, 223–27; Robson, *One Legged Rebel*, 56.

42. Bean, *Liberty Hall Volunteers*, 159.

43. Worsham, *Jackson's Foot Cavalry*, 112–13; Bradwell, "Grand Review," 17; *Grayjackets*, 229–32; Terrill and Dixon, *Stewart County*, 1:273–74; Jeb Stuart to wife, 11 Sept. 1863, Stuart Papers, VHS; Sandie Pendleton to mother, 11 Sept. 1863, folder 35A, WNP.

44. Hotchkiss diary, 21 Aug. 1863, R1, HP; Jedediah Hotchkiss to wife, 21 Aug. 1863, R4, HP; James Smith to sister, 22 Aug. 1863, Smith Papers, FRSP.

45. Worsham, *Jackson's Foot Cavalry*, 113–14; Hotchkiss diary, 9 Aug. 1863, R1, HP; Sandie Pendleton to mother, 11, 15 Sept. 1863, folder 35A, WNP.

46. Freeman, *Lee's Lieutenants*, 3:224 n.

47. Sandie Pendleton to mother, 23 Sept. 1863, folder 35B, WNP; Susan P. Lee, *Memoirs*, 302; Howard, *Recollections*, 223; Jedediah Hotchkiss to wife, 7 Oct. 1863, R4, HP; Terry L. Jones, *Lee's Tigers*, 180. In contrast to the Shaw house, where they stayed outside, Ewell and his officers occupied Morton's Hall. According to Hotchkiss they still left tents up in the yard "for show." For the location of Morton's Hall, see *Official Military Atlas*, plate 81, no. 1, and plate 87, no. 4.

48. Freeman, *Lee's Lieutenants*, 3:220–24; William D. Henderson, *Bristoe Station*, 69–71; Peter W. Hairston to Fanny, 5 Oct. 1863, folder 53, Hairston Papers, SHC; HB to LE, 2 Oct. 1863, WM; Sandie Pendleton to Ned Lee, 3 Oct. 1863, folder 35B, WNP; HB to LE, 12 Oct. 1863, WM. Lizzie had left some time earlier.

Chapter 23

1. William D. Henderson, *Bristoe Station*, 71–72; Jubal A. Early, *Autobiographical Sketch*, 303; *OR* 29(1):439.

2. *OR* 29(1):404, 29(2):637.

3. Sandie Pendleton to mother, 10, 16 Oct. 1863, folder 35B, WNP; ELB, 6; William D. Henderson, *Bristoe Station*, 84–85; Howard, *Recollections*, 232–33.

4. Walter H. Taylor, *Four Years*, 115; Jubal A. Early, *Autobiographical Sketch*, 303; *OR* 29(1):417; William D. Henderson, *Bristoe Station*, 122; Freeman, *Lee*, 3:174.

5. ELB, 6; Sandie Pendleton to mother, 16 Oct. 1863, folder 35B, WNP; Robert G. H. Carroll to Ella T. Carroll, 13 Oct. 1863, Carroll Papers, MHS; William D. Henderson, *Bristoe Station*, 122–34.

6. Howard, *Recollections*, 233; Sandie Pendleton to mother, 16 Oct. 1863, folder 35B, WNP; A. D. Kelly to brother, 23 Oct. 1863, Kelly Papers, DU.

7. Sheeran, *Confederate Chaplain*, 58.

8. Ibid., 62–63; Sandie Pendleton to mother, 16 Oct. 1863, folder 35B, WNP.

9. William D. Henderson, *Bristoe Station*, 150–61.

10. Ibid., 155–61; ELB, 7–8; Leon, *Diary*, 50; Robert G. H. Carroll to Ella T. Carroll, 15 Oct. 1863, Carroll Papers, MHS.

11. ELB, 7–8; Sandie Pendleton to mother, 16 Oct. 1863, folder 35B, WNP; *Official Military Atlas*, plate 45, no. 6; *OR* 29(1):246; Jubal A. Early, *Autobiographical Sketch*, 304.

12. *Official Military Atlas*, plate 45, no. 7; *OR* 29(1):426–27.

13. Susan P. Lee, *Memoirs*, 304; Chamberlaine, *Memoirs*, 82; Sandie Pendleton to mother, 16 Oct. 1863, folder 35B, WNP.

14. *OR* 29(1):429; ELB, 7–8; Jubal A. Early, *Autobiographical Sketch*, 305–6; Jubal Early to William Mahone, 30 May 1871, vol. 6, Early Papers, Library of Congress. According to Early, Lee and Ewell were present superintending the movement of his division, and Lee himself gave the orders for the flank attack.

15. ELB, 9; Jubal A. Early, *Autobiographical Sketch*, 306; Jedediah Hotchkiss to wife, 15 Oct. 1863, R4, HP. Sandie Pendleton claimed Stuart's cavalry captured 500 to 600 additional stragglers (Sandie Pendleton to mother, 16 Oct. 1863, folder 35B, WNP).

16. Chamberlaine, *Memoirs*, 83.

17. *OR* 29(1):406, 411; A. D. Kelly to brother, 23 Oct. 1863, Kelly Papers, DU; William D. Henderson, *Bristoe Station*, 193.

18. Leon, *Diary*, 51; William D. Henderson, *Bristoe Station*, 194; ELB, 9; Sandie Pendleton to mother, 16 Oct. 1863, folder 35B, WNP; Jubal A. Early, *Autobiographical Sketch*, 306; Nichols, *Soldier's Story*, 129.

19. ELB, 9; Susan P. Lee, *Memoirs*, 304; Freeman, *Lee*, 3:185–86.

20. Arrel Marsteller to RSE, 29 June 1863, Minor Family Papers, VHS; note in folder 23, WM; HB to LE, 23 Oct. 1863, WM. A passing Confederate estimated that the land at Stony Lonesome, which was never very fertile, was worth only about $2.50 per acre (Abram Miller to wife, 19 Oct. 1863, Miller Papers, Handley Library).

21. ELB, 9; Walter H. Taylor, *Four Years*, 116; RSE to BSE, 18 Feb. 1864, LC.

22. Sandie Pendleton to mother, 16 Oct. 1863, folder 35B, WNP. Elsewhere Pendleton remarked that Ewell had moved promptly during the late campaign and had handled the corps well.

23. Hotchkiss diary, 20 Oct. 1863, R1, HP; ELB, 10–12.

24. Hotchkiss diary, 22 Oct. 1863, R1, HP; CB to HB, 26 Oct. 1863, FC; Sandie Pendleton to Ned Lee, 30 Oct. 1863, folder 35B, WNP; Leon, *Diary*, 51; Casler, *Four Years*, 195.

25. *Official Military Atlas*, plate 44, no. 3; Hotchkiss diary, 20 Oct. 1863, R1, HP; Sandie Pendleton to Rose, 28 Oct. 1863, folder 35B, WNP.

26. Sandie Pendleton to Ned Lee, 30 Oct. 1863, folder 35B, WNP; CB to HB, 26 Oct. 1863, FC; Sandie Pendleton to mother, 1 Nov. 1863, folder 36, WNP.

27. *OR* 29(1):612.

28. *OR* 29(1):612, 618–20; Jubal A. Early, *Autobiographical Sketch*, 308–9. Lizinka and Hattie arrived at Brandy Station on 7 November. Ewell was on his way to the train station to meet them when he learned that the Union army was in motion. He hurried to Kelly's Ford while the ladies returned to Orange Court House to await the issue of the battle (HB to LE, 17 Nov. 1863, WM, and McMullen, *A Surgeon*, 57).

29. *OR* 29(1): 612, 632.

30. *OR* 29(1): 555–57, 632.

31. *OR* 29(1): 632; Hotchkiss diary, 7 Nov. 1863, R1, HP; Casler, *Four Years*, 196.

32. *OR* 29(1): 620–21, 631.

33. *OR* 29(1): 612–13, 616, 620–21, 623–24; Jubal A. Early, *Autobiographical Sketch*, 309; Everard H. Smith, "Peter W. Hairston," 69.

34. *OR* 29(1): 616, 632, 29(2): 435.

35. *OR* 29(1): 613, 618–20, 625.

36. Lyman, *Meade's Headquarters*, 45; Jedediah Hotchkiss to wife, 9 Nov. 1863, R4, HP; Hotchkiss diary, 9 Nov. 1863, R1, HP. A Union map shows Ewell's headquarters in a grove of trees south of the Brandy Station Road (*OR* 29[1]: 557). For a map showing the Confederate line on 8 November, see *OR* 29(1): 614.

37. *OR* 29(1): 625; Everard H. Smith, "Peter W. Hairston," 73. See also McMullen, *A Surgeon*, 59.

38. Bean, *Stonewall's Man*, 151; Sandie Pendleton to Mary, 25 Nov. 1863, folder 36, WNP.

39. LCB to TTG, 1 June 1866, TN; HB to LE, 17 Nov. 1863, WM; Hotchkiss diary, 11 Nov. 1863, R1, HP.

40. Everard H. Smith, "Peter W. Hairston," 71, 73; Hotchkiss diary, 13 Nov. 1863, R1, HP; Bean, *Stonewall's Man*, 173.

41. Hunter McGuire, in *Medical and Surgical History*, 2(3): 242; HB to LE, 17 Nov. 1863, WM. Ewell's first wooden leg was made by Dr. Bundy of New Orleans, La. (Richmond *Sentinel*, 19 Aug. 1863).

42. Everard H. Smith, "Peter W. Hairston," 74–75; Hunter McGuire, "Gun-shot Wounds of Joints," 262.

43. HB to LE, 17 Nov. 1863, WM; Hotchkiss diary, 16 Nov. 1863, R1, HP; Everard H. Smith, "Peter W. Hairston," 79; Mary R. Hoge to LE, 26 Nov. 1863, WM; Jedediah Hotchkiss to wife, 22 Nov. 1863, R4, HP.

44. G. Peyton to Dr. Lefar, 14 Aug. 1863, Ewell Papers, DU; John Esten Cooke, "Humors of the Camp," 560; James Conner, *Letters*, 111.

45. HB to LE, 17 Nov. 1863, WM; Everard H. Smith, "Peter W. Hairston," 79; *OR* 29(1): 13, 846–47.

46. Hotchkiss diary, 29 Nov. 1863, R1, HP; Everard H. Smith, "Peter W. Hairston," 85.

47. Everard H. Smith, "Peter W. Hairston," 85.

48. Hotchkiss diary, 3 Dec. 1863, R1, HP; Everard H. Smith, "Peter W. Hairston," 85–86.

49. Hotchkiss diary, 4 Dec. 1863, R1, HP; CB to HB, 5 Dec. 1863, FC.

Chapter 24

1. McPherson, *Battle Cry*, 676–80.

2. *OR* 29(2): 861, 866; Freeman, *Lee*, 3: 208.

3. Jubal A. Early, *Autobiographical Sketch*, 341; *OR* 29(1): 928, 970–71, 51(2): 598, 793–97. For a map showing Averell's route, see *Official Military Atlas*, plate 135-C, no. 1.

4. Freeman, *Lee*, 3: 207, 216–19; *OR* 42(2): 1293.

5. *OR* 31(1): 467–68, 33: 1074–75; Sanger and Hay, *Longstreet*, 252–53.

6. RSE to BSE, undated letter (ca. Jan. 1864), WM.

7. RSE to LE, 8 Jan. 1864, LC; Hamlin, *Letters*, 122–23.

8. RSE to James A. Seddon, 16 Jan. 1864, RG 109, M437, R126, F426, NA.

9. *OR* 33:1095–96; RSE to James A. Seddon, 16 Jan. 1864, RG 109, M437, R126, F427, NA; Ewell's compiled service record, RG 109, M331, R89, NA.

10. Dowdey and Manarin, *Wartime Papers*, 662–63.

11. Bean, *Liberty Hall Volunteers*, 175; Everard H. Smith, "Peter W. Hairston," 80; Robert G. Stephens Jr., *Clement Anselm Evans*, 347–48; Charleston *Mercury*, 21 Nov. 1863.

12. *Official Military Atlas*, plate 81, no. 1, and plate 87, no. 4; Howard, *Recollections*, 262–63.

13. Robert Stiles, *Four Years*, 232.

14. RSE to BSE, 18 Feb. 1864, LC; Dame, *Rapidan to Richmond*, 40–41; Frederick S. Daniel, *Richmond Howitzers*, 105–6; *OR* 33:114–17.

15. Dame, *Rapidan to Richmond*, 41–42.

16. Robert Stiles, *Four Years*, 236.

17. Nichols, *Soldier's Story*, 132–35; Robert G. Stephens Jr., *Clement Anselm Evans*, 348–51; Thomas P. Devereux Jr. to father, 10 Feb. 1864, Devereux Letter Book, pp. 41–42, North Carolina Department of Archives and History; Charles W. McArthur to "Sister Mary," 21 Jan. 1863, Kennesaw Mountain National Military Park. Thomas Devereux of the Forty-third North Carolina Infantry, who related this story, misidentified General Ewell as "Ben Ewell" and General Hays as "Gen Hazen." There was a Gen. William B. Hazen in the Union army, but he was then serving in the western theater. Alexander Hays, on the other hand, commanded the Union forces at Morton's Ford and was seen riding his horse in the vicinity of the Morton house at sunset.

18. Robert G. Stevens Jr., *Clement Anselm Evans*, 364.

19. Ibid., 348–51. For a map of the Morton's Ford battlefield, see *OR* 33:117.

20. RSE to BSE, 18 Feb. 1864, LC; *OR* 33:118.

21. RSE to BSE, 18 Feb. 1864, LC.

22. Francis A. Walker, *Second Army Corps*, 395–96.

23. Gallagher, *Ramseur*, 94.

24. Sheeran, *Confederate Chaplain*, 74–75.

25. For information on Ewell's efforts to rent a portion of the house for Lizinka and Hattie, see RSE to LCB, 20 Dec. 1863, PBE, and Hurst, *The War*, 37–38. Ewell paid approximately $150 to rent the rooms for the winter. His monthly salary at that time was $337 (Ewell's compiled service record, RG 109, M331, R89, NA).

26. RSE to Samuel Cooper, 24 Aug. 1864, in Alexander S. Pendleton's compiled service record, RG 109, M331, R196, NA; James P. Smith's compiled service record, RG 109, M331, R229, NA; Bean, *Stonewall's Man*, 182, 187; Hotchkiss diary, 21 Dec. 1863 to 10 Apr. 1864, R1, HP.

27. HB to LE, 19 Jan. 1864, WM; RSE to LCB, 20 Dec. 1863, PBE.

28. James Conner, *Letters*, 114; Rev. B. T. Lacy and War Recollections, Nov. 11, 1892, in "Jackson's Staff" file, R39, containers 38–39, HP.

29. RSE to LCB, 20 Dec. 1863, PBE.

30. James Conner, *Letters*, 114–15; Freeman, *Lee's Lieutenants*, 3:331–32; Bean, *Stonewall's Man*, 152; Susan P. Lee, *Memoirs*, 338. For additional evidence of Ewell's anxiety about Campbell Brown's safety, see RSE to BSE, undated letter (ca. Jan. 1864), folder 9, WM. In the spring Ewell recommended Brown to command a Tennessee brigade, a strange occurrence in light of his comments to Lizinka. Like Pendleton, Brown declined the promotion, preferring to be a major on Ewell's staff than a lieutenant colonel of the line (*OR* 36[1]:1075).

31. Bean, *Stonewall's Man*, 189; HB to LE, Jan. 1864, 19, 30 Jan. 1864, WM; RSE to BSE, 18 Feb. 1864, LC. Brig. Gen. John Pegram, Dr. Hunter McGuire, and Col. Henry C. Cabell were frequent guests at Ewell's headquarters that winter.

32. RSE to LCB, 5 June 1865, PBE.

33. RSE to LE, 8 Jan. 1864, LC; Howard, *Recollections*, 252–53; Gallagher, *Ramseur*, 90.

34. *OR* 29(2):760–61. This is the same Northrup who had been Ewell's nemesis in the Old Army. Although a friend of Jefferson Davis, Northrup was roundly disliked in the army.

35. *OR* 33:1094–95, 1187; Sheeran, *Confederate Chaplain*, 73, 78; Robert Lee to RSE, 18 Feb. 1864, GWC; Hotchkiss diary, 9 Jan. 1864, R1, HP; RSE to LE, 8 Jan. 1864, LC.

36. Gallagher, *Ramseur*, 92–93; Robert G. Stephens Jr., *Clement Anselm Evans*, 347–48; Hunter McGuire to mother, 3 Feb. 1864, McGuire Papers, VHS.

37. Hickerson, *Echoes of Happy Valley*, 75.

38. Freeman, *Lee*, 3:224.

39. *OR* 33:161–63, 182–87; Howard, *Recollections*, 259–60; Worsham, *Jackson's Foot Cavalry*, 121; Casler, *Four Years*, 206.

40. Richardson, *Grant*, 194. According to Richardson, Ewell said, "There is one West Pointer, I think in Missouri, little known, and whom I hope the Northern people will not find out. I mean Sam Grant. I knew him well at the Academy and in Mexico. I should fear him more than any of their officers I have yet heard of. He is not a man of genius, but he is clear-headed, quick, and daring." Ewell and Grant crossed paths on one or two occasions, but there is no evidence to suggest that they knew each other well. Barring prophetic inspiration, this statement must be dismissed as apocryphal.

41. *OR* 36(1):1070; Freeman, *Lee*, 3:25. Walter Taylor stated that Ewell's corps numbered closer to 17,000 men (Walter H. Taylor, *Four Years*, 124–257).

42. RSE to BSE, undated letter (ca. Jan. 1864), folder 9, WM; Jedediah Hotchkiss to wife, 1 May 1864, R4, HP.

Chapter 25

1. *OR* 36(1):1070; Law, "Wilderness to Cold Harbor," 118; Evans, *Confederate Military History*, 3:432; Wynn, "Lee Watched Grant," 68.

2. Wynn, "Lee Watched Grant," 68; *OR* 36(1):1054, 51(2):888.

3. Evans, *Confederate Military History*, 3:432.

4. Ibid.; *OR* 36(1):1070, 1081; *Official Military Atlas*, plate 81, no. 1.

5. *OR* 36(2):952, 968; Royall, *Some Reminiscences*, 28.

6. Jubal A. Early, *Autobiographical Sketch*, 345; *OR* 36(1):1070. Johnson's division and Lt. Col. William Nelson's artillery battalion pitched their tents two miles south of Locust Grove, Rodes's division bivouacked behind them, and Early's division spent the night of 4 May at Locust Grove itself.

7. Worsham, *Jackson's Foot Cavalry*, 126; *OR* 36(1):1054.

8. *OR* 36(2):948.

9. Hotchkiss diary, 5 May 1864, R2, HP; Robert Stiles, *Four Years*, 244–45.

10. *OR* 36(1):1070; CB, "Memoranda—Campaign of 1864," TN.

11. *OR* 36(1):1070. The Union troops seen by Ewell probably belonged to Maj. Gen. George W. Getty's division of the Sixth Corps.

12. Ibid.; George Wise, *Campaigns*, 310; Steere, *Wilderness Campaign*, 155–56.

13. *OR* 36(1):1070; Steere, *Wilderness Campaign*, 157–61; Brainard, *Campaigns*, 275–76.

14. Steere, *Wilderness Campaign*, 161–62; CB, "Memoranda—Campaign of 1864," TN; Battle, "Third Alabama," 98, Alabama Department of Archives and History; *OR* 36(1):1070; George Wise, *Campaigns*, 310.

15. Frederick L. Hudgins memoir, DU; John B. Gordon, *Reminiscences*, 40–41; *OR* 36(1):1077; John W. Daniel manuscript in folder titled "The Wilderness, May 5, 1864," box 24, Daniel Papers, UVA. Frederick L. Hudgins of the Thirty-eighth Georgia Volunteers remembered Gordon saying, "I think I can change the situation here," to which Ewell replied, "Try your hand."

16. *OR* 36(1):1070, 1077.

17. CB, "Memoranda—Campaign of 1864," TN. Brown reflected on the ambiguity of Lee's orders. "I had frequently noticed before & have also since this occasion, that Gen. Lee's instructions to his Corps Comrs. are of a very comprehensive & general description & frequently admit of several interpretations—in fact will allow them to do almost anything, provided only it be a *success*. They caution them particularly against failure & very frequently wind up with the injunction to 'attack whenever or wherever it can be done to advantage.'"

18. *OR* 36(1):1084–85. Brig. Gen. Armistead Long commanded the Second Corps' five artillery battalions. Under Long were Cols. J. Thompson Brown and Thomas H. Carter. Brown had charge of Hardaway's, Braxton's, and Nelson's battalions; Carter controlled those of Cutshaw and Page. When the campaign opened, Page's and Nelson's battalions were guarding the Rapidan fords, and the other three battalions were camped near Gordonsville. Ewell called on Long to bring the Gordonsville battalions to the front on 4 May. By the next day Long had the artillery concentrated at Locust Grove.

19. Terry L. Jones, *Lee's Tigers*, 196–97; Handerson, *Yankee in Gray*, 69–70; *OR* 36(1):1070; Richmond *Daily Whig*, 9 May 1864.

20. *OR* 36(1):1070–71, 1081; Richmond *Sentinel*, 24 May 1864; Driver, *52nd Virginia*, 48–50; Jubal A. Early memoir, p. 4, Early Papers, VHS.

21. Royall, *Some Reminiscences*, 30; Steere, *Wilderness Campaign*, 136–37, 203–42.

22. *OR* 36(2):952–53, 51(2):889–90. Ewell wrote his reply from "Dempsey's," a house that stood on the north side of the Orange Turnpike approximately one-half mile west of Saunders Field. This building may have served as his headquarters during the day, though there is no specific evidence to that effect. Dempsey's appears in the *Official Military Atlas*, plate 83, no. 2.

23. *OR* 36(1):1071, 1077, 1081.

24. *OR* 36(1):1085; Howard, *Recollections*, 281–82.

25. Hotchkiss diary, 6 May 1864, R2, HP; *OR* 36(1):18, 51(2):889–90; Evans, *Confederate Military History*, 3:439; Jubal A. Early, *Autobiographical Sketch*, 347; Richmond *Sentinel*, 24 May 1864; Steere, *Wilderness Campaign*, 319–23; Rhea, *Battle of the Wilderness*, 318–19. Rhea's *Battle of the Wilderness* is the definitive secondary source on the battle.

26. *OR* 36(1):1081; Gallagher, *Ramseur*, 99–103; Steere, *Wilderness Campaign*, 323–28.

27. *OR* 36(1):1077.

28. Thomas Jones to John Daniel, 3 July 1894, box 22-G, Daniel Papers, DU.

29. Hotchkiss diary, 26 Apr. 1863, R1, HP; Robert E. Lee to Adjutant and Inspector General's Office, 27 Apr. 1864, Museum of the Confederacy; Percy Hamlin to Douglas Freeman, 3 July 1943, in "Letters from D. S. Freeman to P. G. Hamlin," Collection #9435-B, UVA. Ewell placed Early under arrest on 26 April on charges of conduct subversive to good order and good discipline after Early made disrespectful remarks about Ewell in connection with the execution of an order. Lee mildly chastised Early for his conduct and released him from arrest the following day.

30. *OR* 36(1):1071, 1077–78, 36(2):962; Thomas Jones to John Daniel, 3 July 1894, box 22-G, Daniel Papers, DU; John B. Gordon, *Reminiscences*, 255–56; Richmond *Times-Dispatch*, 8 Oct. 1905; Jubal A. Early, *Autobiographical Sketch*, 348; note by John Daniel in folder titled "Wilderness—May 6, 1864," in box 24, Daniel Papers, UVA. By this time Brig. Gen. Robert B.

Potter's and Brig. Gen. Orlando B. Willcox's Ninth Corps divisions were facing Ramseur in the woods south of the turnpike, Brig. Gen. Thomas G. Stevenson's division was in reserve at Wilderness Tavern, and Brig. Gen. Edward Ferrero's division guarded the pontoon bridges at Germanna Ford. The movement seen by Cowles may have been a minor demonstration by Ferrero against Confederate scouting parties near the river.

31. John B. Gordon, *Reminiscences*, 255–56; *OR* 36(1):1071; Thomas Jones to John Daniel, 3 July 1904, box 22-G, Daniel Papers, DU.

32. Ewell letterbook, box 2, folder 2, TN. The substance of this meeting is not known, but its basic outline can be inferred both by the tactical situation at that time and by Ewell's subsequent undated dispatch to Lee found in Venable Papers, SHC.

33. RSE to Robert E. Lee, undated, Venable Papers, SHC; Jubal A. Early, *Autobiographical Sketch*, 348; Robert Johnston report of the Wilderness Campaign, "1849–1879" folder, box 1849–1904, Daniel Papers, DU; Robert Johnston to John Daniel, 30 June 1905, Daniel Papers, DU.

34. Thomas Jones to John Daniel, 3 July 1904, box 22-G, Daniel Papers, DU.

35. Seymour, *Memoirs*, 114; Jubal A. Early, *Autobiographical Sketch*, 348.

36. *OR* 36(1):1071, 1077–78; Jubal A. Early, *Autobiographical Sketch*, 349. Gordon later wrote that the order to attack came directly from Lee, who, he claimed, visited Ewell's headquarters at 5:30 P.M. Neither Gordon's own report nor other contemporary documents bear this out. In an 1868 letter to Lee, Gordon specifically stated that he did not remember seeing Lee on the left flank prior to 7 May. "Indeed," he wrote, "I was not aware of your desire to make a movement on that flank until after the 6th. I am glad to know that such was your wish" (John B. Gordon, *Reminiscences*, 258, and Eckert, *John Brown Gordon*, 68).

37. Thomas Jones to John Daniel, 20 June 1904, Daniel Papers, DU; Robert Johnston report of the Wilderness Campaign, "1849–1879" folder, box 1849–1904, Daniel Papers, DU; William Smith to John Daniel, 26 Oct. 1904, Daniel Papers, DU; Steere, *Wilderness Campaign*, 440–43; Richmond *Sentinel*, 24 May 1864.

38. *OR* 36(1):1077–78; Jubal A. Early, *Autobiographical Sketch*, 350.

39. *OR* 36(1):1075; Hotchkiss diary, 6 May 1864, R2, HP. Estimates of Union losses on Ewell's front are derived from figures in *OR* 36(1):119–33.

40. *History of the 118th Pennsylvania Volunteers*, 404–5; *OR* 36(1):1071.

41. *OR* 36(1):639–40, 1075–76; Hotchkiss diary, 7 May 1864, R2, HP; Howard, *Recollections*, 280–81. The captured guns—two twelve-pounder Napoleons—belonged to Capt. George B. Winslow's Battery D, First New York Light Artillery.

42. John B. Gordon, *Reminiscences*, 268–69; *OR* 36(1):1085, 36(2):970; Worsham, *Jackson's Foot Cavalry*, 130. Freeman, perhaps misled by Gordon's inaccurate assertion that Lee visited Ewell in the morning, states that Lee visited Ewell twice on 7 May (Freeman, *Lee*, 3:302).

43. *OR* 36(2):968.

44. J. F. J. Caldwell, *"McGowan's Brigade,"* 135–36.

45. Matter, *If It Takes All Summer*, 48.

Chapter 26

1. William C. Davis, *Confederate General*, 1:28–29.

2. *OR* 36(1):1071, 51(2):902; Seymour, *Memoirs*, 118; Matter, *If It Takes All Summer*, 72; *Official Military Atlas*, plate 80, no. 1; Evans, *Confederate Military History*, 3:445; *OR* 36(1):1056; John William Jones, *Memorial Volume*, 54.

3. Clark, *Histories*, 3:45–46; Montgomery *Daily Advertiser*, 28 May 1864; Hotchkiss diary, 8 May 1864, R2, HP; OR 36(1):1071; Worsham, *Jackson's Foot Cavalry*, 132.

4. *OR* 36(1):1071, 1078, 36(2):974–75, 51(2):902–3; Jubal Early to Charles Venable, 31 Oct. 1879, Venable Papers, VHS.

5. *OR* 36(1):1071; Evans, *Confederate Military History*, 3:445; Matter, *If It Takes All Summer*, 91–95; *OR* 36(1):1071, 1801; Battle, "Third Alabama," 102, Alabama Department of Archives and History; Clark, *Histories*, 3:45–46.

6. Howard, *Recollections*, 284–85.

7. Clark, *Histories*, 1:152.

8. Thomas Doyle memoir, Doyle Papers, Library of Congress.

9. Stine, *Army of the Potomac*, 617.

10. *OR* 36(1):1078; Old, "Trees Whittled Down," 20–21. See also Howard, *Recollections*, 286; Thomas H. Carter, "Colonel Thomas H. Carter's Letter," 241; Seymour, *Memoirs*, 120.

11. Henry A. White, "Lee's Wrestle with Grant," 59; Evans, *Confederate Military History*, 3:446–47; *OR* 36(1):1071–72; Seymour, *Memoirs*, 120; Old, "Trees Whittled Down," 21.

12. Old, "Trees Whittled Down," 20–21; *OR* 36(1):667, 1042–43, 1071–72; Gold, *Clarke County*, 191; Howard, *Recollections*, 286; Worsham, *Jackson's Foot Cavalry*, 132. Ewell personally directed the Stonewall Brigade to add a headlog to its works and to place abatis in front of the line.

13. *OR* 36(1):1072, 1056, 51(2):905; Terry L. Jones, *Lee's Tigers*, 203; Seymour, *Memoirs*, 121.

14. *OR* 36(1):1072, 51(2):911.

15. *OR* 36(1):667, 1072.

16. *OR* 36(1):668; Asbury Jackson to Luticia Jackson, 11 May 1864, Harden Papers, DU.

17. Seymour, *Memoirs*, 119; CB to LCB, 11 May 1864, PBE; Clark, *Histories*, 3:47–49.

18. Clark, *Histories*, 3:47–49; Battle, "Third Alabama," 103, Alabama Department of Archives and History; William W. White, "Diary," 245–46.

19. Howard, *Recollections*, 290; Evans, *Confederate Military History*, 4:237; Matter, *If It Takes All Summer*, 164–65.

20. Robert Johnston to John Daniel, undated letter, 6 Aug. 1895, and 30 June 1905, Daniel Papers, DU.

21. Frank Moore, *Rebellion Record*, 11:480; CB to LCB, 11 May 1864, PBE.

22. *OR* 36(1):668, 1072; Matter, *If It Takes All Summer*, 167.

23. *OR* 36(1):1072, 1075; CB to LCB, 11 May 1864, PBE.

24. *OR* 36(2):983; Howard, *Recollections*, 290–92.

25. *OR* 36(1):1072; Jubal A. Early, *Autobiographical Sketch*, 355; Matter, *If It Takes All Summer*, 173–74; Robert Johnston, "Gen. Lee's Story," unidentified newspaper article in Ramseur Papers, North Carolina Department of Archives and History. Johnston remembered this conversation as having occurred on the night of 10 May, but the circumstances instead point to the Harrison House on 11 May.

26. CB, "Memoranda—Campaign of 1864," TN. Brig. Gen. A. L. Long submitted his report of the May 1864 operations to Ewell on 25 November. On the back of the report Brown wrote, "By Gen. Ewell's direction I wrote to Gen. Long immediately on rec't of this, asking him to specify *from whom* came the orders for withdrawal of his guns from Gen. Ed. Johnson's lines. No answer ever rec'd. Wrote a second time—with same result. I *heard Gen.* R. E. Lee give the order to Gen. Long in person in Gen. Ewells presence." Long's report appears in folder 11, PBE.

27. *OR* 36(1):1044. For a map of the Muleshoe Salient and its roads, see Matter, *If It Takes All Summer*, 203.

28. *OR* 36(1): 1079–80; Richmond *Daily Whig*, 23 May 1864.

29. *OR* 36(1): 1079–80; Robert Hunter to John Daniel, undated letter, Spotsylvania folder, box 23, Daniel Papers, UVA; Hunter, "Johnson at Spotsylvania," 336–37; Douglas, *I Rode with Stonewall*, 269.

30. Thomas H. Carter, "Colonel Thomas H. Carter's Letter," 240; Page, "Captured Guns," 535; *OR* 36(1): 1086–87.

31. *OR* 36(1): 1078.

32. Seymour, *Memoirs*, 123–24; Howard, *Recollections*, 295–98; Terry L. Jones, *Lee's Tigers*, 205; Huffman, *Ups and Downs*, 85; Parramore et al., *Before the Rebel Flag Fell*, 81; Robert Carroll to Ella Carroll, 15 May 1864, Carroll Papers, MHS; Richmond *Daily Whig*, 19 May 1864; *OR* 36(1): 192. Ewell optimistically estimated the number of Johnson's men who had been captured at 2,000 (*OR* 36[1]: 1072).

33. Thomas H. Carter, "Colonel Thomas H. Carter's Letter," 241; *OR* 36(1): 1044, 1079–80; Page, "Captured Guns," 536; Howard, *Recollections*, 295–98; Frank Moore, *Rebellion Record*, 11: 480.

34. *OR* 36(1): 1072; Clark, *Histories*, 3: 50–51.

35. CB, "Memoranda—Campaign of 1864," TN; John Gordon to Charles Venable, 24 Nov. 1878, Venable Papers, VHS; Robert Johnston to John Daniel, 6 Aug. 1895, Daniel Papers, DU.

36. *OR* 51(2): 922; John B. Gordon, *Reminiscences*, 40–41.

37. John Gordon to Charles Venable, 24 Nov. 1878, Venable Papers, VHS. For evidence of Ewell's presence at this famous episode, see Peyton, "Pegram's Brigade," 60–61, and Snider diary, 12 May 1864, West Virginia University.

38. Julius Schaub to O. C. Whitaker, 5 June 1909, Schaub Papers, Troup County Archives; Clark, *Histories*, 3: 51–52; *OR* 36(1): 1082; Grimes, *Extracts of Letters*, 52.

39. *OR* 36(1): 336.

40. John William Jones, *Memorial Volume*, 58; Matter, *If It Takes All Summer*, 206.

41. Alfred Lewis Scott, "Memoir," VHS.

42. Ibid.; Matter, *If It Takes All Summer*, 206–7.

43. *OR* 36(1): 1073, 1091; Cohen, "Modern Maccabean," 31–37. Harris remembered reaching the field at 7:00 A.M. Arthur T. Watts, a soldier in the Sixteenth Mississippi, estimated the time of arrival at 8:00 A.M. Ewell, in *OR* 36(1): 1073, stated that Harris's troops went into battle at 9:00 A.M.

44. Cohen, "Modern Maccabean," 31–37; Julius Schaub to O. C. Whitaker, 5 June 1909, Troup County Archives.

45. *OR* 36(1): 1091–92; Philadelphia *Weekly Times*, 3 Sep. 1881.

46. *OR* 36(1): 1092–94.

47. J. F. J. Caldwell, *"McGowan's Brigade,"* 145; *OR* 36(1): 1093–94.

48. Horace Porter, *Campaigning with Grant*, 110–11; *OR* 36(1): 1091–92; Richmond *Daily Whig*, 19 May 1864; Clark, *Histories*, 3: 51–52.

49. Quoted in Hale and Phillips, *Forty-Ninth Virginia*, 124. The field desk mentioned may be the one on display at the Virginia Military Institute Museum in Lexington, Va.

50. Ibid.; Robert Stiles, *Four Years*, 259, 262.

51. Seymour, *Memoirs*, 125. See also Casler, *Four Years*, 323–24.

52. Columbus (Ga.) *Daily Sun*, 22 Dec. 1864.

53. Montgomery, *Days of Old*, 28; Allan, "Conversation with General Lee," 3: 8–9, Allan Papers, SHC.

54. Long, *Memoirs*, 342; *OR* 36(1):1073; Casler, *Four Years*, 213; Hotchkiss diary, 12 May 1864, R2, HP.

55. William McWillie Notebooks, Mississippi Department of Archives and History; Page, "Captured Guns," 535–40.

56. *OR* 36(1):1057, 1067; Robert Stiles, *Four Years*, 262.

57. *OR* 36(1):1057; Stringfellow, "Account," 250–51; George P. Ring to wife, 15 May 1864, Louisiana Historical Association Collection, Tulane University.

58. RSE to Nathaniel Harris, 27 Dec. 1864, published in Philadelphia *Weekly Times*, 3 Sep. 1881. Ewell's report of the Overland Campaign appears in *OR* 36(1):1069–75.

59. Hotchkiss diary, 14 May 1864, R2, HP; RSE to LCB, 16 May 1864, FC; Jedediah Hotchkiss to wife, 19 May 1864, R4, HP; CB, "Memoranda—Campaign of 1864," TN.

60. *OR* 36(1):337, 431, 1057, 51(2):929–30.

61. RSE to Charles Venable, undated dispatch (16 May 1864), Venable Papers, VHS; *OR* 36(1):431. The field hospital stood at the Couse house, about a mile north of the Muleshoe Salient.

62. *OR* 36(1):337–38, 1072; Matter, *If It Takes All Summer*, 305–6. Ewell began the campaign, by his own account, with 13,500 infantry (not counting Robert D. Johnston's brigade) and lost 1,250 men in the Wilderness. Subtracting from this figure the 4,000 men he lost as prisoners on 10 and 12 May, and adding 1,000 men for Johnston's brigade, this suggests that he lost approximately 3,250 men killed and wounded between 8 and 19 May.

63. *OR* 36(1):1046, 1088; William S. White, "Diary," 255.

64. Seymour, *Memoirs*, 128; Hotchkiss diary, 18 May 1864, R2, HP; *OR* 36(1):337–38; Robert Carroll to Ella Carroll, 18 May 1864, Carroll Papers, MHS; Matter, *If It Takes All Summer*, 311; Richmond *Daily Whig*, 20 May 1864. Compare William S. White, "Diary," 255.

65. Hotchkiss diary, 19 May 1864, R2, HP; *OR* 36(1):1073.

66. *OR* 36(1):1046, 1073, 1088. On the condition of the roads, see William Allan memoir, folder 11, Allan Papers, SHC.

67. Horace Porter, *Campaigning with Grant*, 122.

68. *OR* 36(1):1082–83; Gallagher, *Ramseur*, 113–14; Richmond *Sentinel*, 25 May 1864; Matter, *If It Takes All Summer*, 325–27; Peyton memoir, p. 33, FRSP; *OR* 36(1):1073.

69. Richmond *Sentinel*, 25 May 1864; Roe and Nutt, *History of the First Regiment*, 162; Ewell's compiled service record, RG 109, M331, R89, NA; Peyton memoir, p. 33, FRSP; Bosang, *Memoirs*, 7. Ewell valued the horse at $500, more than the mare he lost at Gaines's Mill ($200), but far less than the one he lost at Gettysburg ($1,200). According to Henry Wingfield, Ewell also lost a horse at Port Republic, but if he did, he never submitted a claim for it (Wingfield, "Diary," 12).

70. Allan was Lee's secretary at Washington College after the war (William Allan, "Conversation with General Lee," 3:9, and William Allan memoirs, folder 11, both in Allan Papers, SHC).

71. Peyton memoir, p. 33, FRSP; Matter, *If It Takes All Summer*, 327, 330; *OR* 36(1):338, 471, 36(3):3.

72. *OR* 36(1):1073, 36(3):3.

73. *OR* 36(1):337, 1074–75.

74. *OR* 36(1):1075; CB to LCB and HB, 20 May 1864, PBE.

75. Sandie Pendleton to mother, 2 June 1864, folder 39, WNP; Jedediah Hotchkiss to wife, 11 May 1864, R4, HP; *OR* 36(2):910, 36(3):8. Ewell wrote Lizinka on 22 May, "The position of Grant's army is this—Beaten—terrible losses—worn out. His chances are in his numbers that might stand killing untill we are worn out & he has still some left to use. But the chances are

against this. I trust in Providence with the firm belief that the issue, whatever it may be, will be to the best" (RSE to LCB, 22 May 1864, PBE).

Chapter 27

1. Hotchkiss diary, 21 May 1864, R2, HP; Susan P. Lee, *Memoirs*, 335. The Stanard house stood just east of the Telegraph Road, north of the Po River. Stanard's Mill stood at the point where the Telegraph Road crossed the river. There were several Beasley houses in that area. The one closest to the Telegraph Road was the D. Beasley house. For the location of these structures, see *Official Military Atlas*, plate 91, no. 1.

2. "A. P. Hill," p. 10, in R49, HP; *OR* 36(3):823–24.

3. Hotchkiss diary, 21 May 1864, R2, HP; RSE to LCB, 22 May 1864, PBE; Richmond *Sentinel*, 25 May 1864; J. Michael Miller, *North Anna*, 31.

4. *Official Military Atlas*, plate 81, no. 7; Evans, *Confederate Military History*, 3:460.

5. Venable, "Wilderness to Petersburg," 535.

6. RSE to LCB, 26 May 1864, FC.

7. McPherson, *Battle Cry*, 735.

8. For evidence of Ewell's good health at this time, see RSE to LCB, 22 May 1864, PBE, and CB to LCB, 25 May 1864, FC. Ewell described his malady as diarrhea, while Lizinka referred to it as "something of the nature of scurvy" (*OR* 36[1]:1074; LCB to BSE, 8 June 1864, in Hamlin, *Letters*, 127).

9. *OR* 36(1):1074, 36(3):838.

10. Robert Lee to RSE, 29 May 1864, PBE; RSE to LCB, 1 June 1864, PBE; *OR* 36(1):1074, 36(3):846.

11. Robert Lee to RSE, 31 May 1864, PBE.

12. Robert Lee to RSE, 1 June 1864, PBE; RSE to Walter Taylor, 1 June 1864, PBE; Walter Taylor to RSE, 1 June 1864, PBE.

13. *OR* 36(3):863.

14. Robert Lee to RSE, 1 June 1864, PBE; *OR* 36(1):1074.

15. CB to RSE, 13 June 1864, PBE; William Allan memoir, folder 11, Allan Papers, SHC; RSE to LCB, 1, 2 June 1864, PBE.

16. Jubal Early to RSE, 5 June 1864, PBE; CB to RSE, 13 June 1864, PBE. A sense of guilt seems to have nagged Early. On learning of his former commander's death, he wrote a note of condolence to Benjamin Ewell in which he apparently referred to the break in the friendship between himself and General Ewell. Ben replied diplomatically that his daughter, Lizzie, had often heard General Ewell speak of Early "but never except in terms of respect and confidence; that she had heard him when he seemed to be communicative, and even confidential, but always in this strain. She was in the family a great deal, & would know if he had ever spoken otherwise" (BSE to Jubal Early, 30 Jan. 1872, box 1, "Biographical" file in Benjamin Ewell faculty file, CWM).

17. RSE to BSE, 20 July 1864, in Hamlin, *Letters*, 130.

18. Ewell related the details of the conversation to Lizinka, who in turn related them to Benjamin Ewell in a letter dated 8 June 1864 (Hamlin, *Letters*, 126–31). Ewell's offer to accept a demotion rather than leave the army shows his attachment to active field service. Twenty years earlier he had written Ben, "Of all things promotion downwards is the most disagreeable" (RSE to BSE, 17 Oct. 1844, LC).

19. John B. Gordon, *Reminiscences*, 267.

20. William Allan, "Conversation with General Lee," 3:9, Allan Papers, SHC.

21. This raises an interesting point, for Ewell's removal made A. P. Hill the army's senior corps commander, and Hill's performance at the corps level had been no better than Ewell's. Hill had not performed well at Gettysburg; his rashness had resulted in the slaughter of two Confederate brigades at Bristoe Station; and his negligence in preparing his troops for battle on 6 May in the Wilderness nearly led to catastrophe. Moreover, Hill's health was so precarious at this time that he often could not ride a horse, and he had to relinquish command of his corps for two weeks during the battle of Spotsylvania. In spite of this, Lee allowed Hill to return to command when he was well enough to do so, a privilege he did not accord to Ewell.

22. Sorrel, *Recollections*, 247.

23. *OR* 36(3):897–98; Gorgas, *Diary*, 116.

24. David Woodruff to D. H. Woodruff, 7 June 1864, Talcott Family Papers, VHS; William S. White, "Diary," 266; Alexander, *Military Memoirs*, 397.

Chapter 28

1. RSE to BSE, 20 July 1864, LC. For Department of Richmond returns, see *OR* 40(3):670–71, 822, 42(2):1213, 1266, 42(3):1197, 1248, 1358, 46(2):1112, 1274, and ser. 4, 3:1182.

2. *OR* 40(2):652.

3. The compiled military service records for these individuals may be found in the National Archives in RG 109, M331 on the following rolls: (George) Campbell Brown, 35; Isaac Carrington, 49; Robert G. H. Carroll, 50; Theodore Chestney, 53; Frances T. Forbes, 96; James Ker, 148; Legh Page, 192; John H. Parkhill, 193; James Pegram, 195; Harry Seldon, 221; Thomas P. Turner, 252; and Thomas T. Turner, 252. For a full list of officers on Ewell's staff, see Appendix E.

4. Dowdey and Manarin, *Wartime Papers*, 783.

5. RSE to BSE, 20 July 1864, LC.

6. *OR* 40(3):745, 794, 811, 51(2):1026.

7. *OR* 40(3):755–56, 794–95. See also 51(2):1033.

8. Humphreys, *Virginia Campaign*, 247–49.

9. RSE to LCB, 29 July 1864, FC.

10. *OR* 40(3):808–10; Sulivane, "Fall of Richmond," 725.

11. *OR* 40(3):811–13; John B. Jones, *Rebel War Clerk's Diary*, 2:256; Freeman, *Lee*, 3:465.

12. *OR* 40(3):814–15, 819.

13. RSE to LCB, 30 July 1864, PBE.

14. *OR* 40(3):818.

15. Robert Carroll to Ella Carroll, 5 Aug. 1864, Carroll Papers, MHS; *OR* 42(2):1164.

16. Gallagher, *Ramseur*, 135; Stephen Ramseur to RSE, 10 Aug. 1864, PBE.

17. *OR* 42(2):1173–74.

18. Michie, "Account," 575.

19. Robert Lee to RSE, 10 Aug. 1864, Gunther Family Papers, Chicago Historical Society; Robert Lee to RSE, n.d., Smith Papers, VHS; *OR* 42(2):1169, 1173.

20. HB to LE, 16 Aug. 1864, WM; Humphreys, *Virginia Campaign*, 267–72; *OR* 42(2):1180–81; J. F. J. Caldwell, *"McGowan's Brigade,"* 176–78.

21. *OR* 42(2):1200.

22. Bean, *Stonewall's Man*, 219–20.

23. *OR* 42(2):1293; Chapman, "Benjamin Stoddert Ewell," 157, CWM; Benjamin S. Ewell's compiled service record, RG 109, M331, R89, NA.

24. Sommers, *Richmond Redeemed*, 5.

25. Ibid., 5–7, 9–10, 17–18. Ewell later wrote that he had just 4,000 men in his department to meet the onslaught, including "citizens, furloughed soldiers, Locals &c." (RSE to Walter Taylor, 8 Nov. 1864, Ewell Papers, DU; ELB, 15).

26. Sommers, *Richmond Redeemed*, 22; Humphreys, *Virginia Campaign*, 284–94.

27. ELB, 16; Sommers, *Richmond Redeemed*, 28.

28. Sommers, *Richmond Redeemed*, 29.

29. Ibid., 41–49; ELB, 16–17; Humphreys, *Virginia Campaign*, 290–94.

30. *OR* 42(2):1303; Rock, "War Reminiscence," 505.

31. Humphreys, *Virginia Campaign*, 285–86; Sommers, *Richmond Redeemed*, 62–64; CB, "Notes of Campaign before Richmond," TN.

32. Charles Johnston, "Fort Gilmer," 440; ELB, 17; Sommers, *Richmond Redeemed*, 62–68.

33. *OR* 42(2):1303; Sommers, *Richmond Redeemed*, 79, 82–89.

34. Sorrel, *Recollections*, 256–57; Sommers, *Richmond Redeemed*, 91–92; Humphreys, *Virginia Campaign*, 288; Edward A. Moore, *Story of a Cannoneer*, 263–64; Charles Johnston, "Fort Gilmer," 441; John McAnerney Papers, p. 32, VHS.

35. ELB, 18; *OR* 42(2):1304.

36. *OR* 42(2):830; Comstock diary, 30 Sep. 1864, Petersburg National Battlefield; Humphreys, *Virginia Campaign*, 289.

37. In a private letter, Ewell branded as absurd charges that the Federals had taken him by surprise at Fort Harrison. "When a place has more than the wonted garrison, has two hours notice, & uses all the means intended for its defence, its loss can hardly be called a surprise. When the authorities received due notice—When for months the almost certainty of such a movement by the enemy had been stated—When able officers who saw the position of affairs thought the fall of R[ichmon]d must follow the expected move of the enemy's[,] What sane person could be surprised that two army corps of the enemy could, being able to fall on any point unexpectedly, of a line four miles in length held by less than 1500, be able to carry whatever they went against?" (ELB, 19–20).

38. Charles Johnston, "Fort Gilmer," 439; Harriot Stoddert Turner, "Ewells of Virginia," 47, CWM; ELB, 19.

39. Sommers, *Richmond Redeemed*, 63.

40. Sorrel, *Recollections*, 259–60; Sperry diary, 30 Sep. 1864, Handley Library; CB, "Notes of Campaign before Richmond," TN.

41. Gregg died leading his troops in the 7 October attack. "He was a brave & able officer," wrote Ewell, "& no individual of his rank has been more directly instrumental in saving our capitol [*sic*]" (ELB, 18).

42. Sommers, "Dutch Gap Affair," 51–64; Catton, *Grant Takes Command*, 370–74; *OR* 42(3):184–85, 216–17; John B. Jones, *Rebel War Clerk's Diary*, 2:311.

43. Longstreet, "Report of Affair," 541; *OR* 42(1):871; Sorrel, *Recollections*, 265; Longstreet, *Manassas to Appomattox*, 574.

44. *OR* 42(3):1295–96.

45. *OR*, ser. 4, 3:970–74; *OR* 42(3):1310–11.

46. *OR* 46(2):1163; Weddell, *St. Paul's Church*, 2:229; LCB to Dr. David Pise, 6 Apr. 1865, Pise journal, University of the South. A Richmond woman described the ceremony, in which one of her family members was also confirmed: "How I wish you could have been with me last

night when I saw the Bp. [bishop] lay his hands on dear Dave's head. . . . Beside him knelt Gen. Ewell, so maimed and hurt that he could hardly stand. there were four others confirmed, but I dont know who they were" (Bessie ? to Katherine Marshall Bastable, 30 Sep. 1864, Thornton Family Papers, VHS).

47. Pollard, *Lee and His Lieutenants*, 461–62.

48. William McWillie notebooks, Mississippi Department of Archives and History.

49. Stott diary, 10 Jan. 1865., USAMHI. The author of this biography has taken the liberty of correcting two obvious typographical errors in the quoted portion of the typescript.

50. Edward A. Moore, *Story of a Cannoneer*, 266, 271–72; Robert Stiles, *Four Years*, 314–15; Heinichen memoir, MHS; William Pegram to BSE, 21 Jan. 1865, RG 109, box 13, entry 112, NA.

51. Edward A. Moore, *Story of a Cannoneer*, 271–72; Robert Stiles, *Four Years*, 313.

52. Edward A. Moore, *Story of a Cannoneer*, 271–72; Robert Stiles, *Four Years*, 313; *OR* 42(3):1179; John B. Jones, *Rebel War Clerk's Diary*, 2:315; Sorrel, *Recollections*, 263.

53. William L. Nuckolls to Rowland, 10 Jan. 1918, BV 30, FRSP. Because no records survive, the actual number of deserters in Ewell's department can only be surmised, although fragmentary evidence suggests that it was large. Custis Lee alone reported forty-five men of his command deserting to the enemy between 4 and 27 October 1864 (*OR* 42[3]:1179).

54. BSE to "Dear Sir," 30 Jan. 1865, PBE.

55. Longstreet, *Manassas to Appomattox*, 645; *OR* 46(2):1259–60; H. E. Wood, "Last Defense," 397.

56. McPherson, *Battle Cry*, 837.

57. Charles Marshall to RSE, 30 Mar. 1865, LC. Lee urged Ewell to impress this point on the city leaders, the inference being that if the South did not use black troops to help even the odds against the Federals, Richmond would be captured.

58. *OR* 46(2):1318, and ser. 4, 3:1144. Ewell later appointed his provost marshal, Maj. Isaac Carrington, to superintend black enlistment on a statewide basis. The War Department authorized other officers to raise black companies in late March and early April 1865, but the Confederacy collapsed before anything came of these efforts (*OR*, ser. 4, 3:1193–94).

59. Richmond *Daily Enquirer*, 23 Mar. 1865. Smith's factory stood between Main and Cary Streets.

60. RSE to Robert Lee, 29 Mar. 1865, LC; RSE to LCB, 12 May 1865, FC; Charles Marshall to RSE, 30 Mar. 1865, LC. Thomas P. Turner wrote about the reluctance of Virginians to allow their slaves to enlist in the army. "Their wives and daughters and the negroes are the only elements left us to recruit from, and it does seem that our people would rather send the former even to face death and danger than give up the latter" (*OR*, ser. 4, 3:1194).

61. Charles Marshall to RSE, 27 Mar. 1865, LC.

62. McPherson, *Battle Cry*, 837; Tomlinson, "Advance into Maryland," 141. The fact that half of the black troops came from Jackson Hospital suggests that Ewell had a direct role in the recruiting process. The hospital's director, Dr. Francis W. Hancock, had been the medical director of Ewell's division in 1862, and Ewell had lodged at Hancock's Richmond home for several months in 1863 following the amputation of his left leg. In February 1862, more than a month before the Virginia legislature authorized the enlistment of slaves, Ewell had questioned Hancock about the willingness of the black hospital workers to fight for the Confederacy. Hancock polled the workers and found that sixty of seventy-two men questioned were willing to take up arms for the South. Therefore, when Lee asked Ewell to raise a few black companies, he had a solid nucleus with which to begin (*OR*, ser. 4, 3:1193, and George Christian to the editor of the Richmond *Times-Dispatch*, 4 Nov. 1904, Christian Papers, VHS).

63. Samuel Moore to RSE, 11 Mar. 1865, RG 109, box 13, entry 112, NA; Flournoy, *Calendar of Virginia State Papers*, 11:263–64. According to Campbell Brown, Ewell feared Sheridan might slip behind Longstreet's forces at Hanover Junction and penetrate the city's defenses. "Gen. E. made every effort to get troops into the Intermediate Line," wrote Brown, "sending out among others three batt'ns. of Convalescents from the Hosp'ls. A negro company of volunteers attached to one of these battns. were the first & only black troops used on our side" (CB, "Notes of Campaign before Richmond," TN).

64. Harriot S. Turner, "Recollections," 172–74. According to Hattie, assassin John Wilkes Booth stopped at the Stuart house after shooting President Abraham Lincoln.

Chapter 29

1. Freeman, *Lee's Lieutenants*, 3:675; Freeman, *Lee*, 4:41; *OR* 46(1):1293, 46(3):1376.

2. *OR* 46(1):1295, 46(2):1259–60; Freeman, *Lee*, 4:30, 41.

3. *OR* 46(1):1293, 46(3):1380; Alexander, *Fighting for the Confederacy*, 517; Haskell, *Memoirs*, 84; Patrick, *Fall of Richmond*, 38; Howard, *Recollections*, 365.

4. Latrobe diary, 2 Apr. 1865, VHS; John William Jones, *Personal Reminiscences*, 171. On another occasion Lee received a batch of strawberries, of which only a few were ripe. Lee ate the ripe ones and gave the others to Ewell, saying, "General, Dr. ——— says acid fruit is good for our health" (William McWillie notebooks, Mississippi Department of Archives and History).

5. Howard, *Recollections*, 362–63; Lossing, *Pictorial History*, 3:544–45; McCabe, *Lee*, 609–10.

6. *OR* 46(1):1293; RSE to LCB, 20 Apr. 1865, PBE; Lossing, *Pictorial History*, 3:545–46 n.; McCabe, *Lee*, 610; William S. White, "Diary," 280.

7. *OR* 46(1):1293. See also H. E. Wood, "Last Defense," 397.

8. *OR* 46(1):1293. See also BSE to the editor of the Richmond *Daily Whig*, Apr. 1865, Ewell Papers, DU.

9. Pollard, *Lee and His Lieutenants*, 695–96; Lossing, *Pictorial History*, 545–46; Richmond *Daily Whig*, 14 Apr. 1865.

10. Lossing, *Pictorial History*, 545–46; Pollard, *Lee and His Lieutenants*, 695–96; Patrick, *Fall of Richmond*, 43 n.

11. *OR* 46(3):1380; *Official Military Atlas*, plate 78, no. 1; Calkins, *Petersburg to Appomattox*, 20.

12. *OR* 46(3):1380–81.

13. Howard, *Recollections*, 365–67; *OR* 46(1):1296; Robert Stiles, *Four Years*, 322.

14. Dwight, *Recollections*, 4.

15. Ibid., 5–6.

16. *OR* 46(1):1283, 1293; Duke, "Burning of Richmond," 135; Watehall, "Fall of Richmond," 215; Alexander, *Fighting for the Confederacy*, 519; Sulivane, "Fall of Richmond," 725; RSE to LE, 28 May 1865, in Hamlin, *Letters*, 141; McCabe, *Lee*, 612 n.; *OR* 46(1):1293–94; RSE to LE, 18 May 1865, LC; Lossing, *Pictorial History*, 545–46 n. Soldiers of the Local Brigade comprised the guard, although Sulivane himself was a member of Custis Lee's staff.

17. Lossing, *Pictorial History*, 546 n.; Handy, "Fall of Richmond," 17–18.

18. Handy, "Fall of Richmond," 18; Sulivane, "Fall of Richmond," 726; Dwight, *Recollections*, 3; Edward A. Moore, *Story of a Cannoneer*, 275–77; Lossing, *Pictorial History*, 546; Susan Hoge to husband, 4 Apr. 1865, section 18, folder 3, Hoge Papers, VHS; Robert Stiles, *Four Years*, 322; Howard, *Recollections*, 367.

19. Boykin, *Falling Flag*, 8–14. Lee had ordered Ewell to hold the picket lines until 3:00 A.M. (*OR* 46[3]:1380; Sulivane, "Fall of Richmond," 726).

20. Susan M. Hoge to husband, 4 Apr. 1865, section 18, folder 3, Hoge Papers, VHS. See also Sulivane, "Fall of Richmond," 725; RSE to LCB, 20 Apr. 1865, PBE; RSE to RLE, 18 Apr. 1865, LC; Ewell to LE, 18 May 1865, LC; Ewell to LE, 28 May 1865, in Hamlin, *Letters*, 141.

21. CB note, 14 Apr. 1865, LC; Reed, *Hospital Life*, 162–63.

22. BSE to the editor of the Richmond *Daily Whig*, Apr. 1865, Ewell Papers, DU; Benjamin Taylor, "Reminiscence."

23. *OR* 46(1):1283, 1293–94.

24. RSE to LCB, 20 Apr. 1865, PBE.

25. RSE to RLE, 18 Apr. 1865, LC. For similar statements by General Ewell to Lizzie on this matter, see his letters of 18 May 1865 (LC) and 28 May 1865 (Hamlin, *Letters*, 141).

26. Benjamin Taylor, "Reminiscence"; CB to Charles Venable, 13 Jan. 1888, Venable Papers, VHS; RSE to LCB, 20 Apr. 1865, PBE.

27. RSE to LE, 28 May 1865, in Hamlin, *Letters*, 141; TTG to RSE, 3 Mar. 1871, TN; BSE to RSE, 16 Mar. 1871, WM; Judge Crump to RSE, 30 Mar. 1871, TN; BSE to RSE, 6 Apr., 2 May 1871, TN; BSE to LCB, 18 Apr. 1871, TN.

28. Benjamin S. Ewell's compiled service record, RG 109, M331, R89, NA; Rouse, "'Old Buck,'" 20.

29. Harriot Stoddert Turner, "Ewells of Virginia," 35 fn., CWM; Ewell's compiled service record, RG 109, M331, R89, NA.

30. *OR* 46(1):1283, 1294, 1296; Calkins, *Petersburg to Appomattox*, 22; Duke, "Burning of Richmond," 136.

31. William S. White, "Diary," 281; Howard, *Recollections*, 370–71; undated anonymous note in box 2, folder 44, PBE; *OR* 46(3):1382; Calkins, *Petersburg to Appomattox*, 22; *Official Military Atlas*, plate 78, no. 1.

32. *OR* 46(1):1296; Alexander, *Fighting for the Confederacy*, 520; Howard, *Recollections*, 370–71. For Lee's dispatches to Ewell on the matter of crossing the river, see *OR* 46(3):1382, 1384–85. Lee's 3 April dispatch notifying Ewell that there was no pontoon bridge at Genito Bridge probably reached Ewell sometime before noon, 4 April, after he had made the discovery himself.

33. *OR* 46(1):1265; Blake, "Retreat from Richmond," 213–14.

34. Calkins, *Petersburg to Appomattox*, 26; *OR* 46(1):1296; Blake, "Retreat from Richmond," 213–14; Howard, *Recollections*, 372; Edward A. Moore, *Story of a Cannoneer*, 279; William Miller Owen, *In Camp and Battle*, 375. Ewell probably lost his baggage at Paineville or possibly Sailor's Creek. Among the items he lost were a pair of buckskins he had had since his days on the frontier, a daguerreotype of Lizinka, and important headquarters papers (RSE to LCB, 20 Apr. 1865, PBE; RSE to LCB, 5 May, 11 June 1865, FC; RSE to LCB, 22 June 1865, TN).

35. *OR* 46(1):1296; Howard, *Recollections*, 372–73; Robert Lee to RSE, 5 Apr. 1865, PBE.

36. *OR* 46(1):1265, 1283, 1294, 1296; Walter C. Watson, "Sailor's Creek," 140–41; Calkins, *Thirty-six Hours*, leaf 3. Ewell, with characteristic hyperbole, supposedly said that "he had never witnessed such gallantry on any battle field" as he had witnessed in Gordon's handling of the Confederate rear guard (Rast, "Fisher's Hill," 124; compare CB to Charles Venable, 13 Jan. 1888, Venable Papers, VHS).

37. CB to Charles Venable, 13 Jan. 1888, Venable Papers, VHS; Howard, *Recollections*, 377.

38. *OR* 46(1):1294.

39. *OR* 46(1):1298.

40. *OR* 46(1):1283–84, 1294; CB to Charles Venable, 13 Jan. 1888, Venable Papers, VHS.

41. *OR* 46(1):1284, 1294–95; Timberlake, "Siege of Richmond," 413.

42. *OR* 46(1):1295. Capt. McHenry Howard, a member of Custis Lee's staff, stated that Lee had approximately 1,300 men at Sailor's Creek, while Kershaw claimed that his division had fewer than 2,000 effective troops. More recent calculations place the size of Ewell's command as high as 5,300 men (Howard, *Recollections*, 377; *OR* 46[1]:1284). Ewell, with gross exaggeration, told his sister Rebecca that his corps had fought more than ten times its number of Federal troops at Sailor's Creek (RSE to RLE, 18 Apr. 1865, LC).

43. *OR* 46(1):1284, 1295, 1297; Edward A. Moore, *Story of a Cannoneer*, 280–81; Johns, "Sailor's Creek"; Howard, *Recollections*, 380–81; Robert Stiles, *Four Years*, 330.

44. Colston, "Lee's Ordnance," 24; Duke, "Burning of Richmond," 137.

45. *OR* 46(1):984, 1284, 1297; Dwight, *Recollections*, 12–13; Calkins, *Thirty-six Hours*, leaf 9; Robert Stiles, *Four Years*, 331–33.

46. *OR* 46(1):1295; RSE to LCB, 20 Apr. 1865, PBE; Robinson, "Sailor's Creek."

47. *OR* 46(1):1284.

48. *OR* 46(1):1295, 1297; Robert Stiles, *Four Years*, 331–33. Longstreet stated that just 287 of Ewell's command remained to surrender at Appomattox three days later. E. P. Alexander put the number of Ewell's men who escaped Sailor's Creek at an even 200 (Longstreet, *Manassas to Appomattox*, 631; Alexander, *Fighting for the Confederacy*, 523). Ewell estimated that Anderson lost approximately 1,000 men in the battle. Horatio Wright reported losing 442. Sheridan's casualties during the day are not reported but have been estimated at 1,000 (RSE to LCB, 20 Apr. 1865, PBE; *OR* 46[1]:909; Walter C. Watson, "Sailor's Creek," 150). Andrew Humphreys estimated that Ewell had 3,600 men at Little Sailor's Creek and lost 3,400 of them (Humphreys, *Virginia Campaign*, 383–84).

49. *OR* 46(1):1295. Ewell encountered Capt. William F. Dement's artillery battalion while visiting Anderson's front, a fact Dement mentioned to Ewell's sister Elizabeth when he saw her a couple of weeks later. In a letter to Dick written on 25 April, Elizabeth wrote, "Capt. Dement spoke in the kindest manner of you, telling that your care for his command caused your capture" (ESE to RSE, 25 Apr. 1865, FC).

50. *OR* 46(1):1295; CB to Charles Venable, 13 Jan. 1888, Venable Papers, VHS; Harriot Stoddert Turner, "Ewells of Virginia," 47, CWM. Custer claimed credit for the capture in his report of the battle (*OR* 46[1]:1132). In an 18 Aug. 1887 article published in *The National Tribune*, F. C. Robinson of the First West Virginia Cavalry stated that he "was the first Union officer or soldier to meet with THAT ONE LEGGED GENTLEMAN, Gen. Ewell." Although some of Robinson's details about the capture are suspect, his claim may be valid. In any case, no better claim has yet come to light.

The Sixth Corps likewise claimed credit for Ewell's capture. But Ewell's report, as well as later statements by Campbell Brown and Hattie Turner, make it clear that he surrendered to Custer's cavalry rather than to the Sixth Corps. For a full discussion of the various claims surrounding Ewell's capture, see Appendix K.

51. *OR* 46(1):1295; Tremain, *Last Hours*, 153–55. The officer who permitted Ewell to send the message may have been one of Custer's subordinates rather than Custer himself. The messenger, who seems to have been Maj. James W. Pegram, never reached Custis Lee (*OR* 46[1]:980, 984, 1284).

52. Tremain, *Last Hours*, 155.

53. *OR* 46(1):1295; article by a man who served on Wright's staff, identified only as T.H.F., taken from the 11 Mar. 1920 Union College *Alumni Monthly*. A copy of the article is in the John Stone Bradley file, Special Collections, Union College.

54. RSE to LCB, 20 Apr. 1865, PBE; *OR* 46(1):1295.

55. Newhall, *With General Sheridan*, 187–88; Todd, "Reminiscences," SHC.

56. Horace Porter, *Campaigning with Grant*, 459; Ulysses S. Grant, *Memoirs*, 2:477–78; Lyman, *Meade's Headquarters*, 354; Newhall, *With General Sheridan*, 187–88; CB to LCB, 3 July 1862, PBE.

57. Westbrook, *49th Pennsylvania Volunteers*, 420. For a good map of the area between Burkeville and City Point, see *Official Military Atlas*, plate 93, no. 1.

58. RSE to LCB, 20 Apr. 1865, PBE; RSE to LE, 18 May 1865, LC. "He contrasted with the fat northern horses," wrote Ewell of Rifle. "I expect when he got his fill of good oats & hay he thought the millenium [*sic*] had come." For other references regarding Ewell and Rifle at this time, see Timberlake, "Last Days," 119; Johns, "Sailor's Creek"; and Lawrence, "Capture of General Ewell."

59. Patrick diary, 9 Apr. 1865, Library of Congress; Badeau, *Military History*, 3:577–78 n.

60. Muffly, *Our Regiment*, 179; Patrick diary, 9 Apr. 1865, Library of Congress; Badeau, *Military History*, 3:577–78 n.; Hunton, *Autobiography*, 124–25; Howard, *Recollections*, 390.

61. Hunton, *Autobiography*, 125–26; Benjamin Taylor, "Reminiscence."

62. Benjamin Taylor, "Reminiscence."

63. Howard, *Recollections*, 391.

64. Reed, *Hospital Life*, 162–63; Mobley diary, 8–9 Apr. 1865, FRSP.

65. Bates, *History*, 2:677 n.; *OR* 46(3):692–93.

66. *OR* 46(3):675; *Official Military Atlas*, plate 93, no. 1; Orlando Willcox to wife, 11 Apr. 1865, in possession of William H. Willcox of Washington, D.C.

67. Raup, *Letters*, 26–27.

68. Hunton, *Autobiography*, 128; Robert Stiles, *Four Years*, 238–39; Howard, *Recollections*, 392.

69. George Lewis, *Battery E*, 431; *History of the Fifth Massachusetts Battery*, 954; Ewell's compiled service record, RG 109, M331, R89, NA.

70. Collis, *Woman's War Record*, 71–73. Barringer was a brother-in-law of both Stonewall Jackson and D. H. Hill, having married one of the Morrison sisters. He had been captured on 3 April near Namozine Church.

71. Lucien Hall, "Prison Sketchbook," 5001–2.

72. Hunton, *Autobiography*, 129.

73. Lucien Hall, "Prison Sketchbook," 5002; G. B. Russell diary, 15 Apr. 1865, Davis Papers, SHC.

74. Montgomery Blair to TTG, 17 Apr. 1865, PBE.

75. Lucien Hall, "Prison Sketchbook," 5002–3; Howard, *Recollections*, 393–95.

76. Montgomery Blair to TTG, 17 Apr. 1865, PBE; RSE to LCB, 20 Apr. 1865, PBE.

77. HB to LCB, 20, 23 Apr. 1865, FC; RLE to CB, 1 May 1865, FC.

78. Lucien Hall, "Prison Sketchbook," 5002–3; Howard, *Recollections*, 393–95; Montgomery Blair to TTG, 17 Apr. 1865, PBE; HB to LCB, 23 Apr. 1865, FC; RSE to LCB, 20 Apr. 1865, PBE.

79. G. B. Russell diary, 15 Apr. 1865, Davis Papers, SHC; Hunton, *Autobiography*, 130; Butler, *Butler's Book*, 908; Harriot Stoddert Turner, "Ewells of Virginia," 51, CWM.

80. Hunton, *Autobiography*, 130; G. B. Russell diary, 15 Apr. 1865, Davis Papers, SHC.

81. Hunton, *Autobiography*, 130; Harriot Stoddert Turner, "Ewells of Virginia," 47, CWM; G. B. Russell diary, 15 Apr. 1865, Davis Papers, SHC; RSE to LCB, 20 Apr. 1865, PBE.

82. Hunton, *Autobiography*, 130; G. B. Russell diary, 15 Apr. 1865, Davis Papers, SHC.

83. Ewell's compiled service record, RG 109, M331, R89, NA.

Chapter 30

1. McLain, "Fort Warren," 136.

2. Ibid., 136–50; Harriot Stoddert Turner, "Ewells of Virginia," 49, CWM; Alexander H. Stephens, *Recollections*, 127, 133, 167, 175; RSE to LCB, 21 May 1865, PBE.

3. Hunton, *Autobiography*, 137; *OR* 46(3):787. The signatures are in Ewell's 1865 diary, box 3, PBE. Hunton erroneously lists a General Wilson among the prisoners.

4. Alexander H. Stephens, *Recollections*, 162; RSE to LCB, 27 May, 13 July 1865, PBE; CB to LCB, 23 June 1865, PBE.

5. HB to LE, 23 Apr. 1865, WM; CB to HB, 23 Apr. 1865, PBE.

6. HB to LCB, 23 Apr. 1865, PBE; ESE to LE, 23 Apr. 1865, WM; RSE to RLE, 18 Apr. 1865, WM; RSE to LCB, 20 Apr. 1865, PBE; HB to LE, 7 May 1865, WM; CB to HB, 23 Apr. 1865, PBE. Brown was transferred to Ewell's casemate on 7 May 1865 at the order of Brig. Gen. William Hoffman, the commissary general of prisoners in Washington, D.C. (CB to HB, 8 May 1865, PBE; LCB to CB, 21 May 1865, FC).

7. *OR* 46(3):1013.

8. RSE to LCB, 20 Apr. 1865, PBE.

9. Hunton, *Autobiography*, 137–38.

10. RSE to Ulysses Grant, 16 Apr. 1865, PBE. This letter has been reproduced in *OR* 46(3):787; in *Southern Historical Society Papers*, 39:4–5; and in the 8 May 1865 edition of the *Commercial Bulletin* (Richmond, Va.). Acting post commander Maj. John W. M. Appleton forwarded the resolution to General Hoffman, who sent it to Grant. At the bottom of the page, Appleton wrote the following postscript: "The general officers confined at this post as prisoners of war have, from the moment of the reception of the news, expressed their regret for the loss of President Lincoln, and their utmost horror of the act and detestation of his murderers."

11. Alexander H. Stephens, *Recollections*, 137; *OR* 46(3):1052; Heitman, *Historical Register*, 1:158; RSE to LE, 18 May 1865, LC; Hunton, *Autobiography*, 139; HB to LE, 23 Apr. 1865, WM; RSE to LE, 20 Apr. 1865, PBE.

12. CB to HB, 23 Apr. 1865, PBE; CB to LE, 22 June 1865, LC; RSE to LCB, 31 May 1865, FC; RSE to LCB, 22 June 1865, TN; RSE to LCB, 24 June 1865, PBE.

13. Alexander H. Stephens, *Recollections*, 220, 244; CB to LE, 22 June 1865, LC; RSE to LCB, 27 May 1865, PBE; RSE to RLE, 27 May 1865, LC; RSE to LCB, 31 May 1865, FC.

14. Alexander H. Stephens, *Recollections*, 152, 178, 220.

15. CB to HB, 8 May 1865, PBE; RSE to LCB, 21 May 1865, PBE.

16. RSE to RLE, 8 May 1865, LC; CB to HB, 23 Apr. 1865, PBE. See also Alexander H. Stephens, *Recollections*, 178–83.

17. Alexander H. Stephens, *Recollections*, 128–32, 137; RSE to LCB, 21 May 1865, PBE; RSE to RLE, 8 May 1865, LC.

18. RSE to RLE, 8 May 1865, LC.

19. Newnan (Ga.) *Herald*, 9 Sept. 1865.

20. RSE to LCB, 12 May, 11 July 1865, FC; RSE to LE, 18 May 1865, LC; RSE to LCB, 19 May 1865, PBE; RSE to RLE, 27 May 1865, LC; CB to LCB, 14 July 1865, FC. Drs. Joseph C. Greenfield Jr., Marvin Rozear, and G. Ralph Corey of Duke University Medical Center believe that General Ewell's medical condition may have been chronic sinusitis.

21. RSE to LCB, 5 May 1865, FC; CB to LCB, 10 June 1865, PBE; RSE to RLE, 27 May 1865, LC. For Ewell's views on the reason the South lost the war and the policy it should adopt toward black suffrage, see RSE to LCB, 17, 24 June 1865, PBE.

22. RSE to RLE, 27 May 1865, LC; RSE to LCB, 18 June 1865, PBE; CB to HB, 18 June 1865, PBE; RSE to ESE, 25 June 1865, LC; RSE to LCB, 22 June 1865, TN; HB to LE, 7 May 1865, WM.

23. CB to LCB, 23 June 1865, PBE; RSE to LCB, 12 May 1865, FC.

24. Alexander H. Stephens, *Recollections*, 132; CB to HB, 23 Apr., 8 May, 18 June 1865, PBE; RSE to LCB, 22 June 1865, TN; Hunton, *Autobiography*, 139.

25. RSE to LCB, 27 May, 24 June 1865, PBE; RSE to ESE, 25 June 1865, LC.

26. RSE to LCB, 29 June, 13 July 1865, PBE; Harriot Stoddert Turner, "Ewells of Virginia," 50–51, CWM; CB to HB, 18 June 1865, PBE.

27. RSE to LCB, 11 June 1865, FC.

28. Harriot Stoddert Turner, "Ewells of Virginia," 50, CWM.

29. RSE to LCB, 5 May 1865, FC; Joseph Lewis to RSE, 20 June 1865, FC; RSE to LCB, 29 June 1865, PBE. For Lewis's letter to Ewell, see Hamlin, *Old Bald Head*, 195–96.

30. CB to HB, 23 Apr. 1865, PBE; H. O'Brien to RSE, 12 July 1865, PBE; ESE to RSE, 2 July 1865, PBE; RSE to LE, 28 May 1865, in Hamlin, *Letters*, 139–41.

31. RSE to LCB, 22 June 1865, TN; RSE to LE, 28 May 1865, in Hamlin, *Letters*, 139–41; Mabel Appleton to RSE, 22 May, 22 June 1865, FC; RSE to RLE, 28 June 1865, LC.

32. RSE to LCB, 22 June 1865, TN; RSE to ESE, 25 June 1865, LC; RSE to LCB, 13, 16 July 1865, PBE; Hunton, *Autobiography*, 138–39. If Hunton is correct, Fort Warren's commander must have given the prisoners special leave to remain outside all day.

33. RSE to LCB, 22 June 1865, TN.

34. RSE to [Montgomery Blair?], undated letter, FC.

35. CB to Montgomery Blair, 14 May 1865, FC; CB to HB, 17 May 1865, FC.

36. RSE to LCB, 21 May 1865, PBE; RSE to LCB, 31 May 1865, FC; RSE to LCB, 22 June 1865, TN.

37. CB to HB, 14 May 1865, FC; RSE to LCB, 12 May 1865, FC.

38. RSE to LCB, 27 May, 17 June 1865, PBE.

39. *OR*, ser. 2, 8:578–80; RSE to LCB, 31 May 1865, FC; Alexander H. Stephens, *Recollections*, 187.

40. CB to LCB, 9 June 1865, PBE.

41. *OR*, ser. 2, 8:578–82.

42. CB to HB, 17 May 1865, FC.

43. RSE to LCB, 17 June 1865, PBE; RSE to Andrew Johnson, 16 June 1865, LC. Signed copies of the oath are in box 1, folder 14, PBE, and in LC.

44. RSE to LCB, 8 June 1865, FC; TTG to RLE, 4 June 1865, WM.

45. RSE to LCB, 28 May, 8 June 1865, FC; Thomas Turner to CB, 5 July 1865, PBE; David Meriwether to RSE, 30 June 1865, PBE. Ewell wrote Lizinka that he had known "Genl. Grant for many years—our relations have always been pleasant & I think he would be friendly disposed. General Sherman was a classmate at West Point. We were also on friendly terms while there, though I have not met him since."

46. CB to HB, 18 June 1865, PBE; Harriot S. Turner, "Recollections," 174.

47. Basler, *Collected Works*, 8:372; Harriot Stoddert Turner, "Ewells of Virginia," 55, CWM; note in box 20, folder 6, TN. Gantt lived at the corner of 15th Street and Lucas Place (LCB to John Pope, 19 June 1865, FC).

48. LCB to Rev. Dr. David Pise, 6 Apr. 1865, Pise journal, University of the South.

49. Ibid.; LCB to RSE, 25 May 1865, PBE; note in box 20, folder 6, TN.

50. Harriot S. Turner, "Recollections," 174; LCB to RSE, 28 June 1865, PBE; Graf and Haskins, *Papers of Andrew Johnson*, 7:561, 567, 597. Compare LCB to RSE, 25 June 1865, PBE.

51. Harriot S. Turner, "Recollections," 174.

52. Montgomery Blair to [TTG?], 10 May 1865, GWC, quoted in Harriot S. Turner, "Recollections," 174; Montgomery Blair to RSE, 17 May 1865, FC; LCB to RSE, 25 May 1865, PBE. For other evidence that Lizinka wished to go to Europe, see LCB to RSE, 4 May 1865, PBE. Johnson later changed his views. On 4 June he wrote Edwin Stanton that if the Ewells "were to go beyond the limits of the United States and there remain it would no doubt be the best disposition we could make of them at this time" (Graf and Haskins, *Papers of Andrew Johnson*, 8:180).

53. *OR*, ser. 2, 8:501; Harriot S. Turner, "Recollections," 175; LCB to Montgomery Blair, 4 May [*sic*; June] 1865, PBE; Graf and Haskins, *Papers of Andrew Johnson*, 7:601; LCB to RSE, 4 May 1865, PBE. Lizinka later told General Pope that she had been arrested on 22 April (LCB to John Pope, 19 June 1865, FC).

54. LCB to RSE, 25 May 1865, PBE. Johnson's arrest of Lizinka at the time that his family was occupying her house casts suspicion on his motives.

55. HB to LE, 7 May 1865, WM; Montgomery Blair to LCB, 29 Apr. 1865, PBE; Harriot S. Turner, "Recollections," 174.

56. LCB to RSE, 25 May 1865, PBE; LCB to RSE, 13 June 1865, FC. Lizinka wrote to her land manager in Tennessee instructing him to collect rents from black families living on her town lots only if they were willing to pay; otherwise he was to let them stay there free (LCB to W. L. Murfree, 4 May 1865, TN).

57. RSE to Mrs. M. Ringgold Archer, 23 June 1865, LC; RSE to LCB, 18 June 1865, PBE.

58. Hunton, *Autobiography*, 129; RSE to LCB, 29 June, 2 July 1865, PBE.

59. LCB to John Pope, 19 June 1865, FC; John Pope to LCB, 19 June 1865, FC; John Pope to LCB, 21 June 1865, PBE. On Pope's civility toward Lizinka while she was in St. Louis, see HB to CB, 24 June 1865, PBE.

60. HB to CB, 24 June 1865, PBE; LCB to RSE, 25 June 1865, PBE; LCB to Andrew Johnson, 21 July 1865, FC; RSE to LCB, 21 May 1865, PBE; Harriot S. Turner, "Recollections," 174–75.

61. TTG to LCB, 6 July 1865, FC; Harriot S. Turner, "Recollections," 175; LCB to RSE, 28 June 1865, PBE. For a summary of Lizinka's efforts to secure Dick's and Campbell's releases, see Dorris, *Pardon and Amnesty*, 161–66. Before leaving Washington that day, Lizinka stopped at the adjutant general's office, where she learned that the attorney general had received recommendations "of the highest & strongest character" for her husband's release. Officials there told her that all of the Confederate generals still being held in confinement would soon be released. They also assured her that, with one exception, no one would be put on trial for treason. The exception was Jefferson Davis.

62. Dorris, *Pardon and Amnesty*, 164. A copy of the petition that Lizinka presented to Johnson is in Graf and Haskins, *Papers of Andrew Johnson*, 8:320.

63. HB to CB, 2 July 1865, PBE; Harriot Stoddert Turner, "Ewells of Virginia," 55, CWM; Harriot S. Turner, "Recollections," 175; ESE to RSE, 2 July 1865, PBE. Lizinka had written to Grant on 28 May enlisting his help in securing her husband's release. As a result of her letter, Grant went to see Johnson about General Ewell, but he was unsuccessful in securing his release (LCB to Ulysses Grant, 28 May 1865, FC; Montgomery Blair to LCB, 29 May 1865, FC; RSE to LCB, 8 June 1865, FC).

64. LCB to RSE, 9 July 1865, PBE; CB to LCB, 14 July 1865, FC; CB to LCB, 9 June [*sic*; July] 1865, PBE.

65. LCB to Andrew Johnson, 13 July 1865, PBE. This letter also appears, with slight changes, in Graf and Haskins, *Papers of Andrew Johnson*, 8:403.

66. Andrew Johnson to LCB, 7 July 1865, PBE; LCB to RSE, 14 July 1865, FC.

67. Notes in GWC; Harriot S. Turner, "Recollections," 176; addenda to Ewell's compiled service record, RG 109, M347, R125, NA; Ewell's compiled service record, RG 109, M331, R89, NA; Alexander H. Stephens, *Recollections,* 356; G. W. Gordon to CB, 24 July 1865, TN; Eppa Hunton's compiled service record, RG 109, M331, R136, LC; Hunton, *Autobiography,* 139.

68. LCB to Andrew Johnson, 21 July 1865, FC; also found in Graf and Haskins, *Papers of Andrew Johnson,* 8:442–43.

Chapter 31

1. LCB to CB, 7 Aug. 1865, TN.

2. CB to LCB, 10 Aug. 1865, PBE; CB to LCB, 17 Aug. 1865, TN; CB to LCB, 13 Aug. 1865, FC; LCB to Rebecca Hubbard, 21 Aug. 1865, Hubbard Papers, TSLA; LCB to CB, 7, 17, 21 Aug. 1865, TN; LCB to RSE, 19 June 1868, TN. For a list of farms visited by Brown, see his 1865 notebook at FC.

3. CB to LCB, 10 June 1868, TN.

4. CB to LCB, 29, 31 Aug. 1865, PBE; LCB to CB, 6 Sept. 1865, TN; Graf and Haskins, *Papers of Andrew Johnson,* 9:19–21.

5. LCB to CB, 6 Sept. 1865, TN; note in GWC; TTG to RLE, 9 Sept. 1865, WM; TTG to LCB, 15 Sept. 1865, TN; RSE to BSE, 19 Sept. 1865, LC.

6. LCB to CB, 17 Aug., 6 Sept. 1865, TN; RSE to the Assistant Adjutant General, Headquarters of General Meade, 17 Oct. 1865, in Ewell's compiled service record, RG 109, M331, R89, NA; RSE to LCB, 27 Sept. 1865, PBE.

7. LCB to CB, 18 Aug. 1865, TN; TTG to RSE, 8 Sept. 1865, TN.

8. RSE to Andrew Johnson, 23 Sept. 1865, PBE; RSE to LCB, 27 Sept. 1865, PBE; RSE to E. W. Clark Jr., 28 Sept. 1865, PBE. Lizinka also brought the matter of her husband's parole to President Johnson's attention at her 5 September meeting at the White House (LCB to CB, 6 Sept. 1865, TN).

9. Ewell's compiled service record, RG 109, M331, R89, NA; E. D. Townsend to RSE, 13 Oct. 1865, TN.

10. LCB to CB, 6 Sept. 1865, TN; LCB to RSE, 26 Sept. 1865, TN; RSE to LCB, 27 Sept. 1865, PBE.

11. RSE to Assistant Adjutant General, Headquarters of General Meade, 17 Oct. 1865, in Ewell's compiled service record, RG 109, M331, R89, NA; 28 Oct. 1865 receipt for prosthesis, FC; Meade, "Meade-Sickles Controversy." Ewell's new limb must have suited him well, for he never again complained of abrasions to his stump (*Medical and Surgical History,* 2[3]:242; Hunter McGuire, "Gun-shot Wounds of Joints," 262).

12. CB to LCB, 31 Aug. 1865, PBE; CB to Rebecca Hubbard, 7 Sept. 1865, Hubbard Papers, TSLA; RSE to Dr. Samuel Jackson, 10 Dec. 1865, Milligan Papers, MHS; E. P. Hotchkiss, Register of Descriptions of Abandoned & Confiscated Property, Freedman's Bureau Records, RG 56, p. 47, NA. See also "Copy of List of Abandoned Lands by E. P. Hotchkiss, Assistant Special Agent Treasury Department at Murfreesboro, Tenn.," RG 105, box 10, NA, and note in box 19, folder 3, TN.

13. Survey map, 1866, in box 19, folder 1, TN; E. P. Hotchkiss, Register of Descriptions of Abandoned & Confiscated Property, Freedman's Bureau Records, RG 56, p. 47, NA.

14. CB to LCB, 31 Aug. 1865, PBE; legal statement in box 20, folder 6, TN; RSE to BSE, 25

Jan. 1866, LC; RSE to LE, 22 Apr. 1866, LC; RSE to Dr. Samuel Jackson, 10 Dec. 1865, Milligan Papers, MHS.

15. Ewell 1866 diary, 3, 4, 8, 11, 12, 13 Jan., 15 Feb. 1866, FC.

16. RSE to LE, 4 Jan. 1865 [*sic*; 1866], LC; CB to Jedediah Hotchkiss, 15 Mar. 1866, R49, HP; RSE to Jedediah Hotchkiss, 14 Mar. 1866, R49, HP; LCB to CB, 17 Jan. 1866, TN.

17. RSE to ESE, 28 Oct. 1866, LC; RSE to LE, 7 Jan. 1866, LC. See also RSE to ESE, 7 Apr. 1867, LC; CB to LCB, 7 Jan. 1866, FC; CB to LCB, 10 Jan. 1865 [*sic*; 1866], PBE.

18. Agricultural Schedule, 1870 Census, 22nd District, Maury County, Tenn., pp. 5–6, NA; CB to LCB, 27 Dec. 1869, TN; CB to Susan Brown, 6, 9 Aug. 1869, TN. Ewell principally grew Catawba grapes, with lesser amounts of the Ives, Harford, Prolific, Delaware, and Concord varieties.

19. LCB to CB, 27 Feb., 19 Mar., 5, 19 Apr. 1867, 12 Apr., 7 June 1869, 21 Nov. 1870, 22 Mar. 1871, TN; LCB to RSE, 27 Sept. 1871, PBE.

20. A. S. Horsley to RSE, 17 Mar. 1871, TN; LCB to CB, 2 Mar. 1871, TN. In 1870 Lizinka's dairy produced 1,500 pounds of butter and 200 pounds of cheese (Agricultural Schedule, 1870 Census, 22nd District, Maury County, Tenn., pp. 5–6, NA).

21. LCB to CB, 24 July 1866, TN; RSE to LCB, [Oct.?] 1870, box 9, folder 7, TN; Ewell 1870 appointment book, box 1, folder 3, PBE; RSE to LCB, 23 May 1868, TN; RSE to CB, 14 Feb. 1871, TN. The 1870 census lists Ewell as having forty mules at Spring Hill. This probably represented only a fraction of his total stock. By then most of the animals had probably been taken to Mississippi for use at Melrose and Tarpley (Agricultural Schedule, 1870 Census, 22nd District, Maury County, Tenn., pp. 5–6, NA).

22. LCB to CB, 19 May 1867, 30 Dec. 1869, TN; RSE to John Cooke, 21 June 1871, Cooke Family Papers, VHS; RSE to Robert Chilton, 3 Jan. 1871, Chilton Papers, Museum of the Confederacy; CB to RSE, 30 July 1866, PBE; BSE to RSE, 28 July 1871, WM; Gardner, Buckner, & Co. to RSE, 6 Apr. 1871, PBE. Ewell sold 2,500 pounds of wool in 1870 (Agricultural Schedule, 1870 Census, 22nd District, Maury County, Tenn., pp. 5–6, NA).

23. Agricultural Schedule, 1870 Census, 22nd District, Maury County, Tenn., pp. 5–6, NA; CB to Susan Polk, 10 July 1866, TN; LCB to Susan Brown, 29 Jan. 1867, TN; LCB to CB, 5 Apr. 1867, TN; George W. Polk, "Some Reflections and Reminiscences," Polk Papers, TSLA.

24. LCB to RSE, 27 Sept. 1871, PBE; *Historical Sketch*, 33; *Southern Home* (Charlotte, N.C.), 5 Feb. 1872; LCB to CB, 8 Feb., 19 Mar., 5 Apr. 1867, TN; RSE to CB, 15 [month?] 1867, box 1, folder 13, TN; J. F. Smith to RSE, 2 May 1867, TN; RSE to CB, 14 Feb. 1871, TN; RSE to John Cooke, 21 June 1871, Cooke Family Papers, VHS.

25. Agricultural Schedule, 1870 Census, 22nd District, Maury County, Tenn., pp. 5–6, NA.

26. Ibid. The shepherd's name was Cross. He must have been skilled at his job, for the Ewells later rehired him despite his ongoing bouts with the bottle (LCB to RSE, 25 Nov. 1870, TN).

27. Agricultural Schedule, 1870 Census, 22nd District, Maury County, Tenn., pp. 5–6, NA; RSE to CB, 10 Mar. 1867, TN. Two sharecropping agreements, dated 29 Feb. 1868 and 18 Apr. 1869, are in box 20, folder 1, TN.

28. Agricultural Schedule, 1870 Census, 22nd District, Maury County, Tenn., pp. 5–6, NA. This figure may include only Lizinka's Tennessee lands. Two years later, when she died, her real estate holdings alone were valued at $240,000. For a breakdown of her various landholdings, see Appendix C.

29. 17 Jan. 1870 note in box 20, folder 5, TN; CB to LE, 10 Apr. 1872, WM; CB to BSE, 28 Feb. 1872, WM; note in box 19, folder 10, TN; 10 Aug. 1872, Chancery Court Minutes, Nashville, Tenn., book U, pp. 289–302; deed in folder 19, PBE.

30. Deeds 2T325 and 3F246, Register of Deeds, Maury County Land Records, Columbia, Tenn.; CB to LE, 10 Apr. 1872, WM; CB to RSE, 5 Feb. 1871, PBE; LCB to RSE, 29 Oct. 1871, PBE. See also information contained in box 19, folder 9, TN.

31. LCB to CB, undated letter, box 11, folder 5, TN; Ewell 1866 diary, 30 Jan. 1866, FC; LCB to CB, 8 Feb. 1869, 17 Nov. 1870, TN; J. & J. Stuart & Co., Bankers, to RSE, 26 Apr. 1871, TN; American Merchants Union Express Company to RSE, 13 Dec. 1871, TN; William Reynolds to RSE, 17 Nov. 1865, 3 May 1866, 2 Nov. 1867, TN; 30 May 1871 note in box 18, folder 8, TN; Henry Heath to RSE, 2 June 1871, TN. Among General Ewell's investments was the purchase of forty shares of stock in John B. Gordon's University Publishing Company.

32. Lizinka Ewell legal statement in box 20, folder 6, TN; CB to LCB, 18 Sept. 1865, PBE; William Reynolds to RSE, 15 Jan. 1866, TN; Stephens & Smith, Attorneys at Law, to LCB, 27 Dec. 1867, PBE; CB to LCB, 6 Apr. 1869, TN; LCB to CB, 6 Dec. 1870, TN; TTG to LCB, 7 July 1871, PBE.

33. LCB to RSE, 19, 21 June 1868, TN. For examples of loans between family members, see Ewell 1866 diary, 30 June 1866, TN, and CB to LCB, 6 Mar. 1870, TN.

34. RSE to ESE, 7 Apr. 1867, LC; TTG to RSE, 20 Feb. 1866, TN; LCB to CB, 17 Jan. 1866, 27 Feb. 1867, TN; ESE to RSE, 22 Jan. 1867, TN; RSE to LE, 22 Apr. 1866, LC; RSE to CB, 10 Mar. 1867, TN.

35. HB to CB, 29 July 1866, TN; LCB to CB, 28 May 1866, TN; HB to LCB, 19 Mar. 1870, TN.

36. Richard Taylor, *Destruction*, 78. The Ewells visited New Orleans again in January 1871. Lizinka wrote Elizabeth Ewell about "the agreeable qualities 'of the rebels'" whom she met there "and their witty conversations." "She and Richard seemed charmed with the encounter with these Generals," remembered Elizabeth, "especially Genl. Beauregard was mentioned, as supplying the wear and tear of nature by art, hair, &c also his agreeableness" (ESE to CB, 4 May 1885, FC; LCB to CB, 8 Jan. 1871, TN).

37. LCB to CB, 18 July 1866, TN; Ewell 1866 diary, 20 July 1866, FC.

38. Ewell 1866 diary, account ledger for 21 July 1866, FC; LCB to CB, 24 July 1866, TN; HB to CB, 29 July 1866, TN; Goldsborough, "With Lee at Gettysburg."

39. BSE to RSE, 9 Aug. 1867, TN; BSE to ESE, 9 Aug. 1867, WM; LCB to BSE, 26 Aug. 1867, WM. For information on the William and Mary cemetery where Rebecca is buried, see Appendix D.

40. LCB to CB, 12 Aug. 1866, TN. For the locations of Millborough Springs and Bath Alum Springs, see *Official Military Atlas*, plate 94, no. 1. Ewell had seen Johnston during his stay in Baltimore a few weeks earlier (LCB to CB, 1 Aug. 1866, TN).

41. CB to LCB, 19 July, 8 Aug. 1866, PBE; CB to LCB, 23 July, 6 Aug. 1866, FC; CB to RSE, 17, 30 July, 2 Aug. 1866, PBE; CB to RSE, 12 Aug. 1866, TN; LCB to CB, 28, 29 July 1866, TN; RSE to BSE, 25 Jan 1865 [*sic*; 1866], LC.

42. CB 1866 (and 1867) diary, 18 Apr., 13 Aug. 1866, 17 Mar. 1867, box 4, GWC; HB to CB, 27 Apr. 1866, TN; CB to LCB, 15 Oct. 1866, PBE; RSE to ESE, 8 Jan. 1867, LC; Campbell Family Bible Records, box 4, item 5, GWC. For Benjamin Ewell's estimation of Susie Polk, see BSE to LCB, 3 Oct. 1866, TN. See Appendix F for a genealogical chart of the Campbell family.

43. Chapman, "Benjamin Stoddert Ewell," 186−87, CWM; BSE to LCB, 1 Jan. 1868, WM; Ewell Bible Records, folder 23, WM. Beverly S. Scott had served in Company K, 34th Virginia Infantry, during the Civil War (Beverly Scott's compiled service record, RG 109, M382, R49).

44. Notes on this property are in box 19, folders 1 and 2, and in box 20, folder 1, TN. See

also CB to LCB, 14 Oct. 1869, TN; CB to LCB, 29 Dec. 1871, PBE; and RSE to CB, 17 Mar. 1869, TN.

45. RSE to CB, 17 Mar. 1869, TN; Charles Field to LCB, 18 May 1865, 23 Aug. 1866, TN; CB to LCB, 6 Mar. 1870, TN.

46. Hugh Reynolds to RSE, 31 Mar. 1871, PBE; CB to LCB, 3 Nov. 1870, TN; William Randolph to RSE, 2 Dec. 1868, TN; Thomas Allen to CB, 14 Nov. 1870, TN; Thomas Allen to CB, 16 Sept. 1871, TN. Randolph had commanded Company B, Thirty-ninth Virginia Cavalry Battalion (Wallace, *Guide*, 68).

47. CB to RSE, 18 Jan. 1870, TN; LCB to CB, 11 Dec. 1868, TN; CB to LCB, 2 Jan. 1869, TN.

48. RSE to Robert Carter, 18 Dec. 1868, TN; note in box 20, folder 1, TN. Ewell hired Randolph despite indications that he may have mismanaged Tarpley's cotton crop the previous year (CB to LCB, 2 Jan. 1869, TN).

49. Ewell 1869 diary, 5 Jan., 14 Mar., 3 June 1869, folder 3, PBE; CB to Susan Brown, 9 July 1869, TN; RSE to CB, 5 Dec. 1869, TN.

50. William Randolph to RSE, 5 June 1869, TN.

51. RSE to LCB, 30 Dec. 1869, TN; C. V. Snell to RSE, 30 Mar. 1870, TN.

52. RSE to CB, 30 Dec. 1869, TN; RSE to LCB, 30 Dec. 1869, 2 Jan. 1870, TN.

53. RSE to LCB, 2 Jan. 1870, TN; CB to LCB, 29 Jan. 1870, TN; note in box 20, folder 1, TN. Ewell and Randolph jointly owned all the stock, farming implements, and other personal property at Tarpley.

54. CB to LCB, 26 May, 10 June 1868, TN; LCB to RSE, 27, 28 May 1868, TN; LCB to CB, 13 June 1868, TN.

55. LCB to CB, 17 May 1869, TN.

56. LCB to CB, 8 Jan. 1870, TN.

57. LCB to RSE, 19 Dec. 1869, TN; RSE to LCB, 22, 30 Dec. 1869, TN.

58. LCB to RSE, 31 Dec. 1869, PBE; LCB to RSE, two undated letters, box 6, folder 13, TN.

59. LCB to RSE, 19, 31 Dec. 1869, PBE; RSE to LCB, 22, 30 Dec. 1869, TN; LCB to RSE, undated and 3 Jan. 1869 [*sic*; 1870], box 6, folder 13, TN.

60. Campbell Family Bible Records, box 4, item 5, GWC.

61. Ewell 1870 appointment book, 9, 11, 14 Feb. 1870, folder 3, PBE; CB to LCB, 18 Feb. 1870, TN.

62. RSE to LCB, 14 Feb. 1870, TN.

63. CB to Susan Brown, 25, 27 Feb. 1870, TN; William C. Davis, *Confederate General*, 6:8–9; Robert Carter to RSE, 2 Feb. 1871, TN; CB to LCB, 16 Apr. 1871, TN; RSE to CB, 14 Feb. 1871, TN.

64. CB to LCB, 8, 14 Apr. 1870, TN; CB to LCB, 3 Mar. 1870, PBE.

65. CB to LCB, 6 Mar. 1870, TN; Lizinka Ewell's will, Maury County, Tenn., Records, R184, book F, pp. 414–16, TSLA; Carter Stevenson to RSE, 3 Aug. 1870, 30 Mar. 1871, TN; A. W. Garber to RSE, 16 June 1870, TN.

66. RSE to John Cooke, 21 June 1871, Cooke Family Papers, VHS. The Ewells' destination is based on letters sent to them during their vacation by Campbell Brown (CB to RSE, 25 July 1870, TN; CB to LCB, 25, 28 July 1870, TN).

67. RSE to LCB, 14, 16, 21, 29 Oct. 1870, TN.

68. RSE to LCB, 8, 26 Nov. 1870, TN.

69. CB to LCB, 29 Jan. 1870, TN; RSE to LCB, 27 Oct. 1870, TN; RSE to CB, 1 Nov. 1870, TN. For additional comments by Ewell on his managers, see RSE to LCB, 26 Nov., 1 Dec. 1870, TN.

70. RSE to LCB, 21 Oct. 1870, TN; CB to LCB, 25 Nov. 1870, TN.

71. RSE to LCB, 3 Nov. 1870, TN. Compare RSE to LCB, 2 Dec. 1870, TN.

72. LCB to CB, 4, 29 Dec. 1870, 5 Apr. 1871, TN.

73. Robert Carter to RSE, 2 Feb. 1871, TN; CB to RSE, 5 Feb. 1871, PBE; Hugh Reynolds to RSE, 12 Feb. 1871, PBE; LCB to CB, 22 Feb. 1871, TN; CB to LCB, 8 Apr. 1871, TN. See also CB to LCB, 5 Jan. 1871, TN, and Hugh Reynolds to RSE, 9 Jan. 1871, TN. Ewell made Reynolds his legal attorney at Tarpley (note in box 20, folder 1, TN). Ewell traveled to Tarpley in November 1871 to oversee the harvest. On the way he stopped in Memphis, Tennessee, where he paid a visit to Jefferson Davis (RSE to LCB, 16, 25 Nov. 1871, TN).

74. CB to LCB, 29 Dec. 1870, PBE; Hugh Reynolds to RSE, 27, 31 Mar. 1871, PBE; Hugh Reynolds to RSE, 28 Apr. 1871, TN; LCB to CB, 5 Apr. 1871, TN; Carter Stevenson to CB, 8 Sept. 1871, TN. Ewell employed between thirty and fifty pickers (RSE to LCB, 4 Dec. 1871, TN).

75. RSE to CB, 8, 22 Dec. 1871, TN; LCB to CB, 24, 27 Dec. 1871, TN.

Chapter 32

1. Nashville *Republican Banner*, 26 Jan. 1872; *Southern Home* (Charlotte, N.C.), 5 Feb. 1872.

2. Columbia *Herald*, 2 Feb. 1872; LCB to CB, 5 Jan. 1872, TN; Nashville *Union and American*, 26 Jan. 1872.

3. LCB to CB, 21, 24, 27 Dec. 1871, 5 Jan. 1872, TN; M. S. Caruthers to LCB, 26, 29 Dec. 1871, TN; John L. T. Snead to RSE, 2 Apr. 1870, TN. In at least one letter, Lizinka referred to the school as the Spring Hill Academy.

4. "Bivouac 18," 566; Isham W. Harris to RSE, 28 Oct. 1869, TN; Anna von Kasoff(?) to RSE, 25 May 1866(?), box 8, folder 8, TN; RSE to Mrs. E. H. Brown, 14 Apr. 1867, Smith Papers, FRSP.

5. Robert Lee to RSE, 3 Mar. 1868, TN. This letter is quoted, with some changes, in John William Jones's *Personal Reminiscences*, 117–18. Ewell apparently never followed through with the pledge. Following his death in 1872, Brig. Gen. Robert D. Lilley wrote to Campbell Brown inquiring whether General Ewell had included the endowment in his will. He insisted that the pledge had been unconditional and urged Brown, as executor of the will, to honor it. Brown disagreed. He believed his stepfather had pledged the money for the purpose of increasing General Lee's salary. Now that Lee was dead, he argued, the pledge was no longer valid, and he was not obliged to honor it (CB to BSE, 12 Apr., 12 July 1872, WM).

6. HB to Mildred Lee, 30 April [year?], section 23, Lee Family Papers, VHS; William Allan to RSE, 22 Oct. 1870, TN; "Sketch of the Lee Memorial Association," 390; LCB to RSE, 30 Nov. 1870, TN. William N. Pendleton was elected chairman of the executive committee, John C. Breckinridge was the association's president, and Joe Johnston was its vice-president. Other vice-presidents included Jubal Early and Walter Taylor (Va.), P. G. T. Beauregard (La.), D. H. Hill (N.C.), Wade Hampton (S.C.), William Hardee (Ala.), Stephen Lee (Miss.), John Hood (Tex.), Isaac Trimble (Md.), John Marmaduke (Mo.), William Preston (Ky.), and James Tappan (Ark.).

7. Robert Lee to RSE, 31 July 1865, Milligan Papers, MHS; Robert Lee circular letter to generals, 31 July 1865, PBE.

8. Edward Pollard to RSE, undated letter, box 7, folder 9, TN; RSE to LE, 22 Apr. 1866, LC; Jedediah Hotchkiss to RSE, 1 Feb. 1866, TN; Henry Dawson to RSE, undated letter, box 6, folder 9, TN; Ewell manuscript fragment, box 1, folder 20, PBE.

9. Campbell Family Bible Records, box 4, item 5, GWC. See Campbell genealogical chart in Appendix F.

10. CB to LE, 10 Apr. 1872, WM.

11. HB to ESE, 15 Apr. 1872, WM; HB to LCB, 19 Mar. 1870, TN. See also LCB to RSE, 30 Nov. 1870, TN.

12. For examples of the general's 1869 ailments, see RSE to LCB, 5 [Dec.] 1869, box 9, folder 5, TN; RSE to LCB, undated 1869 letter, box 9, folder 5, TN; LCB to CB, 20 Mar. 1869, TN; CB to Susan Brown, 15 Aug. 1869, TN; TTG to RSE, 6 Oct. 1869, TN; RSE to ESE, 11 Nov. 1869, LC. For information on Ewell's health in 1871, see LCB to CB, 12 Feb. [1871], 12 Dec. 1871, box 12, folder 7, TN; LCB to CB, 28 Feb., 31 Mar. 1871, TN; LCB to RSE, 27 Sept. 1871, PBE; CB to LCB, 1 Dec. 1871, PBE.

13. LCB to CB, 21 Dec. 1871, TN; Susan Brown to CB, 22 Dec. 1871, TN; Nashville *Union and American*, 26 Jan. 1872.

14. LCB to CB, 8 Jan. 1872, TN.

15. HB to LE, 31 Jan. 1872, WM; Nashville *Republican Banner*, 26 Jan. 1872; WS to BSE, 25 Jan. 1872, WM; LCB to CB, 10 Jan. 1872, TN. Drs. Joseph C. Greenfield Jr., Marvin Rozear, and G. Ralph Corey of the Duke University Medical Center believe Ewell and the other members of the household may have suffered from a particularly deadly strain of influenza.

16. Nashville *Republican Banner*, 26 Jan. 1872; WS to BSE, 25 Jan. 1872, WM; HB to LE, 31 Jan. 1872, WM.

17. HB to LE, 31 Jan. 1872, WM.

18. Ewell's will and codicil are registered in Maury County Records, R184, book F, pp. 414–16, TSLA. The wills were probated on 13 June 1872 (Nashville, Tenn., Chancery Court Minutes for that date in book V, pp. 390–98, TSLA). Ewell could not remember the name of Jesse Ewell's grandson, which suggests that his bequest to him was motivated by charity rather than from any personal consideration. The boy (Jesse Ewell V) was the son of Dr. Jesse Ewell's eldest son, John Smith Magruder Ewell. His mother died at an early age, and he was reared by his grandparents at Dunblane (Alice M. Ewell, *Virginia Scene*, 40, 52, 56, 68, 107).

19. WS to BSE, 25 Jan. 1872, WM; HB to LE, 24, 25, 31 Jan. 1872, WM; LCB to CB, 8 Jan. 1872, TN; Nashville *Republican Banner*, 23 Jan. 1872; CB to BSE, 26, 28 Mar. 1872, WM.

20. HB to LE, 24, 25, 31 Jan. 1872, WM; CB to BSE, undated letter (ca. 1872), folder 1, WM.

21. LCB to CB, 10 Jan. 1872, TN; HB to LE, 24, 25, 31 Jan. 1872, WM; WS to BSE, 25 Jan. 1872, WM.

22. Nashville *Republican Banner*, 23 Jan. 1872; CB to ESE, 23 Jan. 1872 telegram, WM.

23. WS to BSE, 25 Jan. 1872, WM. See also an unidentified newspaper clipping in Campbell Brown's scrapbook, box 20, folder 13, TN.

24. Henry S. Foote, *Bench and Bar*, 172; Nashville *Republican Banner*, 25, 26 Jan. 1872; HB to LE, 24, 25, 31 Jan. 1872, WM. The Campbell family plot is in section NE-28, lot 9, south of and adjacent to Oak Avenue. Others now buried in the plot include Harriot Turner, David and Rebecca Hubbard, and Lizinka's brother Benjamin Stoddert Campbell, who had died as an infant in 1822.

25. Nashville *Republican Banner*, 26 Jan. 1872; WS to BSE, 25 Jan. 1872, WM; HB to LE, 31 Jan. 1872, WM.

26. WS to BSE, 5 Feb. 1872, WM. In addition to the bequests made by General Ewell in his codicil, his brothers and sister also received title to the Barrancas, his 260-acre farm in Maury County, which they were able to sell for $6,500. The Ewells' wills were probated in Nashville Chancery Court on 13 June 1872. In a highly complex and tedious legal decision, the court decreed that Lizinka's estate (valued at more than $240,000) and that portion of General Ewell's

estate not specifically bequeathed to members of his family be evenly divided between Campbell and Hattie (Maury County Records, R184, book F, p. 416, TSLA; Deed 3F246 between Thomas Gibson and Benjamin Ewell registered 7 Oct. 1880, Register of Deeds, Maury County Land Records, Columbia, Tenn.; and Chancery Court Minutes, Nashville, Tenn., book U, pp. 298–302, and book V, pp. 390–98, TSLA).

27. Nashville *Republican Banner*, 26 Jan. 1872; undated notes in box 2, folder 44, PBE, and in folder 22, WM; Harriot S. Turner, "Recollections," 176.

28. HB to LE, 24, 25, 31 Jan., 27 Feb. 1872, WM; HB to ESE, 15 Apr. 1872, WM. "Major Yeatman" may have been Capt. William E. Yeatman of the Second Tennessee Infantry.

29. WS to BSE, 25 Jan. 1872, WM; Nashville *Republican Banner*, 26 Jan. 1872; William Reynolds to CB, 27 Jan. 1872, PBE.

30. HB to ESE, 15 Apr. 1872, WM; WS to BSE, 25 Jan. 1872, WM; Nashville *Republican Banner*, 26 Jan. 1872.

31. Nashville *Republican Banner*, 26 Jan. 1872; Nashville *Union and American*, 26 Jan. 1872; *New York Times*, 26 Jan. 1872; Richmond *Daily Dispatch*, 27 Jan. 1872.

32. Memphis *Daily Appeal*, 26 Jan. 1872; *Southern Home* (Charlotte, N.C.), 5 Feb. 1872.

33. Joseph E. Johnston to BSE, 30 Jan. 1872, LC.

34. Record of funerals, St. Peter's Episcopal Church, Columbia, Tenn.; Nashville *Republican Banner*, 27 Jan. 1872; Nashville *Union and American*, 27 Jan. 1872.

Epilogue

1. *Southern Home* (Charlotte, N.C.), 5 Feb. 1872. John William Jones also used this phrase to describe Ewell in "Career," 84.

2. Jubal A. Early, "Review," 260. See also Fremantle, *Three Months*, 184–85, and John William Jones, *Personal Reminiscences*, 187.

3. Edward Reeve to wife, 21 Jan. 1862, Reeve Papers, SHC. James Longstreet, in a newspaper article, told a reporter that "Ewell was greatly [A. P.] Hill's superior in every respect; a safe reliable corps commander, always zealously seeking to do his duty. In execution he was the equal of Jackson, perhaps, but in independent command he was far inferior" (Richmond *Times-Dispatch*, 12 Nov. 1911).

Appendix C

1. LCB 1866–67 notebook, box 1, folder 3, PBE; LCB to CB, 21 Aug. 1865, TN; CB to LCB, 18 June 1868, 28 Feb. 1869, TN; note in box 8, folder 5, Provine Papers, TSLA.

2. CB 1868 diary, 22 Apr., 17 June 1868, box 14, folder 1, TN.

3. CB 1868 diary, 8 Oct. 1868, box 14, folder 1, TN.

4. Ibid.; Chancery Court Minutes, Nashville, Tenn., 10 Oct. 1872, book U, pp. 298–302, TSLA.

5. Chancery Court Minutes, Nashville, Tenn., 10 Oct. 1872, book U, pp. 298–302, TSLA.

6. Campbell Brown's notes on George W. Campbell's will, box 20, folder 6, TN; copy of the Property Book of the Freedman's Bureau, box 1, folder 16, PBE; CB to LCB, 10 Sept. 1865, FC; CB to LCB, 11 June 1868, TN; Chancery Court Minutes, Nashville, Tenn., 10 Oct. 1872, book U, pp. 298–302, TSLA.

7. Chancery Court Minutes, Nashville, Tenn., 10 Oct. 1872, book U, pp. 298–302, TSLA.

8. Ibid.

9. Ibid.; note in box 19, folder 5, TN; Campbell Brown's notes on George W. Campbell's will, box 20, folder 6, TN.

10. Chancery Court Minutes, Nashville, Tenn., 10 Oct. 1872, book U, pp. 298–302, TSLA.

11. LCB to CB, 21 Aug. 1865, 6 Feb. 1868, TN; CB to LCB, 10 Sept. 1865, FC; CB to LCB, 24 Apr. 1868, TN.

12. Copy of Property Book of the Freedman's Bureau, box 1, folder 16, PBE; CB diary, 17 June 1868, box 14, folder 1, TN; CB to LCB, 28 Feb. 1869, TN; Chancery Court Minutes, Nashville, Tenn., 10 Oct. 1872, book U, pp. 298–302, TSLA.

13. E. P. Hotchkiss, Register of Descriptions of Abandoned & Confiscated Property, Freedman's Bureau Records, RG 56, p. 47, NA; Campbell Brown's notes on George W. Campbell's will, box 20, folder 6, TN; Chancery Court Minutes, Nashville, Tenn., 10 Oct. 1872, book U, pp. 298–302, TSLA; note in box 19, folder 1, TN.

14. Chancery Court Minutes, Nashville, Tenn., 10 Oct. 1872, book U, pp. 298–302, TSLA.

15. Ibid.

16. Campbell Brown's notes on George W. Campbell's will, box 20, folder 6, TN; notes in box 19, folders 5 and 8, TN; TTG to LCB, 1 Feb. 1854, TN; LCB to Jonathan L. McKay, undated letter, box 9, folder 1, TN.

17. Chancery Court Minutes, Nashville, Tenn., 10 Oct. 1872, book U, pp. 298–302, TSLA.

18. Campbell Brown's notes on George W. Campbell's will, box 20, folder 6, TN.

19. Newsom, Horton & Co. to LCB, 22 June 1871, TN; Chancery Court Minutes, Nashville, Tenn., 10 Oct. 1872, book U, pp. 298–302, TSLA.

20. Chancery Court Minutes, Nashville, Tenn., 10 Oct. 1872, book U, pp. 298–302, TSLA.

21. Campbell Brown's notes on George W. Campbell's will, box 20, folder 6, TN; LCB to CB, 17 Feb. 1867, TN.

22. Chancery Court Minutes, Nashville, Tenn., 10 Oct. 1872, book U, pp. 298–302, TSLA.

23. James A. Robey to CB, 26 Sept. 1865, PBE; Campbell Brown's notes on George W. Campbell's will, box 20, folder 6, TN.

24. Jan. 1867 entry in CB's 1866 diary, GWC; LCB to CB, 12 Jan.(?) 1867, box 11, folder 2, TN.

25. LCB to CB, 17 Mar. 1869, TN.

26. A sketch of the property appears in box 19, folder 1, TN, and notes on it may be found in box 19, folders 2 and 7, and in box 20, folder 1, TN; CB to LCB, 14 Oct. 1869, TN; CB to LCB, 29 Dec. 1871, PBE.

27. A note on the property appears in box 19, folder 1, TN.

28. J. T. Ward to RSE, 4 Aug. 1866, PBE; LCB to CB, 19 Nov. 1867, TN; R. A. Hooe to RSE, 28 Oct. 1867, TN; R. A. Hooe to LCB, 8 Sept. 1871, TN.

Appendix G

1. Alfred Roman to P. G. T. Beauregard, 29 Dec. 1884, Palmer Papers, Western Reserve Historical Society.

2. George F. Harrison, "Ewell at First Manassas," 357.

Appendix H

1. Ewell account of the Valley Campaign, box 1, folder 18, PBE.
2. *OR* 12(1):704–5.
3. *OR* 12(1):609.
4. *OR* 51(2):562.
5. *OR* 12(3):899.
6. *OR* 12(3):899.
7. *OR* 12(3):899.
8. CBM.

Appendix I

1. 1860 Virginia census records.
2. Interview with William O. Hutchison.
3. CBM.
4. Interview with William O. Hutchison.
5. Alice M. Ewell, *Virginia Scene*, 62; CBM.
6. Interview with William O. Hutchison.
7. E. R. Conner III, *One Hundred Old Cemeteries*, 167.

Appendix J

1. John B. Gordon, *Reminiscences*, 157.
2. Hoke, *Great Invasion*, 494 n.
3. Mary Johnston, "Gettysburg," 395.
4. Note in box 23, Daniel Papers, UVA.
5. Seymour, *Memoirs*, 79.
6. CBM.
7. Hotchkiss diary, 3 July 1863, R1, HP.

Appendix K

1. *OR* 46(1):1132, 1295; CB to Charles Venable, Venable Papers, VHS; Robinson, "Sailor's Creek"; Tremain, *Last Hours*, 153–55.
2. *OR* 46(1):953.
3. *OR* 46(1):915, 942.
4. *OR* 46(1):984; Day, "Gen. Ewell."
5. T.H.F. article.
6. W. A. Watson, "Fighting at Sailor's Creek," 148.
7. Robinson, "Sailor's Creek."
8. Lawrence, "Capture of General Ewell."
9. *OR* 46(1):1295; CB to Charles Venable, 13 Jan. 1888, Venable Papers, VHS.

★ ★ ★

Bibliography

Manuscript Sources

Alabama Department of Archives and History, Montgomery
    Cullen Andrew Battle, "The Third Alabama Regiment." In the Reverend J. H. B. Hall
        Papers.
    Lida Bestor Robertson Papers
Chicago Historical Society, Chicago, Ill.
    P. G. T. Beauregard Papers
    Henry Kyd Douglas Papers
    Richard S. Ewell Papers
    Gunther Family Papers
    Thomas J. Jackson Papers
    William L. Jackson Papers
    Robert E. Lee Papers
    Alexander S. Pendleton Papers
    Earl Van Dorn Papers
College of William and Mary, Manuscript Department, Williamsburg, Va.
    "Buildings and Grounds—College Cemetery." Subject file.
    Anne West Chapman, "Benjamin Stoddert Ewell: A Biography." Ph.D. dissertation,
        1984.
    Benjamin Stoddert Ewell Papers
    Faculty File, Benjamin Stoddert Ewell, biographical file
    Faculty Minutes (1859)
    Harriot Stoddert Turner, "The Ewells of Virginia, Especially of Stony Lonesome"
Davidson College Archives, Davidson, N.C.
    William E. Ardrey Diary
Duke University, William R. Perkins Library, Manuscript Department, Durham, N.C.
    William B. G. Andrews Papers
    Patrick H. Cain Papers
    Confederate Veterans Papers
    John Warwick Daniel Papers
    Benjamin Stoddert Ewell and Richard Stoddert Ewell Papers
    Richard Stoddert Ewell Letterbook
    Richard Stoddert Ewell Papers
    Samuel Wragg Ferguson Memoir

Edward Harden Papers
David B. Harris Papers
John Cheves Haskell Memoir
F. W. M. Holliday Papers
Benjamin Hubert Papers
Frederick L. Hudgins Papers
Bradley Tyler Johnson Papers
Williamson Kelly Papers
Munford-Ellis Family Papers
G. Peyton Letter
Fairfax County Land Deeds Office, Fairfax, Va.
Deed Books L3 and V2
Filson Club, Manuscript Department, Louisville, Ky.
Brown-Ewell Family Papers
Fredericksburg and Spotsylvania County Battlefields Memorial National Military Park,
Fredericksburg, Va.
Alexander Betts Autograph Book
Seaton Gales Letter
Radford Eugene Mobley Diary
William L. Nuckolls Letter
F. M. Parker Letter
George Quintus Peyton Memoir
James Power Smith Papers
Georgia Historical Society, Atlanta
Hilton Papers
Gettysburg National Military Park, Gettysburg, Pa.
Kathleen R. Georg, "The John Blocher Farm Historical Report"
Handley Library, Winchester, Va.
Mary Lee Diary
Abram Schultz Miller, "Civil War Letters of Abram Schultz Miller Written to his Wife,
Julia Virginia Miller, 1861–1864"
Kate S. Sperry Jr., "Surrender? Never Surrender! The Diary of a Confederate Girl"
Huntington Library, San Marino, Calif.
J. E. B. Stuart Papers
Kennesaw Mountain National Military Park, Kennesaw, Ga.
Charles W. McArthur Letter
Library of Congress, Manuscript Division, Washington, D.C.
George Washington Campbell Papers
Thomas S. Doyle Papers
Jubal Anderson Early Papers
Richard Stoddert Ewell Papers
Jedediah Hotchkiss Papers
Henry J. Hunt Papers
Marsena R. Patrick Diary
Manassas National Battlefield Park, Manassas, Va.
Hamberton Belton Letter
Robert E. L. Krick Report on Ewell's Wounding
Maryland Historical Society, Baltimore
Robert Goodloe Harper Carroll Papers

Civil War Collection
Edward L. Heinichen Memoir
Milligan Papers
John Eager Howard Post Papers
Ringgold Papers
Walker Papers
Maury County Courthouse, Columbia, Tenn.
Register of Deeds, Maury County Land Records
Mississippi Department of Archives and History, Jackson
William McWillie Notebooks
Museum of the Confederacy, Eleanor S. Brockenbrough Library, Richmond, Va.
Chilton Papers
Ewell Letters to Lizinka C. Brown (folder E-332)
Ewell Letter to George W. Randolph (Maryland Room, folder 613G, leaf #1)
Robert E. Lee Letter
Hunter McGuire, Address on General T. J. Jackson Delivered at V.M.I.
Pendleton Papers
Peyton Letter (folder S-767A)
William B. Taliaferro Papers
National Archives, Washington, D.C.
1830, 1840, 1850, 1860, 1870 Census Records, including Agricultural and Slave Schedules
Applications for Army Promotions, Record Group 107
Compiled Service Records of Confederate Generals and Staff Officers, and Nonregi-
mental Enlisted Men, Record Group 109, microcopy 331
General Records of the Department of the Treasury, Record Group 56
Index to Letters Received by the Office of the Adjutant General (Main Series), 1846,
1861–1889, Record Group 94, microcopy 725
Inspection Reports and Related Records Received by the Inspection Branch in the
Confederate Adjutant and Inspector General's Office, Record Group 109, micro-
copy 935
Letters Received by the Confederate Adjutant and Inspector General, 1861–1865,
Record Group 109, microcopy 474
Letters Received by the Confederate Secretary of War, 1861–1865, Record Group 109,
microcopy 437
Letters Received by the Office of the Adjutant General (Main Series), 1822–1860,
Record Group 94, microcopy 567
Letters Received by the Office of the Adjutant General (Main Series), 1861–1870,
Record Group 94, microcopy 619
Miscellaneous Letters of the Department of State, 1789–1906, Record Group 59, micro-
copy 179
Orders and General Orders, Department of New Mexico, 1849–1868, vol. 36, Record
Group 393, pt. 1, entry 3170
Records of the Bureau of Land Management, Record Group 49
Records of the Bureau of Refugees, Freedmen, and Abandoned Lands, Record Group 105
Records of the Virginia Forces, 1861, Record Group 109, microcopy 998
Register of Letters Received, and Letters Received by Headquarters, Ninth Military De-
partment, 1848–1853, Record Group 393, microcopy 1102
Registers of Letters Received, and Letters Received by Headquarters, Department of
New Mexico, 1854–1865, Record Group 393, microcopy 1120

Returns from Regular Army Cavalry Regiments, 1833–1916, Record Group 94, microcopy 744

Returns from U.S. Military Posts, 1800–1916, Record Group 94, microcopy 617

Special Orders, Department of New Mexico, 1849–1868, vol. 27, Record Group 393, pt. 1, entry 3172

Unified Papers and Slips Belonging in Confederate Compiled Service Records, Record Group 94, microcopy 347

U.S. Military Academy Cadet Application Papers, 1805–1866, Record Group 94, microcopy 688

New Hampshire Historical Society, Concord

John B. Bachelder Papers

New York State Library, Manuscript Division, Albany

Diary Kept by a Confederate Artilleryman, 1861–January 1864

North Carolina Department of Archives and History, Raleigh

Henry A. Chambers Diary

Eli S. Coble Papers

Thomas Pollock Devereux Jr. Letter Book

F. M. Parker Papers

Stephen D. Ramseur Papers

Petersburg National Battlefield, Petersburg, Va.

Diary of Cyrus B. Comstock, typescript edited by Merlin E. Sumner

Donald C. Pfanz, Personal Correspondence

Mildred H. Ewell Letters

William D. Matter Letter

Harry Myers Letter

Noah Andre Trudeau Letters

Prince William County Land Deeds Office, Manassas, Va.

Deed Book 34

Rice University, Houston, Tex.

Jefferson Davis Association Papers

Rockbridge Historical Society, Lexington, Va.

Theodore Barclay Letters

St. Peter's Episcopal Church, Columbia, Tenn.

Record of Communicants

Record of Funerals

Tennessee Historical Society, Nashville

William Alexander Provine Papers

Tennessee State Library and Archives, Manuscript Department, Nashville

Campbell Brown and Richard S. Ewell Papers

Chancery Court Minutes

David Hubbard Papers

Sara T. McKennon, "Maury County, Tennessee 1870 Census"

Maury County Records

Polk Papers

William A. Provine Papers

Felix Robinson Smith, "Alphabetical List of the Dead in the City Cemetery, Nashville, Tennessee"

Yeatman-Polk Papers

Troup County Archives, Troup County, Ga.

Julius L. Schaub Papers

Tulane University, New Orleans, La.
    Jefferson Davis Papers
    Louisiana Historical Association Collection
Union College, Special Collections, Schaffer Library, Schenectady, N.Y.
    John Stone Bradley File
United States Army Military History Institute, Manuscript Department, Carlisle Barracks, Pa.
    Carlisle Barracks Collection
    Gregory A. Coco Collection
    Robert E. Lee and George Washington Custis Lee Papers
    Lewis Leigh Papers
    John W. Stott Diary, Civil War Times Illustrated Collection
United States Military Academy Library, Special Collections, Manuscript Collection, West
    Point, N.Y.
    Richard S. Ewell Papers
    Abraham R. Johnston Papers
    Journal of the Dialectic Society, 1840–1844, and membership roll, vol. 8, 1839–1842
    Library Circulation Records, 1836–1841
    Post Orders, 1832–1842
    Record Group 404, Series 14, 96, 101, 102, 105, 176, 178, 242, 245, 299
    Register of Punishments, 1837–1847
University of Georgia, Manuscript Department, Athens
    John Brown Gordon Papers
University of Michigan, William J. Clements Library, Ann Arbor
    Seymour Papers, Schoff Civil War Collection
University of North Carolina, Southern Historical Collection, Chapel Hill
    William Allan Papers
    Thomas F. Boatright Papers
    Thomas Claiborne Papers
    Burke Davis Papers
    Peter Wilson Hairston Papers
    Heartt-Wilson Papers
    Joseph M. Kern Papers
    Noble-Attaway Papers
    William Nelson Pendleton Papers
    Polk-Brown-Ewell Papers
    George Washington Polk, "Some Reflections and Reminiscences." Polk Papers.
    Edward Payson Reeve Papers
    Westwood A. Todd, "Reminiscences of the War Between the States, From April '61 to
        July '65"
    Charles S. Venable Papers
University of South Carolina, Columbia
    Milledge L. Bonham Papers
    Samuel Wicliff Melton Papers
University of Texas, Manuscript Department, Austin
    Jesse Ewell Papers
University of the South, Manuscript Division, Sewanee, Tenn.
    David Pise Journal
University of Virginia, Manuscript Department, Charlottesville
    Lawrence O'Bryan Branch Papers
    John Warwick Daniel Papers

Ewell Family Papers
Douglas Southall Freeman Papers
Washington Hands Memoir
James L. Kemper Papers
Virginia Historical Society, Richmond
Willie Walker Caldwell, "The Life of General James A. Walker"
George Llewellyn Christian Papers
Confederate States of America, Army, Department of Northern Virginia, Special
Orders
Cooke Family Papers
John Warwick Daniel Papers
Early Family Papers
Jubal Early Memoir
Thomas Ewell Papers
Achilles Whitlocke Hoge Diary
Hoge Family Papers
Watkins Kearns Diary
Lacy Family Papers
Osmun Latrobe Diary
Lee Family Papers
Mary Custis Lee Scrapbook
Lyons Family Papers
McCarthy Papers
Hunter McGuire Papers
Minor Family Papers
Pegram-Johnson-McIntosh Papers
St. Paul's Church Records, Richmond, Virginia
Alfred Lewis Scott Manuscript, "Memoir of Service in the Confederate Army"
George Edgar Sipe, "Civil War Recollections"
F. W. Smith Papers
James Ewell Brown Stuart Papers
Talcott Family Papers
Thornton Family Papers
Charles Scott Venable Papers
Georgia Callis West Papers
Charles Wight Memoir
Western Reserve Historical Society, Cleveland, Ohio
Cooke Papers
William P. Palmer Papers
West Virginia University, Manuscript Department, Morgantown
Henry J. Mugler Diary
Joseph C. Snider Diary
William H. Willcox, Washington, D.C.
Orlando Willcox Letter

Newspapers

Abbeville (S.C.) *The Medium*
Atlanta (Ga.) *Southern Confederacy*

Carlisle (Pa.) *Evening Sentinel*
Charleston (S.C.) *Mercury*
Charlotte (N.C.) *The Southern Home*
Charlottesville (Va.) *Progress*
Columbia (Ga.) *Daily Enquirer*
Columbia (Tenn.) *Beacon*
Columbia (Tenn.) *Herald*
Gettysburg (Pa.) *Star and Sentinel*
Lexington (Va.) *Gazette*
Lynchburg (Va.) *Daily Republican*
Macon (Ga.) *Daily Telegraph*
Montgomery (Ala.) *Daily Advertiser*
Nashville (Tenn.) *Republican Banner*
Nashville (Tenn.) *Union and American*
Newnan (Ga.) *Herald*
New Orleans (La.) *Daily Picayune*
New York (N.Y.) *Herald*
Philadelphia (Pa.) *Record*
Richmond (Va.) *Commercial Bulletin*
Richmond (Va.) *Daily Enquirer*
Richmond (Va.) *Daily Whig*
Richmond (Va.) *Sentinel*
Richmond (Va.) *Times-Dispatch*
Richmond (Va.) *Whig*
Staunton (Va.) *Spectator*
Staunton (Va.) *Vindicator*
Tucson (Ariz.) *Weekly Arizonian*
Washington (D.C.) *National Tribune*

Books, Articles, and Pamphlets

"About the Burial Services of Capt. Latane." *Confederate Veteran* 10 (1902): 62.

Acuna, Rudolph F. "Ignacio Pesqueira: Sonoran Caudillo." *Arizona and the West* 12 (1970): 139–72.

Alexander, Edward P. *Fighting for the Confederacy.* Edited by Gary W. Gallagher. Chapel Hill: University of North Carolina Press, 1989.

———. *Military Memoirs of a Confederate.* New York: Charles Scribner's Sons, 1907.

———. "Tribute to Confederate Veterans." *Confederate Veteran* 19 (1911): 227–28.

Allan, William. "History of the Campaign of Gen. T. J. (Stonewall) Jackson in the Shenandoah Valley in Virginia." *Southern Historical Society Papers* 43 (1920): 113–294.

———. *History of the Campaign of Gen. T. J. (Stonewall) Jackson in the Shenandoah Valley of Virginia from November 4, 1861, to June 17, 1862.* Philadelphia: Lippincott, 1880.

———. "Letter from Colonel William Allan, of Ewell's Staff." *Southern Historical Society Papers* 4 (1877): 77–80.

Allen, C. T. "Fight at Chaffin's Farm, or Fort Harrison." *Confederate Veteran* 13 (1905): 418.

Altshuler, Constance W., ed. *Latest from Arizona! The Hesperian Letters, 1859–1861.* Tucson: Arizona Historical Society, 1969.

Alvey, Edward, Jr. *History of the Presbyterian Church of Fredericksburg, Virginia, 1808–1976.* Fredericksburg, Va.: Session of the Presbyterian Church, 1976.

Amason, Mrs. H. W., ed. *This They Remembered.* Washington, Ga.: Washington Pub. Co., 1965.

Ambrose, Stephen E. *Duty, Honor, Country: A History of West Point.* Baltimore: Johns Hopkins University Press, 1966.

Anderson, D. W. "Major D. W. Anderson's Relation." *Southern Historical Society Papers* 21 (1893): 251–54.

Andrews, J. Cutler. *The South Reports the Civil War.* Princeton: Princeton University Press, 1970.

Andrews, Marietta M. *Scraps of Paper.* New York: Dutton, 1929.

Averell, William W. *Ten Years in the Saddle: The Memoirs of William Woods Averell.* Edited by Edward K. Eckert and Nicholas J. Amato. London: Presidio, 1978.

Avirett, James B. "Sketch of General Ashby." *Land We Love* 5 (1868): 287–90.

Bachelder, John B. "Letter from John B. Bachelder, Esq." *Southern Historical Society Papers* 5 (1878): 172–80.

Badeau, Adam. *Military History of Ulysses S. Grant.* 3 vols. New York: Appleton, 1881.

Bancroft, Hubert H. *History of Arizona and New Mexico: 1530–1880.* San Francisco: History Company, 1889.

Barnes, Will C. *Arizona Place Names.* Revised by Byrd H. Granger. Tucson: University of Arizona Press, 1960.

Barton, Randolph. *Recollections, 1861–1865.* Baltimore: Thomas & Evans, 1913.

Basler, Roy P. *The Collected Works of Abraham Lincoln.* 8 vols. New Brunswick, N.J.: Rutgers University Press, 1953.

Bates, Samuel P. *History of Pennsylvania Volunteers, 1861–5.* 5 vols. Harrisburg: B. Singerly, 1869.

Bean, William G. *The Liberty Hall Volunteers.* Charlottesville: University Press of Virginia, 1964.

———. "Stonewall Jackson's Jolly Chaplain, Beverley Tucker Lacy." *West Virginia History* 29, no. 2 (Jan. 1968): 77–96.

———. *Stonewall's Man: Sandy Pendleton.* Chapel Hill: University of North Carolina Press, 1959.

Beauregard, Pierre Gustave Toutant. *A Commentary on the Campaign and Battle of Manassas of July, 1861.* New York: G. P. Putnam's Sons, 1891.

———. "The First Battle of Bull Run." In Johnson and Buel, *Battles and Leaders*, 1:196–227.

"Bivouac 18, A.C.S. and Camp 28, U.C.V." *Confederate Veteran* 5 (1897): 566.

Blackford, Susan L. *Letters from Lee's Army, or Memoirs of Life in and out of the Army in Virginia during the War between the States.* New York: Charles Scribner's Sons, 1947.

Blackford, William W. *War Years with Jeb Stuart.* New York: Charles Scribner's Sons, 1945.

Blake, Thomas B. "The Artillery Brigade at Sailor's Creek." *Confederate Veteran* 28 (1920): 213–16.

———. "Retreat from Richmond." *Southern Historical Society Papers* 25 (1897): 139–45.

Boatner, Mark M., III. *The Civil War Dictionary.* New York: David McKay, 1959.

Bond, Frank A. "Company A, First Maryland Cavalry." *Confederate Veteran* 6 (1898): 78–80.

Booth, Andrew B. *Records of Louisiana Confederate Soldiers and Louisiana Confederate Commands.* 3 vols. New Orleans: Privately published, 1920.

Booth, George W. *Personal Reminiscences of a Maryland Soldier in the War between the States, 1861–1865.* Baltimore: Privately published, 1898.

Borcke, Heros von. *Memoirs of the Confederate War for Independence.* 2 vols. New York: Peter Sm. h, 1938.

Bosang, James. *Memoirs of a Pulaski Veteran of the Stonewall Brigade, 1861–1865.* Pulaski, Va.: B. D. Smith & Brothers, 1930.

Bourke, John G. *On the Border with Crook.* New York: Charles Scribner's Sons, 1891.

Boyd, David F. *Reminiscences of the War in Virginia.* Edited by T. Michael Parish. Austin, Tex.: Jenkins, 1989.

Boykin, Edward M. *The Falling Flag. Evacuation of Richmond, Retreat and Surrender at Appomattox. By an Officer of the Rearguard.* New York: E. J. Hale & Son, 1874.

Bradwell, I. G. "First Lesson in War." *Confederate Veteran* 33 (1925): 382–83.

———. "From Cedar Mountain to Sharpsburg." *Confederate Veteran* 29 (1921): 296–98.

———. "Gordon's Ga. Brigade in the Wilderness." *Confederate Veteran* 16 (1908): 641–42.

———. "The Grand Review." *Confederate Veteran* 31 (1923): 16–18.

———. "Morton's Ford, January 4, 1864." *Confederate Veteran* 33 (1925): 412–14.

Brainard, Mary G., comp. *Campaigns of the One Hundred and Forty-Sixth Regiment, New York State Volunteers.* New York: G. P. Putnam's Sons, 1915.

Brooks, Clinton E., and Frank D. Reeve. *Forts and Forays.* Albuquerque: University of New Mexico Press, 1948.

Brown, George Campbell. "General Ewell at Bull Run." In Johnson and Buel, *Battles and Leaders,* 1:259–61.

———. "Notes on Ewell's Division in the Campaign of 1862." *Southern Historical Society Papers* 10 (1882): 255–61.

Brown, George R. *Washington: A Not Too Serious History.* Baltimore: Norman Pub. Co., 1930.

Brown, Varina D. *A Colonel at Gettysburg and Spotsylvania.* Columbia, S.C.: State Co., 1931.

Browne, J. Ross. *Adventures in the Apache Country: A Tour through Arizona and Sonora, with Notes on the Silver Regions of Nevada.* New York: Harper & Brothers, 1869.

Bryan, Wilhelmus B. *A History of the National Capital from Its Foundation through the Period of the Adoption of the Organic Act.* 2 vols. New York: Macmillan, 1914.

Buck, Samuel D. *With the Old Confeds: Actual Experiences of a Captain in the Line.* Baltimore: H. E. Houck, 1925.

Buckley, Cornelius M. *A Frenchman, a Chaplain, a Rebel: The War Letters of Pere Louis-Hippolyte Gache, S.J.* Chicago: Loyola University Press, 1981.

Bulletin of the Dialectic Society, 1840.

Bushong, Millard K., and Dean M. Bushong. *Fightin' Tom Rosser, C.S.A.* Shippensburg, Pa.: Beidel, 1983.

Butler, Benjamin F. *Butler's Book.* Boston: Thayer, 1892.

Caldwell, J. F. J. *The History of a Brigade of South Carolinians Known First as "Gregg's," and Subsequently as "McGowan's Brigade."* Philadelphia: King & Baird, 1866.

Calkins, Christopher M. *From Petersburg to Appomattox.* Farmville, Va.: Farmville Herald, 1983.

———. *Thirty-six Hours before Appomattox.* Farmville, Va.: Farmville Herald, 1980.

"The Captured Guns at Spotsylvania Courthouse—Correction of General Ewell's Report." *Southern Historical Society Papers* 7 (1879): 535–40.

Carleton, J. Henry. *The Prairie Logbooks: Dragoon Campaigns to the Pawnee Villages in 1844, and the Rocky Mountains in 1845.* Edited by Louis Pelzer. Chicago: Caxton Club, 1943.

Carmichael, Peter S. "'Oh, for the Presence and Inspiration of Old Jack': A Lost Cause Plea for Stonewall Jackson at Gettysburg." *Civil War History* 41 (June 1995): 161–67.

Carrington, James M. "First Day on Left at Gettysburg." Richmond *Times-Dispatch,* 19 Feb. 1905.

Carson, William Clark. *My Dear Jennie.* Edited by Blake W. Corson Jr. Richmond: Dietz Press, 1982.

Carter, Harvey L. *"Dear Old Kit": The Historical Christopher Carson.* Norman: University of Oklahoma Press, 1968.

Carter, Thomas H. "Colonel Thomas H. Carter's Letter." *Southern Historical Society Papers* 21 (1893): 239–42.

———. "Letter of Colonel Thomas H. Carter." *Southern Historical Society Papers* 39 (1914): 5–7.

Casler, John O. *Four Years in the Stonewall Brigade.* Marietta, Ga.: Continental Book Co., 1951.

Catton, Bruce. *Grant Takes Command.* Boston: Little, Brown, 1968.

"Cause of Confederates in Maryland." *Confederate Veteran* 1 (1894): 17–19.

Chamberlaine, William W. *Memoirs of the Civil War between the Northern and Southern Sections of the United States of America, 1861–65.* Washington, D.C.: Byron S. Adams, 1912.

Chambers, Henry A. *Diary of Henry A. Chambers.* Edited by T. H. Pearce. Wendell, N.C.: Broadfoot's Bookmark, 1983.

Chambers, Lenoir. *Stonewall Jackson.* 2 vols. Wilmington, N.C.: Broadfoot Pub. Co., 1988.

Chesnut, Mary B. *Mary Chesnut's Civil War.* Edited by C. Vann Woodward. New Haven: Yale University Press, 1981.

Chisolm, Samuel H. "Forward, the Louisiana Brigade!" *Confederate Veteran* 27 (1919): 449.

Clark, Walter, ed. *Histories of the Several Regiments and Battalions from North Carolina in the Great War, 1861–'65, Written by Members of the Respective Commands.* 5 vols. Goldsboro, N.C.: Nash Brothers, 1901.

Cleaves, Freeman. *Rock of Chickamauga: The Life of General George H. Thomas.* Norman: University of Oklahoma Press, 1948.

Cockrell, Thomas D., and Michael B. Ballard. *A Mississippi Rebel in the Army of Northern Virginia.* Baton Rouge: Louisiana State University Press, 1995.

Coddington, Edwin B. *The Gettysburg Campaign.* Dayton, Ohio: Morningside Bookshop, 1979.

Coffin, Charles C. *The Boys of '61: or Four Years of Fighting.* Boston: Estes and Lauriet, 1881.

Coffman, Edward M. *The Old Army: A Portrait of the American Army in Peacetime.* New York: Oxford University Press, 1986.

Cohen, Henry. "A Modern Maccabean." *Publication of the American Jewish Historical Society* 6 (1897): 31–37.

Coker, James L. *History of Company G, Ninth S.C. Regiment, Infantry, S.C. Army and of Company E, Sixth S.C. Regiment, Infantry, S.C. Army.* Charleston: Walker, Evans & Cogswell, 1899.

Collis, Septima M. *A Woman's War Record.* New York: G. P. Putnam's Sons, 1889.

Colston, Frederick M. "Efficiency of General Lee's Ordnance." *Confederate Veteran* 19 (1911): 22–26.

———. "Recollections of the Last Months in the Army of Northern Virginia." *Southern Historical Society Papers* 38 (1910): 1–15.

Confederate Veteran Magazine. 40 vols. Nashville: 1893–1934.

Conley, Brian A. *Cemeteries of Fairfax County, Virginia: A Report to the Board of Supervisors.* N.p., 1994.

Connelly, William E., ed. "A Journal of the Santa Fe Trail." *Mississippi Valley Historical Review* 12 (1925): 72–98, 227–55.

Conner, E. R., III. *One Hundred Old Cemeteries of Prince William County, Virginia.* N.p., 1981.

Conner, James. *Letters of James Conner, C.S.A.* Edited by Mary Conner Moffett. Columbia, S.C.: R. L. Bryan, 1950.

Cooke, John Esten. "Humors of the Camp." In King and Derby, *Camp-Fire Sketches*, 560–65.

Cooke, Philip St. George. *Scenes and Adventures in the Army: or, Romance of a Military Life.* Philadelphia: Lindsay & Blakiston, 1857.

Coulling, Mary P. *The Lee Girls.* Winston-Salem, N.C.: John F. Blair, 1987.

Corson, William C. *My Dear Jennie.* Edited by Blake W. Corson Jr. Richmond: Dietz Press, 1982.

Couper, William. *One Hundred Years at V.M.I.* 4 vols. Richmond: Garrett & Massie, 1939.

Coxe, John. "The Battle of Gettysburg." *Confederate Veteran* 21 (1913): 433–36.

Crabtree, Beth G., and James W. Patton, eds. *"Journal of a Secesh Lady": The Diary of Catherine Ann Devereux Edmondston.* Raleigh: Division of Archives and History, 1979.

Cremony, John C. *Life among the Apaches.* Glorieta, N.M.: Rio Grande Press, 1969.

Crute, Joseph H. *Confederate Staff Officers, 1861–1865.* Powhatan, Va.: Derwent Books, 1982.

Cullum, George W. *Biographical Register of the Officers and Graduates of the U.S. Military Academy.* 7 vols. Boston: Houghton, Mifflin, 1891.

Curtis, Newton M. *From Bull Run to Chancellorsville: The Story of the Sixteenth New York Infantry, Together with Personal Reminiscences, by Newton Martin Curtis.* New York: G. P. Putnam's Sons, 1906.

Dabney, Robert L. *Life and Campaigns of Lieut.-Gen. Thomas J. Jackson (Stonewall Jackson).* New York: Blelock, 1866.

———. "Stonewall Jackson." *Southern Historical Society Papers* 11 (1883): 125–35, 145–58.

Daly, Louise H. *Alexander Cheves Haskell: The Portrait of a Man.* Norwood, Mass.: Plimpton Press, 1934.

Dame, William M. *From the Rapidan to Richmond.* Baltimore: Green-Lucas, 1920.

Daniel, Edward M. *Speeches and Orations of John Warwick Daniel.* Lynchburg, Va.: J. P. Bell, 1911.

Daniel, Frederick S. *Richmond Howitzers in the War, Four Years Campaigning with the Army of Northern Virginia, by a Member of the Company.* Richmond: Privately published, 1891.

Davis, Jefferson. *The Rise and Fall of the Confederate Government.* 2 vols. New York: Appleton, 1881.

Davis, William C. *Battle of Bull Run: A History of the First Major Campaign of the Civil War.* Garden City, N.Y.: Doubleday, 1977.

———, ed. *The Confederate General.* 6 vols. Harrisburg: National Historical Society, 1991.

Day, H. W. "Gen. Ewell." *National Tribune,* 3 Mar. 1887.

"The Death of Ashby." *Confederate Veteran* 32 (1924): 156.

Dobbins, Austin C. *Grandfather's Journal.* Dayton, Ohio: Morningside Bookstore, 1988.

Dobyns, Henry F. *The Mescalero Apache People.* Phoenix: Indian Tribal Series, 1973.

Donohoe, John C. "The Fight near Front Royal, Va." *Confederate Veteran* 22 (1914): 308–9.

Dorris, Jonathan T. *Pardon and Amnesty under Lincoln and Johnson.* Chapel Hill: University of North Carolina Press, 1953.

Douglas, Henry Kyd. *I Rode with Stonewall.* Atlanta: Mockingbird Books, 1976.

———. "Lee and Ewell at Gettysburg." *Nation* 54 (1892): 87.

———. "A Ride for Stonewall." *Southern Historical Society Papers* 21 (1893): 206–12.

Dowdey, Clifford. *The Land They Fought For.* Garden City, N.Y.: Doubleday, 1955.

———. *The Seven Days: The Emergence of Robert E. Lee.* New York: Fairfax Press, 1964.

Dowdey, Clifford, and Louis H. Manarin. *The Wartime Papers of R. E. Lee.* Boston: Little, Brown, 1961.

Driver, Robert J., Jr. *52nd Virginia Infantry.* Lynchburg, Va.: H. E. Howard, 1986.

Duke, R. T. W. "Burning of Richmond." *Southern Historical Society Papers* 25 (1897): 134–38.

Duncan, Bingham, ed. *Letters of General J. E. B. Stuart to His Wife, 1861.* Atlanta: Emory University Press, 1943.

Dunlop, W. S. *Lee's Sharpshooters.* Little Rock: Tunnah & Pittard, 1899.

Durham, Walter T. *Nashville: The Occupied City.* Nashville: Tennessee Historical Society, 1985.

Dwight, Charles S. *A South Carolina Rebel's Recollections.* Columbia, S.C.: State Co., n.d.

Early, John C. "A Southern Boy's Experience at Gettysburg." *Journal of the Military Service Institution of the United States* 48, no. 169 (Jan.–Feb. 1911): 415–23.

Early, Jubal A. *Autobiographical Sketch and Narrative of the War between the States.* Philadelphia: Lippincott, 1912.

———. "A Review by General Early." *Southern Historical Society Papers* 4 (1877): 241–81.

Eaton, W. Clement. "Frontier Life in Southern Arizona, 1858–1861." *Southwestern Historical Quarterly* 36 (Jan. 1933): 173–92.

Eberlein, Harold D., and Cortlandt V. Hubbard, *Historic Houses of George-Town & Washington City.* Richmond: Dietz Press, 1958.

Ecker, Grace D. *A Portrait of Old Georgetown.* Richmond: Garrett & Massie, 1933.

Eckert, Ralph L. *John Brown Gordon: Soldier, Southerner, American.* Baton Rouge: Louisiana State University Press, 1989.

Edmonston, James K. *My Dear Emma.* Edited by Charles W. Turner. Verona, Va.: McClure Press, 1978.

Eggleston, George C. *A Rebel's Recollections.* New York: Hurd and Houghton, 1875.

Eliot, Ellsworth, Jr. *West Point in the Confederacy.* New York: G. A. Baker, 1941.

An English Combatant. *Battle-Fields of the South.* New York: John Bradburg, 1864.

Estergreen, M. Morgan. *Kit Carson: A Portrait in Courage.* Norman: University of Oklahoma Press, 1962.

Evans, Clement A., ed. *Confederate Military History: A Library of Confederate States History . . . Written by Distinguished Men of the South.* 13 vols. Atlanta: Confederate Pub. Co., 1889.

Ewell, Alice M. "Life in Old Bel Air." Newspaper clipping in genealogical collection of Mrs. Nathaniel McGregor Ewell Jr., Charlottesville, Va.

———. *A Virginia Scene or Life in Old Prince William.* Lynchburg, Va.: J. P. Bell, 1931.

Ewell, Benjamin S. "Jackson and Ewell." *Southern Historical Society Papers* 20 (1892): 26–33.

Ewell, Richard S. "Letter of General R. S. Ewell to General Grant." *Southern Historical Society Papers* 39 (1914): 4–5.

Executive Documents Printed by Order of the House of Representatives, during the 1st Session of the Thirty-Fourth Congress, 1855–56. 16 vols. Serial 840. Washington, D.C.: Cornelius Wendell, 1856.

Farish, Thomas E. *History of Arizona.* 2 vols. Phoenix: Filmer Brothers, 1915.

Faulk, Odie B. *The U.S. Camel Corps: An Army Experiment.* New York: Oxford University Press, 1976.

Field, Charles W. "Campaign of 1864 and 1865." *Southern Historical Society Papers* 14 (1886): 542–63.

Fleming, Thomas J. *West Point: The Men and Times of the United States Military Academy.* New York: William Morrow, 1969.

Florin, Lambert. *Ghost Towns of the West.* New York: Promontory Press, 1971.

Flournoy, Henry W., ed. *Calendar of Virginia State Papers and Other Manuscripts from January 1, 1836, to April 15, 1869; Preserved in the Capitol at Richmond.* 11 vols. Richmond: R. F. Walker, 1893.

Foote, Henry S. *The Bench and Bar of the South and Southwest.* St. Louis: Soule, Thomas, & Wentworth, 1876.

Foote, Shelby. *The Civil War: A Narrative.* 3 vols. New York: Random House, 1958–74.

Forbes, Robert H. *The Penningtons, Pioneers of Early Arizona.* N.p.: Arizona Archaeological and Historical Society, 1919.

Fravel, John W. "Jackson's Valley Campaign." *Confederate Veteran* 6 (1898): 418–20.

Frazer, Robert W. *Forts and Supplies: The Role of the Army in the Economy of the Southwest, 1846–1861.* Albuquerque: University of New Mexico Press, 1983.

———, ed. *Mansfield on the Condition of the Western Forts, 1853–54.* Norman: University of Oklahoma Press, 1963.

Freeman, Douglas S. *Lee's Lieutenants.* 3 vols. New York: Charles Scribner's Sons, 1942–44.

———. *R. E. Lee: A Biography.* 4 vols. New York: Charles Scribner's Sons, 1934–35.

Fremantle, James A. L. *Three Months in the Southern States: April–June 1863.* New York: J. Bradburn, 1864.

Gache, Louis-Hippolyte. *A Frenchman, a Chaplain, a Rebel: The War Letters of Pere Louis-Hippolyte Gache, S.J.* Edited by Cornelius M. Buckley. Chicago: Loyola University Press, 1981.

Gallagher, Gary W. *Stephen Dodson Ramseur: Lee's Gallant General.* Chapel Hill: University of North Carolina Press, 1985.

Gardner, Hamilton. "Captain Philip St. George Cooke and the March of the 1st Dragoons to the Rocky Mountains in 1845." *Colorado Magazine,* Oct. 1953, pp. 246–69.

Garrett, Jill K., ed. *Confederate Soldiers and Patriots of Maury County, Tennessee.* Columbia, Tenn.: Cpt. James M. Sparkman Chapter of the U.D.C., 1970.

Gibson, J. Catlett. "The Battle of Spotsylvania Courthouse, May 12, 1864." *Southern Historical Society Papers* 32 (1904): 200–215.

Gilmor, Henry. *Four Years in the Saddle.* New York: Harper & Brothers, 1866.

Gold, Thomas D. *History of Clarke County, Virginia.* Berryville, Va.: Thomas D. Gold, 1914.

Goldsborough, William W. *The Maryland Line in the Confederate Army, 1861–1865.* Baltimore: Press of Guggenheimer, Weil & Co., 1900.

———. "With Lee at Gettysburg." Philadelphia *Record,* 8 July 1900.

Gordon, John B. *Reminiscences of the Civil War.* New York: Charles Scribner's Sons, 1903.

Gordon, Eugene C. "Controversy about Gettysburg." *Confederate Veteran* 20 (1920): 465.

Gorgas, Josiah. *The Civil War Diary of General Josiah Gorgas.* Edited by Frank E. Van Diver. University: University of Alabama Press, 1947.

Govan, Gilbert E., and James W. Livingood. *A Different Valor: The Story of General Joseph E. Johnston, C.S.A.* Indianapolis: Bobbs-Merrill, 1956.

Grace, C. D. "Rodes's Division at Gettysburg." *Confederate Veteran* 5 (1897): 614–15.

Graf, Leroy P., and Ralph W. Haskins, eds. *The Papers of Andrew Johnson.* 12 vols. Knoxville: University of Tennessee Press, 1967–1995.

Grant, Bruce. *American Forts Yesterday and Today.* New York: Dutton, 1965.

Grant, Ulysses S. *Personal Memoirs of U. S. Grant.* 2 vols. New York: Charles L. Webster, 1886.

The Grayjackets: and How They Lived, Fought and Died, for Dixie. Richmond: Jones Brothers, n.d.

Green, Wharton H. *Recollections and Reflections.* N.p.: Edwards and Broughton, 1906.

Grimes, Bryan. *Extracts of Letters of Major-General Bryan Grimes, to his Wife.* Edited by Pulaski Cowper. Raleigh: Alfred Williams, 1884.

Grimsley, Daniel A. *Battles in Culpeper County, Virginia.* Culpeper, Va.: Raleigh Travers Green, 1900.

Grunder, Charles S., and Brandon H. Beck. *The Second Battle of Winchester, June 12–15, 1863.* Lynchburg, Va.: H. E. Howard, 1989.

Hairston, Peter W., ed. "J. E. B. Stuart's Letters to His Hairston Kin, 1850–1855." *North Carolina Historical Review* 51 (July 1974): 261–333.

Hale, G. W. B. "Recollections of Malvern Hill." *Confederate Veteran* 30 (1922): 332–33.

Hale, Laura V., and Stanley S. Phillips. *History of the Forty-Ninth Virginia Infantry.* Lanham, Md.: S. S. Phillips, 1981.

Hall, James E. *The Diary of a Confederate Soldier.* Edited by Ruth Woods Dayton. N.p.: Elizabeth Teter Phillips, 1961.

Hall, Lucien. "Prison Sketchbook by Lucien Hall." *Northern Neck of Virginia Historical Magazine,* Dec. 1993, pp. 4988–5006.

Hall, W. R. "First Confederate Killed." *Confederate Veteran* 6 (1898): 320.

Hamlin, Percy G., ed. *The Making of a Soldier: Letters of General R. S. Ewell.* Richmond: Whittet & Shepperson, 1935.

———. *Old Bald Head.* Strasburg, Va.: Shenandoah Publishing House, 1940.

Hammond, George P., ed. *The Journal and Letters of Colonel John Van Deusen DuBois.* N.p.: Arizona Pioneers High School, 1949.

Hancock, Cornelia. *South after Gettysburg: Letters of Cornelia Hancock from the Army of the Potomac, 1863–1865.* Edited by Henrietta Stratton Jaquette. Freeport, N.Y.: Books for Libraries, 1971.

Handerson, Henry E. *Yankee in Gray.* Cleveland: Western Reserve University, 1962.

Handy, Moses P. "The Fall of Richmond in 1865." *American Magazine and Historical Chronicle* 1, no. 2 (Autumn–Winter, 1985–86): 2–21.

Hardy, A. S. "Terrific Fighting at Winchester." *Confederate Veteran* 9 (1901): 114.

Harrison, Constance C. *Recollections Grave and Gay.* New York: Charles Scribner's Sons, 1916.

———. "Virginia Scenes in '61." In Johnson and Buel, *Battles and Leaders,* 1:160–66.

Harrison, George F. "Ewell at First Manassas." *Southern Historical Society Papers* 14 (1886): 356–59.

Hart, Herbert M. *Old Forts of the Far West.* New York: Bonanza, 1965.

Haskell, John C. *The Haskell Memoirs.* Edited by Gilbert E. Govan and James W. Livingood. New York: G. P. Putnam's Sons, 1960.

Hassler, William W. *A. P. Hill: Lee's Forgotten General.* Richmond: Garrett & Massie, 1957.

———, ed. *The General to His Lady: The Civil War Letters of William Dorsey Pender to Fanny Pender.* Chapel Hill: University of North Carolina Press, 1965.

Hatton, Clarence R. "Gen. Archibald Campbell Godwin." *Confederate Veteran* 28 (1920): 133–36.

Hawks, A. W. S. "Maj. Wells J. Hawks, C.S.A." *Confederate Veteran* 19 (1911): 386–87.

Hayden, Horace Edwin. *Virginia Genealogies.* Wilkes-Barre, Pa.: E. B. Yordy, 1891.

Hayes, James. *War between the States: Autographs and Biographical Information.* James Island, S.C.: Palmetto Pub. Co., 1989.

Headley, J. T. *The Life of Ulysses S. Grant.* New York: E. B. Trent, 1868.

Heitman, Francis B. *Historical Register and Dictionary of the United States Army.* 2 vols. Washington, D.C.: U.S. Government Printing Office, 1903.

Henderson, G. F. R. *Stonewall Jackson and the American Civil War.* 2 vols. New York: Longmans, Green, 1919.

Henderson, William D. *The Road to Bristoe Station.* Lynchburg, Va.: H. E. Howard, 1987.

Hennessy, John. *Return to Bull Run: The Campaign and Battle of Second Manassas.* New York: Simon and Schuster, 1993.

Heth, Henry. *The Memoirs of Henry Heth.* Edited by James L. Morrison Jr. Westport, Conn.: Greenwood Press, 1974.

Hewes, M. Warner. "Turner Ashby's Courage." *Confederate Veteran* 5 (1897): 613.

Hickerson, Thomas F., ed. *Echoes of Happy Valley.* Chapel Hill, N.C.: Thomas F. Hickerson, 1962.

Hill, Daniel Harvey. "Lee's Attacks North of the Chickahominy." In Johnson and Buel, *Battles and Leaders*, 2:347–62.

Historical Sketch of Maury County Read at the Centennial Celebration in Columbia, Tennessee, July 4th, 1876. Columbia, Tenn.: Excelsior Printing Office, 1876.

History of the Fifth Massachusetts Battery. Boston: Luther E. Cowles, 1902.

History of the 118th Pennsylvania Volunteers. Philadelphia: J. L. Smith, 1905.

Hodge, Hiram C. *Arizona As It Is; or, The Coming Country.* New York: Hurd and Houghton, 1877.

Hoehling, A. A., and Mary Hoehling. *The Day Richmond Died.* San Diego: A. S. Barnes, 1965.

Hoge, Peyton H. *Moses Drury Hoge: Life and Letters.* Richmond: Presbyterian Committee of Publication, 1899.

Hoke, Jacob. *The Great Invasion of 1863; or, General Lee in Pennsylvania, Embracing an Account of the Strength and Organization of the Armies of the Potomac and Northern Virginia. . . .* Dayton, Ohio: W. J. Suey, 1887.

Hotchkiss, Jedediah. *Make Me a Map of the Valley.* Edited by Archie P. McDonald. Dallas: Southern Methodist University Press, 1973.

Houck, Peter W. *Confederate Surgeon: The Personal Recollections of E. A. Craighill.* Lynchburg, Va.: H. E. Howard, 1989.

Houghton, W. R., and M. B. Houghton. *Two Boys in the Civil War and After.* Montgomery, Ala.: Paragon Press, 1912.

Howard, McHenry. *Recollections of a Maryland Confederate Soldier and Staff Officer under Johnston, Jackson, and Lee.* Baltimore: Williams & Wilkins, 1914.

Huffman, James. *Ups and Down of a Confederate Soldier.* New York: William E. Rudge's Sons, 1940.

Humphreys, Andrew A. *The Virginia Campaign of '64 and '65.* New York: Charles Scribner's Sons, 1907.

Hunt, Henry J. "The First Day at Gettysburg." In Johnson and Buel, *Battles and Leaders*, 3:255–84.

———. "The Second Day at Gettysburg." In Johnson and Buel, *Battles and Leaders*, 3:290–313.

———. "The Third Day at Gettysburg." In Johnson and Buel, *Battles and Leaders*, 3:369–85.

Hunter, Robert W. "Major-General Johnson at Spotsylvania." *Southern Historical Society Papers* 33 (1905): 335–40.

Hunton, Eppa. *Autobiography of Eppa Hunton.* Richmond: William Byrd, 1933.

Hurst, Patricia J. *The War between the States, 1862–1865, Rapidan River Area of Clark Mountain, Orange County, Virginia.* Rapidan, Va.: Patricia J. Hurst, 1989.

Hutchins, James S. "'Bald Head' Ewell, Frontier Dragoon." *Arizoniana: The Journal of Arizona History* 3 (1962): 18–23.

Hutton, Ralph B. *The History of Elkton.* N.p., 1958.

Imboden, John D. "The Confederate Retreat from Gettysburg." In Johnson and Buel, *Battles and Leaders*, 3:420–29.

———. "Stonewall Jackson in the Shenandoah." In Johnson and Buel, *Battles and Leaders*, 2:282–98.

Jackson, Mary Anna. *Memoirs of Stonewall Jackson.* Louisville, Ky.: Prentice Press, Courier-Journal Job Printing Co., 1895.

Jensen, Les. *32nd Virginia Infantry.* Lynchburg, Va.: H. E. Howard, 1990.

Johns, B. F. "Sailor's Creek." *National Tribune,* 28 Apr. 1887.

Johnson, Allen, and Dumas Malone, eds. *Dictionary of American Biography.* 20 vols. New York: Charles Scribner's Sons, 1928–36.

Johnson, John L. *The University Memorial.* Baltimore: Turnbull Brothers, 1870.

Johnson, Robert U., and Clarence C. Buel, eds. *Battles and Leaders of the Civil War.* 4 vols. New York: Century, 1887–88.

Johnston, B. S. "Battle of Sailor's Creek." *Confederate Veteran* 8 (1900): 538.

Johnston, Charles. "Attack on Fort Gilmer, September 29th, 1864." *Southern Historical Society Papers* 1 (1876): 438–42.

Johnston, Joseph E. *Narrative of Military Operations, Directed, during the Late War between the States.* New York: Appleton, 1874.

———. "Responsibilities of the First Bull Run." In Johnson and Buel, *Battles and Leaders,* 1:240–59.

Johnston, Mary. "Gettysburg." *Confederate Veteran* 21 (1913): 394–97.

Johnston, Robert D. "Gen. Lee's Story." Unidentified newspaper article in Stephen D. Ramseur Papers, North Carolina Department of Archives and History, Raleigh.

Jones, John B. *A Rebel War Clerk's Diary at the Confederate States Capital.* 2 vols. Philadelphia: Lippincott, 1866.

Jones, John William. *Army of Northern Virginia Memorial Volume.* Richmond: J. W. Randolph & English, 1880.

———. "The Career of General Jackson." *Southern Historical Society Papers* 35 (1907): 79–98.

———. *Christ in the Camp, or Religion in Lee's Army.* Richmond: B. F. Johnson, 1888.

———. "Down the Valley after 'Stonewall's Quartermaster.'" *Southern Historical Society Papers* 9 (1881): 185–90.

———. "From Port Republic to the Chickahominy." *Southern Historical Society Papers* 9 (1881): 362–69.

———. "Gen. A. P. Hill: Partial Sketch of His Thrilling Career." *Confederate Veteran* 1 (1894): 233–36.

———. *Personal Reminiscences, Anecdotes, and Letters of Gen. Robert E. Lee.* New York: Appleton, 1875.

———. "Reminiscences of the Army of Northern Virginia." *Southern Historical Society Papers* 9 (1881): 557–70.

———. "'Stonewall' Jackson." *Confederate Veteran* 12 (1904): 174–75.

———. "Stonewall Jackson." *Southern Historical Society Papers* 19 (1891): 145–64.

Jones, Terry L. *Lee's Tigers: The Louisiana Infantry in the Army of Northern Virginia.* Baton Rouge: Louisiana State University Press, 1987.

Jones, Thomas O. "Last Days of the Army of Northern Virginia." *Southern Historical Society Papers* 21 (1893): 57–103.

Jordan, Weymouth T., ed. "Diary of George Washington Campbell: American Minister to Russia, 1818–1820." *Tennessee Historical Quarterly* 7, no. 2 (June 1948): 152–70.

Kane, Randy. "Policing the Plains: The Dragoon Expeditions of the 1840's." *Gone West!* 3, no. 3 (Fall 1985): 11–14.

Kean, Robert G. H. *Inside the Confederate Government: The Diary of Robert Garlick Hill Kean.* Edited by Edward Younger. New York: Oxford University Press, 1957.

Kelly, Henry B. *Port Republic.* Philadelphia: Lippincott, 1886.

King, W. C., and W. P. Derby. *Camp-Fire Sketches and Battlefield Echoes, 61–5.* Springfield, Mass.: King, Richardson, 1889.

Krick, Robert K. *Conquering the Valley: Stonewall Jackson at Port Republic.* New York: William Morrow, 1996.

———. *Lee's Colonels.* Dayton, Ohio: Morningside Bookshop, 1979.

———. *Ninth Virginia Cavalry.* Lynchburg, Va.: H. E. Howard, 1982.

———. *Stonewall Jackson at Cedar Mountain.* Chapel Hill: University of North Carolina Press, 1990.

LaBree, Benjamin, ed. *Camp Fires of the Confederacy.* Louisville, Ky.: Courier-Journal Job Printing Company, 1898.

Lacy, William S. *William Sterling Lacy: Memorial, Addresses, Sermons.* Richmond: Presbyterian Committee of Publication, 1900.

The Land We Love. Edited by Daniel Harvey Hill. 6 vols. Charlotte, N.C.: N.p., 1866–69.

Lane, Mills, ed. *"Dear Mother: Don't grieve about me. If I get killed, I'll only be dead." Letters from Georgia Soldiers in the Civil War.* Savannah, Ga.: Beehive Press, 1977.

Lankford, Nelson D., ed. "The Diary of Thomas Conolly, M.P.: Virginia, March–April 1865." *Virginia Magazine of History and Biography* 95, no. 1 (Jan. 1987): 75–112.

Law, Evander M. "From the Wilderness to Cold Harbor." In Johnson and Buel, *Battles and Leaders,* 4:118–44.

———. "The Struggle for 'Round Top.'" In Johnson and Buel, *Battles and Leaders,* 3:318–30.

Lawrence, James M. "The Capture of General Ewell." *National Tribune,* 7 Apr. 1877.

Ledford, P. L. *Reminiscences of the Civil War.* Thomasville, N.C.: News Printing House, 1909.

Lee, Fitzhugh. "Letter from General Fitz. Lee." *Southern Historical Society Papers* 4 (1877): 69–76.

Lee, Robert E., Jr. *Recollections and Letters of General Robert E. Lee.* Garden City, N.Y.: Garden City Pub. Co., 1924.

Lee, Susan P., ed., *Memoirs of William Nelson Pendleton, D.D.* Philadelphia: Lippincott, 1893.

Leon, Louis. *Diary of a Tar Heel Confederate Soldier.* Charlotte, N.C.: Stone Pub. Co., 1913.

Lewis, George. *The History of Battery E, First Regiment Rhode Island Light Artillery, in the War of 1861 and 1865, to Preserve the Union.* Providence, R.I.: Snow & Farnham, 1892.

Lewis, Lloyd. *Sherman: Fighting Prophet.* New York: Harcourt, Brace, 1932.

Long, Armistead L. *Memoirs of Robert E. Lee.* New York: J. M. Stoddert, 1887.

Longstreet, James. *From Manassas to Appomattox.* Philadelphia: Lippincott, 1896.

———. "General James Longstreet's Account of the Campaign and Battle." *Southern Historical Society Papers* 5 (1878): 54–86.

———. "General Longstreet's Report of Affair of October 27th, 1864." *Southern Historical Society Papers* 7 (1879): 541–43.

———. "Lee's Invasion of Pennsylvania." In Johnson and Buel, *Battles and Leaders,* 3:244–51.

———. "Lee's Right Wing at Gettysburg." In Johnson and Buel, *Battles and Leaders,* 3:339–54.

Longworthy, Franklin. *Scenery of the Plains, Mountains, and Mines: or, A Diary Kept Upon the Overland Route to California, by Way of the Great Salt Lake.* Ogdensburg, N.Y.: J. C. Sprague, 1855.

Lossing, Benson J. *Pictorial History of the Civil War in the United States of America.* 3 vols. Hartford, Conn.: Winter, 1866–68.

Lyman, Theodore. *Meade's Headquarters, 1863–1865.* Edited by George Aggassiz. Boston: Atlantic Monthly Press, 1922.

McCabe, James D., Jr. *Life and Campaigns of General Robert E. Lee.* Atlanta: National Pub. Co., 1866.

McCarthy, Carlton. *Detailed Minutiae of Soldier Life in the Army of Northern Virginia, 1861–1865.* Richmond: Carleton McCarthy, 1882.

McClendon, William A. *Recollections of War Times.* Montgomery, Ala.: Paragon Press, 1909.

McDaniel, Henry. *With Unabated Trust.* Edited by Anita B. Sams. Monroe, Ga.: Walton Press, 1977.

McGrath, Francis S. *Pillars of Maryland.* Richmond: Dietz Press, 1950.

McGuire, Hunter. "Clinical Remarks on Gun-shot Wounds of Joints, delivered January 10, 1866, at Howard's Grove Hospital." *Richmond Medical Journal* 1, no. 2 (Mar. 1866): 260–65.

McGuire, Hunter, and George L. Christian. *The Confederate Cause and Conduct in the War between the States.* Richmond: L. H. Jenkins, 1907.

McGuire, Judith W. *Diary of a Southern Refugee during the War.* Richmond: J. W. Randolph & English, 1889.

McIntosh, David G. "Review of the Gettysburg Campaign." *Southern Historical Society Papers* 37 (1909): 74–143.

McKim, Randolph H. "The Gettysburg Campaign." *Southern Historical Society Papers* 40 (1915): 253–300.

———. *A Soldier's Recollections.* New York: Longmans, Green, 1910.

———. "Steuart's Brigade at the Battle of Gettysburg." *Southern Historical Society Papers* 5 (1878): 291–300.

McLain, Minor H. "The Military Prison at Fort Warren." *Civil War History* 8 (June 1962): 136–51.

McMahon, Martin T. "From Gettysburg to the Coming of Grant." In Johnson and Buel, *Battles and Leaders,* 4:81–87.

McMullen, Glenn L., ed. *A Surgeon with Stonewall Jackson: The Civil Letters of Dr. Harvey Black.* Baltimore: Butternut and Blue, 1995.

McPherson, James M. *Battle Cry of Freedom: The Civil War Era.* New York: Oxford University Press, 1988.

"Maj. Chatham Roberdeau Wheat." *Confederate Veteran* 19 (1911): 425–28.

Manarin, Louis H., ed. *Richmond at War: The Minutes of the City Council, 1861–1865.* Chapel Hill: University of North Carolina Press, 1966.

Mansfield, Edward D. *The Mexican War.* New York: A. S. Barnes, 1849.

Manson, H. W. "A. P. Hill's Signal Corps." *Confederate Veteran* 2 (1894): 11–12.

Marshall, Charles. *An Aide-de-Camp of Lee.* Edited by Frederick Maurice. Boston: Little, Brown, 1927.

Martin, J. H. "Forts Gilmer and Harrison Forces." *Confederate Veteran* 14 (1906): 409.

Martin, Samuel J. "The Complex Confederate." *Civil War Times Illustrated* 25, no. 2 (Apr. 1986): 27–33.

———. *The Road to Glory: Confederate General Richard S. Ewell.* Indianapolis: Guild Press of Indiana, 1991.

Matter, William D. *If It Takes All Summer: The Battle of Spotsylvania.* Chapel Hill: University of North Carolina Press, 1988.

M'Dowell, W. G. "Gen. R. E. Lee at Gettysburg on First Day." *Confederate Veteran* 21 (1913): 126.

Meade, George G. "The Meade-Sickles Controversy." Pt. 1. In Johnson and Buel, *Battles and Leaders,* 3:413–14.

The Medical and Surgical History of the War of the Rebellion. 6 vols. Compiled by George A. Otis and D. L. Huntington. Washington, D.C.: U.S. Government Printing Office, 1883.

Meriwether, David. *1855 Report to Congress.* Washington, D.C. Series 840, pp. 506–7.

Merrill, James M. *Spurs to Glory: The Story of the United States Cavalry.* Chicago: Rand McNally, 1966.

Message from the President of the United States, to the Two Houses of Congress, at the Commencement of the First Session of the Thirtieth Congress. Serial 503. Washington, D.C.: Wendell and Van Benthuysen, 1847.

Michie, Peter S. "Account of Dutch Gap Canal." In Johnson and Buel, *Battles and Leaders,* 4:575.

Miller, Fanny W. "The Fall of Richmond." *Confederate Veteran* 13 (1905): 305.

Miller, J. Michael, *The North Anna Campaign: "Even to Hell Itself."* Lynchburg, Va.: H. E. Howard, 1989.

Miller, William J. "Major Wells J. Hawks: Jackson's Commissary of Subsistence." *Color Bearer* 2, no. 2 (July 1993): 8–9.

———. *Mapping for Stonewall: The Civil War Service of Jed Hotchkiss.* Washington, D.C.: Elliott & Clark, 1993.

Mixson, Frank M. *Reminiscences of a Private.* Columbia, S.C.: State Co., 1911.

Montgomery, Walter A. *The Days of Old and the Years That Are Past.* N.p., n.d.

Moore, Alison. *The Louisiana Tigers or the Two Louisiana Brigades of the Army of Northern Virginia, 1861–1865.* Baton Rouge: Ortlieb Press, 1961.

Moore, Edward A. *The Story of a Cannoneer under Stonewall Jackson.* New York: Neale, 1907.

Moore, Frank, ed. *The Rebellion Record.* 12 vols. New York: G. P. Putnam, 1863.

Moore, James B. "The Attack of Fort Harrison." *Confederate Veteran* 13 (1905): 418–20.

Morrison, James L., Jr. *"The Best School in the World": West Point, the Pre-Civil War Years, 1833–1866.* Kent, Ohio: Kent State University Press, 1986.

Morton, Lewis. *Robert Carter of Nomini Hall.* Williamsburg: Colonial Williamsburg, 1941.

Mowry, Sylvester. *Arizona and Sonora.* New York: Harper & Brothers, 1864.

Muffly, J. W., ed. *The Story of Our Regiment: A History of the 148th Pennsylvania Vols. Written by the Comrades.* Des Moines, Iowa: Kenyon Printing & Manufacturing, 1934.

Munford, Thomas T. "A Confederate Cavalry Officer's Reminiscence." *Journal of the U.S. Cavalry Association* 4 (1891): 276–88.

———. "Reminiscences of Jackson's Valley Campaign." *Southern Historical Society Papers* 7 (1879): 523–34.

Murray, Alton J. *South Georgia Rebels.* St. Mary's, Ga.: Alton J. Murray, 1976.

Myers, Franklin M. *The Comanches: A History of White's Battalion, Virginia Cavalry, Laurel Brig., Hampton Div., A.N.V., C.S.A.* Baltimore: Kelly, Piet, 1871.

Myers, Harry. "Guardians of the Middle Border." *Gone West!* 3, no. 3 (Fall 1985): 8–10.

Neese, George M. *Three Years in the Confederate Horse Artillery.* New York: Neale, 1911.

Nevins, Allan. *Frémont: The West's Greatest Adventurer.* New York: Harper & Brothers, 1928.

Newhall, Frederick C. *With General Sheridan in Lee's Last Campaign.* Philadelphia: Lippincott, 1866.

Nichols, George W. *A Soldier's Story of His Regiment.* Jessup, Ga.: Privately published, 1898.

North, Diane M. T., ed. *Samuel Peter Heintzelman and the Sonora Exploring & Mining Company.* Tucson: University of Arizona Press, 1980.

Oates, William C. *The War between the Union and the Confederacy and Its Lost Opportunities.* New York: Neale, 1905.

O'Connor Richard. *Thomas: Rock of Chickamauga.* New York: Prentice-Hall, 1948.

"Official Diary of First Corps, A.N.V., while Commanded by Lieutenant-General R. H. Anderson, from May 7th to 31st, 1864." *Southern Historical Society Papers* 7 (1879): 491–94.

The Official Military Atlas of the Civil War. Compiled by Calvin D. Cowles. New York: Fairfax Press, 1978.

Old, William W. "Trees Whittled Down at Horseshoe." *Southern Historical Society Papers* 33 (1905): 16–24.

Oliva, Leo E. "Fort Scott: 'Crack Post of the Frontier.'" *Gone West!* 3, no. 3 (Fall 1985): 2–6.

Opher, Morris E., and Catherine H. Opher. "Mescalero Apache History in the Southwest." *New Mexico Historical Review*, 25, no. 1 (Jan. 1950): 1–36.

Owen, Thomas M. *History of Alabama and Dictionary of Alabama Biography.* 4 vols. Spartanburg, S.C.: Reprint Co., 1978.

Owen, William Miller. *In Camp and Battle with the Washington Artillery of New Orleans.* Boston: Ticknor, 1885.

Page, Robert M. C. "The Captured Guns at Spotsylvania Courthouse—Correction of General Ewell's Report." *Southern Historical Society Papers* 7 (1879): 535–40.

Park, Joseph F. "The Apaches in Mexican-American Relations." *Arizona and the West* 3 (1961): 129–46.

Park, Robert E. *Sketch of the Twelfth Alabama Infantry.* Richmond: William Ellis Jones, 1906.

Parramore, Thomas C., F. Roy Johnson, and E. Frank Stephenson Jr., eds. *Before the Rebel Flag Fell.* Murfreesboro, N.C.: Johnson Pub. Co., 1968.

Patrick, Rembert W. *The Fall of Richmond.* Baton Rouge: Louisiana State University Press, 1960.

Pendleton, William N. "Official Report of General W. N. Pendleton, Chief of Artillery, A.N.V." *Southern Historical Society Papers* 5 (1978): 194–201.

"Personne" [Felix G. DeFontaine]. *Marginalia; or, Gleanings from an Army Note-Book.* Columbia, S.C.: Steam Power Press, 1864.

Peters, DeWitt C. *The Life and Adventures of Kit Carson, the Nestor of the Rocky Mountains.* New York: W. R. C. Clarke & Meeker, 1859.

Peyton, George Q. "Pegram's Brigade at Spotsylvania." *Confederate Veteran* 38 (1930): 58–62.

Pfanz, Harry W. *Culp's Hill and Cemetery Hill.* Chapel Hill: University of North Carolina Press, 1993.

Pollard, Edward A. *Lee and His Lieutenants.* New York: E. B. Treat, 1867.

———. *Southern History of the Civil War.* 4 vols. New York: Blue and Gray Press, n.d.

Pope, John. "The Second Battle of Bull Run." In Johnson and Buel, *Battles and Leaders*, 2:449–94.

Porter, Fitz John. "Hanover Court House and Gaines's Mill." In Johnson and Buel, *Battles and Leaders*, 2:319–43.

Porter, Horace. *Campaigning with Grant.* New York: Century, 1897.

Powell, Henry F. *Tercentenary History of Maryland.* 4 vols. Chicago: S. J. Clarke, 1925.

Proceedings and Report of the Board of Army Officers Convened by Special Orders No. 78, Headquarters of the Army, Adjutant General's Office, Washington, April 12, 1878, in the Case of Fitz-John Porter. 3 parts. Washington, D.C.: U.S. Government Printing Office, 1879.

A Provisional List of Alumni, Grammar School Students, Members of the Faculty, and Members of the Board of Visitors of the College of William and Mary in Virginia, from 1693 to 1888. . . . Richmond: Division of Purchase and Printing, 1941.

Pumpelly, Raphael. *Pumpelly's Arizona.* Edited by Andrew Wallace. Tucson: Palo Verde Press, 1965.

Purifoy, John. "Battle of Gettysburg, July 3, 1863." *Confederate Veteran* 32 (1924): 16–18.

————. "Ewell's Attack at Gettysburg, July 2, 1863." *Confederate Veteran* 31 (1923): 454–56.
————. "In Battle Array at Williamsport and Hagerstown." *Confederate Veteran* 33 (1925): 371–73.
————. "With Ewell and Rodes in Pennsylvania." *Confederate Veteran* 30 (1922): 462–64.
————. "With Jackson in the Valley." *Confederate Veteran* 30 (1922): 383–85.
Ramey, Emily G., ed. *The Years of Anguish: Fauquier County, Virginia, 1861–1865.* Warrenton, Va.: Fauquier Democrat, 1965.
Rast, P. J. "Fisher's Hill." *Confederate Veteran* 23 (1915): 123–24.
Raup, Hallock F., ed. *Letters from a Pennsylvania Chaplain at the Siege of Petersburg, 1865.* Kent, Ohio: Kent State University Press, n.d.
Redwood, Allen C. "Jackson's 'Foot Cavalry' at the Second Bull Run." In Johnson and Buel, *Battles and Leaders*, 2:530–38.
Reed, William H. *Hospital Life in the Army of the Potomac.* Boston: Privately published, 1891.
Reeve, Frank D. "The Apache Indians in Texas." *Southwestern Historical Quarterly* 50 (Oct. 1946): 189–219.
Regulations Established for the Organization and Government of the Military Academy. . . . New York: Wiley & Putnam, 1839.
"Reminiscences of the Gettysburg Battle." In *Lippincott's Magazine of Popular Literature and Science*, o.s., 32; n.s., 6. Philadelphia: Lippincott, 1883.
Report of the Adjutant General of the State of Kentucky. 2 vols. Utica, Ky.: McDowell, 1980.
"Reunited at Gettysburg." *Confederate Veteran* 30 (1922): 445–46.
Reynolds, Philip. "Early Texas Forts: Lost but to History." *Journal of the Council on America's Military Past* 17 (1989): 43–50.
Rhea, Gordon C. *The Battle of the Wilderness, May 5–6, 1864.* Baton Rouge: Louisiana State University Press, 1994.
Richardson, Albert D. *A Personal History of Ulysses S. Grant.* Hartford, Conn.: American Pub. Co., 1868.
Ripley, Roswell S. *The War with Mexico.* 2 vols. New York: Harper & Brothers, 1849.
Roberts, James W. "The Wilderness and Spottsylvania, May 4–12, 1864." *Quarterly* (Florida Historical Society) 11 (Oct. 1932): 58–72.
Robertson, James I., Jr. *General A. P. Hill: The Story of a Confederate Warrior.* New York: Random House, 1987.
————. "Stonewall in the Shenandoah: The Valley Campaign of 1862." *Civil War Times Illustrated* 11, no. 2 (May 1972): 4–49.
————, ed. *Proceedings of the Advisory Council of the State of Virginia.* Richmond: Virginia State Library, 1977.
Robinson, F. C. "Sailor's Creek." *National Tribune*, 18 Aug. 1887.
Robson, John S. *How a One-Legged Rebel Lives.* Richmond: W. H. Wade, 1876.
Rock, R. S. "War Reminiscence." *Confederate Veteran* 9 (1901): 505–7.
Roe, Alfred S., and Charles Nutt. *History of the First Regiment of Heavy Artillery Massachusetts Volunteers, formerly the Fourteenth Regiment of Infantry, 1861–1865.* Worcester, Mass.: Commonwealth Printers, 1917.
Roman, Alfred. *The Military Operations of General Beauregard.* 2 vols. New York: Harper & Brothers, 1884.
Ropes, John C. *The Army under Pope: Campaigns of the Civil War.* New York: Charles Scribner's Sons, 1881.
Rouse, Parke, Jr. "'Old Buck'—A Hero in Spite of Himself." *William and Mary Alumni Gazette*, Jan.–Feb. 1983, pp. 18–20.
Royall, William L. *Some Reminiscences.* New York: Neale, 1909.
Russell, Charles W., ed. *The Memoirs of Colonel John S. Mosby.* Boston: Little, Brown, 1917.

Sacks, Benjamin. "The Origins of Fort Buchanan: Myth and Fact." *Arizona and the West* 7 (1965): 207–26.

St. Louis Star. *The City of St. Louis and Its Resources.* St. Louis: Continental Printing Co., 1893.

Sams, Anita B., ed. *With Unabated Trust.* Monroe, Ga.: Walton Press, 1977.

Samuels, Green B. *A Civil War Marriage in Virginia.* Edited by Carrie Esther Spencer, Bernard Samuels, and Walter Berry Samuels. Boyce, Va.: Carr Pub. Co., 1956.

Sanger, Donald B., and Thomas R. Hay. *James Longstreet.* Baton Rouge: Louisiana State University Press, 1952.

Schildt, John W. *Hunter Holmes McGuire: Doctor in Gray.* Chewsville, Md.: John W. Schildt, 1986.

Scott, Winfield. *Memoirs of Lieut-General Scott, LL.D.* 2 vols. Freeport, N.Y.: Books for Libraries, 1970.

Scribner, Robert L. "Reconnaissance through Fairfax." *Virginia Cavalcade* 6, no. 1 (Summer 1956): 18–21.

Sears, Stephen W. *To the Gates of Richmond: The Peninsula Campaign.* New York: Ticknor and Fields, 1992.

Serven, James E. "The Military Posts on Sonoita Creek." *Smoke Signal* 12 (Fall 1865): 26–48.

Seymour, William J. *The Civil War Memoirs of Captain William J. Seymour.* Edited by Terry L. Jones. Baton Rouge: Louisiana State University Press, 1991.

Sheeran, James B. *Confederate Chaplain: A War Journal of Rev. James B. Sheeran, c.ss.r., 14th Louisiana, C.S.A.* Edited by Joseph T. Durkin. Milwaukee: Bruce Pub. Co., 1960.

Shevchuk, Paul M. "The Wounding of Albert Jenkins, July 2, 1863." *Gettysburg Magazine,* 1 July 1990, pp. 51–63.

Shotwell, Randolph A. *The Papers of Randolph Abbott Shotwell.* 3 vols. Edited by J. C. DeRoulhac Hamilton. Raleigh: North Carolina Historical Commission, 1931.

Singletary, Otis A. *The Mexican War.* Chicago: University of Chicago Press, 1960.

"Sketch of Major General S. D. Ramseur." *Land We Love* 5 (1868): 1–10.

"Sketch of the Lee Memorial Association." *Southern Historical Society Papers* 11 (1883): 388–417.

Smith, Adelaide W. *Reminiscences of an Army Nurse during the Civil War.* New York: Greaves Pub. Co., 1911.

Smith, Eugenia B. *Centreville, Virginia: Its History and Architecture.* Fairfax, Va.: Fairfax County Office of Planning, 1973.

Smith, Everard H., ed. "As They Saw General Lee." *Civil War Times Illustrated* 25, no. 6 (Oct. 1986): 20–25.

———. "The Civil War Diary of Peter W. Hairston, Volunteer Aide to Major General Jubal Early, November 7–December 4, 1863." *North Carolina Historical Review* 67 (Jan. 1990): 59–86.

Smith, James Power. "General Lee at Gettysburg." *Southern Historical Society Papers* 33 (1905): 135–60.

———. "With Stonewall Jackson in the Army of Northern Virginia." *Southern Historical Society Papers* 43 (1920): 1–110.

Smith, William. "An Eye-Witness Account of the Skirmish at Fairfax Courthouse." In *Fairfax County and the War between the States,* 1–10. Vienna, Va.: Fairfax County Civil War Centennial Commission, 1961.

Sommers, Richard J. "The Dutch Gap Affair: Military Atrocities and Rights of Negro Soldiers." *Civil War History* 21 (Mar. 1975): 51–64.

———. *Richmond Redeemed: The Siege of Petersburg.* Garden City, N.Y.: Doubleday, 1981.

Sonnichsen, Charles L. *The Mescalero Apaches.* Norman: University of Oklahoma Press, 1958.

Sorrel, Gilbert Moxley. *Recollections of a Confederate Staff Officer.* New York: Neale, 1917.

Southern Generals, Who They Are, and What They Have Done. New York: Charles B. Richardson, 1865.

Southern Historical Society Papers. 52 vols. Richmond: 1876–1959.

Steere, Edward. *The Wilderness Campaign.* Harrisburg: Stackpole, 1960.

Stephens, Alexander H. *Recollections of Alexander H. Stephens.* Edited by Myrta Lockett Avary. N.Y.: Doubleday, Page, 1910.

Stephens, Robert G., Jr. *Intrepid Warrior: Clement Anselm Evans.* Dayton, Ohio: Morningside Bookshop, 1992.

Stiles, John C., comp. "In the Year 1862." *Confederate Veteran* 25 (1917): 414–16.

———. "An Unsung Hero." *Confederate Veteran* 23 (1915): 437.

Stiles, Maynard F. "Maj. J. Coleman Alderson." *Confederate Veteran* 21 (1913): 87.

Stiles, Robert. *Four Years under Marse Robert.* New York: Neale, 1903.

———. "Monument to the Confederate Dead at the University of Virginia." *Southern Historical Society Papers* 21 (1893): 15–37.

Stine, J. H. *History of the Army of the Potomac.* Philadelphia: J. B. Rodgers, 1892.

"Stonewall Jackson at Prayer." *Southern Historical Society Papers* 19 (1891): 111–13.

Stringfellow, M. S. "Rev. M. S. Stringfellow's Account." *Southern Historical Society Papers* 21 (1893): 244–51.

Sulivane, Clement. "The Fall of Richmond." Pt. 1. In Johnson and Buel, *Battles and Leaders,* 4:725–26.

———. "Last Soldiers to Leave Richmond." *Confederate Veteran* 17 (1909): 602.

Sweeney, Edwin R. "Cochise and the Prelude to the Bascom Affair." *New Mexico Historical Review* 64, no. 4 (Oct. 1989): 427–46.

Talcott, T. M. R. "Stuart's Cavalry in the Gettysburg Campaign." *Southern Historical Society Papers* 37 (1909): 21–37.

Taliaferro, William B. "Jackson's Raid around Pope." In Johnson and Buel, *Battles and Leaders,* 2:501–11.

Tankersley, Allen P. *John B. Gordon: A Study in Gallantry.* Atlanta: Whitehall Press, 1955.

Tanner, Robert G. *Stonewall in the Valley.* Garden City, N.Y.: Doubleday, 1976.

Taylor, Benjamin. "Reminiscence of Gen. Ewell." *National Tribune,* 12 Dec. 1912.

Taylor, Richard. *Destruction and Reconstruction.* New York: Appleton, 1879.

Taylor, Walter H. *Four Years with General Lee.* New York: Appleton, 1877.

———. *General Lee: His Campaigns in Virginia, 1861–1865, with Personal Reminiscences.* Norfolk: Nusbaum Book and News, 1906.

———. "Memorandum by Colonel Walter H. Taylor, of General Lee's Staff." *Southern Historical Society Papers* 4 (1877): 80–87.

———. "Second Paper by Colonel Walter H. Taylor, of General Lee's Staff." *Southern Historical Society Papers* 4 (1877): 124–39.

Terrill, Helen E., and Sarah R. Dixon. *History of Stewart County, Georgia.* Columbus, Ga.: Columbus Office Supply, 1958.

Tevis, James H. *Arizona in the '50's.* Albuquerque: University of New Mexico Press, 1954.

T.H.F. Article in Union College *Alumni Monthly,* 11 Mar. 1920.

Thomas, Henry W. *History of the Doles-Cook Brigade, Army of Northern Virginia, C.S.A.* Atlanta: Franklin, 1903.

Thompson, Mangus S. "From the Ranks to Brigade Commander." *Confederate Veteran* 29 (1921): 298–303.

Thorndike, Rachel S., ed. *The Sherman Letters.* New York: Charles Scribner's Sons, 1894.

Thwaites, Reuben Gold, ed. *Early Western Travels, 1748–1846.* 31 vols. Cleveland: Arthur H. Clark, 1906.

Timberlake, W. L. "In the Siege of Richmond and After." *Confederate Veteran* 29 (1921): 412–14.
———. "Last Days in Front of Richmond, 1864–1865." *Confederate Veteran* 20 (1912): 119.
———. "The Retreat from Richmond in 1865." *Confederate Veteran* 22 (1914): 454–56.
Todd, George T. "Gaines's Mill—Pickett and Hood." *Confederate Veteran* 6 (1898): 565–69.
Tomlinson, A. R. "On the Advance into Maryland." *Confederate Veteran* 30 (1922): 141.
Toney, Marcus B. *The Privations of a Private.* Nashville: Marcus B. Toney, 1905.
Townsend, George A. *Campaigns of a Non-Combatant, and his Romaunt Abroad during the War.* New York: Blelock, 1866.
Tremain, Henry E. *Last Hours of Sheridan's Cavalry.* New York: Bonnell, Silver & Bowers, 1904.
Trimble, Isaac R. "The Battle and Campaign of Gettysburg." *Southern Historical Society Papers* 26 (1898): 116–28.
———. "The Campaign and Battle of Gettysburg." *Confederate Veteran* 25 (1917): 209–13.
———. "General I. R. Trimble's Report of Operations of his Brigade from the 14th to 29th of August, 1862." *Southern Historical Society Papers* 8 (1880): 306–9.
Trudeau, Noah Andre. *Bloody Roads South.* Boston: Little, Brown, 1989.
Truett, Randall B., ed. *Washington, D.C.: A Guide to the Nation's Capital.* New York: Hastings House, 1968.
Turner, Harriot S. "Recollections of Andrew Johnson" *Harper's Monthly Magazine,* Dec. 1909–May 1910, pp. 168–76.
U.S. Congress. *Report of the Joint Committee on the Conduct of the War at the Second Session, Thirty-Eighth Congress, Army of the Potomac, General Meade.* . . . Washington, D.C.: U.S. Government Printing Office, 1865.
U.S. Secretary of War. *Annual Report of Secretary of War.* 1838–39. Serial 340. Washington, D.C., 1839.
———. *Annual Report of Secretary of War.* 1847–48. Serial 503. Washington, D.C., 1848.
———. *Annual Report of Secretary of War.* 1855–56. Serial 811. Washington, D.C., 1856.
———. *Annual Report of Secretary of War.* 1856–57. Serial 876. Washington, D.C., 1857.
———. *Annual Report of Secretary of War.* 1857–58. Serial 920. Washington, D.C., 1858.
———. *Annual Report of Secretary of War.* 1858–59. Serial 976. Washington, D.C., 1859.
———. *Annual Report of Secretary of War.* 1859–60. Serial 1024. Washington, D.C., 1860.
———. *Annual Report of Secretary of War.* 1860–61. Serial 1079. Washington, D.C., 1861.
U.S. War Department. *Reports of Explorations and Surveys, to Ascertain the Most Practicable and Economical Route for a Railroad from the Mississippi River to the Pacific Ocean.* 6 vols. Washington, D.C.: A. O. P. Nicholson, 1856.
———. *The War of the Rebellion: A Compilation of the Official Records of the Union and Confederate Armies.* 128 vols. Washington, D.C.: U.S. Government Printing Office, 1880–1901.
Utley, Robert M. *Frontiersmen in Blue: The United States Army and the Indian, 1848–1865.* New York: Macmillan, 1876.
———. *The Indian Frontier of the American West, 1846–1890.* Albuquerque: University of New Mexico Press, 1984.
Vandiver, Frank E., ed. *The Civil War Diary of General Josiah Gorgas.* University: University of Alabama Press, 1947.
Venable, Charles S. "The Campaign from the Wilderness to Petersburg." *Southern Historical Society Papers* 14 (1886): 522–42.
———. "General Lee in the Wilderness Campaign." In Johnson and Buel, *Battles and Leaders,* 4:240–46.

Virginia Magazine of History and Biography. 104 vols. Richmond: Virginia Historical Society, 1893–1996.

Virginia Writers Program. *Prince William: The Story of Its People and Its Places.* Manassas, Va.: Bethlehem Good Housekeeping Club, 1941.

Walker, Francis A. *History of the Second Army Corps in the Army of the Potomac.* New York: Charles Scribner's Sons, 1891.

Walker, Henry P., ed. "Colonel Bonneville's Report: The Department of New Mexico in 1859." *Arizona and the West* 22 (1980): 343–62.

Wallace, Lee A., Jr. *First Virginia Infantry.* Lynchburg, Va.: H. E. Howard, 1984.

———. *A Guide to Virginia Military Organizations, 1861–1865.* Lynchburg, Va.: H. E. Howard, 1986.

Ware, John N. "Second Manassas: Fifty-eight Years Afterwards." *Confederate Veteran* 30 (1922): 60–62.

Warner, Ezra J. *Generals in Blue.* Baton Rouge: Louisiana State University Press, 1964.

———. *Generals in Gray.* Baton Rouge: Louisiana State University Press, 1959.

War Was the Place. Bulletin 5 (Nov. 1961). N.p.: Chattahoochee Valley Historical Society, 1961.

Watehall, E. T. "Fall of Richmond, April 3, 1865." *Confederate Veteran* 17 (1909): 215.

Watson, W. A. "The Fighting at Sailor's Creek." *Confederate Veteran* 25 (1917): 448–52.

Watson, Walter C. "Sailor's Creek." *Southern Historical Society Papers* 42 (1917): 136–51.

Wayland, John W. *Stonewall Jackson's Way.* Dayton, Ohio: Morningside Bookshop, 1984.

Webb, Alexander S. "Through the Wilderness." In Johnson and Buel, *Battles and Leaders,* 4:152–69.

Weddell, Elizabeth W. *St. Paul's Church, Richmond, Virginia: Its Historic Years and Memorials.* 2 vols. Richmond: William Byrd, 1931.

Welch, Spencer G. *A Confederate Surgeon's Letters to His Wife.* New York: Neale, 1911.

Wellman, Manley W. *Rebel Boast: First at Bethel—Last at Appomattox.* New York: Henry Holt, 1956.

Welsh, Jack D. *Medical Histories of Confederate Generals.* Kent, Ohio: Kent State University Press, 1995.

Westbrook, Robert S. *History of the 49th Pennsylvania Volunteers.* Altoona: Altoona Times Print, 1898.

Wharton, Anne H. *Social Life in the Early Republic.* New York: Benjamin Blom, 1969.

White, Henry A. "Lee's Wrestle with Grant in the Wilderness, 1864." In *The Wilderness Campaign.* Vol. 4 of *Papers of the Military Historical Society of Massachusetts.* Boston: Military Historical Society of Massachusetts, 1905.

White, William S. "A Diary of the War or What I Saw of It." *Contributions to a History of the Richmond Howitzer Battalion.* Pamphlet no. 2. Richmond: Carlton McCarthy, 1883.

Wilcox, Cadmus M. *History of the Mexican War.* Washington, D.C.: Church News Pub. Co., 1892.

———. "Letter from General C. M. Wilcox." *Southern Historical Society Papers* 4 (1877): 111–17.

Williams, T. Harry. "General Ewell to the High Private in the Rear." *Virginia Magazine of History and Biography* 54, no. 2 (Apr. 1946): 157–60.

Wilson, William L. *A Borderland Confederate.* Edited by Festus P. Summers. Pittsburgh: University of Pittsburgh Press, 1962.

Wingfield, Henry W. "Diary of Capt. H. W. Wingfield." Edited by W. W. Scott. *Bulletin of the Virginia State Library* 16, no. 2 (July 1927): 9–47.

Wise, George. *Campaigns and Battles of the Army of Northern Virginia.* New York: Neale, 1916.

———. *History of the Seventeenth Virginia Infantry, C.S.A.* Baltimore: Kelly, Piet, 1870.

Wise, John S. *The End of an Era.* Boston: Houghton, Mifflin, 1902.

Wood, H. E. "More of the Last Defense of Richmond." *Confederate Veteran* 16 (1908): 397.

Wood, John S. *The Virginia Bishop: A Yankee Hero of the Confederacy.* Richmond: Garrett & Massie, 1961.

Worsham, John H. *One of Jackson's Foot Cavalry.* Edited by James I. Robertson Jr. Jackson, Tenn.: McCowat-Mercer Press, 1964.

Wright, Marcus J. "Bushrod Johnson's Men at Fort Harrison." *Confederate Veteran* 14 (1906): 545.

———. *List of Staff Officers of the Confederate States Army, 1861–1865.* Washington, D.C.: U.S. Government Printing Office, 1891.

Wynn, B. L. "Lee Watched Grant at Locust Grove." *Confederate Veteran* 21 (1913): 68.

Year Book, 1883: City of Charleston, So. Ca. Charleston: News and Courier, n.d.

Young, Anna M. *The Soldier of Indiana in the War for the Union.* 2 vols. Indianapolis: Privately printed, 1866.

Young, Otis E. "Dragoons of the Santa Fe Trail in the Autumn of 1843." *Chronicles of Oklahoma* 32, no. 1 (Spring 1954): 42–51.

641